The Spirit of Uppsala

The Spirit of Uppsala

Proceedings of the
Joint UNITAR-Uppsala University Seminar
on International Law and Organization
for a New World Order (JUS 81)

Uppsala 9–18 June 1981

Edited by
Atle Grahl-Madsen and Jiri Toman

Walter de Gruyter · Berlin · New York 1984

Library of Congress Cataloging in Publication Data

Joint UNITAR-Uppsala University Seminar on International Law and Organization for a New World Order (1981 : Uppsala, Sweden)
The spirit of Uppsala.

English and French.
Includes index.
1. International law-Congresses. 2. International organization-Congresses. I. Grahl-Madsen, Atle. II. Toman, Jiří. III. United Nations Institute for Training and Research. IV. Uppsala universitet. V. Title.
JX54.J57 1981 341 83-5232

ISBN 3-11-008822-3

CIP-Kurztitelaufnahme der Deutschen Bibliothek

The **spirit of Uppsala** : proceedings of the Joint UNITAR Uppsala Univ. Seminar on Internat. Law and Organization for a New World Order (JUS 81), Uppsala, 9–18 June 1981 / ed. by Atle Grahl-Madsen and Jiri Toman. – Berlin ; New York ; de Gruyter, 1983.
ISBN 3-11-008822-3
NE: Grahl-Madsen, Atle [Hrsg.]; JUS <1981, Uppsala>; Institute for Training and Research <New York, NY>

Dust Cover Design: Rudolf Hübler, Berlin. – Printing: Georg Wagner, Nördlingen. – Binding: Verlagsbuchbinderei Dieter Mikolai, Berlin. – Printed in Germany

In Memoriam:

Abdullah El-Erian
Mustafa Kamil Yasseen

Preface

It all started with Music. Allan Pettersson's mighty Twelfth Symphony toned through the Great Aula as Uppsala University celebrated its half-millennium, accompanied by the challenging words of Pablo Neruda's Canto General: I do not want them to reach me their hand . . . I do not want to see them as ambassadors . . .

Impression gave way to thought; and thought led to further thought; one added to another in a chain reaction.

Neruda's indictment of State positivism, of the way of thought whereby human beings are reduced to objects, pawns who do not really count in the game which the Great Ones – the Powers that be – are playing: that was the starting point.

Thoughts raced back to the period between the two World Wars, when "das Land der Dichter und Denker" had become "das Land der Richter und Henker", and one pensive German reflected, how could it come that once a murderous villain manoeuver himself into the position of Head of State, opposition against him becomes "high treason".

Our mental time machine takes us even further back, to the time when men like Hugo Grotius pondered the question: is there not something which may guide the Sovereigns, the Mighty Ones, in their mutual relations and in their conduct towards the Nations they are ruling, when there is no Earthly authority – temporal or spiritual – above them?

And after this journey back in time, the next was a *tour d'horizon* of our modern world, with its great hopes and great despairs. The greatest hope of all: the final recognition of the right of all Peoples to govern themselves, this being the final acknowledgement of the Human Being as subject, not an object, not a pawn. But gone is the relatively uniform and limited world of a Hugo Grotius; facing us is the diversity of all mankind.

What rules may guide the Peoples in their mutual relations, their co-existence as well as their co-operation? How can we combine the newly won Freedom with a measure of Equity and Equality, how can we build a true Community of goodwill among Humans? How can we prevent villains from usurping power over fellow men and women, a power that rightfully belongs to the People, and should be exercized solely for the benefit of the People?

If the Free Man and the Free Woman are what we proclaim, what we strive for, if this dream could come true, how should then the Community of Nations be organized, in order that we – the Peoples of the World – can live together in peace and under conditions where the elementary needs of all members of the human race will be satisfied?

Such were the visions. It was only too clear that it was not for one person to give the answers, not even to pose the questions.

And so the idea of the great Joint UNITAR-Uppsala University Seminar on International Law and Organization for a New World Order (JUS 81 for short) was born.

The idea was to bring together leading international scholars from all over the world to a brain-storming session to ponder the questions and perhaps try to indicate some directions where the answers might be sought.

It was in the nature of things that the gathering should be as diverse as possible, bringing in so many angles, so much knowledge, as manifold experience as possible. That meant that the different regions of the world should be as equally represented as possible. It meant that we should draw men and women from as diverse responsible positions as possible. And it meant that different age groups should be represented.

Once the potency of such a gathering was realized, support was forthcoming, as the acknowledgements below will testify. And the response to the invitations to participate in this great endeavour was magnificent. It proved to be an idea whose time had come. As Professor William Michael Reisman later expressed it in his General Report of the Seminar: In the past the project might have seemed ambitious, even grandiose. Today no one questions its realism, gravity or urgency.

And then for ten full days seventy leading international legal scholars – judges, ambassadors, legal advisers, professors, attorneys – from fifty countries participated keenly in this quest for pertinent questions and possible ways to answer them.

The outcome is this great volume.

The Seminar was designed to allow and to ensure the active participation of all participants. A General Rapporteur and five Main Rapporteurs were selected, together representing all major regions of the world, to digest the outcome of the collective effort and to contribute their own views as influenced by the common experience of the Seminar. It was intended that six different scholars with widely different backgrounds should perceive the problems in different ways: this easily explains why there may be discrepancies between their reports. Better understanding, not consensus, was the goal.

The following papers are a *mélange;* as is to be expected when persons of profound knowledge, yet with so diverse experiences are hurled together and try to find bearings in uncharted territory. There emerged, quite perceptibly, a Spirit of Uppsala. But it was a spirit not of accomplishment but of endeavour. JUS 81 was but a beginning, a shared sense of starting out together on a great quest in search of new trails for humankind to tread, after so many of the old ones have proved to be dead ends.

It was but natural that the search should go in many directions, in very different directions, and that not all could lead to fruition.

Nothing which appears in this volume is irrelevant. But of course, the book is no ready-made recipe for a New World Order. It is merely the modest contribution of a very good Collective Brain addressing some of the more pressing problems of our time and age.

The proceedings of the Seminar were not recorded, and it was up to each participant if he would submit a resumé of his intervention or not. Therefore the reproduced interventions represent merely a fraction of the interesting discussions that took place in the course of the ten days the Seminar lasted. To make up for this, the five Main Rapporteurs have endeavoured to give the reader an impression of what directions the discussions took and the different opinions which were voiced.

It is important to stress that all participants were invited in their personal capacity, and that they never spoke as representatives of any government or institution.

Acknowledgements

Thanks are due, first of all, to His Majesty Carl XVI Gustaf, King of Sweden, for dignifying the Seminar and honouring its participants by opening the Seminar and participating during its first day, and also to His Excellency Dr. Kurt Waldheim, Secretary-General of the United Nations, for his important message, read at the opening ceremony of the Seminar, stressing the urgency of the topics and the importance of coming to grips with them.

Moreover, thanks are owed to His Excellency Chief Judge Gunnar Lagergren, Marshal of the Realm of Sweden, for accepting to be the Honorary President of the Seminar and for taking an interested and constructive part in its proceedings, to His Excellency Dr. Davidson Nicol, Under-Secretary-General of the United Nations and Executive Director of the United Nations Institute for Training and Research, and to Professor Martin H:son Holmdahl, Rector Magnificus of Uppsala University, for supporting the idea of the Seminar from the outset and for taking decisive part in its realization throughout. In the same breath thanks are expressed to Professor Stig Strömholm, Vice-Rector of Uppsala University, for the absolutely essential task he performed, and for the time and efforts which he invested, as chairman of the Organizing Committee. His contribution was of vital importance – indeed a conditio sine qua non – for the happy realization of the Seminar.

Profound thanks are extended to the members of the Uppsala Organizing Committee and of the UNITAR Liaison Committee. By giving of his or her time and experience, each member made an important contribution to the success of the Seminar. In this connexion it seems fitting to mention in particular the great work of Dr. Åke Vinterbäck, the Secretary-General of the Seminar, whose meticulous planning and unsparing efforts were decisive for the faultless execution of all the great and small things which spell the difference between failure and success. Here I would also like to extend my thanks to Dr. Issa Diallo, who as "our man in New York" and as Deputy Seminar Director played an essential role in the realization of the Seminar idea.

Special thanks are addressed to the Åland Host Committee, in which connexion the Speaker of the Åland Parliament Olof Jansson, the Governor of Åland

Martin Isaksson, and the Premier Folke Woivalin deserve particular mention along with Ambassador Osmo Lares, the representative of the Government of the Republic of Finland.

The Seminar owes much to Dr. Hans Blix, who both as Foreign Minister and as Under-Secretary of State was an active promotor of the Seminar, as well as to Mr. Anders Forsse, Director-General of the Swedish International Development Agency (SIDA) for his engaged co-operation, and to his Agency, which was the most important contributor to the budget of the Seminar.

Other contributors were Marianne and Marcus Wallenberg's Foundation, the Fritz Thyssen Stiftung, and the Swedish Ministry of Education. Profound thanks are expressed to them all.

The Seminar would never have become a success had it not been for the many persons who – in executive positions or as members of the Seminar secretariat – worked so hard and with such devotion towards that success. I may be forgiven for mentioning in particular Dr. Vinterbäck's right hand, Ms. Ingrid Fagerström, and my own untiring personal assistants, Mr. Magnus Beer and Mr. Göran Lindholm, my amanuensis Mr. Lars Wahlund, and last but not least Mr. Rafal Lekach, the intendent and librarian of the Swedish Institute of International Law (SIFIR), who with unfailing zeal and loyalty lent his support from the very beginning to the glorious end.

A very special mention deserve the many graduate and post-graduate students who willingly gave of their time and in various capacities made a vital contribution to the success of the Seminar.

The Swedish Research Council for Social Sciences is thanked for its contribution towards the publication of this volume. A very special appreciation is reserved for Dr. Jiri Toman, my co-editor. He and I extend our thanks to Ms. Micheline Severis and Ms. Christine Seydoux for their valuable assistance in the preparation of parts of the manuscript, and no less to Mr. Harald van Rees Rotler for his meticulous attention to the proofs. We would finally like to express our gratitude to Dr. H. Hassenpflug and Mr. Franzkowiak of Walter de Gruyter & Co. for their valuable co-operation and understanding throughout the period of preparation of the present book.

Bergen, July 1983.

Atle Grahl-Madsen

Table of Contents

IV. General Papers

V. International Law in a Multicultural World
Working Group I

I. Greetings

1.1. Opening Speech

H. M. King Carl XVI Gustaf of Sweden

Your Excellencies,
Distinguished guests,
Ladies and Gentlemen:
It is a great honour for Sweden and Uppsala University to host this conference, assembled to study and discuss present international order and how to adapt and improve it to new demands. This is of utmost urgency and calls for persistent efforts to master.

However, these problems will never be solved once and for all. Every generation has to tackle them anew. This conference is one part of these efforts.

Sweden has been spared the devastation of war for 167 years. One basic reason for this is our situation on the Northern rim of Europe, separated from the European mainland by a large inland sea, the Baltic. Also to-day we believe our territory not to be a main target in a strategic conflict. This together with our means and strong determination to defend our nation are the fundaments for our policy of non-alignment in peace, aiming at neutrality in the event of war.

This position, non-committed between the two blocs, however, does not imply that we neglect conflicts. On the contrary, we believe that the small nations have a right to be heard.

Therefore, Sweden takes active part in the international exchange of views and opinions. We believe in peace, justice and freedom for all mankind and try – within our limited resources – to aid other countries. We support the work of the United Nations, always reminding the equal right of all nations, big or small, and the dignity of the human being. Principles often stressed by Dag Hammarskjöld, the former United Nations Secretary-General, whose name should be mentioned in this context here in his hometown.

We recognize that environmental problems, increasing energy prices, the limited capacity of the globe to provide necessary essentials and to take care of waste must be mastered in a way that gives all nations a fair deal. The lack of equality of to-day's world is tragic. It is human, yet regrettable, that frustration and difficulties shall lead to irrational responses and actions, and in some cases serve as an excuse for setting aside basic human rights.

The material and human problems confronting mankind should be vigourously attacked by men and women of good will in all parts of the world. In order to do so it must be useful to look over our present system in international law for solving conflicts.

I understand that these are themes of your seminar. I am happy that neutral

Sweden can provide a meeting ground for so many distinguished lawyers and scholars discussing these important problems. I think it has a special value that you participate in your own capacity and not as representatives. The individual voice must be heard through the sharp and loud official debate.

I wish you all success in your fateful task. I hereby declare the Joint UNITAR-Uppsala University Seminar on International Law and Organization for a New World Order 1981 opened.

1.2. Message from the Secretary-General of the United Nations

Read at the opening of the Joint UNITAR-Uppsala University Seminar on International Law and Organization for a New World Order, Uppsala, 9–18 June 1981

I should like to express to His Majesty, Carl XVI Gustaf, King of Sweden, and to the Government and People of Sweden, my sincere gratitude and deep appreciation for their generous hospitality in hosting the Joint UNITAR-Uppsala University Seminar on International Law and Organization for a New World Order. It is indeed fitting that this seminar is taking place in Sweden, a country which has shown consistent commitment to the aims and acitivities of the United Nations.

It also gives me great pleasure to extend my warm greetings to the participants in this important seminar. The eminent international reputation of Uppsala University augurs well for the success of your deliberations.

The issues which you will be discussing are of critical importance to the international community. In an ever changing world, it is necessary to keep under constant review the role of international law and organization so as to ensure its continuing effectiveness and responsiveness to newly emerging needs.

The authors of the United Nations Charter realized that in order to create the conditions of stability necessary for peace the world Organization would have to help solve the great social and economic problems of the day. They could not, of course, have foreseen the extent and complexity of the difficulties that would arise and the crucial position that these questions would take in our work. But they indeed understood the close relation between the ideals of peace and of social and economic progress. These concepts are clearly indivisible. Over the 36 years since the signing of the Charter severe tensions and dangerous confrontations have grown out of the despair and misery engendered by economic and social injustice. Conversely, the disastrous effects of war and conflict on development have, unfortunately, been known to most of mankind.

Your initiative in holding the present seminar is therefore particularly appropriate in the context of one of the foremost objectives of the United Nations today, that of establishing a new international economic order. The aim of this endeavour is to create a new order based on equity, sovereign equality, interdependence and common interest and co-operation among all States.

Your deliberations in this seminar can generate the ideas we need for fostering new and better means of international co-operation and contribute towards a framework for international law and organization for a new world order. I send you my best wishes for a most successful and fruitful meeting.

KURT WALDHEIM

II. Introduction

2.1. International Law and Organization for a New World Order*

ATLE GRAHL-MADSEN

The present paper reflects some ideas behind the Joint UNITAR-Uppsala University Seminar on International Law and Organization for a New World Order (JUS 81), scheduled to take place in Uppsala in June 1981.

Rapporteurs and other participants will deal with the matters in any way they see fit, and in this preparatory paper one has merely tried to formulate certain thoughts in order to identify some of the problems to be encountered in the discussions at the seminar.

1. International law in a multicultural world

1.1. A realistic approach to international law

At the beginning of modern history, international law was conceived as an instrument regulating the relations between the sovereigns in a Europe where no earthly or spiritual authority could any longer claim any kind of supremacy.

Until the middle of the twentieth century, the world scene was dominated by European or European-inspired States. Only a very few States of non-European origin were able to persevere, and even those few had, to some extent, to abide by rules laid down by the European powers.

The basis for international law was sought in the Law of Nature; and as the Christian faith loosened its grip on the rulers and the peoples of Europe, custom became the recognized law-making factor besides treaties.

In our modern times the international community comprises a majority of non-European sovereign nations. Like the old Law of Nature, a customary law and legal principles developed in Europe can no longer serve as s solid basis for international law.

Yet the fact remains that treaties bind only the Contracting States, and the thought that a State could be unbound by any international rule is repulsive and indeed unacceptable.

Our experience tells us that besides treaty law there exists a general international law, binding on all States, globally or regionally.

In a multicultural and multireligious world the binding force of this general

* The following Memorandum was sent to rapporteurs and other participants and formed the basis for the proceedings of the Seminar

law cannot be based on belief in any particular deity. We must search for a non-metaphysical basis. The mere existence of certain rules and the fact that they are being observed by a large majority of States most of the time, may be a less than persuasive argument *vis-à-vis* a new State which desires to go its own ways.

But perhaps we may find a basis in Necessity? If peace and international security are going to be preserved, it is necessary that States abide by certain basic – and a number of not so basic – rules. And if humankind is going to prosper, additional equations enter the picture.

When it comes to the actual contents of international law – general and conventional – we shall gain only limited insight from the study of texts and textbooks: the effective implementation of the rules is a decisive factor. Just as the principle of effectiveness is applied to States and governments, we shall have to apply it to the rules of international law, too.

In formulating the rules, we should not be blind to moral values. The principles of equality, reciprocity, and equity seem to have validity in all cultures and all religions, and they should consequently not be ignored when attempting to describe modern international law.

A law based on necessity, effectiveness, and basic moral values may perhaps not solve all the world's problems, but the realization of such a common basis may at least help to create better understanding and enhance goodwill between States, and in the world's present predicament, those benefits may prove essential.

1.2. Growth of the international community and qualitative shift in international legal relations

Our generation has witnessed an unprecedented growth of the international community.

There are now more than one hundred and fifty States Members of the United Nations, and we have not seen the end yet. The majority is non-European in every sense of the word.

The new States are very sensitive to power politics, and it is a prerequisite for lasting and friendly relations that the principles of national sovereignty and equality are scrupulously respected and honoured.

At the same time we have witnessed the growth of multinational corporations, some with a budget many times that of many States. Attempts to regulate the life of such giant corporations by national legislation are bound to fail. Only international regulations based – to some extent, at least – on the consent of the corporations themselves, may stand a chance of success.

Also non-profit, voluntary, non-governmental organizations operate internationally on a scale which forbids our ignoring them.

And the individual has come into the international limelight as never before, thanks not least to the many conventions pertaining to human rights in a broad sense.

Just as the rules governing intergovernmental organizations, important rules affecting multinational corporations, voluntary societies, and individuals may best be dealt with within the framework which traditionally has been that of international law, this being, of course, a matter of convention and convenience.

The discussion about who should be considered "subjects of international law" has hardly been a very fruitful one, autotelic and circular as it too often has been.

We may get rid of some of the more emotional overtones if we substitute "international person" for "subject of international law". But perhaps it would be advisable to speak merely of "actors" on the international scene.

We may then in a detached, completely natural and factual way describe the relations between different actors and classes of actors and the norms applicable to these relations.

1.3. Customary law: from "universal" in a European system to "regional" in a world system

We may doubt whether custom really is a constitutive element in the creation of legal norms, yet a general practice may provide good proof as to the existence of a particular rule of general international law.

International lawyers have to take note of the criticism levelled against international customary law, to the effect that new States cannot be bound by old customs, which they have had no chance to influence and which has come about in conditions entirely different from those prevailing today and in their part of the world.

Some rules, such as those concerning territorial integrity and diplomatic immunity, new States are as eager as anyone else to uphold.

Other rules, like those relating to investments abroad, are sometimes fiercely attacked.

The status of customary law, the requirements for the creation of customary rules, and the territorial applicability (global, regional) of such rules need unbiased reassessment.

2. Independence and interdependence

2.1. Sovereignty, independence, and interdependence of nations

Sovereignty may, perhaps, usefully be defined as the fact that the source of power in any one State is to be found within the State itself, and not in some external will.

It is important for peaceful and friendly co-existence that States should respect and honour each other's sovereignty and independence.

However, in the modern world States are also dependent on each other. The modern industrial society is based upon a division of labour between individuals as well as between nations.

But the industrial development in the Northern parts of the world has created an economic gap between North and South which poses flagrant dangers for the maintenance of international peace and security, and also a challenge to our conscience.

The idea of a New International Economic Order has so far brought few tangible results. Perhaps the matter may be usefully approached in terms of interdependence between nations? This begs the question, not only what the rich countries may do to help the poor, but also how the different countries should adjust to the requirements of optimal utility of new economic equations.

Independence and interdependence are both necessary for a benificial development. One cannot do without the one or the other. Is it possible to define in more precise terms where the one ends and the other begins?

2.2. Natural resources: heritage of nation and mankind

Natural resources are unevenly distributed. For some time now Third World countries have placed emphasis on the national sovereignty over natural resources. This was a natural and justified reaction to the exploitation by foreign interests.

But the time may now be ripe to look a bit further. The uneven distribution of important resources creates considerable inequalities between States. Moreover, the unhampered consumption of natural sources by some nations is likely to cause problems in others. Some resources cannot be depleted without causing problems for all mankind, especially for future generations, e. g., the rain forest in Brazil and the living resources of the sea.

Could some resources be defined as belonging to all mankind, and what legal rules would be necessary in such a context?

2.3. Material, economic, and human limits to activities of humankind: legislating for a new international economic order in an ecological context

At the same time as the nations of the Third World are pressing for their fair share of the riches of the world, humankind is becoming aware of the limitations of our globe, with respect to resources as well as resorptive capacity. The lesson seems to be that welfare for all will only be possible if one adopts a life-style less dependent on the use of energy, consumption of raw-materials, and production of waste. This does not necessarily mean an end to the division of labour between nations. But as the present world crisis shows, any readjustment to new Economic equations is bound to be painful. Do the plans for a New International Economic Order correspond to economic and ecological realities? What can international lawyers do to help to formulate a viable strategy for the painful period of transition ahead of us?

3. Sovereignty and humanity

3.1. A natural or moral basis for international law?

It has been suggested under heading 1.1 that general international law may perhaps find its basis in principles of necessity, reciprocity, and equity.

Is it indeed possible to fit moral values into a legal system whose validity is based on its "*être*"?

Some suggestions in this respect have been put forward in my paper "International Law at the Crossroads", notably at pp. 185 ff.

3.2. Sovereignty and humanity: can they converge?

Humanitarian intervention was considered to be dead. And yet we have recently seen some remarkable events where the justification given is strikingly similar to the argumentation for humanitarian intervention: the Entebbe raid, the interventions in Uganda and Kampuchea.

Could it be that Vattel's distinction between sovereign and tyrant, legitimate ruler and usurper, is still valid, and that only the sovereign, but not the tyrant, is protected by international law, provided that the other party acts out of acceptable motives?

More generally, what is the status of international protection for human rights today, including the right to self-determination, and what can be done to improve it?

3.3. Suppression of tyranny: a feasible task?

The proposal for a Torture Convention is interesting, in particular as it may make torture an international crime and subject the torturer to prosecution, judgment, and punishment whenever he enters the territory of a Contracting State.

In connexion with the growing refugee problems, impatient statesmen have suggested that one has to strike at the root causes. This is, of course, easier said than done in a world based on sovereign equality of States.

But could the draft Torture Convention point to a way: would it be possible to draft a convention for the prevention and punishment of tyranny?

As international law is constituted today, any general or colonel may seize power, declare himself president, and once firmly established claim recognition by all other States as the legitimate Head of State.

Could it not be possible for an important number of States to agree that once a regime was found to be a tyrannical one, ambassadors would be withdrawn and diplomatic relations maintained at the level of chargés-d'affaires?

And when the tyrant was deposed, he would be an outlaw everywhere, subject to jurisdiction in every Contracting State.

There are certain instruments already, which point in this direction: the Genocide Convention, the Red Cross conventions and protocols, the Refugee Convention, also provisions of extradition treaties which allow, for example, the extradition of a former president to his home country in order to let him stand trial for economic crimes allegedly committed while he was in a position of power.

Of course there are difficulties: the definition of tyranny; how a *coup d'état* may be justified by subsequent events (e. g., referendum under the control of the United Nations?); the introduction of a date-line excepting present regimes, provided they mend their ways.

But the idea seems well worth exploring. Or are there other ways?

4. International organization for a new world order

4.1. New ways for treaty-making and international legislation

The progressive development of international law depends on a smooth machinery for the adoption of new conventions.

It seems to have become increasingly costly and difficult to achieve treaty-making by means of diplomatic conferences.

And there is serious opposition to accepting resolutions of the General Assembly of the United Nations and other similar organs as legally binding instruments.

The middle way, that draft conventions are prepared and submitted to the General Assembly for scrutiny and thereafter opened for signature by governments, seems to be an acceptable procedure.

Would it be feasible and worthwhile to establish – on an orderly basis – specialized commissions to supplement the International Law Commission, which could draft texts for the consideration of the General Assembly? One might envisage that the General Assembly might give the text a first reading, and then return it to the commission for reconsideration in light of the remarks made. After a second reading the General Assembly might then open the convention for signature by governments.

Or are there other and more attractive solutions to the problem of multilateral treaty-making?

4.2. Organs for conflict resolution and execution

The resort to orderly procedures for conflict resolution and execution is of great importance for the effectiveness of international law.

What is the status in this respect today?

And what can be done in this field? Is it possible to get more States to trust the judicial or arbitral process?

What else can be done?

4.3. Universalism and regionalism

Certain problems are of a global character, others may best be resolved on the regional level, as is proved over and over again by such organizations as the Council of Europe, the Organization of African Unity, and the Organization of American States.

Is there a case for reorganizing the United Nations – or at least the Security Council – on the basis of regions rather than States, giving each region one vote, and reducing the veto-power to a kind of "opting out" for the different regions?

5. Legal and organizational problems of small states

Small States – those with less than one million inhabitants – face certain problems, not least in connexion with their representation in international organizations.

Some States are so small that they are not allowed to become members. How can the interests of such States be taken care of?

Would it be an idea that small States jointly created some sort of secretariat, providing their delegates with all necessary facilities, so that they better might take care of their interests?

Would it also be desirable and possible for small States to co-operate in other ways, e. g., by creating universities and other facilities which they hardly can maintain alone?

Could also autonomous territories be admitted to such co-operation?

2.2. International Law at the Crossroads*

Atle Grahl-Madsen

We live in a time of crisis. Every day the press, radio, and television bear fresh testimony of this fact. We live in an era of great changes, and we are heading towards even greater changes. The crisis, and the changes too, are largely of a global character; in almost every instance we find, at least, a global dimension.

The study of global conditions, of international relations, has therefore become vitally important. Lawyers, in particular, are facing enormous challenges. Every issue at the international level demands legal expertise: legal knowledge, experience, and understanding. But this expertise must be coupled with a true insight into the material, the economic and – not least – the psychological factors which provide the framework, and spell the limits, for the activities of humankind on this planet of ours.

International law, too, is in a state of crisis. But this is a crisis of a different kind, a crisis at the intellectual level. Three hundred and fifty years after Hugo Grotius wrote his great work, *De jure belli ac pacis,* we face the task of adapting this honourable branch of the science of law to the demands which a profoundly new world situation imposes upon us.

In 1945, the United Nations had about fifty member States. Today, there are three times as many. Most of them are new States, created in the course of the last twenty years. The States vary in population from several hundred million to less than one hundred thousand inhabitants. We have become conscious of the enormous differences in the standard of living between the industrialized societies in our part of the world and the more primitive economies and the vast oceans of human beings in what is often referred to as the Third World.

The new States have been admitted not only to the United Nations but also to the so-called international community, the community of international law. Thereby both the world organization and international law have been subjected to strains which, of necessity, have caused, at least to some degree, a change in their character. Many time-honoured ideas have had to be scrapped. We have

* This paper was annexed to the preceding Memorandum. Originally the author's inaugural lecture in Uppsala University, it was first published (in Norwegian) in *Svensk Juristtidning,* vol. 63 (1978), pp. 321–330. This English version was originally published in *Scandinavian Studies in Law,* vol. 24 (1980), pp. 175–186, but is reproduced here for handy reference.

acquired a new perspective on many problems which often are of profound importance.

In many of the new States, there has been a tendency to question the old customary law as a basis for the resolution of conflicts between nations. How, it is asked, can the new States be bound by a custom which has been developed in the interaction between a limited number of States in a different part of the world and on the basis of conditions differing from those which exist today? Little by little we have been forced, even in our part of the world, to admit that not all customary law can claim to be of global validity. We mut differentiate, and accept that many established rules must be given a new interpretation, and that in part they are of merely regional relevance.

On the other hand, it was once an uncontested maxim that resolutions adopted at international conferences or by international organizations were not legally binding. Neither the League of Nations, nor the United Nations, was conceived of as an organ for international legislation. And yet we see today how many international legal scholars have advocated that such resolutions – and even proposals which have not been formally adopted as expressions of an international consensus, and for that reason must be recognized as guidelines for the intercourse between States.

The attitude which States adopt towards an issue under discussion at an international conference is being accorded a new importance. To some extent, the statements made by delegates are taken as signals and may add momentum to a quite revolutionary development, such as the one we experienced in 1976–77 with respect to the law of the sea. All important coastal States realized almost simultaneously that they could dare to take the step of unilaterally proclaiming economic zones up to two hundred nautical miles (370.4 km) wide. Attempts have been made to explain the legality of this step on the basis of the international law which existed up to 1975. But it is probably better to admit that what happened was a leap in the development, which has come to be accepted by operation of the mechanism of estoppel, because, as we know, a person who has taken the law into his own hands cannot protest against others doing the same thing.

The efforts towards a new economic world order have very clearly demonstrated the belief that substantial results can be achieved by way of resolutions in international fora. With great sincerity delegates from all nations have engaged in veritable battles over hairsplitting formulations in drafts for General Assembly resolutions.

In some areas formal agreements have been concluded, for instance concerning tariff reductions, in order to improve the competitiveness of the poorer nations. A classic instance is the so-called Kennedy Round regarding the exemption from duties on textiles from developing countries. The agreement is now openly circumvented in a number of industrialized countries, by means of internal discriminatory measures aimed at safeguarding employment in the industrialized countries themselves.

What had, however, a dramatic impact on the economic relations between the continents was the establishment of the oil cartel – the Organization of Petroleum-Exporting Countries (OPEC) – and the subsequent quadrupling of energy prices. Other raw-material-exporting countries contemplate similar cartels, but so far they have not succeeded in creating a sellers' market.

What happened to the oil prices has, nevertheless, been sufficient to trigger off an economic crisis, which undoubtedly will lead to changed structures in the western as well as the global economy.

The fact that the demands for a new economic world order came at a time when we became aware in earnest of the limitations of the world's potential for economic growth and regeneration – the basic conditions for our very existence – makes the problems seem overwhelming.

At the same time we experience – and not only with respect to the law of the sea – what we may describe as a retreat to national egoism. We observe in far too many places a more or less articulated distrust of other nations as well as of international solutions, coupled with a belief that the nation State in the proper framework for the resolution of the more pressing problems. The word "sovereignty" is being used, not as a neutral term for a certain concept in international law, but as a justification for demands as well as a basis for conclusions which often have far-reaching consequences.

We are sometimes confronted with expressions of doubt as whether the law of nations has any reality – whether there really exists anything that deserves the name of international law.

It is pointed out that international law is not effective; that when we come to the crucial questions, the individual States often do as they think fit. And people point in that connection to the balance of terror, but also to a number of other examples, from the Connally Amendment[1] to the Vietnam war, from the Security Council's incapacity to act to the powerlessness of the international community with respect to even flagrant violations of human rights.

It is quite true that there are important areas where the rule of international law is not efficacious – or is not efficacious enough.

But such lacunae are not peculiar to international law. Even in the municipal law of the national States there are important areas where much is left to the free interplay of forces. Let me mention labour law, where important questions are decided by struggle and negotiation between the big organizations of employers and employees. I may also mention the law of corporations, which in many countries has remained rudimentary, owing to the resistance of powerful organizations and pressure groups to any kind of legislative control.

Some will deny international law the quality of law, because there are no organs for compulsory conflict resolution and execution.

1 A clause by which a State excludes from its acceptance of the jurisdiction of the International Court of Justice disputes with regard to matters essentially within its domestic jurisdiction *as determined by the State itself;* named after the US Senator Thomas Terry Connally.

And it must be admitted that problems arise from the fact that a number of nations, large and small, have consistently refused to submit themselves to any form of international jurisdiction.

On the other hand, this has not prevented those nations from fulfilling, to a great extent, their international obligations. To be sure, the fulfilment has been on their own premises, as is exemplified by the incident immortalized by the great Finnish poet, Johan Ludvig Runeberg, in the poem "Sandels" in *The Tales of Ensign Stål.*[2] The Swedish General Sandels entertains a guest at a leisurely and convivial breakfast:

> "Today, at *one*, the battle starts,
> It will rage near Virta bridge. –
> . . .
> Tutschkoff has sent me a friendly note,
> That our truce is to an end.
> . . ."
> A message came, an urgent one:
> "Our convention has been breach'd:
> Brusin's forepost back is thrown,
> It's too late to tear the bridge.
> Our watch was *twelve,* and we't stood upon,
> But by the Russian clock it's *one*".

If international law is to be a useful instrument for international progress in the years ahead, a realistic understanding of what international law is and what international law can achieve is necessary.

This presupposes a realistic understanding of the matter of law in general.

I do not consider myself a fully-fledged legal philosopher. But I have received strong impressions from the Uppsala School[3] and Scandinavian realism in general.

2 Author's translation from the original Swedish. For a different translation, see Johan Ludvig Runeberg, *The Tales of Ensign Stål (Fänrik Ståls Sägner),* translated by Clement Burbank Shaw, New York (G. E. Stechert & Co.) 1925, p. 97. The problems raised by the poem are discussed by Professor Yrjö Holm, "Sandels: Ett problem i Runebergs-tolkningen", in Societas Scientiarum Fennica, *Årsbok – Vuosikirja,* XI B no. 1, Helsinki 1933.
In *The Tales of Ensign Stål* Runeberg highlights in heroic poems events and persons in the Finnish war (between Russia and Sweden) 1808–09. The Swedish General Sandels had made a truce with the Russian General Tutchkoff. The truce was due to end at 1 p.m. However, Tutchkoff, going by Russian time, which was one hour earlier, ordered his troops to commence their attack at 12 noon Swedish time. Runeberg's poem relates the dramatic events that ensued.

3 For an account of the Uppsala School, see Folke Schmidt, "The Uppsala School of legal thinking", 22 *Sc. St. L.,* pp. 151–75 (1978). I fully share Professor Schmidt's criticism. Another author who meant much to me in my formative years was Ingemar Hedenius, in particular his *Om rätt och moral,* Stockholm 1941.

Metaphysical notions or explanations of the legal phenomena are not adequate; least of all in a world that stretches far beyond the frontiers of Christendom.

I do not believe in any "valid law" *(geltendes Recht)*, if by "validity" *(Gültigkeit)* is meant something else and something more than the fact that people abide by certain rules, or can be expected to abide by them, should a certain situation arise. An expression such as "the obligatory power of the law" *(die verpflichtende Kraft des Rechts)* is to me empty words, if thereby it is intended to state anything beyond the fact that the individual considers himself compelled (on grounds which I shall discuss presently) to abide by certain rules.

I do not believe in any "basic norm" *(Grundnorm)*, from which one may deduce a hierarchy of subordinate norms.

On the other hand, I cannot accept that the science of law can be reduced to the science of judicial behaviour. The reality is much more complex.

I think that in every organized community there exists a legal system – a system of rules which are being upheld by organs of the state, and which the individual, for one reason or other, takes into account in many of the situations which he faces during his lifetime.

I think that legal phenomena may best be explained by the opposition: the One against the Many. We are all, each by himself, born into a society where a number of rules are practised an enforced.

The breach of certain of these rules is met with purely social sanctions: a higher or lower degree of disapproval by the offender's fellow citizens, or at least by certain individuals or groups of citizens. These rules are often referred to as moral rules; I think it is better to call them social norms, because I should like to reserve the word "morals" for certain ethical conceptions, which make a person feel obliged to commit or omit certain acts, irrespective of other people's reaction or other personal consequences.

Certain other rules are administered by the organs of the State, and non-abidance may lead to sanctions by those organs. These are what we call legal rules.

It should be stressed that sanctions are relatively rare and affect only a comparatively small number of persons. Thus, the sanctions have mostly exemplary importance. The vast majority of people abide by the rules out of habit, out of a sense that "one ought to obey the law", or out of fear for the consequences. Here I may add that our cultural heritage and our upbringing play very important roles.

The legal system consists of a multitude of norms. Some of those norms are created spontaneously in the society and may after some time be recognized as customary law. Some rules are shaped by the practice of the authorities – perhaps in particular that of the courts. And some come into being by decisions of persons or collectives which are generally considered competent to make such descisions, such as the nation's parliament, goverment, and administrative authorities.

The relative importance of the different legal norms is not clear and unequivocal. We often speak of a hierarchy, in particular with respect to the written norms: constitution, statute, order in council, administrative decree, But such a hierarchy cannot be assumed automatically. Norms at all levels may be interpreted and applied in different ways, and some are considered so old-fashioned, unpractical, or inconvenient that they are either explained away somehow or quite simply ignored.

From what has been said, it will be realized that the legal system is in a process of continuous change. Each of us is born into the system. At some point in time we may come into positions which enable us to influence the rules, to a greater or lesser extent, by participation in the work of parliament or government, as judges or civil servants, by activities in different political parties, or simply by obeying or ignoring the various rules. But irrespective of the influence any one individual may possess, he or she remains subjected to the legal system as it is constituted at any particular time.

International law is – like the internal law of a country – a system of rules, which are considered to be legal rules. These rules are formulated and interpreted by lawyers.

What more than anything else sets international law apart from municipal legal systems is the fact that the number of actors is so much smaller. While each of us, as an individual, is but one among several million fellow citizens, the State to which we belong has only a couple of hundred co-actors, if by that we mean the other States that make up the international community. Another difference is apparent in the fact that – in traditional international law, at least – there is not the division between the authorities and the public which we know from the internal life of the states.

The small number of actors gives each single actor – each separate State – a much greater opportunity than any citizen in the municipal society to influence the system. Moreover, as we have seen, the States differ enormously with regard to size. The big States have many more opportunities to satisfy their ambitions than the small States have. On the other hand, small States frequently have considerable freedom of action precisely because of their smallness and relative unimportance.

The States are not, however, the only actors in the international arena. International organizations, too, are today generally accepted as co-actors. And we cannot exclude others from taking part. There are today rules which affect – and are influenced by – multinational corporations, nongovernmental organizations, and indeed private individuals. And if we consider the development of the rules, we shall have to admit that both arbitrators and legal writers play far from unimportant roles.

I shall not here take sides in the discussions of the question whether or not any of the categories just mentioned may be considered subjects of international law. The concept of "State", just as well as the concept of "subject of international law" (or "international person", which means about the same), is of little, if any, value in modern international law. Instead of definitions of concepts, we need a description of actually existing relations. And like municipal law, international law is in constant development. What was true yesterday is not necessarily true today or tomorrow.

At the international level, too, legal rules may develop spontaneously – by the practice of the actors concerned. The development may be slow, but it may also be quick: the Truman doctrine on the continental shelf was proclaimed in 1945. Already at the Conference on the Law of the Sea in 1958, the right of the coastal States to lay claim to the continental shelf was considered to have become customary law! There are clear indications that the international doctrine will very soon recognize the economic zones of two hundred nautical miles.

Nor are decisions in international fora, which are followed up in the practice of States and international organizations, to be ignored by those who attempt to describe or analyse today's international law in some particular area.

The decisions of the International Court of Justice are read, discussed and commented upon, and they undoubtedly influence the development of international law. Arbitral awards and legal writing are, of course, not to be neglected.

But just as legislation is of great importance within the national society, the written agreements between States or possibly other actors occupy a central position in international law. Such agreements span from administrative and executive agreements between administrations and governments, to formal, ceremonial treaties and conventions – bilateral as well as multilateral.

Pacta sunt servanda – agreements shall be fulfilled – is a basic maxim in traditional international law. And on the whole, agreements are respected. But, like constitutions and laws, treaties are subject to wear and tear. One often speaks of *clausula rebus sic stantibus,* but this is in fact only a concession to what we may consider a universal principle of attrition.

As I have said, the rules of international law are considered to be legal rules. The States and other actors interpret and abide by the rules, in much the same way as authorities and citizens do within the individual country. And like the citizens in the municipal society, the actors in the international arena have a tendency to be law-abiding, provided, with respect to both categories, I am tempted to add, that the abidance by the law does not cost too much compared with the risk connected with non-abidance of the rules.

It is always advantageous for a government to be able to show that it has international law on its side. Otherwise it risks protests from many quarters, both at home and abroad, and it may easily become necessary to provide explanations, often of a very embarrassing character. In extreme cases there may even be a question of retaliation or reprisals, or possibly sanctions under the United Nations Charter.

It is no accident that all ministries of foreign affairs have legal departments and advisers on international law, who are seriously concerned with the task of spelling out the rules of international law pertinent to the international problems with which the respective governments are faced at any particular time.

Sometimes it is authoritatively decided by the International Court of Justice or an arbitral tribunal what is right and what is wrong in a particular relation. And it is interesting to note that in the sensitive atmosphere in which States lead their lives, the fact that a State has lost its case may, indeed, be considered a fully adequate sanction in itself.

When I spoke about the municipal legal system, I placed more emphasis on the actual law-abidance than on the relatively rare instances when sanctions imposed by the authorities hurt lawbreakers. The sanctions of international law are different from those of municipal law. But I firmly believe that the international legal system is sufficiently effective to justify our considering it a true system of law.

As lawyers, we operate within a triangle, whose three sides are Law, Power, and Morality.

That international law must make concessions to Power is obvious. We saw this in connection with the unilateral declaration of economic zones by the coastal States. It is clearly expressed in the principle of effectiveness, which is a cornerstone of international law. Should a new State be born somewhere, the international community will have acquired a new member. Should anyone seize power in an existing State, his government will be recognized under international law, no matter how repugnant his regime may appear to be.

In Allan Pettersson's mighty Twelfth Symphony, which was first performed at Uppsala University's 500th anniversary celebration on 29. September 1977, the following words by Pablo Neruda are sung: "I do not want them to reach me their hand . . . I do not want to see them as ambassadors"[4] Yet the world's governments do not ask whether the ambassadors they receive are not the henchmen of dictators with bloodstained hands. Neither historical nor democratic legitimacy is required for the recognition of a new Government.

Perhaps it cannot be otherwise, if international law is to be relevant to the real world. An international community consisting of dethroned monarchs and ousted presidents would serve no useful purpose.

But how can we fit moral values into a system whose "validity" is based on its mere existence?

It is often said that human rights, as they have been expressed in the existing international conventions, are based on a modern law of nature. There is a grain of truth in this. But whereas the old law of nature claimed that it was able to resolve any kind of legal problems, this modern law of nature is more modest.

It is based on a few simple experiences: People are generally better off if those in positions of power have to respect the life, freedom, and physical integrity of individuals. Freedom of expression and freedom of assembly are preconditions for this. Also, there should be no discrimination without just cause. At least from the point of view of a democratic society, it is a great advantage if as many States as possible have a government based on the active participation of those governed.

4 "No quiero que me den la mano . . . No los quiero de Embajadores": Pablo Neruda, *Canto General* (Buenos Aires: Biblioteca Ayacucho, 1955), p. 178 (V. La Arena Traicionada: iii. Los muertos de la plaza: Los enemigos). The text used at the quincentennial celebration in Uppsala was from a Swedish version by Artur Lundkvist and Francisco J. Uriz.

It is, so far as I understand the matter, not necessary to seek metaphysical explanations in order to justify such points of view: we want to live, and to live as free persons. And this we shall achieve best if as many others as possible can do the same. One may speak of "relativity morals" and "reciprocity morals". But I believe we can find an empirical basis for certain fundamental human rights.

However, it follows that the desire for universal respect for human rights must be fitted into a larger reality, where those considerations which form the basis for the principle of effectiveness also have their place. At a time when the great powers have arsenals of weapons which can wipe out every living being on the entire globe, preservation of peace must be a paramount consideration.

We do not need to hide our ideals. Indeed, it would be dangerous to do so. But if we want to spread them, we must proceed with caution, and we must not be afraid of detours.

For example, one could imagine a convention which would make it an international crime to become a despot, and which would make the deposed tyrant an outlaw on the earth. Embryos for such rules exist in the Genocide Convention of 1949 and the Refugee Convention of 1951. We may also mention the American Government's extradition of a former Venezuelan president to his home country, where he was wanted for serious economic crimes, which he had allegedly committed while he was president. So the idea of such a convention is not merely utopian. A Convention for the Prevention and Punishment of Tyranny would undoubtedly have far-reaching psychological and political consequences, if it were ratified by an important number of States. Whether this is feasible, only the future can tell.

In an imperfect world we shall have to live with imperfect rules which are applied in an imperfect manner. We must admit the shortcomings and limitations of the international legal system. But at least we shall then have a sound basis for achieving whatever is to be achieved.

III. General and Group Reports

3.1. International Law and Organization for a New World Order: The Uppsala Model

General Report of JUS 1981

William Michael Reisman

We have been convened by Professor Atle Grahl-Madsen under the auspices of Uppsala University and UNITAR to consider the nature of – and impediments to – an optimal world order. We have been selected because we represent diverse views from different parts of the globe. Whatever our provenance – be it the university, the government office, private practice or the courtroom – we know that we must approach our task not as representatives or proponents of a particular national view but as individuals and citizens of the world community. We form, in Judge Lachs' phrase, "a small parliament of lawyers of the world".

In the past, Professor Grahl-Madsen's project might have seemed ambitious, even grandiose. Today no one questions its realism, gravity or urgency. The need for such a project is clear; the reasons compelling. Designed for a less complex world, the world community's formal institutions are being subjected to major and unforeseen stresses; the recent 200% increase in membership in governmental organizations has changed the constellation of world political power in ways that are as yet only imperfectly understood; the production and distribution of weapons of mass destruction is booming; financial and trade institutions are undergoing shock after unexpected and unsettling shock; the planet's resource base has diminished; and our ecosystem is deteriorating at an alarming rate. Meanwhile, the universal demand for human rights and a life of dignity has become urgent, intense and potentially explosive. And while international law continues to work in innumerable ways, it is simply not working well enough in many of the most critically important sectors of the world order.

In this report, I will not seek to summarize the rich variety of viewpoints which have been expressed in our plenary sessions and in committee. The rapporteurs have done that in admirable fashion. Instead, I propose to try to organize, explicitly, the major conceptions that have emerged during our conference and address the key intellectual and professional tasks that – in anticipation of the 21st century – should be shouldered by international lawyers everywhere. Though I have drawn freely on the ideas of many of our members, this is an individual statement for which no one but myself is responsible.

In our plenary discussions and groups, we identified three major tasks for international lawyers and the international community: (1) identifying the goals toward which the community should be mobilized (goals for individuals as well as basic institutions); (2) improving the international community's basic decisionmaking institutions; and (3) improving the components of an international public order. We shall treat these in order.

I. Goals for a new world order

Law is not a supernatural or even "natural" phenomenon. It is a human creation, an artifact, a tool. It is created by people in a coordinate political process for the realization of social goals. To use this tool intelligently, we must first decide what social consequences we desire, then, how to bring them about. As international jurists interested in bringing about an optimal world order, we must therefore occasionally be willing to think not like legal archivists but like international legislators. This is not to suggest that we can operate asocially or ahistorically. The metaconceptions of a legal system are usually deeply embedded in its society and culture and, as Professors Dimitrijević, Theutenberg and Saxena pointed out, have important subliminal functions as regards legal innovation and general effectiveness. As our largely Euro-centered and essentially monarchical system was fragmented by popular revolution and then stretched by a rapid increase of non-European membership, the heterogeneity of its myth system increased to the point where there was no longer a single base of common myths to legitimate the system. Grotius could justify his theories by reference to a literature and traditions common to all the elites he addressed. However still vibrantly relevant his conception of common interest, his sources now seem quaint and parochial. Some contemporary scholars have sought to find metaconceptions anew either in common features of the world's civilizations or in novel legitimizing myths emphasizing cooperation and peace. For mass mobilization, characteristic symbols on the new flags emphasize integration. Compare, for example, the UN's emblem with its theme of global unity expressed in a recurring and almost tender circularity with the bold lines emphasizing vector in 18th and 19th century national flags.

Other scholars have sought to rework natural law to create new bases of legitimacy. But in this context, the term is misleading. As Professor Dimitrijević observed, nature *is*, while law involves *choices* about how it is to be used. No law is natural. Nor do law and its goals "evolve". The passive voice is wholly inappropriate. Changes in the law have been proposed and agitated for by individuals. Future law will be formed by the same process. The human agency in inventing the goals for the process must be emphasized. It is much more than a search for values common to the diverse cultures of the world. While commonality is relevant, goals are *invented*, especially in radically new situations.

We stand at a crossroad. There are few precedents for our species and our planet. Humanity as a whole is moving rapidly toward an increasingly homogenous industrial and science based global culture which is providing, though at different time rates and at the moment unevenly, new levels of material comfort and enhanced opportunities for individual development – in politics, wealth, skill, education, life expectancy, sexual fulfilment, religious choice and so on. While these changes have many positive and desirable aspects, they inevitably bring about the disintegration of social arrangements and their supporting ethical systems, systems that evolved for entirely different socio-technological arrangements. Thus we are witnessing the collapse of the extended family in civilizations where it had been a fundamental social unit for thousands of years; we have seen the subjection of the nuclear family and the nation-State to new and formidable stresses; we are witnessing the redefinition of social roles in even the most intimate sectors of life; we see the depreciation of old values, the transformation of intense nationalism from a civic virtue to an international pathology, and the superannuation of religious and ethical systems that were important mooring points for psychological coherence and personal integrity. These are radical changes and therefore can be calamitous events for us. But radical as these earth-bound changes might be, they are sure to be matched by humanity's move from earth into space. Plans for human settlements in space – curiously often referred to as colonization – are now viewed as realistic. The commercial use of space is already a reality. And the major powers are exploring the military potential of "killer" satellites and other space-borne craft.

Given the sharp disjunction between our conceptions of the past and the certainty that the future will be very, very different, probably surprising, perhaps unpleasant, nostalgia for the past is understandable. Politically, this nostalgia is sometimes translated into an intense veneration of old value systems and a rejection of new alternatives and at times an almost hysterical and atavistic embrace of archaic religious doctrines. At such times, the jurist must provide the balm of perspective, and he must redirect our attention to a spectrum of probable futures, for each of which a set of principles or policies or basic norms must be developed. Insofar as possible, those principles should be consistent with older and still intensely held values, but there is no reason to assume that old values are necessarily desirable, that they are inherently good or that they should be projected into the future. Indeed, in the multi-cultured international environment in which the international jurist finds himself, helping communities clarify goals and principles will be facilitated by minimizing the alleged diversity and sacro-religious quality of the norms of diverse cultures and focussing on policies that address the actual aspirations of contemporary people.

A first goal and one that in our zeal for reform often gets overlooked is the need for the maintenance of minimum world order. In a world of potentially instant armageddon, the old Roman maxim *fiat justitia pereat mundus* – let there be justice even though the world should perish – carries the seeds of self-destruction. Efforts at change and our choice of the appropriate tempo of change must take into account the distribution of power in the world.

Our discussion has assumed an unbroken projection of current trends – a continuation of the present into the future. This is an easy and reassuring assumption because these are trends that seem to allow for an increase in the welfare function. Yet it is most dangerous. Radical disjunctions are just as likely as organic continuations. Global war, a world wide economic collapse, plague or epidemic, a nuclear disaster triggered by terrorism or accident or an ecological disaster are all quite thinkable and would completely change the straight line projections we have been working with. Incremental developments could have similar effects. The exhaustion of hydro-carbon resources before a substitute is found or, as is quite likely, a technological breakthrough leading to the radical diminution of the cost per energy unit would completely reshuffle the cards in the global political deck.

Any one of these contingencies would lead to radical changes in future decision processes. Virtually all of them underline the fact that our discussions and implicit images of the future and its possibilities assume that these things will not happen. That is not a certainty. But because we have assumed it, many current political activities aimed at averting such crises have been characterized as themselves pathological and appropriate targets for change.

Consider the arms race: It may be viewed as an unnecessary exercise in greed by the military industrial complex or as a necessary way of enhancing security in an ugly but unyielding reality. Economic measures taken by the industrial states may be viewed as devices to deprive the world's poor of their due or as desperate efforts to stave off economic collapse in the industrial States themselves. The point here is that the discipline of a systemic view still sometimes reveal positive aspects of activities otherwise viewed as pathological or pathological aspects of activities otherwise viewed as positive. Thus a comprehensive and systemic view is an important step in the determination of goals.

Another realistic constraint which the function of clarification of goals must contend with is the world political system and, in particular, the super-power rivalry. This is something our discussions appear to have actively ignored. Two mighty powers with different social and political structures and essentially incompatible views of how societies should be organized confront each other in a strategic arena which includes both the earth and near space. Because both are industrial and science-based and have current and potential resource requirements that extend far beyond their own territories, political arrangements throughout the world which assure one's supplies or deprive one's adversary are appraised with great care. From the perspective of each Power, every change in the world – political, legal, social, economic – has a military valence. Conversely, the perspective of everyone else in the world, allies as well as neutrals, must take account of the strategic moves of the giants.

Most observers believe that a major deterrent to overt and probably globally catastrophic conflict between the superpowers has been the rough equivalence of the capacity of each to wreak unacceptable havoc on the other. This has been aptly described as the balance of terror. This sterile balance was established and is maintained by the arms race, an intensely competitive armaments process which has sometimes included a mutually balancing arrangement optimistically called "arms control". Given the reciprocal distrust of the superpowers, there appears to be no alternative to a continuation of the arms race, with its painfully expensive diversion of funds from more productive and socially desirable activities to the bolstering of already unbelievably destructive arsenals. Paradoxically, its systemic function seems to be a world security maintenance device.

Changes in legal, social, and economic arrangements which are perceived as compromising the security or power positions of the superpowers will be strenuously resisted. The more the proposed changes take on a security dimension, the more stoutly will they be resisted. In planning for the world welfare system, these systemic considerations must be carefully weighed, for in addition to all the usual restraints on planned social change, these aspects of contemporary world politics set a limit to change potentials.

For the next several decades, those committed to moving the international community to a new world order have several options. One is to confront the First and Second Worlds in adversarial fashion; another, is to accept the concerns of the First and Second Worlds as given and to accommodate them, seeking change where possible, but remaining alert to special opportunities occasioned by shifts in international political circumstances. We might call this the "Hammarskjöld approach", for it was characteristic of the diplomatic technique of that great statesman whose accomplishments are too often attributed to an alleged international political constellation rather than to their architect's imagination, courage and judiciousness. The Hammarskjöld approach recognizes that there are areas of substantive agreements between the different power groups of the world. Where there are not, it finds whatever room for maneuver exists and exploits it creatively.

Our discussions expressed substantial agreement on the goals or objectives toward which the international system should aim. Whether derived from older cultural and religious traditions or postulated in a secular and existential manner, the key principle is the dignity of the individual. Nineteenth century philosophical radicalism and twentieth century liberalism were content to view the organized community's responsibility to the dignity of the individual as limited to the provision of merely civil and political rights. The international consensus and indeed the consensus of our colleagues here is that international responsibility extends beyond the political realm to economic, cultural, and as we shall see, even ecological rights. We demand of political systems that they provide their citizens abundance and opportunity in wealth, education, the acquisition of skill, affection, respect, health and life expectancy, in addition to political rights. It has become common to refer to these as the welfare functions of the State, and they may be described in terms of all the components of a world public order. The aggregate of human rights demands and prescriptions are crystallizing into a conception that this international welfare system is a type of minimum standard of acceptable government. Man is the measure.

But not the only measure. World order is made up of many social constellations for each of which a degree of recognized distinctive competence is necessary if it is to discharge its functions with regard to its constituents. This was a subject of some misunderstanding in our discussions, a misunderstanding which may have derived from the term sovereignty itself.

It is curious that a discussion about the design and construction of a new world order should rely on a term crafted centuries ago in a different context and for purposes quite different from ours. Jean Bodin and Thomas Hobbes meant something quite different by "sovereignty". Over the centuries the term has become encrusted with layer upon layer of connotation. Instead of side-tracking ourselves with analytical and etymological exercises, I suggest we eschew the term and address ourselves to the empirical questions which are really at issue.

Our task is to design an international system which will best achieve the goals expressed in the United Nations and in other authoritative international fora by

1. protecting the political integrity and the coherence of the internal, social and economic processes of territorial communities from unlawful pressures by other communities;
2. ensuring the subordination of national territorial communities to the international community in those social, economic and human rights matters for which the international community has prescribed;
3. establishing the competence of the international community to oblige individual States to act affirmatively or forebear from acting in ways deleterious to others.

If we address ourselves to these questions, there is no need to pursue the historical meaning of the term "sovereignty".

All of this may be described as the emerging constitutional law of a world community which allocates competence to different communities subject to review for conformity with fundamental human rights norms, not because States, as such, have rights, but because as Professor Bernhardt suggested, States are useful and often indispensable instruments for achieving human rights. The world community must make this allocation because its centralized organs lack both the resources and the decisional infrastructure to do everything. Who indeed would even want an international bureaucracy of that magnitude? Rather than being in conflict with human rights, this system of "sovereignty", if we must use that troublesome term, must serve as an instrument for the realization of human rights.

Though the goals of an international welfare system reach most aspects of world public order and need not be set out at this point, attention should be drawn to one matter of particular importance: the environment. It is increasingly viewed as a common resource, as well it must, and must be considered in more detail in later remarks.

II. Institutions

Since the time of Aristotle, we have thought of government in terms of three branches or organs: the legislature, the executive and the judiciary. In complex societies, particularly those in which technology plays an important role, this venerable categorization overlooks a number of important functions which loomed large in many of our discussions. To account for them, I propose to organize the review of our work under five functions and to refer to international organizations when appropriate under each.[1] The functions are

Intelligence – the gathering of information relevant to law-making, its evaluation and timely transmission to law-makers;

Pre-Legislation – lobbying and drafting;

1 Ordinarily, one would examine seven functions; see McDougal, Lasswell and Reisman, "The World Constitutive Process of Authoritative Decision" reprinted in McDougal and Reisman, *International Law Essays* (1981).

Prescribing – actual law-making;
Applying – the application of law in specific disputes and its implementation or enforcement;
Appraising – making general assessments of the performance of the entire international legal system, the extent to which it is achieving its objectives and, if not, the reasons why.
We will consider these seriatim.

Intelligence

Rational reaction to the challenges of our rapidly changing milieu requires a timely flow of accurate and usable information about political, economic, social and environmental matters. In developed legal systems, law-makers and other decisionmakers are served by government research centers, research staffs, hearings, and those various intelligence agencies generally unmentioned in polite company. If the international system is to legislate effectively, it too will require enhanced flows of information. Some is already provided by existing services within the United Nations and other specialized agencies and some by the network of non-governmental agencies. But much more is required.

We have been instructed about the research activities of UNITAR, which is slowly becoming the center of a network of international "think tanks" scattered about the world. In addition, a new and effective world order will require a comparable network of world observatories for environmental monitoring as well as a World Human Rights Observatory. Some of these institutions exist in nascent form at the national and international level. Similarly, the United Nations University may play some role in this effort and may coordinate activities with the great national universities such as the one whose guests we are at this moment.

Pre-legislative functions

The modern state is characterized by institutionalized processes for determining policy and expressing it in legislative terms which can be made operational. One often forgets that much of the mass of legislation produced each year by national legislatures is shaped in processes anterior to the formally legislative. Indeed, without these anterior processes, it is unlikely that legislatures could even begin to discharge their functions. Pre-legislative functions may be performed by legislative committees, drafting committees, private lawyers and so on. In the United States, law student organizations sometimes do all the onerous research and drafting of bills which are then submitted by formal legislators.

Internationally, the pre-legislative function is performed by entities such as the International Law Commission, UNCITRAL, by UN and specialized agency committees, by scholarly organizations such as the Institut de Droit International and the International Law Association and by individual scholars. Many participants here have emphasized the need for enhanced pre-legislative activities and some have suggested quantitative and qualitative changes in the ILC. Many suggested more ILC's as well as an expanded ILC operating in chambers and other specialized commissions producing drafts in their own arcane areas. One would also hope that there will be more activities by law students in different countries, acting transnationally, in the researching and drafting of international legislation.

Prescription or law-making

Much of our discussion focussed in one form or another on law-making. Procedures for the establishment of authoritative and effective policies are the *sine qua non* of a community undergoing rapid change. As the group reports indicate, there was wide agreement on the need to improve this process, in some cases by more institutionalization and, in others, by less. While the United Nations General Assembly has become more democratic, its effective focus, as a number of participants observed, has shifted increasingly from security, the organization's original *raison d'être*, to social and economic matters. Security agreements have increasingly been regionalized and strategic policy, a matter affecting all, has increasingly been arrogated by a two-member cartel.

A number of papers appraised treaty-making and codification from different perspectives. Some observed that the enchantment with codification was a phenomenon which flourished strongly after World War II, especially among the new States, who viewed it as a way of enhancing their role in the reshaping of inherited law. More radically, new States and some older non-European States have sometimes claimed that they are not bound by traditional international law because they did not participate in its creation; rather, they insist that international law was a European creation that was imposed upon them. Unfortunately, it is impossible to make such clean breaks with the past. As the American novelist William Faulkner put it: "The past is not dead; it is not even past." In fact, given the numerous additions to the corpus of international law during the past 30 years, the assertion that international law is a European product is, as Judge Elias stated, no longer factually correct. As for those norms that are legacies of the imperial period, they must, as Judge El-Erian contended, be judged on their merits and their contemporary utility, not on their provenance. As the Chinese proverb puts it, the color of a cat does not matter; the important thing is that it can catch mice.

In the future, more formal arenas will be making law, some of it akin to "rule-making" in national systems. Specialized arenas will be producing what may be called international statute law for highly technical areas. Moreover, regions may be expected to produce more prescriptions to regulate the more intense interactions in their own global sectors. Despite its express authorization in the Charter, for many the word regionalism has ominous connotations of spheres of influence, derived from experience with such regional principles as the Monroe Doctrine, the Brezhnev Doctrine and their many corollaries. But it is worth remembering that regionalism has also been a useful banner for national collaboration in keeping both superpowers out. The challenge is to design legal principles which will enhance the positive aspects of regionalism while minimizing its abuses. There will hence be a need *first* to develop a set of jurisdictional principles, akin to those found in advanced federal systems, allocating competence as between the international community as a whole and regions, specifying in which matters the regions may prescribe and in which more general norms are peremptory and cannot be deviated from, *second*, to develop jurisdictional principles for allocating competence for law-making as between regions and *third* to draft principles regarding the susceptibility of regional states to regional competence in matters in which a particular regional State dissents. And, of course, as Ambassador Theutenberg noted, the exclusivity of regionalism must be balanced by an increased exchange of information and perspectives between regions.

The General Assembly of the United Nations, as the international institution with certain similarities to and aspirations to be a world parliament, will no doubt continue to try to extend its law-making competence. Professor Puig admonished us to avoid assuming that "one State – one vote" equals "one man – one vote". Aside from numerical disparity, the quality of the governments voting might be considered. Numbers themselves have created illusions. Because the Assembly has frequently gone beyond its base of effective power, it has often endangered *pro tanto* its international law-making function. The issue cannot be concealed by mystical invocation of the word 'consensus', which has of late infiltrated the international lexicon. Consensus is frequently used as a code word for the outcomes of a very complex parliamentary political process in which the more conventional parliamentary techniques of voting no longer fit a uniquely assymetrical constellation of power. Because of the very agreeable connotations of the word 'consensus', redolent of venerated concepts such as "sovereign equality" and "consent", there is a tendency to assume that consensus is the basis of contemporary international law. This is misleading. We have law precisely because we do not always agree; hence an indispensable indicator of law is a sanction, an attendant communication to those who are less than happy with the law that the community intends to enforce it.[2] Even where there is a consensus, there may be resistance. Frequently, the word 'consensus' is employed in a self-delusory way precisely because a proposed norm enjoyed insufficient support and would not otherwise have been passed.

A number of members of the seminar could not agree with Professor Suy that so-called indirect sanctions – "informal pressures and general opprobrium" – were enough to make resolutions of the General Assembly "a modern tool for standard setting and rule creation". Law-making involves not only determining policy, but also communicating authority and, equally important, communicating the capacity and willingness to make the normative assertions effective. Because there is often no congruence between a majority, even a consensus in the General Assembly, and a power base sufficient to make particular policy effective, it is delusory to contend that the Assembly is making law in cases where it lacks such a base. But it would be equally wrong to assume that power is the only ingredient of law. Majority and consensus in organs like the General Assembly may often perform latent law-making functions. As Professor Yasseen noted, traditionally the concept of "practice" as evidence of general custom was sought by painstaking investigation of the archives of the world. In the contemporary

2 See generally Reisman, "International Law-Making: A Process of Communication", *Proceedings of The American Society of International Law*, 1981.

world, voting in the General Assembly may be a more accurate and simpler method for assessing the extent and depth of a general *opinio juris*. And even in the absence of an effective control base, Assembly resolutions, by virtue of the central role of the United Nations in the world community, may be less than legally binding, as Professor Yasseen put it, but more than only morally binding.

One of the commonest methods of law-making today (and one on which we were instructed most usefully by Ambassador do Nascimento e Silva) is the multi-lateral treaty. This modality recommends itself when the problem addressed is common to many States, when the treaty-makers seek to create common standards or as in the problem of terrorism, when it requires for its effectiveness homologous behavior. This modality might be improved by lowering the numerical threshold for entry-into-force and by emphasizing the Vienna Convention's good faith obligation of signatories to comport themselves in ways that do not frustrate the treaty until such time as they have indicated that they do not intend to ratify it.

The multilateral law-making conference, in addition to its manifest function, has also demonstrated an extremely important latent function: the acceleration of the crystallization of customary norms that have not attained adequate parliamentary support in the conference but which win wide adherence in practice. As was noted, this is both useful and potentially perilous.

Despite a variety of opinions, the general view was that formal legislation will not totally supplant custom, since custom is an allpervasive and inevitable feature of any social process. We might restate the old Roman maxim to read *ubi societas ibi mos*. Custom is proto-law, i. e., it reflects the expectations of members of a community about appropriate behavior. The traditional indicators of custom were practice and subjectivities, *opinio juris sive necessitatis*. But, in fact, any indicator may serve. Practice, one might add, includes both actions as well as protests of action, condemnations and other indications of appraisal of actions in terms of law.

Application

All of us recognize the fact that the most dramatic and urgent problem of contemporary international law is its inability to apply existing law to disputes in effective and timely fashion. Part of the problem derives from the distribution of power in the world political arena and the unwillingness of actors to submit to law. Yet there are things that international lawyers can do. Many of them were explored in our discussions. Since some of the suggestions involved perforce constitutional changes in the formal international system, discussions of application necessarily brought our attention to techniques for change at the most basic constitutive level.

In functional terms, application involves the designation of the norms appropriate to a particular dispute, their specification, a decision, implementation and enforcement. In a developed system, the application function is generally performed by specialized institutions such as courts. Given the special jurisdictional problems of courts in the international system, application here is often performed by political agencies such as the Security Council or General Assembly, by specialized agencies or by international courts and tribunals.

It was Georges Scelle who taught us that national agencies are also international decisionsmakers in what he felicitously called *le dédoublement fonctionnel*. Our discussions tended to focus almost exclusively on the weaknesses and structural defects of international institutions. More attention, *pace* Scelle, might have been given to national institutions, particularly to the current and future role of national courts in matters of the protection of human rights, as argued by Professors Lillich and Chandrahasan.

A preliminary problem in application is the confirmation of salient facts. In domestic systems this can be done by means of subpoena powers. Internationally, this is not yet the case. Much attention has been directed at developing a better fact-finding procedure, particularly one which is not subject to a veto in the Security Council. Fact finding is also important in the activities of many other international organizations. One might note in passing the adoption by the International Law Association at its Belgrade meeting of the Model Rules on Fact-Finding drafted by Professor Franck.

While many institutions must of necessity apply law in the international system, it is difficult to imagine substantial gains in world order without an enhanced role for the International Court of Justice. Professor Suy noted the precipitous decline in the number of accessions to the compulsory jurisdiction of the Court; Professor Broms suggested a variety of reasons which might account for this bleak development. Equally disturbing is the fact that when the Court renders a judgment under its contentious jurisdiction, enforcement action under Charter Article 94(2) may apparently be frustrated by the veto. While a mandatory enforcement by the Council would appear too mechanical (since this would prevent that body from reappraising the matter in a new context), the notion that a single state can nullify an authoritative decision made in The Hague by a veto in New York seems incompatible with an acceptable world order.

Many of the innovations discussed would involve changes in the United Nations Charter, a process which is indeed contemplated by the Charter itself at periodic intervals. Alas, any changes that would seriously restrict the powers of those states that benefit from the Yalta formula may be expected to be strenouously resisted and, in formal procedures, to be blocked. Happily, there are alternative modalities for securing change. Interpretation by a UN organ of its own competence was suggested by Judge Jimenez de Aréchaga. Another possibility proposed by Judge Elias and explored in a number of discussions was the increased use of the advisory jurisdiction of the International Court. Thus, the General Assembly, for example, could pose a question to the Court on the proper interpretation of a provision or the propriety of an innovative practice and then accept its authoritative interpretation of the Charter. In the *Namibia* case, the Court affirmed its own general competence to conduct what we in the United States call "judicial review". In the *Admissions* cases, early in the history of the United Nations, the Court demonstrated an acute sensitivity to the power restraints of the world arena; and in the *Expenses* case, it actually tried, perhaps unsuccessfully, to change constitutional practice despite Great Power opposition. The point here is that there are alternative ways of securing Charter revision.

In too many cases, the organized international community proves unable to apply and/or to enforce, a problem which is likely to continue into the future. May a State then resort to self-help measures, sometimes using high levels of coercion? As would be expected, a range of sentiments about the utility to future world order of unilateral humanitarian interventions was expressed. And coercion initiated by non-state entities? Dr. Diallo observed that the individual's resort to violence against the apparatus of the State has been most important in terminating colonialism and seemed unwilling to condemn it prospectively and in general. Professor Grahl-Madsen cited Vattel in support of such a right, adding that in an interdependent world, local violence often transnationalizes. Hence Judge Jimenez de Aréchaga contended that the international system cannot revert to even the most minimal theory of just war. In fact, there would appear to be such a theory with regard to anti-colonial struggles. The Declaration on Friendly Relations would appear to permit an entity in such a struggle to claim the aid of other states and permit if not oblige other states to help it.

Appraisal

It may seem strange to suggest that appraisal is an indispensable decision function, but alas, even the best designed mechanism, as Professor Grahl-Madsen observed, must be examined from time to time to make sure that it is performing adequately and, if not, why not. Appraisal involves reconsideration of goals as well as an assessment of the aggregate performance of the institutions of decisions in achieving those goals. The United Nations Charter provides for periodic review, as we observed, and the International Court untertakes review and revision of its rules from time to time. Yet there are few institutional arrangements for appraising the aggregate performance of the varied interwoven practices and institutions that constitute the international system.

In national systems, appraisal is conducted by a controller-general, by specially appointed review panels and often by scholars. To a large extent this function has been performed internationally by individual scholars and by some institutes. Few of them, however, have been able to maintain sustained efforts, and even fewer have worked with a breadth as comprehensive as the agenda Professor Grahl-Madsen designed for us. In the general debate on 17 June, many noted that this is a decision function which could be improved by further international meetings of scholars, during which careful consideration of the adequacy of the performance of different parts of the international system be undertaken.

III. Components of a world public order

The projected and preferred constitutional arrangements we have been exploring have little value *per se* but exist essentially as instruments for shaping all the social arrangements in which human beings participate: internal political and civic arenas, domestic economies, educational systems, health systems, domestic human rights and so on. A comprehensive review and projection of these arrangements would consider every value process within the territorially-based community. Our discussions at the Seminar touched on some of these arrangements: self-determination, human rights, economic order and the environment.

Self-determination

Self-determination has been one of the rallying points of contemporary international law and politics and the banner under which almost two-thirds of the States of the world have marched to independence. In fact, self-determination is often confused with de-colonization, a historical process, now largely completed, in which the results of Western European imperial expansion (other empires formed at the same time have apparently been excluded) were undone, with indigenous elites displacing European ones. The few examples that remain are viewed as pathological and the progress is likely to be all but concluded by the end of the century. But while decolonization is finite, self-determination is virtually infinite, for modern nation-States are patchworks of religious, linguistic, and ethnic groups which could be "peoples". Moreover, the process of personal individuation and group formation which is encouraged by contemporary international law, as Professor Kimminich noted in the general debate, has the potential for generating new "peoples" all the time. In this respect, self-determination may fragment existing communities into components that are not viable and invite irredentist diplomacy and mischievous ethnic manipulation as a form of intervention by other States. The *Western Sahara* opinion of the International Court reflects authoritative thinking concerning this problem.

Many have asked whether the classic doctrine of self-determination leading to full statehood should be projected into the 21st century without some reconsideration. In the future, one would hope that discussion will shift from arguments about whether particular aspirants do or do not constitute a "people" (and hence are entitled to self-determination) to the development of a set of procedures and a spectrum of institutional arrangements which will allow international supervision of the protection of group rights and their political and social integrity in ways that meet that group's needs as well as the needs of other affected communities. It is now clear that in an interdependent world, self-determination is never a purely internal, politically autistic act, but a major international event with intense and potentially grievous effects on other States and non-territorial groups and long term consequences on the world community. No one wants a rigid theory of self-determination which precipitates rather than resolves conflict.

The challenge to the jurist at this crossroads is to transform self-determination from a rigid doctrine which must *eo ipso* lead to a single form of political organization into a policy which seeks in each idiosyncratic context to enhance the continuity, integrity and quality of group life in ways compatible with the interests of others. Thus self-determination may be realized in the future by any of a wider spectrum of institutional arrangements than that envisaged in Resolution 1514 (XV), from internationally supervised minority guarantees through different forms of autonomy and association on through to formal independence. The "right" form of self-determination will be that which in its context, best approximates the international principles and the needs of all concerned actors. The

Åland experience, of which we are all especially conscious, is an instructive example of a supple and creative approach to self-determination.

The same analysis may be useful with regard to the increasingly urgent problem of mini-States. There are four especially pertinent problems here:

1. Should existing mini-States be deprived *ex post facto* of the rights of an existing state?
2. Should mini-States be admitted – and under what terms – to the United Nations and other international organizations?
3. How should mini-States that lack the infrastructural capacity to fulfill the basic requirements of their citizens be helped by other States and by the international community?
4. Should very small territorial communities be encouraged in the future to seek full statehood?

The first three questions were thoroughly discussed in the papers and comments. The fourth – which may be the most important – has been ignored but may serve as an object lesson of the point discussed above. Perhaps we should no longer expect the principle of self-determination to lead invariably to full statehood. The real thrust of policy is self-determination of people and not of States. Since international law now has a welfare function which establishes, as of right, human standards, a threshold self-determination question must be whether a candidate community has the capacity to provide its inhabitants with those minima. If not, then that community should be urged to achieve self-determination in a different fashion – association, autonomy, integration, minority guarantees and so on. General Assembly Resolution 1541 (XV) is suggestive of the direction which we may wish to pursue here.

As for the existing mini-States, there can be little question of international responsibility to help them achieve the conditions of human dignity. Professors Amoah and Schram developed a number of creative suggestions for enhancing self-reliance as well as for infrastructural supports through the United Nations.

Human rights

Human rights, like law-making, were a leitmotif in our discussions, for human rights, most broadly understood, have been taken as the major goal and the major justification of world order. At the same time, one must note, as Professor Cervenka and Mr. Nobel said, the growing brutality of power and the use of torture and violence to suppress all dissent. Precisely because of this, a key concern in our discussion was that of making human rights effective by limiting the atavistic conception of state sovereignty, subjecting it to an international human rights jurisdiction and, as Professor Grahl-Madsen suggested, in the Vattelian mode, delegitimizing thugs who seize power. Some attention was given to the possibility of incremental non-recognition, for example by refusing the envoys of a government, acting in gross violation of international human rights, *exequatur* and of denying such rulers themselves the perquisites of sovereignty. The conflict between effectiveness and *de jure* authority is, of course, quite venerable. In the *Tinoco* arbitration, Chief Justice Taft decided in favor of effectiveness. In the *Namibia* case, the International Court was asked to indicate how third States should behave with regard to the continued unlawful presence of South Africa in Namibia and indicated that the question of the denial of the perquisites of recognition to an unlawful occupier is much more complex than it might at first appear.

There was relatively little discussion of the possibility, raised by Professor Bernhardt, of mobilizing people in non-governmental operations to sanction international law-breakers, but there seemed to be high hopes for a role for domestic courts in this area in the future.

Wealth

A key part of the new world order, in some ways its engine of change, has been the self-styled New Economic Order, a systematic effort to revise the legal regime over resources, trade and industrial technology in ways which consciously discriminate in favor of the weakest and least developed States of the world. Though this program is attributed to the 6th Special Session of the General Assembly, the roots of efforts in this area go back, as Professor Ohlin was at pains to emphasize, to discussions at the end of the Second World War, were manifested in the abortive International Trade Organization, and are reflected in the GATT and in a variety of other early efforts.

One would of course have to be morally defective not to recoil from the maldistribution of resources and life opportunities about the globe and the dreadful poverty and life expectancy reduction that so many of our fellow human beings are subjected to. There must be change in the most basic institutions of production and distribution. Nor is there any reason to treat the "market" as sacrosanct. The doctrine of the free market is misleading; the market is not natural but is a complex artifact which has been carefully crafted to indulge some and deprive others. It can be changed. The problem is whether the proposals put forward are optimally designed to achieve that end.

In the process of establishing a New International Economic Order (NIEO), two tendencies, apparent in the papers by Dr. Hossein and Minister Deng, have operated in almost dialectic contradiction. One involves the increasing internationalization of approach with emphasis on such code words as "common heritage", a planetary approach to planning and so on. The second involves an increasing nationalization, epitomized in the claims for national sovereignty over resources. It is precisely here that some of our colleagues encounter a problem with the NIEO in its current phase. I, for one, wish to limit state sovereignty not only in human rights matters but in matters which influence other States or the entire planet. I would have thought that the Third World, controlling as it does, the major international fora, would now be quite willing to do this. But, *mirabile dictu,* NIEO is in many ways a celebration and extension of state sovereignty in matters with potentially devastating consequences for the world economy.

To me this seems a serious misperception of common interest which is unlikely to endure into the 21st century. Like it or not, there are, as Professor Grahl-Madsen put it, certain elements and processes which are essential to the survival of the planet and of our species. If we ask a nation not to use certain things, there should, of course, be a compensation scheme. But an international competence over these resources and processes is the essential point. Can the planet survive without these resources and processes being subjected to, at least, international supervision?

At a lower level of intensity, there are resources which are "vital". Should not processes for their use, pricing, conservation and distribution also be subjected to some supervision? As Professor Ohlin observed, the economic unity of the world means that certain responsibilities must be observed if harm is not to be caused to others. One wonders, for example, whether cartels approved by the Charter of Economic Rights and Duties of States may enhance the economic development of 14 or 15 states while causing enormous injury to others.

One of the more unpleasant aspects of NIEO has been its confrontational character. Both sides share responsibility for this. From the days of the Bandung Conference through a decade of UNCTAD, the industrial States were insufficiently responsive to their poorer and weaker neighbors. The 1973 October War and the effect of the oil boycott were perceived as indications of a new Third World supremacy. As the Declaration of May 1, 1974 put it, "The developing world has become a powerful factor that makes its influence felt in all fields of international acitivity." Now the shoe was on the other foot and the declarations and resolutions took on a more strident tone which still seems to infect and frustrate efforts at North-South dialogue. But the change in world power was not as sweeping and clear cut as it had seemed. With the exception of petroleum, as Professor Ohlin noted, NIEO was suffering a lot of stalemates.

We are in one boat. The key focus of the economic component of a New World Order should be the development of a system that enhances production everywhere as well as improving equitable distribution. It will require compromises. Multinational corporations will have to accept the effective jurisdiction of host States in the Third World as they do in the First World. Third World States will have to abide by agreements, particularly those subjecting disputes to impartial arbitration. The notion that compensation – whether it be full or, as Article 2 of the Charter of Economic Rights and Duties of States puts it, 'appropriate' – need not be paid will simply stop the inflow of private capital. Insofar as that capital source is an important adjunct to scarce public funds, the no-compensation position would appear to be an ill-considered strategy for a New Economic Order.

Overall one must bear in mind that there is a systemic dimension to equity. Not only the equities of certain individuals and groups but also the viability of the system which sustains the lives of many others. Changes that bring about a world-wide collapse will benefit no one. Should not change be regulated at a tempo that takes account of the consequences on others of the changes?

The New Economic Order is also supposed to be international in the sense that it seeks combinations of developing states so that the weakest as well as the more advanced can advance rapidly in economic and social matters. The Declaration's substitution of "preferential and non-reciprocal treatment for developing countries" for equality should indeed have benefitted the very weakest. Unfortunately, it has not always worked that way. The rapid increase in the price of petroleum which accelerated the development of some 15 nations caused hardships to all of the industrialized developed States but was catastrophic for almost 100 other developing States. The doctrine of the "common heritage of mankind", as Judge Oda delicately observed, which might have been used to redress the capriciously unequal distribution of land-based resources, has been increasingly arrogated by coastal and geographically advantaged States, with less and less left as a common heritage.

It would seem most appropriate for the world community to view the New Economic Order not as a conclusion, but only the beginning of an effort to redesign resource use and trade patterns so that all the peoples of the world may ultimately share the benefits of the planet. This may require an international taxing power and may be helped at some point by revenues from ocean mining. Whatever the international changes, here more than elsewhere, we must bear in mind that we are not concerned with securing justice for States. No one has ever seen a State starve or get kwashiorkor. We are concerned with social justice for people. Here, then, is the place to pierce the corporate veil and disaggregate national statistics to be assured that all people actually benefit.

Environment

In response to the criticism that we are dealing with 30 different issues, Judge Lachs said that we are dealing with 30 different aspects of one issue. In many ways, the increasing concern of the world community with its comprehensive environment is inextricably linked to the New International Economic Order and basic conceptions of human rights. In the same way that NIEO ist replete with environmental statements, the Stockholm Conference on the Environment a year before expressed many of the concerns of NIEO. The reason for this apparent replication is that the more intense application of science and technology to resources in the hope of increasing the material conditions of all human beings has put stresses on the ecological balance of our planet which, though imperfectly understood, are feared to threaten grave long term consequences. This is the problem: pollution and, more generally, environmental deterioration are not severable evils that can be exorcised, but inevitable by-products of intense and otherwise desirable resource uses.

Several points are clear. Acid rain has no nationality. Dramatic examples like acid rain and the global ecological function of the Brazilian rain forests, only two of a host of others, underline the international aspects of problems for which there are simply no national solutions. Insofar as the resources being used are a *res communis,* there is already a growing sense of international competence for dealing with the problems associated with use. A prime example may be found in the maritime environment provisions of the draft Law of the Sea Treaty and, in more complex fashion, in the *Nuclear Tests* case. Insofar as the resource being used is located within the territorial confines of a nation-State, claims of sovereign control truculently meet international demands. The international responsibility of the State with the resource for injuries to others, even in the absence of fault, could be derived from general principles as expressed in the *Lake Lanoux* and *Trail Smelter* cases. Unfortunately, the injuries contemplated may be of a magnitude beyond monetary reparation. My own view is that national control must yield here to planetary planning and control, with, as Professor Grahl-Madsen has suggested, appropriate compensation to the State concerned for losses from the use of a resource it has forsworn. The gap here between aspiration and realization may prove unbridgeable. For the near future, let us hope that nations comport themselves according to the maxim *sic utere tuo ut alienum non laedas.*

IV. The future

Looking toward the future, a number of lessons can be drawn. First, as the King observed in his speech of greeting to us, the project which we have set ourselves to does not end with a single conference or a single report. We are in a process of ceaseless change, hence the tasks we have posed for ourselves must be performed continuously. The project should be made a more explicit part of our international legal duties, for in the future, international lawyers must play an even larger role than in the past in the redesigning and refinement of world order. In performing this function, as Professor Sheng Yu put it, international lawyers must be champions of international justice. And there must be more of them! Dr. Toman exhorted us to increase the "army of international lawyers". The *Institut* in a recent meeting urged that the teaching of international law be made a compulsory subject in law schools; one would hope that that teaching will include a component devoted to the ongoing appraisal and redesign of world order. As in so many other areas of the New World Order, there must be a simultaneous increase in production and distribution. We must have more students, more regional meetings and, as Dr. Toman suggested, more transfer of technology in the teaching of international law, by international teaching seminars, international seminars on how to establish and manage that unique and indispensable instrument of legal scholarship, the law journal, and more sharing of information about the most efficient methods for documentation, information storage and retrieval.

It is a tribute to the foresight of Professor Grahl-Madsen and Uppsala University that this seminar was arranged to facilitate the performance of our task. Above all, there should be more meetings on the Uppsala model. They may be undertaken within individual countries, within regions, or, as our own, attempt to be universal in recruitment as well as in scope. Encounters and opportunities to interact, exchange ideas and debate positions are indispensable for us better to fulfill our mission of creating a new world order of human dignity.

3.2. International Law in a Multicultural World
Report of Working Group I

TASLIM O. ELIAS

The theme discussed by the Group was "International law in a multicultural world". It was noted that this theme was of a very general nature and that the best way to structure the work of the group was to discuss the various reports (falling under the theme of the group), in the same order in which they were presented during the plenary sessions.

1. The first subject discussed was consequently the "Growth of the international community and qualitative shift in international legal relations" and the rapporteur and co-rapporteur (Professors Jimenez de Aréchaga and Franck) offered some introductory comments based on their respective reports (see papers 5.3 and 5.4).

The ensuing discussion was focused on the principle of self-determination of peoples. The rapporteur reiterated what was said in his report, namely that although UN practice in this field had primarily concerned peoples under colonial rule, the right to self-determination was not limited to those cases. The Friendly Relations Declaration of 1970[1] thus made clear that the principle of self-determination also applied to peoples within independent and sovereign States. In this respect, however, it was important to note that the Friendly Relations Declaration of 1970 also contained "safeguard clauses", aimed at protecting the national unity and the territorial integrity of existing States.

One participant felt that the principle of self-determination should be given a narrow interpretation, restricting its application to cases of decolonisation. A wider interpretation would be extremely dangerous and could threaten the integrity of new States. Instead, the efforts of new States to create a feeling of national unity within their countries should be supported by the international community.

Another participant pointed out that the recognition and protection of a national identity was the essential element of the principle of self-determination. The right to liberation should not be restricted to colonial movements, there also existed post-colonial suppressors.

1 Declaration on Principles of International Law concerning Friendly Relations and Co-operation among States in accordance with the Charter of the United Nations. United Nations General Assembly Resolution 2625 (XXV) of 24 October 1970.

The non-applicability of the right to self-determination was illustrated by one participant with the example of the civil war in Nigeria. Nigeria had been a political homogeneous entity since 1914. Those who called themselves Biafrans were treated in the same way as other citizens, in fact the first president of Nigeria had been indigene of the area called Biafra. One of the distinguishing features of the secession attempt of Biafra was that one ethnic group wanted to bring with it other ethnic groups in a carved-out territory which lacked ethnic homogeneity.

It was pointed out that the United Nations always supported the integrity of Nigeria: that the "safeguard clause" was working. The safeguard clause could in the future protect states like Yugoslavia and Belgium. An independent and sovereign State which possesses a government representative of the whole of its people is always safeguarded from any claim for self-determination by a part of its population. Many participants felt, however, that it was undesirable to apply the principle of self-determination to sovereign States.

One participant felt it was possible to throw light on the application of the principle of self-determination by relating the principle to standards of treatment, i. e. to the quality of treatment given to peoples. If the treatment was good (as in Biafra), the principle of self-determination was not applicable. If the treatment was in violation of civil, political and human rights (as in former East Pakistan), there was a right to self-determination for the oppressed people. In the latter case, however, it had to be noted that the United Nations was opposed to the Indian intervention in what was to become Bangladesh.

Another participant thought that the focusing on quality of treatment was a feasible approach. He wondered whether one could or should also discuss a criterion of geographical distance in this connexion.

It was strongly felt by one participant that the only correct approach to the problem was to start from a formula which was included in the two International Convenants on Human Rights of 1966. According to the Covenants "*all* peoples have the right to self-determination". Hence, every people was entitled to self-determination and not only an oppressed or suppressed people. This was the only correct interpretation of the Covenants. It was quite true that the provisions of the Covenants were dangerous for existing States since there were very few homogeneous States around in the world community. That did not, however, alter the legal position. In this context article 2 par. 4 of the UN Charter was of paramount importance and it constituted a categorical prohibition for States against the use of force. Nevertheless the prohibition applied only to inter-state conflicts and not to internal conflicts. Admittedly, States could not intervene on behalf of insurgents and sometimes when a state of belligerency was recognized they could not even give military assistance to Governments. As long as the United Nations Charter was not amended, any attempt in a General Assembly resolution to admit the use of force by one State against another on behalf of a national liberation movement was unconstitutional. It was important to remember that the Friendly Relations Declaration, although adopted with consensus, was not in its totality declaratory of existing law.

Another participant agreed that the Friendly Relations Declaration perhaps might not reflect existing law in all instances, but he was of the opinion that the 1970 Declaration had introduced new elements in the classical international law and that these elements had to be taken into account. Thus, the Friendly Relations Declaration states that peoples fighting for their right to self-determination "are entitled to seek and to receive support in accordance with the purposes and principles of the Charter"'. He was not, however, of the opinion that such support could include *military* assistance, unless that was authorized by competent organs of the United Nations.

The problem of the definition of "peoples" was then brought up in the discussion. There was general agreement that no clear-cut definition of this concept existed. It was pointed out that one had to look at the practice of United Nations organs. Unilateral interpretations of States were not helpful, while, on the other hand, an authoritative interpretation by the International Court of Justice would be most useful. Already today there existed a United Nations practice in these matters. The United Nations dealt with the problems of the Togoland, the Cameroons and Ruanda-Burundi. Different criteria could be taken into account by United Nations organs. In the case of South Africa a "quality of treatment-standard" would illuminate the non-equal treatment of different parts of the population (exemplified by the Bantustans). In the Katanga case a "common resources standard" would show that the whole population of the Congo had during a long time shared the natural resources of the Katanga region (indicating that a right to self-determination for that region was not warranted).

It was maintained that a criterion of legitimacy was established in international law. The right to self-determination was considered as realized if a State had a Government that represented the whole people and such a state was safeguarded from any claims for self-determination by a part of its own population. In the view of one participant the question of continuity of legal title should also be taken into consideration when restricting States to their present boundaries. In Sri Lanka – which used to be three kingdoms – the British handed over the power to one of the races of the country. The case of Sri Lanka showed that boundaries were not always inviolable. The principle of self-determination applied also in cases of post-colonial domination.

One participant felt that the discussion was somewhat unrealistic. In his opinion it was not possible to base a right to self-determination on the concept of "peoples". For new states – as he had pointed out before – it was an important task to create a united people, a national identity. "People" was not only a cultural-historical-linguistic concept, above all it was a social concept. He also expressed some doubts whether the safeguard clause really was workable. Even if the United Nations General Assembly functioned as a "judge" in the matter, the problems of interpretation would be difficult to handle. It was an interesting suggestion that denial of human rights could serve as a potential criterion, all the same, he doubted whether considerations of this kind could fruitfully be related to the principle of self-determination. Since this principle was in the United Nations used as a political strategy, one could well ask whether it at all should be characterized in legal terms.

Another participant reiterated his view that the principle of self-determination was not limited to colonial situations. The Scottish people and the Welsh people could – if they so wished – exercise the right to self-determination. Geographical distance was not important from a legal point of view, although it had practical repercussions (as in Bangladesh). Geographical proximity did not mean that for example the Lapps in the Scandinavian countries did not have a right to self-determination.

This statement induced another participant to put the question whether the Lapps could be said to have an *absolute* right to self-determination. The question could also be phrased in a different way. Since the Lapps had the right to vote (and were treated in accordance with international humanitarian standards), could it not be argued that they already exercised their right to self-determination.

2. The group then went on to discuss the subject of "Customary law: From 'Universal' in a European System to 'Regional' in a world System" (see papers 5.5 and 5.6). The rapporteur and co-rapporteur offered some introductory comments. It was agreed that in a conflict between general and regional norms, general norms prevail if they constitute *jus cogens,* while in other situations the concept of *lex specialis* played a prominent role.

The rapporteur (Dr. Feliciano) noted that general and regional norms could coexist (without any conflict) and that regional norms could fill out empty spaces in the legal system.

The co-rapporteur (Professor Rosas) noted that he (in his report) was more inclined to favour universal law than the rapporteur was. The question to be answered was: should international lawyers be more universalists than regionalists. In his opinion there was a clear danger in the "regionalization" and "particularization" of customary law since one would run the risk of losing important common elements in the legal system. From a terminological point of view, "special law" was a more apt expression than "regional law", since special custom was not always limited to certain geographical areas. Special custom could apply between industrialized states or other states, united by a common ideology.

One participant expressed the view that with regard to the conflict between general and regional law, primacy should be given to universality – that was in line with the United Nations Charter. At the same time it should be noted that the International Court of Justice had (as in the *Asylum* Case) recognized regional norms as part of international law.

It was pointed out that the term "region" or "regional" had to be interpreted in a flexible way in this context. It was agreed that separate rules (bilateral or multilateral) could be established as *jus dispositivum,* as long as norms of *jus cogens* were not affected. One participant stressed that the only way to bind third States in international law, was through universal custom.

Reference was again made to the *Asylum* Case where the International Court of Justice offered a standard for determining the scope of regional or local custom: "The Party which relies on a custom of this kind must prove that this custom is established in such a manner that it has become binding on the other

Party [and] . . . that it is in accordance with a constant and uniform usage practised by the States in question". The Court did not find that Colombia had proved the existence of a regional custom with regard to unilateral qualification of the offence of a person seeking diplomatic asylum. The Court went on to say that, "even if it could be supposed that such a custom existed between certain Latin-American States only, it could not be invoked against Peru which, far from having by its attitude adhered to it, has, on the contrary repudiated it . . .".[2]

One participant stressed the need for consent. States which persistently object can "opt out" of a developing customary law, not only in cases of regional law, but also (according to some authors) in cases of general law. However, if in a clearly defined region, nine out of ten States create special custom, there is a strong *presumtion* that State number ten also has accepted the regional norms.

Another participant asserted that such a presumtion could always be rebutted in a regional context but not in a universal one. In respect of general customary law the consent of the defendent State need not to be demonstrated. General customary law was binding for all States. It was also pointed out in the discussion that the International Court of Justice had confirmed this view in the *North Sea Continental Shelf* and *Namibia* cases.

The *Anglo-Norwegian Fisheries* Case was also brought up in the discussion. One participant felt that the Court had applied a principle that had a certain generality, others felt that the circumstances of the case were too specific to lend themselves to any general conclusions. In any event the 1958 Geneva Convention on the territorial Sea established a general rule on the basis of that judgment.

The question was then raised whether States could derogate from multilateral conventions through bilateral or regional custom. To take a concrete example: Could two States agree to derogate from the Vienna Convention on Diplomatic Relations, admitting the opening of diplomatic bags on a bilateral basis? One participant felt this was unlawful since it could undermine the multilateral convention and thus affect the situation of third States. Others, however, felt that derogations were perfectly possible as long as they were not in conflict with *jus cogens*. One participant also pointed out that derogation by custom always could be made from a convention if the concept of *desuetudo* was applicable with regard to the convention.

It was finally pointed out that the era of general conventions might be coming to a halt. Some participants felt pessimistic about the possibility of achieving universal lawmaking conventions in the 1980's. What was to come instead?

One possibility was that custom would play a more important role in the future. The need for identification of regional rules would be highlighted. Interaction between different kinds of customary rules could reshape and change the law as we now know it.

Another possibility – in the view of one participant – was that consensus resolutions of the General Assembly might be looked upon as a source of law. Such resolutions could be seen as a perception of existing practice – or as com-

2 *Colombian-Peruvian Asylum Case, Judgment of November 20th, 1950: I. C. J. Reports 1950*, pp. 276–278.

mitments with regard to future practice. On the other hand the speaker felt that General Assembly Resolutions might fall into disrepute, if they did not correspond to the actual practice of States.

3. The third subject discussed was "A realistic approach to International Law" (see papers 5.1 and 5.2). The rapporteur (Judge Lachs) stressed the following points:

a) International law as a code of conduct between States has been a necessity in relations between States since they came into contact with one another.
b) The impact of Europe on the law shaped by nations of other continents came to an end with the birth of universal international law, including all nations.
c) Contemporary international law is a reality, which exercises an important impact on the life of nations and States.
d) Though violated and transgressed on many occasions, on the whole it is being complied with. This is the result of the self-interest, the element of reciprocity, desire for self-preservation and fear of possible sanctions, though they are rarely applied.
e) The progressive development of international law has been a continuous process, to which we have committed ourselves by Art. 13 of the Charter. This progress is reflected in its universal character, the recognition of the principle of self-determination, the birth of the international community of *jus cogens*, the outlawry of war, the development of ever new institutions – the enrichment of treaty, customary law and general principles of law.
f) Yet its operation and progress face great difficulties resulting from conflicting interests of States. However, it must be recognized that the Adam Smith model of international law belongs to the past: it constitutes a network of rights and obligations, in which the weakest and poorest have to be protected: there is no conflict between the economic and social development and the community as a whole.
g) Faced with the deniers and the cynics, the task of the international lawyer is to work for a further strengthening of the law; show further inventiveness and seek further influence on Governments, to make them more responsive to the needs for the development and compliance with international law.

It was noted that the co-rapporteur on the subject (Professor Dinstein) had asserted the view that General Assembly Resolutions could never *per se* create law, but that they could be declaratory of pre-existing law or that subsequent State practice might reaffirm the principles of such resolutions, thus transforming them into law. The general practice of States accepted as law was the decisive element. If a norm which is *in statu nascendi* is followed by a practice of States that runs counter to it, it will die.

One of the participants felt that this approach was too rigid. He, for his part, distinguished between three types of General Assembly Resolutions that could express or initiate customary law. First, a resolution could restate or "codify" a pre-existing rule of custom (e. g. the Friendly Relations Declaration). Second, a resolution could crystallize an emergent rule, developing a norm *in statu nascendi*

(e. g. the 1963 Declaration on Legal Principles in Outer Space); and third a resolution *de lege ferenda* could initiate a corresponding practice of States and harden into a customary rule (e. g. Resolution 1514 (XV) and the principle of self-determination). – State practice was not always that decisive.

The co-rapporteur asserted, contrary to what the previous speaker had implied, that Resolution 1514 was a rule *in statu nascendi* in 1960. Ghana gained its independence in 1957 and the process of decolonisation had begun before 1960. Resolution 1514 only formed the basis for new law finalized in the subsequent practice of States. One participant pointed out that Resolution 1514 was followed by a series of resolutions creating bodies to monitor and speed-up the decolonisation process.

Another speaker maintained that, on the other hand, the principle that the resources of the high seas and the ocean floor was to be regarded as the common heritage of mankind, had been accepted at the Law of the Sea Conference without any preceding State practice.

3.3. Independence and Interdependence
Report of Working Group II

ENDRE USTOR

Group 2 has dealt with six papers. Professor Gros Espiell and Professor Saxena submitted papers on "Sovereignty, independence and interdependence of nations". Professors Kimminich and De Seynes presented papers on "Material, economic and human limits to activities of mankind: legislating for a new economic order in an ecological context" and Professor Hossain's and Minister Deng's papers tackled the problems of "Natural resources: heritage of nations and mankind."[1]

My present report is intended only to give a short review of the main ideas put forward in the course of the discussions in Group 2. I cannot be exhaustive as I am unable in this brief report to refer to all of the views expressed during the debate. Here and there I shall add my own comments.

Sovereignty

Most members of the group accepted the view of the rapporteurs of the topic. According to this view the concept of sovereignty was a necessary and fundamental part of international law and of international life and politics. To seek to eradicate the concept and confirm its incompatibility with international law as certain doctrinaire schools had attempted, constituted a useless and antihistorical effort not compatible with the world as it exists and the inescapable and undeniable political and mythical force of the idea of sovereignty. The elimination of the concept and the term was – according to this view – utopistic, without sense or reason.

Others referred to the view – expounded in the plenary meetings – according to which the term sovereignty was crafted centuries ago in a different context and for purposes quite different from ours. Jean Bodin and Thomas Hobbes meant something quite different by sovereignty; over the centuries the term had become further encrusted with layer upon leayer of connotation. Instead of analytical and etymological exercises international lawyers would be well advised to eschew the term and address themselves to the empirical questions which are really the issue.

Your rapporteur would like to recall in this connection the four propositions

1 See papers 6.1 through 6.7.

which Jenks[2] borrowed from the English edition of the text book on International Law of the Institute of the Academy of Sciences of the USSR, edited by Kozhevnikov. They go as follows:

1. Sovereignty may be defined as the right of the State freely and at its own discretion to decide its internal and external affairs without violating the rights of other States or the principles and rules of international law.
2. A sovereign State must not in its international relations behave in an arbitrary fashion, without taking account of the recognized principles of international law and the international undertakings which it has voluntarily assumed. To do so would mean to violate the principle of sovereign equality of all the members of the international community. It would undermine the international community and lead to the unlimited rule of force and violence.
3. Entry into an international organization or the conclusion of a treaty involves certain obligations which are to a certain extent a restriction on sovereignty.
4. The violation or arbitrary, unilateral repudiation of freely assumed undertakings cannot be justified by reference to sovereignty.

Stating that he subscribes to these propositions in full, Jenks held that they appear to be reducible to two fundamental principles: first, sovereignty is limited and does not override law; secondly, sovereignty is an essentially relative concept, subject to a process of constant erosion by the assumption of new obligations.

When we have agreed upon these principles – said Jenks – we have in effect agreed that the term 'sovereignty' as it is used in international law and international relations *has little or no relationship with sovereignty in the etymological sense in which the term was originally used in the days of absolute monarchy. In this context, whether we should retain or abandon the term becomes a matter of practical convenience rather than of fundamental principle* – concluded Jenks.

While he was ultimately in favour of abandoning the term, the general feeling of the group was that the fight against an expression so deeply entrenched in the vocabulary of international law and relations and so frequently used and stressed by States and their representatives would not serve any useful purpose and would remain a futile exercise in semantics.

Interdependence

The Charter of the United Nations refers to the sovereign equality of all member States, to their territorial integrity and political independence. The term interdependence cannot be found in the language employed by the Charter. Nevertheless interdependence forms one of the constitutive elements of the international community and follows from the principle of international cooperation which has been repeatedly invoked by the United Nations Charter.

Your rapporteur ventures again to quote Jenks, who wrote as follows in 1963:

"Interdependence can no longer be regarded as a political, economic or sociological concept too general and imprecise to be of any substantial value to the

2 Jenks, C. W. *Law in the World Community.* London, Longmans, 1967, pp. 5–6.

lawyer; it is in process of crystallising into a legal concept which lies at the heart of contemporary international law."[3] In his view "we no longer have 'coexisting independent communities', but communities whose coexistence depends on the full recognition of their mutual interdependence. We are evolving towards a position in which it is the denial of the interdependence which 'cannot be presumed'. This general approach now has far-reaching application throughout the law. Interdependence for peace, justice and freedom, interdependence for prosperity and technological progress, interdependence in coexistence and for defence, have superseded the sovereignty as the seedbed of the law."[4]

The idea of interdependence leads obviously to the creation of a new international economic order. Does it further lead to international planning? The views were divided. Some were of the opinion that the plight of the developing countries justified the call for managed economy on a global scale. For them the problems of energy, raw materials and ecology were equally pressing in this direction. For others such ideas were found unacceptable as they might lead to a world superstate dictatorship. The holders of opposing views agreed more or less that the keeping to a middle course would be advisable and all were impressed by the dictum that: Economic interdependence that outruns too far the extent of common political control, can be an element of international friction rather than harmony. Keeping a little apart can at times be the best way of keeping together.

A particularly conspicuous case of interdependence is the situation of States whose territory is located in the same drainage basin. Here the relevant Helsinki rules provide for an equitable utilisation of the waters of the basin.

Equality

Equality of States was also brought into the discussion; equality in the sense of Vattel, who said that a dwarf is as much a man as a giant, a small republic is no less a sovereign State than the most powerful kingdom. The factual inequality existing between States cannot be, however, disregarded. The existence of big and small, rich and poor States gives special importance to the principle of solidarity of States which commands that the richer ones aid and assist the poor so that the latter enjoy an equal dignity in their existence. Hence the idea that a breath of socialism should penetrate into the international community and inspire the interstate relations. It might be added, however, that this is without prejudice to the special responsibility of the developed States vis-à-vis their former colonies.

Members of the group were rightfully reminded of the fact that States have a function within this world community, which they do not exercise on their own behalf – for the State is not an aim in itself – but on behalf of an order for the community of the human race, in accordance with given principles.

3 Jenks, C. W. *Law, Freedom and Welfare*. London, Stevens, 1963, p. 71.
4 *Ibid.*, p. 72.

Material, economic and human limits to activities of mankind

The world made enormous progress form the idea of co-existence to that of co-operation, from the simple obligation of refraining from the use of force to the duty to co-operate peacefully. Vattel considered it a natural duty of States to help each other in case of famine or other calamities up to the limit of endangering their own existence (f. "Il faut s'entr'aider, c'est la loi de nature" La Fontaine, Fables, VIII. 17, "L'Ane et le Chien".) At Vattel's time this was considered an imperfect right of States, it seems, however, logical to press for the transformation of this imperfect right – to make it a perfect one.

Among the limits to human activities the problem of food was discussed. The recognition of the fundamental human right to food was claimed. The nutritional level of the population of no State should be permitted to sink below a certain standard. This standard should improve proportionally with the increase in production. States bear common responsibility that no man remains hungry.

The question of population growth was felt to be a domestic matter which cannot be regulated by international law notwithstanding the fact that it has close connection with problems of ecology, scarce raw materials and energy. The latter call for international action and in this relation the importance of concluding the planned commodity agreements was stressed.

The view was held that a new international economic order must not only deal with matters like buffer stocks, preferential tariffs, drawing rights and other technicalities but also with the tremendous problems connected with the unheard of dimension of the migration of populations in our era. The details may still be debatable: are there conceivable measures which might induse people to refrain from migration? What measures could be taken to make migration unnecessary? A host of similar questions could be asked.

Ecology was defined as a grandiose mind-expanding concept which, to those who feel responsible for economic policies might become a veritable nightmare. New obligations to nature, not directly related to human welfare, are in the emergence. Such obligations are as yet alien to western culture and more natural in some civilizations of the East where a belief in the transcendental character of the Laws of nature is supposed to protect ecological cycles and balances.

The principles of the 1972 Stockholm conference were recalled and more particularly the dictum that "man has the fundamental right to freedom, equality and adequate conditions of life, in an environment of a equality that permits a life of dignity and well-being and he bears a solemn responsibility to protect and improve the environment for present and future generations."

The information received at Uppsala that 10,000 of the lakes of Sweden had already been destroyed by acid rain coming from Central Europe was found particularly shocking. New approaches and new strategies were called for to solve the problems of ecology and to make amends for the inactivity of the past.

Natural resources: heritage of nations and mankind

Members were aware of the utmost importance of the resource problem. The statement of the rector of the UN University was quoted: A growing consciousness of increasing resource scarcities – and not only energy sources but also other key minerals or food sources – will trigger increased competition between industrialized countries, between the North and the South, and in the third world itself . . . We are entering a period when what one might call "the geopolitics of resources" will become a major feature of international relations.[5]

There is an obvious antinomy existing between the principle of permanent sovereignty over natural resources (heritage of nations) and the notion of a common heritage of mankind. It was held that the latter notion, which was not to be construed extensively, related to resources not yet under national jurisdiction. This notion can be assimilated to what was called in the domestic laws public property in contradistinction to the resources under national sovereignty which can be looked at as private property of the given nation. These latter resources however are connected with social obligations of an international character just as social obligations burden the private property in progressive legislations of individual countries. Hence resources under national jurisdiction must not be depleted, the environment must not be polluted, raw materials must be equitably used. Speaking in general, resources belonging to the sovereign domain must be subject to the duty of international co-operation.

This applies also to technology in regard of which it is accepted that it does not belong to the public property of mankind but to the private property of nations. It is, however, subject to the duty of co-operation to the duty of transfer under reasonable and fair conditions.

Co-operation was also needed to explore mutually satisfactory ways of increasing the security of investment on the one hand and the supply of resources on the other; without such co-operation and security neither producers nor consumers can derive the full benefits from the resources of the world.

Legislation for a new economic order

In the field of domestic law: It was pointed out by some members that the self-reliant strategies of developing countries had been mostly fashioned on the Marxist model. The cases where such strategies were successful made it probable, that only a revolutionary creed was capable of mobilizing the energies needed for a significant transformation of society. According to others this was not a certainty, it might be that this relation was not an inherent one but rather a case of historic accident.

In any event the development of law should also have its rightful place in the investigetation and introduction of effective poverty-oriented policies. Much research work must be done also in the history of law and its relation to Socialism in general.

In the field of international law: It was found that within the United Nations several institutions, bodies and organs were dealing with the legal aspects of the New International Economic Order. There was no single organ entrusted with co-ordination. The United Nations Commission on International Trade Law

5 See paper 4.7.

(UNCITRAL) made a survey of the trade law aspects and decided recently to concentrate on industrial development contracts in order to elaborate uniform clauses for the various types of contracts. In elaborating international conventions on transport of goods by sea and on the international sale of goods, and in drafting the Arbitration Rules, UNCITRAL has, indeed, contributed to some important aspects of the New Order. (Your rapporteur is still proud of the Hungarian initiative – his brain-child – which led to the establishment of UNCITRAL)

The United Nations Conference on the Law of the Sea will by the drafting of a new convention contribute to a certain extent to the restructuring of the international economic relations.

The work of UNCTAD in the field of eliminating the so called flags of convenience, in setting up a common fund for raw materials, in drafting the various conventions on primary products (commodity agreements) etc., has to be seen also as important contributions to the law of the new international economic order.

There is a pending item on the agenda of the Legal Committee of the General Assembly entitled "Consolidation and progressive development of the principles and norms of international economic law relating in particular to the legal aspects of the new international economic order". This topic was taken up by the General Assembly on the initiative of the Philippines. The Assembly has asked the United Nations Institute for Training and Research (UNITAR) to make a survey of the said legal aspects.

The view was expressed by some members that the creation of a special new law commission could be envisaged for solving the legal issues of the new international economic order. This could be put, possibly, under the aegis of ECOSOC. According to this view the issues involved were too vital and too vast to be left exclusively to our friends, the economists.

International law-making serves obviously the interests of the developing countries. "Between the weak and the strong it is liberty that oppresses and the law that liberates" – it has been recalled. Hence it is to be expected that these countries will continue to make further initiatives and support the initiatives of others in the field of the development of international law.

3.4. Sovereignty and Humanity
Report of Working Group III

HERNÁN MONTEALEGRE

This discussions of the third group, which concentrated on the theme of sovereignty and humanity, were developed against a basic background which was also the permanent presupposition of the debates: that is, that a new world order envisaged from the standpoint of international law has to deal not only with the organization of the conditions of nature, as expressed in the problems of natural resources, ecological matters and others but also, and specifically, with man himself i. e. the human person and the conditions that are necessary to preserve and promote his basic rights.

This basic concern stimulated the discussion of four main issues:

First, does the nature or character of contemporary international law help us in the promotion of the human person and his basic rights as the touchstone in a new world order?

Second, how can we advance, on a universal level, the support of the basic rights of the human person without overriding his particular regional and cultural attributes?

Third, how should we react towards the violations of the basic rights of the human person, violations that today more than ever shock the conscience of mankind?

Fourth, what can be done in order to improve the international protection of these basic rights at a moment when we are moving towards a new world order?

The character of contemporary international law

The group agreed that international law is not a neutral and empty field which States can sow according to their unlimited will and power, but that there are objective values that orientate the process of contemporary international law.

A distinction was made between the source and the general content of these values. While in the last aspect there was a general agreement among the participants, differing opinions were expressed as to the origins of these normative aspects of international law.

For some the values that orientate the process of contemporary international law are rooted in cultural and ideological factors and accordingly can be explained by references to these. For others, on the contrary, some basic values of contemporary international law are a reflection of essential and universal characteristics of human nature, a position which implies a remitance to concepts of natural law.

What should be stressed here is that, although based on different grounds, there was a fundamental agreement on three matters: first, that the process of contemporary international law is in fact orientated by specific values; second, that these values can be objectively described in general terms; and third, that there is a significant basis to criticise the extreme positivism of traditional or classic international law which relies almost exclusively on the power and unrestricted will and sovereignty of States for the generation of international law.

The group estimated that international law had shifted from the narrow horizon of an extreme consideration of analogous though conficting national interests to the perception of universal values which are emerging today as the recognised foundations of this international law.

These commonly held values are not only related to matters such as the prohibition of the use of force, the distribution of wealth in the world, ecological imperatives, but also to the conditions of personal human dignity.

This latter universal concern gives to contemporary international law a specific characteristic which is the emergence of the human person as a subject of international law through the recognition and protection of his basic human rights, and also of peoples themselves as specific international actors, through the recognition of the right to self-determination. It was underlined that this was in direct contrast with classic international law in which the human person is only an object of the law, and in which governments are given a dominant position in the matter of defining sovereignty and international recognition.

The tension between universalism and regionalism

The particular set of universal values which specifically concerned the group was that relating to human rights.

Although there was a consensus that basic human rights are universally acknowledged at present, it was estimated that, at the point of defining those rights precisely, it was necessary to introduce regional, cultural and ideological aspects. This "regionalisation" of human rights, it was said, would emphasise different priorities. This in turn could be linked to the emergence of what some call "new" human rights such as the right to peace and the right to development.

On the other hand, this regionalisation was not meant to suppress the universal character of certain rights, and particular support was given to the efforts at the United Nations to promote the widest internationalisation of these rights through the Covenants on Civil and Political, Economic, Social and Cultural Rights.

The matter, however, of how the different levels, i. e. universal and regional, interact, converge and diverge with each other was not pushed further, in particular the specific image that human rights acquire in a transcultural world, which is an emphasis of this seminar, was not directly approached. I direct your attention to this as one of the specific issues to be followed up from this seminar.

Some examples of basic rights with an admitted universal character were highlighted, and in this connection the prohibition of summary execution (the right to life), torture (the right to personal integrity), unfair trials (the right to a just trial) and arbitrary detentions (the right to personal freedom) were mentioned. In the same universal context, certain economic and social rights were also mentioned, such as the right to food and shelter.

It was also stressed that this universal condition of human rights made them a part of *jus cogens* and of world public order.

Violations of human rights

From the debates on this matter a dual situation appeared for consideration:

a) the problem of individual cases of violations of human rights where attention is concentrated on the victim himself, and
b) the problem of collective or massive violation of human rights where attention does not stop at the individual victim but is directed towards the victimizer, that is, the peculiarities of a government that puts itself in the position of systematically violating the human rights of the people it is supposed to represent.

The basic question that arose within the group was whether international law, in both cases, allows the international community to be concerned only with the victim and not to react specifically, particularly in the second case, against the government.

Nobody denied that in both of these situations it is legitimate in international law for the international community to act in favour of the victims whose rights are being violated through the specific means and competences that have been established in the various international instruments that recognise and protect human rights.

Certainly in these cases, be they individual or collective violations of human rights, the international organs that react, whether quasi-judical or judicial, express their condemnations in different ways, of the governments responsible. But a specific question raised in the group debates was whether there existed cases when the international community should radically oppose the government concerned so as to deny them international legitimacy.

Some arguments were raised against the latter possibility. First, it was said that no rigid model of democracy was imposed either by the United Nations Charter or by the human rights international agreements. Second, ideological and cultural differences made it difficult to have an objective approach to the matter. Third, the prohibition of intervention in the internal affairs of another State was a basic principle of international law. Fourth, it was stated that the specific machinery contemplated in the international agreements on human rights, with the specific measures envisaged in those instruments, constituted the only means by which the international community was permitted to act, thus hindering resort to other and more radical methods of suppressing the violation of human rights. There was a consensus in the group that the concern for human rights and the reaction of the international community *vis-à-vis* their violations should not, as a general rule, aim at the outlawing of the governments responsible from the international community, with all the radical consequences that this would entail. The present national and international situation of different countries and regions in the world shows that this consensus is a realistic view as a general rule. Many participants, though, underlined their interest in considering this action in exceptional cases.

The exceptional case that aroused interest was the situation where a government becomes systematically involved in and institutionalises the violation of human rights relating to personal security, i e., the right not to be summarily executed, the right not to be tortured, the right not, be incarcerated for long periods of time without prior conviction by a fair procedure and the right not to be detained at all under brutal conditions. This particular situation was precisely defined by the group as a situation of tyranny or State terrorism; as such, it was said to pose important questions of international law that concerned the government in itself. Vattel was quoted in his sentence that international law protects only legitimate sovereigns and not tyrants.

The real meaning and implications of the concept of sovereignty were developed by one participant who insisted that its base and the criteria for its legitmacy rested on the free will of the people who were governed and not on the mere fact of a government controlling a society by force.

It was stressed that international law had moved from the exclusivity that it gave to governments as the only legitimate representatives of States and as such as the only subjects of international law, to the consideration of peoples as subjects of this law.

In particular the human right of self-determination was an international criterion for determining international legitimacy. A tyrannic government proves to be incapable of fulfilling its international obligations in the vital field of human rights, and due to its juridical incapability exposes itself in particular to the eventuality of expulsion from the United Nations Organization. When a tyrannic government approaches the point of threatening international security the United Nations has the power to resort even to the use of collective force against that government.

Certain specific sanctions against these regimes were mentioned, e. g., nonrecognition, severance of multilateral and bilateral financial support etc.

It was stated that the new international legal order, already envisaged in the Charter of the United Nations, was essentially linked with the suppression of tyranny and that a new world order based on the respect of the human being cannot be conceived as a community that admits tyrannic governments as proper members and partners in that community.

Promotion of human rights

Present trends in the international community to promote the legal protection of human rights were welcomed and encouraged by all participants as the irreplaceable basis of a new world order.

The United Nations machinery for the promotion of human rights through its different organs and the mechanisms envisaged in the different universal and regional instruments on human rights should now be complemented with a stronger political will.

Although in the particular case of tyranny there should be punishment analogous to that received by aerial pirates, hijackers and other international terrorists, it was not felt that the promotion of a specific convention on tyranny would be opportune at the present moment.

The development of the concept of crimes against humanity in the context of human rights was encouraged. Particular reference was made to the urgency of implementing an international convention on torture and regional conventions on human rights in Africa, Asia and Eastern Europe.

Consideration was given to the issue of humanitarian intervention as a collective action taken by competent international organs in exceptional circumstances.

Stress was also given to the fact that some positive developments were taking place in law, regionally and nationally, for the promotion of human rights, as in the case of aliens and migrant workers.

It was the duty of international lawyers to encourage these important trends in the law.

3.5. International Organization for a New World Order

Report of Working Group IV

MUSTAFA KAMIL YASSEEN †

Working group 4 focused its work on the problem of implementing the New World Order through a strengthening of the international organization. The following main topics were discussed in the group:

1. Possibilities for achieving actual amendment of the Charter or strengthening the United Nations through *"de facto"* amendment using the methods of interpretation and practice.
2. Methods for increasing the binding effect of the General Assembly resolutions.
3. Voting practice and the rôle it plays in the subsequent effectiveness of General Assembly resolutions.
4. Statute of the International Court of Justice:
   a) Ability of States to request advisory opinions;
   b) International organizations as parties in contentious cases before the International Court of Justice.
5. Division of competence between universal and regional organizations.

1. Possibilities for achieving actual amendment of the Charter or strengthening the Charter through "de facto" *amendment using the methods of interpretation and practice*

The United Nations Charter has been amended in a most significant way: the expansion of the membership of the Security Council from 9 to 13 members has made it easier for non-permanent members to cast a "collective veto".

Although aware that the Charter presupposes amendments, some participants in the working group considered that in the present circumstances an amendment would be inappropriate and the equivalent of opening Pandora's Box, as was demonstrated at the Law of the Sea Conference. Once Pandora's Box is open it cannot be closed. In their opinion an amendment would be necessary only in two instances: when trying to achieve something contrary to the provisions of the Charter, or when wishing to impose new duties on States.

Other participants favoured the improvement of the work of the Organization without amendments through the search for means in full agreement with the Charter. Moreover, opposition to revision of the Charter also means no amendment of the Statute of the International Court of Justice as expressed during the discussions in the Special Committee on the Charter of the United Nations and on the Strengthening of the Rôle of the Organization.

An area in which the revision of the Charter seems appropriate is the field of peace-keeping operations. There is nothing in the Charter about peace-keeping operations. However, through assumption and conviction we have managed to introduce a new device. How do we achieve general guidelines in this area? Perhaps by adding a new Chapter to the Charter, as for example a Chapter VI bis? Perhaps the need for guidelines in this area could be filled through an increase of the power exercised by the Secretary-General.

Another question will be the future destiny of the Trusteeship Council. Should we amend the Charter and abolish the Trusteeship Council when it no longer has a function and replace it, for example, by a Council on Human Rights? Or should we be more reticent and leave the Council intact in its present form but change its functions?

According to some participants the amendment of the Charter has to be considered not as a revolution, but as a normal process of evolution of the Organization. Those who accept the revision of the Charter, call for realism and the recognition of political realities, and as such, accept the amendments in respect of Chapters IX, X and XI. Nevertheless, the revision should avoid affecting the basic foundations of the Organization such as the veto of the great powers without which the process of international relations would not be possible.

2. *Methods to increase the binding effect of the General Assembly Resolutions*

It has always been an established fact that the international organizations make a law for themselves, a law which constitutes the internal law of an international organization.

However, many discussions have taken place on the competence of these organizations to create a law for States or to contribute to its formation. The doctrine of international law underlines the non-compulsory character of resolutions, recognizing in them only the character of recommendations. But the international judicial and political bodies as well as the States' organs and courts give to these recommendations more value than would be expected. For those who draft them the resolutions have different degrees of value: some consider a resolution analogous to a treaty, others see it as an element of custom-building or an expression of general legal principles.

The members of the group stressed the importance of the General Assembly resolutions and the problem of their implementation. Some members criticized the fact that the resolutions dit not receive from States the respect and recognition which is appropriate and necessary. It may be considered as a discredit if delegations speak and vote only for the newspapers and governments.

The group also focused its discussion on a proposal by Professor Finn Seyersted, who referred to the discussion by the preceding speakers, and in particular by Professor Jimenez de Arechaga, of the status of resolutions of the

General Assembly and of the United Nations as sources of legal obligations. Under present law, these could not be considered direct sources of rights and duties unless they reflected existing customary law. However, even new rules contained in resolutions could easily become binding after having been applied and thus confirmed by State practice.

In certain fields referred to by Professor Jimenez de Aréchaga, however, a resolution could be given a direct binding force on the basis of the rules of general international law relating to *occupation of territory*. The *high seas*, including the bottom of the high seas, and *outer space* belong to no country. The United Nation resolution and treaty on outer space state expressly that outer space is not subject to *national* appropriation. Professor Seyersted suggested that this does not preclude appropriation by the United Nations. Accordingly, the Organization could appropriate these territories and thereby assume legislative powers in respect of them. This would enable the Organization to enact, by a qualified majority, rules binding on all States. With regard to the high seas, a treaty is under preparation. But even if this can be achieved, we may need the legislative method on the basis of territorial appropriation to make the rules binding upon States which do not accede to the treaty.

The General Assembly makes descisions with respect to its own jurisdictional competence. Can this jurisdictional competence be expanded? The General Assembly cannot make binding decisions without a legal basis. If we cannot find it in the Charter we must look in general international law. The two questions that we must ask regarding this proposal are:

(1) would it be possible to authorize a decision taken by the General Assembly with a qualified majority;
(2) are there certain aspects where members of the United Nations would confer upon the United Nations the right to make binding decisions.

Several members of the group disagreed with this proposal by Professor Seyersted. The resolutions are not binding *per se* and are not entitled to become legal. They are only the evidence of opinions, the first step in the creation of the rules of customary international law. They express and often accelerate the development of customary international law. To go beyond this and say that the General Assembly resolutions can become legally binding by virtue of another General Assembly resolution, would destroy the ability which the Assembly currently possesses. It is impossible to give legislative power to the General Assembly through the mechanism of the United Nations resolutions. Moreover it will not be possible to ensure compliance when the Security Council is not able to provide it.

Authority to adopt binding resolutions may be confirmed only by a Charter amendment. If this is done through an international convention (such as the Law of the Sea Convention), parties may be others than members of the United Nations. In such a case, only member States would decide whether they could accept the obligations. In case of a treaty which would probably be ratified, the General Assembly should declare it binding on all States. This idea was opposed by other members who thought that it would not be possible to extend an obligation after a treaty had been ratified.

Introduction of the binding force of the resolutions will require a new attitude by States. If it is binding by a $^2/_3$ majority vote, it will have as result the reluctance of the minority of States to relinquish these subjects to the General Assembly, resulting in no advantage over the present system.

The fact that the General Assembly of the United Nations has assumed in some respects a quasi-legislative power, does not mean that it can claim sovereignty over certain parts of the world. Such an opinion is going too far. Even if we assume that the United Nations could appropriate certain areas, which organ will be capable to exercise sovereign power? The General Assembly was not created to be a world government. Appropriation of property requires occupation. The United Nations has no technical capacity to occupy the high seas or outer space. It has in some degree recognised that outer space and the high seas do not belong to States. As far as concerns the acquisition of property by the United Nations, this acquisition must be agreed by the States in the same way as the States have to agree that the area cannot be appropriated by any single State. The aim behind the current reasoning prohibiting the appropriation by a single State, is that these areas belong to mankind, to a new subject of international law which has now appeared on the scene. Who should represent mankind and how will this distribution be carried out?

As rapporteur, Professor Seyersted based the idea of expropriation on the rules of general international law of occupation. He stated that he was hesitant about the competence of the General Assembly to appropriate. A General Assembly resolution has no binding force, it has only the value of recommendation. The General Assembly has no right to appropriate anything. There is no doubt, that the role of the United Nations General Assembly in outer space has been very efficient. Many resolutions adopted on this subject are considered as binding, not because of their value of General Assembly resolutions, but because of the context of the customary rules of international law. When all the members of the United Nations General Assembly state that they will use outer space, and the two great powers – who are actually the only ones who can do anything in this field – agree, then the resolutions are binding.

Other members supported Professor Seyersted's idea of the binding force of the General Assembly resolutions in certain specific matters. They based their argumentation on the example given in previous resolutions, for example, on the fact that the Security Council has been deprived of its exclusive competence in peace and security matters. According to some members, joint responsibility of the Security Council and of the General Assembly in this area does not exist. Moreover, it should be reaffirmed in this context, that the primary responsibility belongs to the Security Council which only means that the Security Council has no monopoly, but only the non-exclusive but primary responsibilitiy. When the Security Council discusses a matter, the General Assembly cannot discuss it. If the Security Council is unable to act, the Uniting for Peace resolution is then applied.

Professor Seyersted reaffirmed that the idea he had presented is legally possible and that the United Nations Charter is not exhaustive. The General Assembly resolutions could be used as a mechanism. Through the resolutions it would be possible to give the General Assembly the power to legislate. In the context of peace-keeping operations, the obligations do not arise because of the consent of all parties. These resolutions would impose legal obligations on States so there must be a legal basis in either the Charter or in customary international law. If this has not been done already by the customary international law, then we have this as a potential legal basis, and the resolutions may create a new right to exercise jurisdiction in this area.

The opinion was also expressed that there are some areas where we can obtain binding resolutions more easily than in others. According to one member of the group, the treaties affecting the general interests of humanity *(jus cogens)* should be binding. Since the General Assembly adopted, for example, the principle of self-determination, this principle is binding. There is a tendency at present to consider the New International Economic Order as binding. If resolutions continue to be adopted by consensus in the General Assembly, this would create customary international law, and this would meet the requirements of *opinio juris* and of practice. According to this member, the time element is not necessary.

Some members of the group mentioned the problem of the content of the resolutions of the General Assembly. Very often, the General Assembly adopts the same resolutions every year. Should we rather look at the compliance with the resolutions which have already been adopted? By failing to analyse compliance, are we acquiescing in non-compliance? One of the members of the group suggested that we should discourage the passage of resolutions on the same issues and concentrate on compliance with resolutions that have already been passed. He doubted whether setting higher standards resulting from the Charter amendment, necessarily leads to a better record of compliance.

3. *Voting practice and the rôle it plays in the subsequent effectiveness of the General Assembly resolutions*

At the beginning of the discussion the question was raised of the possibility of having a majority voting system in international organizations. At one time, States did not enter an organization where decisions had to be reached by a majority vote. This was not at all against the sovereignty of the State. When a State enters the organization and agrees by this act to bind itself to the basic provisions including the procedure of deciding and voting, the State is not giving up its sovereignty, on the contrary, it is merely applying its sovereign right.

In some organizations the system of weighted voting is introduced. This is not taken seriously by the great powers. The great powers use weighted voting as a reaction to the suggestions that the permanent members of the Security Council restrict their use of veto. Until now, the only organizations which have been using a weighted voting system are those which have a competence concerning particular commodities and the financial organizations. Many proposals for weighted voting systems have been suggested, such as voting based on the population, economy or the extent of the railway system. All these proposals have been rejected. The only weighted voting system which is possible refers to the mini-States and their voting rights in the United Nations.

Discussion in the group was concentrated on two main subjects in this field, namely:

a) Limits to the power of veto
b) Consensus

a) Limits to the power of veto

In order to enable the Security Council to take prompt and effective action as the organ vested with "primary responsibility" for the maintenance of international peace and security, the group felt that it would be desirable to limit the scope of application of the rule of unanimity of the permanent members to exclude all matters other than those directly relating to the maintenance of international peace and security.

This limitation would bring the use of the so-called "veto power" in harmony with the objectives envisaged at the San Francisco Conference. If the permanent members were to agree to refrain from exercising their veto power, as they have sometimes voluntarily done in the past, this would enhance the ability of the Security Council to take prompt and effective action on behalf of the United Nations.

The members of the group suggested several areas where they felt it would be especially desirable for the permanent members to refrain from exercising their veto power. These areas include, but are not limited to matters dealing with the peaceful settlement of disputes, such as the establishment of fact-finding commissions and the organization of observer groups.

b) Consensus

The group noted the emergence of a trend towards the use of consensus as a device to reach agreement in organs of the United Nations and various international fora.

It is important that this trend not becomes institutionalized as a replacement of the majority rule because this might allow a certain minority, or even an individual member, to impede or veto the adoption of any decision.

However, the use of the consensus method should still be accepted as a means of facilitating negotiations in order to reach an agreement, but when all efforts at consensus are exhausted the final recourse must be to the voting procedure.

The question was raised at the beginning of the discussion as to whether it is a sign of evolution or rather of regression. The idea of consensus was hailed as a great success at the beginning. It is only recently that people have stopped to think that if you follow this principle you will get the lowest common denominator.

Even if one of the members accused the Western powers of having the idea of consensus to avoid compliance with the resolution which would be against their will, it was pointed out by other members of the group, that the Eastern European States are striving towards consensus. The trend to adopt resolutions by consensus occurred ten years ago. During the last General Assembly, many resolutions were adopted without vote, without objection or by acclamation. These methods are not the same as consensus. All resolutions once adopted become valid resolutions whatever the form of their adoption. The resolutions adopted by consensus are based on the lowest common denominator. They are often accompanied by reservations of the Member States. The method of consensus has grown in popularity because of a wish to extend agreement. However, this is not a voting method but rather a means to use every effort to reach an agreement. Consensus is used to agree on something which is not final. One of the members from a developing country stressed that it is not appropriate to say that one group of States favours consensus and all others not. Non-aligned countries use consensus. Consensus has to be understood as a method used to facilitate movement towards decision, and should not be pushed beyond this point. It has never been accepted that consensus is a binding principle. As mentioned by Professor Broms, the vote took place only once in the Sixth committee and on a procedural point. It occurred when the non-aligned States wanted to show their power and give the great powers a reminder of voting. On that occasion the vote was carried by an overwhelming majority. In the minds of members there is always the tactical strategy of resorting to the vote. Consensus is a means of pressure on the conference from both sides. But consensus may affect the preparedness of the parties to adopt a Convention. Very important documents have been drafted through consensus and then later the Convention adopted by this system has not been ratified.

Naturally consensus is justified by the idea of not allowing a majority abuse its rights. What is even more unacceptable is that the minority abuse the rights of the majority. It is a fact that the small minorities tend to exploit this use of consensus to block agreement on certain matters.

The idea of consensus has often been exaggerated and it has to be stressed that consensus may be justified only by the principle of good faith. Those who view the idea of consensus negatively think that consensus is a way of reaching agreement where agreement no longer exists.

4. *Statute of the International Court of Justice*

a) Ability of States to request advisory opinions

The proposal allowing States the right to seek advisory opinions may be accepted if its objective is to clarify points of law concerning the States' conduct in international relations.

However, this must not be a means to avoid the application of the fundamental principles underlying the jurisdiction of the Court or indirectly to promote a settlement that would prejudice the rights of other States, whose rights have been protected by the procedures of contentious cases.

The question was raised whether any State can obtain an adivisory opinion or should this be done as it is now, which means with the Security Council's or the General Assembly's approval. Otherwise, if any State can ask for an advisory opinion, this would imply a heavy burden on the Court.

b) International organizations as Parties in contentious cases before the International Court of Justice

Professor Seyersted proposed in the discussion an amendment to the Statute of the International Court of Justice, which will permit States to request advisory opinions from the Court, but which will also allow the international organizations to appear as parties in contentious cases before the Court.

This amendment to Article 34 of the Statute of the Court was formulated as follows:

"States and organizations of States may be Parties in cases before the Court".

The author of this proposal explained that there is a need for such an amendment because of the growth of the number of international organizations. He stressed that both the international organizations composed of States and those composed of organs of States would be entitled to appear as Parties in the contentious cases. This proposed amendment which exludes non-governmental organizations, refers from the many bilateral agreements concluded between governmental international organizations and States in areas such as privileges and immunities and technical assistance.

In the light of the growth in the number of international organizations the only expedient procedure that will enable settlements in these matters, is to allow these international organizations to appear as parties before the Court.

Even if legally possible, this amendment will require, according to some members of the group, a study in relation to the international personality of the organizations. As is well known, the constitution of an international organization places a decisive limit on the scope of its personality. It is therefore necessary to study this proposal in the context of the constitution of each organization. A right cannot be granted without taking this important aspect into consideration.

Professor Seyersted was thinking of all intergovernmental organizations in case of the amendment of the Article 34 of the Statutes. It would be preferable, according to him, not to refer to the constitution of an organization, as this would be too restrictive. The organizations engage in many areas that are not covered by their Charters and he would prefer rather to limit it by the reference "within the scope of their functions".

In this respect the legal adviser of the United Nations raised the question of the form of the realization of such transformation and doubted the necessity of making the amendment of the Charter or of the Statute. He asked if the jurisdiction is exclusively based on the Charter and the Statute? Is it not possible to have *ad hoc* jurisdiction without changing the Charter? Is it not possible to imagine that both the organization and the State might agree on the jurisdiction?

This rather pessimistic attitude was not shared by other members of the group who suggested a careful approach to this problem. The Court might not be willing to accept such conferred jurisdiction.

Although the group was in general agreement that the proposed change in the Statute would be useful, there were three distinct views expressed relating to the scope of this new right.

Some members of the group expressed the view that international organizations, as subjects of international law, should be allowed to be parties in contentious cases before the Court, without any limitation, other than that applied to States (concerning, for instance, the acceptance of the optional clause); while other members of the group expressed the view that an international organization may only be a party in a contentious case before the Court, if this competence to be a party can be deduced from interpretation or the application of the implied powers doctrine to the constituent document of the organization.

Still another view was expressed by some members of the group, that the only international organizations, which should be allowed to participate as parties in contenious cases, are those organizations that are presently allowed to seek advisory opinions of the Court pursuant to Article 65, paragraph 1 of the Statute of the Court. In the light of the Statute, the jurisdiction of the Court cannot be assumed. Therefore, the amendment has to be limited according to this proposal: instead of speaking of all international organizations, the proposal should be limited to "those which are entitled under the present arrangement" to go to Court and ask for an advisory opinion. Such limitation would make the acceptance of this modification easier.

5. Division of competence between universal and regional organizations

Under the New World Order regional organizations have an important part to play in the development of international law. A division of labour must be made between purely global concerns and those which are regional in character and can be more efficiently handled in regional organizations.

However, the scope of competence and the rules that govern these regional organizations must be in accordance with the fundamental principles of the United Nations Charter and general international law. For example, in the area of enforcement action, the Charter provides in Article 53, paragraph 1, that "... no enforcement action shall be taken under regional arrangements or by regional agencies without the authorization of the Security Council ...". Uncontrolled development in this area could lead to a dangerous fragmentation of the world order.

3.6. Legal and Organizational Problems of Mini-States
Report of Working Group V

Philip K. A. Amoah

Mini-States or the very small nations of the world are located in all parts of the globe – Africa, Asia, the Caribbean, Europe and the Pacific. On the attainment of independence most of them (over thirty) have been admitted to the membership of the United Nations and its related agencies. A few of them, however, have sought neither United Nations membership nor the membership of other international organizations because of their inability to fulfil the obligations of membership. Several dependent territories are on the threshold of political independence and are likely to seek United Nations membership and that of other international organizations on the attainment of independence. Indeed, it has been estimated that by the year 2000, the number of independent States in the world community would have reached the 200 mark. As members of the global community in an era of inter-dependence and co-operation, international lawyers concerned with a new world order are naturally interested in the future of these States. Such interest must go beyond the mere issue of their United Nations membership to the broader questions of their relationship with other mini-States in particular and States of the international community as a whole.

Recent attention drawn to the problems of mini-States has been focused on four main areas; viz,

1. Whether legal restrictions should be placed on their United Nations membership, in particular by limiting their right to vote in the General Assembly and other organs of the United Nations.
2. Whether mini-States are viable entities which can exist and operate independently of more powerful neighbours in the international community.
3. Whether in the light of their organizational problems associated with their smallness they have the capacity to influence the conduct of world affairs?
4. What problems do mini-States pose for their more powerful counterparts in the community of nations?

Areas covered by the reports

The two reports covered substantially the same ground. Both reports concentrated mainly on the membership of small States in the United Nations. In the view of the rapporteurs, unlike the United Nations Charter which is based on the concept of sovereign equality of States and consequently does not discriminate between States, the constitutional provisions of several international organizations contain obligations which may be too onerous for some mini-States to fulfil. They consequently do not seek membership of the organizations concerned; problems of membership do not therefore arise.

The reports touched upon the problem of definition and addressed the question: What is a mini-State? The criteria of population, size and resources applied to sovereign independent States were considered to be arbitrary standards which were neither fixed nor immutable and could lead to further problems. The main thrust of the arguments put forward by the rapporteurs was that in spite of the numerous organizational problems of mini-States, having been launched into independent statehood and admitted to full membership of the United Nations it would be unjust to expel them or relegate them to some other subordinate or second class status. For the future, however, the rapporteurs agreed that in the light of the problems presently being experienced by mini-States, provision could be made for a limited participation in the United Nations of newly independent small territories if they themselves so desired, either from financial or other reasons. To this end, three options were canvassed: observer status, limited membership and joint membership. Various problems associated with the suggested options, in particular the need for Charter amendment, were also discussed. As part of proposed solutions the co-rapporteur (Professor Schram) made a convincing case for the need to convene conferences of mini-States from time to time for the discussion and evaluation of their common problems and issues.

Discussions on reports

In recognition of the fact that problems of mini-States have political and economic implications for designing international law norms to meet the challenges of the future, a number of interventions were made by participants. Professor Reisman expressed the view that there were four problems pertinent to the formulation of future policy about mini-States. These were:

1. Should mini-States that now exist be deprived *ex post facto* of the rights of an existing State?

2. Should mini-States be admitted – and under what terms – to the United Nations and other international organizations?

3. How should mini-States that lack infra-structural capacity to fulfill the basic improvement of their citizens be helped by other States and by the international community?

4. Should very small territorial communities be encouraged in the future to accede to full statehood?

Professor Reisman submitted that the papers and comments had concentrated on the first three questions and ignored the fourth which was probably the most important. He contended that we should no longer think that the principle of self-determination must invariably lead to full statehood. He argued that since international law now has a welfare function which establishes as of right human standards, a preliminary question in the future is whether a candidate community has the capacity to provide its inhabitants with those minima. If not should not that community be urged to achieve self-determination in a different fashion – association, autonomy, integretion, minority guarantees and so on. He concluded that the real thrust of policy was self-determination of peoples and not of States.

Professor Saxena, on the other hand, maintained that in the area of settlement of disputes by States by peaceful means (Article 2(b) of the United Nations Charter), the purpose of the Charter would be better served even if mini-States are members of the organizations and that there should be no attempt to block the membership of such States. He also pointed out that an increase in the membership of the General Assembly would not affect the distribution of power in the United Nations system. He argued that large numbers alone do not necessarily lead to effective action and that the examples of lack of action on General Assembly resolutions on the new international economic order and the law of the sea conference revealed weaknesses in the present system.

Professor Grahl-Madsen emphasised the need to identify areas of cooperation among mini-States themselves. Such cooperation could take several forms. In order to increase their effectiveness in the United Nations, Professor Grahl-Madsen called for the establishment of a common secretariat and service staff by the mini-States themselves. He did not favour the idea of the United Nations itself being involved in that exercise since such involvement might be seen as undue interference in the affairs of mini-States. Other areas of cooperation based on efforts at self-reliance by mini-areas could be in the educational, technical and medical fields.

Professor Hingorani raised the issue whether the international community could reconcile the emphasis on universalism with the move to exclude some States from membership of the United Nations. He found it rather unusual to speak of universalism and at the same time exclude the participation of some States.

Dr. Thapa's intervention was based on an analogy of States forming a family of nations. He reasoned that just as all members of a family received equal treatment irrespective of age, size and other natural characteristics, all nations large and small, were entitled to be granted equal status.

Professor Lillich welcomed the idea of holding the session on mini-States on Åland Islands and suggested that participants might gain some good ideas from the Åland experience since it was a classic example of an autonomous entity linked to a sovereign State, which had achieved the maximum of rights – political, economic, social and cultural – for its inhabitants. He pointed out that the Åland Islands could serve as a model for other small territories or areas of existing States currently flirting with the idea of seeking independent State status. With respect to the two reports, Professor Lillich drew attention to the fact that it had been assumed that small territories emerging from the colonial experience should be admitted to the United Nations, the Organization of American States and other international and regional organizations. He maintained that such contentions, appealing to the elites of the territories concerned, carried few benefits and many burdens for their inhabitants.

The problem of voting rights was touched upon by Professor Lillich. He argued that the admission of mini-States to the United Nations or the Organization of American States frequently distorted the voting pattern and the acitivities of such international organizations. Consequently, seeking a reasonable degree of autonomy within the formal legal structures of an existing sovereign State – as the Ålanders had done – might in his view, present a more appealing and certainly more rational alternatives to statehood in many if not all cases. At the very least entities contemplating statehood also consider the option of autonomy, which could be tailored to suit the size, needs and volumes of inhabitants of the area. In conclusion, he agreed with Professor Reisman's earlier intervention that there could be no "roll-back" or revocation of statehood status to already existing mini-States, nor could their membership in the United Nations or the Organization of American States be easily withdrawn. He, however, maintained that mini-States should be encouraged, politically and financially to relinguish statehood status in their own interests and in the overall interests of the international community.

Professor Manigat dealt with the Caribbean experience with regard to the problems of mini-States. He referred to the 1974 Barbados conference on "Size and Self-determination, the small States in International Relations in the Caribbean". He argued that although mini-States undoubtedly had problems relating to their *credibility, viability, security, capacity to fulfil international obligations*, drawing on the Caribbean experience the international community would be better-off adhering to the concept of national sovereignty and the one-State-one vote principle. Following Professor Broms' question "What do the mini-States want?", a number of concrete proposals and suggestions were put forward.

Concrete suggestions and proposals

1. Conference of Mini-States:

A conference under these auspices of the United Nations was suggested. Such a conference would be participated in by existing Mini-States as well as very small territories desirous to seek independence and apply for membership of international organizations. Such a conference will be an appropriate forum for ascertaining the needs and aspirations of mini-States as a group, and their views on limited or full United Nations membership.

2. Joint Membership of the United Nations and other International Organizations.

In view of the difficulties encountered by very small nations with regard to obligations of membership, it is proposed that a number of mini-States from one region could apply for joint membership. By so doing they retain their independence and are accorded *one vote* in the deliberations of the organization.

3. Cooperation and Common Services.

Such areas of cooperation as a common secretariat at the United Nations and common educational, medical and technical services were proposed.

4. Asurvey should be undertaken to ascertain the attitude of the mini-States themselves towards various forms of United Nations membership and participation in other international organizations.

5. It was suggested in the discussion on the five reports that small dependent territories should be urged not to choose full sovereignty with subsequent unrestricted United Nations membership, but rather another form of autonomy or independence better suited to their needs.

IV. General Papers

4.1. International Law for Our Times
Speech at the Opening Ceremony of JUS 81

ATLE GRAHL-MADSEN

We live at a crucial time in the history of all mankind. The economic crisis afflicts not only Sweden but all other countries as well, albeit in different ways and in different degrees. Yet this crisis reflects but a single aspect of a process of transformation which is most profound and which can leave no-one unaffected, and for whose consequences we all shall be – and be held – responsible in some way or other.

As international lawyers we are in particular faced with four problem areas – which we may label as the military, the material, the humanitarian, and the constitutional.

The nations of the world are spending tremendous sums of money to keep up their military establishments and to supply them with ever more sophisticated and costly military hardware. We all know – although we like to suppress the fact from our consciousness – that the great powers have lined up against each other, and against other countries as well, nuclear weapons capable of turning the good Earth into a wasteland and of destroying all higher orders of life in the process.

Millions of men are day in and day out serving in armies, navies, and air forces in practically all countries. The possession of armed forces has become a symbol of national sovereignty, and national security is a major concern in most countries. It is apparent, however, that for many States the threat from foreign powers is negligible; the armed forces are maintained to protect the existing power structure against elements of opposition within the country itself.

In any case, the problem is confounded by the fact that many important countries depend economically on the trade in arms; this may be their major commodity exportable on a substantial scale, and we see all too often heads of proud nations prostituting themselves by acting as super-salesmen for arms from their country's weapon factories.

The problem is further complicated by the fact that if a country takes the opposite position and refuses to sell any arms to other countries, it may lose both goodwill and influence among the only all too eager customers.

The lack of trust between the great powers is in itself an impediment to successful arms limitations on a large scale: the non-ratification of the carefully negotiated Strategic Arms Limitation Treaty – SALT 2 – reminds us of this.

Indeed, the mixture of economic interests with internal as well as external power interests makes it extremely difficult to reach international agreement on any kind of reduction of armaments.

I am afraid that this problem area can only be attacked in a round-about way, by creating an international environment where military power and military hardware become less attractive. This is one reason why we have left this area out of our deliberations in this great Seminar. But let us not for one single moment be led to forget that the area is one of the utmost importance. We should not for a second forget that we live in the shadow of mutual assured destruction, that we in fact live on borrowed time. The military threat is a real one, and it adds significantly to the urgency of our discussions on any other aspect of international law and international relations.

The problem area, which we may call the material one, encompasses economy, technology, and ecology.

This is an area where we can find a great number of international agreements; and several international organizations, both inside and outside the United Nations system, are at work in this area.

On the economic side there are trade agreements, monetary agreements, development agreements, and so on, and so on, up to mighty organizations such as the World Bank, apexed by the integrated system of the European Communities.

Some sort of international accommodation in this field is a necessity for all States. As long as agreements or organized efforts are for the mutual benefit of the parties concerned, on short or intermediate term, it is apparently not difficult for the States to agree. Even programmes which are more charitable than for reciprocal benefit have not been too difficult to negotiate, especially since it may be a question of giving of one's surplus.

But what we are faced with today is a demand for a New International Economic Order. This has regularly been conceived in the North-South context, but its real scope is considerably broader, since it has to encompass our entire ecological situation.

The accumulation of waste – known as pollution – is as ominous as the threatening exhaustion of resources and the unequal distribution of means of livelihood.

The concept of a New International Economic Order calls for a redistribution and – more generally – for a readjustment of wealth and income throughout the world. It is not only a question of trimming the fringes; it will cut into the substance of our economic existence; and then things are not so easy any longer.

An essential requirement for a successful therapy is a precise diagnosis of the ailment. When we listen to our politicians, we realize that we are still far from a realistic understanding of the economic crisis we are faced with. People still talk about recovery and renewed growth, as if this crisis was a cyclical one, something resembling the one which hit the world fifty years ago.

On the other hand, some persons speak lightly and without profound concern about our standing on the threshold to the post-industrial era. If they knew how right they are, their tone would undoubtedly be less unconcerned.

I am no pessimist nor doomsayer. I see the present crisis as a challenge, more than anything else. It is indeed the greatest challenge of our lifetime, and that says much.

It is important that we should not prescribe a cure for an ailment which does not exist, and above all that if such a cure fails, we should not panic.

Of course, there is reason for concern; our greatest enemy is the lack of understanding of what is happening around us and the absence of a political will to tackle the situation. But this may come.

As lawyers we are, like physicians, used to face reality – our profession concerns by its very nature the human predicament in all its aspects. We know from experience that if we drive a car at full speed into a wall, the consequences for the car and all who are in it will be disastrous. But if we ease the car to a stop before it hits the wall, we are safe.

With such a metaphor in mind, we may more easily tackle the economic and ecological problems which are towering before us.

International law is born out of necessity. Once we realize the true necessities of our times, we may start our search for a way out.

Whereas economic considerations may prove to be of paramount importance with respect to our material problem area, it is power interests which provide the obstacles in the humanitarian area.

The Charter of the United Nations obliges the Member States to promote respect for human rights, and already the Third General Assembly adopted that unique instrument, the Universal Declaration of Human Rights, which in lasting words spells out the rights and freedoms which would enable us to live peacefully together and which ought to be the heritage of all humankind, in particular the generations to come.

I shall not raise here the contentious issue whether the Universal Declaration is law or not. It has been followed by international agreements which without doubt satisfy the traditional criteria of sources of international law, such as the European Convention for the Protection of Human Rights and Fundamental Freedoms and the two International Covenants, on Civil and Political Rights, and on Economic, Cultural, and Social Rights, and also other, more specialized instruments.

The fact remains, however, that in a great number of States, actually Members of the United Nations, human rights are more or less systematically throdden under foot, often in the name of high interests of State, which, however, often are nothing but a front for the most egoistic interests of persons clinging to power to which they may have only the most tenuous of claims.

This is one of the most serious of the problems besetting the modern world.

We do not need any great gift of perception to observe how important national sovereignty is – not only in the actual intercourse of States, but also in our minds. The new States place particular emphasis on the recognition of and respect for their sovereign equality, and any step which may be considered to jeopardize this conception will no doubt prove counterproductive.

If we go back to the foundations of international law, we may, however, possibly find a basis for some constructive ideas. No lesser an author than Emmerich de Vattel drew a fine distinction between sovereigns, who should always be respected and obeyed, and tyrants, who by their deeds had become enemies of their own nation and consequently not worthy of the privileges and immunities due to legitimate rulers.

We may also search for other solutions. At the same time as we must accept – at least for the time being – a world divided into some 150 to 200 sovereign entities, there is a growing consensus to the effect that flagrant abuses in the name of sovereignty should not be tolerated.

What will come out of our probing into this delicate area is by no means certain. But unlike the situation in the military area, we are not faced here with an unholy alliance between money and power. Power has to struggle alone, and it need not be victorious in a confrontation with a rising demand for respect for basic moral values and the dignity of the human being.

Our last problem area is that which we are calling the constitutional one. It deals with international law itself.

We know that international law has developed in Europe, in order to provide a framework of rules for the relations between princes in a world which did not any longer recognize any spiritual or temporal overlord.

In a time more religious than our own, international law could rest on a common faith – call it Divinity, call it Nature. But as the Occident became secularized, a new basis had to be found, and Custom was recognized as the creator of law. However, the customary international law grew up in the intercourse between European and European-inspired States.

Our generation has broken the old bonds. We have now a majority of States that are not European, and they naturally react against the thought that European custom should dictate the world of today and tomorrow.

Of course, States may conclude agreements and accept to be bound by them. But so long as we have no international legislative machinery, States may avoid the obligations laid down in conventions by the simple expedient of not ratifying or acceding to any convention.

Yet we find it abhorrent that States could avoid all international responsibility simply by refusing to accept it.

What then can be the basis for binding rules in the absence of treaties and recognized custom, in a world with no common faith?

Could it be Necessity? We cannot allow the world to be blackmailed by posing rockets in the territory of a State unbound by any treaty stipulation; that is clear. But how far does Necessity carry us? Does it bring us much further than what is essential for the maintenance of international peace and security?

Of course, we have also the time-honoured principles of Reciprocity and Equity. But they, too, have their limitations.

I cannot see that we have any alternative to attempting to create new and more efficient machinery for the progressive development of international law.

I believe that much may still be achieved within the system of sovereign and equal States. One possibility would be to supplement the International Law Commission with other, specialized committees, which could prepare drafts for the consideration of the United Nations General Assembly or of regional organizations, so that these organs could work somewhat like parliaments, even if they do not possess the legislative power of parliaments but merely would have to open the instruments for accession by States.

But in the final analysis the most important thing is to try to create an atmosphere of good will among men and women of all nations. Once they realize that our predicament is a real one, I believe that responsible statesmen and experienced international lawyers may lay the foundation for a breakthrough in co-existence and co-operation between all Nations.

If the spirit in which we meet at this Seminar is an omen, then I am not talking about Utopia.

After all, we are all in the same boat.

4.2. Can World Order be Negotiated?

GÖRAN OHLIN

The discussions about comprehensive reforms of the international economic system to create a New International Economic Order have now gone on for so long as to seem almost a permanent and unchanging feature of the life of the United Nations organisations.

How should one explain the failure of this massive political and economic effort?

The record of these negotiations and the substantive issues are well known and I shall not restate them here. Briefly, the perspective in which they will be seen is the following:

In one sense, the existing international economic order, characterized by the unequal economic relations between the unindustrialized countries in Africa, Asia, and Latin America on the one hand and the industrialized world in America and Europe on the other, established itself, as Arthur Lewis has argued, in the last quarter of the nineteenth century when tropical countries entered international trade in a significant way. Its political roots in Western colonialism go even farther back.

In another sense, the international economic order is often taken to be the system of rules and institutions created after the Second World War to avoid a repetition of the collapse of the international economy in the 1930s. The economic constitution then laid down for nation States was, for all its imperfections, a new and remarkable achievement. But its political premises were faulted by discord among major industrial powers which resulted in relaxation of international monetary discipline. Then the developing countries, which had consistently sought changes and amendment in the postwar system, were greatly increased in numbers when Asian and African countries became independent. The pressure for renegotiation of the postwar arrangements and their enlargment to take fuller account of the interests of the developing countries went into a new phase with the creation of UNCTAD in 1964 and were intensified in the 1970s.

These efforts have so far yielded very little.

Conflicts of interest?

The easiest explanation of the general stalemate in North-South talks might seem to be that the developing countries are pressing for such profound changes in the international economic system that they conflict too violently with the national interests of the rich countries to be acceptable to them. The steamy rhetoric that envelops so many North-South encounters fosters this view. The proposals for change are, for instance, called a bid for power which the North is unwilling to surrender, and the diplomatic offensive is made out to be more of a demonstration or a confrontation than a quest for negotiated change.

In actual fact, the core of the proposals to modify the prevailing regimes in international trade and investment, capital flows and other areas are far from revolutionary. Many have their origins in proposals that were part of the Anglo-American plans for the postwar world, such as commodity price regulation. A great many academic assessments have long concluded that there are extensive mutual interests in proposals for international economic reform. Such views have drawn support from the stagnation of world trade and industrial growth in the 1970s, from the energy crises in rich and poor countries alike, and from the new concerns with global food supply prospects, ecological and environmental deterioration – all of them issues that can be said to demonstrate the malfunctioning or the inadequacy of the existing world economy to the harm of industrial countries as well as to the young countries for whom national development is an imperative. The interdependence of the world economy, which reveals not only the dependence of the poor countries on the rich ones but also the opposite, is used to support the claim that the call for a new world economic order is a proposal that the rich cannot refuse, as it is in fact in their own vital interest.

Why then do the industrial countries' governments and negotiators fail to recognize this? Economists seeking to press their own conceptions upon recalcitrant policy-makers are frequently inclined to interpret past history in terms of national interests infallibly pursued while they ascribe to the governments of the present nothing but the most shortsighted and obtuse perception of their own true interests. Those who argue that industrial countries act counter to their own interests in resisting suggestions for world economic reform tend to assume that a preoccupation with serious domestic difficulties or a failure to understand the new premises and needs of the postcolonial world are to blame. There may be much in this. My premise is only that there is a potential for negotiation and arrangements. It should be possible to translate at least some of the mutual interests into mutually satisfactory accords even if it proves impossible in others.

Now, the peculiarity of the North-South talks that have been going on for so long is precisely that they have led practically nowhere. The contrast with major negotiations of the past is staggering. It took two or three years to prepare Bretton Woods – in very exceptional conditions, to be sure – and even after the war some international agreements have been negotiated successfully in reasonable time. The North-South talks rather lead the mind back to the desultory international economic conferences of the 1920s and 1930s culminating in the World Economic Conference in 1933.

Facile references to lacking political will or insuperable conflicts of interest in North-South issues tend to deflect attention from the very special setting and circumstances in which these issues are tackled. This is a pity as the multilateral diplomacy within which the reforms of the international economic order are discussed is a novel phenomenon.

Even the general implications of multilateral diplomacy in international organizations are not easily assessed. For major powers it may for the most part be a marginal adjunct to classical diplomacy, but to smaller and weaker countries it may offer opportunities they would not otherwise have had. Its greatest contribution has perhaps been to provide new forms for settlement of disputes that arise between States. The belief implicit in the schemes for postwar international economic organization that the time had come for universal systems of rules and international law has taken some knocks, especially in the monetary field. Although based on charters internationally negotiated, it is far from clear whether multilateral diplomacy as presently practiced in international organisations is suited for, or even capable of, reforms that would set new and different rules for governments.

Size and diversity

It cannot be denied that it must be very much more difficult to engineer agreement among 150 States than among the 50 or less that reached at least partial agreement on the post-war system for international cooperation. And at the time conditions were peculiar indeed. The participants were allied in an ongoing but victorious war. American or Anglo-American leadership was readily acquiesced to, and it was exercised with rare vision and openmindedness. In the monetary and financial discussions extraordinary personalities like Keynes and Harry Dexter White dominated the proceedings.

The present situation is obviously different on all counts. Apart from the addition of close to a hundred new States there has been a great diffusion of power frequently commented upon, and the complexity of negotiation has been compounded.

International organizations as negotiating forums

It was the control of the agenda of the United Nations that made it possible for developing countries to force talks about these matters against the reluctance of major industrial countries. The latter have frequently recalled that the United Nations is a deliberative body only, and that its proceedings should not be described as negotiations in any proper sense.

Everyone recognizes that declarations adopted by international organizations will not necessarily be abided even by States that vote for them, let alone by those who oppose them. When such declarations are nonetheless pursued, it is presumably because they are expected to have an impact on world opinion, to exercise some pressure on reluctant governments, and to guide the course of future diplomatic efforts. That they are of some importance must be the view also of governments investing considerable effort in forestalling the adoption of declarations and pronouncements which they oppose.

Such conflicts, the portentous and extensive statements, and the massive machinery of documentation and meetings lend to contemporary international assemblies an aura of importance and seriousness even when it is widely known that at best only insignificant results are to be expected. The solemnity of the proceedings appear as little more than a celebration of the fortunate circumstance that there is a shared will to confer and consult, which probably serves a role of its own and to some extent takes the place of the binding treaties often aspired to which are, after all, not the only means of ordering relations among States.

Too much has perhaps been made of the voting rights of the United Nations that enable countries contributing less than five percent of the budget to take decisions with a two-thirds majority. It threatens the very survival of the organizations if declarations are voted through in a discordant manner, but this is not a reason why genuine negotiation could not take place under the auspices of the United Nations. There are a few instances of such negotiation, but there are many grounds for suspecting that the North-South dialogue will not be crowned by grand settlement arising out of the profusion of meetings that now succeed and repeat one another in New York and Geneva.

Neither governments and delegates nor the secretariats are committed to seeking agreements that would have to involve concessions on all sides. It is hardly even envisaged, and government instructions are not framed as negotiating mandates. It is widely recognized that the present financial disorder, the alarming food prospects, the precarious energy supply arrangements and many other aspects of the world situation call for a far greater measure of international cooperation but in the proceedings of the international organizations the impulses to joint action are mostly ground asunder.

The permanent secretariats of those organizations are not necessarily well suited to drive proceedings toward positive conclusions. They have a vast range of administrative and technical tasks. They operate in a heavily bureaucratized and politicized environment leaving little scope for active and flexible brokerage, and their perception might well be swayed by their interest in the survival and enlargment of their organization and its responsibilities. The qualities that lead to promotion to high posts are not, and should perhaps not be, those wanted in a group servicing negotiations that aim at quick and forceful action. In standing bodies, with permanent delegates and secretariats, negotiations tend to become permanent too.

The group system

The division between rich and poor countries in the United Nations was established long before UNCTAD I, and the emergence of the group system was probably inevitable, especially after the setting up of an *ad hoc* working party at the OECD in 1963 in order to prepare a joint strategy for the forthcoming Geneva meeting in 1964. The only surprising thing is that it was then possible to maintain the unity of such a large and diverse body as the Group of 77.

There has been much complaint about the inherent tendency of the group system to widen rather than narrow the gaps in positions, as each of the two groups strives for agreement by yielding to its hard-liners.

In games and bargains among more than two participants coalitions will always be of decisive importance, and if such coalitions become too rigid the chances of reaching agreement will be very small. Unless the consequences of failure are perceived as so disastrous or costly as to seem worth much concession, a coalition marked by widely divergent interests might well exhaust its negotiating capacity internally and have no room for bargaining with outsiders.

Negotiators from industrial countries sometimes complain that this is precisely the trouble with the Group of 77 and that it, on its side, attributes to Group B a unity of interests and attitudes which does not exist. Southern negotiators believe that industrial countries coordinate their policies effectively in such bodies as the OECD and the EEC, and many think that if the Third World had a secretariat of its own it would make for better negotiation. It is perhaps significant that this proposal has not gained wide adherence.

In bargaining about concrete and tangible matters the group system breaks down. In specific commodity markets many Group B countries are producers and exporters which aligns them with individual members of the Group of 77. In the Law of the Sea Conference similar North-South alliances frequently arose. But in general discussions about global arrangements the group system has become institutionalized in most international organizations except the International Monetary Fund and the World Bank where the structure of decision making bodies and the weighted voting make for a different environment.

The adoption of the group system as a quasi-constitutional feature has contributed an element of structure that conferences of 150 States badly need. Third World non-alignment, of which the Group of 77 can be seen as a manifestation, has also been a contribution to international political stability. But this has been at the cost of effective multilateral negotiation. As a seasoned Swiss diplomat has concluded,

> the consulations within the respective caucuses must not be allowed to monopolize the time of international conferences to the point of relegating the real negotiating process between the groups to the eleventh hour. This has frequently happened in the past. Much more time has been spent on elaborating common platforms than on narrowing down the differences between them and on seeking to solve specific issues across the negotiating table.

The North-South dichotomy in international organizations further mesmerizes many political commentators into thinking that it is also the expression of a world-wide confrontation and stalemate in political and economic relations outside of these assemblies, and it has led to extravagant speculations about future strategems of North and South that wildly exaggerate the will and capacity of both groups to pursue united policies. There is more to the world than that, and the consequence of sustained failure to progress through multilateral diplomacy is more likely to be that it is bypassed by events and that elements of international order grow on less overarching bilateral and regional links.

Lack of individual leadership

It is undeniable that personal qualities matter greatly in international negotiation. In postwar development cooperation the vitality, determination, and charisma of some outstanding personalities is recognized to have been of decisive importance in overcoming the inertia of governments and rallying them to greater commitments in the joint interest. Robert McNamara has enhanced the standing and capacity of the World Bank. In North-South relations Raúl Prebisch played a singular role as a supplier of ideas, militant leader and persuasive mediator.

With the routinization of North-South talks they seem to have lost towering personalities who might incarnate the will to achieve what is possible and necessary and help to lead a way out of the stalemate. That is not to say that there is a lack of able and talented negotiators. The spectacular growth of multilateral diplomacy raises a great demand for delegates and negotiators, and it is understandable that governments may be reluctant to spare their best negotiators for such blocked situations. Especially for smaller and poorer countries the strain and expense of covering the sprawling agendas of current international conferences and meetings is quite unreasonable. In view of all this it is remarkable how much ability is still invested in these Byzantine proceedings.

But the circumstances do not favour the emergence of personalities commanding general respect and confidence. The task of conciliating the groups internally requires able diplomacy, and occasionally delegates from minor countries who have received no precise instructions may attain considerable influence by their freedom to manoeuvre. But the institutionalized distrust is hard to overcome, and prolonged immersion in the rarefied athmosphere of those talks is likely to impair the sense of their role.

The issue of non-reciprocity

From the outset North-South discussions have been couched in terms that could not be conducive to negotiations in a traditional sense. As Ambassador K. B. Lall of India remarked at the occasion of UNCTAD II, a negotiating technique based on mutual concessions could not easily be applied to economic development.

The basic difficulty that little or nothing could be expected to come out of strategy based on unilateral demands was recognized by Raúl Prebisch who at the end of the 1960s attempted to promote a doctrine of "convergence" under which developing countries would pledge themselves to certain policies of development which the rich countries would in return commit themselves to support, in the interest both of international solidarity and ultimately of their own welfare.

This doctrine had little impact and many Third World negotiators remained convinced that reciprocity was alien to these proceedings, either because developing countries were too poor to have anything to offer or because they were only asking for rights and dues that should not be bargained for.

That the group system also made it more difficult to offer concessions than to make demands is obvious. However, in the GATT where negotiation along group lines has been less suitable and less common developing countries have also tended to refrain from offers and thus from active participation in genuine negotiation. And in the monetary field, individual developing countries in the Committee of Twenty were so aware that their own actions had a negligible feedback on the international monetary system that they failed to realize that this was not true of them collectively and that they would therefore be expected to accept the obligations and disciplines of the proposed SDR standard if they were to collect the benefits. They were thus reduced to an attitude of "all asking and no bargaining".

The failure or unwillingness to put North-South issues in a negotiable form may have been welcome to those who did not want the talks to turn serious. Mahbub ul Haq has recently argued that in retrospect it is clear that mistakes were indeed made on both sides, that the call for a New Order should not have been launched as a "demand" of the developing countries but with more emphasis from the start on the global needs of the world economy and more attention to the interests of the North – and that the North should similarly have been wiser and more far-sighted. Such things bear saying, and the Brandt Report is an elaboration on that theme, but the trouble is that by now the habits and postures have become engrained and encrusted.

The prospects of world order talks

After reviewing these handicaps of multilateral diplomacy one must conclude that the chances of negotiating substantive change through such channels are not very great. The setting for the negotiations is so stained with failure, and the conduct of them is so cumbersome and flawed that they are heavily biased against agreement. Even such shifts in attitudes and political will as can reasonably be expected in North and South would not be likely to survive the crunching treatment of the negotiating system which has become an engine of frustration.

If the mere continuation of such talks, in Global Rounds or in other forms, will not lead anywhere, what are then the prospects?

Many both in North and South have seen the need too for a face-lifting of the agenda to make it more appropriate to the present and future needs of the world, which do not today appear quite the same as when North-South talks started. One such view as expressed by Peter Jay in an appeal to the US where he was then British Ambassador:

> There is scope indeed for an imaginative approach. It must start from the indivisibility of the globe, from the need for nations to coexist peacefully on it; from the threat to that posed by extreme inequality and absolute poverty; and from the enlightened self-interest of the developed countries in tackling poverty and extreme inequality in ways that are politically acceptable to the beneficiaries . . . the West will also to have to identify more clearly with the general and specific goals of the Third World. It will have to offer a world political and economic order that makes small countries feel secure, poor countries confident of development, aggressive countries fearful of retribution, and all countries properly independent within their necessary interdependence. The order must offer better prospects than disorder.

The Brandt Commission with its large and heterogenous membership of prominent political personalities agreed on a similar view of world needs and proposed, as an attempt to mobilize the political will and the mutual interests necessary to meet the many signs of ciris and disorder, a limited North-South summit.

Such a meeting should not be expected to strike at once a global bargain. But if approached in general awareness of the need for greater trust it could go a long way toward installing that notion of a compact which Prebisch once thought of as an "international commitment to development". The Brandt Commission, alarmed by the present trends of disorganization and mounting conflicts in a nuclear world, even saw it as a commitment to survival.

On the political foundation of a shared determination to turn the trends, multilateral diplomacy might again serve the great historical purposes that were hoped from it at its inception.

What if this does not happen? Some possibilities may be sketched. One is that the present paralysis of multilateral diplomacy is gradually overcome. The world is changing rapidly. The economic dynamism of some parts of the Third World, the financial and geopolitical role of the oil exporters, and the participation of China have not yet been fully reflected in multilateral diplomacy. With new and more numerous foci of power the possibility of more flexible and shifting alliances might restore a greater degree of mobility. Whether it would then be possible to resume the global economic constitution building of the early postwar years, which has dominated the minds in the discussion of a New Order, is an open issue. Events in the monetary field have already marked a retreat from schemes for universal rules, and the monetary non-system may be a portent of the general shape of things to come. Already several years ago, Richard Gardner suggested that

> the hope for the foreseeable future lies, not in building up a few ambitious central institutions of universal membership and general jurisdiction as was envisaged at the end of the last war, but rather in the much more decentralized, disorderly and pragmatic process of inventing or adapting institutions of limited jurisdiction and selected membership to deal with specific problems on a case-by-case basis, as the necessity for cooperation is perceived by the relevant nations.

This building of world order "from the bottom up rather than from the top down" is already under way and breaks through North-South barriers in the forging of vertical links, as in the Japan-ASEAN-Australia nexus in the Western Pacific basin, the European Lomé connection, and many messier and more confusing ones. That this development conflicts with the plans for global order drawn up in international organizations is not a serious objection. The issue is whether this decentralized approach suffices to meet the needs of a world economy in which mutual dependence is already global in so many ways. Will it enhance the risks of conflict and tension, will it leave global needs unmet, or will it make it possible to achieve the necessary trimming of national sovereignty more smoothly than the direct reach for global order? And would the Third World lose its bargaining power in a more pluralistic world, as many fear?

The conflict is probably more apparent than real. Multilateral global diplomacy would in any case stand to gain from paring its agenda down to essentials which would restore its capacity for the double task of political dialogue and technical negotiation.

4.3. A New International Law for a New World Order

Erik Suy

The title of my topic unavoidably raises a question which many are asking: Do we have a new world order? An objective survey of the international scene would indicate that we are indeed witnessing the emergence of a new order, which differs in many respects from the old. One important difference is the universal character of the present world community, as compared to what it was prior to, or even immediately following, 1945. The new world order is universal in membership, in outlook and in purpose. The old order was predominantly European and the active international community consisted almost exclusively of European States and their dependencies across the oceans.

Among the original Members of the United Nations there were only 12 Asian and African States out of a total of 51; a mere 24% representing more than two-thirds of humanity. Today the United Nations has 89 Asian and African Member States out of 154; a more reasonable 58%. Nations that had been excluded from the select community of the old order are now active members of the new, with a voice in all matters of import to the global family of nations. Universal in membership, the new order is also universal in outlook. The old elitist mentality of "we" and "they", which characterized the old order, is being replaced by a new self-image and a new world-view of the international community. Although immediate individual and group interests may still diverge, the pervading spirit is one of universality transcending those individual or group differences. States or groups of States no longer look at themselves in isolation. Ours is indeed becoming "one world" with bonds of solidarity and interdependence among its members never felt so strongly before.

The new order is also universal in purpose. The main concern is no longer the preservation of good relations among a limited number of States. The aims of the new order are global and its attention is turned, beyond the traditional objectives of peace and security, to such questions of universal concern as co-operation, development and environmental control, to mention only a few. Universal good – or the *bonum commune humanitatis* – is the proclaimed aim of all, although there may be disagreement on how to achieve it. In the old order States were hardly concerned with the universal good and did not hesitate to pursue their narrow self-interest to the detriment of others or even of an unrecognized universal good that might be shared by all.

Beyond its universality expressed in those three dimensions, the new order has other characteristics that set it apart from the old. That old order was committed to stability rather than to progress, was not concerned with true equality among the nations of the world on a global scale and was so self-satisfied that doubts seem never to have disturbed its passive tranquility. By contrast, the new order is committed to change, is egalitarian in more than a formal sense and is highly self-critical in the search of a better world for all.

One of the more evident characteristics of the new order is its recognition of the social, economic and political interdependence of the world community. It is now widely acknowledged that our entire earth-space environment is an ecological unit both in a basic scientific sense and in terms of the social processes by which we exploit it. Although this physical interdependence has always existed, its intensity, as well as the general perception thereof and of the necessity to protect and preserve it are characteristic of the new order.

The new order is also *economically* interdependent. The limited availability of natural resources and the need for certain human resources make the idea of economic self-sufficiency appear more and more unrealistic and outmoded. The unbalanced distribution of natural resources and of population in earth-space in conjunction with the steadily more insistent demands by people for a better and a more prosperous life are also realities of the new order. By now the more prosperous States have realized that their economy and prospects depend upon events occurring in other countries and that their own stability requires stability in areas beyond their territorial jurisdiction.

Political interdependence is another characteristic feature of the new order. Events in one country may alter the internal political and social processes of another country. A national crisis in country A may well cause internal crisis in country B, in a region or in the world.

In all these respects the emerging new order appears to be the antithesis of the old. True, the old order did not completely disappear and it may be contrary to the nature of human affairs that it would do so overnight. The important thing is that a process, seemingly irreversible, has been set in motion. The two orders still co-exist, the old on the wane, the new on the rise. They overlap in certain areas and are in diametric opposition in others. But the mere fact that the change from the old to the new has started indicates that the process so commenced is likely to achieve its end and that the new order will one day displace the old.

*

The emerging new order is characterized by a complexity which derives from an intricate world social process. The pattern of international relations is undergoing rapid and important changes through the advent of new actors whose behaviour was only occasionally taken into account in the past. Non-State actors, such as transnational corporations and individuals, have a growing impact on inter-State relations and their activities have become of growing concern to States. The increasing number of international treaties dealing with those new actors transform international law and relations. The Convenants on human rights, the treaty outlawing apartheid, the convention on the elimination of all forms of racial discrimination, recent efforts to curb aerial hi-jacking, the taking of hostages and the activities of mercenaries and the elaboration of a convention on the protection of diplomats clearly indicate the concern of the international community to deal with potential threats to international peace and security which are of a non-State origin.

International law is by and large observed by States. But the activities of individuals and groups tend more and more to affect and destabilize the fabric of orderly relations between States. The international community is therefore called upon to deal with those activities, which have to be controled on a national level through criminal legislation. Accepted general principles of international law already compel States to take measures to prevent violations of established rules by individuals and to prosecute those who destabilize interstate relations. But it seems necessary to start a process of harmonization and even unification of criminal law in certain areas. Therefore the possibility of creating a United Nations Commission on International Criminal Law might be examined.

Similarly, efforts are under way to regulate activities of transnational corporations in order to achieve at least two goals: first, that they contribute to the development of the less developed parts of the world, and second, that they be prevented from using their power and influence to destabilize or interfere in the internal affairs of States.

In addition to the traditional non-State entities, there are now different governmental and non-governmental organizations such as organizations of raw material exporting countries, and various regional associations.

Even the more traditional non-State entities such as the United Nations and its specialized agencies have expanded the scope of their activities; they have adopted resolutions, decisions, and declarations on many important social, economic, political and technical issues. Many of these resolutions, decisions and declarations have been adopted without a vote, by consensus or by acclamation. Contemporary international law must deal with these new "prescriptive norms". There are a number of questions that must be examined. For example, to what extent are the decisions of those various intergovernmental organizations creating new norms? Are they legal norms? Are they generally binding legal norms, or are some of them binding and some not? How are the binding norms determined? These are only a few examples of the complex issues that an adequate international law of the new order has to face.

What role does international law play in this process of the emergence of a new order? Could it in any way help in the evolution and the consolidation of this new world order? This raises the recurrent question of whether law, in general, is only a reflection of social realities, which supports the existing order and helps preserve it?

According to this view, law is a mere superstructure which undergoes change only as prior changes in the infrastructure require it. A different view sees law not only as an expression of what is but also as an indicator of what ought to be or even as an instrument for attaining it; according to that view law can and should be a tool for change in society's search for higher values and for a better deal for all its members.

Actually, law operates in a structure of reality, which exhibits elements of stability and of change. With regard to the elements of stability, law exemplifies the principle of order. But law also strives for the principle of justice and thereby the elements of change come into the picture. Admittedly, the most urgent aim of international law is the achievement of order and security. However, justice is increasingly asserting itself as a highly important, though more remote, objective of international law. In fact, the absence of at least a modicum of justice has an impact on the legitimacy and thus the validity or even the existence of any legal system, at least in relation to groups that are deprived of fundamental rights or whose just expectations are flagrantly ignored. To such members of the community the particular legal order would appear as wholly arbitrary and oppressive – and therefore, illegitimate and unacceptable. Hence the need in international law for a judicious balance between the principle of order and the principle of justice. To a considerable extent international law has to be a tool for a change in a world order where new claims are being pressed that cannot simply be ignored. Continued disregard of such new claims might well affect the principle of order itself with deplorable consequences for all members of the international community.

There are undoubtedly limits to the use of international law as an instrument of "social engineering" on a global scale. Those limits stem mainly from the still largely consensual nature of international legal norms. Recent developments, however, point to the emergence of a living international law that is not purely consensual in nature.

Examples of the principles of this new living international law are decolonization, eradication of racial discrimination, assistance in development and sharing of global resources. In all these areas, and in others, principles have emerged or are emerging which cannot be traced to a formal source based on State consent in the traditional manner. In fact, the States against whom claims in these areas are made would be expected to withhold formal consent while going along with a general consensus on the necessity for establishing these principles.

Resolutions of the deliberative bodies of international organizations, and specially of the United Nations General Assembly, are important instruments in this new process of formulating international norms. It would be possible to contend that the General Assembly is only giving formal expression to what the majority of its membership has come to regard as obligatory. This has effected a deep change in the nature of the process by which customary rules of international law emerge. The time factor in lawmaking through custom has become insignificant while the *opinio juris* factor, being self-evident in the resolution itself, is no longer subject to speculation or to differences of opinion as to whether it exists or not. Thus the General Assembly has carried customary lawmaking much further than before and has found a measure of support for the legitimacy of its activities in the recent jurisprudence of the International Court of Justice.

Technical opposition to this trend, based on the consideration that General Assembly resolutions are recommendations and not decisions, no longer appears to be overwhelmingly convincing. If it is true that legal norms must carry sanctions, the nature of the sanction itself is a different matter. Under the influence of domestic law, lawyers have come to regard sanction as institutionalized coercion ensuring compliance. But in the international arena, sanction may well take a different form consonant with the different nature of international society. There the coercion is non-institutionalized, but informal pressures or general opprobrium, and actual or potential adverse effects on membership status, more often than not result in compliance with even "non-binding" resolutions. Such "indirect" sanctions may thus be just as effective as a directly imposed specific sanction built into the legal system. It is therefore no exaggeration to say that the general will of the international community has acquired a certain legislative status when manifested through formal actions of international institutions. In this sense the General Assembly resolution is becoming a useful modern tool for standard-setting and rule-creation in an expanded international society that requires more rapid formulations of standards governing the conduct of its members.

Whatever the importance of the standards and norms created through this novel process may be, sovereign consent naturally still remains a very important basis of international lawmaking. But conventional rules have contributed to the emergence of the new world order and should be enabled to play a still larger role in defining its future course.

*

With the active participation of all States, conventional international law will by definition become truly universal, reflecting not only the views of all States and embodying the concepts of all legal systems. That it must also secure universal implementation may sound rather idealistic, but there can be no other solution. A glance at the volume of multilateral treaties concluded over the last thirty-five years clearly indicates how global interdependence affects international law-making. The trend towards a truly universal world order is clear. However, in order to achieve this goal several conditions must be fulfilled.

First and foremost there must be a genuine willingness of all States to proceed with the codification and progressive development of international law through international conventions.

Second, all States must be given the opportunity to participate in this exercise. Such universal participation in the elaboration of international instruments was not realized in the past (except in some recent instances, such as the Third Law of the Sea Conference). Even after the membership of the United Nations became almost universal, one of the major obstacles has been that many countries did not have the material possibility of participating in law-making conferences because these exercises took place in cities where they did not have a diplomatic representation. It would seem therefore that New York is the most suitable place for this type of gathering, unless other UN centers (perhaps Geneva or Vienna) become equally representative.

A third and major difficulty seems to be that not all countries have at their disposal the necessary qualified manpower to deal with often simultaneously conducted law-making conferences. One should therefore have a close look at the feasibility of organizing the international conference calendar in a way that maximum attendance can be achieved. This would mean that international law-making gatherings may have to be spaced (in the case where a diplomatic conference is being called) and that these conferences could only be organized if and when maximum attendance can be secured. It may therefore be necessary to hold those meetings within the framework of sessions of the General Assembly of the United Nations, and one may envisage that efforts to draft a multilateral convention of a universal nature could extend through several sessions of the General Assembly. At the same time, serious efforts should be made to help strengthen the capacity of new nations to deal with the growing demands for expertise in the various fields of international law.

Fourth, even if legislative activities continue primarily at diplomatic conferences, the rules of procedure should provide that non-participating delegations be entitled to submit texts or amendments.

Fifth, since many duly adopted conventions are not signed or ratified by a sufficient majority of States to enter into force or, even if formally in force, to achieve world-wide effectiveness, and it seems difficult for the United Nations to exercise pressure on States to become parties to a particular treaty, efforts should be made to concentrate on the difficulties that cause these delays and develop some means of assuring faster universal participation.

Finally, is it not timely to think about implementation procedures? For example, States that have become parties to a treaty might be induced to report on the way they have implemented it – a procedure that has been adopted in the field of human rights and of the protection of diplomats. Reports of implementing measures, as well as reports on violations of treaties, have gradually become acceptable. One could perhaps examine the feasibility of inserting such reporting requirements in the final clauses of all multilateral treaties. A compulsory reporting system on both the implementation and the breaches of a treaty, combined with an appropriate control and settlement mechanism, seems to be a feasible next step in the development of international law.

In this context, I wish to refer to two recent experiences that may very well have set striking precedents. At its 35th session the UN General Assembly adopted a resolution on "Consideration of effective measures to enhance the protection, security and safety of diplomatic and consular missions and representatives" (35/168), which establishes a control mechanism under which States are invited to report to the Secretary-General serious violations of the protection, security and safety of diplomatic and consular missions and representatives. States where such violations took place are invited to report on measures they have taken to bring the offenders to justice and to prevent repetition; the Secretary-General is to circulate these reports to all States and submit an annual report to the General Assembly.

On a similar matter the Assembly adopted a resolution on the "Respect of the privileges and immunities of officials of the United Nations and the specialized agencies" (35/212). Under this resolution all organs, organizations and bodies of the United Nations system are requested to furnish information on cases in which there are clear indications that the protected status of a staff member has not been fully respected. The Secretary-General is to submit a report to the General Assembly on those cases.

It may confidently be expected that these reporting practices will serve as an incentive towards a more complete respect for the international obligations States have undertaken in these fields. The reports, which may receive appropriate publicity, may also appear as a device worthy of further exploration as a means of enhancing the respect for international law.

*

In the course of a debate in the Sixth Committee during the General Assembly's last session it was observed that the work of the United Nations on the codification and progressive development of international law played a significant role in the Organization's efforts to implement the principles of the Charter by promulgating fair and equitable legal rules to ensure the peaceful development of international relations, to strengthen peace and security, to encourage the peaceful settlement of disputes and to promote co-operation among States and to further the establishment of a new economic and political world order.

In its universality, complexity and interdependence, the new order doubtless needs such support. As far as the *peaceful settlement of disputes* is concerned, one must of course start with Article 33 of the United Nations Charter, which sets out various modalities for settling disputes. These methods have long been the object of numerous and detailed international treaties and other instruments. Major world-wide instruments include the First Hague Convention on the Peaceful Settlement of International Disputes (18 October 1907), the General Act for the Pacific Settlement of International Disputes (26 September 1928), and the Revised General Act (28 April 1949); similar regional treaties were concluded among the American States (Pact of Bogotà, 30 April 1948) and among Western European States (29 April 1957). However, on the universal level, no relevant major treaty has been developed for more than thirty years, although the membership of the international community has tripled. Moreover, a closer look at the status of participation in the universal treaties on the peaceful settlement of international disputes, reveals the very small number of States having either ratified or adhered to those instruments. For example, only 22 States acceded to the General Act of 26 September 1928 and only seven States to the Revised General Act of 28 April 1949, which the General Assembly of the United Nations adopted as a universal convention.

One may wonder if, in view of the achievement of all but perfect universality in the international community, a new effort should not be undertaken to negotiate a comprehensive universal treaty on the peaceful settlement of disputes.

But even if such an initiative is undertaken, one should not forget that specific disputes cannot always be resolved by existing stand-by machinery. Territorial disputes are not identical with disputes concerning the application or interpretation of treaty provisions; disputes concerning trade or economic agreements have little in common with environment agreements. Some settlement provisions are more suitable to some types of disputes than to others.

Territorial disputes, however, seem to be of a growing concern to the international community although they are, by definition, of a local or regional character. In the future development of international relations, many territorial conflicts will no doubt be the consequence of former colonial situations reflecting boundaries that were established withouth taking into account important factors. It is true that in the immediate post-colonial era the principle *uti possidetis iuris* was accepted both in Latin America and in Africa, in order to avoid territorial disputes, but in the long run it may not always provide an absolute guarantee of territorial stability. This seems to be an area where judicial settlement has proov-ed useful, and one could explore further means of improving methods for settling territorial disputes through judicial or arbitral proceedings. But would it not be worthwhile to examine the possibility of establishing within regional organizations a permanent expert body charged with monitoring and studying territorial and boundary situations in all their aspects: historical, geographical, economic and legal, as well as taking into account the views of the governments concerned; such studies or surveys could be most useful as background material in further efforts towards settling future conflicts.

The limited participation in disputes settlement conventions is exemplified by the very low rate of acceptance of the compulsory jurisdiction of the International Court of Justice. In 1950, when the international community of States had some 60 members (including some non-members of the UN), 36 (exactly 60%) had accepted the compulsory jurisdiction of the Court, though some of these acceptances were weakened by serious reservations. Today, 157 States are parties to the Statute of the Court, but only 47 (30%) have made declarations under article 36, para. 2 of the Statute, which is just half the former rate. It would seem that the more universal the community of States becomes, the weaker is the tendency towards compulsory jurisdiction, whether through arbitration or judicial settlement. If this is the crux of the problem, why not convene a universal conference to discuss those issues? What are the obstacles to genuine peaceful settlement? Why is it that the overwhelming majority of States does not accept the compulsory jurisdiction of the World Court, even though they are parties to its Statute? What is wrong with the conciliation procedures established more than half a century ago? If it is true that judicial settlement is more appropriate for territorial disputes, what about the settlement of conflicts in the many other fields of international interaction? Confrontations have been avoided and conflicts solved through a variety of other means, some of which are only just now being developed. Is there some merit in new procedures such as consultations? It seems to me that these questions ought to be addressed first of all in a forum of experts before being broached on an official level.

*

The progress of *science and technology* during the forthcoming decades can only be a matter of speculation and guesswork to those who in their lifespan have witnessed tremendous developments that have transformed international relations and brought about new fields of international law, such as space law and nuclear law, while revolutionizing others, such as the law of the sea, patent law and telecommunication law. Additional and still more drastic technological developments will require urgent consideration of their international implications. It is likely that, quite soon, the current discussions on the definition of outer space will sound as archaic as the classic delimitation of the territorial sea on the basis of the reach of coastal batteries.

It seems to me that one of the major consequences of the impact of scientific and technological developments on international relation will be the growing importance of specialized agencies. The predominance of the mainly political organization, the United Nations, will probably have to yield to the ever-growing role of specialized institutions in dealing with the regulation of international developments one can expect in those fields. It is of course to be hoped that this increased responsibility will not lead to an increasing politization of these agencies. Although there has been such a trend, it now seems that governments have come to realize that the benefit for the whole of mankind of sensibly regulating the growing progress in science and technology should not be overshadowed by petty nationalistic interests.

*

I have dealt very briefly with some, and only some, of the questions posed by the recent qualitative changes on the world scene that are the harbingers of a new order. The challenge now facing international law and organization is that of keeping pace with the shifting realities of international relations. Members of the international community appear to have realized that long-term stability, which is the classical concern of the law, can only be achieved through timely responsiveness to change. Changes have indeed taken place in the structure of the world community and in the power relations among its members. The success or the failure of those involved in the law-making process at the international level will be measured by the degree to which they can adapt international law and organization to the changing realities of our times. Their crowning success would be the elaboration of a new international law for a new world order. W. Friedman used the expression "international law of cooperation". Today, nearly twenty years later, we could perhaps accentuate this notion by using the term: "international law of solidarity"!

4.4. Changes in the Norms Guiding the International Legal System – History and Contemporary Trends

BO JOHNSON THEUTENBERG

An old treatise in international law, compiled by Baron Demmel de Carels Croon and printed in Amsterdam in 1732, clearly indicates that orderly inter-State relations existed in the distant past. It gives proof that rules of conduct were also codified in treaties then as they are today. This work is worth reading. In one part, ancient documents from "les temps les plus reculez jusque à l'Empereur Charlemagne" are to be found – most astonishing – documents signed by the pharaohs of ancient Egypt, the Persian king Xerxes, Alexander the Great, various muslim rulers, caliphs and sultans. The other part contains documents from Charlemagne up to the "present time", i. e. the year 1732.

In these days, when debates are going on about the nature of international law and its shape for the future, it is useful to read treatises of the kind I have just mentioned. It is important, almost a *sine qua non*, to get back to the historic perspectives in international law. It is primarily necessary for occidental experts in international law to become orientated in history – political, economic and religious history. In its striving for material perfections, the occidental world has overlooked these foundations. But we shall never be able to understand trends in the rest of the world unless we try to "get away" from the Euro-centric aspect of international law. We must recognize the fact that other parts of the world had their own functioning systems in the past, even sophisticated law systems, and that these systems somehow are in the background when former colonies now return to the Society of States. It is a sort of come-back. The "new States" are not new in the sense that they entered into statehood from a vacuum. Of course not, all the time they have existed in the historical, cultural and religious sense. But military-political constellations cut them off from participating in the shaping of "modern" international law.

But when all these "newer States" are now in a position freely to express their own opinions and safeguard their own interests, it seems quite natural that they to a large extent base their actions on their old historical, cultural and religious traditions. Thus, there is in my opinion a clear link between the history of inter-State relations in its broad sense and the future shape of international law. We witness new tendencies in present-day international law and these tendencies are more understandable when put into their correct historical perspectives. Almost every country in the Afro-Asian world, sometimes called developing countries (the term "developing" applies only in its industrial sense, because the occidental world has scarcely anything to teach the developing world about moral values, religion and justice), has rich historical sources to draw from when taking decisions in different spheres. The interests and needs of one country are always formed out of a complex past. When Europe dominated the world on the strength of its colonial system, the then existing European States played their roles – both internally and externally – taking their common European background into consideration. There were no clashes between different systems, quite simply because the "European Concert" made its own external rules. The States decided themselves how to behave towards one another. Nowadays it is more complicated. The Society of States is now, at long last, universal. Many different systems are to co-exist. Different historical, religious and cultural systems should interweave with one another. To do this, all different regions of the Society of States should penetrate deeper into one another's thinking and traditions. A better understanding of the details of the different systems would help us to preserve peace. The Occident, on its part, has much to learn in this respect.

We must realize that new tendencies in international law may often be deeply rooted in the history, culture and religion of one particular region. We must also remember that in the past law and religion were one and the same. Religion shaped and sanctioned the laws. The laws then became divine and unchangeable. The god formed the internal legal rules, but since internal laws and rules always are reflected in the external relations between countries, inter-State relations were also affected by the divine legislation, whether it was the Egyptian Ra, the Babylonean Shamash, the Israelian El Aeljon or Jahve, the divine Emperor of Japan or China, the Allah of Islam, the Greek and Roman gods who gave the commandments. We must remember that although all modern States have typical interests to safeguard – development, trade, commerce, economy, etc. – all States are products of their respective systems. They cannot remove themselves from their traditions, albeit they are formally trying to adhere to modern ideologies. It is also vital to take modern ideologies into account when analysing the norms of international law; otherwise the analysis would be incomplete. We must be realistic. Not only must historical, cultural and religious factors be taken into consideration, but modern doctrines and ideologies, like Marxism and socialism, must be included in our analysis of changes in the international system of norms.

Rules governing inter-State, or at least inter-community, relations have existed in one form or another for milleniums. International law is surely not an invention by Europe. We know, for example, that a treaty existed already between Pharaoh Ramses II and the King of the Hethites, Hattusili III, pertaining to the frontiers of the province of Canaan, done in the year 1284 B. C. There are early Egyptian rules of warfare, prohibiting the poisoning of wells and governing the treatment of prisoners of war which date back to 1400 B. C. The Persian King, Cyrus, forbade his soldiers to loot Babylon when he conquered the site in the year 538 B. C. The same regulations are known from Alexander the Great's conquest of Western Asia.

It is also interesting to note that the States in Asia and the Far East developed rules of inter-State conduct, which are deemed to have survived in their legal and cultural heritage.

The ancient Chinese world order, for instance, although it is described as a Sinocentric hierarchy, recognized neighbouring peoples and even other States as equal adversaries. A complicated inter-State system developed, where inner and outer zones played an important role. The *nei-fu* was the inner or royal domain (or in another term"all-under-Heaven") and *wai-fu*, areas of the outer lords. The outermost zone was named *fan*, which is transliterated as "foreign", "barbarian", i. e. outside the domain of the Emperor. Those concepts can be dated back to the first millenium B. C. Ancient Chinese views on inter-State relations are founded on the teachings of Confucius, which even today influences the Chinese thinking. In Confucius' work *Ch'un-ch'iu* there is a kind of balance between the ideal way of dealing with the *fan*-world, i. e. the barbarians; either by pacifism or militarism. The barbarians were considered external; sometimes they were militarily strong and then a policy of appeasement was followed; just as today the balance of power makes it urgent to construe a principle in international law named peaceful co-existence. Otherwise, the Chinese ideal was the principle of *Wang-che wu-wai* – the principle of universality – "the King leaves nothing and nobody outside his realm". In other words, a truly universal King. This idea we recognize generally as a red thread running through the history of mankind. Many systems have claimed universality: a *Pax Romana* governing the world, a *Pax Islamica, Pax Christiania;* and why not a *Pax Communistica?* The claims of universal adherence to the one and only system leads sooner or later to confrontations in international law and to the outbreak of wars, out of which situation a principle of *modus vivendi* such as "peaceful co-existence" usually develops.

In our days the doctrine of "just war" is essential. Nowadays "just war" is described in Article 51 of the UN Charter. Only a war in self-defence is *bellum justum*. But this is by no means something new. The same idea can be traced back through history, both in the *shari'a*-law and Roman law, and the first historic signs thereof are probably to be found already with Confucius in the first millenium B. C. Confucius distinguished between five kinds of military force. Forces used to settle chaos within the realm and to punish the turraneous are righteous forces, which will dominate "all-under-Heaven", i. e. all China. Forces that are used with reluctance for the purpose of self-defence are responsive forces, which will win. Forces used to release minor grudges or resentments are resentful forces, which will suffer defeat. And, now we hear an echo from history: forces used to seize territory and wealth are greedy forces, which will meet destruction. Finally, forces used to display great power and numerical strength to save the enemy are arrogant forces, which will meet extinction. Confucius claims that these five are not only "matters of man" but also the ways of Heaven; again a religious sanction with regard to inter-State relations.

It is very interesting to make a connection here between the doctrines of Confucius and the international law-materia within the Islamic *shari'a*-law. Divine Islamic law also restricts the use of force. In the Islamic world order, wars could only be launched for righteous purposes, purposes blessed by divine law. Here we have the doctrine of *djihād*, which was circumscribed by strict rules. We have almost the Confucian five principles enunciated here: forces against chaos and heresy within the realm; the concepts *ridda, bāghī, muhārībūn,* and the very essential one – *ribāt* – defence of the holy territory of Islam. These are righteous forces, *bellum justum,* and these principles should still today govern the use of force, since they are part of the unchangeable *sharī'a*-law.

A special observation must be made here. All the ancient systems have a flexible border between morals, or ethics, and the law. The different systems contained an all-embracing "way of life", not only strict legal rules. Today it is perhaps the moral and ethical aspects that are the stronger part of the heritage from these ancient systems. This also goes for the *Buddhist* system. This is really an ethical system – a way of thinking – although even here a canonic law system is to be found, namely the 227 rules of the *Vinaya,* the "Guidance". Medieval China respected Indian States as equals because they were the home of Buddhism, a sort of respect and *modus vivendi* between religious systems. In this region of the world the *Hindu*-system also denotes dominance. The *Code of Manu* dating from 500 B. C. is interesting from the point of view of international law, e. g., it prohibited the use of poisoned weapons against enemy forces (contained in book No. 7 dealing with the rules of government, including the art of war). Buddhism and Hinduism are still the foundations of societies in the Far East, and thus somehow influence their basic outlook on what form relations between States should take. Of course, from the strictly scientific point of view, this subject must be analysed, perhaps by case studies, but all the same, we could probably agree that these systems form the historical, cultural and religious foundations of a great part of the world.

It is true that Confucianism, Buddhism and Hinduism, even Islam, in a sense upheld the principles of universality. The eternal "truth" was one and the same and that "truth" should be propagated all over the world. However, if this really was the basic doctrine, I believe it is fair to say that the ethical-religious systems now mentioned were in the main liberal in their attitude to adversaries and neighbouring peoples. Their doctrines did not require them to blot out enemies and adversaries from the earth. Co-existence with other peoples was possible; one example is the Islamic principle regulating the positions of *dhimmis* – believers in another faith – within the realm of Islam. Other faiths were accepted within Islam, something that has been forgotten in world politics for quite some time.

Many principles in international law can thus be traced back through history. Even before a powerful Europe existed ancient cultures hailed basically the same principles, or perhaps rather ideas, that are purported to have been invented by the occidental world. One conclusion can be drawn from this: the different systems in the world today may be based on the same theoretical foundation when we get down to the real essence of our common values in international law. For instance, the protection of foreign envoys and embassies is something that was recognized in ancient cultures, even primitive societies. Sophisticated rules about their protection are to be found in ancient Egypt, China, Greece, Rome and the Empire of Islam. Authors of the ancient world talk about foreign envoys as "*jure gentium sancti*" and the one who violates these basic rules is by these authors considered as *"violator juris gentium"*, i. e. offenders against the Law of Nations.

I believe it is fair to purport that some different elements are flowing into the corpus of rules regulating relations with foreign peoples when the doctrines of the Greek philosophers are coming into existence some hundred years B. C. We notice now a nationalistic, almost elitarian trend. The cities of Greece develop a sophisticated inter-State law system; here the old customs of taking hostages are even regulated by treaties. A "Greco-centric" inter-State system is being shaped; a common cultural and religious background crystallizes the law system into a highly developed "inter-family" law system, exactly as happened to the Roman *"juris gentium"* and the so-called modern international law or the Euro-centric international law that has survived until now. Because of an elitist educational system among the Greeks the benefit of the inter-State laws were never extended to the peoples outside the frontiers of the Greek amphictyon. Is not this *mutatis mutandis,* also a characteristic of the Euro-centric international law that has developed during the last hundred years? The Hellenistic people had, says Paul Fauchille, "une haute opinion de leur race: race, a leur yeux, supérieure, appelée à exerser la suprématie sur les autres peuples, sur les barbares: telle était l'opinion de Platon, celle d'Aristote". The "barbarians" were outside the law; the political duty was to conquer them. This is, regrettably, a good definition also of the Euro-centric attitude to interstate relations less than one hundred years ago.

These trends continue and are even strenghtened in the laws developing during the epoch of the Roman Empire. All the imperfections, so to say, in the Greek system are now being transformed into an extremely meticulous and sophisticated system of laws – the Roman Law. This is actually the very foundation of the European schools of law. Principles from Roman Law have been taken up by most occidental legal systems. During medieval times Roman Law was revived by the glossatores and transformed into the internal systems of most of the European States. Even Roman Law had a religious background; it was considered as *jus naturale,* emanating from a divine mind. But it is important to note that this legal foundation for all Europe continues on the harsh and elitist path from the Greeks. Now the notion of *jus gentium* develops, i. e. one all-embracing universal law governing the world – *Pax Romana.* The Romans took a harsh, even cruel stand against foreign peoples, the barbarians. They should be conquered. "Le désir, la volonté de la domination universelle régit et gouverne tout le développement politique de la puissance romain", says Fauchille. "Elle ne put souffrir ni rivales, ni égales". With the Roman Law – spread over the world by the Roman legions – the principle of pacifism and peaceful co-existence disappears from the corpus of law. And another very important factor – the excellent Roman lawyers with their sophisticated rules of law pertaining to *private and civil rights* have deeply influenced the international corpus of laws in this particular direction. Ideas about private rights, rights of ownership, procedural and formal questions were not transformed also into the public international law. This is important to note. The preoccupation of modern occidental international law with "rights" to territories, rights to air-space, rights to the sea, rights to the territorial sea, rights to their colonies etc. have most surely much to do with the ownership-oriented trend in Roman private law, where the rightful owner was always protected; he had a sophisticated procedural system to hand by which he, the owner, sustained his proper rights of ownership. This is actually an idea that has survived until now in Euro-centric law, internal as well as external. Man owns his territory; he does what he likes with it, because he owns it by right. Man even thought he owned the Earth by heritage and right. Only in these days, with the evolvement of international environmental law, has man come to realize that he has no rights to anything. He is only the guardian, the caretaker of what has been entrusted to him.

This survey of the normative system regulating inter-State relations has so far shown that many systems have contributed to the product. There are more common goods than we thought. We have now come to the point in our analysis of the history of international law where part of present-day international law is taking shape. We have actually to go that far back to understand the underlying elements in our respective systems. We, the Europeans, must see what has influenced us. Why have we treated the rest of the world as we have over the centuries? We must go far back to understand the foundation of Buddhism, Hinduism and Islam. These religions are still governing a greater part of the world in many respects, and now, when the European domination of the world system tends to fade out in many respects, these ancient systems are free to come to the surface again, after many centuries of political oppression by the colonial system. These ethical and religious systems, also containing the law, have existed for centuries and centuries, but not until today – in the year of 1981 A. D. – are they again free to develop in separate directions, if these countries choose to do so. We do not know what will happen with the corpus of international law. Recent evidence has shown that Islam again acts with strength, and naturally the rest of the world asks the question whether this means that some doctrines of the Islamic *shari'a*-law in the long run will influence the corpus of international law with regard to inter-State relations; and in that case what interpretation of the *shari'a*-law will be the guiding one. Is it going to be an orthodox interpretation, as we now see in some parts of the Islamic world?

It is a strange thing for peoples of the Occident to see, in these days, how a theocracy is being formed in the name of Allah. The occidental observer suddenly sees how Islam as a religion and system of ethics, is back in an influential and powerful position. But the view is distorted. This is not a sudden thing, not a real revival in the correct sense. Islam has been there all the time as a system, the fact of the matter is that the Occident, by virtue of its political power, has had no need to penetrate into the Islamic system, because it was of no real relevance other than from the theoretical point of view. But now, matters have changed. Because political circumstances and the decolonization period have brought back ancient cultural systems into real world politics, the Occident is forced to gain insight into strange areas like religious and ethical dogmas. A materialistic world has to understand that life is conducted in accordance with "higher values", in accordance with a strict religious system, also affecting the legal world of the regions. In my opinion this is quite a natural historical and political process. When the European domination and the European bonds now are being lifted from the colonial world, it is natural that these countries revert to their own "values". The interesting thing is, however, that it is not only one single country that takes recourse to its own cultural system, but a big part of the world, the whole Afro-Asian group of countries. Acting in the same direction, those countries can most surely influence the evolution of international law.

The Occident with its materialistic, industrialized society, where generally speaking all values are being measured in terms of physical welfare, assets and money is in many aspects approaching a crisis of identity. When industries cannot grow bigger, when profits decline, the Western advanced society is trembling. It is perhaps a crisis of ideals and values that has been characteristic of that part of the world since the First World War. The norms are missing. The legal rules have lost their original connection with "normal and higher justice", and that goes for internal rules as well as for rules in the external field; how States should behave towards one another. A true civilization is really not a technological but an ethical phenomenon. When the ethical basis disappears, a civilization will face problems of identity. Against this very background the Occident meets other, totally strange phenomena, even influencing world politics. Against a standpoint of materialism and even atheism, men in the Occident cannot get it into their heads that a great part of the world basically hails other values, morals, ethics, religions. That they, for example, act in accordance with religious commandments.

This is strange, we maintain, but the Occident should be aware of its own history. History links us up with our own past systems, and in those systems, cultural and religious – we in fact meet the same features. Even the Occident has emerged from a strict religious system. We should therefore be able to recognize and even understand the basic elements in the legal systems of other parts of the world. We must be in a position to realize that other regions might have different wishes and needs with regard to the shape of international law. And that these wishes have something to do with the identity of those countries. Striving for independence and nationalism usually contains more than just pure political independence. It involves the revival of the indigenous culture and traditions, and a rejection of cultural elements which are considered foreign.

At about the same time as the legal heritage from the Antique and Roman epochs is taken over by the Roman Catholic Church for further development, another religion and law system is coming into being, namely Islam. Both systems have the dogmas of universality built in, and thus, unfortunately, the systems have been fighting each other down the centuries. These two systems have taken up arms against one another. We could here refer to the *djihād*-doctrine, the duty of believers to strive for the spreading of Islam. Today, when Islam is acting in world politics with strength, the doctrine of *djihād* is again being brought up. The notion is used in various ways, sometimes leaving room for questions about what it really stands for. Since it is a part of the *sharī'a*-law it has divine origin, and is consequently guiding the thoughts of believers and true Islamic countries in their inter-State relationships. But what will the effects be of this doctrine, because this doctrine might, in its essence, have effects on the very principles of the U.N. Charter. This question is quite vital for future international law. I believe it is important that the different systems try to allow a just analysis of their respective legal norms. Only so can misunderstandings be avoided as to the true contents of the norms. Islam and the Occident have much to talk about, much to inform each other about, but now on an equal footing. We must be fully aware of the fact that political-military circumstances and constellations may "push" the dogmas towards a clear distortion, and after that much is destroyed. The distorted and misunderstood dogmas will exist as "eternal" barriers to rapprochement between the systems.

Just as the dogma of *djihād* once became involved in political-military entanglements, so the Christian message of universality "Go and teach *all* nations" became disturbed by the medieval political constellations. The divine missionary message was misused in the name of Christianity. Unfortunately, we still suffer the effects of this; the suspicion is even today sometimes obvious in the relationship between the Occident and Islam, for instance, just as in the broader relations between the developing Third World and the occidental industrialized world. It is fair to state, I believe, that historical developments temporarily confused the notion of "universal human brotherhood" and its logical implications. Because the Christian message had from its origin a purely theological-religious meaning, the conquest of minds, instead of a conquest by arms.

As to the Islamic *djihād*-doctrine a distortion has most surely come about to some extent because of linguistic difficulties to give an adequate translation of the very complex dogma of *djihād*. It has become equivalent to the "holy war". This expression is, also nowadays, used more in its physical sense mainly in Western literature, but also, to a large extent, by the Islamic countries themselves. Apart from the classical order of law, and the Islamic tradition of law *(hadīth)* in this field, it is important to note, I believe, that several modern Islamic treatises and scholars differ as to the interpretation of the real meaning of *djihād*. In order to counter the general idea of a "holy war", modern Moslems profess that *djihād* is essentially defensive warfare, striving to protect Islam, its territory and its believers and to guarantee the propagation of the Islamic mission. Here the element of "conquest of minds" is again strong. This modern interpretation is built upon the mechanism of *idjtihād*, the specific mechanism of interpretation of the Islamic *sharī'a*-law. It might very well be the case that this modernistic interpretation, serving well the aim to converge with present-day international law as embodied mainly in the U.N. Charter, has a good foundation in the teachings of the Prophet Muhammad himself. It was actually after the death of the Prophet that *djihād* became a feature apprehended as "the holy war". Surely, other more orthodox interpretations exist.

It is important to deepen the analysis further in this respect. Why did it go wrong, so to say? Why this historical misunderstanding between two religions, so near each other in their basic belief in one and the same God? Why all the repercussions in the field of international law, where for instance the Islamic world was not allowed to benefit from "the Law of Nations", as it was put during the last century. It is difficult to say, but an effort to answer this question might do some good for the future relationship between the different systems of the world. For the next millenium, for the future international normative system, it is impossible to maintain all the ancient misunderstandings and grudges. The future world cannot afford such a state of affairs. A piece of the answer might lie in the very construction of the Christian dogmas. The *Old Testament* of the Bible containing the *Decalogue* or the *Ten Commandments* is a divine, strict, unchangeable and even, to our minds, a cruel system of law. The one and the only law regulates everything, the whole conduct of life. The atmosphere of this religious law is rigid: "an eye for an eye, a tooth for a tooth". The principle of revenge is visible, the notion of *tu quoque*, "what you do, I will do". The *tu quoque*-principle is actually a fundamental principle in the international law system that started to form during the 15th and 16th centuries. Reprisals and revenge were factors that deterred an aggressor from action. This was not a principle of pacifism or peaceful co-existence; it was the divine law that demanded strict adherence from believers. These basic principles have to a great extent influenced the materia of modern international law. And combined with the elitist and ownership-directed norms from the Greek and Roman spheres, the outcome was not all that positive. But the strict principles of the Old Testament are being superseded by the human messages of the *New Testament;* the principles of brotherhood among all the peoples of the world; the human and forgiving principles. The Christian messages of the New Testament give no room whatsoever for brutality and cruelty in international relations. It is a very interesting factor in this connection, namely that the law system of the Roman Catholic Church, the *Canonic Law* that was guiding both the internal laws of the Christian medieval States and their relations towards each other, only recognizes the New Testament as a primary source of law, i. e. the spiritual and humanitarian messages of Christ. Among the *fontes ivris canonici scripti* are first of all the New Testament. Strangely enough the Old Testament with its system of reprisals and revenge, the "eye for an eye" principle, is not considered a source of Christian canonic law at all; at most an *adminiculum.* The positive law of the Old Testament was actually abolished by the preaching of the gospel, and therefore it is easy for the Catholic Church to denounce that misuse of force that occurred during history in the name of Christianity. Inter-State relations were at low ebb and the reigning pontiffs declared even then that the misuse must be banned, and that other peoples of the world were "true men, capable of the Faith". Beginning with the New Testament and the teaching contained in it, a minimum doctrine or tradition of international "rights" has been evolved by the Church, thus forming a sort of Roman Catholic tradition in international law, being under the guardianship of the Pontiff and the Holy See. One commentary to "Catholic international law" says explicitly that the history of the last four centuries is filled with shameful tragedy. How many millions of native peoples in Africa and America have suffered unspeakable miseries and ultimate annihilation through the instrumentality of colonial conquerers, Catholic and Protestant alike, who have only used the added powers and greater skill which civilization has given them as occasions for greater sin. It cannot be stated more clearly that the principles of the Christian system on inter-State relations were greatly abused. Not until our era, when the Church has lost its central position of a wordly power, it can truly pursue a "spiritual tradition in international law" based solely on the Christian messages of the New Testament. If ever the Church has been successful in inducing social reforms, in promoting political peace and unity, it has been through insistence upon the rights of God, the claims of the supernatural life, the primacy of the spiritual, says one commentary in this field. Whenever attempts have been made to treat Christianity as being mainly a pacifist or humanitarian system the desired effects have not ensued.

This is something that is very true of today. The efforts of the Pontiff, John-Paul II, follow this pattern exactly. To enhance the Christian ideals on inter-State relations, which also include the spiritual situation within the States, he keeps strictly to the "primacy of the spiritual". New aims are set; new efforts are being made to further develop if not an international law on the spiritual field, so international bonds over the frontiers, bonds of spiritual solidarity, and to a great extent based on the old Roman Catholic tradition of inter-State relations. It seems quite obvious that these bonds of spiritual solidarity play an important role in world politics today. Many new contacts are established, new areas penetrated, in the cause of establishing a spiritual front against totalitarian ideas and materialism. Further, for the first time in history ecumenical and friendly contacts are established between Christianity and Islam, two religions that are united in the same basic belief, namely in one and the same God.

It seems quite obvious that all this will bring something new into the sphere of international relations. It is important also to take this factor into account when discussing changes in the normative system in the world. I should very much like to put the question whether the period of decolonization during the middle of the 20th century has not led us back to a sort of natural law, a *jus naturale,* that existed as a concept before the development of the positive and rationalistic modern international law. The strengthening of Islam must definitely be seen as a strengthening of the concept of "natural law". The influence of the Afro-Asian world might lead to a new, more intensive discussion on the question of the sources of international law. Here the ethical, moral and religious aspects forming the base for the concept of "natural law" will clash with the occidental and why not even the Marxist secularistic view on the nature of international law. Even if there are constructions such as "Islamic Socialism", it seems quite clear that there is a definite frontier between the religion of Islam and atheistic Marxism and Socialism. From that point of view there seems to be more common base between Islam and the Occident – frenetically looking for norms and ideals to hold on to – although for the time being all the waves from the colonization period have not ebbed out. But there should be a basis for common understanding in the future, and even common rules in international law. This depends, however, perhaps more on what outcome the Occident crisis will have. Either the Occident will find its way back to common humanitarian and ethical ideas, retrace its way to a firm normative system both legally and morally. Of course, much of the Occident still has all these ideals, while the rest, an obviously increasing part, is moving towards pure materialism. A collision could eventually take place between materialism and ethics, where the "new" developing world has the great advantage of a rich, uninterrupted cultural and spiritual heritage. These opposing forces will be at cross-purposes in much the same way as the two sides now are in the North-South dialogue between the industrialized and the developing world.

The foregoing gives evidence that common roots are to be found in the far distant past as to the essential general norms regulating inter-State relations. These norms have somehow, in their original shape, once again entered the world political scene and international law after the period of decolonization. The world has been made almost painfully aware of the religious and legal power of Islam following the recent events in the Middle East and Iran. The formation of a theocracy is a reminder for the Occident. If it is going to be like this, says the man in the West, what will happen to my own life in the long run, what will happen to the norms of international law which have "protected" our system for so long and to which we are so accustomed? He even maintains that no matter what happens we shall stick to the recognized rules of international law, and the others can do what they like. This line of argument seems impossible. International law is formed by the actions and customs of separate sovereign States. Their actions always reflect their inner wishes and needs. If several States recognize the same wishes and needs, based on their own ambitions and their own legal traditions, these traditions will form a customary pattern, and will eventually be recognized as customary international law. This was what happened when the so called modern international law came into being during the 16th and 17th centuries in Europe. The then emerging powerful European nations formed a "family of States" and developed among themselves a customary law, mainly serving their own interests as conquering powers, regulating the conduct of law and neutrality, the status of envoys etc.

We have already noted that the basis for this development was the Greek and Roman legal traditions, with their strong elitist emphasis, the disregard for other tribes and peoples and the strong private ownership ideals. To this was added the "eye for an eye, tooth for a tooth" principle from the Old Testament. And through the big schism in the history of the Church during the 16th century, the existing pattern of supremacy and reign over *Communitas Christiana* was broken. States came to emerge as sovereign and independent entities, and they adopted successively a pure nationalistic and eventually even a secularistic stand on inter-State relations. In the corpus of international law the Christian message of the New Testament was somehow completely forgotten and overshadowed by politics and the use of military forces in the name of defending the true faith.

This is the point at which the occidental system for inter-State relations embarks on its path towards nationalism and secularism eventually ending up in the Marxist-Socialist system, with its specific positivistic stand on questions pertaining to international law. Medieval Catholic Western Europe had its constitution in the *Communitas Christiania* with its two highest powers, Emperor and Pope. Beginning in the late Middle Ages, the gradual decentralization of this Christian community brought about the appearance of national, territorial, sovereign States and the *international community* as the successor to the loosely linked medieval Christian community. The emerging sovereign States came to disclaim any allegiance to Emperor and Pope. This could have resulted in anarchy and the constant threat of war. To prevent that, international law came into being to guarantee relative peace among the now sovereign States. These new states, insisting on their own exclusive sovereignty, recognized the sovereignty of the other members of the West European Christian community. The most important task of the "new international law" was to secure the relatively peaceful coexistence of the sovereign States. And this was actually done by delimiting the jurisdiction of the sovereign States and their legal orders through rules of a general international law, mainly developed by custom and customary law. So the first and most important source of this "international law" is the custom of States. And the development of custom was furthered because of the common background of this family of States. Just as the Greeks and Romans had once done, the western block also had serious difficulty in allowing outside countries to participate in their exclusive system. The urge to conquer them became strong, and the system of laws came to serve as a basis for the principle of universality, for military conquest and the economic suppression of the colonial world. It is this kind of a secularistic, elitist and harsh system that, for example, meets the politically declining Islamic world during the 15th and 16th centuries. The European domination of the world seemingly became a permanent feature, the Euro-centric international law became universal in the sense that its rules were applied by European States as relevant to the whole world.

There is no need to go into the particular structure of the modern Euro-centric international law. We have seen that it differs from the religious laws previously mentioned. From its emergence as a modern European feature it caused many learned authors to penetrate deep into the structure. Many questions were posed as to the nature of international law. At the beginning, modern international law took recourse to the well-known doctrines of *Communitas Christiania*. All laws are formed by an eternal divine will. All men and all States have a duty to follow – internally and externally – certain basic tenets because this is imprinted in human conscience. All men know, or may know, what is essentially right, or wrong, by the dictates of their conscience. In seeing things this way, it was not difficult to explain the legal force behind international law. It was regulated by the eternal will, as all other rules of the society of men. The founders of the European modern international law, authors like *Grotius* (1583–1645), *Pufendorf* (1632–1694) and *Vattel* (1814–1767), all emphasize that international law is founded in natural law. The nations are obliged to act against one another as is prescribed by this "natural law". Here we still have a clear link between European modern international law and the ancient and, as we have shown, also the present schools of thought of th Afro-Asian world. The basis for international law is here one and the same, namely an idea that all guidance for men and States are to be found in "higher values and ideas", in the conscience of man himself, in the eternal will or divine commandment, or why not in concepts like "justice", "the idea of justice", "human values", "humanitarian principles", "international solidarity" and so on.

What are these nowadays so commonly used concepts but references to "higher ideas" that should be inherent in the actions of men and States. If we look through all the documents that have been adopted by the UN General Assembly, particularly in recent years when the Organization has reflected the universal opinion of States, we find numerous references to abstract norms like those just mentioned. Is this the influence of the developing world on the policy of the UN that has changed the trend again towards the thinking in terms of *natural law?* Because these signs cannot be interpreted otherwise. Either there *is* some meaning behind them, and then States are for some mystic reason *obliged* to follow them, or they are only some "lofty bubbles" without any content but hot air. This last is surely not what the society of States means when it speaks in terms of this nature. Humanitarian principles, the concepts of human rights, to take some examples, mean something to us all, and these principles are supposed to be followed by States because they are binding upon them apart from all nice conventions worked out in this field. The principle of "solidarity" among nations is also frequently referred to. What does it mean? Probably the same thing as we found when discussing the "brotherhood among all peoples" in the true Christian sense. Thus we are back to "natural law" somehow. "International solidarity" is something that is frequently used even by Marxists and Socialists. You often hear this expression in their pronouncements. Are they also referring to a sort of "higher natural will", or what do they mean? Probably they are. Even these positivistic and materialistic doctrines resemble in their essence the ancient religious dogmas in so far as they are built up in the same manner. They have the dogmas, the faith in the dialectic, materialistic apprehension of the world. Their *credo* is the commandments of Marx, Engels and Lenin. Through the higher idea of the "class struggle" a new order will materialize both internally, within the States, and internationally. Here again, through world revolution – the basic dogma of the faith – they will acquire universality. As a *Pax Romana* once ruled the world, a *Pax Communistica* is the dogmatic fulfillment of this "materialistic faith". So from these points of view even Socialists and Marxists refer to some inevitable "higher truths" when they speak about, for instance, "solidarity". But usually the term has also some more concrete political implications, as now and then has been evident in world politics.

Just like the ancient divine unchangeable law systems of the world, the Socialist-Marxist system has also turned into a strict, unchangeable, untouchable dogmatic system. The surrounding doctrine of interpretation of the "will" is assuming the same proportions as the most complicated divine "law system". It is static, the dogmas seem to have become finally crystallized, both within their societies and in the *"Socialist School of International Law"*. This might be termed the third main feature of the international normative system of the world of today. There are always risks involved in a numerical classification of systems, but a general view on the structure of the international norms may justify the conclusion that these main systems are visible in the "corpus of international law": *first* the so-called traditional international law, based on the Euro-centric system, *second* the system of the emerging Third World, based on ancient cultural and clear religious values, even a divine will, which elements heavily influence the "law", and *third* the atheist and materialistic Marxist-Socialist views on inter-State relations, also in some way influenced by "higher dogmas" of a specific kind. It should be emphasized, however, that in reality it is extremely difficult to maintain a clear-cut division of the systems like this. They are interwoven. Traditional European international law receives goods from the Socialist school of thought, foremost through the exchange of views which takes place when trying to codify a common international law through treaties, and work at the United Nations. The exchange between the system of the Third World and European international law has so far been limited, even though there have been clear signs in fields like the law of the sea, the right to natural resources, the terms of the international economic system, the self-determination of peoples and the struggle for national liberation and independence. In those fields, as well as in others, the emerging "laws" of the developing world have pushed back the frontiers of traditional international law. This is partly done by applying the methods of development of customary law, where the expression of a *opinio* in the UN Assembly by resolutions and declarations has come to play a great role in the formation of customary law; partly by way of treaty-making, where strict written rules bind the States parties that sign a particular treaty. In this connection it must be said, too, that strangely enough the law systems of the Third World and the school of Socialist international law also intermingle. Bilateral treaties bind countries in the Third World in some way or another to the Socialist-Marxist doctrine of international law. This is probably due to purely political considerations and constellations, and during our recent history many countries in the Third World, particularly the Islamic, have erected a "mental frontier" between their own system, founded on ethics and religion, and the atheistic Marxism. Therefore, in the long run, difficulties must arise in adjusting these opposing systems to one another.

Out of a strict, common system of divine law, through the special contributions of the Antique and Roman schools of law, through the Christian – Catholic and Protestant – application of this system, through the notion of a "natural law", the European system approaches a critical line of thought. Is it true? Is there a divine will, is there a "natural law"? European thinkers are linking up again with the rationalist thinking of the Antique philosophers. Everything must have a rational explanation. There must be a rational will behind everything or put in another way, a "visible and concrete" dimension of the will. The world is here and now, and there is no divine will. International law therefore has no foundation at all, it is not even a law, since there is no international legislator any longer, no supranational power above the numerous sovereign and independent nations. This brings us to the *positivistic way* of looking at international law. There must be a ground for "international law". It must be based on something. If there is no God or eternal "will", there must, when all is said and done, be a base somewhere.

The *positivism*, developing at the beginning of the 18th century, with representatives *Moser, von Martens* and *Austin*, purports that all foundation for international law is to be found in an expressive act of will by the States themselves. As *Hobbes* put it: "Law, properly is the word of him that by right hath command over others". But how could equally sovereign States bind each other by "an international law" when no one is commanding them to do so. Several answers were given; the will of the State to follow the law is enough, says one school. Here we meet ideas like the "auto-limitation" of States. They limit themselves in their actions against other States. Then, *Jellinek*, for example, explains the foundation of international law by the "consent of States". States have a *collective will* which forms the foundation of international law. All rules of international law are founded on the concept of "consent and agreement" by the States, either explicitly by way of treaty-making, or tacitly, by a silent acceptance or adherence to a specific rule of international law. The whole construction is open to criticism. This means actually that if a State does not *want* to adhere to a rule of international law, it is not at all obliged to. Consequently, the ultimate result of this kind of argument is that there is no international law in the binding sense, since all statutes are subordinated to the idea of the exclusive sovereignty of the individual States. But *pacta sunt servanda* says another school: agreements should be kept. This principle – the way of treaty-making – is the foundation of international law. But the next question is why should agreements be kept? What is the foundation of this maxim? We are back to ethics, somehow. Because this is a universally recognized general principle of international law, a postulate! Or this is, as *Kelsen* and *Verdross* maintain, a basic objective norm, anchored in the "realm of objective values". We are back again to ethics and morals. Is then *pacta sunt servanda* basically a moral norm? Even modern writers tend to agree on this, but in saying so, one approaches again the track of "natural law". And why is it that States are for some reason expected to follow the guidelines given in the majority resolutions of the UN General Assembly? They have no formal legal force, but an often-heard argument – especially nowadays – is that States should follow them because there is some kind of moral or ethical obligation to do so. The politicians deciding the policy of their respective State obviously have some "moral obligation" to act in a certain direction. In the final analysis, the principles anchored in "natural law" or ethics are somehow always present, even in modern world politics.

The rationalist thinking of European philosophers in this field even led to a formal denial of the idea of international law. Nothing of this kind can ever exist. The State is sovereign, its will decides its external relations. In case of conflict there is only one way out, to resort to force and war. The States, says *Hegel*, have only to consider their own needs, their own interests. *Lasson* maintains that "international law" is nothing more than the pursuance by the individual States of their own selfish interests. International law and treaties are nothing but expressions of temporary constellations of power. All these ideas continue on the path staked out by Antique rationalist thinking and diverge away from the religious, moral or ethical ideals towards Marxist dialectisism and materialism. All the positivistic ideas, all ideas about the sovereignty of the States, their individual needs and interests, the denial of the existence of an international law are elements that form the basis of the doctrines of a *revolutionary State*. The opposition against the existing system, the Marxist dogmas of a class struggle and class law become leading features towards the end of the 19th century, and are predominant today in a large part of the world. "The law is an instrument of the ruling class", says Marx. Even international law, based on customs between capitalist and bourgeois States, is used to promote the interests of the capitalist western system. Euro-centric international law was of the nature of "class law", and it was quite evident that a new State that emerged out of a revolution and representing another class, namely the proletariat, was not bound by the existing norms of international law. New norms in international law became absolutely necessary, norms reflecting the needs of the proletariat, represented by their State, in the first place, the Soviet Union. In accordance with the Marxist dogmas the world revolution would one day make international law unnecessary since the Marxist system would then prevail over the world. The principle of universality – *Pax Communistica* – is here visible, just as we during our review have met the same features but under different headings: *Pax Romana, Pax Christiana, Pax Islamica.* All the nations of the world would be bound together by the dogmas and principles of Marxism, basically the principle of *proletarian internationalism;* solidarity between States founded on proletarian ground and united by the same wishes and needs. Use of force and wars cannot take place between States of their kind, according to the theories and dogmas, and no instruments are needed to settle a state of affairs so bourgeois as conflict or crisis.

The ultimate aim must therefore be a world-wide system applying the Marxist rules; but, as history has taught us, reality and the military-political constellation of power has to be taken into consideration. Dogmas and doctrines cannot be implemented, if reality stands in the way. If anyone tries, the dogmas will disappear altogether, and with them the whole system. Even pure and extreme revolutionary States wake up and realize that the world around them still exists, just as before. Even the revolutionary State must start dealing with the rest of the world sooner or later. This goes for all revolutions, whether Communist or religious. They will always assert their dogmas and their faith, and their gospels may be accepted by others, maybe not, but while waiting for the coming of this "realm of the idealistic State" a "vehicle of compromise" must somehow be worked out with the rest of the world. So, the realities of this world seem to demand international law, rules regulating the intercourse between States with different systems of society. Since no one is strong enough to conquer the other, they have to deal with each other in a certain manner. A *modus vivendi* has succeeded the dogmas of universality, a principle of *peaceful co-existence* has evolved as a basis for the inter-State relations between the different systems. But the principle of peaceful co-existence is only present as long as it has to be; if political-military constellations are changed in favour of one system, the dogmatic way of looking upon things might revert. Then the dogmas are given free play. And we should be aware of one thing: the principle of peaceful co-existence does not apply to the ideological struggle. That struggle continues as always, but more as a "conquest of mind", sometimes, however, supported by other more concrete measures.

The difficulties of adjusting two opposing ideas to each other, namely, on the one hand the idea of revolution, and on the other, the political-military necessity of peaceful co-existence with the other systems of the world, are evident in the development of the "*Socialist School of International Law*" as it started to evolve in the Soviet Union in 1917, the year of the revolution. At the side of all the Marxist ideological dogmas reality existed in form of the peace treaty of Brest-Litovsk and all other treaties and arrangements with the occidental international law system. The Bolshevik government was bound from the very beginning by the language and methods of occidental international law, though they tried hard to avoid it. But the realities were there, and ideology could not influence the shaping of international law. During this period, from 1917 to 1923, "the period in search of a theory of reconciliation", the Russian Commissar of Justice, *Stuchka*, maintained "we assign a relatively unimportant sphere to international law". That was true even of the domestic legal system. No codes were promulgated during this first revolutionary period, and "justice" was administered by "judges of the people" using their own *credo*, namely their "revolutionary legal sense". Parallells could be drawn with recent events in the Middle East. Even the most dogmatic revolutionary State, however, has to undergo a development into some kind of order. Chaos cannot exists indefinitely. It cannot deny the existence of commonly used rules of international law, at least a minimum standard. If it does, the consequences will affect the State itself. This goes for events of today, and it was true of revolutionary Russia. The nihilism of *Stuchka* was replaced around 1925 by the thesis of *Korovìn* in his "International Law during the Transitional Period", where he emphasized the importance of international law. International law had developed and continues to develop, he maintained, only when there is really a need for international law. He saw international law as a "bridge" between the two systems, the bourgeois and the Socialist. The law was used by both systems, but as time passed it would evolve into a pure Socialist international law, in accordance with the dogmatic aims, the so called "*two-line formula*". Korovin continues along the positivistic track of European thinkers and consequently he is inclined to deny the existence of a customary law. Custom cannot be the foundation of an international law used by a proletarian State, because custom was originally formed by "hostile forces". Only through *treaties* can a base for the new international law be found. International rules are coming into being by the explicit will of the sovereign State. Even though the Soviet Union could not do away with the customary law entirely, it has since this period always hailed the importance of treaties. Through negotiations and conferences the Soviet Union and its Socialist companions are in a position to influence the crystallization of the new international law system, evolved by a treaty-making process. All rules for international intercourse should be codified in writing, and in doing so the Socialist States are in an excellent position to further a replacement of the old traditional customary rules of international law with new strict rules, reflecting the basic ideological ideas of the Marxist system. There is a sort of "*trading*" in international law between the systems, and the products are materialized in written documents of different kinds: treaties, conventions, agreements, declarations, resolutions and even communiqués, following meetings and visits of different kinds. The language of communiqués is important, since it reflects a special method of working with a strict semantic-legal-political doctrine.

The views of the Soviet Union on the international law system are pretty well in line with the aims of Soviet foreign policy through time, where due consideration was always given to the strength of the Socialist system and the military-political balance in the world. In 1935 *Pashukanis* in his policy oriented "Essays in International Law" says that although the two world systems can formally use the same traditional bourgeois system of international law, they could always utilize that system for their own purposes. The international law, both *custom* and treaties, could, remarkably enough, be used by the Soviet Union as an instrument for *class struggle*, in accordance with ideology, and in defence of Soviet interests. The principle of "socialist legality" is strengthened around 1938 by *Vyshinski* against a background of true Marxist ideological dogmas; in enhancing this truth he violently repudiates *Pashukanis* for having attempted to undermine the Soviet State and its law by admitting into its thinking both "custom and the bourgeois international law". Only through treaties could the interests of the Soviet Union be safeguarded. In the 1950's the "two-line formula" is back in legal thinking. *Korovin*, now appearing again, and *Koshevnikov*, talk about *"struggle and co-operation"* as a sort of basis for all international law. This is a basic theme in Socialist thinking, coming back now and then, when political constellations so allow. Korovin defines the "two-line formula" in Soviet law as follows: "Like any other law, international law reflects the will of the ruling classes. The reality of international law, however, ist not precluded by the fact that for the time being there are on the international stage bourgeois States as well as feudal and Socialist ones. Each of them, carrying out its own line and directed by its own motives, might be interested in supporting and preserving a certain amount of generally binding legal norms in international relations". In other words Socialist and bourgeois States *interpret* the principles of international law differently because of their different class backgrounds. When talking about the same concept, perception can differ enourmously; of course, given such a state of affairs, the essential question is whether it is at all possible to uphold defined norms in international law; it is even justifiable to ask whether there actually *is* a common international law really binding the two different systems.

In 1956 the Communist Party of the Soviet Union adopted the principle of *peaceful co-existence* in relation to other systems of the world. Co-operation between the systems became possible. But to make co-operation possible the views on the nature of international law also had to be changed. How, otherwise, could co-operation be established with other States if one insisted on denying the existence of the law system applied by these States. Occidental States were certainly not prepared to engage in mutual beneficial co-operation without some assurances that their own legal system on inter-State relations would be respected. In this connection a new theory is launched by the famous Professor *Tunkin*. In 1956 he advocates his *"oneness theory"*; one single international law, based both on treaties and custom. It was even possible for the Soviet Union to accept *custom* as a source of international law, because as Tunkin maintains, treaty and customary norms of international law are the result of agreements between States; either by the participation of States in a clearly expressed or tacit agreement, or in other words "treaties" or "custom". These ideas must be somewhat difficult to reconcile with ideology, even though Tunkin himself urged his colleagues to free themselves "from dogmatism, from the use of citations of Marx instead of creative thought, from crying hallelujah and from the isolation from actual reality which interferes with the development of the Soviet science of international law". These ideas are perfect as a basis for the views on a commonly used international law system, as long as the principle of peaceful co-existence remains in force. But since this principle has never applied to the ideological sphere, where the "struggle" goes on, the question is at what point will the "continuing struggle" between the systems in fact do away with this view on the international law? A change in the military-political balance, as perhaps indicated during events, for instance, in Afghanistan, may even lead to a basic change in the Soviet view on the nature of international law. Then the *Korovin-Koshevnikov* "two-line formula" may return as a leading principle and replace the Tunkin "oneness theory formula". That means in concrete terms that the ideological idea of "struggle" between the systems will be supreme to the idea of co-operation, even in the corpus of international law. Or, as Richard Ericksson puts it in his *International Law and Revolutionary State*: "Should peaceful co-existence as a foreign policy fail, should international or domestic conditions supporting that policy alter, should Soviet policy return to an emphasis of 'struggle over co-operation', then the Korovin alternative will again become relevant. Korovin's 'two-line formula' represents a continuing potential alternative to Tunkin's approach". The decline of détente policy, and the events in southern Asia and the Gulf area, the Soviet actions against Afghanistan, a neutral country, give rise to apprehensions that this is what is happenning, that another older and harsher line in the Soviet view on inter-State relations is somehow back in operation where the acceptance of *common* rules in international law is being underminded.

Even though the Soviet doctrine of international law since 1956 has developed a principle of *peaceful co-existence* in relation to States belonging to *other* systems of society, this principle is by no means applicable to countries belonging to the Socialist system. Countries that have become Socialist, are, some way or another, within the "realm of Socialism", where special inter-State "rules" are valid, based on the principle of *proletarian internationalism and Socialist internationalism.* The latter concept has in the rest of the world come to be known as the "Breszhnev doctrine". These principles, which take precedence of all other principles in international law, are usally enshrined in the treaties concluded between the Socialist States. For example, the East European States are bound to each other by such a treaty system, resting upon the principle of Socialist internationalism, or as it is stated in Article 1 in the Soviet-Czechoslovak treaty of 1970: "The high contracting Parties shall in keeping with the principles of *Socialist Internationalism,* continue to strengthen the everlasting indestructible friendship between . . ." Such formulations are common in these kinds of treaties. The principle of *Socialist Internationalism* has formed a *bond of solidarity* between countries united under the banner of the Marxist-Leninist principles, and the practical implications are that Socialist countries should come each others' "help" when the "conquests of Socialism" are for some reason threatened. The main purpose is to hold this "family of States" together; reference could here be made to the same principles prevailing in other, ancient, empires of the world. It is interesting to see the firm connection between this principle of the *Inter-Socialist School of Law* and the treaty-making mechanism. By analysing written documents like communiqués and treaties much is revealed about the relationship between one particular country and a Socialist State. For example, the Soviet action in Afghanistan was explained from a very legalistic point of view and the treaty of friendship and co-operation of 1978 was explicitly referred to.

When considering the changes in the normative system of international legal relations it is of the utmost importance to keep this *Inter-Socialist School* under close observation; to analyse its structure, its principles and specific legal concepts, and how these are used in relation to other States. Where the "thresholds" are, so to speak; or to put it in another way, *when* does a particular country come under the "shadow" of the principles of Socialist internationalism? Here we see the clear connection between the law and the Marxist ideology.

A large part of the world lies under the aegis of the *inter-Socialist* system of law. It is natural that these principles are interpreted with reference primarily to the Soviet doctrine on this issue. However, the special development of the Socialist principles of law in *China* should be borne in mind. The question is which principles of international law are followed by China today. Even though China at one stage had to pay attention to the Soviet views on international law, it has always taken a pragmatical point of view on traditional international law. *Ying T'ao*, for instance, maintained in 1960 that "owing to its technical rules and institutions, bourgeois international law has its utility as a means for facilitating international intercourse. It may and should be given necessary introduction in China's domestic training". Although discussing the questions pertaining to international law in terms of "class-struggle" and "class-law", Chinese scholars seem to take a considerably less regid attitude towards traditional international law as it has developed throughout history. One should here bear in mind that China has ancient traditions to draw from when it comes to the real essence of international law. The ancient ethics and moral system of China might even influence today's thinking in this regard, especially now after the basic changes that have taken place there since the death of Chairman Mao. With regard to the sources of international law, China tends to give treaties priority as the major source of international law, but Chinese jurists do not seem to emphasize treaties as much as their Soviet counterparts do. So, even traditional custom is acceptable by China as a source of international law. This trend seems to have strengthened in recent years: a new and strong interest in international law is developing in China. One sign of this is the formation of China's Society of International Law. Considering the above, further analysis of the position of China in international law would be interesting. The country seems now to have moved even farther away from the Socialist School of International Law. Whether it is approaching other more traditional values, even morals and ethics, as in its ancient history, it is perhaps too early to say anything about.

The 19th and 20th centuries have brought about structural changes in the world affecting both politics and the norms guiding the international legal system. The society of States has become universal. This reflects the realities of the world of today and all regions, including the Occident, have to live with it. Traditional international law in its Euro-centric sense will most surely undergo changes with the passage of time. Influence will most surely be exerted by a religious force like Islam, by other ethical and moral values both in the Afro-

Asian world and in the Occident, and, naturally, by Socialist and Marxist ideas. Further, the thinking of Latin America has always been extremely important for the development of international law. Basic norms in these different systems will probably "clash" with one another, but on the other hand, we should be aware of the fact that the different systems of the world have more in common than we think. General principles of modern international law – fragments of them at least – are to be found far back in the history of the developing world. If these countries apply ancient basic principles today a rapprochement will, perhaps surprisingly, take place with the present day legal systems. A common understanding between the different systems is essential. If the distance between them broadens too much international relations will get into difficulties and eventually chaos. Suddenly there is no common denominator, and nations cannot communicate with each other through the recognized channels of international law, including the United Nations. The only alternative, then, is to resort to armed force and war. But if that happens all the principles, which have guided world politics and international law since the Second World War, and which are enshrined in the U.N. Charter, will be undermined or even destroyed.

The conclusion of this exposé of historical and contemporary trends in the domain of international relations – what is that? Renewed competition between different ideas and ideologies, perhaps even a "struggle" between the systems? Or a *modus vivendi* based on another kind of "balance of terror"? Or an acceptance of one another based on ethical, moral or religious values? Who knows? We can only ask the questions. The future will supply the answers.

4.5. International Law and Organization for a New World Order

Hans Blix

The title of this paper is not a modest one. The following comments will fall far short of suggesting how a new world order should be designed. I doubt that any such design is meaningful. Visions, dreams, aims are needed, but comprehensive designs tend to become utopian, theoretical. In my view, influenced by my work both in theoretical and the practical internationalism, it is the immediate and intermediate goals that we should concentrate on: the progress that can conceivably be made, given the starting point. My analysis and remarks will aim at identifying scattered areas around the international horizon, where such progress might be made.

The world is constantly evolving, whether we want it or not. It is evolving politically, economically, ecologically, militarily, culturally; and the evolution has much accelerated during this century through science and communications.

World trade has expanded to volumes and values unbelievable fifty years ago. The movement and migration of people has multiplied. Massive burning of hydrocarbons and emissions of chemical industry and waste from modern society poison our atmosphere, our land and our oceans. The natural resources of the earth are being plundered by the ever resource-hungrier industrial States and by rapidly increasing poor populations to cover their basic needs. Over us all hangs, like the sword of Damokles, military and nuclear resources of destruction which are possibly capable of snuffing out human civilization.

The question which billions of people ask themselves is whether and how we can steer this evolution in such ways that fundamental needs are fulfilled. These needs are not difficult to identify:

First, security against armed conflicts between States and inside States.
Second, development, especially for the poor countries.
Third, security against environmental destruction and depletion of natural resources.
Fourth, respect for human rights.
Fifth, protection of cultural diversity.

To answer these questions we need the participation of different crafts: economists, military men, ecologists, lawyers and many others. Social architecture at the international level – even more than at the national level – is a multiprofessional task.

The lawyers have a particular role in this task, for they are the experts of a social instrument – the law – which is needed in most society building. They are, likewise, experts on the construction of international organizations. Yet, they can only provide partial answers to the big questions.

We are familiar with some of the basic concepts in this philosophy: sovereignty and independence, non-use of force and non-intervention, equality and cooperation, peaceful settlement of disputes. Much headway has been made in the definition, respect and application of these principles, but much more evidently remains to be done.

No principles could have been applied on a grander scale than those of sovereignty and independence in the post World War II era, during which colonialism has been dismantled and the number of sovereign, independent States has almost trebled. The great significance of this revolution, of course, lies in the circumstance that only governments emerging from the people itself can be true exponents of the people and provide leadership that genuinely responds to the interests of the people.

Respect for sovereignty and independence has increased in many ways. The crude gun boat diplomacy of the last century, when a convention could be concluded against the use of force in the collection of contract debts, has disappeared. Instead we may find that international institutions, like the International Monetary Fund and the World Bank – sometimes on stiff conditions – seek to assist countries in economic difficulties. We see, further, how much of the international dialogue and negotiation centers on ways to strengthen the independence of the new States, by bringing about a new international economic order. Formidable problems await their solution, however.

While it is a signal and positive development that membership is now almost universal in the global organizations, this vast increase raises new questions. An example is the participation of mini-States, which do not possess enough resources to play a full part in the organizations. While in the long run some of these States may perhaps merge with other entities, the creation of associate membership of some kind could be an avenue to explore.

More serious is it that most procedures become cumbersome with a vast membership. Conferences tend to hold more sessions, longer meetings. The law of the sea conference is but one example. In parliamentary systems party allegiences simplify decision making. At the same time they inject a measure of rigidity. A similar phenomenon can be discerned in the international organizations, where regional groups and political groups of various cohesion begin both to simplify decision making and to stiffen positions. In part this is the price one has to pay to obtain universal adherence to the norms which are worked out.

The problems connected with sovereignty and independence lie less in the formal participation in intergovernmental organiziations than in day to day international intercourse. Economic and military weakness will inevitably translate into weaker negotiating positions *vis-à-vis* other States and corporations – both national and transnational.

The modern law of treaties provides some answers by protecting against duress; and the code of conduct which is being worked out under UN auspices regarding transnational corporations is also relevant. Basically, however, the remedies lie in economic measures, strengthening the weakest members of the international community. Most of these measures fall within the developing countries, but others are or can be taken by the international community, e. g., GATT preferences, soft loans through IDA and regional banks, technical assistance through UNDP etc. The conference on the problems of the least developed countries to be held in Paris in August 1981 will grapple with some of these problems. The discussion of so called graduation is the other side of the coin, suggesting that States that have attained adequate economic strength should cease to enjoy special advantages.

In this context it must be noted that the target of 0.7% of GNP in aid from the industrialized States has been attained only by a few small States, despite the fact that practically all States are ready to testify to the need for resources of that magnitude to promote sustained development. The time has come, it is submitted, to discuss what is euphemistically termed "automatic transfer of resources" or in plainer language an international system of taxation. It is, indeed, absurd that institutions like the United Nations Development Programme, the United Nations High Commissioner for Refugees and – to a somewhat lesser extent – the World Bank and the regional banks should have to devote so much of their time to a search for voluntary contributions for programmes which have been drawn up by common agreement. It is also evident that the effectiveness of these institutions is reduced by the unpredictability of available funds. The Brandt Commission raised the issue of international taxation and it needs to be examined by lawyers and economists. In the Swedish Foreign Ministry various models are actively studied and we urge other governments to do the same.

In the development field, it is difficult to distinguish between measures that strengthen independence and those that lead to increased equality between States. Evidently the whole complex of rules governing concessions and investments are of interest in this regard. The non-concessional flows of resources to the developing countries are much greater than the flows of soft money.

While it is clear that traditional international law bore the imprint of the capital exporting countries, a universally accepted new order has not yet emerged. This would seem desirable. Judging by the difficulties which seem to arise in all discussions which are undertaken at a global level on the issue of "permanent sovereignty over natural resources", it may be that wide areas of this law will have to find its development through court cases and bilateral or regional agreements. It should be noticed that with the emergence of some developing countries as major capital exporters, the issue is no longer a clear-cut North-South matter. Indeed, the safeguarding of assets of oil-exporting countries may well turn out to be an important matter in forthcoming negotiations.

Another issue which directly concerns the sovereignty and independence of States is how to discourage the threat or use of force between States as well as intervention and civil war. Most armed conflicts since World War II have been non-international. Such conflicts, tragic in themselves, nowadays frequently risk to attract Great Power involvement, directly or indirectly, and thereby to escalate into international conflicts.

If the most fundamental requirement of a new world order – that of eliminating armed conflict – is to be fulfilled, many difficult conditions must be met. In the internal spheres equitable conditions must be aimed at economically, socially, racially and in the fields of language and religion. The right of minorities, a central issue in the League of Nations, needs to be paid particular attention within the broader field of human rights.

There has been no lack of attention to the risk of large international armed conflicts and to the armaments race. The public debate abounds in figures demonstrating how much social good could be had for the cost of a fighter or a sub-marine and abounds in appeals for disarmament. It is said with justification, I think, that the armaments race does not lead to greater security and that the superpowers have enough means to obliterate each other. An innocent reader might be driven to the conclusion that it is only out of evilness that this mad race continues. I fear, however, that such simplistic conclusions would only reduce our ability to participate constructively in the debate.

Let me suggest a few issues that could be explored.

First, the issue of confidence building measures merits to remain in focus. It is fundamental that the big powers do not misinterpret each other's military steps. Greater openness and mutual information can help to avoid this.

Second, advanced and effective measures of control need to be linked to most disarmament schemes. The big powers do not trust each other and it is questionable whether they have any good reasons to do so. Reports about alleged use of gas in recent conflicts and an outbreak of anthrax in the Soviet Union point to the need for accepted procedures of effective inquiry in order to deter from violations and to dispel unfounded suspicions.

Third, more discussions would be needed of what is sometimes termed "the rules of the game". What is suggested are some limitations upon the methods by which the great powers compete for influence in third countries. As we know, the Charter rules about non-use of force and non-intervention have been developed in documents adopted by the General Assembly. Considering the difficulties which such definitions encountered one might perhaps be sceptical about the possibilities of going further. Yet, it is realistic to expect that in a world characterized by growing economic and industrial integration and shortage of natural resources, the great powers will be increasingly vying for influence. Indeed, no-one is in doubt that it is precisely this factor that led to the escalation of the Indochina war, that makes the conflict in the oil rich Middle East the potentially most dangerous one in the world and that has invested the various local conflicts in the Horn of Africa with international dimensions.

What then can be done to keep this rivalry within bounds that entail less risk for the sovereignty and independence of the States object of the rivalry and less risk for an internationalization of conflicts?

Some of the answers to this question lie in the realms of law, others in the sphere of economics. An increasing scarcity of natural resources caused by high demands and wasteful uses in industrial States and increasing demands of growing populations in the poor countries must prompt many important changes. We might take the example of oil. The scarcity, apart from causing tension between present importers and other potential users, stimulates the exploration of new sources of oil and alternative sources of energy as well as the emergence of less wasteful methods of using oil.

But there is more! Already the current scarcity has prompted ideas about global arrangements which would guarantee availability and make price increases more predictable. Whatever the outcome of such suggestions, it seems likely that in a not very distant future primitive arrangement may emerge, which seek to assure supply, to stop waste, and to stabilize the prices of various commodities. I have no doubt that many negotiators will find a stable livelihood in such negotiations. Nor do I doubt that arrangements of this kind will be needed to reduce the risks of friction and conflict. The population issue will, likewise, present itself to us in ever starker light.

The remedies in the sphere of law would seem to lie in more precise definitions of impermissible intervention and interference. Ideological competition, of course, should continue. It is not limited to the relative merits and demerits of capitalism and communism but covers other schools of thought as well.

The question becomes more difficult – and also more interesting – when we begin to look at other methods than ideology to achieve influence, e. g., economic subsidies to political parties, training of political or trade union leaders, support for strikes, the gift of arms to a shaky government faced with broad popular uprisings, the selling of arms to rebels, outright military assistance to government or rebels at their request etc. Present rules are fragmentary: a foreign ambassador's direct participation in the domestic political debate of the host country would constitute impermissible interference by the terms of article 41 (1) of the Vienna Convention, but the sending government's infusion of a billion dollars to prop up the government of the host State would not be interference . . .

Better border lines between permissible – indeed inevitable – interdependence and impermissible interference and intervention will not be easy to achieve. Yet, it might be feared that if such "rules of the game" are not attained, there is a risk that blocs and superpowers might seek to minimize their frictions by understandings of what constitute their respective zones of influence. The Brezhnev doctrine which seeks to maintain a right for communist countries to intervene, if necessary with arms, to maintain orthodox communist governments – at least in Europe – seems to be a case in point. American attitudes in the Western hemisphere do not seem to form a doctrine but to go sufficiently far to be a source of concern. Nowhere is the attachment to the principle of non-intervention so strong as in Latin America. From the view-point of the sovereignty and independence of States, the assertion – formalized or not – of zones of influence is thoroughly repugnant.

The independence, equality and diversity of States is affected by the massive domination of the industrial States of the means of communication and news dissemination. There is relatively little that can be done in the sphere of law to reduce this near monopoly. It is questionable whether diversity and truth will be much helped by the growth of government controlled Third World news agencies. Only the long term development of media techniques and independent media management will give hopes for the desired diversity.

The other side of the independence coin is the interdependence and its requirements of cooperation, law and international institutions.

I have already touched on some of these matters. All States are now interdependent for peace. The armed conflict anywhere risks spreading and escalation. The security system of the United Nations is wholly inadequate but expressive of the present structure of the international community. It points to the joint responsibility of the States which were considered great powers in 1945. Where these powers are incapable of exercising joint responsibility, the security of States is in their own hands or in those of alliances. There is no room for sarcasm about this situation, nor, probably, much room for change. The veto power of the superpowers at any rate is but an expression of their actual power. Some limitations upon the exercise of that power could be discussed to prevent abuse, but such limitation could not cover really vital issues. It would seem reasonable, for instance, that a veto should not be available to stop proposals for inquiry, e. g., into alleged violations of arms control agreements like the Convention on the prohibition of the development, production and stockpiling of bacteriological (biological) weapons and their destruction of 10 April 1972, the Convention on the prohibition of military or any other hostile use of environmental modification techniques of 18 May 1977, the Geneva Protocol for the prohibition of the use in war of asphyxiating, poisonous or other gases and of bacteriological methods of warfare of 1925, etc.

It is not likely, in my view, that a reliable international security system can be established until regional and global integration and interdependence have gone much further and mutual confidence is more justified than today. A dismantling of the national security systems of States as foreseen in 1962 in the US and USSR schemes for complete disarmament will require the establishment of an internationally managed security system. Rudimentary beginnings can be seen, by those who so wish, in the peace-keeping UN forces which are sometimes sent but rarely withdrawn and in the resident representatives of the Secretary-General, who are found in more than one hundred States. The world organization could and should undoubtedly slowly proceed on this path. UN forces might perhaps be given the task of managing borders, where friction is likely. But when it comes to more substantive security tasks, States will not abdicate their control. Who would command UN forces? What would happen if the political instances of the UN were not agreed on instructions?

In no area is the interdependence of States greater than that of natural resources and environment. I have already referred to the need, that I believe will make itself increasingly felt, for global arrangements concerning stability of supply and pricing of some primary commodities. While some States may have got too big doses of central planning, the world community in my view has go too little of it.

Several environmental developments are thoroughly disconcerting. Water resources in rivers, lakes and seas are subjected to degradation and destruction due to emissions of chemicals and waste. Deforestation and desertification take place due to extensive logging, to burning and fuel collection by rapidly increasing populations. The carbondioxide rate of the atmosphere is growing, presumably due to extensive burning of hydrocarbons.

These and various other environmental changes pose direct or indirect threats to all States. While this is broadly recognized and international monitoring programmes have been mounted, legal obligations to desist from or to scale down activities which are globally detrimental to the environment are lagging. In my view, the term "heritage of mankind" is wholly justified to describe important properties of the earth. It should be impermissible for any State or group of States so to conduct themselves that they tamper with these properties. A large number of specialized conventions have, of course, been concluded concerning emissions from ships and dumping of particular substances. Conventions protecting specific parts of the high seas have similarly been made and a European convention has been reached providings a basis for restrictions in activities causing transboundary air pollution, notably acid rains. Despite these beginnings it is evident that there are grave inadequacies in the concertation and action regarding global environmental threats. The circumstance that effective action involving regulation, for instance of the use of hydrocarbons, fertilizers or fuel wood, has enormous economic ramifications makes such action more difficult but not less necessary.

Together with the dismantling of colonialism, the elevation of human rights to become matters of legitimate international concern regulated by conventions are among the truly great achievements of the United Nations. It is easy to point to the daily, grave and widespread violations of human rights. Yet, the norms that have been adopted and the mechanisms that have emerged within the UN to examine charges offer an important beginning. While fulfilment of economic and social rights require economic development and fair distribution, civil and political rights can be strengthened by legislative action. There still remains much to achieve in this area. It stands out as a deficiency that there is no international authority with the task of supervising respect for the norms and of setting procedures in motion for inquiries. A UN commissioner for human rights appears still to be unacceptable to a majority of UN members. As a result private organizations, like Amnesty, have an important role to play as fact-finders and watchdogs.

A special and awesome problem relates to countries where the violations of human rights have assumed the character of terror as in the recent cases of Kampuchea, Uganda and Equatorial Guinea. In such cases, resolutions of the UN and pressures by other States seem to have little or no effect. Is the world merely to be a by-stander? Have past abuses of the concept of humanitarian intervention so discredited this institution that no revival in any form is thinkable? Or could there be some form of regional action based on regional consensus? I raise this question, not with enthusiasm, but out of concern that a vital principle like non-intervention must not prevent vitally needed action to protect against massacres – genocide –, in cases where such action could be possible.

I should like to conclude with two comments dealing squarely with international law and organization.

The first is this. We find from time to time that long negotiations take place on the issue whether a new set of rules are to be laid down in legally binding conventions or in codes which are adopted as resolutions and have the nature of recommendations. The strength with which the conventional form is advocated demonstrates the greater faith placed by many in law. As against that advantage, however, one has to weigh the advantage that States are often ready to accept more comprehensive and far-reaching rules, if there is the leeway which the recommendatory nature offers.

A matter which is almost as important as this conceptual question, however, is whether the norms are supplemented by mechanisms for continuous monitoring or periodical review of application or specific machinery for complaint or, indeed, some form of sanctions against departures from the recommended norms. It is submitted that while a traditional international law with few and relatively simple precepts could be self-administered by the subjects – the States – this is impossible for the advanced and detailed system of norms – whether strictly legal or recommendatory – which is emerging in many fields. For their viability and reliability most of these systems – whether they concern the application of the principle of *jus cogens* or escape clauses in GATT, the ban against the production and possession of biological weapons, the regulation of whaling, air safety systems etc. etc. – require mechanisms assisting in or supervising application. International lawyers and others involved in legislation have a duty, I submit, to try to supplement the norms they elaborate with mechanisms that enhance and improve loyal application.

The final comment I should like to make concerns the fragmentary character of the international organizations network that we have created. It is like having a handful of government departments and institutions without any central government. This development is the result, of course, of the strong needs in various national government departments – agriculture, meteorology, health, aviation, trade, finance etc. – to concert and cooperate with their homologues internationally. The lack of cohesion, the overlapping, the gaps, the rivalries and the heaviness of the international institutional system is an evident defect. The ECOSOC can hardly be said to have succeded in its coordinating task. Perhaps only the General Assembly, the Security Council and the Secretary-General would have enough authority to hold the system together. It is now so big that few people – whether in the national or the international sphere – have an overview of it.

One of the most interesting new departures in this field may, however, come about through the global round of negotiations which, hopefully, will start next year. For the first time in the history of UN institutions it would enable governments sitting in a central, universal international forum to direct and coordinate negotiations which take place in various specialized fora such as the World Bank and the IMF, GATT and the FAO. Such a negotiation would no doubt be difficult and complicated. At the same time it could start from the realistic premise of a triple interdependence: the interdependence of States, notably developed and underdeveloped, the interdependence of international institutions and the interdependence of issues.

4.6. International Law and the Categorial Exigences of a World in Dramatic Transition

JUAN CARLOS PUIG

1. Introduction

Nowadays, it is commonplace to say that the world is undergoing a deep crisis and that international law should change in order to take into account the structural transformations that the international situation shows. Having started my studies in the University after the Second World War, I recall that even at that time my teachers spoke of the crisis and that I read scholarly works on the subject, such as for instance the one by Joseph L. Kunz.[1] But I must say, too, that I was amazed as a student when others books on the "crisis" came to my hands dating back to the inter-war period . . .[2]

With the experience accumulated over the years, – as a University professor, a civil servant, an international lawyer, a foreign minister – it is possible for me to say now that the "crisis" of international law is twofold. On the one hand, there is the problem of knowing whether international norms accurately describe the juridical international reality; on the other, there exists the question of the intrinsic injustice of those norms (or of the juridical reality in a broad sense).

Moreover, the international doctrines we currently use, do not give a valid answer to those questions, and hence they distort the comprehension of the international legal order. I realize only too well that this is not the place to analyse them exhaustively; in fact, I have already tried to discuss the subject in some of my previous works.[3] In this paper I would rather make only a few very general comments about main doctrinal trends and their analytical inadequacy. I shall deal afterwards with some concrete cases in which it will be possible to appreciate the distortion and to discuss the ways to overcome it.

2. Main doctrinal trends

For the purpose of this paper, let us group the international legal doctrines in three main currents of thought: normativist, distributionist and jusnaturalist,

1 Kunz, Josef L., La crise et les transformations du Droit des gens. *Recueil des cours, Académie de Droit international;* Tome 88, II, 1955, pp. 1–104.

2 Politis, Nicolas, *Les nouvelles tendances du Droit international,* Paris, Hachette, 1927, pp. 17 ff.

3 See specifically, Puig, Juan Carlos, *Doctrinas internacionales y autonomia latinoamericana.* Caracas, Institute of High Studies on Latin America, 1980, pp. 15–121.

according to the emphasis they place in each dimension of the juridical phenomenon: norm, distribution[4] and justice.

Starting with normativism, its main problem is that it does not take into account the international social reality. This is particularly deplorable in a period of "crisis", since neither revolutionary behaviour nor the conduct of international entities which are not "persons" of international law, and hence have no capacity under the law, could not be described according to international norms. Therefore, approximately 50% of juridical international life does not fall within the realm of the international jurist.

On the other hand, normativism is axiologically aseptic, since justice is a value which does not pertain to the sphere of the law. But this approach is still more blameworthy, because we live in a world which strives desperately for justice, not for abstract justice but for justice on this earth. We do not contend that perhaps a normativistic approach (or a positivistic one) could be analytically valid in a status-quo world, but definitely our epoch is essentially dynamic, the world striving to survive in a process of dramatic adjustments and changes. Trying to be aseptic and "pure", as Alfred Verdross has rightly pointed out, "the critical juridical positivism is in fact founded on an artificially restricted axiology, since it takes as a starting point only the values of external tranquility and order".[5] So, an inhuman order is still a "valid" order for a normativist, which is unfortunate from a moral standpoint, and also scientifically misplaced in a world of profound changes urged by justice.

Sociological (distributionist) approaches to international law would have to minimize at least the distortion between norm and social reality. But in my opinion, however, none of these define the question in its real terms, that is to say, the terms we consider most suitable in order to appreciate the international reality as it is now. For instance, Georges Scelle's solidarism is in fact a kind of concrete jusnaturalism, since the "objective" law is natural law in the sense of "given" law; a law arising from a concrete conception of social human nature, which gives rise to social solidarity and division of labor. The point is that as Scelle does not give acceptable criteria to discover what the "objective" (natural) law establishes, the frontier between "objective" law and "positive" law is a fickle one. The objective law, as Joseph Kunz used to say, is a "cryptic" natural

4 The conduct of distribution of potency and impotency (synthetically, the "distribution") is the sociological support of the juridical world. What really matters from this standpoint is to know who and how is distributing potency (i. e., anything that helps to develop human personality) and impotency (i. e., anything that injures such a development), and who are the addressees of such distributions. According to the answers given to those questions, it is possible to single out the main sociological trends in international law. For the sake of brevity, only some of them are being discussed in the text. For more details see Goldschmidt, Werner, *Introducción filosófica al Derecho: La teoria trialista del mundo juridico y sus horizontes*, 5th Ed; Buenos Aires, Depalma, 1976; for a specific reference to international law, Puig, Juan Carlos, *Derecho de la comunidad internacional.* T. I: General Part. Buenos Aires, Depalma, 1975.

5 Verdross, Alfred, *Derecho internacional publico,* 4th Ed., translation to Spanish by Antonio Truyol Serra; Madrid, Aguilar, 1967.

law developed paradoxically by anti-metaphysical scholars who reject natural law.[6] Leaving aside some rather doctrinal generalizations, in general terms, "objective" law coincides with "positive" law.[7]

Other sociological doctrines try to establish the validity of the fundamental principles of international law in social reality (such as, for instance, the jurists belonging to the so-called "Italian school").[8] Although this is a scientific approach the validity of which could be upheld in specific cases, it does not change the structure of normative international law nor does it permit its adaptation to reality. Such a current of thought raises the question of the fundamentals of international law, not the really important question of the correction of normative juridical reality by focusing upon the social environment.

Some theories deal with the question of determining the exact meaning of the judicial decisions in creating the law. This is an acceptable point of view in the specific task of piercing the veil of the judicial process, but, again, the jurists who believe in this doctrine do not question the substance of "legal maxims authoritatively formulated in accordance with certain rules" and "the rules of conduct emerging from the precedents of the courts themselves and from the legal customs"[9].

There is, too, the official Marxist conception of international law and relations which in fact represents what I have called "dialectical autonomism". International law is founded on a permanent agreement among States, specifically in this period of History, among States implementing different systems as to the ownership of the means of production. From the Marxist standpoint, this is a transitional period since capitalism will unfailingly fall owing to its internal contradictions, and thereafter, instead of an international law (the law of peaceful coexistence between capitalist and Socialist States), we shall find the law of proletarian internationalism.

The problem, however, is the same we found in the other sociological doctrines. Formal normative law is taken by "the" law; sociological realities are set aside, perhaps owing to the fact that "basic agreements" are reached between the United States and the Soviet Union, and that they are not at all satisfactory for small and medium Powers.[10]

6 As Josef L. Kunz has pointed out in his study, Natural-Law Thinking in the Modern International Law, in *The Changing Law of Nations*, Columbus, Ohio State University Press, 1968, pp. 151 ff.

7 See Puig, Juan Carlos, *Doctrinas internacionales y autonomia latino americana*. Caracas, Institute of High Studies on Latin America, 1980, pp. 35 ff.

8 For a very able whole presentation of the main trends of the Italian school, in addition to Sereni's classical book, see Pecourt Garcia, Enrique, *Tendencias actuales de la doctrina italiana del Derecho internacional publico*. Valencia, Institucion Alfonso el Magnánimo, 1965, p. 260.

9 The terms used by Ross, Alf, *A Textbook of International Law*, General Part. London, Longmans Green & Co., 1947, p. 81.

10 See the textbook on international law of the U.S.S.R. Academy of Sciences, under the general supervision of Y. A. Korovin (Mexico, Grijalbo, 1963), translated by Juan Villalba. International law is conceived there as a set of norms whose goal is to safeguard

Finally, in the matter of jusnaturalistic doctrines, it is true that there is nowadays a flowering of natural law thinking (the "*éternel retour du Droit naturel*"), but unfortunately that thinking limits itself to demonstration of the fact that general principles of international law are based on justice. But those principles, owing to their abstraction and generality, do not permit the evaluation, in axiological terms, of the legal order. Thus, for instance, Louis Le Fur has said that "natural law contains essentially but two substantive rules, although they could be reduced to only one. The first one is the obligation to execute engagements freely agreed upon. [. . .] The second is the obligation to pay damages in case of injuries unjustly caused. [. . .] In fact, there is only one principle: the obligation to pay damages, since once the breach has occurred, automatically due compensation is required".[11] Verdross himself insists on two principles which derive their validity from natural law: that of reparation and that of the duty of the coastal State to alert ships sailing along the coast regarding possible off-shore dangers.[12]

It is evident that such rules are of very little use for the evaluation of positive law: they deal with the formal structure of justice, not with its content. "Just" pacts must be fulfilled; injuries "unjustly" caused must be repaired . . . The point is that one should previously know when pacts and injuries are "unjust" and, to this effect, from consideration of the above-mentioned principles nothing operative can be derived.

3. The trialistic approach

If my assertions thus far are true, the result should be that to appreciate the international legal order in its full significance, social reality, justice and norm should be put together. Famous internationalists have expressed such a desider-

a pacific coexistence. At the same time, it expresses "the will of the ruling classes of the different States". See too Tunkin, G. I., Le Droit international de la coexistence pacifique, in *Mélanges offertes à Henri Rolin*, Paris Pedone, 1964, p 410. From the standpoint of international relations theory, see Tomashevski, D. *Las ideas leninistas y las relaciones internacionales contemporáneas*, (Trad. M. Julianov), Moscow, Ed. Progreso, 1974, and Silva Michelena, Agustin, *Politica y bloques de poder: Crisis en el sistema mundial.* Mexico, Siglo XXI, pp. 37 ff. In the Spanish literature, it is worth mentioning the recent book by Gonzalez Campos, Julio D. and Sanchez Rodriguez, Luis I., *Curso de Derecho internacional público*, Universidad de Oviedo, Servicio de Publicaciones, 1980. They make a distinction between the socio-historical and the formal structures of international law and explain, for instance, why the actual international law of the pacific coexistence has nonetheless socio-historical and formal contradictions. Such as, "at the political level, the essential contradiction flowing from the power inequalities between the two super Powers, the greatest owners of nuclear power, on the one side, and on the other, the rest of the States, including the other nuclear Powers." (p. 14).

11 Le Fur, Louis, La théorie du Droit naturel depuis le XVIIè siècle et la doctrine moderne, in *Recueil des Cours, Académie de droit international*, Tome 18, III, 1927, pp. 389–390.

12 Verdross, Alfred, *Derecho internacional publico*, Trad. Antonio Truyol Serra, 4th Ed. Madrid, Aguilar, 1967, p. 21.

atum, although some of them in fact follow the main doctrines we have just discussed. Thus, for instance, Josef L. Kunz has said that "sociological and axiological considerations are indispensable for a full understanding of the law; but it is, of course, equally indispensable to recognize the essentially normative character of the law".[13] Atle Grahl-Madsen, in his persuasive paper, speaks of "a law based on necessity, effectiveness and basic moral values."[14] And such a profound thinker as Charles de Visscher, attempted in his books to draw a "revealing curve" of the reciprocal relations between social and juridical evolutions and to incorporate the humanistic approach.[15]

Perhaps, in effect, the real goal in the matter of this trialistic structure of the law is to build a theory that could make possible the establishment of an active and analytically valid relationship among those elements. Synthetically explained,[16] such a relationship could be established on the following basis: Norm is the starting point, since norms describe the juridical behaviour to be followed in a given society. However, that description should be complemented by a reference to social reality. Norms could be incomplete and inexact. Incomplete, because of the fact that not all international conducts of distribution of potency and impotency (the "distributions") can be taken into account by international norms, and inexact, because the contradiction between norms and patterns of conduct flowing from social environment (revolutionary or not) should be resolved by giving primacy to the latter.

If we proceed this way, the image presented by the international community is far from being the coordinated structure that international jurists consider it to be. On the contrary, it comprises a human group, which functions politically as any other "micro" or "macro" human group. This perspective, arising from social juridical reality necessarily means that the group must have its own rulers (supreme and lower) and subjects, as well as supreme criteria – imposed or spontaneous – on which the political régime lies.

It goes without saying that "criteria" or "principles" such as these were, in general, contrary to those subsumed in the international norms. For instance, the principles of non-intervention and self-determination are superseded by the principle of the relative impermeability of the blocks, whereby an intervention accomplished by a super-Power within its own block will not be curbed by the global and regional security systems set up after the Second World War nor by the massive counter-interference of the other block. Intervention then is not an

13 Kunz, Josef L., *The Changing Law of Nations*, Columbus, Ohio State University Press, 1968, p. 5.

14 Grahl-Madsen, Atle, International Law and Organization for a New World, See paper 2.1 *supra*.

15 De Visscher, Charles, Cours général de principes du Droit international public, in *Recueil des Cours, Académie de droit international,* Tome 86, II, 1954, p. 522 ff., see also De Visscher, Charles, *Théories et réalités en Droit international public,* Paris, Pedone, 1955, pp. 114–128.

16 For more details, see Goldschmidt, Werner, *Dikelogia*, Madrid, Aguilar, 1958, and Puig, Juan Carlos, *Derecho de la comunidad internacional*, Buenos Aires, Depalma, 1975.

illegal act but a process, perhaps an "undue" process of law: it will be seen whether the intervening State or the State being intervened finally wins. As international "permissivity", for different reasons, is ever greater, the chances for small and medium States are accordingly broader. As also happens in other human groups, the international régime, as a whole, contains sub-régimes (or sub-systems, in the sense of James N. Rosenau).[17] Among them, the great Powers' clienteles, the "zones of dominance" mentioned by David Singer, which include the old spheres of influence of the nineteenth century and the present "blocks".[18]

To cite another example, the "over-killing power" (i. e., the capacity of massive retaliation) is the content of a dynamic political rule which assures the access to the ruling levels of the international community. Which does not mean that the "ruling few" have absolute power, for the simple reason among others, that nuclear power is politically sterile and that even military power has reduced its political significance.[19]

In this way, the normative order, adequately corrected by the patterns of conduct flowing from the analytical examination of social reality makes up the "real" law of the international community. Non-integration of social and normative systems means that the observer may only have a very partial view of the entire juridical system.

But this integrated system could be unjust. It is therefore necessary then to proceed to add a new element: to integrate justice to the complex normative-sociological order. How is such an integration possible? Again, only certain fundamental facts can be asserted in this respect.[20]

In the juridical world justice is considered an absolute value. As a value, two of its facets are of the utmost importance: its formal structure and its content or substance. From the point of view of its formal structure justice is a pantonomous category. This means that in order to establish permanent justice in this world it is necessary to be aware of all procedures, past, present and future. As this is obviously impossible for a human being, what in fact is done is to select "relevant" procedures. A method known as the method of selective apportionment enables us to retain those known forms of procedure which the one who administers justice, the adjudicator in a broad sense (judge, State, individual,

17 Rosenau, James N., Toward the Study of National-International Linkages, in Rosenau, James N. (editor), *Linkage Politics*, New York, The Free Press, 1969, pp. 44 ff.

18 Singer, J. David, The Global System and its Subsystems, in: Rosenau, James N. (Ed.), *op cit*, p. 29.

19 Although the literature on the subject is very large, see specifically Knorr, Klaus, On the international Uses of Military Force in the Contemporary World, in *Orbis*, Vol. 21, No. 1, 1977, pp. 18 ff.

20 See nonetheless my books already cited, *Doctrinas internacionales y autonomia latinoamericana y Derecho de la comunidad internacional*. The theory of justice synthetically explained in the text has been adapted from Werner Goldschmidt's *Dikelogia*, Madrid, Aguilar, 1958. Rawls, J. *Theory of Justice*, London, New York, Oxford University Press, 1971, XVI, p. 607, is a fine expression of the renovated interest of the scholars for reasonings based on a substantial conception of justice.

etc.) must take into account in order to reach a "just" decision. Normally, discussion as to whether a decision is just or unjust is, in this sense, discussion of the "relevancy" of procedures envisaged by the adjudicator to arrive at his ruling.

For instance, the famous principle *pacta sunt servanda* is based on a radical selection of procedures. Only the present ones are taken into account. But what is to be done when new forms of procedures (i. e., future procedures when the decision is adopted or the pact enters into force) demonstrate that the solution arrived at focusing only on present procedures, is intrinsically unjust in consideration of future forms of procedures? Justice demands then a "reapportionment" (that, is to say, a re-examination of the matter which includes the evaluation of the procedures set aside before) and, consequently, an invalidation of previous decisions, sometimes retroactively. For instance, to understand fully, from an axiological point of view the problems which arise from the so-called New International Economic Order requires an application of the selective apportionment method and the subsequent reapportionment.[21]

As to the substance of justice, mankind's historical experience shows that there is a fundamental guiding principle of justice: a régime is compelled to guarantee to its subjects an environment of freedom (in a broad sense) within which the human being can develop his personality. From this principle, other minor criteria, equally substantial, could be inferred, thus permitting a continuous evaluation of norms and procedures. Although its influence on international law is still small, there are already operative doctrines of substantive jusnaturalism, such as, for instance, Rafael Caldera's doctrine on international social justice,[22] and Werner Goldschmidt's *Dikelogy.*[23] An interesting extrapolation of J. Rawls' theory of justice to the international context has been made by Inamul Haq.[24] In some of my recent studies, I have equally tried to apply to concrete international situations a substantial reasoning flowing from justice.[25]

The importance of integrating justice into the normative-sociological complex in the terms already debated emanates from the fact that international law has been built on the basis of the predominance of the Great Powers, originally European, and, consequently, is extremely unjust to the small States and to

21 See Puig, Juan Carlos, Integracion y autonomia: A propósito de la reunión del Foro Latinoamericano en Caracas, *Revista Argentina de Relaciones Internacionales,* Vol. 1, No: 3, 1975, pp. 5 ff.

22 See specifically Caldera, Rafael, *International Social Justice and Latin American Nationalism,* Translated by Jaime Tello, Caracas, 1974, pp. 85 ff.

23 Dikelogy means "Science of Justice". Diké was the goddess of justice in Ancient Greece.

24 Haq, Inamul, From Charity to Obligation: A Third World Perspective on Concessional Resource Transfers. *Texas International Law Journal,* Vol. 14, No. 3, 1979, pp. 389 ff.

25 See for instance, Puig, Juan Carlos, El caso de la International Petroleum Co., in *De la dependencia a la liberación: Política exterior de América Latina,* Buenos Aires, La Bastilla, 1972, pp. 11–54; and *Caso Ambatielos – Caso de las Pesquerías,* Buenos Aires, Depalma, 1968.

humankind in general. That is why, given certain circumstances, especially the development of new resources of power by small States, its norms (and, subsequently, its accepted patterns of conduct) will not be obeyed in cases of monstruous unjustice. The "will" of the people based on justice thus creates valid law even in violation of unjust norms in force, and this can be dramatically seen when the new patterns of conduct are applied retroactively, as, for instance, in the Nuremberg trials (see *infra,* § 5.6).

Let us see now how this trialistic perspective works in certain concrete cases.

4. Integration of the international social reality

Three basic problems can be explained satisfactorily by emphasizing the social juridical element within a trialistic perspective: (a) the juridical conduct (distributions) of international entities which do not have normative description but do possess an enormous power exercised in a planetary scope; (b) the surge of spontaneous law, especially the instantaneous one when it amounts to a revolutionary creation, and (c) normative inaccuracy, either initial (i. e., from the very beginning of the entry into force of the norm in question), or supervened (i. e., taken place afterwards).

4.1. Entities which are not persons of international law

The analysis of international distributions implemented by entities other than the classic "subjects" or "persons" of international law cannot be included in any of the doctrinal descriptions of international law actually in use. Progressive as some of them may well be, they do not abandon the conceptual framework, whereby the State is the main person of international law together with other minor ones in so far that they may also acquire rights and assume obligations under international law.

In fact, the criterion that permits the incorporation of entities to the scope of the personal validity of international law is the normological criterion of capacity, and that capacity is granted as a result of a political decision finally taken in a conflict within society between "accepted" and "excluded" groups. This is a latent conflict, as old as history itself. It is possible, for instance, to appreciate the main characteristics of such a conflict in the international community of today in the concrete granting of international personality to the Liberation Movements.

The catalogue of "persons" of international law is therefore open. Perhaps some day INGOs and BINGOs will be included. For the moment, however, they have provoked formidable distributions of potency and impotency without having been envisaged by international law norms as such. It goes without saying that, in addition to INGOs and BINGOs, internal pressure groups and factors of power may also protagonize international distributions.

For this reason, if the international jurist persists in the classic conception, he may perhaps acquire knowledge of a substantial part of international juridical life, but by no means will it be complete. In addition, a dichotomy between international "subjects" and "actors" will take place, as thoroughly analysed by Hans-Joachim Leu in a recent study, which is very dangerous for the comprehension of global international phenomena.[26] As Atle Grahl-Madsen has rightly said: "the discussion about who should be considered 'subjects of international law' has hardly been a fruitful one, autotelic and circular as it too often has been".[27] Perhaps the best way to abolish such a useless discussion would be to broaden the catalogue of true sources of international law.[28] As a result of such a broadening, material sources are all procedures of distribution of potency and impotency whether they flow from "subjects" of international law or not, whereas we understand formal sources to be the descriptions of distributions ordered or agreed to by entities with recognized capacity in international law; such descriptions being made by persons belonging to those entities having competence recognized by law to establish formal sources.

It may be said in passing, that this conception of material source is completely different from the one generally prevalent in many international juridical currents of thought. In them reference is made in a very vague way, to sociopolitical circumstances presiding over the adoption of a particular rule. To my way of thinking, the material source is direct: as direct as the formal one since both constitute evidence of the international juridical phenomenon. Therefore, to cite an example, the international lawyer should deal with an agreement between transnational corporations (material source), as well as with commercial treaties between States (formal source). It goes without saying (and this marks the difference from the normological standpoint) that the treaty, as a formal source, will have its material source too: the agreement which took place in the time-space reality, while the private business deal will not have a formal source (at least in international law). As we shall see later on, such a dichotomy between formal and material sources clears up the subject of interpretation (see *infra*, § 5.2).

4.2. The juridical relevance of spontaneous revolutionary law

As is well known, customary law does not raise any major doctrinal problems in international law, since custom was always accepted as a "source".[29] The classicists maintained some discrepancies as to its juridical nature, being for some of

26 Leu, Hans-Joachim, Sujetos de Derecho internacional y actores de la estructura internacional. *Politeia*, No. 5, 1976, pp. 273–289.

27 Grahl-Madsen, Atle, International Law and Organization for a New World Order, paper 2.1 *supra*.

28 For further details, see my book *Derecho de la comunidad internacional*, already cited, pp. 91–188.

29 The problems raised nowadays by custom in the theory of international law have to do with its classification within the system of sources. Generally, it is considered a "formal" source (for instance, Charles Rousseau, *Droit international public*, Paris, Editions Sirey, 1970, T. I., p. 58. Within our reasoning, it is a material source, since custom can not have a "formal" description made by its protagonists. As a result, a customary law cannot be subject to interpretation; it can only be ascertained by sociological methods.

them a "tacit" pact. But nowadays its character of autonomous source seems unquestionable.[30] At the same time, and from the hierarchical point of view, its equivalence with treaties is generally admitted, which in substance means that, given the same scopes of spatial, personal and material validity, a customary norm derogates prior conventional norms and vice-versa.

However, it is possible to detect nowdays a tendency to uphold the superiority of treaties, at least in the practice of States and international tribunals. As pointed out by Nguyen-Quoc-Dinh, the phenomenon of the predominance of written law began to appear in international law.[31] As we have already seen, however within a trialistic perspective, such a situation should be rejected since the hierarchical equivalence of those sources is necessary in order to introduce social reality as an element of the juridical phenomenon and to comprehend the juridical reality as a whole without distortions.

But limitations of the classical doctrine may be seen with more clarity with reference to revolutionary *(contra legem)* spontaneous law (either customary or instantaneous), that is to say, with reference to juridical practices which stem from illegal means in opposition to other accepted ones by the international juridical order.[32] This happens in the following fundamental situations: (a) when the behavior in question infringes upon the "constitution" of an international organization bringing about a reform thereof without applying the reform procedure foreseen in the same constitution; (b) when two or more States regulate by conventional or customary means a given situation in a way opposed to a treaty or a custom whose scopes of personal and spatial validity are broader than the regulation; (c) when a State perpetrates illegal practices, which receive *a posteriori* some sort of "habilitation" by not finding tangible opposition or by express or implied tolerance of the international persons presumably injured by the illegal practice.

The law of the United Nations furnishes good examples of the first case. For instance it is evident that the Uniting for Peace Resolution of the UN General Assembly (377/V) signifies a fundamental modification of the Charter of a revolutionary character.[33] A good example of the second case is the Danube Treaty of 1948, entered into by the riparian States in flagrant violation of the Paris Treaty

30 With the exception of the Soviet doctrine which seems to go back to such a conception owing to its autonomist dialectical position.

31 Dinh, Nguyen-Quoc, *Droit international public* (Ed. by Patrick Dallier and Alain Pellet). Paris, Librairie Générale de Droit et de Jurisprudence, 1980, p. 305.

32 In this connection, Josef L. Kunz has rightly said that "the problems of 'revolutionary' and illegal creation of norms of international law have hardly been considered as yet by the writers on that subject. These problems call for further investigation. They are highly interesting theoretically and, therefore, highly important practically." Revolutionary Creation of Norms of International Law, in *The Changing Law of Nations*, (J. L. Kunz, ed.) Columbus, Ohio State University Press, 1968, p. 384.

33 With reference to the Uniting for Peace Resolution, Michel Virally has said that its constitutionality continues to be, even at present, an extremely doubtful and controversial point. *"L'organisation mondiale"*, Paris, Armand Colin, 1972, p. 116.

of 1856 to which France, Great Britain and Sardinia were also contracting Parties.[34]

As to illegal (but tolerated) unilateral conducts, perhaps the best recent example is the case of the Iranian hostages, undoubtedly an illicit act under international law which did not burden Iran with the demand for reparation.[35]

Again, within the trialistic conception, revolutionary law does not provoke major problems since, from the point of view of global juridical reality, what really matters is to know whether or not those conducts, formally illegal, are in fact tolerated. They are conducts of distribution of potency and impotency and, as such, they enter into the system of sources of international law as material sources, obviously first as illegal conducts (uni- or multilateral) more or less tolerated, and then as revolutionary law through their pragmatic consolidation over a long period of time.

4.3. Initial or supervened normative inaccuracy

Therefore, juridical norms, even in force from the normative point of view, may be trialistically "inaccurate". Inaccuracy is simply a risk that any norm incurs by being a norm, since in its logical formulation any norm assures its own fulfillment. Moreover, norms may be inaccurate from the outset and it is possible then to predict their inaccuracy by analysing the sociological environment. In addition, a situation can arise whereby programmatic (non self-executing) norms and operative norms which are intended to implement the former, are contradictory although they are adopted at the same time. In such a case the contradiction between programmatic and operative norms when, for instance, included in the same treaty, should be resolved in favour of the latter.

If, for instance, a system of collective security is established of which a super-Power is a part, it is possible to say from the start that such a system will not be applied when the "national interest" of the super-Power is at stake, even more so, when the established "program" of collective security recognizes at the same time, on the normative-operative level, the right of veto of the super-Power, even in the case of its own aggressions.

Therefore, the examination of juridical-normative and sociological reality in the present-day world does not permit conclusions other than admission that the basic juridical principle of world organization is not the principle of non-intervention but the one of "impermeability" among blocks. In effect, after the Johnson and Breszhnev "doctrines", could we not question the so-called rules of international law with respect to intervention, in spite of the programmatic norms in force and some rhetorical declarations of the General Assembly? Is it the non-intervention of the dominant Power in the external and internal affairs of other States or the non-intervention between the blocks? This is the fascinating

34 See, as to the absence of "practical effects" of the declarations in favour of the illegality of the new Danubian régime, Nguyen-Quoc Dinh, *op. cit.*, p. 583.

35 See Richard Falk's most interesting and challenging considerations on this episode: The Iran Hostage Crisis: Easy Answers and Hard Questions, *American Journal of International Law*, Vol. 74 No. 2, 1980, pp. 411–417.

question raised pertinently by R. J. Vincent in his challenging study of this principle and its application in the American and Soviet spheres.[36]

It should be pointed out, however, that in spite of this fact, the analysis of normative inaccuracy is seldom made in the textbooks of international law. Whenever a reference is made, what is normally said is that "violations" do not invalidate the law. That is certainly right, provided that violations are small in number, and those violations not sanctioned by law are even less. If what happens is a general violation of the specific norm, that norm is inaccurate: it never was enforced or it ceased to be enforced from a given moment. An additional point is that what has to be considered "the" law is not the inaccurate norm (although valid, since it was incorporated into the normative order through legal means), but the pattern of conduct consistently followed by the specific human group which constantly demonstrates such inaccuracy.

5. *Integration of justice*

The dikelogical dimension, envisaged also trialistically, brings about a real understanding of basic phenomena of present international law. Thus, for instance, its "progressive development"; the different stages of the functionning of the norm, such as interpretation, implementation and elaboration; the content of imperative law; the retroactive application of norms arising from a new set of values, and the problems raised by interventions (and non-interventions) at the present time.

5.1. Progressive development of international law

If we accept the assumption that today's world expresses everywhere an active desire for justice, it seems essential that jurists must possess a thorough knowledge of justice requirements, according to supreme criteria discovered by men through cruel struggles on the road to obtaining ever broader scopes of freedom in order to develop their personality.

We know now perfectly well that the international régime, evaluated on the basis of such criteria, is intrinsically unjust; it has been proved beyond any doubt that machineries whereby the hegemony of the Great Powers, originally European, was spreading gradually throughout the world. That is why it is no surprise that the juridical debate in international conferences as well as in academic circles is not a debate on what positive law is but on what justice should be. It is not the "codification" of international law that really matters but its "progressive development", to use the same terms as in the United Nations Charter.

Such a situation should orient the work of advisory legal bodies, such as the International Law Commission. Clear definition of the boundaries between positive law and the proposals being made *de lege ferenda* is unavoidable if we wish to express concretely the positions of States with respect to the subject being examined as well as the possible modifications proposed in answer to the present

36 Vincent, R J., *No intervención y orden internacional,* Trad. Luis Justo, Buenos Aires, Marymar, 1976, pp. 311 ff.

very unjust international régime. This is, I know, a highly controversial matter.[37] The real truth is that the two functions are strictly separated in the Charter as well as in the memoranda prepared by the United Nations in order to establish guiding principles for the work of the Commission.[38] It is, of course, easier to remove that frontier, at least to maintain it in very indefinite terms, but the results of such an attitude have proved very harmful to the peoples of the world. What happened in the Conferences on the Law of the Sea is an excellent example.[39]

From a trialistic angle, such attachment to the positivist tradition and to the "constructive" interpretation which is its theoretical basis are at least anti-historical. Reformist propositions, even *contra legem*, although based on justice, belong also to the realm of the international jurist in the last third of this century.

5.2. Interpretation

In this field it is also necessary to go back to the simplest ways and methods and to abandon the paraphernalia of "constructive" jurisprudence, "plain meaning", "free choice" of alternatives within a normative framework, and so forth. Much harm has been done to both international relations and mankind in general with all this juggling in an effort to maintain such a line of thought. In effect, if norms not originating in custom, are in substance none other than the description of the legislator's will (in a broad sense), the only aim of their interpretation should be to find out what the content of such a will (or intention) was. Otherwise, one is attributing to the States (or other persons of international law) what in fact never was in their representatives' minds.

If the adjudicator (in a broad sense, all concerned in doing justice) considers that such an intention is dikelogically unacceptable owing to the predominance of a new set of values, that is a very different question. In such a case, the judge has

37 Highly learned opinions are in favour and against. See for instance, Dokhalia, R. P., *The Codification of Public International Law*, Manchester University Press, 1970, pp. 203 ff.; Yuen-li-Liang, Development and Codification of International Law, in *Proceedings of the American Society of International Law*, 1947, pp. 40 ff.; Bin Cheng, International Law Commission. *Current Legal Problems*, Vol. 5, 1952, pp. 251–273. Cheng was emphatic in his assertion that the work of the Commission would gain much "by greater distinction being made than hitherto between its functions of codification and progressive development of international law and by some attention being devoted to the former" (p. 261). But Lauterpacht and Jennings were opposed to this point of view.

38 See Dokhalia, R. P., *op. cit.*, pp. 67 ff.

39 As it was indicated as early as in 1963 in my article La Segunda Conferencia de la Naciones Unidas sobre el Derecho del Mar, Repercusiones de su "fracaso", in *Revista de Derecho Internacional y Ciencias Diplomaticas*, T. 12, No. 23/24, 1963, pp. 87 ff. Similar views on the harmful repercussions of the consolidated procedure applied by the International Law Commission in the specific case of the Law of the Sea, were expressed by Johnson, D. H. N., The Preparation of the 1958 Conference on the Law of the Sea, *The International and Comparative Law Quarterly*, Vol. 8, 1959, pp. 122–145 and Hurst, Cecil, A Plea for the Codification of International Law on New Lines, in *Transactions of the Grotius Society*, Vol. 32, 1946, pp. 135 ff.

to take notice of the vacuum (a dikelogical one) and proceed to the elaboration of a new individual and specific norm in order to fill that vacuum (see *infra,* § 5.3). To act in a different way means essentially to "disguise" the juridical creation and to assume no responsibility for such a creation since the "new" rule being applied is attributed to the original legislator under the cover of a capricious and harmful interpretation. It is worth recalling that one of the most distinguished analysts of the World Court case-law, J. H. W. Verzijl, in commenting upon some of the judgments of the Court, has plainly said that they amounted to a "juridical creation carefully camouflaged".[40]

This is a painful contribution to the discredit of the international adjudication and of the international law that is supposedly applied at all times. That is why the endeavour to "harmonize" some judgments of the International Court of Justice is doomed to failure. In the first place, the majority of the Court disguises their ideological preferences under different interpretations of the same rule, instead of making clear such preferences (although perhaps the obligation to make clear why they are departing from the original intention of the legislator would compel them to decide in terms of strict justice). In the second place, the resulting case-law (even applying the doubtful method of "distinguishing") is contradictory and practically of no use from the point of view of the rule of law in such cases. As put so clearly by Georg Schwarzenberger: "To attempt to harmonize the judgment of the International Court of Justice in South West Africa (Preliminary Objection) case (1962) with that in the Second Phase of the same case (1966) and both with the advisory opinion on Namibia (South West Africa) (1971) would be evading the real issue: to understand the ideological significance of the break that has occurred in the Court's practice".[41]

It is probable that one of the basic reasons for the distrust of international tribunals in general (and, consequently, of the very small amount of "justiciable material" they have) is due to this senseless juggling.

5.3. Elaboration of the norm in case of normative vacuums

The integration of justice to the juridical phenomenon helps in the solution of the problem of vacuums in international law. The chief current doctrines sustain the hermetical character of international law. They base this assumption on the principle of the "sovereignty" of the State or, in the normativist currents, in the basic juridical principle whereby what is not prohibited to the subjects of law, is permissible.

But the hermeticity of a juridical order furnishes satisfactory solutions in a static world, by no means in critical times, when what imperatively requested it is the adaptation of the existing law to the rapidly changing circumstances of a world in dynamic and dramatic transition.

It is true that within the normative dimension, a solution can always be found

40 Verzijl, J. H. W., *The Jurisprudence of the World Court,* Leyden, Sijthoff, 1966, Vol. 2., The International Court of Justice, p. 115.

41 Schwarzenberger, Georg, *International Law as Applied by International Courts and Tribunals,* T. III: International Constitutional Law, London, Stevens, 1976, p. 168.

to conflicts and situations based upon general principles; the real point is to know whether such solutions are "operative", that is to day, whether they really reduce the existing tensions which started the conflict or situation and guarantee that, even if new conflicts arise, these will have less virulence than the one originally resolved.

The trialistic perspective, in integrating the dikelogical element, does not find any objection in the adjudicator (either an international judicial organ or the government of a State acting as such, according to the *"dédoublement fonctionnel"*) of a controversy detecting the vacuum and creating a specific norm for its solution. Moreover, a careful analysis of the international case-law, proving that arbitral tribunals as well as the World Court itself do not hesitate to follow such a method when adjudicating a case according to existing law, does not seem to provide an "operative" solution. It is thus understandable that Hersh Lauterpacht has spoken in plain language of "judicial legislation".[42]

Difficulties in understanding such a phenomenon are due to the custom of disguising the juridical creation by resorting to the so-called "constructive" interpretation. It is Georges Scelle who has said that "arbitration founded in equity is at the same time frequent and rare". It is *rare,* in the sense that governments hesitates in trusting their political interests to the game of an *ex aequo et bono* adjudication, it is *frequent* in the sense that arbitrators have always had an invisible tendency to adjudicate diplomatically and to give to their awards the appearance of a juridical decision in order better to assure its execution."[43]

Thus, in many arbitral and judicial decisions there will be, no doubt, an explicit major premise, but the premise that the adjudicator really had in mind will only appear in "inarticulate" form, using Lauterpacht's fortunate term.[44] Precisely, the error of law (i. e., the erroneous application of the existing law) does not justify, following the majority of the doctrine and even the international case-law itself, the nullity of the award.[45]

All these points confirm indirectly, but nonetheless in a definite form, the adjudicator's competence to adjudicate according to justice, when existing law presents a dikelogical vacuum.[46]

42 Lauterpacht, Hersch, La théorie des différends non justiciables en Droit international, *Recueil des Cours, Académie de droit international,* Tome 34, IV, 1930, pp. 622–625.

43 Scelle, Georges, Règles générales du Droit de la Paix. *Recueil des Cours, Académie de droit international,* Tome 46, I, 1933, p. 567.

44 Lauterpacht, Hersch, *The Development of International Law by the International Court,* London, Stevens, 1958, p. 54.

45 Impressive is the majority of the doctrine in favour of this point of view. From Merignhac and Thevenaz, at the beginning of the century to Castberg and Sørensen. For further details on bibliography, Puig, Juan Carlos, El laudo arbitral británico en el caso del Río Encuentro. *Revista de Derecho Internacional y Ciencias Diplomaticas,* Ts. 15–16, Nos 29–32, 1966–67, pp. 30 ff.

46 Georg Schwarzenberger speaks of "acquiescence by parties in such arrogation of quasi-legislative functions" which "provides a consensual basis for an, otherwise questionable

The real preoccupation comes from the "form" adopted by such decisions. Would it not be better to proclaim the truth and to confess that the applicable law is unsatisfactory?[47]

5.4. Implementation

Nobody doubts that international law, mainly a primitive law, contains a great number of non-self-executing norms. For Verdross, precisely, one of its characteristics is such an indetermination. With this in mind he recalls the Triepel's figure of speech whereby international law would be something like a commander-in-chief whose orders can only be obeyed if they are transmitted by the officers and executed by the soldiers. Such a parallel is descriptive of international juridical reality more than one can imagine. High-ranking officers (the Great Powers) require that the soldiers (medium and small Powers) carry out the orders of the commander-in-chief (international law) in the same way as they do. The technique has consisted in considering as general norms the individual norms they adopt to implement a non-self-executing norm of international law.

The law of the sea offers good examples of that technique. The "three-mile" rule was displayed by maritime Powers as a general norm, but it was only a specific norm implementing the general norm (non-self-executing) whereby each State could determine its maritime jurisdiction according to reasonable criteria. I upheld such a conception as early as 1960 and at that moment it was considered "heretical",[48] although distinguished jurists have sustained similar positions, such as Georges Scelle,[49] D. H. N. Johnson,[50] Mario Giuliano.[51] What is still more important, in practice it became evident afterwards that that point of view was right.

5.5. Content of imperative international law

After its reception by the "Treaty on treaties" as a cause of nullity, the existence of imperative norms in international law does not seem to have been seriously disputed. No valid criteria for ascertaining its content were however advanced. The question therefore remains open.

There are, no doubt, several possible definitions advanced by different cur-

exercise of jurisdiction by international courts and tribunals." *The Dynamics of International Law,* Millor, England, Professional Books Ltd., 1976, p. 26.

47 As Judge Alejandro Alvarez used to say in some if his individual opinions. See for instance, the one on the Fisheries case. *I.C.J. Reports 1951,* p. 146.

48 Puig, Juan Carlos, La República Argentina y la secunda Conferencia sobre el Derecho del Mar. *Jurisprudencia Argentina,* 1960–II, Secc. Doctrina, pp. 33 ff.

49 Scelle, Georges, Plateau continental et Droit international, *Revue générale de Droit International Public,* T. 26, 3rd series, 1955, p. 53. Also his opinion in the International Law Commission, 313rd session, 14 September 1955, UN Doc. A/CN. 4/SR. 313. p. 11.

50 Johnson, D. H. N., The Legal Status of the Sea-bed and Subsoil. *Zeitschrift für Ausländisches Öffentliches Recht und Völkerrecht,* Vol. 16, 1956, pp. 498–499.

51 Giuliano, Mario, *Lo sviluppo e gli aspetti attuali del Diritto del mare,* Valladolid, Cuadernos de la Cátedra "Dr. Brown Scott", 1960, pp. 129–137.

rents of thought.[52] In my opinion, again one of the most acceptable emanates from justice, and it is evidenced by juridical anthropology.[53] In effect, the surge of imperative norms in human groups takes place when the law abandons its primitive phase, and this coincides with the recognition of the individual as such as subject of the law.

In primitive law, the chiefs of accepted minor groups may set aside existing juridical rules, provided an agreement is reached with other chiefs. Even in the criminal orbit, composition commonly displaces the rules establishing penal sanctions. When the law enters a more developed stage, four basic categories undergo radical change. The juridical decentralization is replaced by a progressive organic centralization; collective responsibility, by individual responsibility; individual security by collective security; and, finally, the most important of them all, the disregard of the human being is gradually superseded by a régime of justice.[54]

From that moment on, all rules relating to the new categories being implanted are considered imperative. That is why most distinguished internationalists have stated that the problem of imperative international law is insolvable unless it is accepted that dikelogical criteria are of its root. This is highly important because some of them are far from being jusnaturalists. It is Georges Scelle who spoke of the "common international law",[55] composed of norms reflecting "supreme values".[56] It is Charles Rousseau who recognized that "there will not be a positive answer to that question unless one could invoke considerations of natural law."[57]

5.6. Retroactive application of new evaluation criteria

The triumph of a new set of values, brought about by the progressive knowledge man is able to acquire about justice, normally has the juridical effect of creating a dikelogical vacuum. We have already seen how it is trialistically comprehended and how it is filled (see *supra*, § 5.3). Nevertheless, when the offence to justice derived from past behaviours has consisted in a deep injury to human nature, individual or collective, the "awaking to reality" makes such behaviours appear tinted with injustice from the beginning, that is, from the very moment it took place.

Here is a case of *ex tunc* injustice. What seemed to be just at a certain moment,

52 See for a good presentation of the main alternatives, George Abi-Saab, Introduction, in *The Concept of Jus Cogens in International Law*, Conference on International Law, Lagonissi, April 3–8, 1966, Geneva, Carnegie Endowment, 1967, pp. 7–15.

53 Cf. Hoebel, E. Adamson, *The Law of Primitive Man: A Study in Comparative Legal Dynamics*, New York, Atheneum, 1974.

54 For further details, my book *Derecho de la comuniad internacional*, Buenos Aires, Depalma, 1975, pp. 16–26.

55 Scelle, Georges, *Précis du Droit des gens*. T. II, Paris, Sirey, 1932, pp. 15 ff.

56 Quadri, Rolando, Cours général de Droit international public, *Recueil des Cours, Académie de droit international*, Tome 113, III, 1964, p. 336.

57 Rousseau, Charles, *op. cit.*, p. 151.

and justified a certain distribution of potency and impotency, ceases to be acceptable. New elements give rise to a reapportionment towards the past, and the inevitable result will be that the effects of an unjust juridical situation come to an end. But, then, as Goldschmidt says, retroactivity is inherent in such a disvalued appreciation. At least, the present consequences of the past situation will have to adapt to the new ruling criterion.[58]

Historically, there have been situations whose treatment has been consistent with this scheme. Such has been the case, for example, with the abolition of slavery. The moment that people became aware of the tremendous injustice implied by servile work, the liberation of slaves were not, in the great majority of cases, accompanied by the corresponding compensation to their masters, although – strictly speaking – from the legal point of view, a slave was submitted to ownership and, consequently, had a specific market value.

But there are applications of this criterion in present international law and, to be sure, in certain situations which would deserve similar treatment. Let us clarify the subject, at least very briefly, with some illustrative references.

It seems evident that in the lawsuits against the great criminals of war (Nuremberg and Tokyo) a new set of values was applied retroactively (at least with reference to the crimes against humanity and against peace), simply because the international law *in force* before World War II did not contemplate such crimes, not to mention the individual responsibility for their perpetration.

It is also clear that the feeling of injustice *ex tunc* explains the practical weakening of the principle of "prompt, effective and adequate compensation" in the case of nationalizations, which has been consecrated in a number of known resolutions of the General Assembly,[59] but at the same time in practice[60] and doctrine, even in the case of developed countries. This is how, in the Harvard project of a Convention on the international responsibility of the States for damages caused to foreigners prepared by Louis B. Sohn and Richard Baxter, it is said (clause 4 of article 10) that if the property is taken over by the State in accordance with a general program of social and economic reform, just compensation can be paid in a reasonable lapse of years.[61]

The point is, in fact, that not only has the deferred compensation been accepted a great many times, but also minor compensations on the basis of global agreements (lump-sum payments) entered into by the nationalizing States and the national States of the persons whose property was nationalized, and this, in

58 Goldschmidt, Werner, *op. cit.*, p. 405.

59 Beginning with UN General Assembly Resolution 1803 (XVII) 14 December 1962 *(Permanent Sovereignty over Natural Resources).*

60 See Francisco Orrego Vicu A, Algunos problemas de Derecho internacional planteados por la nacionalización de la industria del cobre en Chile. *Estudios Internacionales,* Tome 6, No 24, p. 88. For a trialistic approach to the subject in a concrete case: Puig, Juan Carlos, El caso de la International Petroleum Co., in *Della dependencia a la liberación. Politica exterior de American Latina.* Buenos Aires, La Bastilla, 1972, pp.11–54.

61 *American Journal of International Law,* Vol. 55, 1961, pp. 553 ff.

essence, means nothing else but the theoretical acknowledgement of the obligation to compensate.[62]

Similar consideration should be given the formidable foreign debt which afflicts the oil importing underdeveloped countries. The anxiety to honour the debt, according to the severe selective apportionment implied by the principle of *pacta sunt servanda* gives rise to what I call the vicious circle of the debt: the payment of that debt requires more and more funds and creates the need for refinancing agreements, but that does nothing but delay the anguish and add a burden to the future. At the same time, the whole economic activity declines, which in turn implies a shorter supply of goods and services, and consequently new debts, and so on. And all this, in the midst of the world economic crisis, which hits the peripheric economies ever more severely.

If, as we can now show, the difficulties experienced by these economies are due to a great extent to artificial asymmetries, it seems only fair that when we consider those asymmetries to be unjust, this new evaluation should expand retroactively and cover the whole process. The conclusion would be that if the affected countries require new terms and more favourable conditions, they are simply asserting what, in just terms, is a right of their own. In other words, the image of an ashamed debtor, who goes, hat in hand, from one international financing group to another, asking to be granted new credits, has to be replaced by that of a debtor who does not ignore his duties but, conscious that – to a great extent – they are not due to his bad administration, sets the new terms of the agreement according to his possibilities without affecting his own process of development. Probably because of this, some industrialized countries have already started to cancel the public credits they had granted the less developed countries.

5.7. Intervention and non-intervention

The principle of non-intervention, plus the prohibition of the use of force, preserves a State from foreign interference. But this intangibility of the internal order is typical of primitive law, whose main function is that of "coordinating" minor political organizations. In primitive Roman law, for instance, this stands out very clearly. The *jus civile* was a law of coordination between families, and that is why the *paterfamilias*, equivalent to the head of State in international law, was guaranteed a "reserved domain" which the coordinating law could not trespass: hence he had the *jus vitae et necis* over the members of his family.

This does apply however, as long as the intrinsic injustice of the régime is tolerated, which consists in ignoring the right of the individual as such to "personalize". As soon as more reasonable or just conceptions begin to permeate the traditional socio-political structure, the "interventions" of the global bodies become progressively more frequent until, legally speaking, the "intangibility" of the reserved domain gives in, or at least it ceases to be an obstacle, to the expan-

62 Cf. Renato Ribeiro: *Nationalization of Foreign Property in International Law*. Washington, D. C., Brazilian Embassy, 1977, pp. 100 ff.

sion of the new beliefs and their cultural symbols. It is fascinating to follow the evolution which in this sense Roman law underwent in the republican era.

This is the reason why in classical international law (up to World War II, just to choose a landmark, which may be a bit arbitrary perhaps, but certainly significant), the idea of justice implied, primarily, non-intervention. In a régime that admitted intervention for political reasons (maintenance of the balance of power between States, self-preservation, and so forth) and considered war to be legal, it seemed only just to preserve, in the first place, the "reserved domain" of the State, sole guarantee of its survival. It is significant that intellectuals and philosophers of the XVIIIth and XIXth centuries fervently advocated in favour of non-intervention (Immanuel Kant, John Stuart Mill, for example).

But such an evaluation was based on a drastic selective apportionment of contemporary practices. It condemned the behaviour of the ruler who intervened, but not his attitude towards his own subjects (except in those extreme cases of "humanitarian" intervention, which was in essence the product of a minor reapportionment).

Nowadays, this basic approach is still valid. Since interventions keep on taking place motivated by questions of power, it also seems valid to protect the intervened State (generally weaker) against the powerful one. Here is the dikelogical basis of all the pronouncements against intervention which were so common in past decades. But the basic right man has to his own personalization has also made a deep impression and constitutes a motor that generates structural transformations within the State and in the international community as well. The consequence has been, this time, a global reapportionment. What is sought is not only to defend the impermeability of the State against the intervening Powers, but also to protect the individual against the despotic ruler, and to give this protection an international nature.

Hence, tension crops up between the classic principle of non-intervention and the new requirements of justice. Because, obviously, any advance in the field of international supervision of the situation of the individual within the State will only be possible at the expense of intervention.

Therefore, we arrive at a paradoxical dialectic: intervention – non-intervention, which can only be satisfactorily solved through a new definition of traditional terms. In the light of the new requirements necessary for the fulfilment of justice in this world; of the overwhelming surge of a negative but applied and personal "ought to be" to redress unjust situations that arise, non-intervention no longer seems to be an adequate instrument: at least it should harmonize with an intervention intending, genuinely, to dignify human existence.[63]

This is why in times of crisis, as the one we are now experiencing, only justice provides a pattern of action to discern between acceptable and intolerable interventions and non-interventions.

63 For an application of these ideas to interventions in Nicaragua, see Puig, Juan Carlos, El principio de no intervención en el Derecho internacional público americano, influencia de la nuevas relationes internacionales, *Inter-American Juridical Yearbook*, Washington, D.C., OAS, 1979.

But this criterion is valid in other questions as well, equally controversial. There are some who distinguish, for example, between a comprehensive doctrine of non-intervention and a restrictive one, depending on whether the consent of the intervened is accepted or not as a legal justification of the interference. Yepes, supporter of the extensive doctrine, pointed out that "intervention exists even when the affected State has given its consent more or less freely, for the essence of intervention does not lie so much in the existence or not of consent on the part of the State which suffers it, but in the will of the intervening party to impose his will through coercion".[64] On the contrary, Robert Redslob in his famous study on the history of the great principles of international law, although he arrived at the conclusion that in the period before World War I intervention was legally excluded, admitted that it can be legitimated when there is mutual agreement. As an example, he mentioned the Panama Canal Treaty, signed in 1903![65]

At present, the terms of this controversy are still the same. For Hermann Mosler, "there is nothing in law or in fact which prevents a State from signing a treaty by which it allows an intervention in its own affairs on the part of another State or other international organization established by the same treaty. Only in the absence of such an agreement is non-intervention a fundamental principle based on the sovereign equality of the States."[66] It is clear that if this treaty has been obtained through coercion it will be null and void. But this does not provide a definitive solution to our problem because, as Eduardo Jiménez de Aréchaga points out, "there is a thin dividing line separating the legitimate persuasion and bargaining with which governments seek to influence each other, from impermissible compulsion or coercion."[67] For Jiménez de Aréchaga it is possible to determine if this line has been crossed, using the general principles of international law, as, for instance, those of good faith, good neighbourliness, the duty to cooperate among States, apart from the unlawful character of the act which motivates the complaint. This approach follows the line of our reasoning in that there is no specific normative answer in these cases. On the other hand, good neighbourliness, good faith, obligation to cooperate, are in fact very vague principles (*most caoutchouc,* as Louis Le Fur would say) as long as they are not enlightened by the vivifing aura of justice.

64 Yepes, Jesús María, Les problèmes fondamentaux du Droit des gens en Amérique, *Recueil des Cours, Académie de droit international,* Tome 47, II, 1934, p. 70.

65 Redslob, Robert, *Histoire des grands principes du Droit des gens: Depuis l'Antiquité jusqu' à la veille de la Grande Guerre,* Paris, Rousseau, 1923, p. 512.

66 Mosler, Hermann, The International Society as a Legal Community, *Recueil des Cours, Académie de droit international,* Tome 140, IV, 1974, p. 151.

67 Jimenez de Arechaga, Eduardo, International Law in the Past Third of a Century, *Recueil des Cours, Académie de droit* international, Tome 159, I, 1978, pp. 115–116.

4.7. Global Transformation: Search for New Understanding*

Soedjatmoko

I am greatly honoured to have been invited to give a public lecture here at the University of Uppsala, a great and ancient centre of learning. You have been about the task of trying to improve the world's understanding of itself for some five centuries. I speak as a representative of one of the world's newest attempts to join that endeavour, the United Nations University. So I make my remarks here with some humility and trepidation.

I want to talk with you today about a world – only a few steps away from entering the 21st century – which is in a rapid, bewildering and often frightening state of profound change. We very badly need to make this process of global transformation more manageable and less frightening, and I would like to explore with you what international science and scholarship – from both old and new centres – might do together to help bring this about.

The central task that confronts us can be simply stated, but will be formidably challenging: how to arrange our lives in a crowded, competitive and limited world of 8 to 10 billion people beyond the year 2000, in ways that are ecologically sustainable and equitably based on a shared moral consensus that is now lacking.

Over the centuries of its existence, scholars and scientists from Uppsala have immeasurably enriched human life and enlarged the human spirit. Perhaps "immeasurably" is the wrong word – for so many of the indispensable measurements by which international science now communicates had their origins in the laboratories and lecture halls of this university. To Uppsala, the world is indebted for the Celsius Scale, the international symbols of chemistry of Berzelius, and the classifications of life itself of Linnaeus – to cite only a few of the best-known contributions.

It was Linnaeus who concluded, in his monumental work of classification, that man, possessor of the ability to think and reason, should be designated as "Homo sapiens" – man the wise. While the long list of human follies attests that man has often abdicated that title, it is clearly imperative that we seek to draw on that ability now. For men and women around the world, in ever-increasing

* Text of public lecture presented on 19 May 1981 at the University of Uppsala by Dr. Soedjatmoko, Rector of the United Nations University, and – with his permission – included as one of the basic documents of JUS 81.

measure, will need to think creatively and reason wisely if humanity is somehow to get through the next few perplexing and turbulent decades and enter a 21st century that is more secure, just and humane.

The signs of deep and fundamental change – of a literal transformation of the global society – are everywhere at hand, in all parts of the world and in all levels of society. One of the most important things we must learn, if we are to survive and progress in an increasingly insecure, perilous and fragile world, is the art of existing, at more than double population density, in a continuing state of rapid social change accompanied by great common vulnerability.

All societies, the strong and the weak, are now exposed to many forces and processes beyond their control, and all national boundaries have become permeable to the transnational impact of economic and political decisions taken somewhere outside one's own country. The pathology of the arms race, feeding on irrationality, mistrust and misunderstanding, continues to pose the ultimate threat of extinction of all life on this planet.

All of this poses the question of how we are going to learn to live and manage our fears in such a global condition of vulnerability. What new kinds of institutions and international arrangements must we devise to manage a world in a constant state of risk from many directions and in which no one is in control?

The slim and precarious measure of stability which characterized the post-war world and the period of detente – built largely on an uneasy and perilous nuclear stalemate – appears to have disappeared. That stability ignored basic issues of structural change and cultural diversity at both global and national levels. It is no longer possible to put off these issues.

The conventional notions of development of the 1960s and 1970s – the belief in economic growth and the "trickle down" theory – have clearly been unable to provide certain minimums of human survival to hundreds of millions around the globe who continue to live a life of squalor, injustice and despair. A restructuring of the world system, one which could offer hope of a life of dignity for all humanity and reduce rather than widen the gap between rich and poor, is long overdue.

The world economy is in a period of markedly slower growth and even stagnation and will manifestly not respond to shop-worn traditional nostrums. More effective instrumentalities for management of the global economy and the international monetary system must be devised.

Major shifts in the global configuration of power are underway, yet several of the major countries seem unwilling or unable to adjust to new political realities. There is great and obvious danger that when major centres of technological and military might find themselves unable to cope with a new situation they may fall prey to some irrational response – including the nuclear response.

The industrialized countries are experiencing great problems in overcoming the strucutral difficulties that stand in the way of adjustment to the post-industrial era and to advancing industrialization of the South. Their political and social institutions were created to solve other, older problems than those we face today. Government bureaucracies, political party machines and trade unions seem increasingly unable any longer to aggregate interests, hold allegiances and mediate between contending forces towards national consensus on many of our present and emerging problems.

Underlying all of these political and economic instabilities in the industrialized countries are very profound cultural changes and value shifts – manifested, for example, in altered concepts of work or changing consumer expectations and savings habits, but also in the rise of a new religiosity, the search for new life-styles and the emergence of single-issue politics. These are shifts that reflect people's changing conceptions about the meaning of life.

These are forces that are frequently beyond the capabilities of institutions or the control of governments. While they are in many ways healthy and commendable, they also contribute to the general sense of fragmentation, vulnerability and loss of control, of a world where "things are in the saddle and ride mankind".

Equally serious and deep-rooted is the fragmentation and disorder in the third world which is caught up in sharp conflict at home and abroad. As someone from the third world, I believe it is high time for its leaders to face up to this deep fragmentation – to continue to not do so is counter-productive to the third world's hopes of overcoming the global disparities that hamper and distort its development.

There is clear and troubling evidence of the developing countries' inability to act in unity. Throughout the Second Development Decade, the Group of 77 countries were unable to set up a joint Secretariat, or agree on the establishment of a single research institution that could undergird and buttress their negotiating stance towards the North.

The third world's situation is further complicated by the rise of the newly-industrialized countries, most notably in Latin America but also in East Asia. The rapidity of economic development in many of these countries has led to regional and social disparities of great magnitude, to which the third world has to make its own adjustments.

And there is also, it must be admitted and faced up to, deep trouble internally within developing societies. Many of the first generation of political institutions in the third world proved to be unable to cope with the needs of their societies and have collapsed. The second generation is now about to be tested by problems of succession. Too many of the third world elites continue to be bewitched by outworn assumptions about economic planning, technology transfer, and the modern technocratic State. Too many still view the problems in old power terms – whereas the real issues are increasingly of a different order, involving social growth, equity, justice, freedom, and alternative industrial trajectories.

All of this fragmentation and strain on political and social systems has put the call for a new international order and the concept of collective self-reliance at impasse – a logjam of competing interests, values and perspectives. This is hardly a position of strength in which to join the North-South dialogue. And yet the need for such dialogue remains imperative – for basic structural changes in the world system must be comprehended, agreed upon, and implemented if the peoples of the third world are to have any hope of lifting themselves out of their present state of poverty, inequity and powerlessness.

Thus everywhere – East and West, North and South – there is evidence of economic stagnation, social breakdown and political impotence. Everywhere powerful and wholly new processes and deep-seated emotional reactions to the status quo seem to emerge that challenge the traditional institutions' capacity to mangement.

Equally challenging to conventional management systems is the heedless plunder of the globe's finite resources, often in the name of progress and the advance of science and technology. In the rush to modernization and industrialization, we have recklessly brushed aside considerations of just how fragile and delicate the earth's life-support system is and how much its misuse ultimately affects us all. We must find ways to adjust our behaviour to the carrying capacity of the planet. At the moment, however, we are seriously lacking in institutional capacity to even monitor the changes we are imposing on the environment, much less successfully manage them on a sustainable basis.

Tragically, we are witnessing this widespread disintegration in human solidarity and environmental degradation at a moment when other, equally compelling forces – such as communications, world trade, and resource security considerations – are rapidly increasing the world's interdependence. We seem to be experiencing the paradoxical and disorienting process of our globe both fusing society together and splitting it apart. Clearly such a defiance of basic laws of nature cannot continue for long without serious consequences.

Ironically – and seemingly even more defiant of natural law – the first process, interdependence, is actually helping fuel the second, fragmentation. For the increase in global interdependence is due in large measure to the post-war scientific and technological revolution in telecommunications, electronics and transport. Which has, of course, fashioned the "global village" that both heightens the aspirations of the poor of the third world, and, at the same time, makes them all the more keenly aware of the inequity of their own lot.

In attempting to extrapolate the global situation in the decades ahead – from the present scene of spreading fragmentation and disarray in the world, with the increasing awareness of hundreds of millions of the unacceptability of their present daily lives – a pragmatist can only conclude that things will undoubtedly get worse before they get better. And the only real practical hope of an eventually better and brighter world seems to me to rest on our ability to make the powers of science and technology serve more consistently humanity's moral and ethical purposes. Certainly one of the most troubling questions of our age is why science and technology, despite their achievements and potential promise, have been unable to make possible the eradication of the hunger, poverty and injustice from which at least half a billion people still suffer.

The problems we face in the years ahead go beyond questions of development and beyond the North-South dialogue. It comes down really to the question of how we are going to act together to learn to live together in a world with 8 to 10 billion people within the lifetimes of our younger children today.

The harbingers of more serious, more entangled and more stubborn problems are all there in the projections of a number of studies with which I am sure most of you are familiar. One needs to touch upon them only briefly.

There is, of course, the reality of soaring populations. Despite remarkable successes in several countries in reducing fertility rates, rapid population increase is expected to continue – to the extent that by the year 2000, the world's absolutely poor will number 600 million, 540 million of whom will live in the low-income countries.

The implications of population growth can be read in many other ways than the appalling enumeration of absolutely poverty, all of which will tax our creative ingenuity, management capabilities, and readiness for moral response. It raises the question, for example, of the impact of this growth on an already disturbingly high rate of youth unemployment in many countries, both industrialized and developing. Another is the question of how we will learn to survive under conditions of extremely high population densities: will we need to somehow increase our sense of "inner space", as against the inevitable narrowing of "personal space", to cope with living conditions in such densities?

Population growth will also cast the energy outlook in a far starker light. The period of cheap energy is over. We will all have to make fundamental adjustments to the high cost of energy for a very long period in the future.

A growing consciousness of increasing resource scarcities – and not only in energy sources but also other key minerals or food sources – will trigger increased competition between industrialized countries, between the North and the South, and in the third world itself.

Resource transfer will become more and more a political weapon. Much as we might deplore it, resource diplomacy – using energy, food, other commodities – will likely be a reality of international negotiation and bargaining.

We are entering a period when what one might call "the geopolitics of resources" will become a major feature of the international scene. We can expect fundamental realignments of regional and national interests based on requirements of resource security. The political alignments which have characterized the post-war period and detente – which are already beginning to crumble – will witness even more profound change as countries reposition themselves in order to make sure they have continued access to resources. This is bound to accelerate the fragmentation, already underway, in the international constellation of power.

A particularly disturbing instability emerges from the global energy and food outlook. Here the projections indicate converging tracks – with spreading and disastrous consequences – as rising fuel prices, boosting fertilizer, transportation and other agricultural costs inevitably push food prices beyond the reach of hundreds of millions of already hungry people.

To combat this, the poorer and most populous countries will have to find ways to grow more food themselves using less energy-intensive methods. They cannot go on buying food *and* oil without inviting bankruptcy – and certain countries are already perilously close to that state.

Advances in biotechnology – biological nitrogen fixation, genetic improvement and the like – offer promise of ways to increase agricultural yield without high-priced energy inputs. But these are already moving from the laboratory to the profit sector in the West. The third world must move quickly lest a whole new range of dependencies emerge from these biotechnological advances. This speaks to their need to strengthen their own capabilities in the basic sciences and for centres of scientific excellence in the West – such as Uppsala – to be willing to co-operate with them in this effort.

Science alone, however, will not provide the solutions to problems such as these. One thing that should have struck us with blinding clarity by now is that science and technology left unchecked – with no links to moral and ethical purposes – have brought us so many of our present problems. Science and technology alone cannot help us to reshape the social structures in which hunger, poverty and injustice are embedded unless we learn to make them serve social and ethical goals.

To do this, however, we must also improve our understanding of the social and cultural dimensions of the problem. We need, for example, to know more about the dynamics of community participation, village selfmanagement and farmers' associations. We must pay fuller attention to many hitherto unheard voices – the marginal farmers, the landless labourers, women and other disadvantaged groups in the countryside.

It is in such groups that one sees today another major force for transformation and value change. Indeed the surging aspirations of the previously powerless are manifest on a worldwide scale. These trace their roots in part to the liberation movements during and after World War II as the peoples of many countries sought to throw off their foreign shackles. The same sort of aspirations fueled the civil rights movements in the United States in the 1950s and 1960s. This new desire to be heard, to have a vote in one's own future, is also in evidence in the environment and peace movements, the women's movement and in the evolution of workers' and peasants' associations in many parts of the world.

As is true with so much of the profound social change now occurring all around us, such movements from below are fraying and eroding the capacities of existing institutions and governments to deal with them. And yet they must be dealt with for they are expressions of very profound value changes of great magnitude. Left untended, these expressions of desire for change can be dangerous – for we have already seen in many parts of the world how easily pent-up dissatisfaction and frustration can explode into violence.

But more importantly, we need to listen to these voices because they may have something very, very significant to say. There is much that is fresh and original in many of these challenges to old assumptions about development and economic growth. We need to think about new instrumentalities that will be more capable of hearing and assimilating into development thinking, these previously unheard voices – for they represent the aspirations and hopes of vast numbers of mankind.

If this very rough sketch of the state of the world – today and in the decades ahead – has seemed excessively gloomy, let me seek to qualify that. For while it is indeed a troublesome and disquieting world scene, it is by no means a hopeless one. For I firmly believe that we may now be beginning to recognize that out of all the confusion, fragmentation and economic disarray, out of the necessity of living with the high cost of energy, out of the recognition that levels of violence must be reduced, out of the challenges to current life-styles, we may come to see development strategies and trajectories of industrialization that are basically different, and more consonant with human dignity and justice, than those we have followed to date.

We may, in fact, be seeing here a historical process unfolding that could lead to the emergence of alternative, non-Western, modern civilizations in various parts of the world – possibly the Sinitic, Hindu and Islamic as well as others. They will wish to take their rightful place side by side Western civilizations on a basis of rough parity. These civilizations have much to offer a world that could be both interdependent and richly pluralistic in cultural diversity.

Before such a vision can become reality, however, we will need to set in train a vast global learning process by increasing the learning capacity of nations and societies. Francis Bacon reminds us that wonder is the seed of knowledge – and so the learning will have to begin with questions. But here we will need the courage and insight to ask ourselves many new and elementary and even disturbing questions. For too long we have been asking the wrong or only partial questions, which of course goes a long way towards explaining why we have been getting the wrong answers.

Perhaps the first question should be: Do we really understand what is happening to us and what the historical processes in which we are involved really signify?

What are we to make, for example, of the reemergence of the spiritual, manifested in many ways, at many levels of society, around the globe? Is it simply another symptom of the flight from rationality and responsibility – or is it a change of a more fundamental character, signaling the end of secularism, "the return of the sacred", and the breaking through of new transcendental conceptions of life?

Are we in the process of abandoning concepts of universalism in favour of smaller, primary units of social organization? What would be the implications of this – economically, politically, culturally, and technologically?

Are we in the first phases of a global transformation that revolves around different kinds of interpersonal relationships – and therefore different kinds of power relations and different uses of technology? What forms would these new relationships and linkages take?

One thing is clear: Science and technology alone cannot answer such questions. Our technological resources cannot be mobilized to solve global problems unless they are related to the sources of morality, and unless our attitudes towards human suffering, justice and violence encompass a spiritual perception as well. Answers to the questions will only begin to emerge, therefore, when they are undergirded with moral and ethical purpose.

But our capacity for moral reasoning is being eroded by the fragmentation of man's perception of himself and his ultimate value. We must refind this moral and ethical capacity and employ it to its fullest in learning how to live in a world of 8 to 10 billion people in common justice and dignity. We must seek to reorganize ourselves to meet new fundamental requirements to honour both human solidarity and human individuality, as well as cultural and social diversity.

This can be seen as both a management problem and a human problem – a crisis of personal growth and interpersonal relationships writ large. A crisis also because our present knowledge is simply inadequate to deal with either the managerial or the human dimension.

Our knowledge base is seriously lacking – too many of our best intentions of helping humanity are beset by fragmented or ill-connected bits of information. Perhaps of all the fragmentation we see around us, the fragmentation of knowledge is the most tragic and consequential – for it is ultimately a shattering of humanity's perception of itself.

To put it bluntly, we don't really know enough about a great many things – at a moment when swift transformation in the framework of global interdependence asks for more hard and relevant knowledge and much more finely tuned and morally perceptive views of the world around us. The explosion of knowledge that has taken place has not necessarily added to our capacity to solve some of the most important problems faced by humankind. What we have learned has often been irrelevant to these problems.

The United Nations University was established as a global institution to help expand the knowledge base on which humankind will have to make its decisions about the future. Its Charter directs it to mobilize the "international community of scholars" in this effort – and thus it seeks to work in close co-operation with such major centres of learning as the University of Uppsala.

We will all have to work together: sifting and weighing existing relevant knowledge, testing the results of empirical hard research in the crucible of dialogue of many cultures and ideologies, and creating new knowledge, new insights, new understandings and new global perspectives.

In our five and a half years of existence, we have benefited greatly from the wisdom of scientists and scholars from Sweden and the other Scandinavian countries and from the support of the Scandinavian Governments. The UNU is now exploring new and different research activities on a number of the problems I have mentioned here today – the international economic system, the process of global and social transformation, peace and conflict resolution, human rights, values and freedoms, the interlinkages of food and energy, and the appropriate role of applied as well as basic science and technology in development. It hopes to develop with academic and scientific communities around the world a mutually beneficial and collaborative process of research and education.

Maybe – just maybe – if we do work together, we can begin to see more clearly the road we all want to travel towards a more viable, peaceful and equitable international order, with much lower levels of armaments and less destructive and insane violence. We can then begin to hope that this troubled, perilous and changing world can in fact rearrange itself with harmony and dignity for all humanity, and can do so before it is too late. If we can accomplish this, then I think we can rightfully and proudly defend the thesis of Linnaeus that the human species merits the title, "man the wise."

4.8. General Debate of the Seminar 17 June 1981

References:

President: MANFRED LACHS

The President: I suggest that we realise the undeniable truth that in order to promote knowledge and to improve the law we have to continue the dialogue – even expand, increase and multiply the parliament of jurists, where men full of vigour and intellectual curiosity, continue the dialogue.

History has shown that in these parliaments more light has been thrown on many problems, many theories subjected to critical evaluation, some rejected by history, many errors revealed, many new problems have found a new approach. Why should they become pioneers of the law to come? I am certain that each of you has in his mind many ideas and is not short of words to give expression to them, to reflections on whether and how to continue the work happily conceived by Professor Grahl-Madsen and splendidly organized under the protective wings of Uppsala University and UNITAR. In many respects an unusual conference, combining small details with great generalizations – bringing together men of many walks of life, of several generations.

Should we continue it in a wider company of representatives of the other sciences? Is it not worth recalling Plato who tried to explain the link between philosophy and technology; or Alembert who linked Archimedes with Homer; or the great Leonardo who personified philosophy, painting, mechanics and mathematics.

Not to continue the debates of the past, I invite you to look into the future, enriched by the experience of this unusual conference.

Law-making and decision-making – in diplomacy or practice on the bench or in the bar – wherever we may be acting, require of us continuous study and research. We should never stop in study and research for whatever we know is inadequate. You will always find that you are ignorant of some details, that your command of facts, law and other sciences has serious lacunae. We may seek certainty but we never reach it, all we attain in more knowledge, is more but not full knowledge.

We meet this morning at what is intended to be the last debating session of this seminar. We have had a most active time in having listened to 14 reports, an equal number of co-reports – not only in this hall but also in the parliament of Åland Islands. We have had lively debate spread over a great variety of subjects of international law. The four Main Rapporteurs will present a summary of it to-morrow – to be followed by the General Rapporteur. Our tasks as members of this assembly have in fact come to an end. We said what we wanted to say. One may therefore ask: what useful purpose may be served by the meeting of this morning.

I suggest that it may be devoted to some reflections on the deliberations in a broad perspective.

F. V. Garcia-Amador

The Seminar has covered a number of current demands and proposals relating to the idea of revision of international law. This has been possible, thanks on the one hand, to the wisdom shown by its organizers in preparing the agenda and, on the other hand, to the excellency of the *travaux préparatoires,* i. e., the papers that have been submitted for the consideration of the Seminar by our distinguished colleagues.

In the course of the discussion, both in plenary and group sessions, some of the current attacks and criticisms upon traditional international law have been reiterated. I say "some" because other attacks and criticisms are not specifically related with any of the agenda's items. The most relevant examples are, perhaps, the attacks and criticisms upon the traditional law of State responsibility, especially the principles governing nationalization and compensation of foreign-owned property. Obviously the revision of international law is a very broad task, and the subject I have just mentioned would require, in itself alone, another 10 days seminar. I refer to this particular subject of international law because it is one of those with respect to which not only the attacks and criticisms are very severe but also because the proposals for revision are often quite far-reaching.

May I, at this point, clarify my position. Not only I have nothing against the idea of an orderly revision of international law, but on the contrary, I am whole-heartedly in favour of it; as a matter of fact I think I have always been. But in any case that is not at all what matters. What does really matter are some specific features that current attacks and criticisms upon traditional principles often show.

The first feature that must be mentioned is found in the shape of a certain degree of misunderstanding of the true meaning of some of the principles of traditional international law. In effect, an erroneous image of traditional international law and its postwar developments seems to be contributing to such misunderstanding, particularly whenever that image is projected in the writings of learned authorities. To illustrate does traditional international law, particularly as developed by the postwar and current State practice in the field of nationalization and compensation, really justify all and every one of the attempts at revision that are being made nowadays?

A second feature of current attacks and criticisms is the inconsistency that one finds, from time to time, between such attacks and criticisms and the corresponding proposal for revision on the one hand, and on the other, the practice actually followed by the same States and vocating for the revision. A striking example of this feature is found in connection with the question of compensation for nationalized foreign-owned property. The position taking in international fora certainly is not consistent with actual State practice. This we all know. Such inconsistency is even more striking where the idea is not of mere revision but rather that of repudiation of a principle or an institution. Arbitration clauses agreed between States and foreign corporations may serve as illustrations. We are all familiar with the position taken by the Group of 77 during the negotiations of the Charter of Economic Rights and Duties of States and the actual practice of many of the members of said Group, without excluding the Latin American countries, which repeatedly and unanimously have repudiated the 1965 World Bank Convention on settlement of disputes between States and foreign corporations.[1] A similar situation is found when completely different positions are taken in various international fora. A significant example is found when we compare the position taken in the aforementioned negotiations and the one taken more recently by the same Group in the course of the discussion of the proposed code of conduct for the transfer of technology. Within the Inter-American System such a situation has also recently taken place.

For a Latin American student of international law, the idea of revision will remind him of the efforts made by Latin American statemen and scholars during the second part of the XIX century and the first part of the present century. The *Doctrine* and the *Calvo Clause* (i. e., the principle of equality of nationals and aliens and the elimination of diplomatic protection in contractual claims, respectively); the *Drago doctrine,* (i. e., the prohibition of coercive collection of public debts); the proscription of the right of conquest; the consacration of the duty of non-intervention, including the concept of "economic aggression", in our regional treaty law) and so forth, are evidences of a succesful process of revision as well as of a substantial contribution to the development and the improvement of international law. The revision of the principle or institution of traditional international law was, in each case, truly needed and, therefore entirely justified; again repudiation was made only where required and fully warranted, as in the case of the rights of conquest and of intervention.

To conclude, may I reiterate my full, whole-hearted support of the idea of revision of traditional international law in order that its principles and institutions become more in conformity with the present needs of the international

1 Convention on the Settlement of Investment Disputes between States and Nationals of Other States of 18 March 1965 (ICSID/2).

community. Notwithstanding the legitimacy of the claim of the developing world to a preferential treatment, as the debate continues on the proposed new international economic order, it is my hope that it takes the direction of the best legitimate interest of both the developing and developed countries.

Davorin Rudolf

Inspired by the opening speech delivered by Swedish Under-Secretary of State Dr. Hans Blix about the position of non-alliance and neutrality of Sweden, and, after that, by a speech delivered by Mr. Olof Jansson, the speaker of the Åland Parliament about the legal history of the islands and – at the same time – bearing in mind certain changes and novelties in modern international law, I would like to say a few words about a relatively new legal institute which I call pax-activity and about an old one – the neutrality and the status of those countries which adopt neutrality in peace-time. What qualitative shifts have taken place?

Neutrality is often associated with war. For many reasons, however, we can speak about neutrality in peace-time. Rights and obligations which permanently neutral States realize and perform in peace-time are becoming increasingly predominant. A permanently neutral State safeguards and consolidates its status by active participation in all areas of international relations during peace-time. Its authentic interest in present international relations is to eliminate the causes of war and prevent war, and not only to remain neutral in case of war. Moreover, such activities of neutral States have far-reaching positive bearings on the whole international community. The obligation of a neutral State, for example, not to join military alliances or similar politically orientated bodies during peace-time reduces the number of States in confrontation, that is the States belonging to different bloc systems. In the same way, the dynamics manifested by the neutral States in their activities – the latest example is the Madrid Conference on European Security where the European neutral countries together with the non-aligned countries and those free from blocs are particularly active – show that neutrality is now far from being considered an egoistic attitude or equated with politics of strict equidistance.

Furthermore, I think that the old question of compatibility of collective security with neutrality, that is of the obligations under the United Nations Charter with those under neutrality agreements, has now been solved.

However, in legal literature on this subject, particularly Austrian literature, the membership of permanently neutral Austria has been explained as follows: the UN member States have accepted Austria with its status of permanent neutrality into the organization and "in this manner all the UN members have assumed the obligation never to involve Austria in coercive measures during a war between third countries" (Alfred Verdross). In my opinion, such explanations should not be accepted. Among other things, they are contrary to the principle of equality of all UN members. It must also be pointed out that the Security Council is not authorized to release particular countries from the obligations under the UN Charter because of their legal or political status. It is much more logical to adopt the view that the norms in the UN Charter have higher legal force and that in the event of conflict between the obligations of the UN members under the Charter and their obligations under any other international agreement, their obligations under the Charter shall prevail. That practically means: in the case where the collective security system becomes inoperative the State may then validly resort to the neutrality status. However, at the moment when the competent organ of the UN Organization decides to take collective coercive measures, the State ceases to be neutral and becomes pax-active, the right of application of pax-activity being accepted.

Now, of course, let me explain very briefly what I mean by pax-activity. The term "pax-activity" has been coined from the Latin "pax" meaning peace and the English "activity" in order to emphasize the difference between the legal position this term denotes and the meaning of either "belligerency" or "neutrality".

The United Nations Charter has ended the traditional division of States into belligerent and neutral ones – as far as international law and neutrality law are concerned. In cases when the United Nations decides to undertake collective measures owing to a threat to peace, a breach of peace, or an aggression, the member States and even non-member States outside the conflict are, like the United Nations in the legal position of pax-activity, which ought to be distinguished from both belligerency and neutrality.

Pax-activity denotes the legal status of the UN Organization and of any State outside the conflict in the course of carrying out the collective measures of the Collective Security Organization for the purpose of maintaining or restoring international peace and security.

Being a component part of international law, pax-activity incorporates the legal rules by means of which mutual rights and duties are regulated in the course of carrying out collective measures by the United Nations:

a) between the United Nations and its member States as well as non-members taking part in carrying out the collective measures, and
b) between the United Nations and the States taking part in carrying out the collective measures on the one hand, and the State or States against which the measures are being taken on the other hand.

Pax-activity presupposes the existence of a cogent norm prohibiting war and a Universal International Security Organization possessing a built-in mechanism for the authoritative establishment of (**a**) the violation of the norm prohibiting war, (**b**) the violator, and (**c**) the decision to carry out collective measures.

This can be illustrated by the examples of the actions the United Nations undertook against Rhodesia and in the case of Namibia and of the behaviour of Austria or Switzerland.

At the end allow me to point out a novel example in international legal relations. The Helsinki Final Act (1975), i. e., the Declaration of Principles, States that every State has the sovereign right of neutrality. On the question as to whether the Helsinki document is a legal act or only a political one, I know that opinions are divided. However, the trends are clear in any case, and they imply that a unilateral act of a State is sufficient for that State to become permanently neutral. Moreover, it seems that permanent neutrality of the Austrian or Swiss type has become very similar to the traditional neutrality of Sweden and Finland,

and according to certain indications there is also more convergence in the wider circle to which the non-aligned countries also belong.

Peter Nobel

To the impressive contributions to and the thought provoking discussions of this seminar I would like to add a "footnote" on torture or "cruel, inhuman or degrading treatment or punishment" (Art. 7 in the 1966 International Covenant on Civil and Political Rights). The intention is not to voice another emotional protest against these evils but to say something about the very function of torture related to some of the seminar's topics.

The rise of tyrants or the emergence of oppressive regimes – as is often said, also at this seminar – are the results of political and economical causes. Which, however, is the main instrument for the implementation of tyrannical power and for the duration and efficiency of terror and oppression? I dare say it is the use of torture. There are few States in the world today which have not during the last decade or are not now at this moment openly encouraging or silently accepting torture being used by their soldiers, police officers, security men or non-official formations. I am one of those who consider the widespread use of torture as one of the gravest social problems in the world today – because torture more than anything else is used to silence free discussion – and thereby real solutions – in the fields of social justice, human rights, a fair distribution of assets and burdens among all men and all countries, a check on the ruthless exploitation by a few of limited resources as well as the protection of our planet, disarmament, and development. For this imperative reason international lawyers and particularly those without political ties should pay full attention to torture, study it and even its social and political effects and describe it as the hideous thing it is – and this in full recognition of all the problems concerned with political and economical conditions, State sovereignty and non-intervention.

Torture is torture and torture is crime when and where it occurs. It is not worse if a person is tortured under one political system than another – it is the same. It is not acceptable that people shall undergo barbaric punishments because some leaders say that this is in response to religious law. It should not be the internal affairs of a State if some of its citizens are allowed to torture others. Torture should be observed as such and not as an inseparable part of that or that regime and its method of administration.

Also support by study and dissemination should be given to projects like the advanced draft Convention Against Torture and the African Draft of the Organization of African Unity Charter on Human and Peoples Rights and to all the existing instruments. More study and research, more publicity – scholarly and popular and more education – not least at the universities on the use of torture, its effects and its legal remedies. Torture is an obstacle on the way to a new world order.

Bo Johnson Theutenberg

We have come to our general debate. The seminar is closing down, and we have to make a summary of our efforts. Has it been worthwhile to gather here in Uppsala? Have we got something out of it? It is not for me as a member of the organizing committee to give any evaluation on this. If for nothing else I believe it has been useful at least for having given us an opportunity to meet with each other and to establish personal contacts with the different "generations" in our common, favourite subject, international law. I, for one, think that this has been extremely important. The purpose of this seminar was to establish a gathering of experts with ability to look into the future, the crystal ball. To see what international law will be for the future, not only in a couple of years but for some decades ahead. It was rightly pointed out from this rostrum that international law was not something that could be solved once and for all. No, all generations will have to solve their specific problems. We, in our generation, have to tackle fundamental problems right now. We see new elements in the materia of international law that took form some 300 years ago among other things stemming from the great fundamental changes of our own generation, namely decolonization. New States are adhering to the society of States in the sense that they are becoming sovereign entities.

I have tried to analyse the historic process leading up to the present period in my paper submitted to this seminar, and there is no need to dwell on this point any longer here. There is though one point that I should like to emphasize. It was said here yesterday, I believe by professor Reisman[1] that it is not the *State* as such that feels and suffers. I think this was a very good point, indeed. It is this point I would make too, namely that our era has brought international law nearer to our hearts. It is not any longer entirely the high sovereign States – the subjects of international law – that are the only "customers" of international law, as in past times. Our time, our technical development, has brought us intensive international relations and thus international law into our TV-rooms, where all events will currently affect the individuals, the families. No one is untouched by severe attacks on civilians, no one is unaffected by cruel actions in other countries, wherever they may occur, when they see it on the TV-screen or hear it on the radio. Individuals react in accordance with their own values, their own terms of reference. Thus, in my opinion, there have been changes in the international law as to the broadness of its scope. There are more active "observers and listeners", more active participants, more active individuals, who would not be prepared at all to be given the answer that international law is nothing for them – only something that is regulating relations between the "high sovereign States".

International law has become individualized in the sense that it will have more and more customers. Individuals have discovered that international law is something that is affecting their own lives, and their conditions of life. They have discovered that international law could even protect them when it comes to fundamentalities of their own lives.

1 See p. 43.

Rules in international law are fundamentally related to human beings. A State as such does not feel anything. A State is nothing without its people, its inhabitants. It is not the State as a concept that performs in international relations. It is the individuals representing the State. A State is led by human beings. The actions of States are calculated in the human mind. Behind the actions of States you have always deliberate considerations by some persons who direct their actions against other persons, either in their own country or in other countries.

The actors in international law have become numerous – either as initiators of State actions or as the targets of State actions. Formerly the targets of the actions – the inhabitants, the individuals – kept silent, but nowadays they react in some way or another.

It is not the State as such that carries the historical, cultural or legal heritage. It is the people of an entity that in generation after generation carries that heritage onwards. Individuals have always roots somewhere – they act and react out of their own values whatever they may be. In the now universal *multicultural* world it goes without saying that the more individual actors there are – basing their acts on their own values – the more differing trends we will have in the corpus of international law.

I am not going to repeat the message of my original paper, only make the point that it is *necessary* for us, international lawyers, to see international law in a broader perspective. Tendencies of isolation have always been obvious in our field, but an isolation today is extremely dangerous. The main theme has been international law in a *multicultural* world. How is it possible for us, the jurists, to talk about a multicultural concept without thorough analysis and studies of what is really meant by this concept. We know that all actions by individuals are rooted in the sphere of cultural origin – this can never be denied, but we still treat international law as an independent body hanging above all other relations, all other spheres of society.

If we are going to be able to understand different trends in international law we must take a more scientific view on this development. Someone mentioned the folkloric view. It is that view that is dangerous. Development in different parts of the world must be looked upon seriously – must be analysed in a scientific way. Thus we must open up our own subject for cooperation with other fields of science – with historians, economists, even experts in religion and religious history, since religion in many parts of the world form the only legal norms, even today.

I would urge the institutes of different kinds, UN bodies like UNITAR etc. to embark on this road. Only by studies, further analysis and further information bridges can be built between the different cultures of the world. Only by broader cooperation and by better information between the regions can misunderstandings be avoided as to the real content of the specific doctrines. By a profound knowledge of the different spheres of our society we will also be in a position better to understand the functions of international law in the future. My view is that future international law must be of a universal kind. A system providing *all* States of our world with a common denominator – rules how to conduct relations with *all* other States and how to conduct its own policy within society.

Thus we are all affected by regional trends because they will involve ourselves sooner or later. If we meet, as we have done here, and conduct an open discussion, like we have done here, we are contributing, I believe, to the orderly development of a universally recognized international law. Because we have – all regions – *more* values in common than we might think. I will here refer to my original paper. Therefore I express the wish that we will soon see each other again. Perhaps then international law will have even "caught up" with our forecasts here in Uppsala.

Shigeru Oda

1. As I was prevented from participating in this Seminar at its earlier stage, I missed, to my great regret, most of the diskussions centred on the concept of the new international economic order. I ask the floor at this stage neither to reopen nor to supplement the discussions on what has been said about the concept of the new international economic order. Rather, I must confess my ignorance, and would seek some enlightenment on this concept from my colleagues. I shall be pleased if I may be allowed to suggest some new aspects which may require further examination at any future international forum such as this Seminar.

In my view, the concept of the new international economic order is important if it is able to suggest new rules concerning the distribution or allocation of access to natural resources among the sovereign nations, each of which naturally wishes to maximize its own share and to minimize restraints on or sacrifices to its economic development. My question is simply whether the very concept of the new international economic order has ever offered an agreeable solution to any of the concrete problems concerning such distribution and allocation. I pointed out thirty years ago, long before the concept of the new international ecnomic order was introduced, that the law of the sea would be faced with the basic problem of how to share the limited ocean resources among the nations whose demand was infinite, but I have never been able to suggest any satisfactory solution.

2. Let me first start with the distribution or allocation of access to natural resources. The global land resources have never been evenly allocated among the sovereign nations; some States are in advantageous positions, while others are not. Yet these unevenly distributed land resources among the sovereign nations are not made the object of redistribution today. While in past colonial ages land resources in Asia and Africa were often grabbed by some colonial powers, the new concept of permanent sovereignty over natural resources – which, I think, opened the new era of the new international economic order in some respects – can now save these resources from exploitation by other nations, and preserve them for the benefit of each sovereign nation. Thus, in the field of international law today, the exclusive control of land resources by each nation is no longer challenged, and access to the land area and to its resources is exclusively reserved in the hands of each sovereign State. On the other hand, however, except for the marginal belt of the narrow territorial sea around the land, the vast ocean had

been left, for a long time, free to access by any nation. The freedom of the high seas had guaranteed the principle of "first come, first served".

3. After World War II, free access to the ocean's resources first met the objection of the United States, the most developed and most geographically-privileged country, which successfully took the lead towards the formulation of the concept of the continental shelf. The law of the continental shelf was, and is, basically aimed at the exclusive use of the off-shore mineral resources for the sole benefit of the geographically-privileged coastal nations, either developed or developing. The arena which was potentially open for free access by any nation was thus diminished in favour of the coastal nations, which tried to maximize their own share of mineral resources under the legal terms of the continental shelf. This claim did not in fact meet with any strong objections in the post-war period. This was probably because, while those States which could benefit from this concept of the continental shelf were limited to a group of the geographically-privileged nations, yet another group of countries had not yet found it possible, technically or economically, to utilize the mineral resources of this vast area for their own benefit. The situation changed, however, with the increasing demand and the advanced technology of the late 1960s, and a group of geographically-handicapped nations, including land-locked and shelf-locked, but not necessarily developing, countries, were able to organize a power to stop the trend towards the gradual expansion of the exclusive use of off-shore mineral resources being reserved only for the coastal nations. Thus the concept of the common heritage of mankind was introduced into international law in connection with the minerals of the vast ocean bed.

4. In the post-war period similar situations also existed in the United States with regard to off-shore fishing. Yet the claim to exclusive fishing in the off-shore areas was more sophisticated, free access to ocean fishery resources having been a far more established belief worldwide, as traditionally understood in terms of the freedom of the high seas. The expansion of coastal fishery jurisdiction for the sole benefit of the geographically-privileged coastal nations easily met with objections by other States which would be entitled, even if potentially, to claim free access, which might be denied as a result of such an extension of coastal jurisdiction. Unlike the concept of the continental shelf, which became widely recognized only some years after the War, a period of nearly thirty years was required for the United Nations Conference on the Law of the Sea (UNCLOS III) to adopt the concept of the exclusive economic zone in international law.

I must draw your attention to the fact that, while on the one hand the new concept of the common heritage of mankind was introduced to stop the unlimited expansion of the exclusive use of mineral resources for the benefit of coastal nations, on the other hand the traditionally-established concept of the freedom of fishing could act as a barrier to the expansion of fishery jurisdiction. Yet I am inclined to think that the concept of the common heritage of mankind as originally introduced, applying solely to the mineral resources of the seabed of the ocean, will eventually become applicable to fishing in the vast ocean areas. Several years ago I predicted: "At the Fourth Conference on the Law of the Sea that might be convened some day in the future, I think that discussions will be held on the new concept of the common heritage of mankind applicable to ocean fishing similar to those discussions now taking place on the seabed mineral resources in UNCLOS III." I think I was not wrong in so predicting.

In fact, in the field of vast ocean fishing, the traditional concept of free access or the "first come, first served" basis has already been modified to a great extent. I do not deem it necessary to give any explanation on the conservation of fishery resources in this respect, because no one objects to the necessity of conservation of living resources. This is a concept of natural science which has never been challenged. The question we are faced with remains how to share the living marine resources, the maximum allowable catch of which is to be determined by the very objective concept of conservation. Antarctic whaling would appear to offer an interesting example of this. Under the 1948 Convention, Antarctic whaling was open to all countries which were able to compete freely for their maximum catch within the total limit set by the International Whaling Commission. However, this "whaling olympic" had already been abandoned by the late 1960s in favour of the quota system which would allocate the catch among nations. This is simply one of many examples in the field of international ocean fishing, but I would like to say that the most well-established principle of the freedom of fishing – in other words, free access to the resources – will eventually be replaced by a new concept, which, one can say, may be assimilated to the concept of the common heritage of mankind, though this concept is not today, at UNCLOS III, regarded as applicable to ocean fishing.

5. Now let me turn very briefly to the issues of the protection of the marine environment beyond national jurisdiction. With regard to marine pollution, the law of the sea, like environmental issues in general, is facing the basic problem of "development or protection of the environment". One of my frieds said at UNCLOS III: "Poor pollution, no one is in your favour". There are always pros and cons to the various topics at UNCLOS III, but certainly no one has ever been in favour of marine pollution. If disposal of waste into the sea were to be completely prohibited, the problem would then be much simpler. However, the disposal of some waste and toxic substances as a result of economic development is unavoidable. In fact the sea becomes ever more attractive to any nation or to any industry for the discharge of waste and toxic substances. If we were to completely prohibit this activity, we would have to stop all industrial and social progress, and the cost would be extremely high. The same applies to the shipping industry. Although no one ever doubts the necessity of environmental protection of the ocean, stringent environmental control could raise opposition from industry. A choice must be made between the two opposite policies, namely the encouragement of economic development and the protection of the marine environment. A further consideration is how to spread the burden between the different nations: the burden of sacrificing economic development for the protection of the marine environment. In the international community each country, in its relationship with other countries, will try to minimize the burden on its industry necessitated by pollution control. Some years ago I predicted that the law of the sea might eventually face problems related as to how to allocate sacrifices imposed in environmental protection and that the concept of the common heritage of mankind

will also be introduced in this respect, and said that this might become one of the topics to be discussed at a future UNCLOS IV.

6. I now come to the conclusion. Or, rather, I now come to the point where I must throw questions to my colleagues. On the one hand, the question of exclusive use being reserved to each coastal nation has now become defined in terms either of the concept of the continental shelf or the exclusive economic zone. On the other hand, in the areas beyond, the concept of the common heritage of mankind has been introduced for the exploitation of their mineral resources. In future, almost without doubt, this concept will apply also to fishery resources or even to protection of the marine environment. What really faces us today is, firstly, how to distribute and allocate the limited amount of ocean resources, mineral or living, among the sovereign nations, each of which will naturally try to maximize its own share; and secondly, how to distribute and allocate among the sovereign nations the sacrifices – each of which will also naturally try to minimize its own – involved in protection of the marine environment necessitated by economic development. Does simply suggesting the concept of the common heritage of mankind provide us with any solution? Certainly not. I know that the concept of the common heritage of mankind has grown in parallel with the concept of the new international economic order. But what does the phrase "common heritage of mankind" mean? What is the substance of this wording? I am not in a position to comment on the legal implications the 1970 United Nations General Assembly resolution might have. The declaration does not necessarily specify by whom and how the deep ocean floor could be developed, nor by whom and how the benefits would be shared. The substance of "the common heritage of mankind" involved various interpretations. Thus today we have confusion in UNCLOS III. Some autonomous principles work within the idea of freedom itself. However, if this idea of freedom is to be denied and replaced by some new idea of justice, then new principles must be worked out. The mere words "common heritage of mankind" are meaningless. Simply to formulate some machinery is also useless. As the issues discussed at UNCLOS III are related to the areas which are considered those of the common heritage of mankind, the positions of the land-resource-possessing and non-possessing countries are so conflicting as to lead to bloody confrontations. What kind of idea in principle can we obtain if we are to put substance into the conceptual wording of "common heritage of mankind"? If we consider the complexities of national interests that are still strongly projected on the common heritage, then it can be said that international society has not yet developed to such a high level that we can talk of the common heritage of mankind. People today appear to be satisfied only with the somewhat beautifully-sounding wording. As I stated at the outset, land resources are unevenly divided among the sovereign nations, developed or developing, and off-shore resources are reserved only for the benefit of the geographically-privileged coastal nations. Considering this, how to implement the concept of the common heritage of mankind with regard to sharing the benefits of the vast ocean resources, and sharing the sacrifices or burdens of economic development for the protection of the vast ocean, must be an important problem which the international lawyers will have to tackle. I thus have

not given any solution, or even a hint of any solution, to this difficult problem of resource-sharing. I intend only to suggest that we should go beyond simply playing with the concept of the new international economic order or with the beautiful wording of "common heritage of mankind".

I thank you for your indulgence in listing to my arguments, which I am afraid may be somewhat misguided.

Bengt Broms

As I understand it, we were not expected to take up in the general debate new problems or to ask new questions requiring perhaps immediate replies by other participants. Therefore, I have asked for the floor merely to express my best thanks to my good old friend Professor Atle Grahl-Madsen together with his staff and to Executive Director Nicol and his staff for their work in arranging this big conference on international law and organization for a new world order. Their task has been both of utmost importance and an ambitious understanding.

Ambassador Bo Johnson Theutenberg asked a moment ago a question concerning the value of this seminar. As I do not belong to the organizing committee I venture to say that the eloquent statement which was made by the previous speaker, Professor Yu Sheng, is already in itself sufficient evidence for the success of the seminar. For my own part, I feel that it has been a most valuable and stimulating meeting enabling us to build bridges between different schools of international law and to meet with many old and some new friends – all of them interested in the advancement of the cause of international law – for a fruitful exchange of views.

The fact that we have had thirteen topics in our debate is a sign of strength because it goes to show that international law of today is indeed about to develop at an increasing pace and that we – as international lawyers, many of us representing the world of diplomacy or research in various fields of international law – are becomming more and more aware of the needs of the international community.

Ten days is not enough to change the course of events in the mainstream of international law, but I think that, due to the fortuitious combinations of the group that has gathered here in Uppsala, we have been able to cover a lot of ground. Furthermore, once we have before us the report of the seminar, we will have ample time to compare and understand better the various views that have been presented and by then we will have had the benefit of a short time for further reflection.

The fruit never ripens immediately after the seeds have been planted, and I do express the hope that the seeds which have been planted during this seminar will be ripe in a not too distant future and that the wise suggestions we have heard will lead to concrete action and finally to the organization for a new world order.

Zdenek Červenka

1. New international economic order and the use of force

Great, profound changes – and the New International Economic Order is by definition a great change – can be achieved through two means: by negotiation or by the use of force.

A number of participants in their papers, as well as in their oral contributions have convincingly shown that the room for negotiation between the North and South has become so small that it is hardly visible. The question arises whether the new international economic order can be achieved by the use of force.

Recent developments haven shown that this is not a very realistic proposition either. The Third World has little economic and even less military power to enforce the changes which it is so emphatetically demanding from the industrial countries at the United Nations, at non-aligned fora and at the North-South negotiating desk. Oil weapon, which at first seemed to be the alternative to negotiation proved to benefit only those holding it. It has hit the poor nations more than the rich. Besides, oil is an exceptional commodity. Similar moves on part of the copper and other metals producers, as well as cocoa and coffee growers utterly failed. There should be no doubt, however, that if the Third World possessed military means to get what it regards is its right it would not hesitate to use it.

Nevertheless, military impotence of the Third World countries does not mean that the West, where, apart from the Soviet Union all the big guns are, is in a position to use them to put the end to the Third World challenge of its economic superiority. The constraints imposed on the Western military strategists who, at various stages of the oil crisis seriously contemplated to "bomb the rebellious oil sheiks and ayatollahs back to the Stone Age" proved to be considerable. The US-Iran confrontation over hostages is a good example.

These constraints are products of the following two factors:

1. The balance of "nuclear deterrents" between the two superpowers created a peculiar stalemate. Although they both sit on arsenals of nuclear weapons for wiping out mankind from the surface of our planet they cannot use it for fear that they too would perish in the holocaust once they dared to use them.
2. The shift in international relations, marked by the emerge of regional centers of economic and political power which began to challenge the concept of superpowers' spheres of influence – Mexico in Latin America, Nigeria in Africa, ASEAN States in Asia and the Islamic Conference in the Arab world.

While these constraints, in particularly those imposed on the US and USSR, work against a possibility of World War III they do not prevent the outbreak of regional conflicts, the number of which continues to rise. The war between Iran and Iraq, the liberation war of Polisario in Western Sahara and SWAPO in Namibia, the simmering conflict between Vietnam and China as well as the revolutionary upsurge in El Salvador point into this direction.

One of the ommissions of our seminar was the neglect for the existing international peaceful machinery. One of our future tasks should be the examination of ways and means how these conflicts could be averted and if they erupt how they could be extinguished.

2. Human rights versus violence

One of the most encouraging results of the seminar was the unanimity of its participants about the need for greater emphasis on the protection of human rights on both national and global scale. Indeed, as numerous participants noted, the respect for human rights has become one of the corner-stones of international relations of our times.

In contrast to this development we are witnessing an alarming growth in what may be described as "brutalization of human relations". It found its expression in the increase of acts of terrorism the targets of which are "random victims", innocent people with no links whatsoever with the plight of various political groups which use terror to draw attention to their cause. I think it needs more than legal measures to combat this development. After all we all know how easily the emergency laws – through repressive legislation and special powers for the police force – can be abused, and how human rights can be violated under the pretext of "suppression of terrorism".

3. Interdisciplinary approach

The above mentioned problem of rising violence as well as many other issues considered by our seminar call for an interdisciplinary approach. Any follow up of our meeting which may address itself to some of the international problems which we tried to identify if not solve, should be joined by economists, sociologists, anthropologists to help us in our search for legal rules of conduct which would pave the way to a better world to live in.

Badr Kasme

I think it useful to sum up, from a personal angle, some of the ideas which have emerged from this seminar. I will be quite straightforward. I shall focus on ideas common not only in many parts of the Third World countries, but, as the discussions at this seminar has proved, also elsewhere.

Within the framework of the global theme of the seminar, Professor Suy, the Under Secretary-General for legal affairs of the United Nations, drew our attention to the declining proportion (30% at present against 60% in the past) of States accepting the compulsory jurisdiction of the International Court of Justice, but he did not say what were, in his opinion, the reasons behind this trend, nor did he suggest a solution for this question.

Professor Broms, in his paper, indicated various possible reasons for the reluctance of the States to have recourse to the Court, in a word, for their distrust of the Court. Among these reasons, he cited the uncertainty of the law, the fear of new States that the developed States can have more effective advocates for their cases, last but not least, the fear "that, the International Court of Justice, due to the division of seats, will not apply the legal principles to a case in a manner which would reflect their own regional rules". Therefore, in the view of the Third World, the present rules applied by the Court are not adequate.

Will then the solution of this problem, i. e. attracting more States to the Court, be in increasing the number of judges from the Third World? As we all know, contrary to the situation in all other principal organs of the United Nations, the number of judges (15) has not varied since the adoption of the Charter. One could say however that adding new judges from developing countries might lead the developed States, fearing what they call a new automatic majority in this important field, to keep away from the Court, but this risk is not a real one, as potential judges from the Third World have – here, we may perhaps say fortunately – a Western education and an excellent knowledge of Western legal systems and cultures in addition to their own, and, after all, judges are not politicians.

As for the rules applied by the Court, one can say that the present wording of art. 38 of the Statute is not satisfactory and should be revised, and I noted with great interest that, in his paper, Judge Lachs, in referring to par. (c) of art. 38 mentioned the general principles of law applied by nations, but he dropped the word "civilised". I dare think that this was not a typing mistake but rather that Judge Lachs has already, in his mind, tacitly revised the article.

Furthermore, concerning the same art. 38 of the Statute, much was said about the role of custom, with emphasis on regional custom (Professor Feliciano) and on custom being formed rapidly. I shall not come back to this question, but still in connection with this art. 38, I would like to stress a point raised yesterday by Professor Dimitrijevic, namely the relevant resolutions of international organizations adopted by consensus and formulating new principles of law, should formally be added to the currently accepted sources of international law. Art. 38 cites "the teachings of the highly qualified publicists of the various nations as a subsidiary means for the determination of rules of law". – Should not the resolutions figure *expressis verbis* among the sources, and then at least on equal footing with, and I even say at a higher place that the teachings of publicists?

Remaining always in the area of the International Court of Justice, I should like now to refer to the statement of Judge Elias on the case of Iran – I think that everybody concurs with him concerning the enforcement of the judgments of the International Court, but I should like to take this opportunity to raise a more general question: Without defending the position of Iran which so obviously violated international law, a position almost nobody would defend, nor trying to be the devil's advocate, I wonder if we should not search the reasons behind this violation of international law in present international law itself? In fact Iran's case reveals a crisis in international law. An international law which averts the eyes from and thus permits the intervention of a given State in the affairs of another State because of the latter's political orientation or economic policy will inevitably lead to the violation of such an international law. We all know that the declaration of economic rights and duties of States prohibits interventions; but if international law had machinery, adequate and effective, for preventing or stopping such an intervention, we might not encounter the kind of violation demonstrated by Iran.

I would go even further. We know that present international law is concerned with the *sovereignty of States*. In the past, according to national law, sovereignty belonged to the Chief, King or Ruler. Nowadays, national law prescribes sovereignty as belonging to *the people*. I wonder if international law could develop so as also to care for the people. Have we not an encouraging precedent in the Charter of the United Nations whose preamble starts with this phrase: "We the *peoples* of the United Nations . . ."? Professor Lillich's penetrating insights on sovereignty showed us how international law can be concerned with the people.

In fact, this concern can take two directions:

1. international law can care for the peoples having no States – this being, yet insufficiently admitted and implemented, the domain of self-determination.
2. international law can also care for the peoples having a State but one which violates their fundamental rights, – this being the domain of human rights. Once more, if international law had the machinery, adequate and effective, to prevent or to stop violations of human rights in any given State – whether this violation, as was the case in Iran under the Shah, was perpetrated with the help or without the help of official or semi-official foreign entities – many events would not have taken place.

The sovereignty of State should not be invoked against the sovereignty of the people. A few minutes ago, I spoke about non-intervention, but I should like to stress the distinction between an individual foreign intervention violating the economic rights of a given State and collective intervention protecting the human rights in a given State. Here I also refer, in addition to Professor Lillich's view to the courageous ideas suggested for consideration and follow-up in the paper of Professor Grahl-Madsen.

I will end this part of my statement with reference to a problem thus far not discussed in this seminar. This problem, particularly due to the developing countries, concerns the principle of compensation by the colonial powers for the exploitation – I will not go so far as saying spoliation – of national resources during their respective colonial rules. The principle of compensation in the present international law is accepted only after wars: the defeated State must compensate the victorious State for losses and damages caused by the war. If this sometimes unjust principle – when for example the defeated State is not the aggressor – is accepted, *a fortiori* we should accept the principle of just compensation for properties and resources unjustly exploited or spoliated. The acceptance of this principle, not as yet general, in international law will legitimize, and I would even say legalize, the nationalization, almost without indemnity, as foreseen in the Resolution 3281 of 1974 of the General Assembly of the United Nations.

Summing up ideas emerging from this seminar of particular interest to the Third World countries, I would say that, the better international law will further the development of the Third World countries, the more the Third World – encompassing our planet – will contribute to the development of international law and will accept its rules.

Now I should like to touch upon a completely different question, less controversial, but also connected with the general theme of this seminar: The United Nations Library in Geneva is preparing a bibliography on "The Third World and International Law", a project which aims primarily at making better known the position, on various aspects of international law, of Third World countries and intends to promote research in this field as well as to contribute to the development of the elaboration of new rules of international law.

The bibliography will consist of the three following sectors:

I. The First section covers studies prepared by Third World authors or Western authors analysing with sympathy or with criticism the attitude of Third World countries towards general international law.

II. The Second section will follow the 3 resolutions of the General Assembly which constitute three landmarks in the recent evolution of international legal order:

1. Resolution 1514 of 1960 concerning decolonisation and self-determination.
2. Resolution 2625 of 1970 on the seven principles of friendly relations between States.
3. Resolution 3281 of 1974 concerning economic rights and duties of States.

III. The Third section of the bibliography covers studies on selected problems of international law as viewed by the Third World.

Contributions from this seminar will find their right place in the bibliography.

Otto Kimminich

I would like to draw your attention to a problem which so far has not been treated by the seminar, although both the general theme of the seminar as well as some of its special topics could have given us an opportunity to raise it. I mean the problem of ethnic groups. It has to do with human rights, it has to do with sovereignty, and above all it is an inseperable part of the facts of the multicultural world which we have been discussing.

In the context of ecology we are concerned with the preservation of species. We take great care that a certain type of butterfly or bird will have adequate living conditions in spite of the changes going on in the industrialized world. We do this because we have the feeling that the multitude of species, the great variety of forms, sounds and colours with which our earth is endowed is indeed a common heritage of great value for all of us.

But what about the multitude of ethnic groups to be found in all parts of the globe? Should not the variety of cultures which they represent and which only those groups can preserve be regarded as something which has to be protected as well?

Unfortunately these questions tend to be raised to the international level only in times of great upheaval, when empires break up, when new frontiers are being drawn and when political decisions are being influenced by deep emotions. The

League of Nations tried to mitigate the harshness of such political decisions by instituting a legal system of minority protection. It did not work very well for many reasons which we do not have to explore here.

One of the consequences of this failure was that the protection of minorities was not a popular theme when the United Nations was founded. In addition the new mood developing in the United Nations era was not conducive to the notion of minorities because it has – to some extent rightly – the connotation of demeaning an ethnic group. Still more important, there were many who thought that the rights of the individual should not only be given priority, but would, if properly developed, render the protection of group rights unnecessary.

Today there is a beginning awareness of the fact that this is not the case. We are beginning to realize that group rights are equally important. Thus art. 27 of the Covenant on Civil and Political Rights expressly mentions group rights, and also the Final Act of Helsinki urges the States to give due consideration to the rights of ethnic groups differing in language and culture from the majority of the population.

Therefore I think that if we are serious about creating a new world order we should follow the lead of the Covenant and of the Final Act of Helsinki and pay more attention to the protection of ethnic groups.

Endre Ustor

The paper submitted by Ambassador Bo Johnson Theutenberg contained a serious study of legal systems of ancient cultures such as Buddhism, Hinduism, Islam and others. However, his statement that the Marxist system turned into a "strict, unchangeable, untouchable dogmatic system", could hardly be upheld even in the light of the further part of the paper in question, were he acknowledged certain developments and changes in the thinking of a series of Marxist authors. While it could not be denied that there were periods when the dogmatic approach was in fashion, modern Marxist thinkers accept only one unshakable dogma: that of constant change in the world in general and in theories in particular. Moreover, Marxist theory which has followers in East and West alike is multicoloured. A survey of these would need a research of vast dimensions. Should the distinguished author undertake such research, his views on Marxist legal theory would certainly mellow. I hope that my friendly criticism would not be taken amiss by Ambassador Bo Johnson Theutenberg, to whom I owe gratitude for his participation in the organization of this memorable Seminar.

Abdullah El-Erian

As pointed out by Professor Broms, the variety and multiplicity of the topics considered by the seminar are in themselves evidence of what has been referred to by Judge Elias as "the changing frontiers of international law".

Judge Lachs, in one of his statements the other day, said that his first reaction when he read the list of topics was that they constituted a collection of subjects which were inter-related, but later saw in them what may be called "a unifying theme".[1] My comments this morning are moved by the search for such a unifying theme. I shall therefore make a few brief observations of a general character for I fully agree that our interventions in the concluding general debate should be addressed to general concepts and problems and not to the specific subjects which we have been examining in the last ten days.

The title of our seminar is "International Law and Organization for a New World Order". Before examining a new world order, it is necessary to reflect a little on the concept of an international order. In the long and slow evolution of international law three phases can be identified. The first phase relates to antiquity and the middle ages. Here one can trace some rudimentary rules of relations between political communities. These rules have a religious character and their observance was dictated by religious edicts.

The second phase started with the emergence of the national State in Western Europe in the aftermath of the dissolution of the Holy Roman Empire. The newly formed political and territorial entities which were independent and not subject to any supreme authority, be it ecclesiastical or secular, were in need of a law which governed their inter-State relations. This law was developed by analogy mainly to Roman law which constituted their legal heritage. This law consisted by and large of rules of a regulatory character and prohibitive injunctions. They were sporadic and fragmentary rules which emanated from the sovereignty of States. Their underlying philosophy was conditioned by the basic character of international relations as relations of conflict between States. The use of force was recognized as an instrument of national policy and conquest was recognized as a means of acquiring territorial sovereignty.

The third phase was set in motion by the Charter of the United Nations which introduced a fundamental change in the structure of international law. It transformed it from a law of conflict to a law of co-operation. It established an international order based on certain principles, conditioned by certain concepts and committed to the fulfilment of common purposes.

The Charter of the United Nations has had its impact on international law and international organization. It has given rise to the "Law of the United Nations". An assessment of its basic concepts and underlying philosophy is necessary for determining the role of international law and international organization in the restructuring of a new World Order.

We as international lawyers face the challenge of contributing to a better understanding which could replace the "confrontation" between the "developed" and "developing" States which has dominated the international scene of late.

I believe that this confrontation is due to some kind of suspicion on the part of both old and new States. While the new States resent traditional international law, the older States view with suspicion anything called "new order" or "new system". I believe it is important that the new States keep in mind that not all the concepts of traditional international law are bad ones. Equality of States is one of the norms of traditional international law. So is the duty of non-intervention. A

1 Cf. p. 263.

distinction should, therefore, be made between the norms of international law and the conduct of States. International law should not be mistaken for the practice of States which is not in conformity with legal principles and rules. The newly independent States have also a tendency to regard international law as Euro-centred. It is true that until the Second World War the newly independent States were not in a position to take part in the formulation of the rules of international law. However it should be kept in mind that during the last third of the century membership in the Community of Nations has become almost universal and older States are now taking part in the international conferences which codify international law. As regards the older members of the Community of Nations they should keep in mind that the Charter of the United Nations has established a new international order and that it is imperative to institutionalize a system of international relations which reflects the new concepts enshrined in the Charter.

Jiri Toman

Discussions at this Uppsala Seminar have revealed the more important problems facing humankind at the end of the 20th century, and which will require the attention of international lawyers and international institutions participating in the law-making process.

During the next twenty years, years of the beginning of the post-industrial society, everyone, including international lawyers, will assume responsibility in the creation of the new world order. If laws are the essence of the rules of behaviour in the human community within States, international law is the basis of the rules of behaviour on the regional and international levels. If these rules have grown slowly over the past centuries, the 20th century, is in itself an explosion of international legal regulations. This explosion will continue. The future of the Earth cannot be conceived any longer within the context of the Nation-State. Today's problems of humankind must be approached globally as a whole. Man can no longer think in terms of family or tribe as he has done for centuries: he cannot even think in terms of the Nation-State as he did a few decades ago. Regional international cooperation is not any longer a Utopian, fictional or imaginative ideal, but a necessity for human survival. These global Earth interests must predominate over the specific problems of individual States, over their prerogatives of sovereignty and over their ideological, political or economic interests. These interests are negligible in comparison with the emergencies which the world as a whole will have to confront.

International law will play an important role in the settlement of problems faced by all the human race. Over the past decades we have witnessed the fundamental transformation and development of international legal rules which will play an even more important role in the reorganization of our future. During the last decades we have seen the development of law in areas never approached by international lawyers and which were a *domaine reservé* of States. The new rules concerning environment, population, food, energy, industrial development, human settlement, science and technology, telecommunications, agrarian reform are developing.

Moreover, this new international law is built upon the existing international legal system. It was stressed several times during this Seminar that contemporary international law is no longer the product of the European setting, that it represents the interests of the whole international community. But the future will require a continuing adaptation and development of these rules as instruments of the transformation of living conditions of humanity. In the future we shall be obliged to look on world problems in terms of human survival. The principle of humanity as such will become more and more the basic principle on which future society will be built.

The compilation of the new rules of international law will be a most important element in the coming decades. We need the participation of everyone in facing the new world problems. The application of new methods of government will no longer be a question of elites. The implementation of new rules, their application and the knowledge of them will be necessary. Education will become ever more important.

This new dimension of the problems to be faced will require the training of new leaders who will be able to face new responsibilities with the appropriate level of competence.

As stressed some time ago by Karl Deutsch, "an increase in interdependence among States creates an increased need for coordination and predictability of their behaviour, while at the same time an increase in the diversity of those States, with their different elites and broader politically relevant strata, makes any closer form of political amalgamation or integration among States more difficult. The greater the increase in the need for limited international coordination, and the greater the domestic political pressures making for national sovereignty and international diversity, the greater will be the danger of international conflicts and disasters, but all the greater will also become the relevance of international law and the potential political support for its development."[1]

The problem which has occupied the minds of generations of international lawyers, has been the implementation of international law. Moreover, compliance with international legal rules is the most important task of the members of the international community, and all those who are in some way concerned with its application in every-day life. This application requires a spirit of comprehension, confidence and understanding which constitutes the basis for respect of legal ruling. The Declaration on Principles of International Law concerning Friendly Relations and Cooperation among States [UN General Assembly Resolution 2625 (XXV) of 24 October 1970] stresses the principle that States shall fulfil in good faith the obligations assumed by them in accordance with the Charter, as well as the obligations under the generally recognised principles and rules of international law and under the international agreements.

1 Deutsch, Karl W., The Probability of International Law. In: Deutsch, Karl and Hoffmann, Stanley, *The Relevance of International Law*. New York, Anchor Books, 1971, p. 80.

The question is how can we contribute to this implementation, how can we develop a spirit of confidence and understanding, and the respect of international law.

Let me mention as an example how this contribution has been carried out over the past years in the area of international humanitarian law applicable in armed conflict. There is no doubt that the implementation of the rules of the law of war require more than any other a spontaneous reaction, and the reflex of those who on the battlefield are under an obligation to respect the rules of this law. This was stressed right from the beginning when Gustave Moynier, one of the founders of the Institute of International Law, codified this part of international law. According to him it is essential that sovereigns "make these laws known among all people, so that when war is declared, the men called upon to take up arms to defend the causes of the belligerent States, may be thoroughly impregnated with the special rights and duties attached to the execution of such a command". To realise this impregnation, the conventions of international humanitarian law imposed on the Contracting Parties the obligation to disseminate these rules as widely as possible in their respective countries. During the past years many international and national institutions have developed a programm of dissemination of the knowledge of these rules by systematic teaching on different levels, by promoting research and studies. The aim of all these efforts is to sensitize the persons directly converned by this application, but also the general public who, by an awareness of their rights and duties, may largely contribute to making these rules a reality.

It seems to me that international law as a whole requires the development of the program of teaching of international law at all levels. We need an "army of international lawyers" which can be constituted only by systematic teaching of international law to all lawyers, and not only lawyers who may be concerned with international relations. The rules of international law must be made known to politicians, political scientists, diplomats, all foreign service officers and advisers. It is important that this knowledge be promoted among journalists who are daily confronted with international legal situations and who furthermore could help in promoting its knowledge throughout the general public, thus contributing to the requirements of its application. We need more international, regional and national seminars and meetings to show the significant role international law can play in the construction of our future.

Before being obliged to apply the rules of the law of war, we must develop a wider knowledge of the methods for the peaceful settlement of disputes. It is necessary not only to improve existing means for this settlement as required by the draft of the Manila declaration drawn up by the Special Committee on the Charter of the United Nations and on the strengthening of the role of the Organization (A/AC.182/L.32/Add.1). It is even more important to know what means and methods already exist and further their use in situations tending to degenerate into international disputes. The Frenche draft of the Manual submitted recently to the Special Committee (A/AC.182/L.24) is a good example of the appropriate promotion of the knowledge of this important part of international law.

Other areas of international law require similar attention.

Efforts must be concentrated on the new members of the international community. This will not only help in making known the existing international legal system, but will create conditions for their wider participation in the law-creating process and will finally contribute to the development of international law according to the wish of the international community as a whole.

The new States concerned with setting up the new world order will understand that international law is the most efficent instrument in the realization of the new rules of conduct, of the new rules of life on the Earth. Only by a thorough knowledge of international law, can States understand that existing international law imposes not only on them duties but on all members of the international community. They will realise that existing international law gives them extensive means in protecting their rights. Different methods may be envisaged. The establishment of a coordinating organ for legal and economic problems is only one step. It will be necessary to pay more attention to the legal aspects of development, establish or develop legal assistance in organizations like UNCTAD. This will be helpful not only in the implementation of international decisions and recommendations by these organs, but will also contribute to the development of their own legal systems by using comparative legal methods and by an exchange of experience between developing countries themselves on different legal matters. We are sure that the improvement of legal approaches to development will greatly contribute to development itself.

It is generally recognised that education in international affairs will widen views and foster concern for the future of nations and for problems of common interest. This also applies to declarations and resolutions of international organizations which will be effective only if they influence the public at large and are known to people in general and in particular to the young generation.

Education will also require a new approach. If we want to create a new international law, we need to understand its evolution more and more, not only in the context of the modifications which have occurred during the past years, but also in the context of the evolution of humanity. If we look at the history of international law during the last two thousand years, we can understand that the problems faced were very often similar to ours and that the solutions which we try to find now, many generations have been trying to solve.

The international organizations contribute even more to the promotion of the knowledge of international law. Recent proposals to create an International Legal Centre and a Human Rights Centre within the structure of the United Nations could be a useful means for developing coordination of legal activities. If the United Nations International Law Commission holds its traditional seminar, the same should be arranged within UNCITRAL, UNESCO, UNITAR and the United Nations University. These organizations must play a more important role, mainly for the developing countries, in the furtherance of the teaching of international law and comparative law. This would contribute not only to a better knowledge of the law, but also to an improvement of the legal system in the new States.

We have not only to limit ourselves, however, to traditional methods. We are speaking at this seminar of the influence and the part played by international law in the creation of a new world order. We see great *technological revolutions* transforming our lives and our professions fundamentally. International lawyers cannot stand outside this process. The transfer of technology from one country to another has been mentioned several times during the seminar, but let us speak also about the transfer of technology into international law itself. How helpful can a wider use be of the new methods of documentation, the use of microfiches which could also provide new States with all the necessary documentation which research and teaching or simply understanding, may require.

If computers start to be extensively used in legal systems, this is not yet the case for international law where computerization seems appropriate in the area of international treaties and international jurisprudence. Even if all these technical means are easily available, we do not yet have a reliable and adequate data bank of international treaties. Let us hope that the United Nations Treaty Information System will soon advance in the realisation of this task. The use of these new technical appliances should free lawyers from documentary research and facilitate access to all existing documents at a speed difficult to imagine some years ago. It will enable them to concentrate on the analysis of situations, on the better application of the law, on the intellecutal approach which has not – so far – been done by computers.

In the forthcoming decades international lawyers will not only benefit from computer systems and telecommunications; the extensive use of new technology on the international level will give rise to various legal problems in inter-State relations which already start to be regularised by international conventions. An example is the Convention for the Protection of Individuals in connection with the Automatic Processing of Personal Data adopted by the Committee of Ministers of the Council of Europe on 17 October 1980. Studies of these problems are carried out within the OECD and the Council of Europe. This new area of legal activity is now being widely developed in many legal systems and seems likely to proceed in the coming future in developing harmonization of national legislation in this area. This very area of international legislation on communications and automatic data processing will play an important part in international cooperation.

The aim of the Uppsala seminar is to provide an independent overview of the problems which will require increased attention by international lawyers in the near future. It is an important starting point to which we shall often refer and which we shall always remember. This seminar, however, is only a beginning which has to be followed by other meetings on specific subjects and on the global viewpoint of lawyers on contemporary problems faced by humanity. The wide participation of international lawyers from all continents is a proof that international lawyers do not want to remain inactive in the building of the new world order, but rather be active participants in the creation not only of a new, but of a better world.

Rudolf Bernhardt

This Seminar is concerned with International Law and Organization for a New World Order. It is obvious that the present World Order has many deficiencies, that the economic order, the protection of human rights and many other parts of law and reality must be improved in order to be really humane and just. These are merely commonplaces which nevertheless have always to be kept in mind.

The task of this Seminar has been and is, in my understanding, to discuss the different parts and problems of the present world order and to find out what proposals can be made for improvement and what changes are necessary. I must confess, that during our discussions I sometimes had the feeling that we are touching the problems only superficially and that we do not take into account adequately the complexity of the world order and the questions involved. This is probably unavoidable in view of the difficulties of the subject and the fact that we are meeting here for the first time.

It has already several times been said and I repeat that one should not discredit the traditional international law in general and one should not call always for new law if the present reality does not conform to our ideals and wishes. There is no sector of international law and of the international order in general in which out-and-out-solutions can be offered or accepted. If one considers the different problems more thoroughly, one always has to state that different and manifold conclusions and suggestions are necessary. I would like to explain this by taking a few examples.

Yesterday we spoke about sovereignty and humanity. I had the impression that nearly all speakers, with a few exceptions who are probably going too far in the opposite direction, considered State sovereignty as an evil in itself which should be abolished. Nothing has been said that the sovereign State not only violates but often also protects human rights, that it is still the State which is responsible for basic human needs, for internal and external security. Nothing has been said about the danger that also a supranational or international authority may abuse its power. What we need is limited State sovereignty as well as a vast amount of humanity and an effective international protection of human rights. In our programme the question is put whether sovereignty and humanity *can* converge. I think that they *must* converge and neither the one nor the other can be neglected if we hope for a peaceful and humane world.

Let us take other examples. Two days ago I already said it is not always the law which is bad but it is often the reality which has to be improved. The use of force and the protection of human rights are outstanding examples. From the League of Nations Covenant to the Briand-Kellogg Pact, from the United Nations Charter to the definition of aggression, many norms and institutions have tried to outlaw the use of force. Some progress has been made, but the real dangers are much greater than the effectiveness of the existing machinery to preserve peace.

In the human rights field the world and the position of the human beings in many States would be much better if the existing rules were respected. New human right covenants or conventions against torture might be useful, but what is much more necessary is the respect of the human rights already enshrined in international customary and treaty law. In this field extralegal means as the mobilization of world opinion might be of more importance than the call for ever new norms.

We have discussed many other topics: The protection and preservation of national resources, the "common heritage of mankind", the relation between universal and regional agencies and solutions, the peaceful settlement of disputes, improvements in the structure of existing organizations. In none of these fields can one say that all the old or traditional law has to be replaced by new norms and new rules for a better world order. In each field much more work has to be done in order to find out what should be preserved and what must be changed.

It is the great merit of this seminar and of its organizers, especially of Professor Grahl-Madsen, that we had the opportunity to exchange views on so many important questions of the international order. There cannot be any doubt that this order must be improved and in many respects changed if mankind should survive and live under humane conditions. I think that all of us, like myself, will leave Uppsala with many new insights and inspirations.

Nirmala Chandrahasan

I would like to address your minds to the question of how we, as international lawyers, can in our individual capacities make some contribution towards the New World Order which has been the topic of this conference. Ambassador Bo Johnson Theutenberg referred to the fact that States are not seperate entities divorced from people, but are made up of individuals, and it is individuals who lead States and shape policies. In this context I would like to point out, that many of us do play a role in the shaping of our countries' policies, as legal advisers to governments, members of delegations to international conferences, and as members of universities who constitute the intellectual elite.

I would suggest that, in these capacities, we should try to influence our governments and attempt to introduce principles of equity and justice in the relations of States to each other, and to the international community. Thus for example in the drafting of international treaties and conventions those of us participating could attempt to work textually into these treaties or conventions principles of equality, reciprocity and equity. To give a concrete example, in the draft convention on the law of the sea in the law relating to the regime of the Exclusive Economic Zone one equitable principle has been worked in, namely that the landlocked and geographically disadvanted States should also share in the resources of the Exclusive Economic Zone. In other areas too this could be done. Professor Kimminich mentioned the subject of ethnic minorities. In relation to the problem of ethnic minorities, we could try to advise our governments or by our writings influence public opinion within our countries, to do what is just and fair to these minorities and to concede the principle of self-determination in those instances, where it is justifiable under the Charter and international law. Hence it is my submission that we, as international lawyers, should not be ego-centric.

We should not look at rules of international law from the point of view of narrow national self-interest, but should consider ourselves as citizens of the world and look to the interests of the international community, and try to introduce into the relationship of States the principles of equality, reciprocity and equity. It is in this way as I see it, that we as international lawyers can make our contribution to a new world order.

There is another matter which I would like to briefly touch on. There has been much talk at this conference on the question of human rights. To my mind it would appear that the effective implementation of human rights lies in the hands of the municipal courts. Because it is only if individuals are able to get redress for infringements of human rights at the national level, that it can be said that the human rights law is being effectively applied. Here again I have a practical suggestion to make, namely that we should try and introduce some kind of system of monitoring the judgments of municipal courts and giving them greater publicity so that the judges of the municipal courts will be aware that their judgments are being scrutinised by their peers throughout the world, and this I think would make these judges more careful in their interpretation of constitutional provisions relating to human rights, and in their application of international conventions dealing with human rights.

In conclusion may I thank Professor Grahl-Madsen and the organising committee of Uppsala University for a splendid seminar. I am sure that if all international lawyers were like Professor Grahl-Madsen the world would be a much better place.

Taslim O. Elias

As we all know the theme of the seminar is International Law in a Multi-Cultural World, and one of the aspects of it with which we are now concerned deals with the growth of the international community and qualitative shift in international legal relations, customary law: from "universal" in a European system to "regional" in a world system, and a realistic approach to international law. In consideration of the matter I wish to draw attention to the fact that in 1961 the United Nations invited some eight or nine of us to contribute chapters to a little book subsequently entitled *International Law in a Changing World*[1]. The title of my own chapter was "The Expanding Frontiers of Public International Law". I must warn you however that at that stage of international relations, we could not have envisaged all the global transformations that later followed those tentative ideas that we promulgated in these essays. It was, however, clear to us as to many international jurists that the United Nations approach was going to the much wider than that of the League of Nations, as its basic assumptions are those of the principle of universality. Whereas the League of Nations was composed mainly of European States and a very small number of associated Asian States, the United Nations Charter envisaged a universal membership embracing African, Asian and Latin American States. This also resulted in the membership of the

1 *International Law in a Changing World.* Ed. by E. Collins, Jnr. New York, 1963.

United Nations rising from 51 in 1945 to its present total of some 154 member States.

Almost from its inception, therefore, the United Nations took two major steps towards enlarging its membership as well as its conceptual orientation. The International Law Commission which was established in 1947 began with a membership of 15 and is now made up of 25 which include representative member States from Africa, Asia and Latin America. The importance of this step has been that this newly established body has in its composition reasonable elements of new States in the initiation and formulation of the codification and progressive development of international law. The second important step taken by the United Nations has been not so much in the enlargement of the membership of the International Court of Justice as in a decisive change in the character of its composition as well as its modus operandi. Here again the Court has gradually transformed itself, at the instance of the United Nations, into a more universally representative body of members from Africa, Asia and Latin America. In this regard, mention must be made of the United Nations resolution of November 1974 which calls upon the Court constantly to have regard to the various changes in international law which have taken place particularly in consequence of various conventions, treaties and other activites of the General Assembly and ancillary organs in the field of codification and progressive development of international law.[2]

The enlargment of the membership of the United Nations has been due in no small measure to the principle of self-determination which has been set in motion by the policy of decolonization which has transformed many previous colonial territories into independent member States of the organization; included in this development has been also the assumption of independent States in previous Trust territories.

If we may turn to positive activities of the United Nations in the field of universality of its membership and participation in its work, we should recall the United Nations Universal Declaration of Human Rights of 1948 and the two United Nations Covenants which complemented and broadened its basic assumptions in the field of political, economic and cultural rights of member States and their citizens. Of great importance also has been the adoption of a General Assembly resolution approving the Declaration on Peaceful Co-Existence and Friendly Relations which embodies some six principles based on and inspired by the Charter of the United Nations, redefining the rights and duties of States in their relations with one another within as well as without the framework of the United Nations system.[3]

In this connection, we may recall the conferences held in Geneva up to 1977 resulting in the adoption of two Protocols on Humanitarian Law making certain

2 United Nations General Assembly resolution 3232 (XXIX) of 12 November 1974.

3 United Nations General Assembly resolution 2625 (XXV) of 24 October 1970 by which the General Assembly approved the Declaration on the Principles of International Law concerning Friendly Relations and Co-operation among States in accordance with the Charter of the United Nations.

concessions to the principles already embodied in the four Geneva Conventions of 1949 regarding the rules and principles that should govern the laws of armed conflict which should also take into account International Liberation Movements and the modern activities of mercenaries, with particular reference to the Third World.[4]

The Third Law of the Sea Conference has no doubt caught the imagination of the member States of the United Nations, especially in the past five years, in that efforts are now being made to reformulate and modify the principles embodied in the four 1958 Conventions on the Law of the Sea, so as to take account of subsequent developments in the uses of the sea and exploitation of its resources. Notable among the leading innovative ideas are of course the principle of the Exclusive Economic Zone, enlarged notions of the Continental Shelf and the exploitation of the seabed and of its resources as a common heritage of mankind.

Finally, we may note that the current vogue is for the establishment of a New International Economic Order (NIEO) which took shape in the adoption of the General Assembly Resolution on the United Nations Charter of the Rights and Duties of States. Important aspects of these are of course the formulation of a new Code of Conduct for Transnational Corporations, the Code of Conduct on the Transfer of Technology, the Sovereignty of States over their Natural Resources and the relations between all these and Human Rights. It will be seen, therefore, that contemporary international law has come a long way towards its visions of 1945 in establishing and propagating the principle of universality in the multi-cultural world of today.

The President (concluding remarks)

In conclusion, in the interventions on specific subjects and those of a general character it has been made clear that you do not want to abandon your responsibilities by refusing to take up the challenge of our days in particular at a time which may be ripe for writing new chapters of law. It is reported of a king that while on his expeditions he kept a copy of Grotius' book under his pillow; other rulers recited its principles. But what we must strive at today is the constant and continuous compliance with its rules.

The study and dialogues should help to give international law the rank due to it and to students of it real fascination. To this you made a notable contribution for which all of us owe a debt. I feel that you will leave Uppsala with the feeling that the days passed so quickly – and the flag symbolizing this conference will soon be planted at another place, equally as attractive as the present one, and the work will be continued. Our task is not only to strengthen the law and our discipline, but encourage its further development – this inter alia could be achieved by increasing the army of international jurists. To achieve this goal we need ever

4 Protocols Additional to the Geneva Conventions of 12 August 1949, and relating to the Protection of Victims of International (Protocol I) und Non-International (Protocol II) Armed Conflicts, signed in Geneva in June 1977.

more recruits: and that means the growth in the number of students. But to be successful we must make them feel that they are themselves helping to shape it so that they have a sense of participation in its future.

What we need is a dialogue between representatives of various schools of law, of various shades of views, but also generations. I think the great advantage of this conference was the participation of the young – they may perhaps have been too timid to speak yet their mere presence was an advantage and I see in it a step towards their future active role in such gatherings. For what we need is not only a bridging of the gap between representatives of various schools, creeds in international law but last but not least of the gap between generations in all dimensions.

V. International Law in a Multicultural World

Working Group I

5.1. International Law in a Multicultural World

MANFRED LACHS

The Rapporteur has been invited to take a realistic approach to international law and reflect on its effectiveness and general role in the world. This is a timely mission at a period when international law is being subjected to challenge from so many quarters, when its very existence is being questioned not only by laymen but even by some lawyers, and when its relevance to international relations and to the regulation of concrete problems between States is constantly belittled. It may be useful to begin with a short analysis of the important stages which have marked the development of international law.[1]

If we are to take a truly historical standpoint, we have to be aware of the necessity for questioning many of the encrusted assumptions which have dominated the teachings and teaching of international law for centuries: in particular the assumption that it is of exclusively European origin and that it developed as a product of European culture which was gradually exported to other regions.

If we view international law as a code of conduct established between States as a necessity, this can be noted as a phenomenon on all continents. The fate of certain extra-European States, however, was determined at one stage or another by confrontation with the Europeans. Some vanished, leaving very few traces, having been destroyed by Europe. An illustration lies in Latin America, where the Aztecs, the Incas and the Mayas were destroyed. Yet historical investigations indicate that peaceful international relations, treaties and contacts between these units, i. e., diplomatic relations, existed. This situation eventually changed through the domination of some of these groups over others, but conquest by the Spaniards put an end to it all. The most puzzling and most misrepresented of all continents is Africa, on which a number of States confronted one another and, though living in isolation, established some kind of relations of a legal and quasi-legal character. The growing relationship between States situated around the Mediterranean, in particular their trade and the establishment of diplomatic missions and treaties, paved the way, somewhere around the 9th century, to a pluralistic community. This resulted, generally speaking, from the interaction of three empires: the Byzantine Empire, Islam with its deep roots in the Caliphate of Baghdad, and the Holy Roman Empire of Charlemagne.[2] There were other important historical developments which played a role in the relationship between States: for example, the existence of contacts within and between the

1 Many of the present reflections were developed by the author in the General Course on International Law, *Recueil des cours, Académie de droit international,* 1980.

Indian, the Chinese and other eastern cultures, and eventually between West and East. Much has remained of the tradition of Asian treaties, even those going back to ancient days, like those between the Hittites and Egypt.

Thus other continents showed phenomena similar to those which developed in Europe and in the Mediterranean, and codes of conduct which, though perhaps less developed in view of the limited character of their relations, nonetheless existed.

The birth of colonial empires and the climax of Europe's domination over other continents came in the 19th century and were reflected in doctrine and jurisprudence.

The truly universal character of international law is of recent origin only: it covers the whole globe to its remotest spots; it reaches deep below the ocean floor and up to outer space. It is universal because it includes all peoples and all nations inhabiting our planet.

However, the question remains: how much impact has this law had on international relations? An analysis of the subject cannot be adequate without taking account of two great revolutions – the economic and the scientific. Economics touch the very roots of international relations. The immense growth of world population; the demand for and the supply of an ever greater number of goods; food on the one hand – industrial products on the other; raw materials and ready-made goods; the mutual, supplementary and competitive character of economies, have brought a host of economic issues into the foreground. All these have required co-operation in finance and transport at sea, on the land, and in the air. Hence the development of an essential part of contemporary law defined as *jus commercii* in which all types of treaties and agreements, thousands of agreements on trade, production, joint production and enterprises, investments, copyright, and other forms of international economic co-operation are brought together. Thus not only have treaties become essential; great strides in economic life, industrial revolutions, have brought nations closer together and created the necessity for ever more extensive and closer ties between them. The daily life of nations has changed.

The impact of science and technology – man's relation to nature has been shaped by his continuous attempts to uncover and use its secrets and riches. The air and the sea are being used by ever more modern means of transport; the depths of the earth and even the subsoil of the ocean floor are being explored; new sources of energy are being harnessed. Technology has become a power which has translated the achievements of science into the means of satisfying the daily needs of man and of nations. Mastery over matter and technical progress have become political factors decisive for social and economic development

2 Cf. the studies of Ago and Paradisi: Ago, Roberto, Sciences juridiques et droit international. *Recueil des cours, Académie de droit international,* tome 90, II, 1956, pp. 849–958; Paradisi, Bruno, L'Amitié internationale: Les phases critiques de son ancienne histoire. *Recueil des cours, Académie de droit international* (La Haye), Tome 78, I, 1951, pp. 329–378.

within societies and in relations among States. As has been said: "The most amazing thing about science and the most surprising and exciting fact about our world is the astonishing connection between highly abstruse theoretical ideas and the matter of fact."[3]

The birth of so many new independent States, the growth of world population – all these processes have caused a feed-back reaction affecting all of them. They have created new dimensions for inter-State relations.

With all this in the background: What is the role of international law? The reply is very simple. International law is there in order to regulate relations between States in all the areas of their contact. Its task has become more complex and more difficult. A limited set of rules suffices no more: their number has grown into volumes. *Ex factis jus oritur,* hence the close link between the realities of life and the rule of law. It is called upon to control not only elementary agreements on purchase and sale, but much more sophisticated forms of economic co-operation. Technology, which has become the "toolmaker" of scientific invention, has made it necessary to establish formal and legal rules for its use on the international level and in co-operation between States. The thousands of inventions which enter the life of nations have become important factors in their daily intercourse. The thousands of ships crossing seas and oceans, planes filling the skies, require regulations; those using them, protection. In all this the helpful hand of the lawyer and law have become essential – the protection of ships in case of disaster, that simple symbol of SOS, the protection of the environment against a pollution which has become acutely dangerous. The growing control of man over nature requires the elaboration of rules in all spheres of the environment. We are, of course, far from having reached the stage at which we can say that the environment is protected.

Here, then, law must play a decisive role. Law is an indispensable element in the world of today, which would be unthinkable without it and maybe cease to be viable without its further development. The evidence that international law exists lies all around us. It is there in the thousands of treaties which have been and are being signed and which find their way into the Treaty Series, a treaty or two being signed every day in any capital of the world. It is there in the increased speed of codification of international law, which has gone on in recent years with unparalleled efficiency. There is the growing body of customary law which has entered so many areas and which binds States of various cultures and various continents. Customary law, as I stated in one of my opinions, develops in some areas with "greater ease" than in others. And I added: "The great acceleration of social and economic change, combined with that of science and technology, have confronted law with a serious challenge: one it must meet, lest it lag even further behind events than it has been wont to do."[4] In addition, there are of course the general principles of law recognized by nations, which have enriched the catalo-

3 Cf. Sir George Thompson in his Presidential Address to the British Association for the Advancement of Science, 31 August 1960.

4 *I.C.J. Reports 1969,* pp. 230 ff.

gue of rules of law binding States. Thus the body of international law as it exists today is very rich and very substantial. And it binds States in all dimensions. The international community has accepted the principle that certain rules have been so deeply enshrined in the body of international law that they cannot be altered by the will of some States even within their mutual relationship: *jus cogens.*

Thus today we face a world in which what has been called the Adam Smith model of international relations is an anachronism. An ever-growing number of rules are agreed upon by States in treaties and other instruments: they call for co-operation. This cross-relationship has brought about a situation reflected in this principle: that the rights of one State end where the rights of others begin. The *Trail Smelter* arbitral award was one telling symbol of this development. We live in a variegated, multi-coloured and multi-cultural world; a world in which nations subscribe to various philosophies but in which not every nation features a uniform philosophy of life. Nations remain divided by political, cultural, philosophical, economic and other kinds of difference.

Is all this an obstacle to the subsistence, further development and, more particularly, effectiveness of international law? Or is it a challenge to it, and its vindication?

To recapitulate: the tremendous increase in intercourse between States, with a vast multiplication of international fora, has by no means changed the world into a uniform clear-cut pattern. It has remained a world of many colours; the number of shades may even have increased. There are States of different economic and political systems; nations whose tradition-based cultures have remained very distinct. There has been much influence, very little assimilation. The growth of independent States as the result of the movement towards the liberation of colonial peoples, the triumph of the idea of self-determination (though it has not yet borne fruit for all nations of the globe), have introduced new elements of distinction and variety. Despite, or rather because of this, the character of international law has been growing even more evidently universal. (How strange that the same philosopher who denied the existence of international law admitted that: "For the first time humanity is living one and the same history.")[5] All attempts to divide humanity into disconnected parts are bound to fail – and those to divide the law reigning over humanity are failing. There are of course some peculiarities characteristic of the law binding States of a defined region, sharing a common political system, or those which have integrated their economies. But any renewal of attempts to split the world almost on the day following its unification are doomed to failure.

Political and philosophical differences between States do not constitute an obstacle to the strengthening of the universality of the law. Nor need they lead to the break-up of the existing system of international law or create unsurmountable difficulties in its application or further development. For at no stage of history have the potentialities of international law been the preserve of any one group of

5 Aron, Raymond, *Les désillusions du progrès: Essai sur la dialectique de la modernité.* Paris, Calmann-Lévy, 1969, p. 191.

like-minded States. Ideological differences are not irreconcilable with the existence of a universal system of international law. Two illustrations substantiate this: "Nine years of experience on the International Court of Justice have led me to conclude that a common basis of jurisprudence and common language exists among the judges whereby they are able to make mutual assertions, discuss, reach agreement, and disagree in spite of their different religious, racial or cultural background."[6] A similar view has been expressed in regard to the work of the International Law Commission on the law of treaties: "Lawyers from different parts of the world, representing different cultures, different philosophies and backgrounds, different thoughts, have managed to find common ground. That was the explanation of the achievement of the Commission. It has been able to create something durable by helping to evolve or develop rules to fit the changing needs of life and by adjusting the law to the impact of dynamic development of the present way."[7] There we have two conclusions based on the practice of a law-making and a law-applying organ of the international community.

The most essential question: effectiveness of international law. Violations of international law, strife and conflict, confrontation between States, fights and shots fired across frontiers dominate the headlines. I made it clear at the onset that this cannot imply that international law is helpless. It is an undeniable fact that tens of thousands of treaties are being applied daily between States; compliance with the law occurs in thousands of cases every day, almost every hour, in different parts of the globe: when ships enter harbours, planes land in foreign airfields, trains cross frontiers, goods are sold and bought. Rules in all domains of economics, science, technology, health, labour, co-operation in other fields are being implemented. Thus the effectiveness of international law in these many areas is not subject to any doubt. These facts are viewed as so natural that no special attention is paid to them. The role of law passes almost unnoticed. Yet to realize it one need only imagine the serious consequences of violations of these rules.

Of course, one cannot ignore the fact that international law is frequently violated in many other areas, frequently concerning important rights of States. (In that context, various theories have been advanced: cf. the so-called "orphan", "harlot" and other theories of international law.[8] But it is at the same time admitted that these theories are the result of "underestimation with over-expectation" of the international legal order.) To follow, for instance, a treaty provi-

6 Judge Tanaka, Kotaro. He referred in this contect to the heritage of Rome, which does not alter the situation. The Character of World Law in the International Court of Justice. *Japanese Annual of International Law,* Vol. 15, 1971, pp. 1 ff.

7 Lachs, M., 94th Meeting of the International Law Commission, 19 July 1966, in *Yearbook of the International Law Commission 1966,* Vol. I, part II pp. 348–349. (UN document A/CN. 4/SER. A (1966).

8 Cf. Fried, John H. E., How Efficient is International Law? In *The Relevance of International law: Essays in Honour of Leo Gross,* ed. by K. W. Deutsch and S. Hoffman, Cambridge, Schenkman Publishing Company, 1968, pp. 93–132.

sion from its birth one has to admit that States negotiate, conclude, sign and ratify treaties with the intention of complying with them, for at the time each has a definite (identical or complementary) interest in doing so. As long as these interests continue the question of effectiveness of the law does not arise: they would comply with the provisions of the instruments even if they did not constitute a legal obligation. The questions arises at the moment when their interests begin to differ: the confrontation between new interests and the obligation solemnly subscribed to. Even so, law may and should prevail.

However, violatation of its rules is not the "monopoly" of international law, for it arises in all systems of law. Attempts to evade its obligations have been known throughout history, in States of all formations and at all stages of cultural development. Even in well-developed countries like the United States, to quote an authority on the subject: "The number of thefts that go unpunished or the breaches of contract that bring no recompense to the wronged parties, make shocking figures." In the world community, it must be admitted, no international sheriff or marshall is available to handcuff a State and no public prosecutor to hale it before an international bar of justice.

In international law the situation is particularly complex, as the violations sometimes concern great principles enshrined by it: basic rights of States, the life of nations. Where are we to seek an answer: are these violations to continue? There remain however forceful motives in favour of compliance: (1) States continue to obey the law, prompted by self-interest: aware that failure to do so may expose them to much greater risks than the possible temporary disadvantage resulting from complying at a given stage with the provision of agreements or other rules of law. (2) There is the element of reciprocity. (3) The element of self-preservation. In the system of interdependence which exists in the world of today, the obligation to comply with the law may outweigh all other considerations in view of the vital interests involved which may be exposed to the danger in case of law being ignored. The obloquy to which States may be exposed by the international community may make non-compliance an expensive luxury. (4) The possibility of sanctions may not be absent (though recent illustrations on the subject are not very encouraging).

When our situation is properly compared with that of the past, we will see the fallacy of the comparison that the "19th contury was a golden age for international law" while ours is an age of relative lawlessness. In the 19th century, in the age of the expansion and consolidation of colonialism, the domination and exploitation of many nations by the European powers, even some nations of Europe were not independent and free. The mere fact that today the number of States has grown to over 150 is a signal tribute to the power of international law as an instrument of liberation. The progressive growth of the body of law in rules codified, conventional or customary is an accomplished fact. Yet the world is still far from the day when international law will be applied in full. Even while the principle of reciprocity is becoming more effective, and the risks run by the violator greater, the temptation to violate is growing also, because the stakes are higher – one of the main reasons of the inefficiency of international law in several dimensions. If international law as a whole is not at present more effective, this is due to the transitional nature of our age.

On the whole its role in the world of today is greater than at any previous stage in history.[9]

However, it is not effective enough. It requires further protection and its influence on international relations must be enhanced. For the world to become truly peaceful, and to put an end to or at least to reduce the gravest of violations, a series of conditions must be evolved – in the field of politics and economics. Law must correspond more faithfully to the vital rights of States and nations – progress more speedily – at a period of convulsions between the dusk of yesterday and the dawn of today. Within a more modest scope, within the province of legal discussions and the family of jurists, to achieve some progress:

a) the body of law must be continuously enlarged;
b) more attention should be concentrated on the role of international organizations, called upon to create and implement the law in their respective field of activities;
c) law should enter fields it has not yet tilled;
d) jurists should show greater inventiveness and initiative; take a greater responsibility not only in law-making but also in the implementation of law;
e) a closer relationship should be established between governments and the representatives of the world of law.

In a wider sense, the words of the constitution of Unesco, referring to wars "beginning in the minds of man" that, therefore, it is "in the minds of man that the defences of peace must be constructed", apply to all international relations and within them to international law. It is in the minds of man that we must construct the defences of international law as a bulwark protecting not only peace but the rights of nations and man.

9 "... the regular observance of international law of peace is explained only too easily; it is generally observed largely because there is little temptation to violate it because its yoke lies too easily on states". Brierly, J. L., "the Basis of Obligation". In *International Law and other Papers.* Selected and edited by H. Lauterpacht, and C. H. M. Waldock. Oxford, Clarendon Press, 1959, p. 54.

5.2. A Realistic Approach to International Law

YORAM DINSTEIN

The argument that international law does not constitute a genuine legal system has been propounded by laymen and lawyers alike on numerous occasions. International law has been compared to the law of the jungle. Cynics have even suggested that, whereas it is clear that there are professors of international law, it is not at all clear that there is such a thing as international law.[1]

Those denying the legal character of international law do not necessarily share a common ground in their line of approach. But many of them are captivated by a dogmatic preconception based on the incompatibility of international law with this or that technical definition of the term "law" to which they adhere. The principal spokesman of this school of thought was Austin who maintained that international law is not law but merely a "positive morality", since it does not consist of a system of commands issued by a sovereign and imposing duties enforced by sanctions.[2]

The mistake inherent in Austin's contention, like in that advanced by others, is that an arbitrary definition of the term "law" is first prescribed as if it were obligatory, and then it is proved that international law does not fit within the Procrustean bed of that definition. In fact, there is – and there can be – no definitive definition of law. Aristotle already pointed out that "not everything demonstrable can be defined".[3] And Glanville Williams justifiably states that the idea of a true definition is a superstition.[4] One may almost say that there are as many definitions of law as there are lawyers. For my part, I believe that the proper definition of law is as follows: Law is a binding normative system that a society creates in order to regulate human conduct. This definition – which I believe is a good as others and better than some – does not exclude international law at all. On the contrary, against the background of the general definition of

1 *See* Holland, Thomas Erskine, *Lectures on International Law* / ed. by Walker, Thomas Alfred, and Walker, Wyndham Leigh. London, Sweet and Maxwell, 1933. XL, 576 pp.

2 Austin, John, *The Province of Jurisprudence Determined.* 2nd ed. New York, B. Franklin, reprinted 1970. Vol. 1., pp. 114 ff., 128.

3 Aristotle, *Posterior Analytics*, Book 2, Chapter 3, para. 90b; The Basic Works of Aristotle, New York, Random House, 1966, p. 161.

4 Williams, G., International Law and the Controversy concerning the word 'Law'. *British Year Book of International Law,* Vol. 22, 1945, p. 146, 159.

law, international law may easily be perceived as a binding normative system that the international society has created in order to regulate human conduct.

It must be emphasized that international law, like all law, is created by human beings for human beings. International law is not derived from preter-natural sources (which are then, paradoxically, represented as "natural law"). The norms of international law are not "found", they are created. Their crucible is the practice of States.

It is often suggested that international law fails to meet some conditions quintessential for the existence of a legal system. The primary conditions which are claimed to be missing are: (a) there is no real international legislature (hence, there is no sense of security as to the identity of international legal norms); (b) there is no international judiciary with compulsory jurisdiction (consequently, there is no sense of security as to the legal outcome of transactions); (c) there is no international police force (therefore, there is no sense of physical security).

The response to this challenge to the legal nature of international law can be made on three different levels:

It must be appreciated that international law has made tremendous strides since its infancy. Whereas it is true that international law is not as well-developed as most national legal systems, it is wrong to believe that international law is entirely helpless when it comes to legislation, judicial settlement of disputes and policing of transgressions.

As for legislation, there is no denying the fact that there does not exist a real international parliament where a majority is entitled to pass legislation which is binding on everyone within the realm. Still, there is now a whole network of multilateral conventions covering a series of very important subjects, to which the overwhelming majority of States are contracting parties. The process of formulation of such new treaties is rather cumbersome, but the results of efforts of codification as well as of the progressive development of international law through treaties in the last half-century are very significant (particularly when compared to the previous record). The outstanding example is that of the Charter of the United Nations which, with 154 contracting parties, is binding well-nigh universally. There are many other instances, ranging from constitutions of international organizations to the four Geneva Conventions of 1949 for the Protection of War Victims. These instruments are not fully legislative in the precise meaning of the term, but, having achieved virtually unanimous acceptance, may be considered quasi-legislative in nature.

In the judicial sphere, we have the experience of the International Court of Justice, the European Courts and other international tribunals to draw upon in assessing the situation. No doubt, the results of the experience are checkered. The regional courts in Europe seem to be thriving. On the universal plane, however, litigations are rare. While the relatively few judgments which the International Court of Justice delivers are of great importance for the evolution of international law, the overall practical impact of the Court leaves a lot to be desired, for the simple reason that States show very little inclination to settle their disputes at The Hague. This is a major obstacle which must be overcome if international law is expected to grow and to play a greater role in the life of the international community. But it must be appreciated that the machinery is on hand. The international legal system as such is quite equipped to deal with litigations between States. It is the lack of the desire on the part of the prospective litigants to avail themselves of the opportunity which is the crux of the issue.

When it comes to an international police force, the international legal system is still lagging far behind. Admittedly, some steps forward have been taken since the birth of the United Nations and the establishment of voluntary UN forces which have been operative, especially in Korea, the Middle East, the Congo and Cyprus. But such forces are few and far between, and their activities are limited. In many respects they bring to mind the sad spectacle of a lone sheriff here and a solitary marshal there trying to impose law and order on a Wild West territory.

All in all, international law has a long way to go before we can take pride in its accomplishments. Nevertheless, we must evaluate its performance in a continuum. Surely, with all the disappointments – and they are abundant – the pattern of progress is clear. As Lord Russell proclaimed almost a century ago, international law is not like the Twelve Tables in ancient Rome: it is not a closed book and it does not stand still.[5]

It must be stressed that, generally speaking, even if the contention about the absence of a legislator, a judge and a policeman in the international arena were entirely accurate in terms of the facts (and, as we have seen, the contention is only partially accurate), this would not necessarily undermine the legal foundations of international law. It is indisputable that the state of affairs characterized by the absence of these three pillars of advanced society is far from ideal. But no one claims that international law in its present form is an ideal legal system. On the contrary, international law is still an undeveloped primitive system.

On the one hand, of course, we must not exaggerate the primitive dimensions of international law. Everything in life, including the primitiveness of law, is relative. There are primitive societies which manifest only nascent indications of legal norms scarcely distinguishable from religion or magic.[6] International law, as compared to the law of such societies, appears to be extremely sophisticated.

On the other hand, the relative primitiveness of international law (as compared to the sophistication of advanced national legal systems) is tragic in an age of scientific and technological revolution. It is exceedingly difficult to live in the era of the jet, the computer and the nuclear reactor with legal instruments that appear anachronistic. Yet, while it is evidently necessary to strive for the further development of international law, this law must not be disqualified as a legal system, even in its current shape. No national legal system has ever sprung forth suddenly and fully grown – like Athene from the head of Zeus – and each has gone through a gradual process of evolution. International law is following the same path at its own pace.

5 Russell, Lord B., International Law. *Law Quarterly Review*, Vol. 12, 1896, pp. 311, 317.

6 Hoebel, Edward Adamson, *The Law of Primitive Man; a study in comparative legal dynamics*. Cambridge, Harvard Univ. Press, 1954, VIII, 357 pp.

The finicky criticis who look with disdain upon the contemporary status of international law usually proceed from the inarticulate premise that the modern national legal systems have reached a degree of progress bordering on perfection. It is therefore important to underscore that law in general – any law – is not an exact science. In a book of law, in contradistinction to a book of arithmetic, there are no binding solutions at the back. Law is based on common estimates, agreed hypotheses and reasonable expectations. There is no sense of total security in law. No legal system is perfect, and law reform is a perennial challenge.

It is advisable to take a closer look at the national legal systems insofar as legislation, the judiciary and the police are concerned.

In principle, legislation is certainly of major consequence in the modern State. However, in all countries there are still legal strata (like customs and conventions) which are not the product of a legislator. This is particularly conspicuous in "common law" countries where legislation in some legal branches is still viewed as mere *addenda et corrigenda* to pre-existing norms which evolved in a casuistic fashion through the courts. International law is much more dependent than the modern national systems on customary law, but the recourse to *jus non scriptum* is by no means uniquely characteristic of the international community.

It may be argued that here is the rub. In "common law" countries it is the courts which give an *imprimatur* to legal norms, whereas in the international legal context courts (at least global courts) are sadly deficient in their workload. However, first of all, it is noteworthy that the judicial framework relevant to international law does not consist only of international courts. International law, especially in some of its branches (e. g., in the sphere of diplomatic immunities), is applied and developed in ordinary national courts not less than in international tribunals. Of course, when domestic courts administer international law they are somewhat in "a position analogous to that of a judge in his own cause", but, as Pollock points out, a judge in his own cause is better and different from a case of total default of justice.[7]

Secondly, though not secondarily, the almost blind faith in courts, which is so predominant in "common law" countries, is to a large extent mythical. Not every legal transaction ends with a dispute, and only a small percentage of disputes reach the courts in any given country. More often than not, disputes are resolved outside the court system by compromise or otherwise. Naturally, the existence of courts is of import in all cases inasmuch as the threat of litigation by itself may produce results. But by themselves courts do not turn law into an exact science. Judges often disagree on fundamental legal points, where any comparable disagreement among scientists would be unthinkable.[8] The operation of courts may make it easier to utter prophecies as to what they will do.[9] But there

7 *See* Pollock, The Sources of International Law, *Columbia Law Review*, Vol. 2, 1902, pp. 511, 515.

8 *See* Chase, Stuart, *The Tyranny of Words*, 4th ed. New York, Harcourt, 1943, p. 213.

9 Justice Holmes, as is well known, viewed all law through the lens of "prophecies of

can never be a sense of total security as to the legal outcome of transactions even where courts with compulsory jurisdiction exist. The sense of security may only be relative because no one can predict with certainty how judges will respond to the facts of a case. The jurisprudential school of "fact scepticism" (developed by the American judge Jerome Frank) goes beyond that and questions the capacity of judges to ascertain the facts of the case.[10] The further development of international case law is very important. But it is wrong to believe that here lies the sole solution to the problems of a legal system.

As regards the absence of an international police force – and the resultant disrespect for international law – the truth of the matter is that there is a great deal of compliance with international legal norms in the international community. Most States actually observe most of their international obligations most of the time.[11] The average person is more cognizant of violations of international law inasmuch as they draw publicity in the mass media, while the observance of international law is not newsworthy. But the very fact that the observance of international law does not merit publicity demonstrates that this is a common and ordinary phenomenon – it is the rule – whereas violations of international law attract publicity because they constitute the exception to the rule.

There is no doubt that inter-State relations are motivated at bottom by extra-legal, more than by legal, considerations and that frequently gross violations of international law take place. Yet, inter-personal relations are also governed by extra-legal considerations, and every national legal system is violated daily without anyone contesting its claim to be treated as valid law. The violations of legal norms does not detract from their legal validity. Even those States which act in contravention of international law never contest its legally binding nature. The denial of the legal character of international law is argued in the abstract by lawyers and laymen: States and statesmen in practice seem to have no doubt on the subject. When the latter transgress against international law, they do not contend that international law is not binding. They make painstaking efforts to justify their behaviour with legal excuses and purport to show that what looks like a violation of international law is not in fact so. This is the reason for such an abundance of information pamphlets published by any Foreign Office worth its salt: these are designed to explain policy against the background of law. Often they represent sheer hypocricy, but it is the very hypocricy with reflects the profound and universal feeling that international law is binding. If States were to have denied the legal character of international law, they could have ignored it without much ado.[12]

what the courts will do in fact". Holmes, O. W., The Path of the Law. *Harvard Law Review,* Vol. 10, 1896–97, pp. 457, 461.

10 *See* Frank, Jerome, *Courts on Trial; myth and reality in American justice.* New York, Atheneum, 1963. 441 p. and in particular the Introduction by Cahn, Edmond, *ibid.*, pp. viii–ix.

11 *See* Henkin, Louis, *How Nations Behave.* 2nd edition. New York, Columbia University Press, 1979, p. 47.

12 *See* Oppenheim, L., *International Law,* Vol. 1, 8th ed. by Lauterpacht, H. London, Longmans, 1955, p. 15.

The paucity of real legal sanctions in the international legal field is lamentable. But, in any event, in every legal system the ultimate – and really effective – sanction is not legal but socio-psychological in nature. It is the pressure of public opinion. Any serious study of international relations denotes that States, too, frequently avoid violations of international law owing to the pressure of world public opinion. Cynics tend to scoff at the efficacy of world public opinion. But there is a wealth of experience which attests otherwise. Clearly, the (non-legal) sanction of world public opinion is not omnipotent, but it is unwise to underestimate its influence in the international sphere. Obviously, world public opinion is not monolithic, but herein perhaps lies its strength. The public whose opinion is of consequence to one State (say, the United States) is not necessarily the same as the public whose opinion is of significance to another (e. g., the USSR). But neihter State can afford to antagonize that public opinion which it holds in esteem.

*

Life does not tolerate a vacuum. The existence of an international community is a fact. And, as the old adage has it, *ubi societas ibi jus.* International law is derived not from metaphysical sources but from the actual social need of the members of the international community to coexist. The alternative in a world based on a plurality of States is *bellum omnium contra omnes.*[13] International law fills an imperative need by enabling States to share the planet.

13 Hobbes, who coined this phrase, actually believed in his day that it reflected accurately the state of affairs prevailing in international relations. Hobbes, *Leviathan* Part 1, Chapter 13. Reprinted from the edition of 1651. Oxford, Clarendon Press, 1909, p. 96.

5.3. Growth of the International Community and Qualitative Shift in International Legal Relations

EDUARDO JIMENEZ DE ARÉCHAGA

I. Legal principles underlying the growth of the international community

The past third of a century has brought unprecedented change in the structure and composition of the international community.

The principle of self-determination of peoples, mentioned in an incidental phrase of Art. 1 (2) of the Charter, has become the constitutional basis for the emancipation of colonial peoples, which is one of the outstanding achievements of the United Nations.

This principle of self-determination of peoples was considered for a long time a moral or political postulate rather than a legal principle. In 1920 Sweden invoked the principle in a dispute with Finland concerning the Åland Islands, but a Committee of Jurists appointed by the Council of the League of Nations advised that "although the principle of self-determination of peoples plays an important part in modern political thought", "there is no mention of it in the Covenant of the League" and it does not constitute "a positive rule of the Law of Nations".[1]

In marked contrast to the Covenant, there is an explicit mention of the principle in Articles 1 (2) and 55 of the Charter of the United Nations.

However, in early studies and commentaries on the Charter it was observed that the expression "respect for the principle of equal rights and self-determination of peoples" is an incidental phrase which refers to self-determination merely as the basis for friendly relations among nations; that although it is described as a principle, it appears in the Article of the Charter defining the purposes of the United Nations, and in the Chapter on Economic and Social Co-operation, and not in Article 2 among the Principles governing the conduct of the Organization and its Members. Consequently, a common view at the time was that the Charter itself stopped short of recognizing this political postulate as a legal principle or of extracting from it consequences in the form of legal rights or legal obligations.[2] Despite these early views, in what probably constitues the most important de-

1 *League of Nations Official Journal*, Special Supplement, No. 3, October 1920, p. 5.

2 See, for instance Kelsen, Hans. *The Law of the United Nations: a critical analysis of its fundamental problems*. London, Stevens and Sons, 1950, p. 51–53; Bentwich, Norman. Martin, Andrew. *A commentary on the Charter of the United Nations*. London, Routledge and Kegan, 1950, p. 1. Goodrich, L. M. Hambro, E. Simons, A. P. *Charter of the United Nations. Commentary and documents*. (Third and revised edition.) New York, Columbia University Press, 196, p. 29 ff.

velopment which has taken place with respect to the law of the Charter, this passing reference to self-determination in Articles 1 and 55 has been shown to possess significant implications and to be pregnant with legal meaning. These eleven words in Articles 1 (2) and 55 have practically swept away the whole of Chapter XI of the Charter and rendered moribund the international trusteeship system established in its Chapters XII and XIII.

Self-determination and decolonization

At the time of incorporating in the Charter the principle of self-determination it was understood by many that this phrase, as a provision in the Charter, had to be interpreted in the light of the remaining provisions and thus such interpretation was without prejudice to what was provided for in Chapters XI, XII and XIII. In the early years of the United Nations the debates on the administration of non-self-governing and trust territories took place within the framework of those Chapters and mainly concerned divergences in the legal interpretation and scope of Articles 73 or 76 to 79 of the Charter. Initial but important steps in favour of decolonization were the setting-up on a permanent basis of the Committee on Information under Article 73, and the establishment by the General Assembly of criteria for the cessation of the transmission of information under this Article. But very soon after these steps were taken, the decolonization movement gained momentum and was placed on a different and wider constitutional basis than a mere liberal interpretation of Article 73 or 76. The movement for the emancipation of colonial peoples succeeded in obtaining recognition of self-determination as a fundamental human right and on that basis asserted that colonialism, by its very nature, constitutes a denial of basic human rights. This identification of the principle of self-determination with fundamental human rights brushed aside the ideology of "enlighted colonial rule", namely, the assumption in Art. 73 that each colonial power should, at its own discretion, lead its dependent territories progressively to self-government "according to the particular circumstances of each territory and its peoples and their varying degree of advancement". The aim was no longer to improve the standards of colonial rule but to liquidate colonialism. It came to be increasingly recognized that no pleas of sound administration, of modern efficiency or kindly paternalism could compensate for the intolerable wrong that is done when a whole race is denied political rights.

Besides the intrinsic justice of this claim, two factors supported this legal development and gave it irresistible force. First, the fact that the decolonization movement is a self-sustaining process, which, through the admission of new Members of the United Nations substantially increases the majority in favour of it.

And the second factor is that the most serious difficulties encountered in the practical application of the principle of self-determination do not arise or are easier to solve in respect of peoples under colonial rule.

What are those difficulties? Sir William Ivor Jennings said of the principle: "on the surface it seemed reasonable: let the people decide. It was in fact ridiculous because the people cannot decide until somebody decides who are the people."[3]

3 The Approach to Self-Government, p. 56.

The proper answer to this criticism was furnished by Hans Blix when he said that the right of self-determination

> "is an example of a rule which for its proper application to concrete cases, requires international institutions. Which people is entitled to self-determination? If, on the one hand, dangerous fragmentation of States is to be avoided, and on the other, the rule is to have practical significance, there needs to be a third party to assess the concrete cases and apply the rule. While a political organ like the General Assembly may not be ideal in this role, it seems to be the only one which has assumed it for the time being."[4]

The task of the General Assembly in this respect has been facilitated in most cases concerning decolonization. The physical separation between metropolitan and colonial territories, the differences in race, customs, religion or language made it easier to determine whether a given population could be regarded as having the identity of a "people" entitled to self-determination. On the other hand, the identity of a "people" entitled to self-determination was denied to the populations of Gibraltar or Malvinas (Falkland) Islands, since the General Assembly refused to accept the effects of a referendum or a consultation of the present inhabitants of those territories.

Resolution 1514 of the General Assembly

From a legal point of view, the decolonization process found its expression in United Nations General Assembly Resolution 1514 (XV) of 14 December 1960 – Declaration on the Granting of Independence to Colonial Countries and Peoples, which proclaimed:

> "All people have the right to self-determination: by virtue of that right they freely determine their economic, social and cultural development."

Since good government is no substitute for self-government, Resolution 1514 further declared in paragraph 3 that:

> "inadequacy of political, economic, social or educational preparedness should never serve as a pretext for delaying independence" and proclaimed "the necessity of bringing to speedy and unconditional end colonialism in all its forms and manifestations".

To this end it was declared that:

> "immediate steps shall be taken in Trust and Non Self-Governing Territories or all other territories which have not yet attained independence, to transfer all powers to the peoples of those territories, without any conditions or reservations, in accordance with their freely expressed will and desire, without any distinction as to race, creed or colour, in order to enable them to enjoy complete independence and freedom".

A complementary resolution, No. 1654, established in 1961 a Watchdog Committee for the implementation of the Declaration. The political pressures exercised by this organ and by the General Assembly have ensured the continuous application of Resolution 1514 (XV) to the point that there is today no State bold

4 Blix, H. *Sovereignity, Aggression and Neutrality.* Stockholm, Almquist and Wiksell, 1970, p. 13–14.

enough to invoke the legitimacy of colonial title or to challenge openly the requirement that all powers must be transferred to the peoples of former colonial territories. Even colonial situations which were described as immovable a few years ago[5] are beginning to crumble under the weight of the new principle, confirming Victor Hugo's dictum that no thing is stronger than an idea whose time has come.

General Assembly declaration and customary law

The principles proclaimed in the 1954 Declaration have become a rule of customary law, recognized as such by the International Court of Justice. Declarations of the General Assembly may constitute customary law in three different ways: a Declaration may merely restate a pre-existing rule of custom; it may crystallize an emergent rule, "*in statu nascendi*"; or finally, a resolution "*de lege ferenda*" may become the focal point of a subsequent practice of States and, in due course, harden into a customary rule.

The 1970 Declaration of Principles of International Law concerning Friendly Relations might be considered an example of a declaratory resolution, expressing the general consensus of States Members in respect of certain corollaries resulting from the basic principles of the Charter; the 1963 Declaration of Legal Principles in Outer Space may be viewed as crystallizing emergent rules which had until then a twilight existence. But Resolution 1514 has been recognized by the International Court of Justice, on the basis of the subsequent practice of States and of the United Nations itself, as having generated a rule of customary law which has abolished the legitimacy of colonial title and of colonial domination.

The 1954 Declaration was already described by the Court in the 1971 Namibia advisory opinion as an important part of customary law[6] and in the Western Sahara advisory opinion the Court had occasion to express more detailed views as to the method through which Resolution 1514 (XV) had become part of general customary law. It results from the Court's pronouncements in this respect that the resolution became a rule of positive customary law through the subsequent action of States, particularly within the United Nations. The Court took into account the fact that since its adoption Resolution 1514 (XV) had been the basis for a development which caused or assisted the independence of many new States which, once they became independent, were accepted as Members of the Organization.[7] Thus, around the nucleus of a General Assembly resolution, the practice of States and of the international organization itself created a rule of customary international law.

II. Qualitative shift in international legal relations

The first qualitative shift in international legal relations to be examined in connection with the principle of self-determination concerns the extension of this principle as a right of all peoples. When the Special Committee which drafted

5 Fitzmaurice, Sir Gerald, in his dissent to the Court's advisory opinion on Namibia, *ICJ Reports*, 1971, p. 298.
6 *ICJ Reports*, 1971, p. 31.
7 *ICJ Reports*, 1975, p. 32.

General Assembly Resolution 2625 on Friendly Relations undertook the elaboration of the principle of self-determination, a view was advanced that since this codification was limited to the rights and duties of States the principle should be defined only as imposing a duty on States to respect and apply it, but should not be proclaimed as a right of peoples, as had been done in Resolution 1514 (XV). In support of this approach the argument was made that only States are the subjects of international law; also the difficulties inherent in the definition of what constitutes a "people" were invoked.

However, the 1970 Declaration, without mentioning Resolution 1514 but adopting its language, provides for a right of peoples that in turn imposes a duty upon States, in the following terms:

> "By virtue of the principle of equal rights and self-determination of peoples enshrined in the Charter of the United Nations, all peoples have the right freely to determine, without external interference, their political status and to pursue their economic, social and cultural development, and every State has the duty to respect this right in accordance with the provisions of the Charter."

Peoples thus appear as proper subjects of international law, together with States and international organizations. This recognition is made in Articles 1 and 55 of the Charter which both refer to the equal rights and self-determination of peoples. Peoples are mentioned as subjects of rights under international law in specific provisions of the Charter, and not merely in the lofty and somewhat rethorical terms of its preamble. In this respect it is necessary to mention Article 80, paragraph 1, of the Charter, which was relied upon by the Court both in the 1950 Advisory Opinion on South West Africa and in the 1971 Opinion on Namibia.

In the latter case, after reciting Article 80 (1) the Court said:

> "A striking feature of this provision is the stipulation in favour of the preservation of the rights of 'any peoples', thus clearly including the inhabitants of the mandated territories, and, in particular, their indigenous populations."[8]

While in the United Nations practice the right of self-determination has primarily concerned peoples under colonial domination, it is by no means limited to them nor circumscribed by a political situation which is disappearing. The generality of the principle may not be evident in Resolution 1514 by reason of its emphasis on anti-colonialism. But the Charter, in Articles 1 and 55, refers to the principle as applying to all peoples and not just to those referred to in Chapters XI and XII. The mention in Article 55 of the universal protection of human rights makes it clear that the scope of the principle is a general one.

Consequently, the 1970 Declaration, while retaining a reference to bringing "a speedy end to colonialism" deliberately broadens the scope of self-determination and provides that the principle applies both to peoples of non-Self-governing and trust territories and also to peoples within independent and sovereign States: that this right is one that must survive the historical function it performed in the dismantlement of colonialism.

8 *ICJ Reports* 1971, p. 33.

The safeguard clause

Paragraph 6 of Resolution 1514 (XV) provides that:

> "Any attempt aimed at the partial or total disruption of the national unity and the territorial integrity of a country is incompatible with the purposes and principles of the Charter of the United Nations."

This provision must be interpreted as a safeguard clause in favour of existing or recently formed sovereign States. The generality of the phrase makes it both a rule for States and also an injunction addressed to the General Assembly as the organ competent to apply the principle of self-determination and decide when a certain population is a people entitled to it. It means that in taking such a decision the General Assembly must pay regard to a fundamental principle of international law and of the law of the Charter, namely that of the territorial integrity of States and the national unity of countries.

Such an injunction was followed, for instance, in the action taken by the United Nations with respect to the secessionist attempt in Katanga, and it determined the attitude taken in regard to the Biafran insurrection in Nigeria.

The fact that the principle of self-determination has been recognized in Resolution 2625 (XXV) as applying also to peoples already forming part of sovereign and independent States obliged the authors of the 1970 Declaration to consider with special care the safeguard clauses in paragraphs 7 and 8 of this Chapter of the Declaration. It is obvious that an unlimited recognition of the principle of self-determination would encourage irredentist and secessionist movements in various parts of the world and even lead to a fragmentation of existing States. Such a possibility could not be contemplated or easily accepted by an international organization composed of States, as the United Nations is, except in very exceptional cases.

Consequently, the two final paragraphs contain certain restrictions designed to protect States against the possibility of secessionist movements by proclaiming the countervailing principle of respect for the territorial integrity and national unity of States and countries. The final paragraph is inspired by paragraph 6 of Resolution 1514 but it is now an injunction addressed to "every State" to refrain from "any action aimed at the partial or total disruption of the national unity and territorial integrity of any other State or country". There is no change in substance since such a prohibition would also include any action of States within an international organization.

The criterion of legitimacy

According to the penultimate paragraph no action is to be authorized or encouraged "which would dismember or impair, totally or in part, the territorial integrity or political unity of sovereign and independent States conducting themselves in compliance with the principle of equal rights and self-determination of peoples". And what are the criteria by which to determine when a State is acting in compliance with this principle?

A criterion of legitimacy is established: this is the State "possessed of a government representing the whole people belonging to the territory without distinction as to race, creed or colour".

An independent and sovereign State which possesses a government representative of the whole of its people is thus safeguarded from any claim to self-determination by a part of its population.

A contrario, a State possessed of a government which does not represent the whole people of the territory and which introduces distinctions as to race, creed or colour, is not protected by the safeguard clause and is exposed to actions which, in the name of the principle of self-determination, may dismember or impair, totally or in part, its territorial integrity or political unity. A denial of equal access to government, but not, for example, a denial of ethnic or cultural autonomy, can give rise to a justifiable claim to self-determination in plural States. The unrepresented sections of the people become entitled to determine freely their own political status.

It is significant for the interpretation of this provision to recall that South Africa, when voting in favour of the General Assembly Declaration made a reservation with regard to provisions "which implied that the rule that a State might not violate the territorial integrity of other States would not apply where that State maintained that the other States did not possess governments representing the whole people".[9]

The position of third States

The 1970 Declaration further provides that:

> "In their actions against, and resistance to, such forcible action in pursuit of the exercise of their right to self-determination, such peoples are entitled to seek and to receive support in accordance with the purposes and principles of the Charter."

This sentence introduces an important change in the traditional rule of international law that foreign States should not interfere in an internal strife or civil war in order to give support to insurgents. It constitutes what may be described as a qualitative shift in international legal relations, since it authorizes States to render moral and material support to peoples fighting for their right of self-determination.

In view of the significance of this qualitative shift, it is necessary to consider carefully the requirements for rendering legitimate such a support which must be given "in accordance with the purpose and principles of the Charter".

It is necessary, first of all, that the General Assembly has found and declared that in a given country there is an unrepresented "people" entitled to self-determination. It would also seem necessary that there are not rival factions fighting for liberation, in which case to assist one against the other would constitute intervention.

The most delicate question is whether such moral and material support may include military assistance in the form of the actual use of armed force by a State against the State opposing self-determination.

9 United Nations, General Assembly, Sixth Committee, 1184th meeting, 28 September 1970 par. 15 A/C. 6/SR. 1184. in *Official Records of the General Assembly, 25th session, Sixth Committee, Legal Questions, Summary records of meetings, 15 Sept. – 4 December 1970*, New York, United Nations 1974, p. 42.

In this respect, it is necessary to recall that in the deliberations of the Special Committee which prepared the 1970 Declaration of the General Assembly a proposal was made by a number of States to declare that the use of force in self-defence was permissible not only if an armed attack occurs but also "in self-defence of peoples against colonial domination in the exercise of the right of self-determination".[10]

The prohibition of the use of force in Art. 2 (4) of the Charter is addressed to States and consequently, in no way hampers the unrepresented people of a territory from taking up arms against the established authority in the pursuit of its own right of self-determination.

Thus, the above proposal, if merely intended to assert the right of a dependent people to use force in implementing its self-determination, was totally unnecessary.

The real issue raised by the proposal was that, through the concept of collective self-defence authorized by Article 51 of the Charter, third States would become entitled to use force against other States despite the prohibition in Article 2 (4).

The acceptance of this exception to the prohibition on the use of force, would have signified an enlargement of the notion of self-defence of virtually unlimited scope, taking it beyond the terms of Article 51, and being in fact a substantial amendment of the Charter.

The juxtaposition of self-determination and self-defence, as suggested by the proposal, would have had explosive consequences. In the absence of an objective and collective decision as to when a "people" is entitled to self-determination, the proposal, if accepted, might have been interpreted and applied as authorizing a State to use force against another on the ground that it was asserting through collective self-defence the self-determination of a part of its people. This would have permitted the use of force in support of irredentist movements or ethnic minorities in many parts of the world, thus destroying the value of the restrictions on the use of force imposed by Articles 2 (4) and 51 of the Charter.

The non-acceptance of the proposals on self-defence in respect of self-determination and the concluding reference in the next to the support being given "in accordance with the purposes and principles of the Charter", indicate that third States, while entitled to furnish moral and material support to unrepresented peoples fighting for their right of self-determination, are not permitted to use armed force against another State, unless such action is ordered or authorized by the competent organs of the United Nations.

10 Report of the Special Committee on principles of international law concerning friendly relations and cooperation among the States, *UN General Assembly, Official records: 24th session supplement No 19 (A/7619)*, par. 29 No. 7 and par. 34 No. 6.

5.4. Growth of the International Community and Qualitative Shift in International Legal Relations
The View from the United Nations

Thomas M. Franck

This paper will seek to examine, in outline form, the assigned topic in the context of the United Nations systems of multilateral diplomacy.

Since the founding of the United Nations in 1945, the number of member States has virtually tripled. Startling as this fact is bound to be, its impact is compounded by the concomitant change in the profile of UN membership. In 1945, the typical member State was located in the temperate zone of the globe, endowed with a sophisticated industrial economy and high per capita income enjoyed by a trained, well-educated and heavily urban population. Today, the profile is completely different. The preponderance of new members comes from tropical or semi-tropical regions, having moderate or low income populations, which suffer from inadequate industrial, scientific, and managerial training.

These changes in the composition of the standing system for multilateral diplomacy has had consequences which were predictable, and others which were not.

At its simplest: the nature of multilateral negotiations have been transformed, fundamentally; so has the agenda of the negotiators.

Inevitably, a negotiation – whether in the General Assembly, leading to a resolution, or in a special conference leading to a treaty – is quite different when it involves some 160 actors (and, sometimes, more than 1,000 delegates), than in a negotiation involving one third that number. This mathematical fact, together with its subtle institutional manifestations, has altogether altered both the process by which international law is made and the contents of that law. The difference is vastly compounded by a qualitative change in the composition of the actors and their perceived self-interest.

Among these changes are the following:

1. The rise in the use of the consensus

New factors militate in favor of norm-creation by negotiation, conciliation, compromise and consensus, rather than by traditional adversarial clause-by-clause voting process. These factors are: the vast increase in membership, the transformation of the UN from a bi-polar to a multi-polar (or tri-polar) system of alignment, the increase in discrepancy between numerical (voting) power and economic and military power, and the greater complexity of the law-making agenda in response to the demand of the Third World for radical change. To some extent, the search for consensus has always been a part of the multilateral treaty-making process. However, with the rise of similar procedures in the General Assembly, the line between the legal effect of treaties and of law-declaring consensus resolutions has become less clear, or has softened. When all States agree on a proposition which, on its face, declares that outer space in the common heritage of mankind, does it matter whether they agree in a treaty or in a UN General Assembly resolution? The Charter, after all, gives the Assembly power to pursue the progressive development of international law. Most of its resolutions are not, and are not meant to be law-making. But, it may be argued, some are. Also, when treaty provisions or law-declaring resolutions are adopted by consensus, these may so affect national conduct as to create "instant" customary law. An example is the concept of the 200-mile economic zone, adopted by consensus at the Law of the Sea Conference, which immediately entered into the repertory of practice of enough States to raise the question whether, quite aside from the treaty, it does not thereby become universally sanctioned as customary law.

2. The invention of new institutions and forms to generate negotiating momentum

The diffusion of power and control in the fora of multilateral diplomacy has inevitably served to necessitate inventiveness. Otherwise, the system would have collapsed by sheer weight of numbers. The creative use of rapporteurs, the use of alternative texts in square brackets, the rise of informal negotiating groups and the proliferation and professionalization of conference secretariats and research capabilities, all represent efforts to overcome the inertia and paralysis that might otherwise accompany such a sharp increase in the number of actors. These inventive innovations or embellishments, in turn, have tended to downgrade the role of the International Law Commission, as diplomats, encouraged to believe that the problems of the large forum were not insuperable, came to rely less and less on the preparations of "first drafts" by an independent agency of legal experts. The new facilitators have thus nudged aside the old, with consequences that have not yet been studied or evaluated.

3. The rise of the negotiation decade

Negotiations for the Law of the Sea treaty have gone on for nearly 10 years. North-South negotiations on the New International Economic Order have gone on intermittently for 5 years and, as yet, have barely begun to produce visible results. We are only becoming dimly aware of the effect of this protraction on the law-making process. For example, are smaller and poorer States placed at a disadvantage in perceiving, let alone pursuing, their national interest if they cannot afford to spare a team of experts for such a long period of time? It is probably demonstrable that the influence of smaller States on the outcome of such negotiations depends upon the personal prestige and knowledgeability of its delegates, which, in turn, in part, depends upon their Governments being able to keep the same team in one forum for the whole course of the negotiations. In part, too, the negotiators' influence will depend upon being supported by an adequate research infrastructure. Few States can afford to assemble and maintain a consistent negotiating team, let alone provide it with research support, for an entire decade in respect of a single subject.

In addition to these and other systemic effects, the growth of the international community has radically altered both the content and the dimensions of the international agenda. Only a few illustrations need be indicated. Economic issues have begun to out-pace security issues, despite the fact that the UN system was designed primarily to deal with the former and has not been wholly successful, as yet, in adapting to the requirements of the new economic priorities. Social issues, such as racism, human rights, and cultural issues are rapidly coming to the fore as subjects amenable to the creation of global norms. Somewhat surprisingly, a recent UNITAR survey of UN delegates identified the conservation, management and distribution of resources (earth, sea and outer space) as having the *top* priority in the minds of diplomats.

This change in the priorities and scope of the global agenda has had two startlingly contradictory consequences, which will make themselves increasingly felt in the law-making fora of the global system. On the one hand, the new order has created a need for greater specialized expertise. Issues relative to energy, anadromous sea species, or outer space require increasing access to, and grasp of, highly technical data, as well as skilled data-interpretation and extrapolation. Intense centrifugal force is thus brought to bear on the negotiating forum, leading to the creation of ever more specialized institutions for negotiation. On the other hand, there has been an increasing tendency – indeed, a necessity – to seek normative solutions in one high-data-intensive area through linkages (trade-offs) in other equally highly complex and specialized areas. Thus, changes in the norms applicable to the terms of trade between North and South are being linked with the creation of new norms assuring a consistent and fairly priced energy supply, to cite but one example.

In summary, changes in the numbers of actors constituting the international community have been accompanied by the most profound changes in the way the international community creates norms and in the number and kind of subjects being addressed normatively.

For the international lawyers, this presents challenges to their institutional and conceptual inventiveness and sensitivity. Less evident, but equally important, is one other rather heartening aspect of the expansion phenomenon. Although normativity, or law, is by its nature biased towards the creation of a stable, systemic status quo, and although revolutionary times usually operate against any rule of law, nevertheless, the quantum leap in community membership has induced a comparable forward jump in efforts to create stable (and progressive) normativity. In a dazzling array of subjects, many of which had previously been governed solely by political vicissitude, the new and essentially underprivileged majority have sought to produce change by normative means, employing negotiation, compromise and the making of new law based on the definition of shared, or intersecting, expectations.

5.5. Regional Conceptions of Public Order

Some Reflections on the Development of an International Law for a New World Order

FLORENTINO P. FELICIANO AND ESTRELLA D. SOLIDUM

We should start with an obvious fact of international life and that is, that notwithstanding the universalist rhetoric which international law professors and practitioners like to use, different conceptions of public order are exhibited in the contemporary arena of international relations. One finds distinct groups of States which share and project relatively distinct social, political and economic goals with varying degrees of explicitness, to be achieved through institutions which may have some measure of organization and specialization. One may perhaps refer to these States as comprising systems of public order, non-global in scope but expecting or demanding realization on a universal or near universal scale. The various systems of public order characteristically reveal varying conceptions of law and of the appropriate goals of law.

What are the systems of public order which are presently observable on the international scene? Happily, we can draw on Ambassador Bo Johnson Theutenberg's very thoughtful paper ("Changes in the Norms Guiding the International Legal System – History and Contemporary Trends") and refer to his quick listing of the Western European system (which presumably includes North America and Latin America), the Socialist family of nations and the Islamic system. We should suggest, along with Prof. Adda Bozeman, that there are other emerging systems: China, so vast as to need consideration as a system by itself; Southeast Asia, the ASEAN nations – Indonesia, Malaysia, Philippines, Singapore and Thailand; and Sub-Sahara Africa. Each of those groupings of States and societies is characterized by order based on some system of belief. The Islamic peoples believe in the Sharia or Revealed Law as the ultimate source of all law. Sub-Sahara Africans who have not accepted Western laws, base laws upon some felt-truths which are derived from the experience of a continuous, intricately regulated participation in the material and the spiritual world. Such felt-truths are carried in proverbs, parables, ritualized speech and the like. ASEAN States use some customary practices such as kinship and kinlike relations, consensus-making low-key diplomacy, mutual consultations, and self-restraint, to regularize their intra-regional relations.

It is useful to have a sense of history in considering the presence of a number of different and competing notions of public order. One needs to recall that general international law as we know it today began as the regional customary law of a small family of nations in Western Europe which drew their fundamental conceptions from Greco-Roman and Judaeo-Christian traditions. When Western Europe exploded with energy and new technology in the sixteenth century and in the next three centuries subjected vast portions of the non-Western world to colonial conquest, its regional customary law achieved quasi-universality. This was of course quasi-universality only in a formal sense: the conquered colonies were characterized simply as possessions of the colonizing power, and not as separate subjects of international law. The effective participants in the system remained the relatively small family of Western European nations. With the impending completion of the decolonization process, we see the re-emergence of ancient communities as once again distinct participants in international processes. One of the important insights offered in Ambassador Bo Johnson Theutenberg's paper is that the socalled "new" but really re-emerged nations may be expected to draw on their ancient and indigenous cultures for their conceptions of appropriate public order for our times.

Drawing once again from Ambassador Theutenberg, it may be stressed that differing systems of public order not only exist in our own time, but have existed at many different points in the deeper past – the Persian, the Roman, the Chinese, the Hindu, the Buddhist and the Islamic empires come readily to mind.

Shifting perspective slightly, we would attempt a statement on trends. The existence of differing systems of public order is likely to persist in the foreseable future. The conditions that lead to peoples maintaining their distinctive public order perspective, including the extent to which peoples may feel threatened by new and alien principles, and correlating the extent to which they feel satisfied by their indigenous system. The relevant arena conditions include the probable persistence of multiple polarities in the international field with respect to political and military power, and to economic wealth and related values. Then too, as long distinct cultures persist, the local system built around and in turn reinforced by such cultures may be expected to persist.

A scholar's responsibility is not exhausted by describing and projecting trends in public systems. He must make explicit to himself and to others his preferable system of public order for the world. The time has now come to try to do that, in very broad and impressionistic strokes and drawing on the work of Prof. Myres McDougal and other members past and present of the New Haven school. We share the widespread demand for a world order that has been described in short hand terms as a public order of human dignity. We understand this public order to be characterized by, among other things,

a) effective acceptance of the principles of basic order – the prohibition of the use of military force and other forms of intense coercion as instruments for effecting value changes in the international order;
b) distributive justice in international relations – achieving the richest possible and sustainable production of economic goods and services and all related values summed up as wellbeing, and the widest and most equitable distribution possible of economic and related values; and
c) recognition of and defence to the spiritual and moral aspirations of peoples.

This last item refers to the rectitude systems of people, their conceptions of order in the relation of man to the universe itself a distinctively human concern. In our view, a purely humanistic or secular view of international law or of a new and preferal world order impart only a partical and limited view, and to that extent an unscientific view. Such a view ignores the fact that religious, moral and ideological factors have historically affected the shape of international law, and that such factors bring important energies to bear upon the task of realizing the preferred shape of public order.

After a summary indication of the principal substantive features of a recommended system of world public order, obviously we move on to consider alternative strategies for bringing about the desired configuration. This is of course a task for several lifetimes and for many institutes and seminars, for lawyers as for those in other disciplines. For international lawyers, we would submit that a primary task is that of improving the strategic capabilities of international legal processes for realizing the desired public order system. One aspect of this task is that of improving the methods and institutions of law creation. It is elementary that there are two general modes of law creation in international law – the method of explicit agreement – treaty making; and the method of implicit agreement – establishment of customary law. It is the latter we would focus on: specifically regional customary law.

We do not consider it necessary to rehearse technical details obviously familiar to you but think it should be enough to refer to the conjoining of physical acts of practice by States and international organizations, and the subjectivities of oughtness with which the physical acts are exercised – the *opinio juris*. The material practice or usage may, and perhaps frequently does, precede the crystallization of the *opinio juris*. Put a little differently, the operating subjectivity during the stage of custom formation may be that of permissibility under international law; when the subjectivities mature into oughtness, the pattern of practice may be characterized as a customary law norm.

The existence of regional customary law on a given subject at any given time is of course a matter for empirical investigation. While we speak of regional customary law, it should be noted that countries observing a given norm or set of norms of customary law may be motivated not by, or not only by, geographic proximity but also by "historical, social, political, religious or other affinities", in short, by shared conceptions of public order. Thus regional customary law may be both reflective of, and integral with, the differing systems of public order that we earlier referred to.

In the hope of promoting discussion, a few points should perhaps be made concerning regional customary law. The first is that the growth of regional customary law, both substantive and procedural, should be encouraged. The general thought here is that States forming part of a region (or some other functional grouping) should have an opportunity to work out approaches and solutions to problems in their own way, to develop normative solutions which take adequate account of a common cultural heritage, shared economic and other interests and common environmental constraints. Our assumption is that the slower, less visible methods of clarifying and specifying goals, and of accretion of consent may, in some contexts, be more viable and efficient then the explicit articulation of both shared and opposed interests which commonly accompanies the process of treaty making.

Because the formation of customary law general or regional is a consensual process, the resulting norms are by definition acceptable to those who developed them and live by them. It is a democratice process which permits those who actively and consistently dissent from a growing practice to be exempt from the thrust of the norm when it emerges. Because it relates to a constitutional principle of the international community, customary law binds even those who were not present at the stage of law formation – the so called new States recently emerged from colonial dependency status. Under contemporary conditions, this is much less of fundamental problem than it might otherwise have been for the new States. For the new States are by and large numerically in a position to change the shape of preexisting customary norms. Further, the process of customary law formation appears now to be significantly more flexible than it did a hundred years back, or even just 50 years back. Proof of acceptance of a customary practice now appears relatively easier – not just treaties and case law and diplomatic correspondence, but also resolutions and declarations and practices of international organizations and international conferences.

It is important to consider the actual and potential relationships between regional or special customary law on the one hand and general international law on the other. It might be useful to think in terms of vertical relationships and lateral relationships.

Consider vertical relationships. General international law could draw new or supporting principles from regional customary law. The general community of nations could derive new ideas, new principles of action, new procedures from existing and potential regional systems. In turn, the conceptions of a just and desirable public order shared within a region may provide religious, cultural or ideological bases for supporting and reinforcing the norms of general international law. This interaction between general international law and regional customary law – between the more comprehensive and the less comprehensive processes – should be a syncretic relationship.

In the event of a conflict between general international norms and regional norms, assuming that both are applicable to a given set of circumstances, which should give way to the other? It is our submission that where the applicable general norm is of the nature of *jus cogens*, the conflicting regional norm must be regarded as superseded or ineffective. In illustration, we may refer to the doctrine or practice within the family of Socialist countries of "Socialist solidarity" which purports to legitimize or justify the use of force by Socialist States against some of their members which wishes to change its internal public order into a non-Socialist system. We might also refer to the doctrines of *jihad* and *dar-al-Islam* found in Islamic law under which the law of peace is applicable only to the domain of Islam, the supreme law rejoining all believers to maintain a state of belligererency *vis-à-vis* all nonbelievers grouped together in the *dar-al-hart*, the domain of war. It is submitted that those internal principles of the Socialist and Islamic groupings respectively are inconsistent with and cannot stand in the face of the prohibitions of the use of force found in the UN Charter and general international law norms forming part of *jus cogens*.

Where, on the other hand, the general international law norm involved does not partake of the nature of *jus cogens*, is not of a fundamental or constitutional nature, it is submitted that the regional customary law can and should be given effect.

Consider next lateral relationships. Regional customary law and general international law, to the extent they are consistent with each other, are applicable at the same time, in respect of the same portion of the globe. There may be, in theory, a need to develop principles for allocating competence over different subjects of legal regulation between general international law and regional law. Analogies are probably available from the domestic law relationships of federal law and state or provincial law. Relationships between members of the same region (or other grouping) could be addressed by regional law. Relationships between members and non-members are presumably to be addressed by general international law, though perhaps not necessarily on an exclusive basis. Possibly analogies from the territoriality and protective personality principles of jurisdiction of national courts over foreigners and non-residents may have some relevance. At all events, one general submission is that regional customary law may flesh out or fill in the intercelestial spaces left by grand international law and, as is well known, those spaces may be large indeed.

Consider finally the areas in which the consensual processes of customary law may be of particular utility in the development of international law as an instrument for a new world order. We can do no more than mention what, in our view, would be these areas: conflict management and conflict resolution; commercial and trade usages or, more generally: resources, technology and capital transfers; protection of human rights; and the development of obligations of assistance to and cooperation with developing and disadvantaged countries.

It is important to close by making very explicit that, to our mind, to encourage the development of regional customary law is *not* to forego or surrender our legitimate aspirations for universality. It is rather merely to recognize that regional or special customary law has a useful function to fulfill in the movement toward our shared vision of a more desirable world order.

5.6. Customary Law: From "Universal" in a European System to "Regional" in a World System

ALLAN ROSAS

This "co-report" deals with the status and function of customary international law in the light of the shift from a Europe-centred international law to a global approach which has taken place especially after 1945. According to one learned author "custom is at the heart of what we mean by international law".[1] According to another "the problem of customary norms of international law is one of the most important and, at the same time, one of the most complex theoretical problems of international law".[2]

It is not surprising, then, that the purpose of the present paper is a very modest one. We are merely trying to present some sketchy notes and ideas on certain aspects of customary law of relevance for our subject. As it does not seem to be possible to isolate the global/regional dimension from certain other problems related to the question of custom we have included some aspects which are central in a general theory of customary international law.

Changes in the international system

The quantitative and qualitative developments which have taken place in the international community are more fully analysed under the theme discussed in papers 5.3 and 5.4 above. Here it is pertinent to ask, what specific problems and perspectives for customary law may have followed from the growth and diversification of the international community? What are the consequences of the fact *that* the number of independent States has quadrupled since the nineteenth century and the number of UN members tripled since 1945, *that* five Asian States were recognized by Europe as forming part of the "civilized" nations at the beginning of this century whereas the African and Asian States today form the majority in the UN, *that* the international community of today consists of States representing manifestly different socio-economic systems, cultures and economic and technological levels of development, *that* the number of international organizations has increased dramatically during this century, etc.?

Without attempting to list all the imaginable consequences of these developments one can mention some obvious repercussions: It is presumably more dif-

1 D'Amato, Anthony, *The Concept of Custom in International Law*, Ithaca and London, Cornell University Press, 1971, p. xii.

2 Tunkin, G. I., *Theory of International Law*. London, G. Allen and Unwin, 1974, pp. 113–115.

ficult today than, say, hundred years ago to reach "consensus" on a given rule. It would also seem to be more difficult today to establish the "practice of States" on a given issue, considering the great number of actors which have to be taken into account (as a factor working in the opposite direction, however, are the improved technological means of registering and tracing instances of State practice). In view of the rapid technological development, and taking into account the tendencies mentioned above, it is also more difficult to "capture" a definite norm when a solution is sought to a concrete dispute. And, of course, the decolonization process has highlighted the question of whether new States are bound by customary law which has emerged before independence.

In view of these and other developments one could easily be inclined to think that general customary law is rapidly losing ground and that custom, at best, can play a role on a regional and local level. It is well-known that treaty law has to a large extent superseded customary law. Still, as we shall argue below, it is not that certain that this development will continue unabated.

The formation and validity of customary law

Facing the abundance of legal writing on the question of the theoretical basis of customary law and the considerable difficulties involved in arriving at coherent and generally acceptable answers one hesitates to enter into the discussion. However, certain problems cannot be brushed under the carpet if one is to have a meaningful discussion on the present function and relevance of customary law.

One fundamental issue may now be considered as settled: The formation of a customary norm requires both a material (State practice) and a psychological *(opinio juris)* element. This point of departure is recognized by the great majority of learned authors, it finds support in the wording of article 38 of the Statute of the ICJ and it has been articulated by the Court, e. g., in the North Sea Continental Shelf cases.[3] This does not mean that there is complete agreement on how State practice or the *opinio juris* are to be determined, or what relative weight should be given to each of these two elements.

It seems to us that one should avoid making a sharp distinction between the two elements, which may interact and be present in one and the same act. This idea, of course, is connected with the question of what type of behaviour should be considered when trying to establish the practice of States (and of international organizations) on a given question. Here we would undoubtedly agree with those who stress that a broad notion of State practice is required, so that not only omissions (passivity) as well as national laws and judgments but also *statements* made, e. g. in the form of resolutions by the UN General Assembly or other similar organs are included as possible constituent elements.[4] This approach seems to enjoy general acceptance today both among States and learned authors. It has also been pointed out that the acceptance of statements *in abstracto* as evidence of practice diminishes the dilemma of changing customary law: "as an

3 *ICJ Reports 1969*, pp. 41–44.
4 Cf., however, D'Amato, A., *op. cit.*, pp. 87–98.

alternative to changing customary law by breaking it, States can change it by repeatedly declaring that the old rule no longer exists – a much more desirable way of changing the law".[5]

Also with respect to the manifestation of an *opinio juris* a flexible approach seems to be in order. Express statements to the effect that a given rule is or should be legally binding are not always necessary; the *opinio juris* may be inferred from other conduct as well,[6] although it is often manifested by the use of normative (legal) language.[7] What matters are not the actual or presumed beliefs of national decision-makers but statements and other manifestations of a normative attitude which can be objectively ascertained.[8]

Traditionally the *opinio juris* is often said to imply that States regard a certain rule as a norm of international law in force *(de lege lata)*. To envisage the creation of a *new* rule would then presuppose that the State which is the first to articulate the new rule has made a mistake or a deliberately false statement as to its binding force. In addition to this possibility, however, one should take into account the possibility of statements *de lege ferenda*. There seems to be no reason why such statements could not evince the necessary *opinio juris*.[9] If they are accompanied by State practice (including perhaps new statements *de lege lata*) which can reasonably be regarded as an application of the proposed rule a new norm of customary international law has emerged. It must be acknowledged, on the other hand, that the relation between statements and acts *de lege late* and *de lege ferenda* in regard to customary law is highly problematical and needs further clarification.

The classical question of the personal sphere of validity of a given customary norm, that is, what States are bound by it and under what circumstances do they become so bound, cannot be entirely disregarded here. Let it be said at the outset that we adhere to the "theory of consent" as a theoretical point of departure. This approach certainly has its shortcomings but it is after all the least dissatisfactory solution. It does not seem possible to State that a State as a general rule may become bound by rules the formation and application of which it firmly opposes. We are not aware of any decisions by international courts which would catego-

5 Akehurst, Michael, Custom as a Source of International Law. *British Yearbook of International Law*, 1974–1975, p. 8.

6 Walden, Raphael M., Customary International Law: A Jurisprudential Analysis. *Israel Law Review*, 1978, p. 98–100; Meijers, H., How is International Law made? The Stages of Growth of International Law and the Use of Its Customary Rules. *Netherlands Yearbook of International Law*, 1978, p. 7.

7 Walden, R. M., *loc. cit.*, pp. 93–100, speaks (with reference to Hart) about the "internal aspect" of customary norms, i. e., a normative attitude which is usually but not always evinced by the use of normative language.

8 See, e. g. Akehurst, M., *loc. cit.*, pp. 36–37; Walden, R. M., *loc. cit.*, p. 95. Cf. Meijers, H., *loc. cit.*, pp. 5–7, who refers to the development *within* States of "the will to make a rule into law". This terminology may lead to unnecessary speculation as to the "real" intentions and beliefs of national decision-makers.

9 See Thirlway, H. W. A., *International Customary Law and Codification*. Leyden, Sijthoff, 1972, p. 55; Walden, R. M., *loc. cit.*, p. 97.

rically State such as principle.[10] Probably all or at least most States would deny the possibility of becoming bound by rules they cannot accept. It then seems impossible to conclude that there exists a "secondary" rule of customary law stating that States become bound by "primary" rules of customary law *against* their will, by a kind a majority voting.[11]

The crucial question, however, is what constitutes "consent" and "opposition". It seems pertinent to speak of *presumed* consent, which means that a State can become bound by a rule the creation of which it has not participated in as long as it has not clearly voiced its opposition.[12] Perhaps this is better terminology than the often used expression "tacit agreement", which despite the word "tacit" seems to connote the idea of specific "understandings" between the parties to a customary norm, something which might not correspond to reality.

It must be acknowledged, of course, that the notion of presumed consent in practice comes close to the view of those who start by rejecting the "consensualist doctrine" of customary law but then go on to say that a customary rule does not bind a State which from the outset has consistently and unambiguously opposed the rule.[13] But if a State has the right to "opt out"[14] of a developing customary rule, is it not more correct to say that it has given its consent by not using this right, in the same way as a State gives its consent to decisions of international organizations using the opting out-system by doing nothing?[15]

The foregoing leads to the conclusion that a norm of general (customary) international law need not bind every State in the world.[16] A rule may well be called a rule of general international law if, say, 150 States have accepted it while a few States flatly reject it (the latter States not becoming bound by the rule).

In fact, there seems to be no dramatic difference between "general" customary law on the one hand and "special", "regional", "local", etc. customary law on

10 On the contrary, the ICJ stated in the Anglo-Norwegian Fisheries case that a certain rule would appear to be inapplicable against Norway "in as much as she has always opposed any attempt to apply it to the Norwegian coast", *ICJ Reports 1951*, p. 131. See also Akehurst, M., *loc. cit.*, pp. 24–26. Some authors, however, (e. g. D'Amato, A., *op. cit.*, pp. 246–252), claim that this and other similar dicta only relate to special (regional) custom.

11 A distinction between primary and secondary rules (secondary rules regulate the creation of primary rules) of customary law is made by Walden, R. M., *loc. cit.*, pp. 87–92.

12 Wolfke, Karol, *Custom in Present International Law*, Wroclaw, Wroclaw Scientific Society, 1964, pp. 158–168. Meijers, H., *loc. cit.*, p. 18.

13 Akehurst, M., *loc. cit.*, pp.23–27; Jimenez de Arechaga, Eduardo, International Law in the Past Third of a Century. *Recueil des cours, Académie de droit international*, Vol. 159, I, 1978, p. 30.

14 This expression is used by Akehurst, M., *loc. cit.*, p. 26.

15 See Brownlie, I., *Principles of Public International Law*. Third edition. Oxford, Clarendon Press, 1979, p. 11, who states that "toleration of the persistant objector is explained by the fact that ultimately custom depends on the consent of States".

16 Cf., however, the dictum by the ICJ in the North Sea Continental Shelf cases, according to which "customary rules . . . by their very nature, must have equal force for all members of the international community". *ICJ Reports 1969*, p. 38.

the other,[17] in the same way as there are no clear-cut legal differences between general multilateral conventions and treaties of a more limited scope. The territorial sphere of validity of a customary rule depends on the nature of the rule and the attitudes and intentions of States participating in its creation. It is also possible to imagine that a usage is "a general practice" for all States but that it is customary *law* in the relations between some States only (the other States opposing the rule as a rule of law).[18] Of course, if a certain rule is followed by a considerable number of States and the rule is by its nature suitable for world-wide application there may be a strong presumption for its development into a general norm, which becomes binding on all States that do not voice their dissent. And as one author puts it, "unless dissenting States are numerous, they seldom maintain their dissent for long."[19]

The "presumed consent" referred to above can only be inferred if the interests of a particular State are in some way affected by the emerging rule.[20] One may argue that a rule intended and suitable for world-wide application should be presumed to affect the interests of all States. Thus, emerging principles of the law of the sea may become binding on land-locked States as well, unless they voice their opposition. If, on the other hand, the rule is clearly intended for regional application only States outside the region do not have to react. It may also be that States outside a region or some other group of States are not even aware of the development of a specific rule within that group. As to States *within* the group it would appear that the requirements for presuming consent become more stringent the smaller and/or the more heterogenous the group is.[21] With respect to bilateral rules it seems difficult to "presume" any consent at all.

It is submitted that the above considerations theoretically speaking also apply to the question of new States. A State which has not existed when a rule has emerged cannot be presumed to have given its consent, and therefore the rule does not seem to become binding on the new State (except in the case of State succession). We would assume – without having conducted any empirical studies – that this is the view not only of the socialist States but also of the majority of States from the Third World.[22] If this is so one could not assert that there is a secondary rule of general validity stating that new States are bound automatically by *all* rules of customary law in force at the moment of independence. But perhaps there is a secondary rule saying that rules of a *ius cogens* nature are today inherent in statehood, and that an entity which claims to be a State has at same

17 Cf. D'Amato, A., *op. cit.*, pp. 246–263; Jimenez de Aréchaga, E., *loc. cit.*, pp. 28–30, who regard consent by a particular State necessary for special but not for general custom.

18 Meijers, H., *loc. cit.*, p. 21–23.

19 Akehurst, M., *loc. cit.*, p. 27.

20 See, e. g., Tunkin, G. I., *op. cit.*, p. 129.

21 See also Akehurst, M., *loc. cit.*, pp. 29–30; Meijers, H., *loc. cit.*, pp. 20–33.

22 Cf., however, Waldock, Sir Humphrey, General Course of Public International Law, *Recueil des cours, Académie de droit international,* Vol. 106, II, 1962, p. 52; Walden, Raphael M., The Subjective Element in the Formation of Customary International Law. *Israel Law Review*, 1977, p. 356.

time given its "consent" to these rules? Moreover, the common interests of States compel the new State to accept (that is, not to rejct) many other norms of customary law as well.

It is true that speaking of consent in the last-mentioned cases may appear as a fiction. But is it not also a fiction to claim that sovereign and independent States become bound by rules of international law against their will, unless such a principle has been established, e. g., in the statute of an international organization? At any rate this discussion may today appear rather academic as the decolonization process is almost completed.

The complexity of the question of customary law is not diminished by the tension which exists between the application and interpretation of *general* principles and rules vs. the creation and subsequent application of *detailed* rules.[23] A State may have accepted a general principle of customary law without accepting its application by way of interpretation to a specific topic. General principles and rules, too, should be interpreted objectively and not as each State bound by them sees fit. On the other hand the consent to a principle cannot be stretched too far to cover specific rules which the State itself does not consider as binding upon it. The problem, which, of course, arises in treaty law as well, can be illustrated by the delicate question of the legality of the use of nuclear weapons. Some (nuclear) States do not recognize a clear-cut prohibition; on the other hand it can be argued that such a prohibition follows from certain general principles and rules of customary as well as treaty law.[24]

Just to mention some other problems which cannot be elaborated here: It seems clear that inter-governmental organizations as subjects of international law can participate in the creation of customary law.[25] But to what extent do rules which, for instance, the organizations have created in their bilateral relations become binding on the member States? And to what extent are the organizations bound by the customary law which has been created by the member States?

Reference must also be made to the temporal sphere of validity of customary norms. If a State *has* given its consent to a customary rule it cannot arbitrarily and unilaterally escape that rule, especially in the context of a dispute concerning the legality of past conduct. On the other hand every State has the right to participate in the creation of new customary rules. As we have argued above this does not necessarily presuppose that the rule is broken by physical actions but can take the form of statements *de lege ferenda* and later *de lege lata.* Is there in addition a right to "withdraw" from a customary rule (except a *ius cogens* rule) comparable

23 See also Geiger, Rudolf, Zur Lehre vom Völkergewohnheitsrecht in der Rechtsprechung des Bundesverfassungsgerichts. *Archiv des öffentlichten Rechts,* 1978, pp. 401–407, who refers to the interpretation of general and uncontested rules of customary law to more specific situations in the praxis of the "Bundesverfassungsgericht" of the FRG.

24 See Rosas, Allan, International Law and the Use of Nuclear Weapons. In *Essays in Honour of Erik Castrén.* Helsinki, Hakapää Editor, 1979, pp. 90–95.

25 Cf. Bökor-Szegö, Hanna, *The Role of the United Nations in International Legislation.* Amsterdam, North Holland Pub. Co. 1978, p. 66, who seems to hold that international organizations cannot through their own conduct create customary norms.

to the denunciation and withdrawal from treaties? According to article 56 of the 1969 Vienna Convention a treaty which is silent on the matter is under certain circumstances subject to denunciation or withdrawal (time-limit: twelve months).[26] One can argue that a similar right with respect to custom would be dangerous for the stability of the international legal order. The question seems to merit further consideration, however.[27]

The function and relevance of customary law

It is important to stress at the outset that there exist different traditions concerning the status and relevance of customary international law. The Anglo-American tradition has underlined the importance of customary law whereas, e. g., the socialist countries have regarded treaty law as the primary source of international law.

Today, against the background of the statutes of international organizations and the "law-making" conventions which have been concluded since 1945, there seems to be a certain consensus on the primacy of treaty law. Still, customary law can be viewed quite differently in different countries. For instance, in Finland, a country which has been rather isolated from the mainstreams of international relations and where the discipline of international law does not play a primary role in legal traditions, a lawyer invoking a norm of customary international law in a lower court would probably be regarded as an odd figure. If he would succeed in convincing the judge that such a norm (and customary law in general) really exists the judge might take refuge in the principle of dualism and refuse to apply the norm on the basis that it has not been transformed into Finnish law.[28]

Speaking on a general level, the function of customary law may be viewed from at least three different angles:

1. The reference to customary law in a concrete dispute. This includes the case when an international dispute-settling organ is called upon to State the content of a customary norm (The "interpretation" of international law).
2. The day-to-day application of customary law by subjects of international law. Innocent passage takes place and diplomats enjoy immunity even if the State in question has not ratified the 1958 Geneva Convention or the 1961 Vienna Convention (The application of international law).
3. The notion of customary law as a "constitutional" law of international relations (particularly customary law of a *ius cogens* nature) and as a bond tying the

26 On this rule see, e. g. Haraszti, György, *Some fundamental Problems of the Law of Treaties*. Budapest, Akademiai Kiadó, 1973, pp. 260–279.

27 It should be noted that according to article 43 of the Vienna Convention a withdrawal from a *treaty* shall not impair the duty of a State to fulfil obligations to which it would be subject under international law independently of the treaty.

28 There is a strong dualist tradition in Finland, see, e. g. Castrén, E., *Suomen kansainvälinen oikens*. Porvoo, W. Söderström, 1959, pp. 9–11; Bengt Broms, *Kansainvälinen oikens*. Helsinki, Suomalainen lakimiesyhdistys, 1978, pp. 51–52. Naturally, the judge is supposed to interpret internal law so that it does not conflict with international law.

different component of international law to a coherent system (The systematization of international law).

It is evident that customary law will continue to play an important role on the levels of points (2) and (3). We feel particularly inclined to underline the importance of point (3). One cannot think of the present international system as a legal order without the notion of customary law. In this connection reference should also be made to the importance of customary law for an understanding of the historical development of international law and of the relationship between international law and societal developments.

With respect to points (1) and (2), however, one could, as was indicated earlier, envisage that the relevance of customary law is diminishing. It would seem that many international lawyers were inclined to draw this conclusion in the sixties. The instances when international tribunals had in fact concluded that a customary norm did exist were comparatively rare. The ICJ, for instance, had often decided that the existence of a customary norm could *not* be established (the Lotus, the Asylum, the Continental Shelf, etc. cases).

Today the picture is not that gloomy for the relevance of customary law. It has been noted that the ICJ during the seventies has had to grapple, "practically in every case", with customary law.[29] This seems to be indicative of a more general trend. According to a Dutch author "customary law appears to be growing in importance for the Netherlands no less than for other countries".[30]

What are the reasons for this trend? The last-mentioned author refers to three different factors which favour the formation of customary law. First of all, the creation of customary law may be the more opportune political option for a State, as it can take place without the formal procedures existing in most countries for the acceptance and transformation of treaties and thus also "out of sight of the electorate". Secondly, customary law may more easily than treaty law achieve virtual universality as it does not require express acceptance – "the inactive are carried along by the active". Many international conventions, by contrast, do not achieve universal adherence and the ratification process is at any rate slow, partly due to the lack of administrative resources in poor and small countries. Thirdly, customary law sometimes emerges more rapidly than treaty law.[31]

Even if one (as the present co-rapporteur is inclined to do) adheres in principle to the requirement of repetition for the formation of customary law it is true that customary law may today emerge during a very short period of time ("instant" customary law[32]).

29 Jimenez de Aréchaga, E., International Law in the Past Third of a Century. *Recueil des cours, Académie de droit international,* Tome 159, I, 1978, p. 9.

30 Meijers, H., *loc. cit.*, pp. 3–4.

31 *Ibid.*, pp. 4–5.

32 This expression has been introduced by Cheng, Bin, United Nations Resolutions on Outer Space: Instant International Customary Law? *Indian Journal of International Law,* No 5, 1965, p. 23. According to Baxter, Richard R., Treaties and Custom. *Recueil des cours, Acedémie de droit international,* Vol. 129, I, 1970, p. 67, "the time

To the above considerations one can today add a factor which is prompted by the experiences of the Third UN Law of the Sea Conference: It appears increasingly difficult to achieve not only rapid and universal ratification of treaties but also approval of the very text of treaties. If the Conference will not, after almost ten years of work, succeed in adopting a new law of the sea convention by consensus there may be an increasing scepticism as to the possibilities of treaty-making on a global level. Obviously the fate of *détente* in the near future will have a bearing upon these perspectives. It is noteworthy that no general disarmament convention has been adopted after the rather marginal ENMOD Convention of 1977 (prohibiting certain environmental modification techniques).

These trends and perspectives indicate that customary law may have a definitive relevance in the future, and precisely on a global level ("general international law"). The formation and evidence of customary law is facilitated by the impressing amount of treaty law which already exists (and which often can be taken as an indication of State practice), the development of the "quasi-legislative" functions of the UN General Assembly and other similar bodies, and so forth. In analysing contemporary customary law it is useful, as has been done,[33] to distinguish between treaties, etc. having (1) declaratory effect; (2) crystallizing effect, and (3) constitutive or generating effect.

But what about special, regional and local custom? As the formulation of our subject indicates there may be a trend towards "regionalism" in the formation and application of customary law. The ICJ has on different occasions envisaged the possibility of special and even of bilateral custom.[34] As an example of a homogenous group of States where special customary rules have emerged one can mention the European Communities.[35] The socialist,[36] capitalist,[37] Latin American[38] and other groupings of States belonging to the same region can be mentioned as other examples.

As these examples show the question of special custom is not limited to geographical areas.[39] The relevant group of States can range from two neighbouring countries to a large group of States united by a common ideology or plainly a common interest in the regulation of a certain topic. As has already been indicated earlier the distinction between general and special custom is not clear-cut.

factor as a separate element in the proof of custom now seems irrelevant". See also Tunkin, G. I., *op. cit.*, pp. 114–115.

33 Jimenez de Aréchaga, E., *loc. cit.*, p. 14.

34 A bilateral custom was recognized in the Right of Passage case, *ICJ Reports 1960*, pp. 39–40.

35 Joutsamo, Kari, *The Role of Preliminary Rulings in the European Communities*, Helsinki, Suomalainen tiedeakatemia: Annales, Dissertationes humanarum litterarum. 16, 1979, pp. 32–33, refers to several customary rules which have emerged within the Communities. See also Meijers, H., *loc. cit.*, p. 4.

36 See, e. g., Tunkin, G. I., *op. cit.*, pp. 427–447.

37 See, e. g., Akehurst, M., *loc. cit.*, p. 28; Bring, Ove, *Det folkrättsliga investeringsskyddet*, Uddevalla, 1979, pp. 254, 287.

38 Asylum case, *ICJ Reports 1950*, pp. 276–278.

39 Akehurst, M., *loc. cit.*, pp. 28–29; Meijers, H. *loc. cit.*, p. 21.

"Where States are divided into two groups of roughly equal size, with one group following one custom and the other following another custom, who can say which is the general custom and which is the special custom?", asks one author.[40] He goes on to note that the fact that custom may exist among some States only may have been lost sight of during the nineteenth and early twentieth centuries, when the international community was small and homogenous, "but in the more heterogenous international community of today the problem is very much alive". Is there, asks the author further, any *general* custom on such topics as the expropriation of foreign property and about the width of the territorial sea and of exclusive fishing zones, "or are there only separate sub-systems of special custom"?[40]

This approach is up to a certain point realistic and maybe attractive. There has probably been too much emphasis on general custom in conjunction with a false belief that old rules created in the nineteenth century by a handful of States claiming monopoly on the denomination "civilized" continue to form part of general customary law binding on all States even if the majority of States clearly does not accept them. On the other hand there is a clear danger in the "regionalization" and "particularization" of customary law. If this development goes too far certain common denominators belonging to customary law and of vital importance for the global world order may be lost. Should we not as international lawyers strive at maintaining as far as possible the universality of international law, while at the same time avoiding to loose sight of reality?

It can be argued that these considerations require the abandonment of the "consensualist" theory of custom and the introduction of a flexible and "sociological" approach[41] to the question of custom-formation. As to the concept and requirement of consent, however, one cannot entirely escape something which does exist. And is it not easier to convince national decision-makers that their State is bound to apply a certain customary norm if they are told that the State has earlier given its consent to the rule compared to the alternative that they are told that they must abide by the rule because other States have created it or because the rule corresponds to some extra-legal values (which the national decision-makers perhaps do not share)?

This leads us finally to the question of the relationship between customary law on the one hand and ethical, religious, etc. considerations on the other. It is self-evident that customary law, as indeed all law, is influenced by (or rather, is based on) common interests and values of States and of mankind. When it comes to legal argumentation in a given situation, however, customary law should be approached as a source *of law* and not as a sociological phenomenon only. Other-

40 Akehurst, M., *loc. cit.*, p. 30. A common denominator for general international law with respect to the nationalisation of foreign property is sought, e. g., by Ove Bring, *op. cit.*, pp. 241–254, 286–287.

41 On the distinction between "positivist", "sociological", etc. theories of custom see, e. g. Rousseau, Charles, *Droit international public*, Tome I. Paris, Sirey, 1970, pp. 311–314; Dinh, Nguyen Quoc, *Droit international public*, Paris, L. G. D. J., 1975, pp. 302–303.

wise the juridical and binding force of customary law may weaken. Relying too strongly on extra-legal considerations may also be unwise in that the concrete basis of a customary rule might collapse if it is shown that the values invoked are *not*, in fact, shared by all the potential subjects of a rule (even if there has been general acceptance of the rule itself). This emphasis on legalism should on the other hand in no way be an obstacle to a flexible and dynamic application and interpretation of customary law, prompted by a desire to guard and strengthen the international legal order of our times.

5.7. International Law as a Law of the World Community

World Law as Reality and Methodology

YASUHIKO SAITO

"Den Glauben müssen Wir festhalten: Über alle Entzweiung der Nationen wird doch der grosse Gedanke der Menschengemeinschaft Kraft gewinnen, sich ausbreiten und wirken – wie ein altes Wort sagt: Sind wir nicht Brüder und hat nicht ein Gott uns alle geschaffen?"

Excerpt from "Die Möglichkeit eines Weltrechts", lecture given by Professor Ernst Zitelmann of Bonn, Vienna, 1888.

1. Inter-State law as a world law

In his famous lecture given in Vienna in 1888, Ernst Zitelmann, professor in Bonn, exhaustively discussed the possibility of a world law.[1] The world law which Zitelmann conceived at the end of the last century was nothing more than the unification of national laws in the fields of some branches of private law, e. g., transport law, economic law, commercial law, etc., namely world law in the narrow sense. The possibility of world law may not nowadays be discussed in this narrow sense; the concept of world law has extended to both public international law and private international law which have remarkedly demonstrated their inherent supranational character.

In the field of public international law, the traditional legal theories, which were generally based on the State's sovereignty and the nationalistic notion of law, were severly criticized after the First World War. If we still abide by the traditional theory and methodology of public international law, discrepancies between the international social reality and its law still never be diminished. It has now become evident that the traditional theories are unable to satisfy the necessities of the new phenomena in international community, and that the theories based on the dogma of the State's sovereignty cannot explain the obligatory

1 This lecture was published the following year (1889) under the title of "'Die Möglichkeit eines Weltrechts', Vortrag, gehalten in der Vollversammlung der juristischen Gesellschaft zu Wien am 20 März 1888". Zitelmann, Ernst, *Die Möglichkeit eines Weltrechts*, Wien, Manz, 1888, 24 p. It is interesting to note that in the same year, Dr. Julius Ofner gave another lecture entitled "Der Grundgedanke des Weltrechts", later published under the same title from Alfred Hölder 1889. Ofner did not discuss the question of *a* World Law as Zitelmann did, but discussed the fundamental question of *the* World Law.

character of international law, as well as a number of new phenomena in international law, such as the status of an international organization as an entity distinct from the States or the international recognition of human rights.[2]

Some prominent internationalists have pointed out the transnational phenomena in international relations and adopted expressions such as "transnational law" (Ph. C. Jessup), "common law of mankind" (C. W. Jenks), "world law" (K. Tanaka).[3] They are all inclined to avoid the use of the term "international" which would apply exclusively to inter-State relations and does not thus represent adequately *jus gentium* as was meant by Roman Law.

Our understanding of world law is therefore different from that of Zitelmann and his successor Peter Klein. They confined their scope of world law within the unification of divers national laws. We understand world law as the law as a whole of the world community or the community of mankind and, therefore, will not confine our observations within inter-State law and relations. We consider world law as the ensemble of laws of the world community, which covers not only traditional legal relations between States, but also embraces all the multifarious traffic across national frontiers of the millions of individuals who compose the populations of States.[4] It includes, therefore, (1) uniform law, (2) international private law, and (3) international public law.[5]

The very basis for world law in this sense should be sought in the existence of the world community itself.

2. *World law as the law of the world community*

Recognition of the existence of the world community starts from the candid observation of the fundamental nature of human beings and its inherent *personne* which is most skilfully defined by Jacques Maritain as *un tout ouvert*. According to Maritain, "La personne est un tout, mais elle n'est pas un tout fermé, elle est

2 It is interesting to note the following observation of Paul Weis, former Director of the Legal Division of the Office of the United Nations High Commissioner for Refugees, who devoted himself for many years to the international protection of refugees: "International law grows slowly. The achievement of this aim (international protection of human rights) would mean the transformation of international law into a 'common law of mankind'. The present phase, we have tried to describe, is but a stage in this long-term development". Weis, Paul. Diplomatic protection of nationals and international protection of human rights. *Human Rights Journal*, Vol. IV, 1971, Nos. 2–3, pp. 643–678.

3 Tanaka, Kotaro, *Sekaiho no riron* (A theory of World Law). 1932–33; 3 vols. Tokyo, Iwanami, 1932–1933, p. 794. Saito, Yasuhiko. La non-discrimination, serait-elle un principe du droit mondial – Opinion dissidente de K. Tanaka dans l'arrêt concernant le Sud-Quest africain, in *Unterwegs zum Frieden, Beiträge zur Idee und Wirklichkeit des Friedens*. Wien, Helder, 1973, pp. 493–510.

4 Parry, Clive, The Function of Law in the International Community, in *Manual of Public International Law*, edited by M. Sørensen, New York, London Macmillan, 1968, p. 2; Cf. Dinh, Nguyen-Quoc, *Droit International Public*, 2e ed. Paris, Librairie générale de droit et de jurisprudence, 1980, pp. 19 ff.

5 Cf. Tanaka, Kotaro, Hoh to sekai (World and Law), in *Zoku Sekaiho no riron* (A Theory of World Law continued edition), Vol. 1, Tokyo, Yuhihahn, 1972, p. 69.

un tout *ouvert*, elle n'est pas un petit dieu sans sportes ni fenêtres comme le monade de Leibniz, ou une idole qui ne voit pas, n'entend pas, ne parle pas. Elle tend par nature à la vie sociale et à la communion".[6] In fact the old Aristotle maxim that "human beings are social animals" is the very foundation of all human societies, including, of course, the international society. As a result of the indefinite and infinite possibilities that an individual has for contact with other individuals, any human society is essentially indefinite in its scope; a society may therefore include all human beings (world society). In other words, the foundation of the world society is this fundamental character of human beings and their society. We have to admit, however, that the world society is not as complete as domestic societies. Its real existence may still remain an ideal. We can, however, observe the emergence of supranational or universal societies as the political, economic and cultural relations of all human beings are gaining in depth, regardless of racial, national and other differences. We simply call the phenomenon of this supranational and universal community the world community, using the term "world" instead of "international" in order to define a community which is free from the concept of nations, States, etc.

The maxim *ubi societas ibi jus* must be applied, not only to the domestic society, but also to the world community. It is impossible to imagine a society without law, whatever the society may be. Law is therefore a condition *sine qua non* also as regards the world community.

3. *Law and enforcement*

Recognition of world law is therefore, in a sense, the natural consequence of the sociological observation of law. The sociological observation of law which starts from the maxim *ubi societas ibi jus* is immune from the traditional way of thinking that law is the function of the State sovereignty, which is called the doctrine of positivism. The doctrine, reflected in the international law, taught that international law is exclusively the sum of the rules by which States have consented to be bound (the consensual theory).[7] We do not think that law is the exclusive prerogative of the sovereignty of States and take the position that every society has its

6 Maritain, Jacques, *Les Droits de l'Homme et la Loi Naturelle*. New York, Ed. de la Maison française, 1942, p. 18 et seq. The understanding of the present author of Maritain's philosophy owes very much to K. Tanaka, who introduced in Japan Maritain's view in connection with the international recognition of human rights as appearing in the above-mentioned booklet, as well as in Maritain, Jacques, *Humanisme intégral; problèmes temporels et spirituels d'une nouvelle chrétienté*. Paris, F. Aubier, 1936. 334 p. (2e édition 1947). See Tanaka, K., *Heiwa no hotetsugaku* (The Legal Philosophy of Peace). Tokyo, Yuhihahn, 1954, pp. 25–27. I quote further from Maritain's work: "Il en est ainsi non seulement à cause des besoins et des indigences de la nature humaine, en raison desquelles chacun a besoin des autres pour sa vie matérielle, intellectuelle et morale, mais aussi à cause de la générosité radicale inscrite dans l'être même de la personne, à cause de cette ouverture aux communications de l'intélligence et de l'amour qui est le propre de l'esprit, et qui exige l'entrée en relation avec d'autres personnes. A parler absolutment, la personne ne peut par être seule". Maritain, Jacques, *Les Droits de l'Homme et la Loi Naturelle*. New York, Ed. de la Maison française, 1942, p. 18.

7 Brierly, J. L., *The Law of Nations*, 6th ed. Oxford, Clarendon Press, 1963, p. 51.

proper law: recognition of law which admits the multiple existence of laws within a State and over States. The doctrine which recognizes only State law and does not, therefore, recognize as laws those rules which are not equipped with enforcement machinery by State authority is that very theory which considers enforcement as a condition *sine qua non* of law.

It is well known that some modern German scholars have tried in vain to reconcile the obligatory character of international law with the full consequences of a pure consensual basis of the law. We do not accept the consensual theory whose logical consequence is that there cannot be a law unless there is specific machinery for its enforcement. We admit, therefore, that there exist *lex imperfecta*, namely, legal norms short of enforcement power, a position which is most clearly illustrated with regard to the respect of human rights.[8] The most of the principles of the respect of human rights may remain *lex imperfecta* at the present stage of development of the international community and the obligations of the States Members of the United Nations may not be manifestly different from *obligatio naturalis*. We cannot however deny the existence of the legal obligations imposed on States Members. The reason for this is simple: the principle of the protection of human rights is derived from the concept of man as *personne* (J. Maritain) and his relationship with society which cannot be separated from universal human nature. The existence of human rights, therefore, does not depend on the will of a State; neither internally on its law or any other legislative measure, nor internationally on treaty or custom, in which the express or tacit will of a State constitutes the essential element.[9] This natural law character of human rights was clearly pronounced in an advisory opinion rendered by the International Court of Justice in connection with the case of "Reservation to the Convention on Prevention and Punishment of the Crime of Genocide", on 28 May 1951:

"The solution of these problems must be found in the special characteristics of the Genocide Convention. . . . The origins of the Convention show that it was the intention of the United Nations to condemn and punish genocide as 'a crime under international law' involving a denial of the right of existence of entire human beings, a denial which shocks the conscience of mankind and results in great losses to humanity, and which is contrary to moral law and to the spirit and aims of the United Nations (Resolution 96 (I) of the General Assembly, December 11th 1946). The first consequence arising from this conception is that the principles underlying the Convention are principles which are recognized by civilized nations as binding on States, *even without any conventional obligation*. A second consequence is the universal character both of the condemnation of genocide and of the co-

8 Cf. Tanaka, K., De droit international au droit mondial, in *Etudes Juridiques offertes à Léon Julliot de la Morandière*. Paris, Dalloz, 1964, p. 560; Wright, Lord Q., Natural Law and International Law, in *Interprétations of Modern Legal Philosophies, Essays in Honor of Roscoe Pound*. Edited with an introduction by Paul Sayre. New York, Oxford University Press, 1947, IX, 807 p:, also with respect to the right to development, Gros Espiell, Héctor, *Derecho Internacional del Desarrolo*. Valladolid, Univ. de Valladolid, 1975, pp. 33–39.

9 Dissenting opinion of Tanaka, K. *I.C.J. Reports 1966*, p. 297.

operation required 'in order to liberate mankind from such an ordious scourge' (Preamble to the Convention)". (emphasis added)[10]

Why cannot we apply the essence of this opinion of the International Court to the cases of the violation of fundamental human rights and the crime of, for example, *apartheid*, in place of genocide?

4. Pacta sunt servanda as the basis of obligation

As so well conveyed by Brierly, the traditional theory of law is based on the dogma of the absolute sovereignty of the State, which gave expression in theory to the growing strength and exclusiveness of the sentiment of nationality during the nineteenth century. By so doing the theory raised a formidable difficulty for international law, for if sovereignty means obsolute power and if States are sovereign in that sense, they cannot at the same time be subject to law. So long as international law is not endowed supranationality, independent from the will of the subordinate State, it was incapable to overcome anarchy in international law and relations. International lawyers have not shrunk from facing the contradiction and have tried to reach a solution in various ways.[12]

Then under what circumstances can we recognize international law as really law? What is the basis of obligation in international law? We have no choice but to meet the basis of obligation of States in international law in the grand principle of natural law *pacta sunt servanda*. In fact from ancient times, recourse to natural law has efficiently contributed to the creation of international law; in international relations, in the absence of any positive law, treaty or customary laws, which was often the case in the early stage of development of the international society and even today, the international order required natural justice for its maintenance and the principles of natural law were often envoked. States were never considered to be free from any obligation in the absence of positive norms of international law. For example, Grotius considered that the positive law depended doubly on natural law: on the one hand its binding force depends on the consent of States in virtue of the principle of natural law *pacta sunt servanda* and on the other hand the validity of positive international law must be examined by its conformity to social justice, or otherwise to the law of higher grade, e. g., natural law. As pointed out by Brierly, natural law, or a like principle under some other name, was considered as an essential underlying principle of the art of legislation. It was also a principle which is necessarily admitted into the actual

10 *I.C.J. Reports 1951*, p. 23.

11 Cf. Gros Espiell, Héctor. No discriminacion y libre determinacion como normas imperativas de derecho internacional, con especial referencia a los efectos de su denegacion sobre la legitimidad de los Estados que violan o desconocen esas normas imperativas. *Separata del Anuario numero 6 del Instituto Hispano-luso-americano de derecho internacional*, VI, 1980, pp. 73–81.

12 Brierly, *op. cit.*, pp. 15–16. The traditional concept of international law has invited a number of criticisms, especially since the end of the First World War. The ciriticisms have been based on the sociological notion of law, or logical structure of a legal system, or the concept of natural law. Cf. Dingh, Nguyen-Quoc, *op. cit.*, p. 93 et *seq*.

administration of law. The court of law appealed to the principle of natural law in case of lacuna in positive law. The life with which any system of law has to deal is too complicated, and human foresight too limited, for law to be completely formulated in a set of rules, so that situations perpetually arise which fall outside all rules already formulated.[13] The function of natural law is much more remarked in the case of the international society than in the domestic societies, for in the international society the deficiency in law is much more striking than in the latter.

5. Natural law and war trials

The function of natural law was illustrated in the case of the punishment of war criminals at the Nürnberg and Tokyo trials. For centuries, members of the armed forces and other persons who committ breaches (or, at any rate, serious breaches) of the laws of war have been liable to prosecution. After the conclusion of the Kellogg-Briand Pact, a war of aggression was clearly illegal, but there was nothing in the Pact to indicate that aggression was a crime, or that the Pact imposed obligations on individuals. It is true that a number of unratified treaties and League of Nations resolutions dating from the 1920s did declare specifically that aggression was a crime. However it was difficult even in this case as in the case of the Pact to apply the principle of individual liability to the international crime of aggression. The Nürnberg and Tokyo Tribunals, which were set up by an inter-allied agreement at the end of the Second World War, tried the German and Japanese leaders not only for traditional war crimes, but also for crimes against peace and crimes against humanity. It was clear that positive law, such as treaty or customary law, was not present to punish them under the name of crimes against peace.[14] In the Tribunal Charter, crimes against peace were defined as "planning, preparation, initiation or waging of a war of aggression or a war in violation of international treaties". This provision was therefore criticized by some people as constituting retroactive legislation. We consider, however, that the trials may be justified by appealing to natural law. In domestic penal law, the rubric *nullum crimen et nulla poena sine lege* is firmly established and appeal to the norm of natural law for the purpose of punishment is out of the question. It is evident that if the application of this rubrical principle should be strictly observed in the domain of international public affairs, punishment under the name of crime against peace may not be permitted. We are convinced, however, that the grand principle of penal law has no basis in justice; it is essentially designed to protect fundamental human rights against any abuse of power by the State. Application of this principle may be justified in domestic societies; we might be able to consider, however, that in an international society where legislature with supra-national competence does not exist, strict observance of this grand principle is not required. In an international society, therefore, punishment may be admitted

13 Brierly, *op. cit.*, p. 23; Tanaka, Kotaro, Hoh to sehai (World and Law), in *Zoku Sekaiho no riron* (The Theory of World Law continued edition). Vol. 1, Tokyo, 1972.

14 Cf. Akehurst, Michael Barton, *A Modern Introduction to International Law*, 3rd ed. London, George Allen and Unwin, 1978, p. 257.

not only in compliance with international law, which is manifestly not as developed as in domestic societies, but also by appealing to natural law and justice. The view expressed by Lord Wright is most pertinent to this point: "All civilized nations have a common interest that offences against International Law and Morality should not go unpunished. All that they can demand is that they should be tried by courts which are duly invested with appropriate jurisdiction and which proceed to the principles of natural or elementary or substantial justice".[15] We consider that the trials under the name of crimes against peace was the most illustrative example of the application of natural law in international law.[16]

6. *International public order and jus cogens*

If the maxim *ubi societas ibi jus* is accepted, and we recognize the existence of the world community, the logical conclusion is that we cannot deny the existence of world law prevailing in this community. Where there is a world society, there is a world law. The world law is, therefore, a kind of product of human society. It is a cultural heritage which is to a considerable degree analogous to science, technology and economics. It is firmly based on those universal elements of law which are to be found in the identity of human nature, in common ethical principles and conditions of expediency in social life. As we confirmed already, rule of law is therefore a condition *sine qua non* of the peace of the world community, which, because of its size, multiplicity and ethnological, cultural, religious, sociological and economic diversity, regulation by law to establish the common basis is indispensable to make international life possible.

However, we are not satisfied with world peace through law,[17] but we require, at the same time, that the content of law be consonant with the universal common good, and particularly with the ideals of justice of the world community. The concept of international public order is nothing but the reflection of this reality of the world community as it is today. As rightly pointed out by Héctor Gros

15 Wright, Lord Q., *op. cit.*, p. 806.

16 It may be possible to consider that the trials constituted an initial practice for the establishment of international customary law, since all positive law, namely, treaty and custom laws are the incorporation or specification of natural law. The initial practice may be explained as the incorporation of a principle of natural law into customary law.

17 Gustav Radbruch does not exclude the question of *Gerechtigkeit* and *Zweckmässigkeit* from his jurisprudence; he recognizes however with priority *Rechtssicherheit* and *Positivität* to *Gerechtigkeit* and *Zweckmässigkeit*. Cf. Radbruch, *Rechtsphilosophie*, 3. Aufl., Stuttgart, K. H. Koehler Verlag, 1932, pp. 70–71. Radbruch cites from Cuche as follows: "La paix, la sécurité sont les premiers bienfaits que la Droit nous procure. Alors même que nous serions en désaccord profond, irréductable sur les fins supérieures du Droit, nous pouvons cependant nous entendre pur lui faire remplir ces fins intermédiaires auxquelles nous sommes tous intéressés". (Cuche, *Conférences de philosophie du Droit*, 1928, p. 19). Our understanding of the legal philosophy of Gustav Radbruch owes very much to K. Tanaka's splendid articles contained in "*Zoku Sakaiho no Riron*" (A Theory of World Law continued edition), Vol. 1. Tokyo, 1972.

Espiell, "the very ideal of public order, both domestic and international, presupposes that in any community ruled by law there must necessarily be norms which take precedence over the wishes of the individuals who make up this community".[18] As a result, it may be held that any act which is contrary to this public order is irregular or illegal. (However many acts may be illegal, e. g., torts and breaches of contract in municipal law, without being crimes.)

We have to revert to the crucial question of "law and enforcement". We are entirely appreciative of the following view of Lord Wright: "I do not accept the view that there cannot be a law unless there is specific machinery for its enforcement. No doubt in practice the two things go together. But the existence of the law is not dependent on the existence of sanctions, that is sanction external to it. The coercive element of the law may be moral. It may be obeyed generally because the conscience of mankind requires obedience".[19]

As further pointed out by Gros Espiell, the concept of international public order is reflected in all areas and themes of international law and included the idea of *jus cogens* which, *prima facie,* specifically relates to the law of treaties. The term "international public order" was first used after the Second World War in considering whether there exists a *jus cogens,* a cogent law limiting freedom of contract. The problem involved in international public policy were discussed in the United Nations International Law Commission when it started its work on the codification of the law of treaties. The Conference of Plenipotentiaries in Vienna in 1970 finally adopted one of the most controversial provisions: article 53 (Peremptory norms of international law). There is certainly a close connection between the two concepts and because of the fact that when *jus cogens* is violated the international public order is necessarily affected, it may be accepted that the expression *jus cogens* should also be used in a broader manner as a term to describe the essential elements of the international public order.[20]

Now we have to discuss the natural law character of a human rights law and reject the so-called consensual theory as the basis of obligation in international law. When we say that we find no special reason to deny that the international norms dealing with human rights have the character of *jus cogens,* we usually use the term *jus cogens* in this broader perspective. Verdross included, among other rules of general international law having the character of *jus cogens,* in particular, "a very important group of norms" which "are all rules of general international law created for a humanitarian purpose".[21] Gros Espiell writes in the same vein:

18 Cf. Gros Espiell, Héctor. No discriminacion y libre determinacion como normas imperativas de derecho internacional, con especial referencia a los efectos de su denegacion sobre la legitimidad de los Estados que violan o desconocen esas normas imperativas. *Separata del Anuario numero 6 del Instituto Hispano-luso-americano de derecho internacional,* VI, 1980, pp. 33–81.

19 Wright, Lord Q., *op cit.,* p. 805.

20 Gros Espiell, *op. cit.,* (note 18), pp. 3–4. Professor Gros Espiell deals in detail with the history of the International Law Commission on the subject of international public order and *jus cogens.*

21 Alfred Verdorss, Forbidden Treaties in International Law, *American Journal of International Law,* Vol. 31, 1957, pp. 571–577; A. Verdross, Jus Dispositivum and Jus

"The essence or basis of *jus cogens* is that the international community recognizes certain principles which safeguard values of vital importance for mankind and that it translates these values into peremptory rules of international law".[22]

We recognize the existence of *jus cogens* in international law for the simple reason which is as follows:[23]

The general theory of law makes a distinction between *jus cogens* and *jus dispositivum*. If we meet no convincing opinion objecting to this general position in jurisprudence, we may admit that distinction in any legal order, not excluding international legal order. The only justification for the objection may originate from the positivist theory of law, which regards the law as an emanation of the sovereign will of a State and nothing else, accepting thus consent as the sole basis in international law, a theory which we have rejected categorically. If we agree with the Aristotelean theory, the existence of *justitia distributiva* and *justitia commutativa*, namely, the interest for both the community and individuals, in an international community, we have to recognize the existence of a growing objective interest for the international community, which may not be at the arbitral disposal of members of the community concerned. This kind of interest or *justitia legalis* contains undoubtedly universal or moral interest. Even under the present stage of development of the international society which is far from the establishment of rule of law, we cannot deny the grand principle of invalidity of agreements *contra bonos mores* which is firmly rooted in any legal community.

This philosophy is clearly made by the International Court of Justice in its advisory opinion concerning the Reservation to the Genocide Convention:

"The Convention was manifestly adopted for a purely humanitarian and civilizing purpose. In such a convention the contracting States *do not have any interests of their own;* they merely have, one and all, a common interest, namely, the accomplishment of those high

Cogens in International Law, *American Journal of International Law*, Vol. 60 1966, pp. 55–63.

22 Gros Espiell, *op. cit.*, (note 18), p. 8.

23 The author of this article presented to the Special Session of the International Institute of Humanitarian Law to commemorate its tenth anniversary, September 1980, a written communication entitled "Humanity transcends Sovereignty – New International Law and its methodology", in which I referred briefly to the *jus cogens* character of a law of human rights. During the session, presided by Dr. Erik Suy, on the subject concerned, this point called for much discussion among the participants, especially between Professor K. J. Partsch of Bonn and Professor H. Gros Espiell. I feel, therefore, obliged to dwell upon this point. However I owe this opinion entirely to chapter 7 of K. Tanaka's article, Heiwa, Jinken oyobi Sekaiho (Peace, Human Rights and World Law) in *Zoku Sekaiho no Riron* (A Theory of World Law continued edition), Vol. 1. Tokyo, 1972. The English translation of this article appeared in *Transnational Law in a Changing Society – Essays in Honor of Philip C. Jessup*, New York, Columbia Univ. Press, 1972, *except for* this key chapter 7 discussing *jus cogens*. I regret this fact deeply, because I consider that this chapter constitutes the most illustrative view on the subject by a contemporary jusnaturalist Tanaka, which would certainly contribute to the development of the theory of *jus cogens* in international law.

purposes which are the *raison d'être* of the convention. Consequently, in a convention of this type one cannot speak of individual advantages of disadvantages to States, or of the maintenance of a perfect contractual balance between rights and duties."[24]

Invalidity of legal acts *contra bonos mores* is undoubtedly a well established principle of any domestic law and we may, therefore, consider this principle as one of "the general principles of law recognized by civilized nations". Recognizing thus the concept of *jus cogens* in international law, we are convinced that fundamental rules at least for the protection of human rights and freedoms constitute the category of *jus cogens*. The application of this category of laws cannot be violated by virtue of agreement between States. The Constitutions of many countries characterize human rights and fundamental freedoms as "inalienable", "sacred", "inviolate", expressions which we do not consider as of a merely decorative character without any substantial significance. The way of characterization of human rights means exactly that a law of human rights exists independently of the will of the State or of individuals and it is deeply rooted in the conscience and high moral order of mankind and of any reasonable man, and it is linked with human nature which is in itself invariable.

7. Obligation erga omnes and actio popularis

The recognition, by the International Court of Justice in the advisory opinion concerning the Reservation to the Genocide Convention, of "a common interest", which was referred to by the International Court as "the accomplishment of those high purposes which are the *raison d'être* of the convention" leads us to the recognition of the interest of the organized international community and the "Bien Commun Universel", the latter having been splendidly defended by Pope John XXIII in his Encyclical *Pacem in Terris*. The concept of the organized international community or the "Bien Commun Universel", unknown until recently to the doctrine of international law, has been advocated by some distinguished international lawyers, among others, Alfred Verdross.[25] Given the present world situation in which economic, political, cultural and other relations between individuals as well as peoples have become so frequent and intense, their interests have become very intricate, international authorities dealing with inter-

24 *I.C.J. Reports 1951*, p. 23. This famous opinion of ICJ was quoted by a number of eminent international lawyers, among others, Verdross, A., Jus Dispositivum and Jus Cogens in International Law, *American Journal of International Law*, Vol. 60, 1966, pp. 58; Tanaka K., Heiwa, Jinken oyobi Sekaiho, (Peace, Human Rights and World Law), in *Zoku Sekaiho no Riron* (A Theory of World Law continued edition), Vol. 1, Tokyo, 1972, p. 355.

25 Verdross, A., Eine neue Völkerrechts-Theorie. *Österreichische Zeitschrift für Aussenpolitik*, No. 4, 1979, pp. 263–269; Verdross, A., Das bonum humanitatis in der christlichen Rechtsphilosophie, in *Festschrift für F. Arnold* (Beiheft zum Österr. Archiv für Kirchenrecht, No. 4, 1963, S. 33 ff.) Cf. Bastid, Suzanne, Place de la notion dans une théorie générale des organisations internationales, in *L'Evolution du Droit Public, Etudes offertes à Achille Mestre*. Paris, Sirey, 1965, especially p. 46 referring to the theory of George Renard.

State and world affairs are growing, the competence of the United Nations and other international agencies is continously strengthened, we have to admit that the traditional doctrine of international law based on the dogma of the State sovereignty and exclusive national interest has already become out of date; the new international law should start from the candid recognition of international reality, namely, the recognition of the interest of the organized international community and the "Bien Commun Universel".

The objectivity of the international legal order was manifestly recognized by the International Court of Justice in its judgment in the case concerning the Barcelona Traction.[26] In this case the International Court unequivocally confirmed the existence of the obligations *erga omnes,* which may be called "Barcelona doctrine", i. e., that States do have obligations towards the international community as a whole and that, in view of the importance of the rights involved, "all States can be held to have a legal interest in their protection; they are obligations *erga omnes*."[27] These rights of the "international community as a whole" which impose the obligation *erga omnes* are the concrete manifestation of the existence of an international public order and a certain area of *jus cogens.* It should be noted, in particular, that the recognition, by the International Court, of the obligations *erga omnes* is fundamentally the product of the jurisprudence of the International Court which, in a series of decisions, has acted as a revelator of its existence.[28]

It has thus become evident that legal relativism without limits, a logical consequence of legal positivism, has been loosing its influence as States have become aware of their common interest which is legalized by the Charter of the United Nations and the constitutions of other international agencies. The United Nations, the highest expression of the international legal community, constitutes the most efficient instrument through which international law will be transformed from the relative instrument to the universal instrument. Jenks did employ the expression "the common law of mankind" to mean the reality of the law of an organized world community which is constituted on the basis of States but discharging its community functions increasingly through a complex of newly established procedures, which have been particularly employed within the UN Family.

The recognition of the obligation *erga omnes* in international law urges us necessarily to consider the question of *actio popularis.* As Egon Schwelb pointed out the term was injected into the 1962 and 1966 proceedings and discussions of

26 Juste Ruiz, José, Las obligaciones erga omnes en Derecho Internacional Público, in *Estudios de Derecho Internacional, Homenaje al Profesor Miaja de la Meula,* Vol. 1, Madrid, Editorial Tecnos, 1979, p. 219 *et seq.*.

27 *I.C.J. Reports 1970,* p. 32.

28 Professor José Juste Ruiz refers to several pronouncements of ICJ starting from the Reparation for Injuries Case of 11 April 1949, Juste Ruiz, José, *loc. cit.*, p. 220 *et seq.*

29 Jenks, C. Wilfred, *The Common Law of Mankind,* London, Stevens, 1958, p. 8, also referred to by Juste Ruiz, José, *loc. cit.*, p. 227.

questions of international law in the course of the South West Africa cases.[30] He concluded that an equivalent to an *actio popularis* was, indeed, "known" to international law in 1919/1920, in 1962 and 1966, but it was however the International Court itself which, in its 1970 judgment in the Barcelona Traction case, gave a comprehensive and most authoritative reply to the question.[31]

The International Court of Justice, in its advisory opinion in 1950, later approved by the Judgment in 1962, on South West Africa, considered that the Mandate system, although its establishment was based on the contractual relations between the organization (the League of Nations) and the Mandate authority, had acquired an international character to which was attached an objective status, and that this status should not be modified by the dissolution of the parent organization. In these two considerations in 1950 and 1962, the International Court recognized in all Member States the legal interest in having recourse to the Court under the clause of "legal protection", despite the dissolution of the League of Nations. In Tanaka's opinion, the International Court thus recognized that the State may become the subject or holder of a legal interest in the realization of social justice and humanitarian ideals. The State which belongs as a member to an international organization incorporating such ideals must, therefore, necessarily be interested in these matters; this interest includes its profound concern with the attitude of other States, particularly member States belonging to the same treaty organization.[32] Tanaka pointed out that Judge Jessup had defended this argument in the following terms:

> "International law has long recognized that States may have legal interests in matters which do not affect their financial, economic, or other 'material' or so called 'physical' or 'tangible' interests. As outstanding examples of the recognition of the legal interests of States in general humanitarian causes, he cited, the international efforts to suppress the slave trade, the minorities treaties, the Genocide Convention and the Constitution of the International Labour Organisation".[33]

As Tanaka further pointed out, from the point of view of purely juridical formalism, there would be the conclusion that, so far as the Mandate was conceived as a contract between the two parties, namely, the League of Nations on the one hand and the Mandatary on the other, the dissolution of the League would produce, as a necessary consequence, the absolute extinction of the Mandate. That pure logicism, the position of the Respondent in the cases concerned, was combined with strict voluntarism according to which all legal consequences attached to juridical act were conceived as the effect of the will or intent of the parties. Tanaka, on the contrary, attached more importance to the institutional side of the Mandate, which, according to Lord McNair, was "valid *in rem* – *erga*

30 Juste Ruiz, José, *loc. cit.*, p. 228 *et seq.;* Schwelb, Egon, The Actio Popularis and International Law. *Israel Yearbook on Human Rights*, Vol. 2, 1972, p. 46.

31 Schwelb, *ibid.*, p. 55.

32 *I.C.J. Reports 1966*, p. 55.

33 I.C.J. Reports 1962, pp. 425–428, also referred to by Tanaka, *I.C.J. Reports 1966*, p. 252.

34 *I.C.J. Reports 1966*, p. 269.

omnes". The 1950 Opinion had already stated that "the object of the Mandate regulated by international rules far exceeded that of contractual relations regulated by national law."[35]

In Tanaka's view, the Mandate, as an institution, was the starting point of the opinion and the most influential reason to justify the survival of the Mandate notwithstanding the dissolution of the League.[36]

Space is too limited to dwell upon the theory of the institution which a generation of distinguished French jurists, le Doyen Hauriou, George Renard, Achille Mestre, G. Burdeau, have elaborated upon. Madam Suzanne Bastid rightly pointed out that "dans l'institution, le Pouvoir est intimement lié à l'idée. Celle-ci a pris un tel ascendant sur les hommes qui assurent le gouvernement de l'institution que leur volonté ne fait qu'un avec elle. Ils extériorisent l'énergie constructive de l'institution. Enfin, le groupe dont la destinée est liée au sort de l'institution ainsi comprise a son terrain d'élection sur le plan politique, participe d'une communion qui survit à la fondation de l'institution."[37] Tanaka considered that as a theoretical construction, the concept of the "organized international community" might be referred to in order to explain the legal position of the mandatary and conceived that, after the dissolution of the League, the mandatary continued to have obligations in relation to an impersonal entity, namely, the organized international community as before, which was personified as the United Nations.[38]

8. *World law as scientific methodology*

The recognition of "the interest of the organized international community" or "Bien Commun Universel" then requires us to adopt a supple and dynamic method of interpretation in a new international law which bases its very existence objectively and independently of the sovereign will of States and fully in conformity with the new trends of thought.[39]

As pointed out by Tanaka, the recognition of the institutional side of the Mandate is nothing else but a product of a scientific method of interpretation of the mandate system, in which the consideration of spirit and objectives as well as

35 *I.C.J. Reports 1950*, p. 132.
36 *I.C.J. Reports 1966*, p. 269.
37 Bastid, S., *op. cit.*, p. 45.
38 *I.C.J. Reports 1966*, p. 270.
39 We remember that Rudolf Jehring lamented the fact that the traditional jurisprudence did not go beyond the framework of "Landesjurisprudenz" and did not study the problem of law in the light of its universal character. We may also mention the names of eminent jurists who discussed the universal character of law, such as Kohler, Sareilles, Lambert, Vinogradoff, Pound, Wigmore from the point of view of the sociology of law or the comperative law; Kohler, Berolzheimer, Del Vecchio from the point of view of the history of law or the legal doctrine; Cathrein, Mausbach, Schilling, Petraschek, Rommen from the point of view of the natural law. These scholars certainly contributed to the idea of world law from their respective legal expertise, but their respective approaches were not comprehensive in considering the relation between the law and the world.

social reality of this system play important roles. This method of interpretation, called teleological or sociological, in contrast with strict juristic formalism, consists in appraising each factor generating customary international law according to the occasion and circumstances, thus considering the formation as a whole as an organic and dynamic process. This method of legal interpretation is particularly relevant to international law; it should be applied to rectify the rigid and formalistic attitude in the recognition of international law, namely, strict voluntarism which emerged from the notion of the absolute State's sovereignty.[40]

As we have already often indicated, discrepancies between law and reality are in no other legal discipline as striking as in the field of international law. We should, therefore, expect the possibility to some extent of a creative role of international lawyers, in particular, in the judicial activities of judges of a court of law.

In interpreting laws, however, it is not permitted to judges to establish law independently of an existing legal system, institution or norm; it is permitted to them to declare what can *logically* be inferred from the *raison d'être* of a legal system, legal institution or norm. With respect to "Succession in international organization", Oppenheim states: "While as a rule the devolution of rights and competencies is governed either by the constituent instruments of the organization in question or by special agreements or decisions of their organs, the requirement of the continuity of international life demands that succession should be assumed to operate in all cases where that is consistent with or indicated by the *reasonably assumed intention* of the parties as interpreted in the light of the purpose of the organizations in question."[41]

This method of interpretation, which is known as the method of "*libre récherche scientifique*" or "*Freirecht*", has been applied mainly in civil law countries for a century with a view to emancipating judges from the rigid interpretation of written laws and their situation of "simple servant of the legislator". The

40 See Saito, Yasuhiko, Une Perspective Téléologique – Opinion de K. Tanaka à la CIJ et Son Origine. Etude offerte au Professeur Haroldo Valladao, Président de la Société Brasilienne de Droit International, in *Area and Culture Studies*, Tokyo, University of Foreign Studies, 1976, pp. 219–230; Friedmann, W. G., The Jurisprudential Implication of the South West Africa Case. *Columbia Journal of Transnational Law*, Vol. 6, 1967, p. 3; Judge Bustamante, *ICJ Reports 1962*, p. 351; Gross, Leo, The ICJ and the United Nations. *Recueil des cours, Académie de Droit international*, Vol. 120, I 1967, p. 321; Professor E. Jimenez de Aréchaga also writes as follows: "Este último método (el método teleologico de interpretacion) pone el enfasis en el propósito general del tratado, al cual se atribuye une existencia propria, independiente del texto y de la intencion original de las partes. De esta manera se llenan vacios, se introducen correcciones, los textos se expanden y completan, siempre que sea en ejecución de fin y objeto atribuido al tratado por el intérprete", Jimenez de Aréchaga, E., *El Derecho Internacional Contemporaneo*. Madrid, Editorial Tecnos, 1980. p. 57. He further indicates as an example of the application of this method the dissenting opinions of Judge Alvarez (*I.C.J. Reports 1950*, pp. 16–19) and of Judge Azvedo (*ibid.*, p. 23).

41 Oppenheim, L., *International Law*. Ed. by H. Lauterpacht, Vol. 1, 8th ed., London, Longmans, 1955, p. 168.

judges of this kind, advocates of legal positivism and voluntarism, wanted to seek the explanation of the obligatory character of law in the sovereign will of States and restricted the object of their jurisprudence to the legislation of States, thus engaging themselves exclusively in the commentary of legal texts; they downgraded legal science and confined it within the strict framework of the established system of law.[42] The situation was the same in the application of international law.

Despite strong persistence nowdays of some schools of international law on the consensual theory of States in the recognition of customary international law,[43] one of the remarkable consequences of the evolution in the jurisprudence of the International Court of Justice in the 1960s was that the consensual theory – which seems to have been affirmed by the International Court in the Lotus case – had been disregarded by the International Court. In fact, the International Court, during the 1960s, had to grap practically in every case, with what Jiménez de Aréchaga described as "la medusa armorfa pero formidable del Derecho Internacional consuetudinario" (the amorphous but formidable jelly-fish of customary international law).[44]

In the North Sea Contential Shelf cases, the core of these cases constituted the question of the opposability or non-opposability vis-à-vis the Federal Republic of Germany, of article 6, paragraph 2, of the 1958 Geneva Convention on the Continental Shelf, which provided for the principle of equidistance in the delimitation of the continental shelf involving several countries. The Federal Republic, although positively participating in the elaboration of the Convention and becoming one of the signatory States on 30 October 1958, did not ratify the Convention. The International Court had to examine the argument by the Kingdoms of Denmark and the Netherlands that the Federal Republic, whatever its position might be in relation to the Geneva Convention, was in any event bound to accept the delimitation on the basis of article 6, paragraph 2, because the use of this method was not in the nature of a merely conventional obligation, and therefore binding on the Federal Republic. The International Court pronounced that the principle of equidistance had a contractual value; it was therefore not binding on the Federal Republic. The International Court held that the relevant rule of customary law required that the parties negotiate in good faith in order to reach an agreement on an equitable delimitation.

The judgment was appended by some dissenting opinions, including that of Judge Tanaka. In his opinion, Tanaka firstly rejected a too rigid interpretation of

42 One may recall the following bitter criticism by Von Kirchmann on the Positivist school in fashion in the middle of the last century: "Drei berichtigende Worte des Gesetzgebers und rechtswissenschaftliche Bibliotheken werden zu Makulator" from *Wertlosigkeit und Unwissenschaftlichkeit des Rechts*, 1948, Cf. *Staatslexikon Herders*, IV, p. 740.

43 Defended for example by G. I. Tunkin, Cf. Jiménez de Aréchaga, *op. cit.*, p. 35.

44 Jimenez de Aréchaga, *op. cit.*, p. 13; Jimenez de Aréchaga, E., International Law in the Past Third of a Century. *Recueil des cours, Académie de droit international*, Tome 159, I, 1978, p. 9.

the two necessary factors of customary law – its *corpus* which constituted a usage or a continuous repetition of the same kind of acts and its *animus* which constituted *opinio juris sive necessitaris* by which a simple usage could be transformed into a custom with binding power. He held that the appraisal of the two factors must be relative to the circumstances and therefore elastic; it required the teleological approach. What was stressed by Tanaka regarding the *corpus* was therefore not the number of ratifications of and accession to the Convention, nor the number of the examples collected from the practice of States, but rather the significance to be attached to the facts and circumstances which necessitated it. Regarding the second factor Tanaka held that there was no other way than to ascertain its existence from the fact of the external existence of a certain custom and its necessity felt in the international community, rather than to seek evidence as to the subjective motives for each example of State practice, which was something impossible to achieve.[45]

Tanaka's legal philosophy in respect to the recognition of customary international law was pronounced in the following terms:

"The attitude which one takes vis-à-vis customary international law has been influenced by one's view on international law or legal philosophy in general. Those who belong to the school of positivism and voluntarism which seek the explanation of the binding power of international law in the sovereign will of States, and consequently, their attitude in recognizing the evidence of customary law is rigid and formalistic. On the other hand, those who advocate the objective existence of law apart from the will of States, are inclined to take a more liberal and elastic attitude in recognizing the formation of a customary law attributing more importance to the evaluation of the content of law than to the process of its formation. I wish to share the latter view. The reason for that is derived from the essence of law, namely that law, being an objective order vis-à-vis those who are subject to it, and governing above them, does not constitute their 'auto-limitation' (Jellinek), even in the case of international law, in which the sovereign will of States plays an extremely important role".[46]

An observation of the same kind was made by a most prominent professor from Louvain, Charles de Visscher, in the following terms:

"The descriptive methods of voluntarist positivism in vogue at the beginning of the century, like those derived exclusively from formal logic, are everywhere in retreat. Contemporary legal thought is intensively alive to the need of a new set of values in the foundations of a positive international law. From now on it refuses to see in that law merely a technical order without moral inspiration or teleological direction".[47]

45 *ICJ Reports 1969*, p. 178. Jimenez de Aréchaga does not fully agree with this position; he writes: "This difficulty may be a little exaggerated" (original in Spanish, E. Jimenez de Aréchaga, La costumbre como fuente del Derecho Internacional, in *Estudios de derecho internacional, Homenaje al Profesor Miaja de la Meula*. Vol. 1, Madrid, Editorial Tecnos, 1979, p. 391.)

46 *ICJ Reports 1969*, p. 178.

47 de Visscher, Charles, *Theory and Reality in Public International Law*, Princeton, N. J., Princeton University Press, 1968, p. 178.

9. Conclusion

The following conclusion may tentatively be drawn from the observation thus far made under the item "A moral or natural basis for international law". The first task is to seek the basis for international law and, therefore, the basis for restraints on the State's sovereignty more than ever in the Community of mankind itself, the existence of which is nowadays recognized as a legal reality. It constitutes the very basis of the legal life of the present world. The community of mankind is in this sense as much a moral as a natural entity. It is possible only through this way to emancipate the concept of law from the State's sovereignty to establish the authority of international law over the States. Every phase of the development of the community of mankind, which we recognize in our daily activities, demand creative progress, which, however great our immediate difficulties may be, justifies a firm conviction in the development of international law as a world law or a common law of mankind.[48]

48 Cf. Takada, Yasuma, *Sekaishakairon* (A theory of world society), Tokyo, Chugaishuppan, 1949, pp. 64–69. Takada discusses the basis of, for example, the international copyright law or the international industrial property law. Takada points out that these international conventions, although having been concluded through formal diplomatic procedures between States, they are essentially the norms of the community of mankind and their basis should be sought in the recognition of and the agreement upon the objectives of the conventions by the individual citizens of the community of mankind. Takada dwells upon this argument in his Die Gemeinschaft als Typus, in *Zeitschrift für die gesamten Staatswissenschaften*, 83. Band. Heft 2. S, 1927, 291 ff.

5.8. International Law in a Multi-Cultural World
Japan's Encounter with the Law of Nations in the Nineteenth Century

SHIGERU ODA

I. The intention of this short paper is to explain how Japan, a non-Christian Asian country which had been secluded from the outside world for more than two centuries, encountered in the middle of the nineteenth century the system of international law which first originated, and was developed, among the Christian nations in Europe, and how she gradually established her status in international society.

In the last century Japan, being a late-comer, adopted the legal norms prevailing among the European nations without questioning their validity or legality, and tried to observe strictly the rules of international law of European origin, Japan never challenged the rule of law based on Christianity and the European tradition. On the contrary, she endeavoured to elevate herself to equal status with other States within the framework of the existing international society. The position taken by Japan was different from the more positive, and sometimes radical, attitudes of non-European nations towards the existing international legal orders today. Two reasons may possibly be suggested for this. First, Japan in the last century, unlike many non-European nations today, was not a country which had been placed under the colonial régime of any of the then-developed European countries. Second, there were few other nations with which Japan could have combined to impose any pressure as a group upon such then-existing norms as might have appeared in her eyes to be disadvantageous for a new nation. Considering the basic differences of situation in which new nations with varying cultures emerge on the stage of the law of nations, I do not intend to imply that Japan can be used as a model for the Third World today. Yet I think that the example of Japan can be the subject of a case study of the application of international law to a different culture.

II. Japan's first contact with Europeans dates back to the sixteenth century, when Christianity, borne along on the current of a flourishing foreign trade, began to filter into Japan. In the middle of the seventeenth century, however, the Shogunate Government, shocked by the rebellion and expanding power of Japanese

* In preparing this paper, the author is indebted to the work done several years ago by his good friend Mr. H. Otsuka of the Ministry for Foreign Affairs, Japan.

Christians, decreed the complecte closure of Japan to the outside world and prohibited entry into Japan of all foreign ships except those of China and Holland, which could only sail into Nagasaki, a port in the far west of Japan. At a time when in Europe an international society was becoming established among the many sovereign States and the modern rule of nations was being formed, Japan was moving in the opposite direction by introducing a policy of exclusion. For a period of two centuries, up to the middle of the nineteenth century, only a trickle of knowledge about Europe and America reached Japan through the tiny window offered by the port of Nagasaki.

In the first half of the nineteenth century, the sea surrounding Japan became the scene of frequent visits by forein vessels and warships on the occasions of the Opium War of 1840–42 between Britain and China and the gold rush and the expansion of the whaling industry of the United States. Under these circumstances, a letter from President Fillmore of the United States, asking for the opening of Japan, was brought to the Shogunate by Commodore Perry. The appearance in 1853 at the mouth of the Bay of Tokyo of a US fleet of four warships under the command of that officer marked the beginning of an era of Japanese participation in the family of nations, and thus symbolizes her first real encounter with the concept of the law of nations. Soon after, in the same year, four Russian warships led by Poutiatin came to Nagasaki and also demanded the opening of Japan and the settlement of the northern border between the two countries. Upon hearing of the visit of the Russian fleet, Commodore Perry rushed back to the Bay of Tokyo with seven warships early the next year to get the Shogunate's reply to the President's letter. This, Perry's second visit to Japan, obliged the Shogunate Government to sign in 1854 a treaty of peace and amity with the United States, the first of its kind between Japan and the West. Having concluded that agreement, the Shogunate Government had soon to conclude similar treaties with Great Britain in 1854, and with Russia and Holland in 1855.

Two years after the conclusion of the treaty with Japan, the United States in 1856 sent a representative to Japan to negotiate a treaty of commerce and navigation. During the negotiations privileges and immunities, such as inviolability of the establishment and immunity of officers, were claimed by the United States as recognized under international law, and the concept of the law of nations was frequently referred to. The people of Japan, where Confucianism predominated, were surprised to learn that there was a law which ruled nations and regulated such matters as the conclusion of treaties and the acceptance of diplomatic missions and their immunity, and that all States were expected to observe such a law.

While application of the law of nations by the government necessarily began during the talks with the American mission in Japan in 1856, study of the law of nations as a science was introduced by some Japanese students who were sent to the Netherlands, Dutch being the predominant foreign language among the students in Japan. Some studied international law, and lectures by Professor Vissering of Leiden were translated into Japanese and published in 1867. In 1864 Wheaton's "Elements of International Law", one of the classics of international law, was translated into Chinese, and this translation was reprinted in Japan the following year. The keen interest of the Japanese in international law at the time is evidenced by the fact that more than ten treatises on international law in the western world had been translated into Japanese and published before 1875.

Realizing the necessity of foreign intercourse, and placing great hope in the law of nations, the Shogunate Government and intellectuals of Japan endeavoured to understand the law of nations through the political theories of natural law inherent in Confucianism and based on the natural principles which ruled the universe. Combining the knowledge of Confucianism with western notions of international law, they interpreted the law of nations as a system of universal justice and righteousness which would eventually bring equal treatment of every nation without distinction between the strong and the weak, or between European and Asian.

III. The faithful attitude of Japan towards the European law of nations resulted in her being quickly granted an honourable status in the international society of Christian origin, in spite of her different religion and culture. Mention can be made of some examples of how Japan quickly adjusted herself to the international law which had hitherto been unknown.

First, the opening of Japan coincided with the outbreak of the Crimean War in 1854; thus at the very outset of her participation in the community of nations Japan had to face the question of neutrality in international law. The authorities in Japan were already aware of the status of Japan as a neutral State under international law, and in a treaty with Russia in 1858 Japan required Russia not to undertake any belligerent action in Japanese ports. Later, at the outbreak of the Franco-Prussian War in 1870, the government issued a formal proclamation of neutrality. It is common knowledge that Japan for the first time adopted the three-mile territorial waters policy suggested by the Minister of France as the established rule of the law of nations, in order to sustain her neutrality during that war.

Second, it was in the *Maria Luz* case that Japan gained her first experience of international arbitration. Influenced by the school of thought of the natural law of nations, Japan successfully fought a case relating to the slave trade arising out of events which took place in the harbour of Yokohama in 1872. Some 230 Chinese on board the *Maria Luz*, a ship of Peruvian nationality, escaped and sought release from the Japanese authorities. The Japanese Government immediately proceeded to release them, regarding slave traffic as a crime against humanity. Strong protest being lodged by the Peruvian Government, the dispute was submitted to arbitration, with the Russian Emperor selected as the arbitrator. The decision given in 1875 was that the Government of Japan was not responsible for the consequences arising from the action which Japan had taken. This case demonstrated that the international law which had developed on the basis of Christianity in Europe was accepted by the public morality which had grown from the ancient Japanese culture.

Third, there were further occasions on which Japan had to face the practical application of the law of nations. During the war with China in 1894 and 1895,

Japan applied the international rules of law and justice which had previously been applied only among the Christian States, or between Christian and non-Christian States. During the war with Russia in 1904 and 1905, Japan again faithfully endeavoured to follow the existing rules and regulations of war. Both in the Sino-Japanese War and the Russo-Japanese War, Japan carefully adhered to the international rules of war by having the expeditionary forces and fleet accompanied by legal counsel to give advice on the legal conduct of warfare. Some monographs on the number of legal incidents and precedents arising out of these wars, published in English and French by Japanese jurists, attracted the interest of western scholars, and the actions of Japan during these two wars enhanced her reputation as a law-abiding nation.

IV. These are only a few examples of how Japan benefited from applying the international law which had to be universally followed. On the other hand, Japan did not always find it easy to get herself accepted as an equal partner in international society. On the opening of the door to the European nations in the middle of the last century, Japan, because of her different religion and culture, and also because of her ignorance of the then-existing rules of law, had been granted less than equal status in various treaties which she was forced to conclude. The diplomatic history of Japan in the last quarter of the nineteenth century may be characterized by her strong exertions to get rid of the burdens imposed on her as a new State.

Shortly after the opening of the door, the Shogunate Government was, in 1858, obliged to conclude a treaty of commerce with the United States, and this was followed by similar treaties in the same year with the Netherlands, England, Russia and France. The opening-up of Japan was then complete. These treaties, however, were distinguished by unequal features, such as the provisions concerning extra-territoriality or consular jurisdiction, restriction of tariff autonomy, and unilaterally imposed most-favoured nation clauses. Although the Emperor's Government which replaced the feudal régime of the Shogunate Government in 1868 was quick to proclaim, in 1869, its accession to the application of the treaties in accordance with the common law of nations, at the same time it expressed a strong wish to revise those provisions which appeared to be unequal. However, the attempts of the Emperor's Government were not directed to challenging the existing legal order by any radical means.

On the contrary, the new Government found it an urgent necessity to improve the internal structure in order to become a modern nation, one civilized in a European way. In many fields Europeanization, without sacrificing the traditional culture based on Confucianism, was regarded as a goal of national policy. The new Government stated, in its declaration opening the country to the world, that all matters of foreign intercourse should be conducted in accordance with the public law of the world, and, in 1868, in order to depart from outmoded customs, it launched a programme of reform, announcing that it was to be based on the principles of universal justice. Thus the Government also adopted the theory of the natural law of nations while carrying out its domestic reforms by introducing western practices. The seclusion policy practised for more than two centuries had kept the country from matching the progress of the western world, but it had enabled the people to foster their own culture, and the internal economy had also gradually developed, even under the feudal system. On the basis of this cultural and economic performance, the Japanese in the last century had reached the stage where rapid modernization of the country was feasible.

First, efforts to organize a democratic government resulted in the promulgation in 1889 of the constitution providing for the separation of the three powers, which remained valid until the end of the Second World War. Though this constitution can easily be criticized from today's viewpoint, it was often quoted as one of the most advanced constitutions in the last century. Thus Japan made a start on the way to a modern civilized State.

Second, the creation of a rich and strong country was accepted by the people as a national goal. The Japanese leaders realized that Japan could only preserve her political independence if she could manage to escape economic control by the western nations. The inauguration of the new era under the Emperor's Government coincided with the time when the Calvo doctrine was being introduced into international law. Being aware of the example of the weak Latin-American nations who suffered from foreign intervention as a result of borrowing from abroad, the Japanese leaders avoided foreign loans and tried to confine direct foreign investment to the areas of the ports which had been opened up to foreigners by the treaties.

Third, at that time Japan was occasionally embarrassed by the actions of some western powers who were demanding, on the basis of State responsibility, excessive indemnity for injuries to their nationals. Japan made the utmost effort not to give foreign powers any pretext for intervention. The judicial system was drastically reformed along western lines and all uncivilized punishment was banned in 1870. The criminal code was promulgated in 1880, and both the civil and the commercial codes in 1890. The basic concept of law was inherited from the civil law countries on the European continent. These codes were replaced by new ones in 1907, 1896 and 1899, respectively, and the fact that these new codes, criminal, civil and commercial, remain with some modification valid until today appears to indicate that Japanese society had already developed to the level of full adjustment to modern and civilized legal concepts.

The University of Tokyo introduced a course on international law for the first time in the nineteenth century, and in 1883 the first Japanese Professor of International Law started giving courses on this subject. The strong Japanese desire for revision of the unequal treaties greatly stimulated interest in the study of the western legal system and, parallel to this, the study of international law was also accelerated in 1897. The Japanese Association of International Law was established, having for its object the study of international law and the diffusion of knowledge of international affairs. This association can boast one of the longest histories of any such body in this field.

Against this background of the reform of internal structures, however, it remained no easy task for Japan to shake off the burdens imposed by the unequal treaties, or to be received into full and equal membership of international society. Negotiations to abolish the consular jurisdiction which Japan had had to endure for the previous decades started in 1871 with Great Britain, the United States, Russia, France, Italy, Holland, Germany and Austria, but it took nearly thirty years, until 1899, to secure complete sovereignty in this respect. Tariff autonomy was finally achieved in 1911 in relation to Great Britain and the United States, in the form of the mutual guarantee of most-favoured nation treatment, yet only in 1937 was agreement reached to abolish the perpetual lease which was first granted in the middle of the nineteenth century.

V. Japan found that she had a thorny path to tread as a new nation in the last century, and she was able to overcome her difficulties, after half a century of efforts, only by elevating herself to the level of the civilized nations of the west, through such domestic reforms as establishing a democratic government, improving the economy and providing a modern system of law. I have thus tried to explore the precedent of a new nation with a distinctive culture being successful in securing the confidence of other nations, and being gradually received into international society as a full member.

5.9. A Reappraisal of the Requirements for the Creation of Customary International Law

Nirmala Chandrahasan

In introducing my topic I would like to explain briefly why I have chosen the law of the sea to illustrate the proposition that the requirements for the creation of customary international law need to be reappraised. This is because in the law of the sea we are able to see at work, before our eyes so to speak, the economic, political and technological factors which are at work in forming new rules of customary international law. Furthemore, it is my contention that in the context of international law rules, the division of the world in terms of racial, cultural or even regional criteria is not always valid, because – as we will see in the law of the sea – geographical, economic and even military criteria could cut across these barriers. For example countries widely seperated as for instance Austria and Nepal may have common interests in relation to the sharing of the resources of the sea by virtue of being landlocked, or countries like USSR and USA – being militarily powerful States – would have common interests in the freedom of navigation and rights of transit of warships through straits. An examination of this subjects also indicates that ultimately rules of customary international law although largely based on self interest must also have the criteria of generality and rationality if they are to gain universal acceptance.

Customary international law is generally described as that body of rules which has evolved from the practices and usages of nations, and which has, by constant repetition and the conviction that the recurrence is the result of a compulsory rule, acquired the force of law. Hence it is usual to break up customary international law into two components: (1) the material element which is made up of the practice of States – i. e. conduct which is recurrent, consistent and general, and which therefore often presupposes a considerable lapse of time; and (2) the psychological element which is constituted by the conviction that the pracitice is obligatory, i. e. the *opinio juris sive necessitatis.* Article 38 of the Statute of the International Court of Justice states that in deciding disputes the court is enjoined to apply *inter alia* "international custom as evidence of a general practice accepted as law." Here there is recognition of the two elements referred to above, namely the general practice representing the material element, and the requirements of acceptance as law representing the *opinio juris.*

We will now examine some of the rules of customary law relating to the law of the sea in order to see how far these two requirements are satisfied, taking examples from both the older established rules, and more recently, some of the emerging new customary rules of the law of the sea. The customary law rule of the freedom of high seas is set out by Colombos[1] as follows: – "that the open sea, lying beyond the limits of the territorial waters of States connot be subject to a right of sovereignty for it is the necessary means of communication between nations and its free use thus constitutes an indispensible element for international trade and navigation." This rule is regarded as being one of the most sacrosant rules of customary international law. But when we examine its origin we find that the doctrine only emerged in and about the 18th century. Until then European States claimed proprietory rights in the seas surrounding them, and countries such as Spain and Portugal made even more extravagant claims over vast areas of the sea. It was the Dutchman Hugo Grotius who first espoused the doctrine of the freedom of the sea – *mare liberum* – at a time when Holland was becoming a powerful maritime nation. In Britain, on the other hand, John Selden espoused the doctrine of the closed sea: *mare clausum*. At that time Britain had not yet reached its position of maritime supremacy, subsequently Britain too espoused this doctrine when she became a great maritime power. This rule is a clear example of how doctrines of international law are fashioned by the national interests of States. For in this instance it was not principles of equity, reciprocity and equality which gave rise to the rule, but rather the commercial and naval interests of the maritime European nations. The element of practice for the evolution of this customary rule was constituted by the practice of the maritime European nations and hence was a regional rather than a universal practice. The conviction, if any, which prompted other nations to follow the rule was not a conviction as to its legally binding nature, but rather the predominant military and economic position of the nations espousing the doctrine. The generality of practice in this instance appears to have arisen out the rule, rather than the other way round.

We might now turn to considering some of the case law on this subject. *The Anglo-Norwegian Fisheries*[2] case is often cited as authority for the proposition that a general practice is a nessesary element in the formation of rules of customary international law. Hence it would be relevant to examine this case. Here Britain contended that the baseline, from which the territorial waters of a State must be measured, was the low water line and that such baselines must follow the sinuousities of the coastline. But the court refused to apply it to Norway for the reason that Norway had consistently followed a different practice, namely the drawing of straight baselines from which the breadth of the territorial sea was measured and further on the ground that this practice had been acquiesced in by Britain, and other States. However, what is interesting here is that the court did not treat the Norwegian practice as being an instance of special customary international law. The approach taken by the court was rather to see whether such practice was in conformity with principles of international law. This approach of the court was largely due to the way in which the issues were framed and to Norway's submission that the court should decide the case on the basis of whether or not her system of delimitation was contrary to international law. The

1 Colombos, C. J., *The international Law of the Sea*. 6th ed. London, Longmans, 1967, pp. 47-48.

2 *ICJ Reports 1951*, p. 8.

court adjudged that Norway's method of delimitation was not contrary to international law, on the ground that this method was an adaption of the general customary international law to suit Norway's particular geographical configuration and economic situation. Here the court said that the drawing of straight baselines by Norway constituted no more than "the application of general international law to a specific case". But the court treated this adaptation as being in itself based on extra-legal and economic criteria.[3] It was the view of the court that where there is a particular type of geographical configuration and an economic dependence on the sea areas, straight baselines may be validly drawn. It is submitted that here the court was in effect notionally deriving a new principle of general customary international law out of certain extra-legal factors, and the presence of the special divergent practice before it. While extra-legal factors are at the basis of all usages and practices, according to the traditional doctrine as set out above, the usages which arise from these extra-legal factors, must acquire the force of a general practice, and furthermore this practice must be carried out in the conviction that it is binding, before it can be regarded as custom. But in this instance the court regarded these extra-legal factors as being of themselves sufficient to validate a departure from an existing rule, and the formation of a new rule of customary international law, in the form of an adaptation of the old rule. Hence it could be argued that a principle of customary intentional law can be notionally derived by the court from extra-legal factors of universal validity, for example certain geographical or economic factors, and the presence of special practice, and that once the court has given such a principle its imprimatur it would become a rule of general customary international law.

The extra-legal factors are also very evident in the evolution of two new rules of customary international law, nameley the law relating to the Exclusve Economic Zone and the law relating to the Continental Shelf. The Exclusive Economic Zone is an area beyond and adjacent to the territorial sea extending up to 200 nautical miles from the baseline from which the territorial sea is measured. This area is subject to the specific legal regime of the coastal State which has a right of exploitation of the natural resources, while leaving unimpared the right of other States to freedom of navigation, and overflight, laying of submarine cables and pipelines, and other internationally lawful uses of the sea related to these freedoms. The concept of this Exclusive Economic Zone may be traced to a regional practice of the South-American States, which had its origin in the Santiago Declaration of 1952 of Peru, Chile and Ecuador, under which these countries made a claim to possess sole sovereignty and jurisdiction over the area of the high seas adjacent to the coasts of their respective States to the extent of 200 nautical miles. The declaration stated that governments are bound to ensure for their people access to necessary food supplies and to furnish them with means of developing their economies. This declaration came to be followed by other nations too, who unilaterally legislated for the establishment of Exclusive Economic Zones. A spate of such legislation was evident in the 1970s, when countries such as Guatemala, Mexico, France, India, Sri Lanka, Norway etc., passed legislation esta-

3 *Ibid.*, p. 133.

blishing a 200 mile Exclusive Economic Zone. The Guatemala legislation is noteworthy as the decree itself states: "The resources of the sea off the coasts of Guatemala constitute a patrimony of the country's inhabitants which needs to be safeguarded for the benefit of present and future generations." There has been some controversy on the question of the legal status of this zone. One view was that this zone was to be regarded as part of the high seas over which the coastal State had certain rights of jurisdiction and exploitation. The other view was that the Exclusive Economic Zone was primarily under the sovereignty of the coastal State with the latter exercising comprehensive rights of jurisdiction and disposition in relation to all forms of exploitation of the resources of the sea, while other States enjoy merely such rights of passage and overflight and laying of submarine cables and pipelines as are consistent with the rights of the coastal State. The doctrine which has now been adopted in Article 55 of the text of the draft convention of UNCLOS III,[4] has been drafted in consonance with the first view rather than the second.

In this context, we might also advert to the role of the 3rd conference on the law of the sea and the draft convention to which it has given rise, on the formation of new customary international law. It has influenced and is in turn influenced by State practice and the behaviour of States at the conference. The inclusion of the Exclusive Economic Zone in Article 55 of the Draft Convention has confirmed its status as a rule of customary international law, while also giving it a more precise formulation. It may be said that conventions in general have a role to play in the formulation of customary law as they often serve as the means by which emerging rules of customary international law are clarified and crystallised.

In the case of the Continental Shelf, too, the same pattern of development is discernible. Till the United States proclamation on the Continental Shelf in 1945, there was no customary international law governing the question of to whom the bed of the sea and subsoil adjoining a coastal State belonged. The US proclamation was followed by a spate of similar proclamations. In 1951 the International Law Commission was unwilling to state that there was a new body of customary international law on this subject, although it recommended the adoption of such rules. By 1958, however, this new body of customary international law had been adopted in the Geneva Convention on the Continental Shelf in Article 76.

In both the above instances we see instances of general custom which had developed from the unilateral act or acts of one or more countries, which has in turn generated a general practice among States. To that extent it may be argued that here there is the element of generality which is required for the formation of general customary international law, but what of the *opinio juris*? We will consider this first in relation to the Continental Shelf. In this case it may be argued that the proclamations or legislation by which States claimed the Continental Shelf was merely declaratory of an already existing right and not constitutive of a new right – see *North Sea Continental Shelf case*,[5] the basis of jurisdiction being

4 Third United Nations Conference on the Law of the Sea.
5 *ICJ Reports 1969*, p. 3.

deemed to be the inherent sovereignty of a State over its territory under the sea and therefore an *opinio juris* as a separate element is not required. But can this be said in respect of the Exclusive Economic Zone? This after all is an assertion of a new right, and as the Santiago Convention boldly states, made in response to certain economic priorities of the coastal State. Hence the evolution of this body of law does not show any evidence of an *opinio juris*, in the sense of a conviction as to its legally binding nature.

These two rules clearly show the inter-relation between economic factors and legal rules. In the case of the Continental Shelf the desire of the coastal States to appropriate the mineral resources, particularly the petroleum desposits lying in these areas, and in the case of the Exclusive Economic Zone the fisheries and living resources of the seas. It thus shows the operation of extra-legal factors in the development of rules of customary international law. The development of this body of law is clearly a development brought about by present day requirements, and economic pressures. Furthermore technological progress has made exploitation of the oceans and ocean depths feasible to a much greater extent. However, while the practice of States has been actuated mainly by self interest, the work of UNCLOS III has helped to introduce certain principles of reciprocity and equity so as to make it acceptable to all nations. Hence, for example the Draft Convention makes provision for the land-locked and geographically disadvantaged States to have the right to participate on an equitable basis in the exploitation of an appropriate part of the surplus of the living resources of the Exclusive Economic Zone of coastal States of the same sub-region or region – see Article 69. It also makes provision for conservation of living resources, and states that the coastal State should not over-exploit these resources. Of course, it could be argued that a convention is only binding on the parties to it, and hence any change or progressive development which it has brought about in the rules of customary international law is not a change in the general body of customary international law, but only applies to the parties to the convention and is hence binding as treaty law. But certainly it must be admitted that a convention apart from its being evidence of the existence of rules of customary international law also clarifies, and progressively develops rules of customary international law giving them a precise formulation, and hence has an effect on the general body of customary international law. In the *North Sea Continental Shelf cases*[6] the court agreed with this proposition. But can we go further and say that a convention itself can give rise to a rule of customary international law? In the *North Sea Continental Shelf cases* one of the arguments put forward by Denmark and the Netherlands was that although there had been no rule of customary international law in favour of the equi-distance method of delimitation, nevertheless subsequent to the Convention such a rule had come into being partly on its own impact and partly on the basis of subsequent practice. Hence the argument was that the Convention was the basis of the rule of customary international law. The court commenting on this said that such a process is a perfectly possible one and does from time to time occur and that it constitutes one of the recognised methods by

6 *Ibid.*, p. 61.

which new rules of international law may be formed although the court was unable to agree that the rule in question had evolved into a rule of customary international law.[7]

Hence it is submitted that in the regime of the law of the sea, the new rules of customary international law which have emerged exhibit a few differences from the old traditional doctrine. To begin with, the underlying extra-legal factors are more evident, and in some instances appear to have directly given rise to rules of customary international law through the court notionally deriving rules of customary international law from them, as well as by unilateral practice based on such factors, as in the case of the Exclusive Economic Zone. Moreover, the time space within which these customary rules have won recognition as being something which is time hallowed. Furthermore, the requirement of practice appears to have taken a somewhat different form and content from the traditional notion of practice as being comprised of usages carried on between States, and has taken the form of unilateral acts by States in the nature of proclamations or legislative enactments. Finally the *opinio juris sive necessitatis* does not appear to be so important or clearly defined in many of these customs. It may also be noted that international conventions, too, have a role to play in the formulation of emerging new rules of customary international law, and to some extent decisions of the International Court also have some part to play in the formulation of customs as the Court's imprimatur gives recognition to an emerging rule of customary internatioal law. We also see how regional practices often evolve into international customs.

Our survey, I would submit, indicates that the traditional requirements for the formation of customary international law, namely the generality of practice, and the conviction as to its binding nature, i. e. the *opinio juris sive necessitatis*, are even in the case of the older established customs as for example the rule regarding freedom of the high seas, largely post-rationalisations of custom which have risen from extra-legal factors based on national interests. But we must keep in mind that all the customary rules of international law to which we have referred, starting with the freedom of the high seas, though established because they advanced the interests of the States propounding them, were also functional and reasonable in their contexts. For it may be said that it is in the interests of all States that the seas should be free for navigation and trade. Hence in the 18th and 19th centuries it was reasonable to limit State jurisdiction over the seas to narrow limits – i. e. 3 miles, and leave the rest of the seas free for all other nations. In the 20th century, however, conditions have changed. Technological advances have made it possible for third States to overfish or pollute the coastal waters of other States. Hence we find that coastal States have to protect their interests and hence the need for an Exclusive Economic Zone. Thus it may be said that self interest and equitable consideration are not necessarily inimical to each other. But while States will necessarily emphasise their individual interests, it is the responsibility of the international community to see that principles of equality, reciprocity and equity are incorporated into developing rules of customary international law, and

7 *Ibid.*, p. 71.

it is here that international lawyers have a role to play. An example which illustrates the above proposition is the inclusion in the Draft Convention of UNCLOS III of the provision for land-locked and geographically disadvantaged States to share in the natural resources of the Exclusive Economic Zone, thus introducing into the concept an equitable principle. Although the concept of the seabed outside the jurisdiction of States as the common heritage of mankind is not a customary international law rule, nevertheless I would like to advert to it as one in which the international community as constituted by the States themselves have consciously introduced equitable principles in sharing the riches of the ocean depths. It is in this way that the principles of solidarity and co-operation can be used to bring about a New World Order.

5.10. International Law in a Multicultural World
Interventions at Plenary Sessions

A Realistic Approach to International Law

References:

Manfred Lachs

Bearing in mind the object and purpose of our gathering, which is due to the splendid initiative of Professor Atle Grahl-Madsen and the hospitality of the Swedish authorities, in this particularly favourable atmosphere of the Uppsala University – the reflections may be both timely and useful.

I rise this morning in order to present to you what, to my mind, is a realistic approach to it: to deal with the reality of law. This I have tried to present in a paper already sumbitted to you, fully aware of its imperfections. I am reminded of a pronouncement of the English Court of Admiralty made 203 years ago: "A pedantic man in his closet dictates the law of nations, everybody quotes and nobody minds him . . . and who shall decide, when doctors disagree."

This obviously referred to your predecessors, the distinguished jurists of those days. It was a harsh statement. But I am also reminded of Fustel de Coulanges, the great historian who, when applauded by his students is reported to have said: "Do not applaud me. It is not I who speak to you but history which speaks through my mouth."

Ours is a much more modest task. I do not wish to abuse your patience by repeating what I said in the paper submitted to this conference. I propose only to recall its main conclusions – and to carry the issue some steps further into the sphere of the tasks it faces; to make some brief comments on how it could live up to the needs and expectations of our age und day, and indicate the trends of its further development. I suggested that its principles and institutions must be seen in a historical perspective. I am grateful to find these views shared by Professors Theutenberg and Feliciano.

The nineteenth and an important part of our century witnessed the so-called "classical" tradition of international law which attained its cruising speed then: most agreed that the law, shaped, developed and influenced by Europe, was binding on other nations; soon other peoples were awakening to claim equal rights. Need I recall that, unlike the laws of nature, man-made law does not operate automatically. It is violated and ignored on many occasions. However, it cannot be denied that most of its rules are complied with – a point so well observed by my friend Erik Suy. They are implemented in circumstances which pass almost unnoticed much more than in the past. This notwithstanding, more attention should be given to the forceful motives which make States comply with the law.

There are of course those who claim that history is a sequence of haphazard events – I do not propose to analyse this or other schools of thought – I am concerned with law. In surveying it, one cannot commit what is rightly described as the fortuitous fallacy: let accident rule and abdicate the responsibility of rational appreciation of events. Here it may suffice to refer to the obligation entered into by our generation: the progressive development of international law (Article 13 of the United Nations Charter).

To remain faithful to the realistic approach, one must be ever mindful of the delicate role of international law. The difficulties it faces are, of course, as serious as the problems it is intended to resolve. The *corpus juris gentium* is being continuously enriched – the International Court of Justice has confirmed this on several occasions – difficulties arise, such as the identification of the birth of new principles and rules – the passage to the world of *lex perfecta*, the identification of the substances and scope of rules of law – and finally their interpretation.

At each of those stages law faces risks of daily distortion and particularly evasion resulting from suspicion and the reluctance to have the structure of law grow.

Whatever the difficulties – and they are a continuous accompaniment to all social processes – we may be able to ascertain the trend of development. This would by no means amount to a metaphysical infatuation with natural science, as a noted philosopher claimed in a different context.

It is essential that the political will should make them part of reality. There is no fundamental conflict between economic and social development and the interests of all men, no such conflict was found by the Stockholm Declaration of 1972 between economic and social development and the preservation and enhancement of the human environment.

These are some reflections on the state of the law and trends towards its further development. They are submitted in all humility. Today the task is much greater than that defined by Mr Justice Gray in the *Paquet Habana* case, who held that the value of the works of jurists and commentators resided not in the speculation "concerning what the law ought to be" but was a "trustworthy evidence of what the law really was". Hence also the conclusions of the paper submitted to you that the law of today is a framework for the New World Order of tomorrow.

Achol Deng

While commending the high quality of the report, I have a few observations to make regarding the position taken by Rector Dinstein on the issue of UN resolutions.

Indeed Rector Dinstein had a point when he observed that international law was as good or as bad as States would like to have it. One of the ways of enhancing the quality of international law is through the resolutions of the United Nations. While resolutions of the UN are not legally binding *per se* they are not necessarily bereft of legal effect. Some resolutions could contribute to the formation of the *opinio juris*.

Much as "what States do in fact" is important it is overstating one's case to relegate "what States say" to the position Rector Dinstein suggests. I would not belabour this point. Suffice it to say that what States say could be important. As Professor Parry Clive pointed out about a decade ago when a State recognises another no overt action is required; "recognition is a mere form of words". Besides we find encouragement for this trend of giving weight to resolutions and what States say in the jugdements and opinions of the International Court of Justice. In the Nuclear Test Case, for example, the ICJ took a unilateral declaration of the French President that his country would not continue nuclear testing in the Pacific as legally binding.

Thus if we give effect to what States say that could contribute to the creation of what Rector Dinstein thought essential for an efficacious International Law for a New World Order.

William Michael Reisman

I am grateful to Judge Lachs for reminding us of the effectiveness of international law in many sectors and of the fact that the reach of international law has now become universal, stretching its enforcement resources to the limit.

With regard to Rector Dinstein's theory of the predominance of practice over resolutions of the General Assembly, I must respectfully disagree. What States do is not necessarily law. In a domestic system, a legislature surveys actual behaviour and its social consequences. It does not then enact laws that confirm or validate that behaviour. It determines what pattern of behaviour is desirable, expresses it normatively and then designs strategies for its implementation. To dismiss normative exercises because they diverge from what their targets are actually doing presses the entire point of law.

Moreover, in international law it is not practice *per se* that creates law. Rather practice is examined as "evidence of custom" to paraphrase Article 38 of the Statute of the International Court of Justice. The practice that is surveyed includes actions as well reactions – protests, evaluation in terms of lawfulness, condemnations and so on. To elevate physical actions alone as practice is to enthrone force as law, an exercise in legal nihilism from which contemporary international law recoils. I do not with to imply that all Resolutions of the General Assembly are prescriptive, but to underline that these Resolutions are an integral and often effective part of the international law-making process.

Growth of the International Community and Qualitative Shift in International Legal Relations

References:

Juan Carlos Puig

We are really fortunate in this Seminar for having with us such distinguished scholars as Dr. Jiménez de Aréchaga and Dr. Franck. Their speeches, so full of challenging and refreshing thoughts, have been a clear demonstration of high academic standing. Although I agree with the core of their conclusions, I would like to make a few comments mainly on a devil's lawyer basis, with the purpose of opening the fire in this debate.

In the first place, I agree with Dr. Jiménez de Aréchaga as to the important role played by the principle of self-determination in the process of decolonisation. But I must confess, too, that in the last analysis I found no visible grounds to be exceedingly proud of it. Because decolonisation did not contemplate the responsibility of the former colonial Powers for the past injuries caused to their former colonies. In fact, decolonisation operated thus in the international level like the French Revolution liberal principles in the internal one. Formal freedom was granted while the people were and continued to be starving.

If the international community reached the conclusion that the colonial rule represented an extremely unjust situation, such an axiological evaluation meant also an *ex-tunc* injustice, that is to say, a situation which was unjust from the very moment of its inception. Therefore, a retroactive claim for damages was legally valid, the term "legal" having been taken in a broad sense. Unfortunately, relations between the colonial Powers and their former colonies were resolved by the application of the succession of States rules, while it seems to me that substantially they raised a case of due compensation for past injuries, and consequently, of a claim for damages. If the United Nations had proceeded this way, perhaps most of the problems brought about by neocolonialism would never have occurred.

In the second place, leaving aside the problem of its application to the decolonisation process, the challenging question posed by the self-determination principle is to find out what is the "real" law, the "positive" law, in the matter. Schwarzenberger and Vincent, among others, have made this point. In effect, is existing international law in favour of the self-determination and the non-intervention principles, or is it determined by the principle of the impermeability between the blocks? Because none of the interventions accomplished by the super-Powers in their own blocks and even in other regions of the world have been checked by the international systems of collective security either global or regional.

With respect to Dr. Franck's contentions, I am asking myself whether such a "qualitative shift in international relations" is good for the law-creating process in the international community. On this matter, I would like synthetically to make three points:

1. It seems to me that advisory bodies such as the International Law Commission should be maintained and enhanced. The problem with the International Law Commission is that it has been unfaithful to the Charter's mandate; the mandate to distinguish clearly between codification and progressive development, whose unavoidability has been pointed out by a set of learned scholars, from Yuen-li-Liang, Johnson, and Hurst to remove that frontier, at least to maintain it in very indefinite terms, but the results of such an attitude have been harmful in the long run.

2. The second point concerns the usefulness of multilateral negotiations when there are no visible grounds for expecting an agreement. The Conferences on the Law of the Sea and on the new international economic order are painful examples of waste of time, resources and prestige of international organizations. Unfortunately, disarmament – a subject still more delicate – is following the same way through special sessions of the General Assembly. Would it not be better to try first in limited fora where main currents of opinion could be well represented through a limited membership? Are we not encouraging a series of useless meetings of diplomats and experts only for the sake of the meetings?

3. As to consensus, the only problem is the problem of "getting a positive consensus". The sessions of the Conference on the Law of the Sea end always in a consensus: they always reach the agreement that no agreement will be reached before everybody agrees on an agreement. . . . Would it not be wise to return, at least for a change, to the majority rule?

Finn Seyersted

I refer to the discussion by the preceding speakers, and in particular by Professor Jiménez de Aréchaga, of the status of resolutions of the General Assembly of the United Nations as sources of legal obligations. Under present law, these could not be considered direct sources of rights and duties unless they reflect existing customary law. However, even new rules contained in resolutions could easily become binding after having been applied and thus confirmed by customary law.

In certain fields referred to by Professor Jiménez de Aréchaga, however, the resolution could be given a directly binding force on the basis of the rules of general international law relating to *occupation of territory*. The *high seas*, including the bottom of the high seas, and *outer space* belong to no country. The United Nations resolution and treaty on outer space state expressly that outer space is not subject to *national* appropriation. However, it does not preclude appropriation by the United Nations. Accordingly the Organization could appropriate these territories and thereby assume legislative power in respect of them. This would enable the Organization to enact, by a qualified majority, rules binding on all States. With regard to the high seas, a treaty is under preparation. But even if this can be achieved, we may need the legislative method on the basis of territorial appropriation to make the rules binding upon States which do not accede to the treaty.

Andrés A. Aramburu-Menchaca

I wish to thank Prof Jiménez de Aréchaga for his brilliant paper on "Growth of the International Community and Qualitative Shift in International Legal Relations". I agree 100% with all he says there and in the summary he has offered us today.

Nevertheless, I would like to make some remarks. In the first place allow me to recall, with Clive Parry, that International Law was not born with the UN. In the field of self-determination we should not ignore two historical manifestations of the same principle: the manifestation of the Ibero-American States and the Principle of Nationalities as conceived in Europe in the past century.

The latter is not exactly the same as "selfdetermination", but both are, I believe, related. Their link is the feeling of irredentismus.

With regard to the Ibero-American revolution (and I say Ibero-American because the expression Latin-American has a different connotation for the lexicon of the United Nations) the expression "self-determination" has had and still has three different meanings. In the first place – and the principal of course – it means emancipation, our "decolonization", movement that started in 1809 -1810 and finished with our total independence some years after.

But it also has – and this will be the second meaning – the option that a certain people had to become sovereign or be attached to another political entity already existing under a unitary or federal organisation or to abandon it afterwards, i. e. through a secession movement.

Finally, we find a third meaning which is related to the right of internal organisation, this is to have the political regime of its choice. This is something that becomes relevant for the policy of ideologic pluralismus, or what we can call "domestic pacific coexistence".

May I stress that I agree 100%, as I have already pointed out, with Prof. Jiménez de Aréchaga's thesis. What I intend to do is just a complementary statement, although I think that self-determination has been in the past something more than a political postulate.

In Ibero-America, the countries have been founded not only on the basis of territories in which they have succeeded Spain or Portugal (the doctrine of *uti possidetis*) but also of the principle of self-determination. Several treaties and arbitration awards, although historical cases, will make evident that self-determination was considered as a legal principle in the area.

Rup C. Hingorani

I take this opportunity to congratulate Professors Jiménez de Aréchaga and Tom Franck for their good presentations.

With regard to Professor Jiménez de Aréchaga's paper, I would say that Resolutions 1514 (XV) of 1960 (Declaration on Decolonization) and 2625 (XXV) of 1970 (Principles Governing Friendly Relations Among States) have confirmed the doctrine of self-determination as a rule of international law. This is despite the fact that self-determination is given as one of the purposes of the United

Nations Charter given in Article 1 and not as one of the principles of international law as given in Article 2 of the Charter.

However, I have some doubts with regard to Professor Jiménez de Aréchaga's premise that no military assistance is possible to people seeking self-determination unless it is authorized by the United Nations. In my opinion, people have the inherent right to seek outside military help against recalcitrant colonial power irrespective of whether it is authorized by the United Nations or not. This is clear from various resolutions passed by the United Nations' General Assembly on decolonization.

I agree with Professor Jiménez de Aréchaga that resolutions of the General Assembly project new rules of international law.

With respect to Professor Tom Franck's paper, I would not say that there is change from temperate weather to tropical weather. This is an over-simplification of the change. I would say that there is change on emphasis of values.

First, there is emergence of real equality among nations. Previously, there was only national equality, although some States were first among the equals. This has also brought the change in a attitude of the Big Powers.

In 1958, these powers were not agreeable to 12 miles territorial sea. But today these powers are too eager to accept 12 miles territorial sea besides 200 miles exclusive economic zone. Again, former big States dictated terms for agreement. Today, there is emphasis on negotiating for agreements. All this would show that it is a real change for better.

Abdullah El-Erian

I am moved to comment on an important point raised by Professor Franck. I refer to what he regarded as a challenge to the international lawyers' institutional and conceptual inventiveness and sensitivity. There is great need for reappraisal in particular of approach and sensitivities of international lawyers belonging respectively to old States and newly independent States.

I have noted with concern what may be called confrontal positions which impeded the attainment of consensus. I wish to note by way of illustration what happened in the United Nations Conferences on the Law of the Sea in 1958 and 1960. The way the supporters of the three miles-formula for the breadth of the territorial sea presented it caused resentment on the part of the representatives of the Third World countries. They regarded it as an attempt to impose upon them a rule which they thought should be replaced by another rule which takes into consideration the needs and interests of the emerging universal community of nations.

I believe the time has come when international lawyers from the Third World should not feel any longer oversensitive about „a Euro-centered international law". First, it is to be noted that the fact that Europe happened to be the repository of the heritage of humanity, this heritage is the aggregate result of the contribution of many cultures in the sense of a long history. Secondly, not all rules of traditional international law are to be viewed with suspicion. After all, equality of States is one of the fundamental rights and positive rules of traditional international law. The fact that is has not always been respected or has been compromised with is another matter which relates to the conduct of States and not the inadequacy of the norms of international law.

Conversely, the time has come for the international lawyers of the old countries to temper their oversensitivity about what they regard as an attempt to do away with traditional international law. They tend to suspect in particular whatever is termed "new order" be it legal or economic. I would like to suggest for their reflection that the Charter of the United Nations envisages a new legal and economic order. Two situations may be in order. In the preamble of the Charter, the peoples of the United Nations express their determination "to establish conditions under which justice and respect for the obligations arising from treaties and other sources of international law can be maintained". Chapter IX of the Charter is devoted to international economic and social cooperation. Article 55 provides that the United Nations shall promote conditions of economic and social progress and development with a view to the creation of conditions of stability and well-being which are necessary for peaceful and friendly relations among nations. When one recalls these important provisions, one wonders how new is the "new international economic order". The conception is established in the Charter and what is needed is the reconstructive way of international institutions to give it effect.

Customary Law: From ,,Universal" in a European System to "Regional" in a World System

References:

Abdullah El-Erian

I wish to congratulate the organizers of this seminar for their choice as one of the topics to be examined the important subject of customary law and its place in contemporary international law. We need a pause for stock-taking and soul-searching in the aftermath of the voluminous work of codification which has taken place during the last third of this century.

It was understandable after the creation of the United Nations that codification generated great enthusiasm. Two factors lay behind such an outcome. First there was a reaction to the failure of the only codification attempt undertaken under the auspices of the League of Nations in 1930. Secondly, the newly independent countries viewed with suspicion customary international law in the formulation of which they did not have the opportunity to participate. They, therefore, saw in the shifting of emphasis to conventional law their long-waited chance to make their voice heard and their views taken account of.

The time has come now for an analysis and thorough reappraisal of the respective roles of general and customary international law. There are topics which are not yet ripe for codification and we are still in need of the evolutionary process of customary law. There are of course instances when it is not possible to wait for the creation of customary law. An example is to be found in the field of outer space where it was necessary to formulate certain principles which govern it.

Achol Deng

I am impressed by the high quality of the papers presented by the Rapporteurs. Regarding the formation of customary international law I am happy to note that the requirement of the temporal element is receding with the background. No present-day international lawer says that practice has to date back to time immemorial before it can be recognised as custom.

The consensual element remains important, however. The presence of international fora, like the United Nations, afford an opportunity for observing the generalisation of practice that could contribute to the formation of customary international law.

However, I believe that consent does not have to be explicit. It could be tacit. To be sure a State that represents a persistent objection cannot be bound by emerging norms. But consent can be constructed through silence. Thus a new State is bound by legal norms to the formulation of which they have not contributed. States that abstain during the adoption of UN resolutions are bound by legal norms that ensue from their adoption.

Rup C. Hingorani

I take this opportunity to thank Professor Feliciano and Professor Rosas for their excellent papers. Here, I will offer a few comments on Professor Rosas' observations.

I would say that it is difficult for me to agree that because of proliferation of the number of States in the world community, it is difficult to reach a consensus. In my opinion, it is just the reverse. In 1930, there was the law of sea conference which failed. But, in 1958, there was agreement on four conventions on the law of the sea. Even now consensus has been reached on 12 miles territorial sea and 200 miles exclusive economic zone despite the number being 154.

It is still difficult for me to agree with Professor Rosas that customary international law is losing ground. In my opinion, real customary law is applicable to new States which have accepted it. The new States have only rejected that part of international law which is inconsistent with their new status as sovereign independent States. Consent being the basis of international law, new States have accepted many rules of customary international law.

Professor Rosas has observed that treaty law has superseded customary law. I think customary international law has not been superseded.

Perhaps it may be right to say that treaty law has strengthened customary international law. We may have to look at the Vienna Conventions on Diplomatic Relations, Consular Relations and Treaties. These Conventions have only strengthened the already existing customary rules of international law.

Customary law being brought into statutory law it is not confined to international law. As society progresses customary law is converted into national statuory law. This is the same case in international law. As the world community progresses, customary international law is brought into treaty law. This is quite reasonable because treaty-law is more certain while customary law is less certain.

Rudolf Dolzer

I wish to point out that it is necessary to recognize the ambivalence which is inherent in an evaluation of regional customary law from the viewpoint of a coherent system of international law. It was indeed correct that regional law had a potential to support and strengthen existing norms of universal law. However, this was not necessarily the case under all circumstances. The possibility that regional law could in effect weaken the consensus reflected in rules of universal law should always be kept in mind: the danger of a fragmentation of the international legal system and the weakening of the contribution of international law to the preservation of a global order through a tendency to recognize regional law in an unqualified name is necessary. In fact, developments within the last decades had revealed this danger. In the area of customary law, the universal rules governing the use of force had been challenged on the ground of regional peculiarities. In the area of treaty law, similar problems had occurred when regional organizations occasionally had made it difficult for the Economic Commissions of the United Nations to perform their functions. Thus, it was necessary in every individual instance to examine carefully whether a regional norm was in fact consistent with the principles and purposes of existing universal law; in case of a discrepancy the member States of the United Nations were bound under Art. 103 of the Charter to recognize and observe the applicable rule of universal law.

Nirmala Chandrahasan

In view of the fact that one of the speakers had mentioned that a regional custom cannot supersede general customary international law, I pointed out that in some instances regional customary international law has done so, e. g., the regional custom of the Latin American countries relating to the 200 miles territorial sea or Exclusive Economic Zone was at the time it was formulated – in the 1950's – contrary to the general customary international law which allowed only a 3 miles limit, but this rule subsequently superseded the general customary rule of international law, and it has today become in fact a rule of general customary international law.

Bengt Broms

After having carefully listened to the two speakers one cannot avoid noting that there is a clear difference in the basic attitudes of the excellent reports by Professor Feliciano and Professor Rosas. While Professor Feliciano seems to stress the importance of regional international law in given instances, Professor Rosas is more reserved as he seems to fear that the developemnt of regional rules may weaken general international law.

In my opinion regional international law is a source of richness for general international law. If regional international law is allowed to flourish – it is rather a sign of strength of the whole system. In this context it is worth while remembering that for the time being the differences between the rules of general and regional international law are not immense – to say the least. All geographic regions have adopted the rules of general international law as the basic principles. International law of today is no longer "European-based" and this has been the case already for a long time. Europe cannot and does not insist on any preference to be given to European legal conventions. And how could it be otherwise? The Charter of the United Nations already indicates a wide acceptance of similar basic principles, and in the extensive codification work that has been undertaken by the General Assembly the representatives of all regions have been well represented. In general, acceptable compromise solutions have always been found.

Having said that I should like to suggest that we look *inter alia* at the following problems. If the rules of general and regional international law coincide – there is no problem. If these rules do not coincide – which rules are likely to lead to new international law? And last but not least – what is the relationship of regional rules to the development of treaty law within the confines of general international law? What is the weight of general and regional rules of international law in the progessive development of the System?

Kamal Hossain

I would like to comment on the role of customary rules as "the constitutional law of international relations", as this was one of the roles correctly identified in Professor Rosas' excellent paper. Constitutional principles can in the international order serve as dynamic principles, which can be invoked in support of proposals for change, just as such principles have played a most important part in promoting change in municipal systems. Thus, for example, the constitutional guarantee of equality before the law and equal protection of the law, in municipal systems, have been effectively invoked by weaker and poorer sections of the community to require the State (the community) to assume a responsibility for adopting special measures in the form of reverse discrimination, preferential treatment, affirmative action to make it possible for such sections *in fact* to enjoy equality. Just as in the municipal sphere, welfare functions were assumed by the State, in recognition of the special responsibility of the community towards the poor, the weak and the disadvantaged, a similar development could be pereceived in the international sphere today as there is emerging a recognition of a responsibility on the part of the international community towards the poorer, the weaker and "geographically-disadvantaged" States. The international community, it could be said, is now in the midst of a transition similar to that which the nation states went through at the turn of the century -- when it began to be recognized that the responsibility of the community (and the functions of the State) should extend beyond merely policing and enforcement of rights to promoting welfare and helping the poor and the weak to realise their rights. International law and international lawyers could thus contribute towards the building of a new world order by identifying the constitutional principles such as equality, equity, international social justice and "mutual and equitable benefit" which could be invoked to support proposals for change, and elucidating the ways in which such principles could provide a basis for claims to re-distribution and re-structuring of existing international institutions.

VI. Independence and Interdependence

Working Group II

6.1. Sovereignty, Independence and Interdependence of Nations

HÉCTOR GROS ESPIELL

I. 1. It is evident that the purpose of my exposition of this topic cannot be that of analysing the historical, doctrinal and juridical evolution of the concepts of sovereignty, independence and interdependence; nor can it be that of making a complete balance sheet of what has been expressed with reference to the theory of International Law. That work would be clearly impossible given that these concepts are among the most complex and polemical of International Law; they have been and are inexhaustible material for theoretical and political controversies which are impossible to summarize in a brief paper; and they are tied to the essence of the constituent elements of international relations yesterday, today and tomorrow.

It is intended, rather, to delineate some concrete conclusions on the current meanings of sovereignty, independence and interdependence based on the Charter of the United Nations, the Declaration on the Principles of International Law Referring to the Relations of Friendship and Cooperation between States [Resolution 2625 (XXV) of 24 October 1970] and other pertinent texts of the United Nations as well as of the present international situation.

Having made this brief analysis and summary and having made the corresponding conclusions, I will try to project them into the reasonably forseeable future given my ideas of what the concepts of sovereignty, independence and interdependence ought to mean for the construction and affirmation of a New International Order capable of assuring peace, security and the integral, unified and harmonious development of the international community and of the subjects inherent to it.

2. We will analyse in accordance with this criterion and in this order the three concepts (sovereignty, independence and interdependence) indicating for each one of them its normative basis, its interrelation with the other two, its meaning and current significance, and its place in International Law and Politics today.

II. 3. The United Nations Charter refers directly to two of these three concepts. In fact Article 2 which enumerates the Principles in accordance with which the Organization and its Members should pursue their goals States that, "The Organization is based on the principle of the *sovereign equality* of all of its Members" (paragraph 1) and that "All Members shall refrain in their international relations from the threat or use of force against the territorial integrity or *political independence* of any State, or in any other manner inconsistent with the Purposes of the Unted Nations" (paragraph 4). On the other hand, the term interdependence is not to be found in the language employed by the Charter.

4. As we have indicated, the Charter does not use the term sovereignty in isolation but refers to this principle in affirming the principle of the sovereign equality of all members of the UN (article 2.1).[1] The content and sense of this principle of sovereign equality has been developed in the Declaration on the Principles of International Law referring to the Relations of Friendship and Cooperation between States [Resolution 2625 (XXV) of 24 October 1970]. This Declaration affirms sovereign equality as one of the "basic principles of International Law" and should be interpreted and applied interrelated to the others, given that "each principle should be construed in the context of the other principles".

Beyond the terminological criticism of the expression "sovereign equality" and the affirmation that the Declaration is, with reference to this principle, tautological,[2] criticisms which we do not share, it cannot be ignored that it is the terminology used by the Charter; that the content of the expression (sovereign equality) cannot be set aside, forgotten or questioned by the interpreter; that sovereign equality is a principle and not a mere "fact" which is the basis of the present International System; and that one must begin with this principle as it results of the United Nations Charter and the Declaration on the Principles, in order to know what today is meant by juridical equality, sovereignty and independence in International Law.

5. The expression sovereign equality (to qualify one of the Principles in accordance with which, according to the Charter, the Organization and its Members must proceed) should be understood in the sense that the juridical equality which the Members of the Organization possess, since these Members must necessarily be States (Article 3), is the equality of sovereign political States.

Eventhough the Declaration approved by Resolution 2625 (XXV) of 24 October 1970 in referring to the Principle of sovereign equality of States has stated that all States "have equal rights and duties, and are equal Members of the International Community, notwithstanding differences of an economic, social, political or other nature", the important point here is the affirmation that all States are equal before the Law[3] as a consequence of their being equal Members of the

1 On the history of the principle of sovereign equality and its inclusion in the Charter of the United Nations in San Francisco: Magarsevic, Aleksander, The Sovereign Equality of States. In: Sahovic, Milan, *The Principles of International Law Concerning Friendly Relations and Cooperation*. Beograd, Institute of International Politics and Economics, 1972, pp. 185-189.

2 Arangio Ruiz, Gaetano, The Normative Role of The General Assembly of the United Nations and the Declaration of Friendly Relations. *Recueil des Cours, Académie de Droit International*, Vol. 137, 1972, III, p. 574, paragraph 83 says: "On the very questionable 'principle'" of sovereign equality of States we find the Declaration too tautological for words. "'Sovereignty' is in our opinion, as well as independence, a Fact".

3 Jiménez de Aréchaga, Eduardo, *Derecho Constitucional de las Naciones Unidas*. Ma-

International Community, whatever their differences of economic, social, cultural, political or of any other nature.

This equality is an equality between sovereign States.

6. The concept of sovereignty is a necessary and fundamental part of International Law and of international life and politics today.[4] To seek to eradicate the concept and conform its incompatibility with International Law as certain doctrinaire schools have attempted, constitutes a useless and antihistorical effort incompatible with the world as it is and the inescapable and undeniable political and mythical force of the idea of sovereignty. In a world constantly and necessarily reminded of the right to existence of national States and the irreducible being of the peoples and which is the result of the rise and organization, since 1945, of nearly one hundred new States born into international life as a consequence of the consecration of their right to self-determination, to seed to eliminate both the concept and the term sovereignty is a utopia without sense or reason. The revindication of their sovereignty by the new States emerged from the struggles of peoples dominated by colonial powers and the affirmation of the sovereignty of those States which had already integrated the International Community which by then possessed it, is a fundamental historical and political element which cannot be forgotten or excluded in any current juridical presentation of the question.

For this reason it is not possible to eliminate the concept of sovereignty of States in relation with the world order. It is only pertinent, possible and logical to accept and include this concept, with a content that would make it compatible with the existence of a juridically organized International Community, with the demands of peace and security and International Cooperation to assure and defend the principles of the Charter.

7. Sovereignty today does not and cannot mean ultimate and supreme State power incompatible with the existence of a new international order regulated by Law. Sovereignty is a characteristic element of State power which typifies this power as supreme in the sense that in internal matters all other sources of authority are subordinated to it and that in external matters, neither the preeminence, superiority nor intervention of any other State can be admitted. Thus the importance of uniting the concepts of sovereignty and juridical equality. Every State is sovereign in the sense that it is not subordinated to any other State and that the other States cannot interfere in its domestic or foreign affairs whatever may be the economic, social or political system which it has adopted in accordance with its unavoidable right.

drid, Escuela de Funcionarios Internacionales, 1958, p. 48; César Sepúlveda. *Derecho Internacional.* 11 a. ed., México, 1980. p. 480.

4 Tunkin, Grigory, International Law in the International System. *Recueil des Cours, Académie de Droit International,* Tome 147, 1975, IV, pp. 30-31; idem, International Law: The Contemporary and Classic. *Essays on International Law in honour of Krishna Rao.* Leyden, Sijthoff, 1976. p. 86; Virally, Michel, Une pierre d'ange qui résiste au temps: avatar et perennité de l'idée de souverainité, *International Relations in a Changing World*, Geneve, Institut de Hautes Etudes Internationales, 1977.

8. The current concept of State sovereignty is compatible with the demand that "The State under the international order should comply faithfully with its international duties and obligations",[5] as was said in the respective report of the San Francisco Conference. The matter is of sovereignty under International Law, a criterion which seems to me undoubtedly acceptable today even though it has been and is inadmissible for an important sector of the doctrine[6] that despite its theoretical value, is not sustainable in the present international and historical situation, as has been recognized not only in another important section of juridical thought, whose authors come from different theoretical currents, but also in international jurisprudence.[7]

The Declaration on the Principles of International Law [Resolution 2625 (XXV)] recognizes and confirms this modern conception of sovereignty by including as one of the integral "elements" of the principle of sovereign equality: "Each State has the duty to comply fully and in good faith with its international obligations and to live in peace with other States."

9. However the Sovereign State does not live in isolation but coexists with other Sovereign States, "immersed in a plurality, The System of States, and even more concretely in a wider and more complex social group, the international society which cannot be reduced to the "inter-State".[8] This cirumstance, which must necessarily be taken into account in considering the topic of sovereignty, explains its content and characteristics.

Moreover, it shows the two aspects of International Law today which is at the same time a right to coexistence as far as it regulates, coordinates and makes possible the existence under the Law of Sovereign States and, in contrast with Classical International Law, of the right to international cooperation.

This right of cooperation, still embryonic and partial, the result of the interdependence of the States and the recognition of the International Community as the appropriate subject of International Law, exists simultaneously with the sub-

5 *United Nations Conference on International Organization. San Francisco, 1945. Documents.* Vol. 6. London, New York, UN, 1945. p. 457.

6 See, for example the position of Georges Scelle, who in 1933 said, "Dès lors, vouloir mauntenir la notion de souveraineté étatique, c'est nier l'existence du droit international", G. Scelle, Regles Générales du Droit de la Paix. *Recueil des Cours, Académie de Droit International,* Vol. 46, IV, 1933, p. 373. Also, among many other examples: Rousseau, Charles, *Droit International Public.* Paris Sirey, 1953, p. 88; Kelsen, Hans, *Principles of International Law.* New York, Rinehart, 1952. p. 114.

7 Basdevant, J., Règles Générales du Droit de la Paix, Souveraineté de l'Etat. *Recueil des Cours, Académie de Droit International,* t. 58, 1936, pp. 577-587; Jiménez de Aréchaga, Eduardo, *op. cit.*, pp. 103-109; Accioly, Hildebrando, *Tratado de Derecho International Público,* Tome I, Madrid, Instituto de Estudios Politicos, 1958. p. 232; Tunkin, G. I., *op. cit.*, pp. 30-31.

8 On this and other questions dealt with in this report the essential reference is to the excellent book by Juan Antonio Salcedo Carrillo, *Soberanía de Estado y Derecho Internacional.* 2nd ed. Madrid, Editorial Tecnos, 1976, which constitutes one of the most intelligent and penetrating current studies of the problems of State Sovereignty. One should also consult van Kleffens, E. N., Sovereignty in International Law. *Recueil des Cours, Académie de Droit International,* Tome 82, 1953, I, pp. 5-131.

stance of the elements of traditional right to coexistence of Sovereign States.[9]

10. The notion of sovereignty has been reduced by many authors[10] to the concept of jurisdiction, which according to them will be simply "the jurisdiction of the State according to International Law". Even though this focus is interesting and positive from the international point of view, it neglects to consider the political and historical factors tied to the idea of sovereignty of the State and the indubitable fact that there is a domain reserved for State sovereignty that, while it varies and evolves in accordance with what I have previously explained, possesses its own nature in every moment of its historical evolution. For that reason even though the contributions of this point of view may be considered, it is not absolutely necessary to rely on them to explain the concept.

11. Sovereignty is, thus, a synonym of irreductible and necessary State jurisdiction,[11] the basis of juridical equality of the States and foundation of their independence and the right of nonintervention. This arises clearly from the Declaration on Principles of International Law [Resolution 2625 (XXV)] which specifies that the principle of sovereign equality encompasses six particular elements: a) the juridical equality of States; b) the possession by all States of inherent rights to full sovereignty; c) the duty of all States to respect the personality of other States; d) the inviolability of the territorial integrity and political independence of the State; e) the right of each State to choose and develop its political, social, economic and cultural system; and f) the duty of each State to comply fully and in good faith with its international obligations and to live in peace with other States.[12]

9 Carillo Salcedo, Juan Antonio, *op. cit.*, pp. 16-17. Friedmann, W., General Course in Public International Law. *Recueil des Cours, Académie de Droit International*, Vol 129, 1969, II, chap. V; Guiliano, Mario, *Diritto Internazionale*. Milano, 1974; Ago, Roberto, La codification du Droit International. *Hommage à Paul Guggenheim*, Genéve, Droz, 1971, p. 95; Tunkin, G. I., International Law: The Contemporary and Classic. *Essays on International Law in Honour of Krishna Rao*. Leyden, Sijthoff, 1976. p. 56.

10 For example, Salvioli, G., La Régle de Droit International, *Recueil des Cours, Académie de Droit International*, Vol, 73, 1948, II, p. 114.

11 Chaumont, Charles, Recherche du contenu irreductible du concept de souveraineté internationale de l'Etat. *Hommage d'une génération de juristes au Président Basdevant*. Paris, Pedone, 1960, I, p. 114.

12 According to the Committee I/1 of the San Francisco Conference, the term "sovereign equality" in Article 2, paragraph 1, of the Charter is composed of the following elements: a) the States are juridically equal; b) each State enjoys the inherent rights of its full sovereignty; c) the personality of each State ought to be respected in its territorial integrity and political independence; d) the States, under the international order, ought to fully comply with their international rights and obligations. *United Nations Conference on International Organization, San Francisco, 1945, Documents*. Vol. 6. London, New York, UN Information Organization, 1945. pp. 69, 88, 230 etc.. This enumeration is, essentially, with editorial changes and some greater development, that which is included in the Declaration of 1970, according to the formulation adopted by the Special Committee in its second session of 1966 (Special Committee Report II, pp. 176-177, Report of the Special Comittee on principles of international law concerning

12. If sovereignty does not today imply the superiority of the internal juridical order over the international order, it is necessary for the full understanding of the concept to determine if this idea of State sovereignty presupposes the existence of "matters"[13] necessarily intrinsic to the internal jurisdiction of States which would be the unavoidable content of the State jurisdiction that can only be regulated by the exercise of the sovereign power of the State or, whether, the content of the concepts of internal jurisdiction or reserved domain are essentially relative and changing, contingent and evolving.[14] This second criterion is, without doubt, the correct one. The limits of the internal jurisdiciton of the State, the determining of that which is its proper, reserved and exclusive domain are derived thus from International Law and it is not possible to attribute to the so-called internal jurisdiction a content by *ratione-materiae*, invariable and necessary, but that this content shall vary and change from one sphere to another as a consequence of whether or not there is an appropriate international norm.

This conclusion is essential to clearly define the concept of sovereignty given the arrangement in paragraph 7 of Article 2 of the Charter which prohibits intervention in matters which are essentially within the internal jurisdiction of the States.[15] In effect, if one accepts – as today the majority recognize – that the interpretation we have given of internal jurisdiction and reserved domain of States is correct, it is possible to arrive at a concept of State sovereignty which would be compatible with International Law and the demands of the juridical organization of the international community such as it results from the Charter of the United Nations.

13. Today, after the doctrinal evolution undergone in the last years and the analysis of international practice and of all the contradictory and polemical cases that have been discussed on this subject, if this question is faced with complete serenity, it must be concluded that there are no matters which by their own

friendly relations and co-operation among States. *General Assembly, Official Records, 25th session, Supplement No. 18* (A/8018), p. 79; Magarasevic, A., *op. cit.*, p. 194.

13 The Spanish text of paragraph 2 of Article 7 of the Charter of the United Nations speaks of "asuntos que son exencialmente de la jurisdicción interna de los Estados"; the text in French "des affairs qui relèvant essentiellment de la compétence nationale d'une Etat", and the English text of "matters which are essentially within the domestic jurisdiction of any States". On the difference between "matiéres" and "questions" relative to this subject, see Bourquin, M., Regles Générales du Droit de la Paix. *Recueil des cours, Acadeamie de droit international.* Tome 35, 1931, I, p. 154.

14 De Visscher, Charles, Cours Général de Principes de Droit International Public. *Recueil des Cours, Académie de Droit International,* Vol. 86, 1954, II, pp. 494-495; Reports of Prof. Charles Rousseau to the Institute of International Law, *Annuaire de l'Institut de Droit International,* vol. 43, t. I, 1950 and vol. 44, t. I, 1952.

15 On the complex problems of interpretation of this norm: Ermacora, F., Human Rights and Domestic Jurisdiction (Article 2.7 of the Charter). *Recueil des Cours, Académie de Droit International,* Vol. 124, 1968. Verdross, Alfred, Le principe de la non intervention dans les affaires relèvant de la compétence national d'un Etat et l'article 2 (7) de la Charte des Nations Unies. *Mélanges Offerts à Charles Rosseau,* Paris, Pedone, p. 367.

nature escape, *a priori*, all possibility of regulation by International Law. And, consequently, from the moment that a subject is regulated by International Law by means of freely accepted conventional norms, it ceases to be a matter reserved for the internal jurisdiction to become a question that is also a matter of International Law.

As was said many years ago, with a criterion that has not only maintained complete force but has reaffirmed its validity: "The jurisdiction of a State is exclusive when no rule of International Law determines how the State ought to exercise its jurisdiction. If a positive rule of International Law exists that determines in what sense this jurisdiction ought to be exercised, this jurisdiction is bound to and is not exclusive of International Law".[16]

This criterion, sustained by the Permanent Court of International Justice[17] and by the International Court of Justice,[18] is perfectly compatible with the Charter of the United Nations and with the reality of today's world.

14. When States celebrate treaties which remove determinate matters from the exclusive national jurisdiction, they do not violate State sovereignty but make use of an attribute of sovereignty which far from being weakened, is reafirmed by this act.[19]

15. State sovereignty, internal jurisdiction and reserved domain are relative, evolving and changing concepts within their limits. Today they imply the idea of a sovereign equality of States which is not incompatible with either the International Order nor International Law but is a guarantee of the independence and equality of States and the principle of non-intervention in accordance with international juridical regulation which, according to the changing circumstances of each moment, determines which matters are of exclusive national jursdiction and which others have ceased to be and have passed to be regulated by both Internal Law and by International Law, or solely by International Law.

16. The recognition that all States are sovereign means that they all equally make up the International Community and are all subject to International Law. This supposes that in external matters they are equal and independent with respect to other States which have no right to interfere in one's domestic or foreign affairs, and that, as members of the International Community, they have the

16 Basdevant, J., Règles Générales du Droit de la Paix. *Recueil des cours, Académie de Droit International,* Vol. 5, 1936, pp. 606 ff.

17 PCIJ, Tunis and Morocco Nationality Decrees Case, Serie B, N 4; Danzig Legislative Decrees, Serie A/B, N 65; See: Pastor Ridrugejo, José Antonio, *La jurisprudencia del Tribunal Internacional de La Haya, Sistematización y Comentario,* Madrid, Ed. Rialp, 1962, pp. 91-98.

18 Peace Treaty Case, *I.C.J. Reports, 1950,* pp. 70-71; Interhandel Case, *I.C.J. Reports,* 1950, pp. 24-25; Nottebohm Case, *I.C.J., Reports,* 1955, pp. 4-65; Right of Passage Case, *I.C.J. Reports,* 1960, p. 33. See: Jiménez de Aréchaga, Eduardo, International Law in the Past Third of a Century. *Recueil des Cours, Académie de Droit International,* Tome 159, 1978, I, pp. 176-177; Podestá Costa, Ruda, *Derecho International Público,* t.I. Buenos Aires, TEA, 1979, p. 73.

19 PCIJ, Wimbledon Case, Serie A, N 1; Blix, Hans, *Sovereignty, Aggression and Neutrality, Three Lectures.* Uppsala, The Dag Hammarskjold Foundation, 1979, p. 11.

complete ability to establish direct relations of any nature whatsoever with other States and international institutions. This implies, finally, that in domestic matters, no other power is higher than the State power exercised by the goverment; and that no other State can exercise any authority whatsoever in the territory of or over the population of another since each State has the right freely to choose and develop its political, social, economic and cultural system "and that each government may exercise, to this end, its legitimate authority without interference or limitation".[20]

III. 17. Independence constitutes an essential characteristic of sovereign States. Although, in my judgement, sovereignty and independence are not synonymous[21] since the concept of sovereignty is broader and more general and refers to both external and internal matters, the two concepts are not only related but may be explained reciprocally. An independent State ought to be sovereign and to be sovereign it must be independent. Political independence, to use the expression of the Declaration on Principles of International Law, is an "element" of the principle of sovereign equality affirmed by the United Nations Charter (art. 2.1). This independence is "inviolable". The inviolability of independence and of the territorial integrity of the State as a necessary consequence brings with it the illicit nature of intervention[22] and the characterization as aggression[23] of the violation of the territorial integrity of the State, which is an aspect or manifestation of its political independence.

18. Political independence of the State, which is, obviously, the opposite of dependence, implies the absence of political subordination to any other State. For this reason, political independence is an element of the principle of sovereign equality in accordance with that already expressed.

20 On the domestic and foreign aspects of State sovereignty, see: UN General Assembly Resolution 724 (VIII) of 27 November 1953 and the Declaration approved by Resolution 2625 (XXV) of 24 October 1970. Diez de Velasco, Manuel, *Instituciones de Derecho Internatcional Público*. t. I. Madrid, Editional Technos, 1980, p. 183.

21 On this question: Rousseau, Charles, L'Indépendeance de l'Etat dans l'ordre international, *Recueil des Cours, Académie de Droit International*, Tome 73, pp. 171-253; Rousseau, Charles, *Droit International Public*. Paris, Sirey, 1953, pp. 90-92; Diez de Velasco Manuel, *op. cit.*, v. I, p. 183; de Accioly, Hildebrando, *Trata do de Derecho Internacional Público*, t. I, Madrid, Instituto de Estudios politicos, 1958.

22 Declaration on the Inadmissibility of Intervention in the Domestic Affairs of States and Protection of Their Independence and Sovereignty, Resolution 2131 (XX) of 21 December 1965. The title uses the term "sovereignty" and the first and second paragraphs of the Preamble "sovereign personality", "political independence", and "sovereign equality".

23 Definition of Aggression, Resolution 3314 (XXIX) of 14 December 1974. Article 1 says: "Aggression is the use of armed force by a State against the sovereignty, the territorial integrity or the political independence of another State or in any other form incompatible with the Charter of the United Nations, as stated in the present Definition".

19. But independence, if it is the opposite of dependence and both concepts are absolutely incompatible, does not indicate the inadmissibility or the repudiation of interdependence which in the International Community unifies and conditions the relations between States.

20. The Charter of the United Nations and the Declaration on the Principles of International Law use the expression "political independence" and do not refer, on the other hand, to the concept of independence without the qualifiying term "political".

This extreme, as well as the fact that always in these two instruments – as well as in the Declaration on the Inadmissibility of Intervention [Resolution 2131 (XX) of 21 December 1965] and the Definition of Aggression [Resolution 3314 (XXIX) of 21 December 1974] – the reference to political independence is tied to the concept of territorial integrity, has an undeniable interpretive transcendence.

In my judgement this was meant to affirm that the independence to which Positive International Law refers in order to confirm and guarantee the same, political independence which implies territorial integrity.

I do not wish to deny or limit the right of all "to freely choose and develop their political, social, economic and cultural systems", to use the formula of the Declaration on the Principles of International Law, nor that these extremes which make up the principle of sovereign equality and, therefore the political independence of the State, be disavowed. The intention is, simply, to make precise the concept of political independence, which is broad and all comprehensive and includes the constitutive elements (strictly political, social, economic and cultural) of the personality of the State; the State personality which, in each and every one of its elements, ought to be respected by other States.

But qualifying independence as political, is to recognize implicitly the interdependence of economic, social and cultural spheres; and interdependence which forms one of the constitutive elements of the International Community and the obligation of all States to cooperate together.

21. In this way the concepts of sovereignty, independence and interdependence of States within the present International Community are interrelated and reciprocally explained.

IV. 22. The principle of international cooperation is repeatedly invoked by the United Nations Charter (articles 1.3; 13.1 a and b, 55 b), and obligates the States to cooperate in conformity with the Charter as expressed in the Declaration of the Principles of International Law adopted by Resolution 2625 (XXV); this principle constitutes the manifestation of the present existence of an International Law of cooperation which is presented in a simultaneous manner with the substance of the classic International Law of coexistence. This International Law of cooperation, to which I have already referred in paragraph 10, was born and has begun to be developed especially as a consequence of the appearance on the international scene of the new developing States. As Roberto Ago says: "The Classic International Community had formed a juridical system which essentially corresponded to the idea of a simple coexistence among relatively strong political formations capable of taking care of themselves. In contrast, the new nations needed above all else a law based on solidarity and cooperation."[24]

23. The International Law of cooperation, result of a new way of conceiving international life – based on the obligation of States to cooperate and on the existence of an International Community ruled by law –, is based on the idea of the interdependence of States.

If all States which make up the International Community are recognized as interdependent in the satisfaction of their needs and the assurance of their just, harmonious, and balanced development, this interdependence obliges, justifies and conditions the international cooperation between States and the International Community and with each of the States.

24. Already in 1948 Alejandro Alvarez in his individual opinion in the advisory opinion of the International Court of Justice in the matter of "Conditions of admission of a State to membership in the United Nations (Article 4 of the Charter)", said: "States no longer have an absolute sovereignty but are interdependent; they have not only rights but also duties toward each other and toward this society" (p. 68). And immediately following he qualified the new International Law as "The International Law of Interdependence" (p. 69).

This International Law of Interdependence is what today the doctrine calls the International Law of Cooperation.

25. It is true that the present International Community is not fully developed as such; but, from the point of view of current law, it cannot be denied that the International Community has been faced as a Legal Community.[25] And it is for that reason and from that point of view, one can and should speak of a true International Community which necessarily implies the independence of the sovereign and legally equal States which form it and which are interdependent one to another and with the International Community itself.

26. The current interdependence of States which is the real basis of the necessary international cooperation[26] and which is projected in all of the areas which this cooperation requires (political, economic, social, cultural, humanitarian, *etcetera*), is the very basis for the idea of international solidarity and hence, of the right to development.

At the recent Congress organized by the International Institute of Humanitarian Law in September of 1980, in my paper on "International Solidarity and Development" I wrote these words which I think it valuable to reproduce now: "If development, a global concept which goes much further than economic growth and social progress and which is ultimately the same as the unfolding of man and his personality, cannot be conceived today without the recognition of

24 Ago, Roberto, *loc. cit.*, p. 95.

25 Mosler, Herman, *The International Society as a Legal Community*. Leyden, Sijthoff, 1980, pp. XV, 15-16, 27.

26 Blix, Hans, *op. cit.*, p. 18; Marin López, A., La Organización Internacional y la Soberanía de los Estados. *Anuario del Instituto Hispano-Luso-Americano de Derecho International*, Vol. I, Madrid, 1959, p. 38; Lowenstein K., Sovereignty and International Cooperation. *American Journal of International Law*, Vol. 48, 1954, p. 225.

the right of development, it must be concluded that there cannot be development without international solidarity. Only solidarity can give to the struggle for development a non-discriminatory, human and peaceful foundation. Only international solidarity supposes the full application of the idea of equality in international relations. It is for this reason that many of the most modern and intelligent studies of the problems of development, are today based on the concept of solidarity. The relation between the concepts of development and solidarity is necessary and unavoidable. Given the present degree of evolution of political and juridical ideas and the situation existing today in the international world, it can be said that solidarity is not merely the basis, but the very essence of the common struggle of Humanity against everything that underdevelopment and injustice mean".[27]

27. In these days the application of the idea of interdependence is particularly important, with reference to the energy crisis and especially in answer to the question of petroleum. The solution to this problem must necessarly be based on the ideas of interdependence, cooperation and solidarity. No partial or selfish view will permit this problem to be resolved. The question will undoubtedly provoke important changes in many traditional concepts and will generate new juridical developments derived from the concepts of interdependence, international cooperation and solidarity.

Not long ago, upon receiving the doctorate *honoris causa* from the University of Toulouse, Professor Roberto Ago expressed the concepts which are quoted below and with which I am in absolute agreement: "J'ai eu quant à moi l'occasion de dire qu'un souffle de socialisme devrait pénétrer aujourd'hui dans l'enceinte de la Communauté internationale et inspirer les relations interétatiques. Je souhaite que vous continuiez à la prôner avec ténacité ces idées. Les Etats, les gouvernements, les peuples mêmes en ont grand besoin, et pas seulement les plus dévelopés d'entre eux, ceus qu'à tort souvent, l'on assimile aux plus riches. Les autres aussi et notamment ceux que la nature a le plus favorisés dans sa distribution inégale des richesses du sol et du soussol, devraient cesser de se conduire à cet égard comme un propriétaire foncier de l'ancienne Rome, comme un souverain absolu '*usque ad sidera et usque ad infera*'. Tous devraient comprendre que seul l'abandon par chacun d'une vision par trop égoiste de ses intérêts, seule une solidarité accrue dans l'utilisation de toutes les ressources, de toutes les forces, de tous les moyens matériels et humains peuvent contribuir à rapprocher l'avènement de ce monde uni dans la paix et dans le progrès que nous souhaitons".[28]

28. The idea of interdependence is a very fertile and dynamic concept which can constitute the engine for the progress and future development of International Law. As jurists this is an aspect of the question that we must not forget but which on the other hand is a subject to which we ought to lend preferential attention.

27 Gros Espiell, Héctor, La solidaridad International y el Desarrollo, paragraph 14, *Congreso del Instututo Internacional de Derecho Humanitario sobre la Solidaridad Internacional y las Acciones Humanitarias*, San Remo, 10-13 September, 1980.

28 Université des Sciences Sociales, Toulouse, Doctorat Honoris Causa de M. le Professeur Roberto Ago, 5 juillett 1979, pp. 13-14.

In a speech by the then Secretary General of the United Nations, U Thant, given in Dublin on 12 July 1968, he spoke on this point with complete reasonableness: "As modern discoveries and technological progress cause a growing interdependence, this ought to accelerate a greater development of international law. The fundamental end ought to be to arrive at that fortunate day when international law occupies in the concert of nations a place so important that it would be as compelling as the law of our present rational societies. But in order to do that, it must be in agreement with the realities of the world, with the necessities of society and with the spirit of Humanity. Just as with national law, it cannot be allowed to ignore the challenge presented to it or to remain static. In the final instance it is the confidence of peoples and nations in the rule of law that can give to International Law its greatest strength, and to deserve this confidence it ought to be as dynamic as the lives of peoples and nations themselves."[29]

V. 29. An analysis of the concepts of sovereignty, independence and interdependence would not be complete and balanced if we limit ourselves to the interpretation of international texts and the current doctrine. As I said in beginning this report, it is necessary to pay particular attention to the present international situation. And the observation of this reality shows, together with the repeated and insistent invocation of these concepts as the necessary bases of current International Law, flagrant and repeated violations of the sovereignty and independence of many States by other States, violations which they try to explain or justify with erroneous and deceitful arguments and words intended to hide the truth. And most grievous is that these violations are not the object of adequate condemnation and the necessary repulsion by the International Community because of momentary political circumstances and because of lamentable weakness and fear. We are observing today a real weakening of these principles, a dangerous lassitude and indifference in the face of undeniable violations of the concepts of sovereignty, independence, non-intervention and non threat or use of force. And I believe that, for jurists and political scientists such as those of us gathered here together, it is not necessary to indicate the tremendous gravity of this situation and the circumstances which it brings.

30. As far as interdependence is concerned, the truth is that all of the practical consequences and conclusions that derive from it have not been extracted from that concept, to pass from the level of words to that of political reality and deeds which the present circumstances demand.

For that reason, the clarification of ideas and precise definition of concepts in this matter are so important today. Devoid of unreal utopias, but with faith in the creative force of International Law and its action – positive, though slow, difficult and complex –, I believe that the dispassionate and serene analysis of concepts such as those we have studied – made in function to the requirements of the New World Order – , constitutes an important contribution to progress, development and the implementation of this New Order.

29 U Thant, El Derecho Internacional y las Naciones Unidas, *ONU, Crónica Mensual.* Vol. V, N. 8, Agosto-Septiembre 1968, p. 133.

6.2. Sovereignty, Independence and Interdependence of Nations

J. N. Saxena

It is desirable to discuss each theme of this Seminar not in isolation, but as an aspect of the general theme, viz., "International Law and Organization for a New World Order", so as to contribute to an in-depth analysis of the status and structure of international law in the world of today and tomorrow. In any discussion concerned with that general theme, it is submitted, the message addressed by WOMP (World Order Models Project) to the world is worth bearing in mind: the present system does not work; it cannot be incrementally repaired; it can be replaced by one that does work, but not quickly or easily; the prospects for replacement are not encouraging, but are themselves a function of the seriousness and representativeness of the search.[1]

There is no dearth of literature dealing with the concept of world order especially within the area of international relations. And still one will not be far from the truth if he asserts that it is also one of the most ill-defined and inadequately conceptualized notions today.[2] The basic issue of international relationship for the foreseeable future is the tension between the quest to retain adequate degrees of national autonomy comprising of sovereignty and independence on the one hand and the imperatives of international interdependence on the other. It is the attempt of this paper to co-relate the concepts of sovereignty, independence and interdependence in the light of the present world order and see if there is any progress towards a new world order where those three concepts take a new shape in international law or, if there is no appreciable change, what can possibly be done in that direction.

Before this august body, neither any useful purpose will be served by going into the historical developments of sovereignty, independence or inter-dependence, nor the space and time permit one to deal with these details. But a brief reference would be necessary as an introduction to co-relate these concepts.

Passing through the developemnt introduced by Jean Bodin, Hobbes, Locke and Rousseau to the present day, sovereignty has meant many things to many men, and has been the subject of much learned discourse and disputation. To give only one illustration, N. Politis was of the view that sovereignty had been viru-

1 Falk, R., The World Order Project and its Critics: A Reply. *International Organization*, Vol. 32, 1978, p. 536.

2 Yalem, R. J., The Concept of World Order. *Yearbook of World Affairs*, Vol. 29, 1975, p. 320.

tally abolished in international relations, and if the expression was still used in official language, it was because of the lack of the visual adaptation, to the disappearance of a light which shone during a very long time, with a bright glow.[3] On the other hand, von Kleffens observed that the notion of sovereignty was not at all a ghost that could be *exorcised* at will but a spirit which was very much alive and very much awake; some may regret it but if they failed to recognise that fact, they abandon the firm foundation of reality.[4]

Sovereignty in the sense of international law can mean the legal authority or competence of a State limited or limitable only by international law and not by the national law of another State.

In the Advisory Opinion Concerning the Customs Regime between Germany and Austria, the majority asserted that Austria as a separate State had the sole right of decision in all matters economic, political, financial or other, and its independence would be lost if its sovereign will would be subordinated to the will of another power or particular group of powers.[5]

In his separate opinion, Anzilotti, J. elaborated the concept of sovereignty, and was of the opinion that external sovereignty or independence meant that the State had over it no other autority than that of international law.[6] While recognizing the concept of independence as the normal characteristic of States as subjects of international law, he pointed out that the legal concept of independence had nothing to do with a State's subordination to international law or with the numerous and constantly increasing states of *de facto* dependence which characterized the relations of one country to other countries.[7]

According to Korowicz, the Court, identifying independence with sovereignty, affirmed that sovereignty implies independence of the State of the will of any other power, and sole right of sovereign decision in all matters concerning the State.[8] He was of the view that even though the terms "sovereignty" and "independence" have been applied in treaties, diplomatic correspondence and writings of some publicists as if the two expressions covered two different and separate legal phenomena, in fact both notions were inseparable; sovereignty meant independence and independence implied sovereignty.[9] The only thing that could be said was that while independence was a negative concept – the State may not receive orders from any one, sovereignty was a positive concept expressing

3 Politis, N., Le Problème des Limitations de la Souveraineté et la théorie de l'abus des droits dans les rapports internationaux *Recueil des cours, Académie de droit international,* tome 6, 1925, I, p. 60. Korowicz, M S., Some Present Aspects of Sovereignty in International Law. *Recueil des cours, Académie de Droit International,* Vol. 102, 1961, p. 5.

4 Kleffens, E. N. von, Sovereignty in International Law. *Recueil des cours Académie de droit international,* Vol. 82, 1953, I, p. 128.

5 *P.C.I.J., series A/B,* No. 41, pp. 45–46.

6 *Ibid.* p. 58.

7 *Ibid.* pp. 57–59.

8 Korowicz, M. S. Some Present Aspects of Sovereignty in International Law. *Recueil des cours Académie de droit international,* Vol. 102, 1961, I, p. 10.

9 *Ibid.* p. 12.

the idea of what was the State's legal competence of what the State was authorized to da.[10] Korowicz emphasises that international courts and tribunals as well as many publicists have used the term sovereignty and independence interchangeably as meaning one and the same thing, and some would go to the extent of even replacing sovereignty by independence (though it would be a futile exercise). In the present submission, the two words, sovereignty and independence, need not be differentiated in a technical sense; they are mostly interchangeable but both of them must be maintained. Even where these terms have been used in the UN Charter [e. g. Art. 2(i) and (iv)] and other resolutions and declarations [e. g. Declaration on Principles of International Law Concerning Friendly Relations and Cooperation Among States in Accordance with the Charter of the United Nations, G. A. Res. 2625 (XXV) of 24 October 1970] the framers never intended to lay down a precise distinction between the two.

Along with sovereignty and independence of States another co-related concept of equality of States developed. The rise of the modern multi-State system gave a great impetus to the doctrine of State equality. The notion of equality is basic, precisely because in actual life individuals and States are unequal in many respects and differ from one another economically, politically and technologically etc. What exactly 'sovereignty' and 'equality' of States meant could not be agreed upon by jurists, still those concepts were accepted as a basis for mutual relations between States. We find both these concepts have been incorporated in the UN Charter, which is based on the principle of sovereign equality of all its Members (Art. 2(1)). The framers of the UN Charter, however, gave legal and practical recognition to the preponderance of great powers and other provisions clearly imply a surrender of sovereignty and equality on the part of the States not permanently represented on the Security Council. Inspite of this, a steadfast respect for the principle of sovereign equality is an essential factor in the development of friendly relations amongst States, meeting the needs of all States, particularly in view of the fact that new members of the international community are attached to their sovereignty and independence with all the freshness and warmth of their national sentiments. That is the reason why it is incorporated in most of the constituent instruments of international organizations. One has to admit however that general principles expressed in diplomatic documents, are frequently not borne out by specific provisions and they are there more for lip service than as an indication of their strength.

It has, however, been argued that when speaking about sovereignty, equality and independence in international law, one has to put aside the problem of factual independence, of factual situations in interstate relations, as international law takes into account exclusivevly the pertinent legal provisions regulating the intercourse of States.[11] Thus in the area of economic development, which is essential for development of human civilization, dependence of one State on another is essential. To a jurist, it will mean dependence of States on the rules of law which they co-created in treaties or customs to govern their intercourse

10 *Ibid.*
11 *Ibid.* p. 14.

and regulate their independence, but otherwise their sovereignty or independence is not touched as economic interdependence does not exist as a legal problem.[12]

While this may be a sound theoretical argument, it is not substantiated by the prevailing practice in the world, or one may say, it would be just stretching the chord beyond elasticity limits. There is an emerging consensus in the modern world that mankind is entering a new phase of human history depicted by such phrases as the "planetary community", the "global village", or "one world". No country in this world can be completely sovereign, for none is an island of self-sufficiency.[13] It can be safely said that even for the most powerful States, experience has shown that "independence" which many were so eager to maintain unimpaired, was merely an illusion (as in the case of the Oil Crisis for the USA and other industrialized States). "Perhaps the only way a country can remain completely sovereign is to avoid the modernization process-to eschew modern education, communication, transportation, and live a bucolic existence. However, the lure of the fruits of modernization are so powerful that all societies are constantly caught in the tension between their desire for a more rapid increase in living standard through borrowing, assistance, trade or other forms of international action, and the incessant nationalistic demand for greater independence and sovereignty."[14]

Of course, there are still those who feel that anything less than self-sufficiency and complete independence are a threat to national sovereignty. Thus the People's Republic of China attempted to be self-reliant and sought no outside help in the case of the massive earthquake of 1977, stoutly maintaining that they could take care of it themselves. But even the Chinese leaders reportedly decided last autumn, though understating their nation's drought and flood calamities, to make their first appeal for international relief aid in more than 30 years.[15] Before quietly approaching the UN last November, Chinese officials carefully weighed both the international and domestic political consequences of seeking foreign relief aid. Their decision to go ahead involved reversing to some extent a policy of selfreliance that had been a source of great pride to them since 1949.

The needs of the national and international community, therefore, are now far greater because of the increasing effects of the interdependence of peoples. Alvarez J. in his individual opinion in the advisory opinion of ICJ in the matter of "Conditions of Admission of a State to Membership in the United Nations", observed:

"States no longer have an absolute sovereignty but are interdependent, they have not only rights but also duties towards each other and toward this society", and

12 *Ibid* p. 15–16.

13 Kleinjans, E., The World as a System – A Framework for Thinking, in Bickley V. & Philip P. J. ed., *Cultural Relations in the Global Community; Problems and Prospects.* New Delhi, Abhinav publications, 1981. p. 29.

14 *Ibid.*

15 Sterba, P. J., Peking had understated disasters in seeking aid, The New York Times News Service (*Times of India,* 23 March 1981).

he qualified the new International Law as "The International Law of Interdependence."[16]

Secretary General U Thant also stated: "No nation, however powerful and wealthy, is now-a-days sufficient unto itself. Interdependence is a vital factor in our world and so is the existence of international machinery to promote an orderly world development."[17]

Mr. Cassen, the principal author of one of the Brandt Commission papers, has very ably described inter-dependence in the following way:[18]

> "Many broad and not necessarily welldefined accounts of interdependence in international affairs can be found, suggesting that it is growing. Events in one part of the world, political events, which earlier might have sent out ripples only over a small local surface, now have wider repercussions. Recognition of the earth as an ecological system with exhaustible resources, disappearing animal species, and a fragile environment, has created an awareness of the harm that can be done by selfish actions or neglect in an unregulated world – harm which may fall on innocent and guilty alike. *Economic interdependence* grows if economies specialize in production and rely increasingly on trade for the supply of necessities and the generation of employment. Above everything looms the question of peace, and wheter some means can be found to preserve it less expensive and more reliable than preparing for war.
>
> "Interdepence" is a term loosely used, sometimes referring to nothing more than frequency of interaction, or to the fact that certain forms of politisation of international relations, together with the growth and acceleration of communications have begun to imply an increase in the impact events in almost any country can have in many others. But the term can be given a more precise meaning in our context: in the *dictionary sense, interdependence means simply that countries rely on each other in various ways; or it could be defined more strongly to imply a relationship between countries such that if it is upset damage is done to all the countries.*"

It is the fact of interdependence which may enhance the possibility of mutual interest in reforming the present world order, and this mutual interest may work perhaps more than anything else as a basis for persuading governments to work for changes not only in the international economic system, but in other fields also like world food shortage, the population explosion, the problem of hijacking, the traffic in drugs, the use of deep sea-beds resources, disarmament, ecology, en-

16 Alvarez A. in his individual opinion of the Advisory opinion of the International Court in the matter of "Conditions of Admission of a State to Membership in the United Nations", *ICJ Report 1948*, pp. 68–69, quoted by Prof. H. Gros Espiell in Sovereignty, Independence and Interdependence of Nations, p. *supra.*

17 Message by Secretary-General on the occasion of the New Year 1967 issued at Headquarters, 23 Dec. 1966, (Press Release SG/SM/632).

18 Cassen, R. H., "Mutual Interests" in the Brandt Commission Papers, Selected Background Papers prepared for the Independent Commission on International Development Issues. Leck, Clausen & Bosse, 1978–1979.

ergy crisis etc. It is a welcome sign that "the UN is preparing to discuss how the sun, the wind, the oceans, not to mention bullocks and donkeys – can help mankind's increasing demands for energy, at a conference on new and renewable sources of energy in Nairobi in August. It will be the first time the world's energy problems be discussed by the entire UN membership, according to Mr. Enrique Iglesias of Uruguay, the Conference Secretary-General."[19] This is a clear manifestation that the idea of inter-dependence is taking deep roots in the present world order.

It is apparent that International Organizations have been playing a vital role in increasing the interdependence among nations and laying down an approach to a different world order in the 20th Century, starting from the Leagues of Nations and manifested at present by the United Nations and its specialized agencies. According to Luard some of the techniques developed by these International Organizations to increase their authority with governments (and thus make them interdependent) are rule-making, standard-setting, co-ordination, administration of common services, development of information, educational or research services, and rapid expansion of activity in assistance. He has very ably indicated certain difficulties in the working of those agencies, e.g., the division of functions between organs within the agencies is sometimes blurred; execution in most political systems is clearly detached from the main deliberative and decision-making process; the Councils, as at present constituted, are badly adapted to the key role they need now to play within each Agency,[21] and suggests that functionalism alone is not enough, what is needed is something over and above functional co-operation if a significant influence on national competitiveness is to be exercised: a deliberate political act of will by member governments, and perhaps by their *publics.*[22]

It may thus be said that international organisations have not been very successful as instruments of world order mainly because they are based upon the principle of sovereign consent for organisational action. No doubt attempts have been made and are being made to remove the short-comings and improve their working, there are no bright prospects in the near future and a sort of lull appears to be prevailing now.

We, therefore, perceive another movement towards the creation of a new world order in this era of inter-disciplinary approach, viz. systems approach to world-order.[23] The basic tenet of this approach is the unity of the world as a system of inter-related parts, and as soon as one part is touched, other parts are affected. The system is composed of subsystems which flow into one another and

19 *Times of India*, 2 June 1981.
20 Luard, D. E. T., *International Agencies: the Emerging Framework of Interdependence*. London, Macmillan, 1977, p. 308–310.
21 *Ibid.* 312–314.
22 *Ibid.* p. 327.
23 Hoffmann, S., International Organization and the International System, *International Organization*, Vol. XXIV, No. 3, 1970, p. 399; Yalem, R. J., "The Concept of World Order", *Yearbook of World Affairs*, vol. 29, 1975, p. 320.

are usually inter-dependent. Thus in the world-order system, there will be an economic subsystem, an international legal subsystem, a political subsystem, a socio-cultural subsystem etc. At one level each of these subsystems is an autonomous entity, but at another level all interact.[24] Kleinjans gives an example of this:

> "The Philippine Government imports approximately 90 per cent of its oil from the Middle East. This is part of their and the world's economic or possibly resource system (sub-system). Internally, problems have arisen with the Moros on the island of Mindanao. This is an event in their political subsystem. The Muslims in Mindanao are supplied arms by Libya – part of the worlds military or arms subsystem – and the Muslims of Mindanao are related religiously to the Muslims of the Middle East wherefrom they get their oil. This is part of the earth's cultural subsystem. Therefore, the Philippine Government sends emissaries to the Middle East to make sure that relationships with the Arab States remain good since they fear that the Arabs, because they are Muslims, may cut off the supply of oil in sympathy with Muslims in Mindanao State.[25] This is a good illustration of how the subsystems work in a world order system. The notable thing is that in this approach, we pass on from interdependence of States to interdependence of sub-systems in a world-order.
>
> Under the systemic view of world order there is a possibility of enhanced human dignity, a feeling of equality, greater self-respect and dignity than it is apparent in the present system. As States, whether large or small, strong or weak, are inter-related, and their actions do affect each other, it would be worth while to think and talk about distributing or redistributing the world's resources in order to make the world system work more effectively for all mankind. Ervin Laszlow has observed: A village is a unit because every one knows everyone else and takes a role *vis-à-vis* the rest. The world will be a true global village when similar conditions prevail."[26]

Thus it may be concluded that the sovereignty of States has a new transformation into the interdependence of States through international organisation, and as that alone may not be fully workable, a wider vision is being given to interdependence under the systemic approach to world order. For this world order system approach what is needed is a completely re-oriented educational system to change the outlook of the youth in all nations and cultures, towards the unity of the world as a system. Perhaps a beginning can be made by opening United Nations Schools and Universities in all the States.

Conclusion

As long as there exists more than one national State, the concept of sovereignty and independence, of the individual State will continue to be an essential qualif-

24 Kleinjans, E., The World as a System – a Framework for Thinking, in Bickley V. an Philip P. J. ed., *op. cit.*, p. 27.

25 *Ibid.*

26 Laszlo, Ervin, *The Systems View of the World; The Natural Philosophy of the New Developments in the Sciences.* New York, G. Braziller, 1972, VIII, 131 p.

ication, in law as in practice, for membership in the international community, for those concepts are the inescapable justification of the authority of the State in an integrated international community. One can believe that sovereignty will continue to be a viable concept without denying that it will continue to fail to fit all the facts for in an international community increasingly composed of developed and undeveloped individual communities, it will indeed be surprising if it is not subjected to frequent distortions, as it has been in the past.[27]

But at the same time it is equally clear that sovereignty and independence cannot have a static, rigid meaning. The question for the future is: how far the sovereign States will learn to control themselves, will they realise that their future must be a shared one? In many fields sovereignty is taking a new dimension in the form of cooperation and interdependence, in the making of decisions that directly affect the citizens' well-being; and international organizations offer a forum for such participation. In other fields, e. g., armament, both traditional and nuclear, no appreciable headway has been made. Rather the world is edging closer to nuclear war, which might mean self-destruction, as has recently been pointed out by the Stockholm International Peace Research Institute (SIPRI) in its 1981 Year Book.[28] The only hope for a new world order lies in the realization that in this world, interdependence is a condition that affects each State's independent status in different ways and in different degrees and at the same time, it is a value that has the capability of developing new insight into mutual understanding. So there must be a continuous search and research for that interdependence. This is possible through international institutions and through a systemic approach to world order. Certain improvements in the international institutional machinery and a restructuring of education for young people in all nations and cultures to make them realise that this world is a system, will go a long way to achieve the desired objective. "Education holds the key to a large number of the world's problems . . . [it] must obviously be linked to the realities of life without being too much overawed by them."[29]

27 Hinsley, F. H., The Concept of Sovereignty and the Relations between States. *Journal of International Affairs*, Vol. XXI, 1967, p. 252.

28 *Times of India*, 5 June 1981.

29 U Thant, Secretary General, Address at the University of Michigan, Ann Arbor, Michigan, 31 March 1967 (Press Release SG/SM/685).

6.3. A Papaya-Seller: Distributive Justice and New World Order

J. N. Saxena

A papaya-seller, carrying a basket full of papayas on his head, comes to my locality every day. When I have to purchase the fruit from him, I call him and help him put down his load on the ground. Every time I call him, the first words he utters even before he starts weighing the fruit, when translated mean: "God, give bread to every-one."

To me that poor man in a developing country is praying to God for distributive justice and for a new world order. He does not know that he has a right (even if not incorporated in the Chapter on Fundamental Rights, at least included in the Chapter on Directive Principles of State Policy in the Constitution of India) to ask his government for what he is praying to God, he is unaware that the preamble of FAO provides for "... ensuring humanity's freedom from hunger" and he is, after all, a human being, he has never heard of the Universal Declaration of Human Rights which in its Art. 25 lays down that "every-one has the right to food", he is ignorant of the fact, that Art. 11 of the International Covenant on Economic, Social and Cultural Rights incorporates that "the States Parties to the present Covenant recognize the right of every-one to ... adequate food ...", and his country has ratified this Covenant, and even if he would have known, there would hardly have been any difference in his attitude. It is remarkable that he is praying to God to give bread to every-one, and not only to him or to his family, and certainly when he is praying for every-one, he is making no distinction between the poor in East or West, North or South. It is also notable that he is praying only for bread, and not for "bread and butter" as the phrase goes in the English language. According to his concept of distributive justice and a world order, at least bread must be available as that is required for "minimal subsistence" or is a basic need, and that should be available to all, for he knows very well, and rightly so, that today he is living in a world where that is not so.

Some may view the above situation as a moral question, courting simply an abstract possibility, having no reasonable answer. Richard Brandt emphasises:

"Any discussion of the basic ethical principles of economic distribution is likely to seem abstract and utopian, unless we see that our usual abbreviated procedure for deciding questions of economic justice really does not go to the heart of the matter. Ordinarily we try to answer questions about economic justice while taking for granted a complex institutional frame-work, and without questioning or assessing the frame-work. If we do this, we over-look the main relevant principles."[1] It is submitted that the real problem falls within the scope of distributive justice as an element of social and economic order towards which sufficient attention has not been paid by jurists either at the national or international level.

Distributive justice embraces "the whole economic dimension of social justice, the entire question of the proper distribution of goods and services within the society".[2] The fundamental precepts of distributive justice, serving as criteria for evaluating the propriety or justice of distribution, have been expressed through a number of aphoristic maxims, such as "To each according to his need", "To each according to his worth", "To each according to his merit", "To each according to his contribution to the common good", etc.[3]

The tasks of distributive justice in an economy of scarcity are obviously far more complex and demanding than in an economy of sufficiency, abundance or super-abundance. In fact, the question of distributive justice becomes of vital importance only in an economy of scarcity and more so in relation to goods required for basic necessity. Reschar has proposed the over-riding principle of distributive justice designed to meet the problems of an "economy of scarcity", stating that the number of individuals whose share of utility falls below the minimal level is to be made as small as possible.[4]

The main problem, therefore, of distributive justice is the choice of a social system so designed that the resulting distribution is just (in the sense of a minimal utility floor below which no one should be pressed) however things turn out.[5] For achieving this end, it is necessary to set the social and economic process within the surroundings of suitable political and legal institutions, for without the proper arrangement of these background institutions the outcome of the distributive process will not be just.[6]

When attempting to employ the concept of distributive justice in international relations, one is confronted with two problems:

(I) its meaning, and

(II) its relevance in interstate relations

Controversy surrounding the concept of distributive justice even in a national society, the job is all the more difficult to formulate its conception at the international level. It is, however, noteworthy that today a very common approach, accepted as the basis of domestic policy of nearby all the States, whether capitalist or socialist, whether democracies or dictatorships, is an attempt to adopt egalitarian premises of the welfare State, such that each member of society has a right to the goods and services minimally necessary to sustain a human life. Thus it

1 Brandt, Richard B., *Ethical Theory: the problems of normative and critical ethics*. Englewood Cliffs, N. J., Prentice-Hall, 1959, p. 411.

2 Rescher, Nicholas, *Distributive Justice; a constructive critique of the utilitarian theory of distribution*. Indianapolis, Bobbs-Merrill, 1966. p. 5.

3 *Ibid.*, p. 73–83.

4 *Ibid.*, p. 28–30.

5 Rawls, J., *A theory of Justice*. Cambridge, Mass., Belknap Press of Harvard University Press, 1971, p. 274–75.

6 *Ibid.*

may be said that there is a common attempt, individually of course, of nearly all the governments that basic needs of each member of their society be fulfilled. With this foundation, there can be an attempt to build a doctrine extending that approach to the whole world and applying those principles cross-culturally to the whole human race, asserting that in a world where some societies enjoy a degree of prosperity, e. g., the industrialized developed States, there is no defensible reason why the basic human needs of all people throughout the world should not be met.[8]

Though the question of equitable sharing among the States of, e. g., river-waters and fisheries has been there for long, the consciousness of inequalities, specially in the economic field that have arisen today in the world, is without precedent. The imbalances and scarcities are such that they have become a danger to the very existence of the social fabric of some areas resulting in a natural demand for distributive justice. So whatever may be the complexities attributable to the concept of distributive justice, one thing is certain that it incorporates even at the international levels, the satisfaction of the basic needs of a State, or "minimal utility floor" below which no State should be pressed.

The relevance of distributive justice, besides its moral worth, is that it is a step towards a better international society where the chances of unrest and upheavels are, to some extent, minimised. It may be said to be a condition leading towards peace. One cannot shut his eyes to the fact that there is a very serious problem of world poverty, and it is likely to aggravate in a not very distant future, giving rise to significant world disorder. This is substantiated by the fact that the majority of violent international conflicts since 1945 have taken place in the developing countries. Therefore it cannot be denied that there is a close relationship between distributive justice as a step towards economic progress that may solve the problem of utter priority, and the existence of political stability and international cooperation. In the words of President Carter,[9]

"More than a hundred years ago Abraham Lincoln said our nation could not exist half slave and half free. We know a peaceful world cannot long exist one third rich and two thirds hungry." It is submitted, it may be difficult to express relevance of distributive justice in a better way.

While the concept of distributive justice is not a new one in international affairs, it caught the attention of the international community with a bang in the first half of the Seventies. On the one hand, the dependence of industrialized countries on the OPEC oil brought to the fore-front the theme of equitable sharing of resources among the nations, and on the other, the demand for a new and just international economic order emanated mainly from the poor and disadvantaged States.

To improve their economic condition, and put pressure on the developed

7 Douglass, R. B., Is Distributive Justice the New Name for Peace? *World Affairs*, Vol. 141, 1978, pp. 155–56.

8 *Ibid.*

9 President Carter's address at Notre Dame University, 22 May 1977, quoted from Douglass, R. B., *loc. cit.*, p. 161.

countries, the developing countries called two special sessions of the General Assembly in 1974 and 1975. These led to the adoption of the Charter of Economic Rights and Duties, and some other resolutions well known to all of us here. Practically nothing was achieved and today virtually there is an impasse on the issue of the new economic order between the developed and the developing States. The developed States are not willing to yield and the developing States are greatly frustrated. They are no longer contented with political freedom, for it has not succeeded in improving their poverty and misery.

It is not unusual today to come across the contention that the real causes of war are closely related with distribution – who gets what, when and how – and therefore it is naive to think that lasting peace can be achieved without addressing the distribution issue directly.[10] There can be no substitute for a just distribution of goods and resources. It has been conceded that pure *laissez-faire* is no longer seriously practiced by any modern government, and the idea of redistribution has long since been accepted as a matter of course by public opinion in the industrialized nations.[11] A new system of distribution has to be adopted if peace in this world is to prevail.

The only viable course is to apply the commitment of the national State – meeting the minimal needs of their citizens, and as a broad normative principle such need is now so widely accepted in national societies as to have attained the status of a general principle – at the international level also. In fact the concept of "minimal needs" has emerged as a widely accepted standard of international distribution in international resolutions and policy statements, supported not only by the developing countries who will be the greatest beneficiaries but also by the developed ones realising a legitimate and sufficient cause for preferential treatment.[12]

It may, therefore, be concluded that the fulfilment of the basic needs of the developing countries has to be recognized as a normative principle and central idea of distributive justice, which in its own turn, can be a foundation stone for a new world order. Schachter has pleaded very cogently that need, after all, can be ascertained in an objective way, and there is a wide-spread consensus on basic requirements of human beings everywhere.[13] Though the criterion of need, it must be admitted, does not provide simple answers even for a single problem like food, it does, however, set a standard, and that can in principle be applied by objective factual enquiry.[14] And this is, after all, the inherent idea of distributive justice – to provide standards and a sense of direction, rather than laying down specific solutions.

It is, therefore, suggested that some such body as the ad hoc Committee of the

10 Schachter, Oscar, *Sharing the World's Resources.* (Part III, Equity in Distribution). New York, Columbia University Press, 1977, pp. 87–142.

11 *Ibid.*, p. 87.

12 Baxi. U., (State of Gujrat V Shantilal), A Requiem for Just Compensation, *Jaipur L. J.*, Vol. 9, 1969, p. 29 at 62.

13 Schachter, Oscar, *op. cit.*, p. 10.

14 *Ibid.*

whole General Assembly on the Restructuring of the Economic and Special Sectors of the UN System may be handed over the job of looking into the needs – the "minimal needs" – of the poor developing countries, and to suggest concrete steps that should be taken by the developed States, and which in good faith, they should abide by, as a first step towards a distributive justice phenomenon for improving the lot of the developing countries. It is important to note what René Dumont pointed out:

"We must not forget that the rich countries are the plunderers of the Third World. They are the ones who 'underpay' for the rare raw materials of the Third World and then sqander them."[15] It is being increasingly felt that the affluent sector of the world "cannot remain a quiet island in the midst of a stormy ocean, an oasis of prosperity in a desert of desperate poverty".

It must be clear that under the concept of distributive justice, the developed States are not required to part with their riches to help the poor nations. What is expected of them is a change in their attitude and to share a small proportion of their continually accruing wealth. The rich industrialized nations realize this, and their representatives have recommended steps in this direction, but mere promises are useless. What is really required is genuine cooperation on their part which will go a long way towards creation of a new world order.

15 Dumont, René, Population and Cannibals. *Development Forum* (Geneva), Vol. 2. No. 7, 1979, p. 2.

16 See Sir Dawada K. Jawara, (President of the Republic of Gambia): *UN General Assembyl, Sixth Special Session, Official Records,* A/PV. 2211, 11 April 1974, pp. 1–3.

17 Anand, R. P., Towards a New Economic Order, in Saxena, J. N. (ed.), *Use of Economic Force by States with Near Monopoly of Special Resources.* New Delhi, Delhi University, 1980. p. 159.

6.4. Natural Resources: Heritage of Nation and Mankind

KAMAL HOSSAIN

> "A growing consciousness of increasing resource scarcities – and not only in energy sources but also other key minerals or food sources – will trigger increased competition between industrialized countries, between the North and the South, and in the third world itself . . . Resource transfer will become more and more a political weapon. Much as we might deplore it, resource diplomacy – using energy, food and other commodities – will likely be a reality of international negotiation and bargaining . . . We are entering a period when what one might call 'the geopolitics of resources' will become a major feature of international relations." –
> SOEDJATMOKO, Rector of the UN University, Public Lecture in the University of Uppsala, 19 May 1981.

I. The problem

The uneven global distribution of certain key natural resources – petroleum and strategic minerals such as iron, tin, nickel, manganese and bauxite – and the increase in the consumption of these resources lead to the projection of a scenario in which the interests of producers and consumers are seen to diverge to the point where they may become a source of potential conflict.

The major consumers are the rich, developed countries (while some of the major producers are developing countries). Thus, though the *per capita* production of minerals in the developed countries is 2.5 times that in the developing world, the former consume sixteen times more than the latter, with the result that developed countries import half of their requirements, principally from developing countries. The developing countries themselves consume only one quarter of the minerals produced by them.[1] Imports of fuel (oil, gas and coal) by developed countries from developing countries in 1972–73 represented around 51% of the average consumption of the developed countries; imports of other minerals – 25%. Some of the developed countries have an even greater dependence on imports from developing countries in respect of certain minerals; Japan and OECD (Europe) import 95% and 75% of their requirements of tin and manganese, and 65% and 43% respectively of their requirements of bauxite (aluminium) and iron-ore.[2] The United States was dependent in 1950 on imports for

1 Nurul Islam, Economic Independence between Rich and Poor Nations. *Third World Quarterly*, Vol. 3, April 1981, p. 230 and 235.
2 *Ibid.*, p. 231.

more than half of its supplies of aluminium, manganese, nickel and tin. By 1970, zinc and chromium were added to that list. Projections indicate that by 1985 the United States will depend on imports for more than one half of its supplies of nine basic raw materials, the further additions to the above list being: iron, tungsten and lead.[3]

II. The changing legal framework

Up until the end of the Second World War, the consumers were in an advantageous position, not only because supply tended to remain ahead of demand, but because the sources of supply were subject to the effective control of the consumer States. These sources were located in colonial territories and the development and production of the petroleum or mineral resources were undertaken by corporations (which subsequently came to be described as "multinationals" or "transnationals") to whom "concessions" were granted on generous terms. Under the traditional concessions, the concessionaire was granted ownership of the resources discovered in concession areas, in return for modest financial payments in the form of royalties to the State. The State thus remained a passive "tax collector", while the concessionaire was vested with ownership and exclusive control over operations.

As the process of decolonization got underway following the end of the Second World. War, the system of "concessions" was assailed as being inequitable inasmuch as the benefits from exploitation of the natural resource concerned were largely appropriated by the concessionaire. This was reflected in the fact that the producer State received only a small proportion of the final price at which the natural resource was sold to the ultimate consumer. Thus, it is estimated that before 1973, governments of oil-producing countries received no more than 16% of the final price[4]; in the case of other primary commodities it was estimated that out of some $ 200 billion paid by the ultimate consumer, only $ 30 billion accrued to the producer States.[5]

It was in this background that newly-independent States claimed the right to alter these inequitable arrangements either through nationalization or re-negotiation.[6] Their right to do so was recognised as being implicit in "the right of peoples to use and to exploit their natural wealth and resources [which] is inherent in their sovereignty" (Resolution 626 (VII) of 21 December 1952). Article 1 of the draft Human Rights Covenants proposed by the Human Rights Commission in January 1955 declared that "the right of peoples to self-determination shall also include permanent sovereignty over their natural wealth and resources". The principle of permanent sovereignty was subsequently reaffirmed in a series of UN General Assembly resolutions, which elaborated on the specific implications

3 Brown, L., *World Without Borders.* New York, Random House, 1972. p. 74.
4 Nurul Islam, *op. cit.*, p. 234.
5 Haq, M. *The poverty curtain: Choices for the third world.* New York, Columbia University Press, 1976. p. 160.
6 Hossain, K. (ed.), *Legal Aspects of the New International Economic Order.* London, Frances Pinter, 1980. pp. 33–43.

of this principle; notable among these resolutions are 1803 (XVII) of 14 December 1962, 2158 (XXI) of 25 November 1966 and 3281 (XXIX) of 12 December 1974, by which the Charter of Economic Rights and Duties of States was adopted. The principle of Permanent Sovereignty over Natural Resources, as elaborated in these Resolutions, provides a number of criteria by reference to which the compatibility with that principle of legal arrangements for exploitation of natural resources may be tested. For a legal arrangement to be regarded as compatible with this principle, it must (1) be in the interest of national development and well-being of the State concerned; (2) be in accordance with the national legislation in force; (3) be *freely* entered into.[7]

The guidelines provided by this principle contributed towards the evolution of new types of legal arrangements for natural resource development which were significant improvements from the producer State's point of view over the traditional concessions. Thus, during the late fifties and sixties, new types of legal arrangements were pioneered in the field of petroleum development. These included equity joint ventures and contractual joint ventures. The latter half of the sixties produced service contracts and a type of joint venture described as a "production sharing contract". While under concessions, ownership of the petroleum or mineral resource effectively stood transferred to the concessionaire, under equity joint ventures these were owned in common, and under contractual joint ventures and production sharing contracts each party owned its portion of the resource. Unlike concessions where the concessionaire had exclusive control over operations, under joint ventures, powers of management were exercised jointly and under production sharing and service contracts, powers of management were exclusively vested in the national oil company. The new types of arrangements thus enabled the producer States to realise such national objectives as retaining ownership over resources, securing control over operations and development of national capabilities, over and above the maximization of financial returns to the State.

The principle of permanent sovereignty was also invoked by producer States to claim re-negotiation of contracts, or alteration of the terms, when changed circumstances had made the original terms inequitable.[8] Thus, for example, financial terms fixed on the basis that the price at which a barrel of oil would be sold was $ 3, if allowed to remain unaltered when the selling price of oil had risen to $ 15 per barrel, would result in "windfall" profits being earned by the concessionaire. In such circumstances, measures such as revision of the financial terms, or the imposition of a "windfall profits" tax, have been resorted to by producer States to secure for themselves a substantial portion of such a "windfall". Indeed, after the sharp rise in prices after 1973, not only did traditional oil-producing countries adopt such measures, but new producing countries, like Britain and Nor-

7 *Ibid.*

8 Asante, S., The Concept of Stability of Contractual Relations in the Transnational Investment Process. In: Hossain, K. (ed.), *op. cit.*, pp. 234–262 and Zakariya, H., Changed Circumstances and Continued Validity of Mineral Development Contracts. In: Hossain, K. (ed.), *op. cit.*, pp. 263–278.

way, rejecting the concessionaire's contention that retrospective alteration of terms was legally objectionable, enacted special legislation in 1975 to impose a "windfall profits" tax.

The principle of permanent sovereignty over natural resources is, thus, not the manifestation of an absolutist concept of State sovereignty which is incompatible with the concept of the supremacy of international law. It is a principle which represents the progressive development of international law in response to the felt need for a legal principle by reference to which traditional concessions and similar arrangements for exploitation of natural resources, which were colonial legacies, could be replaced by more equitable arrangements. Thus, as Schachter has observed: "On the international level, the principle of permanent sovereignty has become the focal normative conception used by States to justify their right to exercise control over production and distribution arrangements without being hampered by the international law of State responsibility as it had been traditionally interpreted by the capital-exporting countries . . . It would be a mistake to consider the idea of permanent sovereignty over resources as anachronistic nationalistic rhetoric. It should be viewed as a fresh manifestation of present aspirations for self-rule and greater equality."[9]

III. New directions

The post-1973 developments, which resulted in substantial increases in the price of oil, and regulation of supplies by producer States, prompted some representatives of consumer States to suggest that a new legal dispensation should be provided by international law whereby consumers might be assured security of supplies of a strategic natural resource such as oil. Some suggested that oil should be made the subject-matter of some kind of agreement between the major producers and consumers, analogous to an international commodity agreement. Others, however, made the more drastic suggestion that a commodity like oil should be treated as part of "the common heritage of mankind" subject to "equitable sharing" – thereby limiting the sovereign right of producers to regulate or withold supplies or unilaterally to determine the price. This approach is one which would not only encounter the unqualified opposition of the producer States, but raises certain basic questions. Given the fact that under the existing international legal order, in which a State has sovereign rights over the natural resources and wealth in its territory, and its continental shelf and Exlusive Economic Zone, it is difficult to justify singling out one particular natural resource and declaring it to be part of "the common heritage of mankind". The question that is raised is: Why should not food, or uranium, or gold, or technology not at the same time also be declared to be a part of the common heritage of mankind? In other words, it is difficult, on the plane of principle to justify the singling out of one particular commodity in isolation from a whole range of others which would have to be brought under consideration if a fundamental change in the existing legal order were to be contemplated, such that resources in respect of which a

9 Schachter, O., *Sharing the World's Resources.* New York, Columbia University Press, 1977. ix, 172 p.

State had hitherto enjoyed exclusive sovereign rights were to be declared to be a part of "the common heritage of mankind". Such a fundamental change would require the establishment of new global institutions for planning and management of the entire range of global resources involved. It would also require the adoption of agreed criteria for equitable apportionment of resources which were considered to be part of "the common heritage".

In the absence of such fundamental changes, any attempt to declare a particular commodity in respect of which a State enjoys sovereign rights to be part of the common heritage is not only likely to be futile, but unless effected with the agreement of the producers concerned, could be well regarded as illegitimate, in as much as such singling out would appear to be both arbitrary and discriminatory. Nor could "interdependenc" provide a basis for designating a single comodity to be part of the "common heritage", for clearly if "interdependence" were to be the basis, then the much wider range of commodities, in respect of which States are interdependent, would have to be brought under the regime of "equitable sharing".

Thus in the present global environment, there would be little prospect of natural resources – in particular petroleum and mineral resources – lying within the territory of sovereign States being treated a "belonging to all mankind". Security of supplies, as well as growth of supplies in the future to meet increasing demand, are objectives which all States – consumer and producer alike – could regard as shared or common objectives. This then could provide a basis on which a programme of international co-operation could be developed for promoting increased exploration as well as alternative energy sources. Studies conducted by the French Petroleum Institute and others have pointed out that there is scope for substantial increase in exploration and development expenditures in the field of petroleum and minerals, and that if the present levels of exploration expenditures are not increased in the developing countries, significant discoveries which could have been made to meet the demands of the nineties would not be made.[10] This is therefore an area where consumer and producer (including potential-producer) governments could effecitvely co-operate to promote international measures aimed at bringing about a significant increase in exploration activities.

This would involve not only more financial resources being allocated by public financial institutions, such as the World Bank for this purpose, but also the devising of new legal frameworks in which capital and technology, not otherwise available under the conventional frameworks, would become available. With regard to mineral resources other than petroleum the Common Fund, established within the framework of UNCTAD, could contribute towards promoting the objective of security of supply by promoting the conclusion of international commodity agreements.

There are, however, natural resources which do not lie exclusively within the territory of a single sovereign State, where a "common heritage of mankind" approach may be fruitfully promoted. Apart from the obvious area of ocean

10 Hossain, K., *Law and Policy in Petroleum Development*. London, Frances Pinter, 1979. pp. 242–252.

resources, this approach could be adopted in respect of the atmosphere and protection of the environment. International regulation could aim to protect the environment from such activities as weather modification and ecological damage resulting from adoption of such practices as destruction of forests, use of chemical insecticides, etc., in the territory of one or more States.[11]

The approach of equitable apportionment may appropriately by applied to resources in respect of which no single State can claim to exercise exclusive sovereign rights, such as the waters of rivers and lakes common to two or more States. The Helsinki Rules, adopted by the International Law Association, provide a basis which carefully balances the equities involved in effecting such apportionment.

Finally, another priority area, in which a new approach is called for is: food. Thus, a plan for World Food Security as approved at the World Food Conference in 1974 provides the basis for purposeful action in this area. The basic elements of the plan are:[12]

"an undertaking by countries of the world to build up and maintain national stocks of cereals, including reserves, on the basis of internationally determined requirements. In combination these stocks would provide a minimum level of basic food stocks for the world as a whole. The Food and Agriculture Organization would assess world needs and supplies, and it would lay down guidelines for the reserves to be maintained by all countries, not only for their own domestic needs but also for export to others in case of crop failure or national disaster. These actions would be supported by procedures for consultation on the adequacy of national stocks of grain and action required to meet any difficulty. To give these collective efforts an adequate factual foundation, the countries would undertake to furnish information on crop conditions, stock levels and prospective exports and imports. In addition, a whole series of international measures would be taken to assist countries, especially in the developing world. This series would include, particularly, expansion of fertilizer production, improvement of water supply, assistance in creating food reserves, and technical assistance in all phases of agriculture."

In addition, certain common interests of this international community in the conservation of natural resources and the prevention of waste could provide the basis for the development of new international legal norms in this area. Also, one can envisage the development of a doctrine of international public policy which would provide a basis for nullification of agreements made in violation of such policy. Thus, a doctrine could be invoked to nullify contexts induced by bribary or procured by duress as well as arrangements which would lead to ecological damage.

11 Schachter, O., *op. cit.*, pp. 37–83.
12 *Ibid.*, pp. 136–137.

6.5. Natural Resources: Heritage of Nation and Mankind

Achol Deng

A. Introductory remarks

To the co-Rapporteur the question of the exploitation of natural resources evokes what would appear, at first sight, the antithesis of independence and inter-dependence.

There is general agreement that a State has sovereignty over the natural resources within its jurisdiction and that the natural resources outside and beyond the limits of State jurisdiction are the "common heritage of mankind." To be sure, there remains some disagreement as to where national jurisdiction ends and the common heritage of mankind begins. Even more important is the disagreement over the practical content to be given to that concept. We shall address ourselves to some of these problems in more detail in Section C of this paper where we make a reassessment of the present situation. In Section D we identify the issues that will preoccupy us in the future and conclude by an examination of whether independence and interdependence are mutually exclusive or whether they could not be complimentary, given the objective of an equitable sharing of the world's resources.

B. General survey

The concept of permanent sovereignty over natural resources owes its genesis to the United Nations Charter,[1] particularly Article 1[2] which upholds "the principle of equal rights and self-determination of peoples". The concept was given form by UN General Assembly resolutions 523 (VI) of 12 January 1952, 627 (VII) of 21 December 1952, 1314 (XIII) of 12 December 1958 which recognised, *inter alia*, the economic self-determination of States.

1 Brownlie, Ian, Legal Status of Natural Resources in International Law (some aspects). *Recueil des cours, Académie de droit international*, La Haye, Tome 162, 1979, I, p. 255.

2 On that issue see Asomoah, O. Y., *The Legal Significance of the Declarations of the General Assembly of the United Nations*. The Hague, M. Nijhoff, 1966, 278 p., Castañeda, J., *Legal Effect of United Nations Resolutions*. New York, Columbia University Press, 1969, 243 p. Jimenéz de Aréchaga, E., International Law in the Past Third of a Century, *Recueil des Cours, Académie de droit international*, Vol. 159, 1978. I, pp. 1–344. Higgins, R. *The Development of International Law through the Political Organs of the UN*. London, Oxford University Press, 1963, XXI, 402 p. Virally, M., La valeur juridique des recommendations des Organisations internationales, *Annuaire Français de Droit International*, Tome II, 1956, pp. 66–95.

It was not, however, until the 1960's that the concept took its present shape. Resolution 1515 (XV) of 15 December 1960 recommended *inter alia*, that the sovereign rights of every State to dispose of its wealth and its natural resources should be respected. A landmark is, of course, Resolution 1803 (XVII) of 14 December 1962 which declares in operative paragraph 1 that the rights of people and nations to permanent sovereignty over natural wealth and resources must be exercised in the interest of the national development and of the well-being of the people of the State concerned. While operative paragraph 1 has it that nationalisation, expropriation or requisitioning should be based on the "grounds of public utility . . .", paragraph 8 calls for the observance of good faith regarding foreign investment agreements freely entered into by or between sovereign States. This is not the place to discuss the legal affects of UN General Assembly resolutions.[2] However, it can be said that subsequent State practice bears out the authority of Resolution 1803 (XVII) as evidence of contemporary international law on matters of nationalisation and expropriation.[3]

The concept of permanent sovereignty over natural resources has been incorporated into the two 1966 General Assembly Covenants on Human Rights. It was further developed and concretised by Resolution 2158 (XXI) of 25 November 1966 (which reaffirmed the inalienable right of all countries to exercise permanent sovereignty over their natural resources), Resolution 3171 (XXVIII) of 17 December 1973 (which condemns coercion against States exercising their sovereignty over natural resources), Resolution 3201 (S–VI) (Declaration on the Establishment of a New International Economic Order), Resolution 3202 (S–VI) (Programme of Action on the Establishment of a New International Economic Order) and Resolution 3281 (XXIX) of 12 December 1974 (The Charter of Economic Rights and Duties of States). Article 2 (1) of the Charter of Economic Rights and Duties of States provides that "Every State has and shall freely exercise full sovereignty including possession, use and disposal over all its wealth, natural resources and economic activities". As we all know, this resolution was adopted by 120 votes in favour, with 6 against (because of strong opposition by Western States to paragraph 2 (c) on nationalisation and expropriation) and 6 abstensions. Intense debate has been generated as to whether this resolution constitutes evidence of *opinio juris*.[4]

I now turn to the notion of the common heritage of mankind, which found earlier expression in the Treaty on Principles governing the Activities of States in the Exploration of Outer Space, including the Moon and the Celestial Bodies, adopted by General Assembly in December 1966. However, the possibilities of the exploitation of the resources of outer space for the benefit of mankind remain, at best, theoretical given our present state of technology.

3 See Award in the Arbitration between Texaco/Calasiatic v. Government of Libya (19 January 1977), R.-J. Dupuy, Sole Arbitrator. *Journal de Droit International* (Clunet), 104 e année, No 2, avril-juin 1977, pp. 378–9, para. 87, or *International Legal Materials*, 1978, p. 30.

4 See views of Bedjaoui, M., *Pour un nouvel ordre économique international*, Paris, UNESCO, 1978, p. 189 and Virally, M., "A propos de la Lex ferenda": *Mélange Reuter*, Paris, A. Pedone, 1981 p. 529.

However, at the initiative of Ambassador Arvid Padro of Malta the UN General Assembly discussed an item entitled "Declaration and Treaty concerning the Reservation Exlusively for Peaceful Purposes of the Sea-bed and the Ocean Floor, underlying the Sea-beds Beyond the Limits of National Jurisdiction, and the Use of their Resources in the Interest of Mankind". This moved the notion of the common heritage of mankind from the realm of the theoretical to that of the practical.[5]

Support for the notion of common heritage of mankind is found in numerous United Nations resolutions and texts of which the latest is the Informal Composite Negotiating Text (Document A/CONF.62/WP.10/Rev.3 of 22 August 1980. According to Article 1 of the Informal Composite Negotiating Text: "Area means the seabed and ocean floor and subsoil beyond the limits of national jurisdiction". Article 136 declares the Area and its resources the common heritage of mankind. According to Articel 140 (1) "activities in the Area shall be carried out for the benefit of mankind as a whole, taking into particular consideration the interests and needs of developing States . . ." Subsection (2) reads: "The Authority shall provide for the equitable sharing of financial and other economic benefits derived from the activities of the area . . ."

It is worth noting that permanent sovereignty is exercised in the "interest of national development and well-being of States concerned" and that under the notion of the common heritage of mankind special consideration would be given to the needs of developing countries.

C. Reassessment of the present situation

The prospects for the application of the notion of common heritage of mankind to the exploitation of the riches of the sea raised great expectations. This feeling was aptly expressed by Professor Virally when he observed that "l'acquisition par l'organisation mondiale de ressources propres résultant de role qu'elle pourrait être amenée á jouer dans l'exploitation des ressources du fond des océans aurait des consequences incalculables. L'autonomie que en résulterait pour le système des Nations Unies, le nouvel élan qui pourrait en être donné a ses activités en changeraient une nouvelle fois le caractère".[6] However, excessive claims by coastal States of continental shelves that extend up to 200 miles (and even beyond) from the baseline from which the territorial sea is measured, have already reduced the area that was originally ear-marked for exploitation in the interest of mankind.[7]

5 Mann-Borgese, E. (Editor), *Pacem in Maribus*, New York, Dodd, Mead & Co., 1972, particularly the contribution of Arvid Padro: New Horizons in Ocean Science and Law p. 249–253, Edward, *The Politics of the Oceans*, Seattle, University of Washington Press, 1972, XVIII, 590 p. particularly Chapter 6: One world, one sea, pp. 250–293, Oxman, B. H, The Third UN Conference on the Law of the Sea: The 8th Session 1979. *American Journal of International Law*, 1980, pp. 1–47, Dupuy, René-Jean. *L'Océan Partagé*, Paris, A. Pedone, 1979, particulièrement Chapitre IV; Les appropriations collectives: Le Patrimoine Commun de l'humanité. pp. 237–248.
6 Virally, Michel, *L'Organisation Mondiale*. Paris, Colin 1972. p. 406.
7 Beer-Gabel, J., L'exploitation du fond des mers dans l'intérêt de l'humanité, chimère ou

Indeed, manganese nodules could still be found in great quantities in the "Area" reserved for the common heritage of mankind. But their exploitation requires sophisticated technology which is only available to a handful of States. Even the exploitation of the economic zones of developing coastal States depends on the aquisition of appropriate marine technology.

There is also disagreement on how to repartition the common heritage of mankind, a disagreement masked by the controversy over the institutional arrangements for the proposed international Sea-Bed Authority. Strong reservations have been registered against the inclusion of "peoples who have not attained full independence or other self governing status" among those who should benefit from the common heritage of mankind.

D. Issues for the future

It would be reassuring if a redefinition of the excessive claims that reduce the scope of the common heritage of mankind were on our agenda for the future. Unfortunately this cannot be so as States would find it difficult to relinquish the rich parts of the sea which they have appropriated. In the circumstances, the best States could do is to facilitate the functioning of the proposed commission on the continental shelf in such a way as to block any further incursions into the common heritage of mankind.

A second outstanding issue, and a cardinal one at that, relates to the "Transfer of Technology" without which developing countries could not exploit the natural resources within their jurisdiction and can but be spectators in the exploitation of deep-sea resources. This concern has been recognized in the UN and has been incorporated in Article 13 of the Charter of Economic Rights and Duties of States which views technology as another "common heritage of mankind". It will be recalled that Article 13 of this Charter was one of those adopted unanimously.[8]

However, when it comes to giving it practical content a host of problems come to the fore. It would seem that Professor I. Seidl-Hohenveldern articulates the position of most Western States when he says that the concept of the common heritage of mankind

"cannot be extended to assets which, like patent rights, are the property of an inventor or of his successors in title. Of course, any inventor has to base his work on the work of his predecessors. Modern Western technology thus is not exclusively due to the inventive spirit of present-day inventors. Like all science it owes a great debt to mediaeval Arab thought transmitting and developing the heritage of Ancient Greece. Yet why should the present-day inventor alone repay a debt

réalité? *Revue Générale de Droit International Public,* Vol. 81, 1977, p. 167–230, Bennouna, Mohamed, Les fonds des mers: de, "L'héritage commun" à la "querelle des héritiers". *Revue iranienne des rélations internationales,* No 5–6, hiver 1975–76, pp. 121–140.

8 See Virally, M., La charte des droits et devoirs economiques des Etats: note de lecture. *Annuaire Français de Droit International,* Tome XX, 1974, p. 74, White, Robin C. A., A New International Economic Order. *International & Comparative Law Quarterly,* Vol. 24, Part 3, July 1975, p. 550.

by accepting a compensating inequality, which is intended to compensate inequalities between States, and hence should be borne by States as such and not by certain individuals only. Moreover such a proposal would be counterproductive. If we were to deprive inventors of parts of their gains we should thereby reduce the incentive for new inventions. Finally, if it were sufficient to declare certain coveted assets to be part of the common heritage of mankind in order to oblige their owners to give them away at less than a fair price, what would prevent industrialised States from placing oil deposits in this category. Thus the common heritage argument could be played both ways".[9]

This appears to be a devastating indictment of the claim that technology is part of the common heritage of mankind. A few comments may be in order, however. Starting from the last point, Ambassador M. Bedjaoui ably demonstrates the incongruity of talking about Middle Eastern oil while oblivious to oil deposits in North America and Europe. In his own words

"la notion de patrimoine commun de l'humanité ne peut donc être affecteé d'un coefficient significatif de credibilité que dans la mesure où elle répartit clairement les droit et devoirs des Etats en tout équité, ou en fonction d'une inégalité compensatrice pour les Etats en developpement. Si le pétrole est un patrimoine commun de l'humanité, il devrait l'être partout où il se trouve et pas en fonction de la localisation geographique. Le pétrole americain, britannique, norvegien ou sovietique devrait tout autant que celui du moyen-orient appartenir à tous."[10]

We might add that this common heritage of mankind has as its objects not only the compensation of inequalities among States but also among individuals (who are after all the basic units of mankind). Besides, developing countries do not want technology at a "throw-away" price. They only demand that the price be reasonable.

If we have quoted Professor Seidl-Hohenveldern at length and have somewhat belaboured this point, it is to underline its significance as a trouble area where a constructive dialogue between States is required.

Another issue is whether mineral exporting developing States would be entitled to compensation for loss incurred as a result of competition with minerals extracted from the Area.

As mentioned in Section B, *supra*, the principal objective for the claims to sovereignty over natural resources and the common heritage of mankind is the development of less economically endowed States. The developing countries would seem to demand the best of both worlds. Indeed one can understand what underlies the acid remarks of some developed States in characterizing Third World claims as "garder son bien et partager celui des autres". It has also been observed that "one can reproach the majority of the UN General Assembly that it wants the international community to carry the losses, for instance in the Sahel

9 Seidl-Hohenveldern, I., International Economic 'Soft Law' *Recueil des cours, Académie de droit international,* Tome 163, 1979, II, p. 189.

10 Bedjaoui, M., *op. cit.*, p. 242–243.

zone, while leaving, in principle at least, the profits of natural resources of an Arab State to that State . . ."[11]

However, if our objective is the equitable redistribution of global resources, one would not see any incompatibilities in the claims of the Third World to sovereignty over natural resources and to benefits from the common heritage of mankind. With appropriate technology and goodwill, the vast potentials of the developing countries could be harnessed for the benefit of all. It would therefore seem that independence and interdependence are not necessarily mutually exclusive if we develop principles of equitable sharing of global resources for a New World Order. This Seminar may therefore wish to contribute towards the construction of the new framework.

11 Seidl-Hohenveldern, I., *loc. cit.* p. 189.

6.6. Material, Economic and Human Limits to Activities of Mankind: Legislating for a New Economic World Order in an Ecological Context

OTTO KIMMINICH

1. *Law and economic order*

1.1. *The framework*

It is certainly safe to assume that the organizers of this seminar meant to give guidelines to the rapporteurs when they formulated the headings under which the various subjects are to be treated. Thus, the heading may serve to justify the exclusion of considerations which, though important and interesting by themselves must be ruled out because they are of minor relevance for the purposes of this seminar. But it is equally clear that all concepts mentioned in the heading are open to scholarly discussion.

There is, first of all, the concept of legislation. We are using it here primarily on the international level, trying to describe the process of formulation of rules of international law in a multicultural world. But we should not forget that in our present international system – and obviously for some time to come – a great proportion of these rules has to be observed and enforced by the organs and authorities of nation States, so that national legislation plays an important role, too. Of course this problem is linked with the question of sovereignty which has to be dealt with by group 3. But it cannot be excluded from considerations in the context of economic world order and ecology.

This brings us to the next concept. For someone who has lived in central Europe for the past 50 years the expression "new world order" has an ominous connotation. But even if we prefer the more modest term "new international economic order" we cannot avoid the following questions: What is an international economic order in the first place? What are the main features of the order which we mean in this specific context? And what is so new about it?

Answering these questions from the viewpoint of international law we have to use legal terms to define the concepts involved, but it is here submitted as a working hypothesis that these definitions by nature are not contrary to those used by economists which of course implies a certain view of the relations between law and economics which must be clarified at the outset.

Textbooks of economics usually define the economic order as a set of organizational principles, norms, decision-making mechanisms, institutions and patterns of behaviour that steer the economic activities in a certain society. They also concede that legal norms contain, reflect, create and shape those principles, institutions and patterns of behaviour. But one cannot establish the same relationship between law and economics on the international level, because "world economy is not an entity on its own like a national economy".[1] Rather, one has to deal with the principles, norms, institutions and so forth governing international economic relations. These in turn are not simply relations between national economies, but (in most cases) at the same time relations between non-governmental decision-making agencies as well. Therefore the legal framework for the whole of these activities consists of a variety of domestic laws, international private law (which is actually part of the national legal systems) and public international law.

Under these conditions it seems rather bold to speak of something like a world order. The problem becomes scarcely less complicated if we narrow our analysis to public international law, because we cannot escape the necessity to explore the question whether this system of legal norms obliges its subjects and organs to engage in certain activities – and refrain from others – in order to facilitate international economic relations with respect to specific goals implicitly or explicitly set by this same system of norms. And again this covers a wide range of State activities including domestic legislation and domestic executive acts – e. g. controlling private enterprises – as well as international treaty making.

At this point we might penetrate deeply into the philosophy of international law asking how and to what extent it is possible for this system of norms to set goals on a global level in a multicultural world. It is the task of group 1 to discuss this question. But the economic aspect cannot be entirely separated from it. On the one hand economic factors play an important role in the process of goal-setting, on the other hand the meta-economic circumstances form a moral, political, social and legal framework for economic life. Again, the additive enumeration of these categories of factors gives a wrong impression, because all of them are mutually intertwined and interdependent, and they are not static, but dynamic. Therefore the correct picture is one of constant interaction.

But those who have analysed this interaction over a long period of time seem to agree on a finding which has been called "the ultimate law of economic history", namely "that under no economic system can economic integration go further than social-political-moral-legal integration which is based on psychological forces, on laws, and on institutions".[2]

Specifically for the relation between international economic order and international law the following conclusion has been drawn: "An intensive and extensive economic exchange cannot exist or last very long without a minimum of mutual trust, confidence in the stability and reliability of the legal-institutional framework (including money), contractual loyality, honesty, fair play, profes-

1 Kapteyn, P. J. G., The basis of the new international economic order. *Netherlands International Law Review*, Vol. XXV, 1978, p. 218.

2 Röpke, Wilhelm, Economic order and international law. *Recueil des Cours, Académie de droit international*, Vol. 86, 1954, II, p. 211.

sional honour and that pride which makes us consider it unworthy of us to cheat, to bribe or to misuse the authority of the State for egoistic purposes."[3]

Is it sheer coincidence that these words were coined by a proponent of liberal economic thought? Taken by themselves they might just as well be used for a code of conduct within a framework of international relations which has nothing to do with liberal thinking. But it is a fact that classic international law in its final stage lasting until World War I was closely interrelated with economic liberalism. There are many who contend that the decline of the cultural tradition of liberalism in our century inevitably meant the end not only of free trade, but also of international law in its classical shape. It is here submitted that although classic international law is a thing of the past the options for shaping the international order have not narrowed down to a winding path inevitably leading to a planned world economy of a collectivistic type. The end of classic international law, initiated by the League of Nations Covenant, hastened by the Briand-Kellogg Pact of 1928 and definitely effected by the Charter of the United Nations, is not due to the decline of liberal thinking in economics and political science. It was brought about by conscious efforts to change the structure of international law irrespective of political philosophies or ideologies.

1.2. Progress from coexistence to co-operation

The motivating force behind this change was the longing for peace which had grown in volume and intellectual maturity ever since World War I had shattered the naive belief that free trade would automatically lead to world peace. Therefore the magnitude of the change is evidenced most distinctly by the attitude of international law towards the problem of war and peace. Whereas classic international law had offered both war and peace as possible modes of conduct on the international level, thus implicitly conceding to the sovereign States a right to wage war *(ius ad bellum)*, international law of the League of Nations era instituted a partial ban on war (cf. art. 11 of the Covenant) which was later broadened to a general ban by the Briand-Kellogg Pact. In a logical continuance of this development the Charter of the United Nations extended the ban to include all forms of violence in international relations. Thus, today nothing is left of the *ius ad bellum* of former times. The right of individual and collective self-defence affirmed by the Briand-Kellogg Pact as well as by the Charter of the UN is not an exception to the general ban on violence, but rather its logical corollary.

There are of course other angles from which this historical development can be viewed. One function of international law which has recently received wider attention is coexistence. Indeed it can be said that it is the function of all legal systems to make possible, within their respective frameworks, the coexistence of various entities and subjects whose rights and duties are defined by the norms of the system. Therefore it is small wonder that we find the term coexistence in textbooks of international law as early as in the 18th century. But under the reign of classic international law, it was either peaceful or warlike coexistence which

3 *Ibid.*, p. 211.

the sovereigns or the leader of sovereign nations could choose according to their whim. Only after the end of World War I did the duty to strive for peaceful coexistence evolve.

The duty to wage positive peace, *"la pacigerence positive"*, was derived from a number of clauses of the League of Nations Covenant even before the Briand-Kellogg Pact.[4] The question today is whether under the impact of the Charter of the United Nations and of the developments initiated by it the duty to work for peaceful coexistence has not been extended to include a duty to establish peaceful cooperation.

2. *Origins of the new international economic order*

2.1. *New international economic order versus free trade?*

Peace and co-operation are the keywords for the New International Economic Order, and one may be surprised that we have been led to it without any reference to economic necessities or changes in the intellectual climate as, e. g., the decline of liberalism. But it is not surpising at all. The quest for a new international economic order is not new, its history goes farther back than the Declaration on the Establishment of a New International Economic Order of 1 May 1974.[5] Like anything else in history its origins are diverse so that any attempt to explain it monocausally would distort reality. In addition, the search for causes may be contested for other reasons. Thus it seems doubtful whether it is true that the quest for a new international economic order was spurned mainly by "the decline of the old bipolar system of world public order".[6] But it is certainly safe to say that the necessity to establish a new set of rules for international economic relations arose at the end of World War I and that the disruption of international trade patterns by the war and its aftermath was only one factor causing this necessity. Therefore the lamentations about "the disintegration of international trade which has gone on ever since the First World War"[7] can show only part of the picture, although it must be admitted that "the end of free trade" plays an important role in the writings of those who have traced the origins of the idea of a new economic world order. There are many who believe that the postwar attempts – led by the United States and at first supported by a majority of UN members – to re-establish "free trade as an ordering principle of an international economic order" has given way to a "UN development ideology" which is intrinsically opposed to free trade.[8]

The kernel of truth in such statements is the fact that the monetary system set

4 Cf. Descamps, Edouard, Le droit international nouveau. *Recueil des Cours, Académie de droit international,* Vol. 31, 1930, I, p. 399 ff.

5 Res. 3201 (S - VI) of 1 May 1974.

6 McWhinney, Edward, The international law-making process and the new international economic order. *The Canadian Yearbook of International Law,* Vol. XIV, 1976, p. 58.

7 Röpke, *loc. cit.* (note 2), p. 214.

8 Kapteyn, *loc. cit.* (note 1), p. 218.

up by the Bretton Woods agreement has collapsed and that "since the general currency float of 1973, free trade has to a great extent lost its meaning".[9] The reason for that is obvious: In the old system free trade was based on the gold standard, the functioning of which in turn depended on the existence of a global clearing center. The Bank of England served this purpose successfully in the 18th and 19th centuries, but when after World War I the center of international finance shifted from London to New York the American Federal Reserve System had still to learn how to manage a currency serving as the prime vessel of international free trade. When the US abolished the convertibility of the dollar into gold in August 1971, the system had actually come to an end even before the floating of exchange rates.

It can be argued that the system of floating exchange rates – which causes considerable difficulties on a global scale, because the erratic fluctuations of parities lead to sudden changes in domestic prices of exported and imported goods, balance of payments, costs of production, and ultimately employment – can be made acceptable by creating a substitute for dollars and gold, i. e. "a reserve unit independent of any particular nation and with its availability subject to strict rules" and by establishing "a control mechanism over international capital flows" as well as "structures for efficient co-ordination of economic policies".[10] But this is exactly what the new international economic order aims at and what the emerging "international law of co-operation"[11] wants to facilitate.

2.2. The UN and the quest for a new international economic order

Thus, closer examination shows that many developments have converged to create the demand for a new economic world order and that practically all of them can be traced to the revolutionary change of international law which began after World War I and which is still going on. Therefore it is not correct to say that "the preoccupation of the UN has shifted from peace and security to economic organisation".[12] Rather the UN efforts in the economic sphere are a logical sequence of previous activities in other fields, not only laid out in art. 55, 56 of the Charter but also necessitated by general international law in its present stage of development. Peace remains the prime objective of international law and of the UN; the legal framework for international economic relations must be shaped accordingly. This simple truth is the basis for the quest for a new economic order.

If this basis is generally accepted, it is not necessary to discuss the various moral arguments for or against the justification of a new international economic

9 de Montbrial, Thierry, For a new world economic order. *Foreign Affairs*, Vol. 54, 1975, p. 62.

10 *Ibid.*, p. 63.

11 Friedmann, Wolfgang, General Course in Public International Law. *Recueil des Cours, Académie de droit international*, Vol. 127, 1969, II, p. 91; Friedmann, Wolfgang, *The changing structure of international law*. London, Stevens and sons, 1964, p. 61.

12 de Waart, P. J. I. M., Permanent sovereignty over natural resources as a cornerstone for international economic rights and duties. *Netherlands International Law Review*, Vol. XXIV, 1977, p. 304.

order. The moral arguments may be interesting by themselves, but they do not advance legal discussion. Although it will always be of great importance to discuss the moral implications of the quest for peace, it is a fact that keeping the peace is a *legal* duty in present international law so that everything that can be based on it can be treated in strictly legal terms.

Seen from this angle, the quest for a new international economic order looks much less dramatic and at any rate free from accusations of greed and guilt. That opens the road for an examination of the substance of the "new" order, as laid down in various declarations of the United Nations and similar international documents. Many writers begin with the Declaration on the Granting of Independence to Colonial Countries and Peoples.[13] Other relevant texts are the Resolutions on Permanent Sovereignty over Natural Resources,[14] the Charter of Economic Rights and Duties of States of 12 Dec. 1974,[15] the Declaration on Principles of International Law concerning Friendly Relations and Co-operation among States in accordance with the Charter of the United Nations of 24 Oct. 1970,[16] the Declaration on the Inadmissability of Intervention in the Domestic Affairs of States and the Protection of their Independence and Sovereignty of 21 Dec. 1965,[17] the resolutions and other accomplishments of UNCTAD and UNIDO, among the latter especially the Lima Declaration and Plan of Action on Industrial Development and Co-operation,[18] and especially the results of the Sixth Special Session of the General Assembly of the UN, viz. the "Declaration on the Establishment of a New International Economic Order" and the "Program of Action on the Establishment of a New International Economic Order".[19] Last not least there are the International Covenants of 16 Dec. 1966[20] whose art. 1 is of prime importance for the subject.

3. Contents of the new order

3.1. The fundamentals of economic relations

The "fundamentals" of economic relations are enumerated in Chapter I of the Charter of Economic Rights and Duties: Sovereignty, territorial integrity and political independence of States; sovereign equality of all States; non-aggression; non-intervention mutual and equitable benefit; peaceful coexistence; equal rights and self-determination of peoples; peaceful settlement of disputes; remedying of injustices which have been brought about by force and which deprive a nation of

13 Resolution 1514 (XV) of 14 December 1960.
14 A/RES1803 (XVII) of 14 December 1962; A/RES/2158 (XXI) of 25 November 1966; A/RES/3016 (XXVII) of 18 December 1972; A/RES/3171 (XXVIII) of 17 December 1973.
15 Resolution 3281 (XXIX) of 12 December 1974.
16 Resolution 2625 (XXV) of 24 October 1970.
17 Resolution 2131 (XX) of 21 December 1965.
18 Adopted on 27 March 1975, cf. *Annual Review of United Nations Affairs*, 1975, p. 168 ff.
19 Resolutions 3201 (S - VI) and 3202 (S - VI) of 1 May 1974.
20 Resolution 2200 A (XXI) of 16 December 1966.

the natural means necessary for its normal development; fulfilment in good faith of international obligations; respect for human rights and fundamental freedoms; no attempt to seek hegemony and spheres of influence; promotion of international social justice; international co-operation for development; free access to and from the sea by land-locked countries within the framework of the above principles.

Each of these principles has been the object of much research which cannot be summarized here. But even someone who deeply abhors sweeping statements will not hesitate to confirm that there is not much that is genuinely new in the whole list. Many of the principles, like sovereignty, equality of States, non-intervention, have been formed in classic international law. Others, like peaceful coexistence, peaceful settlement of disputes, respect for human rights, self-determination of peoples, are the result of efforts during the period of transition since World War I and are well entrenched in present international law. There has been some controversy about the meaning of "mutual and equitable benefit". Many writers associated it with "international social justice" which in turn is deemed to be new, if not revolutionary. But on closer look one finds that there has been talk about international social justice for a long time. Emmerich de Vattel seems to be the first writer mentioning the principle of solidarity, expounding its foundation and explaining its limits. There is, Vattel says, a natural duty of States to help each other in case of famine or other calamities up to the limit of endangering their own existence. But owing to the structure of classic international law, there could only be a "*droit imparfait*" on the part of the States receiving such aid.[21] Again it seems to be logical within the course of development of international law since World War I to press for a transformation of this "imperfect right" to make it a perfect one.

3.2. Old and new legal norms

We all know from our experience in domestic affairs that welfare payments create dependencies which in turn are not conducive to a climate of mutual trust. Therefore it is not enough to make aid a legal duty on the part of the rich and a legal right on the part of the poor – a system which could work only if there was some authority to decide who is rich and who is poor and precisely what specific rights and duties ensue from this decision. Rather it is necessary to establish an international order respecting the dignity and liberty of individuals, groups, nations and subjects of international law. The above enumeration has been chosen deliberately in order to show that this transformation goes beyond the traditional limits of public international law to include subject matters which hitherto were regarded as belonging to the *domaine réservé* of the sovereign States. This does not only mean an increased preocupation with (seemingly) "new" problems like

21 Vattel, Emer de, *Le droit des gens, ou principes de la loi naturelle, appliquées à la conduite et aux affaires des nations et des souverains*, Londres, 1758. Livre II, chap. 1., § 2: "Ce qu'un homme doit aux autres hommes, une Nation le doit, à sa manière, aux autres Nations. Tel est le fondement de ces devoirs communs, de ces offices d'humanité, auxquels les Nations sont reciproquement obligées les unes envers les autres."

the rights of individuals, minority groups, ecology etc., but also some re-thinking about age-old problems like the relation between domestic law and international law. Therefore it would be of little use to sort out "old" and (seemingly) "new" problems in the list of principles governing the new international economic order. Rather it is necessary to see this list – which obviously is not exhaustive – as a composite entity in which each part preconditions and shapes the other. But on the other hand it would be equally wrong to say that we simply leave the form of traditional law unchanged while we fill it with a "new spirit", using "old" international law as an empty shell ready to transport any contents for "new" aims. This may be the illusion of revolutionaries dreaming of "unbloody" revolutions, but it is not the way of thinking of lawyers who know that there is only the choice between peaceful change and violent revolution. The former uses existing legal norms and institutions not as empty shells but as meaningful instruments of change for a clearly defined limited aim while at the same time they continue to perform the prime function of any system of legal norms: maintaining stability.

The problem is not new and it is not limited to legislating for a new economic world order. But perhaps it is posed under the present conditions in a specific, dangerous way. At its core lies the age-old "antinomy between stability and change in law itself" which today raises the question: "Will the present attempts at up-dating or modernisation of classical international law doctrine, in accord with changing societal demands and expectations in the World Community, by making use of existing international institutions and existing international law techniques (multilateral or bilateral treaty; juridical interpretation; developing custom and convention), yield significant incremental change; or will we see, instead, a continuance and extension of resort to extra-legal means – direct action, terrorism –, as instruments of social change in a rapidly evolving World Community?"[22]

Observing world events in our time, one may take a pessimistic or an optimistic position. But as jurists we have no choice. We have to stick to the first alternative, i. e. we have to use existing norms and institutions as instruments of change maintaining peace and stability in a changing world. It has been attempted to show that this approach is not limited to the formalities of the solution of problems, but covers the contents and substance of norms and principles on which the solutions are based. Therefore this view coincides with a political orientation which has been called "pragmatic" in contrast to "an optimistic one" which "is represented by an assortment of jubilant Third World leaders, cheering radicals and self-styled populists" and "an absolutist one" which "is represented in part by romanticists who are unwilling to conceive of a world different from the one they have always known, and in part by some seasonal liberals who do not hesitate to repudiate their liberalism when the shoe is on the other foot."[23]

22 McWhinney, Edward, International Law Antinoies of an Era of Transition, *Homenjae a Miaja de la Muela*, Vol. I. Madrid, Editorial Tecnos, 1979. p. 409.

23 Saddy, Fehmy, A new world economic order: the limits of accommodation, *International Journal*, Vol. XXXIV, 1978/79, p. 17 ff.

3.3. Guiding principles

3.3.1. International solidarity

The postulate to treat all principles pertaining to the emerging order of international economic relations as a whole – i. e. to interpret each principle in the light of all others – is instrinsically related to the further propostion that the new economic order is part of a new system of international law which has been evolving since World War I for reasons far exceeding the sphere of economics. The development has already reached a stage in which public international law is no longer merely a set of rules governing international relations but also the framework of a "public international order".[24] Within this framework old principles preserved from the times of classic international law have attained new meanings, while new principles become ever more important. Among the latter are the principle of co-operation[25] and the principle of solidarity.[26]

24 Cf. Mosler, Hermann, The international society as a legal community, *Recueil des Cours, Académie de droit international,* Vol. 140, 1974, IV, p. 33.

25 Cf. Friedmann, Wolfgang, General course in public international law. *Recueil des Cours, Académie de droit international,* Vol. 127, 1969, II, p. 110 ff., 215 ff; Friedmann, Wolfgang, *The changing structure of international law,* London, Stevens and sons, 1964, p. 61 ff.

26 The principle of solidarity, although mentioned in early writings (see above, note 21), has been (re-) discovered especially in connection with the new international economic order. There is hardly a treatise on this subject not mentioning the principle of solidarity. Cf. Cox, Robert W., Ideologies and the new international economic order: Reflections on some recent literature. *International Organization,* Vol. 33, 1979, p. 257 ff; Feuer, Guy, Les Nations Unies et le nouvel ordre économique international (1974-1976), *Journal du Droit International.* Vol. 104, 1977, p. 606 ff.Gosovic, Branislav and Ruggie, John Gerard, On the creation of a new international economic order: issue linkage and the Seventh Special Session of the UN General Assembly. *International Organization,* Vol. 30, 1976, p. 309 ff; Hirsch, Fred, Is there a new international economic order? *International Organization,* Vol. 30, 1976, p. 521 ; Hossain, Kamal, ed., *Legal Aspects of the New International Economic Order.* London, Pinter, 1980, p. 285. Hubbard, Damian, The International Law Commission and the New International Economic Order, *German Yearbook of International Law,* Vol. 22, 1979, p. 80 ff. Kapteyn, P. J. G., The basis of the new international economic order, *Netherlands International Law Review,* Vol. 25, 1978, p. 217 ff; Kemper, Ria, *Nationale Verfügung über natürliche Ressourcen und die Neue Weltwirtschaftsordnung der Vereinten Nationen.* Berlin, Duncker & Humblot 1976, p. 155. Makarczyk, Jerzy, Le rôle du droit international dans l'instauration d'un nouvel ordre économique international, *German Yearbook of International Law,* Vol. 20, 1978, p. 217 ff; Martin, Pierre-Marie, Le nouvel ordre économique international. *Revue Général de Droit International Public,* Vol. 80, N. 1, 1976. p. 502 ff. McWhinney, Edward, The international law-making process and the new international economic order. *The Canadian Yearbook of International Law,* Vol. 14, 1976, p. 57 ff; Petersmann, Ernst-U., Internationales Recht und Neue Internationale Wirtschaftsordnung. *Archiv des Völkerrechts,* Vol. 18, 1978/80, p. 17 ff; VerLoren van Themaat, Pieter, Some basic legal issues of a new international economic order: A Western point of view. *Netherlands International Law Review,* Vol. 24, 1977, p. 509 ff; Tyler, William G. ed., *Issues and Prospects for the New International Economic Order.* Lexington, Lexington Books, 1977. p. 195.

It seems to be widely accepted that these two principles form the backbone of all efforts to establish a new international economic order, although they are not explicitly mentioned in the Charter of Economic Rights and Duties of States. However, the Charter has been accused of impairing its own implementation by "overstressing national sovereignty".[27]

3.3.2. Sovereignty over national resources

This is in fact the crucial point in the whole discussion. On the one hand the principles of co-operation and solidarity seem to be natural and integral parts of a development which, having been set in motion by the first onslaught on the bulwark of sovereignty in the League of Nations Covenant, should logically lead "beyond the nation-State", as the so-called functionalists proclaimed.[28] On the other hand, the principle of permanent sovereignty over natural resources has been reiterated in practically all documents pertaining to the establishment of a new international economic order.[29] The Charter of Economic Rights and Duties reaffirms it in art. 2 para 1: "Every State has and shall freely exercise full permanent sovereignty including possession, use and disposal, over all its wealth, natural resources and economic activities." Paragraph 2 of this article draws some conclusions and confirms the right of States to regulate and supervise foreign investment and transnational corporations and "to nationalize, expropriate or transfer ownership of foreign property in which case appropriate compensation should be paid by the State adopting such measures, taking into account its relevant laws and regulations and all circumstances that the State considers pertinent."

There has been much speculation as to whether article 2 of the Charter – as the embodiment of the new trends in international law mentioned above – is or is not the repudiation of well-established principles of international law. According to the prevalent view, international law forbids confiscation of foreign property and demands "prompt, adequate, and effective compensation" in case of expropriation.[30] Karl Matthias Meessen believes "that of the five metres of shelf space occupied by literature on expropriation since 1945, 4.50 metres subscribe to the view, that full compensation must be paid for expropriation of any kind."[31]

Wellenstein, E. P. The new international economic order. *Netherlands International Law Review*, Vol. 1978, p. 222 ff.

27 Kapteyn, P. J. G., The basis of the new international economic order, *Netherlands International Law Review*, Vol. 25, 1978, p. 220.

28 Cf. Haas, Ernst B., *Beyond the Nation-State*, Stanford, Stanford University press, 1964, p. 595.

29 Cf. the Resolutions 523 (IV) of 12 January 1952; 626 (VII) of 21 December 1952; 1803 (XVII) of 14 December 1962; 2158 (XXI) of 25 November 1966; 2386 (XXIII) of 19 November 1968; 2692 (XXV) of 11 December 1970; 3016 (XXVII) of 18 December 1972; 3171 (XXVIII) of 17 December 1973.

30 Cf. US Department of State, Statement on Foreign Investment and Nationalization of 30 December 1975, *International Legal Materials*, Vol. 15, 1976, p. 186.

31 Meessen, Karl Matthias, International expropriation law in the conflict between North and South, *Law and State*, Vol. 19, 1979, p. 106. For a factual overview concerning a

Of course it would be possible to argue that the shift from "full compensation" to "appropriate compensation" is not dramatic, especially since it corresponds to a similar shift in the domestic law of "capitalist" States which used to adhere to the principle of full compensation, but have increasingly turned to appropriate compensation under the influence of the idea of the "social obligation of property". But we all know that in litigations concerning expropriations the question whether a certain amount is "appropriate" is the crucial one. Therefore in international law the first question is: who decides upon the amount of compensation? The Charter of Economic Rights and Duties of States gives priority to the domestic law of the nationalizing State and to its tribunals "unless it is freely and mutually agreed by all States concerned that other peaceful means be sought on the basis of the sovereign equality of States".

Exactly that is nothing new. On the contrary, it is this provision in the Charter which most clearly "reflects, so to speak, Western legal history, since it confirms that national legal systems, as juridical exponents of sovereignty, form the basis of the global legal system."[32] Thus it seems that W. Friedmann, writing five years before the Charter was signed, correctly described the new developments as "little more than a natural and organic evolution of an international legal order that has expanded from the International Law of Co-existence to the International Law of Co-operation".[33]

3.4. Sovereignty and property

There are deeper layers of thought on which the relationship between property and sovereignty has to be discussed. There is, e. g., the protection of property as part of a legal culture which in turn is deeply embedded in a specific civilization grown through the ages and intertwined with many beliefs and institutions. This has prompted a leading British economist to say of private property: "It is established and safeguarded by law, and can be modified, diminished or even destroyed by law. But it is no use trying to abolish private property by a stroke of the pen".[34] There is also the role which both private property and sovereignty have played in the evolution of international law. It seems to be no coincidence that again it was an economist who enlarged on the topic. Röpke pointed out that on the same foundation on which classical international law rested, the institu-

special group of countries cf. Kobrin, Stephen J., Foreign enterprise and forced divestment in LDCs. *International Organization,* Vol. 34, 1980, p. 65 ff.

32 de Waart, P. J. I. M., Permanent sovereignty over natural resources as a cornerstone for international economic rights and duties. *Netherlands International Law Review,* Vol. XXIV, 1977, p. 316; cf. also Brownlie, Ian, Legal status of natural resources in international law (some aspects). *Recueil des Cours, Académie de Droit international,* Vol. 162, 1979, p. 245 ff. Elian, Georges, Le principe de la souveraineté sur les ressources nationales et ses incidences juridiques sur le commerce international. *Recueil des Cours, Académie de droit international,* Vol. 149, 1976, I, p. 1 ff.

33 Friedmann, Wolfgang, General course in public international law, *Recueil des Cours. Académie de droit international,* Vol. 127, 1969, II, p. 183.

34 Hawtrey, Sir R. G., *Economic Aspects of Sovereignty.* 2nd ed., London, Longmans, Green and Co., 1952, p. 2.

tion of private property was made independent of the question of what State had sovereignty over the territory where the privately owned property was, and also independent of the question of the nationality of the owner.[35] In economic history this is known as "the separation of dominium (economic power) and imperium (political power)" which 19th century economic thought hailed as bringing freedom and peace by overcoming the barriers which political power had erected. It is an ironic and tragic fact that in the same century colonialism and imperialism reached their heyday, although they had long been refuted by economic thought.[36]

4. Peace and solidarity versus sovereignty and vested rights?

The historic lesson does not seem to be clear. We know that free trade and economic liberalism did not bring peace and freedom for all. But the theory that free economic competition was a major cause of war (especially World War I) has been thoroughly disproved. International law permitted colonialism, but it also permitted and respected the separation of imperium and dominium which in its essence battled against colonialism. The situation becomes clearer only when one considers the one area of legal norms in which the change from classic international law to a new legal order is undisputed, drastic and unequivocal: the realm of exerting political power. It is true that the prohibition of the threat or use of force contained in art. 2 para. 4 of the Charter of the United Nations is quite limited by the wording of this provision as well as by restrictive interpretation in current legal doctrine. But it is equally true that the sovereign States of today do not possess the same sovereignty as the sovereign States before World War I. The re-interpretation of sovereignty which the proponents of the new economic world order are calling for[37] has been under way since the end of World War I with the League Covenant, the Briand-Kellogg Pact and the Charter of the UN acting as catalysts. The resolutions of the General Assembly mentioned above, as well as those of UNCTAD, are logical sequences of a development well founded in present international law going back more than 60 years. Therefore it is of little use to enlarge upon the lack of binding force of such resolutions in general and of the Charter of Economic Rights and Duties in particular. This cursory remark is

35 Röpke, Wilhelm. Economic order and international law. *Recueil des Cours, Académie de Droit International,* Vol. 86, 1954, II, p. 228.

36 It is well known that the leading economists of the 19th century, especially John Stuart Mill, had convincingly proved that colonies were not profitable. Röpke W., *ibid.*, p. 229 cites Leonard Woolf (*Economic Imperialism,* New York, Harcourt, Brace & Howe, 1920): "In the year 1913 all British Colonies in Africa sent less than one per cent of all British imports to the motherland, whereas they received only one per cent of all British exports. As a market for British products Argentina was about three times and as a buyer about six times as important as all African Colonies, without costing the Britsih taxpayer a single penny."

37 Cf. especially the report by the Tinbergen team "Reshaping the International Order". A Report to the Club of Rome. In: *Equality of Opportunity Within and Among Nations.* (Haq, Khadija, ed.) New York, Praeger, 1977. pp. 20-24. (Praeger special studies in international economics and development).

not intended to demean the strenuous efforts of those who have penetrated into the details of the problem.[38] Furthermore one must never forget that the Charter of the United Nations itself has limited the powers of the General Assembly in such a way as to deny it the role of a "world legislator".[39] But nothing is gained by simply using new expressions like "soft law", if they are coupled with the secret intention to ignore the emerging new rules of law whenever national interests seem to be at stake. It may well be that these rules do not yet represent a legal order, but to call them "a mixture of ideological postulates, and some principles of law"[40] does not further the discussion. Putting it bluntly, this might be said of all legal rules throughout their history. All legal systems are, have been and will continue to be, in a permanent process of evolution, with new demands for legislation cropping up, being discussed and either fulfilled or repudiated while old legal norms become obsolete or attain new meaning by admissible interpretation even without new legislation. Thus, ideology and postulates are always mixing with legal principles; their interaction brings forth and preserves what we call the legal culture.

In our time and on the level we discuss here, the postulates of peace and solidarity mingle with a great number of binding rules of international law. Since the latter, as we have seen, is in a period of transition, some of these rules are old ones dating from "classical" times, some of them must and can be interpreted in the light of new developments, others – like the right of self-determination or the ban on violence – have evolved only in the past 60 years. To outside observers this mixture may appear to be the very opposite of an order, but it would be equally wrong to dismiss the present stage of development as a state of disorder or disintegration in contrast to the well-ordered situation of former times or of the national level. At no time did international law – or any national legal system – present the immutable monolithic image which some romanticists may dream of. Of course a legal order must be free from inherent contradictions in its basic system of values. Otherwise it could not endure for a lenght of time. But within this limitation a legal order may give ample room for peaceful change and adaptation to new conditions.

38 Even a limited selection should include Arangio-Ruiz, Gaetano, The normative role of the General Assembly of the United Nations and the Declaration of Principles of Friendly Relations. *Recueil des Cours, Académie de droit international,* Vol. 137, 1972, II, p. 431; Asamoah, Obed Y., *The legal significance of the declarations of the General Assembly of the United Nations.* The Hague, M. Nijhoff, 1966. p. 60; Onuf, N. G., Further thoughts on a new source of international law. *American Journal of International law,* Vol. 65, 1971, p. 778; Tunkin, G. I., The legal nature of the United Nations. *Recueil des cours, Académie de droit international,* Vol. 119, 1966, III, p. 36.

39 Tomuschat, Christian, Die Charta der wirtschaftlichen Rechte und Pflichten der Staaten. *Zeitschrift für ausl. öff. Recht u. Völkerrecht,* Vol. 36, 1976, p. 444 ff. with an English summary "The Charter of Economic Rights and Duties of States – A new legal order of world economy? *Ibid.,* p. 491.

40 This was done in the discussion of the Göttinger Seminar on New Developments of International Law in November, 1980, particularly by Professor F. Münch, Heidelberg.

Thus, provided that the principles of peace and solidarity are not inherently contradictory to the principles of sovereignty and the protection of vested rights, the present image of international law is not one of disintegration or disorientation, but rather one of increasing strength in the direction of peace and international solidarity. To retreat behind the argument that declarations of the UN General Assembly are not binding and that the "development ideology" of the UN has not yet been transformed into a flawless system of legal norms functioning reciprocally is to misunderstand the peaceful change that has taken place within the past six decades and to underestimate the possibilities of further peaceful change still contained in the present system of international law.

Again, this does not mean the abrogation of vested rights – private or public ones – nor the complete destruction of sovereignty. On the contrary, both policies would destroy any hope for successfully legislating for a new economic world order. The first would prevent the creation of the atmosphere of trust which is necessary for any kind of international economic relations.[41] The latter would not be in line with the development since the end of World War I which is obviously not aiming at the immediate substitution of national sovereignty by some kind of world government. But this must not mislead us into believing that the new international economic order is either a new form of disguised colonialism (because it respects property, the sanctity of treaties and vested rights) or a retrogression into the time of unhampered sovereignty.

5. Privileges for developing countries

Some authors are tempted to interpret the new rules of GATT and UNCTAD in terms of a split of traditional international law. The preferential treatment of underdeveloped countries in tariffs and trade and the toleration of their emphasis on national sovereignty has created, they argue, a special, privileged status of developing countries which threatens the unity of international law because it is incompatible with such time-honoured principles as reciprocity and the equality of States.[42] However, this is not true. Neither the principle of reciprocity nor the principle of equality prevents the granting of special rights to certain subjects of international law under certain conditions. Reciprocity does not mean that performance and counter-performance must be exactly equal in given units of money, weight, numbers or any other quantitative measure. Even without having recourse to the principle of solidarity which might oblige the "rich" countries to give out doles to the "poor" ones, we can conceive of an order of international economic relations in which the old system of formal reciprocity, formal non-discrimination and general use of the most favoured nation clause which was characteristic for GATT in its original version, is substituted (for specific groups of States) by a system of preferential treatment as provided in art. XXXIV-XXXVIII of GATT[43] in its new form. It might be called "material reciprocity"

42 Cf. Petersmann, Ernst-U., Die Dritte Welt und das Wirtschaftsvölkerrecht. *Zeitschrift für ausl. öff. Recht und Völkerrecht.* Vol. 36, 1976, p. 492 ff, with English summary "International economic law and the Third World". *Ibid.*, p. 549 f.

43 Added by the Protocol of 8 February 1965.

because it takes into account qualitative measures of performance and counter-performance, including such rewards as safeguarding the world against violence, forceful disruptions, destruction of the very basis not only of international economic relations, but of all relations. This is the true meaning of collective economic security. The premium paid for it in addition to commodity prices and payments for services might be compared to an insurance premium, not a dole, a bribe or a ransom, and not a compensation for injuries inflicted centuries ago.

6. The middle course of action for the new order

Of course these considerations do not solve technical problems in detail. There will continue to be the discussion about revised provisions of GATT or the formulation of UNCTAD resolutions. But there should no longer be discussions about the "legality" of the "new" principles mentioned above, including their technical implementation as, e. g., the waiver for UNCTAD contained in art. XXV of GATT. It is important that the whole body of these "new" provisions not only is a logical continuation of a process of change initiated by the Covenant of the League of Nations and consistently furthered by the Charter of the United Nations, but also is consistent with its own framework.

It may be difficult to ascertain the content and meaning of individual norms in a period of transition, but it is not impossible. The crucial question in this situation always is whether the system of legal norms as a whole remains intact, i. e., without inherent discrepancies and contradictions which would make it unworkable. In that case we would indeed have to say farewell to international law, as has been suggested sometimes in the years past.[44] It is here submitted that on careful examination this pessimism proves to be unfounded. This is true not only with regard to the principle of reciprocity, but also with regard to the equality of States. Again, it is not new to point out that international law has never disregarded factual inequalities and that it has never tried to disguise them by formal equality "before the law". Even before the revision of GATT and the convocation of UNCTAD it was recognised that "the States have a function within this [world] community, which they do not exercise on their own behalf – for the State is not an aim in itself – but on behalf of an order for the worldwide community of the human race, in accordance with given principles".[45]

In fact this is nothing else but the old concept of "universalistic equality" known already to scholastic philosophy. It is inseparably united with what today is called international social justice. Cynics have misinterpreted this amalgamation of principles in terms of a retrogression from the slogan "from each according to his ability and to each according to his need" to "from each according to

44 Cf. Sarup, R. K. P., Farewell to international law. *Nordisk Tidsskrift for International Ret.*, Vol. 36, 1966, p. 3 ff.

45 Kooijmans, Pieter Hendrik, *The Doctrine of the Legal Equality of States.* Leyden, A. W. Sijthoff. 1964, p. 40. Cf. also Ramcharan, B. G., Equality and discrimination in international economic law. *The Yearbook of World Affairs,* Vol. 35, 1981, p. 79 ff.

his vulnerability and to each according to his greed".[46] But in the view presented here, it is neither one. The new international economic order is neither the World Welfare State nor the dissolution of world trade patterns into bilateral or collective relationships of blackmail. As a consequence of the re-interpretation of reciprocity and of the equality of States mentioned above, the States giving and receiving help directly or indirectly (by granting resp. enjoying preferential treatment) retain their equal sovereignty in law. Therefore the emphasis on permanent sovereignty over natural resources found in so many documents is not in the least anachronistic. On the contrary: if the new international economic order is to avoid both the revival of colonialism in a new disguise and the tyranny of a global super-State, it must stress the principle of sovereignty leaving the ultimate responsibility for the welfare of each people where it belongs in accordance with the principle of self-determination of peoples.

This is the only choice for creating a new international economic order on the basis of international law which by definition means basing the order on a concordance of wills between sovereign States and not on some global authority or power. But that does not mean the repudiation of the idea of international planning. The plight of the developing countries is not the only reason for the worldwide call for a "managed economy" on a global scale.[47] Energy, raw materials and ecology are equally pressing, and they cannot be separated from each other.[48] The revision of GATT, UNCTAD, the Charter of Economic Rights and Duties of States, the efforts of the General Assembly and of the various specialized agencies of the United Nations are attempts to create such a management. Without going into details one may say that under the given circumstances the attempts were successful, because they chose the middle course between World Superstate dictatorshop (which many abhor and all believe to be unattainable in the foreseeable future) and free market behaviour (which even in the past was never free from government intervention, and the illusion of which nobody wants to revive). It may become increasingly difficult to keep this middle course in the future. As a general rule, however, one should bear in mind the warning: "Economic interdependence that outruns too far the extent of common political control, can be an element of international friction rather than harmony. Keeping a little apart can at times be the best way of keeping together."[49]

7. Limits and tasks for the managed world economy

So far, material, economic or human limits to any activities have not been mentioned directly. The reason is obvious. If it is true, as here suggested, that the

46 Stanley, Thimothy W., An unorthodox view of the North-South-Dialogue. *The Atlantic Community,* Vol. 18, 1980, p. 315.

47 Cf. VerLoren van Themaat, Pieter, Some basic legal issues of a new international economic order: a Western point of view. *Netherlands International Law Review,* Vol. XXIV, 1977, p. 521.

48 Cf. McWhinney, Edward, The international law-making process and the new international economic order. *The Canadian Yearbook of International Law,* Vol. XIV, 1976, p. 71.

49 Hirsch, Fred. *loc. cit.* (note 41), p. 531.

quest for a new international economic order is an organic part of the transformation of international law which has been under way since the end of World War I, it has no direct connections with limits except one: the ban on war and violence in international law which indeed limits the activities of States and individuals on the international level. Perhaps this is a human limit in the sense the organizers of this seminar used the term. Apart from it, the emerging new international economic order is not primarily designed to limit activities. Its function is to permit international economic co-operation and collective management of the world economy under the conditions of a world in which certain limits have become obvious. Furthermore some of these limits are instrinsically connected with the question of a new economic world order. Among them are those pertaining to food production, supply of raw materials, and energy. All three of them are in turn connected with the ecology problem and thus provide an additional link with the question of economic world order.

7.1. Food and population

The question of food production cannot be discussed in isolation from industrial production (including raw materials) and energy, because even in the less developed countries machinery plays an increasing role in the production and transportation of food. But the most important factor of the food problem is population, since its number determines the magnitude of demand for food; growing population figures automatically lead to the necessity to increase food production. To set artificial limits here would amount to genocide.[50] Enforcing qualitative limits would not help substantially. Therefore most of those who are concerned about the future advocate setting the limits at the very origin of the problem. Limiting population numbers (not just population growth) would help to solve problems of ecology, scarce raw materials and energy as well. But international law has nothing to do with such solutions. A multilateral treaty creating the obligation of States to enforce birth control with certain exactly defined results is an absurdity.

7.2. Migration

International law comes in with the next step: migration. People in distress will leave their homes and try to cross frontiers if they expect a better life on the other side of them. History has witnessed large movements of clans, tribes and even peoples across the continents of Asia and Europe in early times and of large numbers of individuals and families across the Atlantic in modern times. But they were small compared to the alarming magnitude of the migration problem today. Modern means of transportation make it possible for streams of refugees from starvation, poverty and political oppression to reach even distant countries. International law with its rigid mediatization of the individual by "his" State cannot

50 One of the darkest aspects of the discussion about the present global situation is the talk about "food power". Cf. Matzke, Otto, Nahrung als weltpolitisches Machtinstrument? (Food as an instrument of global power politics?) *Europa-Archiv*, Vol. 32, 1977, p. 293 ff.

cope with the ensuing problems. On the one hand the migrants, even if they are political refugees, have no right to be admitted into the territory of a foreign State.[51] On the other hand, the bond between the national and "his" State can be severed either by the individual refusing the (sometimes dubious) protection of the State of his nationality or by the latter, in each case leaving the individual outside the legal system of protection of aliens. If admitted on grounds of domestic law or political expediency, the large numbers of aliens create further problems up to the point of shaking the very foundations of the nation State. But the international order is affected as well. The enormous number of individuals no longer mediatized by any State is a constant reminder of the fact that the nation State is no longer the sole actor on the scene of international relations.

A new international economic order dealing only with buffer stocks, preferential tariffs, drawing rights and other technicalities of managing the world economy without paying heed to the tremendous problem of migration would not live up to the standard which the Charter of the United Nations has set for the transformation of international law in our time. In a certain sense that is a human limit to all activities directed toward this aim. The details may still be debatable: should migration be facilitated or should measures be taken to make it unnecessary? Are there conceivable measures which might induce people to refrain from migration? A host of similar questions must be asked. Obviously they cannot be answered in general terms. But there must be a legal framework for the solution of the manifold problems, and it must be a new framework reaching beyond the old State-centered system of international law.

7.3. Raw materials

From the human factors let us now turn to the material ones. Raw materials have been called "the economic lever" of the Third World.[52] Many believe that with respect to raw materials the clash of interests between North and South is most obvious: the developing countries, as exporters of raw materials, want to raise and stabilize commodity prices; the industrial countries are interested in free access to raw materials on low price levels. Theoretically, this is a situation in which agreement can easily be reached: each side has something it wants and something it offers; both sides have one goal in common, viz. stabilization of prices. In practice the situation is difficult because the formal common ground (stability of prizes) covers an abyss of substantial contrast (the coveted level of prices) and because neither side is monolithic, but consists of a multitude of partners bargaining for a multitude of commodities.

In former times each national economy, by virtue of it specific export and import needs, occupied its own unique position *vis-à-vis* the exporters of raw materials. But developing countries specializing in such exports always were at a disadvantage, because finished goods are by nature more expensive than raw

51 Cf. Grahl-Madsen, Atle, *The Status of Refugees in International Law*. 2 vols., Leyden, A. W. Sijthoff, 1966/1972; Grahl-Madsen, Atle, *Territorial Asylum*, Stockholm, Almquist & Wiksell International, 1980, p. 231.

52 Stecher, Bernd, Der "Gemeinsame Rohstoff-Fonds". *Europa-Archiv*, 1981, p. 57.

materials. In the long run a country may get out of this situation by industrial development. Aid for this effort seems to have dominated the development ideology in its first stages. But the developed countries seem to have dissociated from it not only because they began to fear the competition of newly industrialized countries or senseless global overproduction, but also because they and their partners realized that there were limits to industrialization all over the globe due to economic, human and ecological factors. Furthermore long-range development projects do not solve the immediate problems of a dire lack of foreign exchange needed to feed, house and educate a growing population today.

For a brief historical moment it seemed as if the developing countries might try to offset their disadvantage by forming cartels and raising the price level of raw materials. UNCTAD – especially UNCTAD IV – has changed the situation fundamentally. Recognizing that the fluctuation of commodity prices was detrimental for importers as well as for exporters, the members of UNCTAD cemented the common ground of price stabilization by reaching agreement on the necessity of buffer stocks and their financing through the Common Fund of the Integrated Programme for Commodities.[53] Even more important, it has generally become recognized that bargaining for low price levels, which in former times was taken for granted by the industrial powers, does not fit into the framework of the new international economic order. "Price stabilization or indexation should not form a pretext for avoiding higher prices where these are reasonable."[54]

The principle of permanent sovereignty over natural resources must be taken seriously. That means, first of all, that the share which the suppliers of raw materials receive of the total revenues of finished products must not be dictated by the odds of fluctuating market situations, but must be fixed by the standards of international social justice to represent what truly can be called a fair share. This rules out the old system of bilateral day-to-day bargaining in which the relative power positions of national economies are brought to bear. Rather it calls for global management as envisioned by UNCTAD IV and V. Again, this is not so new as it sounds. It has its precedents in the various commodity agreements, the history of which goes back to the thirties[55] and in the increased efforts to

53 Cf. *Proceedings of the United Nations Conference on Trade and Development, Fourth Session, Nairobi, May 5-31, 1976,* New York 1977, especially vol. I. p. 103 ff., Vol. III, p. 1 ff; Corea, Gamani, UNCTAD and the new international economic order. *International Affairs,* Vol. 53, 1977, p. 177 ff; Koul, Autar Krishnan, *The legal framework of UNCTAD in World Trade.* Leyden, A. W. Sijthoff, 1977, 255 p.; Gatz, Werner, *Auswertung der Dokumentation der vierten Welthandel- und Entwicklungskonferenz Nairobi 1976,* Baden-Baden, Nomos Verlagsgesellschaft, 1978, 635 p.

54 *Reshaping the International Order (RIO - Report):* a report to the Club of Rome/Jan Tinbergen, coordinator; Antony J. Dolman, editor; Jan van Ettingen, director. 1st ed. New York, Dutton, 1976, p. 147.

55 Negotiations for a wheat agreement and the establishment of an international wheat council were begun at conferences in Rome in 1931 and continued in London in 1932 and 1933. The International Wheat Council was finally established in 1949, followed by the International Sugar Council (1953) and the International Tin Council (founded by

stabilize commodity prices in recent times, as illustrated by compensatory financing for shortfalls in export earnings, especially the Export Earnings Stabilization Scheme (Stabex) in the Lomé Convention which entered into force on 1 April 1976.[56]

Also, the corresponding changes on the level of transnational relations concerning the technical implications are well under way. The traditional regime of concessions has been replaced by the new legal arrangement of the "joint venture".[57] New types of contractual agreements are emerging. Though they vary in details they all have one feature in common: they do not confer title to the natural resource on the transnational corporation, but merely engage the latter as a contractor or business partner.

7.4. Transnational corporations

Cynics may argue that new contractual arrangements cannot "effectively deter transnational corporations from realizing their desired return or retaining *de facto* control so long as they enjoy a virtual monopoly of such vital resources as capital, technological and managerial skills, and distribution outlets".[58] Indeed it must be recognized that at this point the whole question of the activities of transnational (or multinational) corporations becomes highly relevant, and that is not only a question of formulating contracts. For many years it seemed dubious whether international law had anything to say about the contractual relations between sovereign States and transnational corporations. The German Association of International Law put this topic on the agenda of its meeting as early as 1963,[59] and the discussion showed a wide variety of opinions. Today there is still

the Tin Convention of 1953, working since 1956). Cf. Fawcett, James E. S., The Functions of law in international commodities agreements. *British Year Book of International Law,* Vol. 44, 1970, p. 157 ff; Seyid Muhammad, V. A., *The Legal Framework of World Trade,* London, Stevens, 1958, p. 3481 Behrmann, Jere R., *Development, the International Economic Order, and Commodity Agreements.* Reading, Mass., Addison Wesley Pub. C., 1978, 152 p.; Seidl-Hohenveldern, Ignaz, Planung im Rahmen internationaler Rohstoffabkommen, in: *Planung IV,* ed. by Kaiser, Joseph H., Baden-Baden 1970, p. 281 ff.

56 Alting von Geusau, Frans A. M. ed., *The Lomé Convention and a new international economic world order,* Leyden, A. W. Sijthoff, 1977, p. 249 (esp. Bishnodat Persaud, Export earnings from commodities, p. 81 ff).

57 Cf. Asante, Samuel K. B., Restructuring transnational mineral agreements, *American Journal of International Law,* vol. 73, 1979, p. 335; Beha, Ralph W., Summary: Mining ventures in developing countries, in: Kirchner, Christian et al., *Rohstofferschließungsvorhaben in Entwicklungsländern,* Frankfurt, A. Metzner, 1977, p. 379 ff.

58 Asante, *loc. cit.* (note 57), p. 370.

59 Cf. Verträge zwischen staatlichen und nichtstaatlichen Partnern ("Contractual agreements between States and non-States"). *Berichte der Deutschen Gesellschaft für Völkerrecht,* Vol. 5, 1964, p. 133 ff. For later developments see Fatouros, A. A., Problèmes et méthodes d'une réglementation des entreprises multinationales. *Journal du Droit International,* Vol. 101, 1974, p. 495 ff.; Rubin, Seymour J., Developments in the law and institutions of international economic relations, Reflections concerning the

a lot of scholarly dispute on the subject, but it is clear, that all attempts to place "transnational law" outside the realm of public international law or to establish a third layer of legal norms between the levels of public and private international law[60] are of no avail. One of the features of the transformation of international law within which the new order of international economic relations is forming is the extension of public international law into the realm of relations between States and subjects of private law across national frontiers. The formulation of a code of conduct for multinational enterprises is only the first step on the way to creating binding rules to be enforced either by the States on whose territory the enterprises are incorporated or by international bodies.[61]

The same holds true for the question of the transfer of technology for which several drafts of a code of conduct have been worked out.[62] In this context the question of vested rights crops up in a special version, viz. patent rights.[63] As in the case of material property, international law cannot tolerate the confiscation of patent rights, but it can and must be reformed in such a way as to give developing countries easy access to advanced technology at reasonable conditions. And again, the principle of reciprocity will have to be interpreted in the light of the superseding principle of solidarity.

United National Commission on Transnational Corporations. *American Journal of International Law*, Vol. 70, 1976, p. 73 ff; (Tharp, Paul A., Jr., Transnational enterprises and international regulations: A survey of various approaches in internationl organizations, *International Organization*, Vol. 30, 1976, p. 47 ff; Vogelaar, Th., Multinational Corporations and International Law. *Netherlands International Law Review*, Vol. 27, 1980, p. 69 ff.

60 Cf. Rengeling, Hans-Werner, *Privatvölkerrechtliche Verträge* (Private treaties under public international law). Berlin, Duncker & Humblot, 1971, p. 272.

61 Cf. Werner, J. Feld, UN proposals for a code of conduct for multinational enterprises and the new international order. In: Tyler, William G., ed., *Issues and prospects for the New International Economic Order*, Lexington, Mass., Lexington Books, 1977, p. 177 ff, Tharp, Paul A., Transnational enterprises and international regulations: A survey of various approaches in international organizations, *International Organization*, Vol. 30, 1976, p. 47 ff. Baade, Hans W., The legal effects of codes of conduct for multinational enterprises. *German Yearbook of International Law*, Vol. 22, 1979, p. 11; Developing and Enforcing Guidelines for Multinational Enterprises. *American Society of International Law: Proceedings of the 70th Annual Meeting 1976*, p. 16 ff.

62 Cf. UN Document TD/B/C.6/14, Annex I and II; Chudson, W. A., *The international transfer of commercial technology to developing countries* (UNITAR Research Report No. 13), New York 1971; Okolie, Ch. Ch., *Legal aspects of the international transfer of technology to developing countries*, New York, Praeger, 1975; UNCTAD, *Guidelines for the study of the transfer of technology to developing countries*, New York, 1972 (TD/B/AC.11/9); UNCTAD, *An international code of conduct on transfer of technology*, New York, 1975, (TD/C.6/AC.1/2 Supp. 1/Rev. 1); UNCTAD IV produced three resolutions (87, 88, 89) on the subject.

63 Cf. UNCTAD, *The role of the patent system in the transfer of technology to developing countries*, New York, 1975 (TD/B/AC.11/19/Rev. 11).

7.5. Law and the integrated program

Facing this variety of problems the United Nations have launched their integrated commodities program, of which only some aspects have been mentioned above.[64] The task of the present paper was not to analyse their feasibility, but only to discuss the question whether they fit into the tendencies which have become apparent in the development of international law since the end of World War I. The answer must be positive. But a word of caution is necessary. It is not enough to know that international law offers the possibility to cope with the problems involved. Many political and moral decisions will have to be made in order to implement the program, shape the new legal system and strengthen the will to enforce its norms.

Thus the legal questions form an integral part of what is usually called "structural change".[65] But legal questions are affected also when this concept is used in its narrower purely economic sense. With some pointedness one observer recently has explained the "structural imbalance" of today's world economy in the following way: "the developing countries have unlimited demand but extremely limited resources, the industrial world has underutilized capacity but low demand, largely as a function of the energy crisis; while the handful of oil producers has most of the money – enough to buy all the companies listed on the New York Stock Exchange in a few years more".[66] This quotation leads us back to a problem area which has been touched upon briefly at the beginning of the present paper: money and the monetary system, which cannot be taken up here except for two concluding remarks. First, this problem area is one in which the idea of a managed economy has its oldest traditions, because it is old bankers' dictum that "money will not manage itself". Second, since the downfall of the gold standard and the abdication of the dollar as the world trade's leading currency the drawing rights against the IMF, the World Bank and similar international credit institutions have become the focus of interest. Again, the special drawing rights of developing countries are compatible with the principle of current international law, including the equality of States, as interpreted in the light of the principle of solidarity. Seen through the "veil of money", to use Pigou's familiar saying,[67] the crucial problems of the new economic world order are those of capital formation in the developing countries and of directing and controlling huge capital flows from one region of the world to others, all of which requires legal norms in accordance with the rest of the new order.

7.6. Energy and ecology

Up to this point the whole question of material assets has been discussed from a short term point of view. Organizing world markets to satisfy the needs of

64 For a summary see Bergsten, C. Fred, Ein umfassendes Programm für internationale Rohstofffragen. *Europa-Archiv,* Vol. 32, 1977, p. 711 ff.

65 Cf. Chenery, Hollis B., Restructuring the World Economy, *Foreign Affairs,* Vol. 53, 1974, p. 242 ff.

66 Stanley, Thimothy W., *loc. cit.* (note 46), p. 317.

67 Pigou, Arthur Cecil., *The Veil of Money,* London, Macmillan, 1949, p. 150.

producers and consumers in the light of international social justice may seem to be a long-term affair, but in the long run there are two additional aspects to be considered: the scarcity of certain raw materials and the protection of the environment. Both are connected with the problem of energy, which in turn is inseparable from the supply of certain raw materials, especially oil. Thus, again, it becomes evident that all sectoral problems of ecology, peace, and economic relations in the new order of international law are interwoven and form a pattern of interactions.

It is interesting to note that until recently the main sources of energy have been treated in international law under different headings. Nuclear energy has been the object of international legislation for decades, at first almost exclusively under the aspect of the threat of nuclear war – although atoms for peace were mentioned in the United Nations as early as 1953 –,[68] later on increasingly under the aspect of protection against harmful radiation. Within the latter context emphasis has shifted from health to ecology in recent years. Coal, natural gas and oil have been the object of international juridical interest mostly as commodities taking part in international trade. Among them, oil has attracted the utmost attention since the crisis of 1973, in which, for the first time, public opinion became aware of some aspects of this particular commodity well beyond purely economic questions.[69] What is still lacking is a comprehensive view of all energy sources not only as commodities in international trade or as potential pollutants, but also in the context of the new order of international law of which the economic order is an integral part. For the production and distribution of energy has created not only dependencies, but also interdependencies, as illustrated by the need of producers to import industrial goods for their production and to ask third parties for assistance in transporting the product across their territory. Building and maintaining permanent facilities for this purpose (pipelines for natural gas and petroleum, power lines for electricity)[70] requires a reliable legal framework. Thus, planning to meet the global energy demands of the future and executing the plans would seem to be a task which should foster international co-operation rather than be a cause of conflict.[71]

68 President Eisenhower's "Atoms for Peace" plan was announced to the Gerneral Assembly on 8 December 1953. Cf. *UN Yearbook 1954,* p. 3 ff.

69 Here it cannot even be attempted to register the vast literature on the subject. Much of it is relevant for the student of international law in spite of the fact that the whole problem is usually treated under economic or political aspects. One sector, however, is especially suited for legal considerations, viz. the forming and using of cartels like OPEC. Cf. Horstmann, Hans-Henning, Der Drang zum Rohstoffkartell (The quest for commodity cartels). *Europa-Archiv,* Vol. 29, 1974, p. 738 ff; Odell, Peter R., The international oil companies in the new world oil market. *Year Book of World Affairs,* Vol. 32, 1978, p. 76 ff; Penrose, Edith, OPEC's importance in the world oil industry. *International Affairs,* Vol. 55, 1979, p. 18 ff.

70 E. g., hydro-electricity from Norway is supplied through Sweden to Denmark and West Germany.

71 Cf. Haseler, Ernest, Energy in decline: A cause of conflict – or forcing international co-operation? *International Relations,* Vol. VI, p. 374 ff; Levy, Walter J., World oil co-operation or international chaos, *Foreign Affairs,* Vol. 52, p. 690 ff.

This holds true especially for the long range efforts to secure the energy supply for the whole world, again within the framework of the new economic world order, i. e. respecting the pinciples of international social justice and solidarity, comprising problems of energy conservation and of substitution. It is generally deemed to be necessary to reach "the optimum development over time of the different sources of energy so that each source can be replaced at the right time by another".[72] Apart from international research and development projects undertaken within the legal framework of existing international organization or on the basis of special agreements, the whole problem area of collective energy conservation and substitution has not yet been made the object of studies in the field of international law. The only exception is solar energy, as far as it implies the use of outer space. Solar energy can be utilized better if it is captured before passing through the Van Allen and ionic filter belts. Therefore the development of suitable outer space technology is most promising. The UN has drawn attention to this fact several years ago.[73] Several colloquiums and seminars on space law have taken up the matter.[74]

Throughout this paper the linkage between the problems of food, raw materials, energy and ecology has been stressed. Energy seems to be the focus of all other problems of the present world. With sufficient energy the production of food and finished goods could be raised to such a level as to satisfy the needs of a far larger world population than today with a far higher standard of living for everybody. Transportation would be no problem. Neither would be raw materials, because synthetic substitutes could easily be produced. But the environmental side effects of producing (or rather converting) such a tremendous amount of energy would be devastating.

Economic and legal analyses of the energy problem very often do not take into consideration that what is called energy production is in reality part of a larger and far more complex network of natural energy flows and that each interference with it has environmental consequences.[75] Very often they are hidden or belated, but that makes them not less grave, only more dangerous. They must be added to the direct damages done to the environment by agricultural and industrial production and transportation. In all cases one could say that environmental damage is wrought not by the activities as such, but by the manner in which they are conducted: in a manner no longer in harmony with nature, depleting natural resources, not allowing for natural regeneration, burdening nature with artificial enemies, destroying cycles of life. All of this is true, but it is not the core of the problem. We cannot be blind to the fact that the present world population would

72 de Montbrial, *op.cit.* (note 9), p. 67.

73 Especially through the efforts of the UN Committee on the Peaceful Uses of Outer Space, whose chairman called for the utilization of outer space for purposes of energy production on June 9, 1975; see UN document A/AC.105/PV.144.

74 Cf. Williams, Maureen, International Law in the pursuance of sun power as a new source of energy. *International Relations,* Vol. 5, 1977, p. 24 ff.

75 Cf. Lovins, Amory B., World Energy Strategies. *Bulletin of the Atomic Scientiests,* Vol. 30, May 1974, p. 14 ff.

be a tremendous ecological burden even if we all lived primitively in perfect harmony with nature. Both the number as well as the standard of living of people, are important factors in the struggle against pollution. But it would be foolish to base any ecological program on the assumption that shrinking world population and the return of the survivors to nature would solve the environmental problems of today and tomorrow. Therefore the insights mentioned above can give only the general direction of the many efforts to be made.

7.7. Protection of the environment

There is scarcely a nation which has not yet started legislation for the protection of the environment. There have also been numerous efforts to co-ordinate the national efforts on regional or global levels. There are the vast areas without national sovereignty in which pollution control is by definition an international task: the high seas, airspace above the high seas, the seabed, outer space. There is finally the problem of transfrontier pollution (air and water). A multitude of bilateral and multilateral agreements have been concluded in each of these problem areas creating a vast number of legal obligations.[76] Even customary law has evolved in the field of pollution control.[77]

76 The literature on this subject is rapidly increasing. For further references the following selection is offered. Abrahamsson, Bernhard J., The marine environment and ocean shipping: some implications of a new Law of the Sea. *International Organization*, Vol. 31, 1977, p. 291 ff; Angelo Homer G., International Environmental Protection: Policy, Legal, and Trade Aspects. *American Society of International Law, Proceedings of the 71st Annual Meeting*, 1977, p. 48 ff; Ballenegger, Jacques, *La Pollution en droit international*. Genève, E. Droz, 1975, p. 268; Barros, James and Johnston, Douglas M., *The International Law of Pollution*. New York, Free Press; London, Collier Macmillan Publishers, 1974, p. 476; Bilder, Richard B., The Settlement of Disputes in the Field of the International Law of the Environment. *Recueil des Cours, Académie de droit international*, Vol. 144, 1975, I, p. 139 f; Bramsen, Christopher Bo, Transnational Pollution and International Law, *Nordisk Tidsskrift for International Ret*, Vol. 42, 1972, p. 153 ff; Contini, Paolo and Sand, Peter H., Methods to Expedite Environment Protection: International Ecostandards. *American Journal of Internatioal Law*, Vol. 66, 1972, p. 37 ff; Douay, Claude, Le droit de la mer et la préservation du milieu marin. *Revue Général de Droit International* Public, Vol. 84, No. 1., 1980, p. 178 ff; Erçman S., *European Environmental Law, Legal and Economic Appraisal*, Bern, Bubenberg Verlag, 1977, p. 508; Handl, Günther, Territorial Sovereignty and the Problem of Transnational Pollution, *American Journal of International Law*, Vol. 69, 1975, p. 54 ff; Hargrove, John Lawrence, (ed)., *Law, Institutions and the Global Environment*. Dobbs Ferry, N. Y., Oceana Publications, 1972; Kay, David A. and Skolnikoff, Eugene B. (eds.), International Institutions and the Environmental Crisis. *International Organization*, Vol. 26, 1972, p. 169 ff; Khan, Rahmatullah, Marine Pollution and International Legal Controls. *Indian Journal of International Law*, Vol. 13, 1973, p. 389 ff; Kiss, Alexandre-Charles., ed., *The Protection of the Environment and International Law*, Leyden, Sijthoff, 1975; 650 p.: Kiss, Alexandre-Charles, *Survey of Current Developments in international Environmental Law*, Morges, International Union for Conservation of Nature and Natural Resources, 1976, p. 141; Kiss, Alexandre-Charles, La pollution du milieu marin. *Zeitschrift für ausländisches öffentliches*

It is not the task of this paper to go into details on the question of international environmental law or even give a summary. The ecological context is inherent in all questions of food, raw materials and energy, as has been shown. In addition however, the overriding goal of the protection of the environment must be respected by the legal rules forming the new order of international economic relations. Otherwise the new order would soon be useless. Generally speaking, this means that the scarcity of raw materials and energy cannot be easily overcome or in some cases is even aggravated, because environmental considerations restrict production resp. conversion. To enforce such rules in the face of population growth and rising expectations will be extremely difficult.

The above statement is phrased in general terms. But although in its essence it does apply to all countries, the factual situation is such that the problem is most sharply accentuated in the Third World. The attitudes towards it vary greatly. For advocates of pollution control it is tempting to say that the less developed state of Third World economies offers a unique opportunity to show that urbanization and industrialization can be effected without repeating the errors of the Industrial Revolution. (In addition there are some who propose to keep the Third World "green" altogether which actually amounts to genocide.) The counterargument is that the developing countries are subjected to discrimination if they are denied the benefit of unhampered use of available technology which the industrial nations enjoyed when they were building up their economic potential.[78]

Recht und Völkerrecht, Vol. 38, 1978, p. 902 ff; Utton, Albert E., International Environmental Law and Consultation Mechanismus. *Columbia Journal of Transnational Law,* Vol. 12, 1973, p. 56 ff; Wilson, Thomas W. Jr., *International Environmental Action, A Global Survey,* London, 1971. For documentations see *International Environment Programmes* (in English, French and German) ed. by Erich Schmidt Verlag, 7 vols. Berlin 1976-1978; *The Basis of the U. N. Environmental Policy – The Resolutions of the General Assembly,* ed. by Erich Schmidt Verlag, Berlin 1973; Burhenne, Wolfgang E, ed., *Environmental Law of the European Communities.* Loose-leaf Edition, Berlin 1973; Burhenne, Wolfgang E., ed., *International Environmental Law* (Multilateral Treaties), 4 vols., (loose-leaf), Berlin, Schmidt, 1974 containing about 600 treaties.

77 Cf. Goldie, L. F. E., Development of an international environmental law. In: Hargrove, John H, ed., *Law, Institutions, and the Global Environment,* Dobbs Ferry, N. Y., Oceana Publications, 1972, p. 104 ff:, esp. p. 131 ff., Handl, Günther, Territorial sovereignty and the problem of transnational pollution, *American Journal of International Law,* Vol. 69, 1975, p. 50 ff., Klein, Eberhard, *Umweltschutz im völkerrechtlichen Nachbarrecht,* Berlin, Dunker & Humblot, 1976, p. 354.

78 Cf. de Aranjo Castro, J. A., Environment and Development: the case of the developing countries. In: *World Eco-Crisis:* international organizations in response, ed. by Kay, David A., and Skolnikoff, Eugene B., Madison, University of Wisconsis Press, 1972, p. 237 ff; Seidl-Hohenveldern, Ignaz, The Third World and the protection of the environment. In: *Estudios de Derecho International, Homenaje a Miaja de la Muela,* Vol. I , Madrid, Editorial Tecnos, 1979. p. 351 ff; Kapp, K. William, Towards a new approach to socio-economic and environmental development. In: Steppacher, R. et al., *Economics in International Perspective.* Lexington, Mass., Lexington Books, 1977, p. 205 ff.

Again, the fundamental legal question is whether the developing countries can be accorded a privileged status in global environmental law. Since in the context of trade and credit rights preferential treatment of developing countries was construed to be in accordance with the principle of equality it seems logical to plead for a similar interpretation of equality in the ecological context, too. However, this is not the case. As will be remembered, the new interpretation of the old principle of the equality of States is based upon the principle of solidarity, which forms the cornerstone not only of the new economic world order, but also of the emerging system of international law. It is also – and must be – the very foundation of global environmental law. Applying the principle of solidarity to the question of global pollution control, one must argue that there can be no privilege to destroy nature.

If the duties laid down by international environmental law place a disproportionate burden on the national economy of a developing country, compensation must be sought for outside the ecological field. Of course this can never be a compensation payment in the strict sense, because the imposition of such a duty is not an expropriation of property rights. In domestic law there may be cases when a certain restriction of private property rights due to the enforcement of regulations for the protection of the environment entitles the private owner to demand compensation. In public international law such a situation is unthinkable because there is no world government acting as the representative of the beneficiary (which in this case would be the world population). It would be possible, of course, to create a world environmental fund to collect and distribute such payments. But the legal norms to define debtors and creditors, the prerequisites and the amount of payments would be difficult to formulate and to enforce. There are easier ways to cope with the problems of just distribution of the burdens created by the enforcement of global environmental law, if the institutions of the new international economic order are used for this purpose. Thus, e. g., developing countries might receive special drawing rights in exchange for their willingness not to undertake certain activities.

The details of such a distribution of burdens will have to be discussed in the future. For the time being, it is important to note that international law doctrine has established a link between environmental law and human rights.[79] Accordingly, the principles proclaimed at the end of the Stockholm conference on 3 July 1972 begin with the dictum: "Man has the fundamental right to freedom, equality and adequate conditions of life, in an environment of a quality that permits a life of dignity and wellbeing, and he bears a solemn responsibility to protect and improve the environment for present and future generations".[80] Neither the right

79 Cf. Gormley, W. Paul, *Human Rights and Environment: The need for International Cooperation*, Leyden, A. W. Sijthoff, 1976, p. 255; Wolman, Abel, Global pollution and human rights. In: *Environmental Policy; concepts and international implications.* Ed. by Utton, Albert E. and Henning, Daniel H., New York, Praeger, 1973, p. 176 ff; Strong, Maurice F., One Year after Stockholm. *Foreign Affairs*, Vol. 51, 1973, p. 690 ff.

80 UN Document A/CONF. 48/14.

nor the responsibility is divisible. The principle of solidarity calls for unequivocal and full respect of the international obligations concerning the protection of the environment, regardless of the economic situation of the country in question. Therefore it is possible to set international ecostandards by multilateral agreement.[81]

As far as internationally shared natural resources are concerned, current international law offers several possibilities. The principle of "equitable use" – which has been confirmed by the Charter of Economic Rights and Duties of States – may be invoked to interdict uses of natural resources which would amount to transfrontier pollution.[82] For goods that are traded internationally or compete with internationally traded goods, GATT concedes exemptions from the principle of non-discrimination, if they are burdened by anti-pollution measures (such as pollution control schemes or pollution rates) which are necessary to protect human, animal or plant life or health (art. XX). Export subsidies to compensate for the cost of environmental regulations applied by the exporting country must be admissible, because otherwise countries which take their global environmental responsibility seriously would be punished. Pollution control measures must not have the effect of trade barriers. On the other hand this policy must not delay the efforts to establish world-wide ecostandards as soon as possible.

The list of problems still to be solved seems endless. And in fact, it is endless, because the advance of science and technology and the continuing deterioration of the environmental situation create new problems every day. There is some comfort in the thought that the emerging new international law can offer solutions for them. Reviewing the efforts of the United Nations during the past two decades one cannot but admire the farsightedness of the organizers and participants of international meetings which have produced convention drafts, declarations, programs of action etc. Yet, at the end of a report which can offer only brief summaries, it cannot be denied that sadness and skepticism are the prevailing emotions, not only because of the deficiencies of the superficial report itself, but also because of the magnitude of the problems still waiting to be solved. All conferences on the subject have ended with stern exhortations appealing to the conscience of political leaders and legislators. More optimistic writers have expressed the view that "environmental deterioration [can be] contained by appealing directly to national interest".[83] International law appeals to both, although in subtile ways.

81 Contini, Paolo and Sand, Peter H., Methods to expedite environment protection: international ecostandards. *American Journal of International Law,* Vol. 66, 1972, p. 37 ff.

82 Cf. Handl, Günther, The principle of "equitable use" as applied to internationally shared natural resources. *Revue belge de droit international,* Vol. XIV, 1978/79, p. 40 ff; McCaffrey, Stephen C., Pollution of shared natural resources: legal and trade implications. *American Society of International Law: Proceedings of the 71st Annual Meeting 1977,* Vol. 71, p. 56 ff.

83 Shields, Linda P. and Ott, Marvin C., The environment crisis: international and supranational approaches. *International Relations,* Vol. IV, 1974, p. 645.

6.7. Material, Economic and Human Limits to the Activities of Humankind

International Law and Economic Paradigms

Philippe de Seynes

From the point of view of international socio-economic order, the present symposium is of enormous importance. To those of us for whom international economics has been a life-long affair, the role of international law remains an unanswered question. Does it facilitate or inhibit economic development, social and cultural welfare?

There is at the outset a question of semantics or definition. In the field of economics, it is certainly more interesting to take the broadest possible concept while recognizing that at the same time, in relation to binding power, one of the essential attributes which the tradition ascribes to law, it is also a "minimalist" concept. But international life and institutions have since World War II proliferated in such an unprecedented manner that law was bound to experience a "qualitative" transformation. The sum total of non-legally enforceable legislation, in the form of resolutions, codes of conduct, final acts of conferences, charters of obligations and rights, comprehensive strategies and plans of action, probably outweighs, in its cumulative impact and influence on the behaviour and mental processes of society the few instances of treaties or conventions endowed with sanctions, mostly of a retaliatory or compensatory nature.[1] As norms negotiated but solidly based on at least two of the three principles identified by Professor Grahl-Madsen, *necessity* and *equity* (the third one, *reciprocity*, cannot very well accomodate the asymmetry inherent in North-South relations) they represent a stage in the evolution of international law, in many cases an ephemeral stage, as some of them become rapidly obsolescent in the light of fast changing behaviour and perceptions.

Therefore, the problem of enforcement seems to me to take second place to that, far more difficult, of formulating correct specific policies in an increasingly complex world. For, in the field of economic order, positive law, whether national or international, confronts other types of "laws", those resulting from the spontaneous mechanisms of nature and social life. Theories or paradigms derived from the knowlegde and understanding of these mechanisms, acquired through the statistical observation of regularities or the scientific identification of causal chains, serve, by virtue of the strength of their rationality, as legitimizing plots,

1 This judgement is likely to remain valid even after the conclusion of a Treaty on the Law of the Sea.

in a somewhat different way but perhaps to a greater degree than positive laws. Their effect is less visible, and more often than not, works unconsciously. Many individuals and institutions, particularly in the last quarter century, have elected, not without some complacency, to categorize their approach to world problems as "international pragmatism". This is of course self-deception as well as a fiction. In one of his witty moods, Keynes wrote that "practical men are usually the slaves of some defunct economist". The dominant paradigm, underpinning practical action in the international field does not have to be repeated every day to serve its purpose. It weaves its way somewhat mysteriously in the mental processes of the political class and the establishment intelligentsia. It is enough that it should not be challenged openly, and in a manner that reaches and unsettles these circles. The dialectical interaction of theory and praxis is part of the great legacy of the nineteeth century, obscured during the period of easy expansion of the last quarter century. In the present and foreseeable circumstances, marked by new, or differently stated problems, it is doubtful whether praxis may successfully develop without a progress in theory. And this has a bearing on International Law.

*

One of the new problems which has yet to be articulated within a coherent framework in relation to the older paradigms is the sudden intrusion of *ecology* in our epistemological universe.

In a very short period the reflexion on ecology has gone far beyond the pragmatic approach to pollution and other environmental hazards. In fact, ecologists are now organizing themselves in social movements, sometimes political parties, and in the search for legitimizing paradigms, they sometimes strive to project a conceptual framework so comprehensive that economics and other branches of social sciences would be viewed as sub-systems of ecology. Ecology is, admittedly, the larger, more comprehensive concept. And it is a grandiose, mind-expanding concept, illustrated at various times of history from ancient Greece to German Romanticism. Such questions as the protection of endangered species involve speculation of a Darwinian type on evolution of the human species and the equilibrium of the universe. It is the delight of philosophers, particularly when they have not been unduly absorbed into the intricacies and rigors of economic imperatives. But to those who feel responsible for economic policies or the further progress of the "dismal science", it may become a veritable nightmare. There are practical dangers, for policy-making at least, in ascribing this kind of primacy to ecology, whatever its inherent transcendental logic. To say that ecology is the larger concept and to understand the desirability of integrating other disciplines with it does not however mean that it can at present be *the* organizing principle for the reflexion on society. To take as a starting point of this reflexion, as was so often the case, the "lifeboat" image has the effect of "evacuating" some of the fundamental mechanisms of history, those involved in the operation of the economic systems, and the interplay of social forces, the tensions and conflicts to which we have been used, with good reason, to look as explanations of changes in human society. If we are threatened with an impending physical catastrophe and concerned with the survival of the human species as such, we need not be too touchy about the flaws in the forms of its social organization.

There is, in the ecological approach, a new consideration of the relations of man to nature, beyond those embodied in the use of land and natural resources through the mediation of labour, capital and technology. This implies new obligations to nature, not directly related to human welfare or the enhancement of human rights and dignity. This is quite respectable in itself, but it is as yet alien to Western culture, although more natural in some cicilizations of the East. It involves a belief in the transcendental character of the "laws of nature", supposed to protect ecological cycles and balances. This clashes with the positivist approach which has provided heretofore the rationality for development, all the more since these laws and balances are not at all well known, nor always well established on a sound ethical basis. For instance, some of them are not quite as exquisite as assumed, more particularly when they involve the extermination of weak animal species by the stronger ones. Nor are they necessarily inevitable, if approached from a positivist world view. With all the preoccupations at one time generated by the depletion of the ozone layer, not enough consideration seems to be given to its possible replenishment through human action. Scientists, prone to explain the phenomenon of depletion and its risks in a language of impecceable objectivity, are also liable to brush off the question of replenishment with the peremptory comment that "it is dangerous to interfere with the laws of nature".

Some of the most crucial situations still affecting a significant portion of humanity in the Third World are in fact part of the "survival" syndrome. There is a vast area where the sustainability of ecosystems and the subsistence of their growing population are totally coincidental. Among them are the degradation of the soils, the depletion of water supplies, the desiccation of forests, the need for new crops, the harvesting of water plants, above all perhaps the micro-biological and viral environment which is still the principal form of pollution of the poor countries.

Elsewhere, the integration of ecology and economy in a comprehensive and well articulated framework, if pursued at too high a philosophical level, would be a trying and exacting task and probably futile for several generations. It is therefore not surprising, and probably unavoidable, although neither quite fair nor absolutely convincing, that planners and policy-makers should still be viewing environmental effects as *constraints* on the development pattern. It is natural for economists to look at pollution, crowding, climate, as "negative externalities", which they have learned to incorporate within economic development models. The treatment of exhaustible resources, although for a long time one of the neglected areas of economic theory, is nevertheless not a new sector of economic science. Concequently, the ecological issue can be, without much effort, brought within a framwork of known quantities.

As hinted earlier, this treatment of environment is somewhat unfair and justified only as long as economists and planners feel that this is the limit of what they are capable of doing. Yet ecology should also be viewed as an opening of *opportunities*. The challenge that the emergence of the ecological school offers to economic science should be particularly welcome as, even in relation to the production subsystems, the most thoroughly ploughed field of the economic discipline, the analysis is much in need of *aggiornamento*. The anguished reaction provoked in Third World countries[2] when zero-growth, or slow-growth is presented as the answer to the ecological problematique, can only find an adequate response if the role of growth in the process of development is seriously re-examined. In this respect, ecology should be seen as a vital element in the renovation of our culture.

*

Indeed, the 1970's appeared to introduce a new outlook on problems of national development and international cooperation. The air vibrated with expressions of dissatisfaction at traditional patterns and prescriptions. Under the cumulative impact of demographic pressure and decades of "disequalizing" policies, attention was shifting from growth to poverty-related issues, employment and distribution, as well as participation of the masses in the decision-making process and reduced "dependencia". The new international economic order legislation emphasized the importance of redressing the South-North balance of power as a condition for sustained economic gains. Yet the great documents heralding the beginning of a new decade, the International Development Strategy for the Eighties adopted by the United Nations General Assembly, and the unofficial but brilliant and highly influential report of the prestigious Brandt Commission, largely reproduce, admittedly with some refinements, the conceptual framework which had served for previous Grand Designs. As is usual in such cases, it is contended that failures are due to lack of political will in the implementation of policies advocated for twenty years. But the "keep on trying" advocacy has a certain hollow ring these days. More and more people think that there are flaws in the traditional approach to development, and question whether what the *Economist* of London calls the "bold international Keynesianism" of the Brandt Commission is the true answer, or the only answer to the problems confronting most countries of the periphery. This is quite apart from the plausibility of such a scheme being implemented in the foreseeable conditions of the 1980's.

It is true that both the International Development Strategy and the Brandt Commission report dutifully and even eloquently mention the whole array of social objectives. They do so, however, in a "declaratory way". They do not analytically relate these objectives to one another, nor to the policies needed for their implementation. The International Development Strategy for the Seventies had a remarkable intuition when it postulated that "Distribution is not only the result but a major determinant of development". This message, curiously omitted from the International Development Strategy of the Eighties, has yet to be absorbed, a matter which requires a great deal of theoretical and empirical work. The old paradigm cannot be changed or repudiated, except with the same sophisticated weapons which established its dominant position. The present lag in theoretical advances places in doubt the compatibility of international law with theory, as a condition of its relevance. The papers of this symposium display a

2 This is also true of Ronald Reagan and François Mitterand.

certain hesitation in regard to the foundations of present international law, which Professor Kimminich at one point seems to relate to an opposite between free trade and the UN development philosophy. The situation is, in my view, somewhat more complex. In fact, the Third World continues in the UN to demand free access to world markets, notably in manufactures, and is hardly satisfied with the so-called "general" but in fact very limited, scheme of preferences. Nor does the introduction of floating exchange rates appear to me such an important watershed in the emergence of the present disorders. The previous regime was not much more stable than the present one. Numerous and somewhat abrupt changes in parities had taken place for some time and they were frequently amplified by a great deal of speculation, which was quite safe as the direction of the fluctuations was entirely predictable in a system of fixed rates. The problem is rather that at no time was there a consensus on rules of adjustment in a world no more prepared to accept automatic disciplines in the context of rising national expectations.

The philosophy underlying the policies of the UN, from an early period, relied on growth transmission from North to South, combined with correctives (now seen as rather minor) through more widely open export markets and through capital transfers, to take in charge a certain recognized asymmetry in the North-South situation. Commodity schemes were a deviation from the pure free trade paradigm, but one which had found its legitimate place in the orthodoxy of the Havana Charter.

Albeit in a somewhat ambiguous formulation, the NIEO, emerging in the new context of the OPEC strategy introduced, as already noted, the important new dimension of power balance, the notion that a correction of the present imbalance is equally important as immediate economic gains, and indeed a condition of sustainable economic gains. Many were hopeful that, after many years of frustrated dialogue, the control of the price of oil would herald a new era of successful negotiation on the catalogue of principles and practical steps elaborated in 1964 at the first UNCTAD Conference. The experience of the subsequent period did not invalidate the OPEC strategy. But it showed that the control of one price, however important, if not butressed by a comprehensive and *adequate* attack on under-development, would not achieve a significant change in the balance of power. It also showed that the control of that price is not an easy matter. Hence, the repeated disappointment of oil producers, and by ricochet of the Third World as a whole, as they realized that the strategy did not produce the full expected results. This also is related to lags in theory as shown in a current UNITAR study on the economics of exhaustible resources.

The debate, from the perspective of Third World countries, must be seen not so much as one between free trade and organized trade or orderly marketing, nor between fixed and floating exchange rates, nor between the use of gold or Special Drawing Rights as currency reserve. The debate is rather one bearing on *how much trade, how much foreign capital and multinational production, what kind of technology and output-mix*, in short what is the desirable degree and nature of the insertion of weak economies in a hostile world system.

The exhaustion of the post-war boom and the uncertainties about stagflation are forcing a widening of the debate. It is the various aspects of the capitalist regime in its present phase and in its total dimension, including its extraordinary resilience (which Marx had so well analysed,) that is under examination. And this is why the reflexion on long-term has now penetrated the political area. This is why the sociological and the historical factors must now enter the discussion, unless the debate becomes futile.

This leads directly to the perspective of "unequal exchange" and "Self-Reliance", as it becomes compulsory to explore whether and how the Third World could disentangle itself from the embrace of the Northern Hemisphere, by more or less radically modifying its own structures which had been historically induced by Northern Capitalism; whether they can become less dependent on international trade (in the current jargon less "outward looking" policies) for the essential goods, including some capital goods, as well as on international capital, and create an economy more oriented toward the needs of the masses. This is advocated not only for reasons of justice, but for the purpose of creating a more viable basis for rapid and sustained industrialization.

It is not the result of a "voluntarist" elaboration but derives from a comprehensive analysis which focuses on the relationship of international and national factors, and seeks to identify the effects – perverse or benign according to circumstances – of international flows of goods and money, on the various dimensions of the economies of the Third World – not just the balance of payments or the volume of investment – but prices, incomes, employment, terms of trade, technological choices, "dependency". In terms of policy prescriptions, the results are significantly different from those which are at present routinely embodied in national policies and schemes of international co-operation. Those arising from UNITAR's study converge with those arrived at under various analytical approaches in a number of studies of the last thirty years. May I simply mention here the prophetic message of Gunnar Myrdal in the early fifties.

The approach marks a clear departure from the neo-classical theory, even in its latest version, with its projection of an International Division of Labour according to comparative advantages, on the assumption of the equalization of factor prices:

- Export-led policies, when the elasticity of labour supply is high, or when the goods exported from the South are wage goods, modify prices and incomes in such a way that income distribution in the South worsens and that, after a time, even the terms of trade, and therefore growth itself are adversely affected. In simple terms, growth cannot durably be based on cheap labour provided by extreme mass poverty, even if in the short-term, total revenues from exports may increase.
- Under specific circumstances, capital transfers may also turn against the terms of trade of the goods exported from the South, thus defeating one of the major objectives of the new international economic order, namely the improvement of the South-North balance, notably through the betterment of the terms of trade.[3]

3 The results in these paragraphs are derived from the theoretical analysis. They are being

- Improvement in the configuration of the production apparatus (or output mix) is therefore, especially in the early stages, the key to a viable economy, providing a sound basis for rapid industrialization oriented towards the needs of the masses. The degree and nature of participation in the world system is a factor crucial to the success of such a policy. Sometimes this objective may be reached through relatively minor changes. But in other circumstances it will require a radical process of "delinking and relinking".[4]
- Massive redistribution through welfare policies are not likely to be stable unless adequate configuration of the system of production is such that the operation of the markets can contribute in creating a situation as close as possible to the desired objectives.
- Tax policies used for redistribution purposes may produce two diametrically opposed outcomes. They may redistribute income against wages for the purpose of maximizing savings. But beyond a certain level of income concentration, they will decrease investment and growth because of reduction in overall demand. On the other hand, a Keynesian type of redistribution in favour of wages may have the initial effect of increasing investment to respond to additional consumers' demand but later may prove to reduce total investment. The UNITAR model and empirical studies may help to determine in various circumstances what policy is likely to be beneficial to growth and distribution.
- The implementation of new self-reliant strategies will to a significant extent depend on new technological options. Since the choice of technologies is not completely free, technological policies must be integrated in overall planning and be compatible with policies designed for other objectives of Society. Usually, this will imply a combination of advanced, even very advanced processes and labour intensive techniques.
- Examined from the point of view of concentration and composition, variability and stability, the operation of international markets demonstrates dramatically, as in UNITAR's study, the extent of the North-South imbalance, as well as certain perverse correlations, as observed between the food and armaments markets. The choice of policies designed to reduce "dependencia" should take into account the control exercised on commodity world markets by certain groups of countries, with a view to minimizing the impact of such controls on national policies.
- With such implications for *national policies*, it is important to devise appropriate international responses. The process of "delinking" and "relinking", essential to national and collective Self-Reliance, is an arduous undertaking which has, at times, been met with embargoes and boycotts. It should instead count on new forms, and adequate provision of liquidity during periods of sufficient duration (that even in its liberalized approach the IMF probably

empirically tested (and are already *partially* confirmed) in the case of a number of countries such as Brazil, Costa Rica, Ecuador, Hungary, India, Malaysia, Nicaragua, Pakistan, Panama, Poland, Tunisia, United Kingdom.

4 Delinking from the North and relinking with the South, and also but in different ways with the North.

cannot afford), and subject to criteria of conditionality inspired by a different philosophy of adjustment, accepting the need for an aggravation of the balance of payment position, during the lengthy period of transition to a more viable self-reliant and egalitarian society.

It is therefore time for the jurists, as well as others, to take note, if not of a change in the dominant paradigm, at least of the emergence of a strong competing paradigm, explored in its practical implications by an increasing body of scholars and policy-makers as well as the "militants of change" in large areas of the Third World, and in important circles of the First World. The recent turn of events in France is having an impact in this respect on several countries of Europe and elsewhere. It is important fo find out how these developments will affect the *evolution of international law*. That they do not as yet find their way into UN or other official legislation because of the inevitable institutional lag is no reason why they should be overlooked by those scholars who contribute to the construction of international law, lest they become the unwilling accomplices of unpleasant geopolitical realities of domination. There are governments which already espouse the findings of the various approaches related to unequal exchange – and given the state of the world, it is a safe bet that there will be more of them. There are also in the UN System large and important programmes of action designed to respond to the aspirations of *all* governments.

The new strategies are also of a nature that will pose to lawmakers difficult conceptual and technical problems. International responses to Self-Reliance policies would have to be attuned to highly differentiated economic and social configurations, notably in the fields of protectionism, subsidies and financial aid. Will the trade rules include more of the usual "tolerable deviations"? Can the International Monetary Fund pursue further its present liberalization policies? Can it change its criteria of conditionality to accommodate "self-reliant strategies" during the lengthy period of balance of payment deficits inevitable in the "delinking" process? In other words, will the International System find an adequate "Niche" for countries pursuing progressive policies?

Finally, Self-Reliant Strategies, up to now have been bent toward the Marxist Model. This is the case with those that have been successful. It may be of course because only a revolutionary creed is seen as capable of mobilizing the energies needed for a significant transformation. But it may be that this relation is not an inherent one, rather a case of historic accident. Among the 19th century authors, Friedrich List is now frequently invoked in the discussion of Self-Reliance. And certainly, the UNITAR model, as previously noted, addresses itself mostly to mixed economies, and focuses on market reactions to different types of international action.

It remains true, however, that the implications of effective poverty-oriented policies for the preservation of liberal political structures have not been convincingly elucidated, and perhaps not even squarely confronted. The development of Law should have its rightful place in this necessary investigation. A young American scholar[5] remarks that it came as a shock to him to find in major libraries of

5 Elliott Eisenberg. Book in preparation.

the United States so few works on the *history of law* and its relation to socialism.

Hopefully, the University of Uppsala, and Professor Grahl-Madsen, to whom we are all so indebted, might decide to make this the topic for a new symposium.

6.8. Independence and Interdependence

Interventions at Plenary and Group Sessions

Sovereignty, Independence and Interdependence

References:

Eero J. Manner

Interdependence may in certain cases be caused by a common interest relating to natural resources. I agree that the concept of interdependence may be applicable also to the shared natural resources. Questions concerning the rise and preservation of the shared natural resources has in recent times been considered by several international organs and conferences, and the idea of interdependence, which in this context meant a regional, or only a bilateral, coherence of interests, could not be denied a legal relevance. The most obvious case of this kind of "Interdependence" concerned international water resources, the coherence of which led to a wide application of the principle of equitable utilization. This principle was adopted by the International Law Association in its 1966 Conference, and was contained in Article IV of the Helsinki Rules. These provided that each basin State was entitled to "a reasonable and equitable share in the beneficial uses of the waters of an international drainage basin".

Leslie F. Manigat

The topic for discussion within group 2 is entitled "Independence and Interdependence". First of all, we should start by *clarifying* and *qualifying* this title in order to *define* the topic of our discussion group. Thereafter, we will consider specific items and problems to be discussed as they emanate from the papers or from our suggestions but all related to the topic as previously defined.

The title suggests an *evolution:* from independence to interdependence (we are in the transitional period from one to the other) and implies a *contradiction:* interdependence as opposed to independence (we have to overcome that contradiction in the new world order).

To understand the relationship between our two notions, we have to take into account that independence, as a goal and as a principle means the contrary of *domination* and *intervention* by one Nation-State in its relations with another Nation-State: the notion of *domination* and its corollary of intervention are central to the theme. It is their rejection as norms which represents a basic context which will have to be preserved in a new world order: that is where and why the word and the notion of interdependence have to be questioned.

Interdependence should not be justification for new forms of domination and intervention. Let us take the example of the relations between the United States of America and Latin America, particularly the Caribbean. Up to 1933, Washington was advocating the thesis of licit intervention by an individual State (namely the US) in the domestic affairs of another State of the western hemisphere. It was only at the Conference of Montevideo (1933) that the principle of non-intervention was accepted, and it was confirmed in 1936. But under the flag of collective intervention the same search for US licit intervention re-emerged as illustrated at the Conference of Caracas (1954) and afterwards. In the same vein, all of us have heard of a certain Brezhnev doctrine of "limited sovereignty" to make Soviet military intervention a licit operation when dealing with "Socialist Eastern Europe". Therefore, we should avoid that, under the cover of the new notion of interdependence, if set up as a principle, we introduce new cases for *licit* intervention by an individual State acting on a unilateral initiative, nullifying the principle of independence coupled with equal sovereignty as rightly conceived in Professor Gros Espiell's paper.

Consequently, the notion of interdependence should be manipulated with caution and not without qualification. The political scientists qualify it as a global and strucutrally *a-symmetrical* interdependence. I do think that international law should avoid using it without a *caveat*. Have we not already the appropriate impression of international law of *cooperation* as a *duty*? Therefore I would like to suggest that we explicitly agree that the title is understood as taking independence as a norm, a principle, a right, while interdependence is rather a *de facto* situation, an actual reality which, to be welcome in international law, should be normalized with qualification and caveat. That is to say that, for us, the title means: *Independence and Consolidated Cooperation in an Interdependent World.*

*

I would like to suggest that we can understand better the challenge that international lawyers have to meet in manipulating old and new concepts, by recalling that we are witnessing the birth of a new civilization through a crisis which corresponds to the passing of an old one (ours).

There is, in this respect, *a striking analogy offered by history.* At the end of the fifteenth century and the beginning of the sixteenth, the final breaking of mediaeval Christendom *(la chrétienté)* paved the way to a new "accidental" order of States becoming Nation-States, from which a new civilization, the modern one, was emerging. And it is then that, accordingly, a new international law corresponding to a new international order, was formulated. In this respect, our twentieth century offers striking signs of resemblances with the sixteenth century, *mutatis mutandis*, new paradigms in science, new technological discoveries, space exploration, new mass communications, a new understanding of man and humanity etc. *By analogy*, we can realize that we are living through a crisis which corresponds to the end of one civilization and to the eve of a new one, and therefore, a new international law is emerging and we should dare to invent new concepts and renew the "acceptation" and context of old ones. This means that we have to take into account when we are manipulating old and new concepts such as independence and interdependence. For example, the notion of ownership as taken from Roman law and applied to the State, may well have to change its content when applied to world natural resources to employ social functions at international level which will be enshrined in the new international law.

Kamal Hossain

The Rapporteur and the Co-Rapporteur have made valuable contributions towards elucidating certain fundamental principles of the existing legal order – sovereignty and independence – and in delineating how these principles should be developed to take into account the principle of solidarity in order to build the foundations of a new world order. The concept of "inter-independence", however, presents certain difficulties – for it is not clear what it implies in terms of specific rights and duties. If a basis is to be found for the *duty to cooperate*, to promote development or other global goals this can be found in the "principle of solidarity" and in the "right to development" which is now widely recognized. Inter-dependence is not a principle: at best it is a description of reality, a fact. To seek to elevate it to a principle could also lead to other difficulties. It may erroneously be thought to qualify the principle of permanent sovereignty over natural resources, and limit the right of producer States to develop their resources in the best interestes of their peoples and their national economies, or to impose duties on them to ensure supplies to other States. It is questionable whether such a principle would serve a desirable purpose except within a framework of global planning and management which would embrace all resources. One must be careful to ensure that a supposed principle of "inter-dependence" is not invoked to justify "intervention" or to limit the freedom of action of weaker States.

Holger Rotkirch

I agree with Dr. Hossain that permanent sovereignty over natural resources cannot be interpreted to make the resources into shared resources, a common heritage of mankind. But I would like this group to add a notion to this concept which relates to the preservation of the environment. In this connection I note that Dr. Hossain mentioned that permanent sovereignty over natural resources does not constitute an absolute right, but is subject to international law. In this respect, I would like to refer to the obligation of preservation of natural resources, which has developed during the 1970's. This concept contains an obligation for each State not to utilize its natural resources to the detriment of others.

As an illustration I would like to mention food, of which there sometimes is an abundance in the developed countries. Food should not be allowed to be destroyed to maintain high prices, for instance. The same applies to other natural resources such as oil, etc. I hope this restriction of the sovereignty right to natural resources could be noted in the report of our group.

William Michael Reisman

It is curious that a discussion about the design and construction of a new world order should rely on a term drafted centuries ago in a different context and for purposes quite different from ours. Jean Bodin and Thomas Hobbes meant something quite different by "sovereignty"; over the centuries the term has become further encrusted with layer upon layer of connotation. Instead of analytical and etymological exercises, I suggest we eschew the term and address ourselves to the empirical questions which are really of issue.

Our concern is designing an international system which can best achieve the goals expressed in the United Nations and other authoritative international fora by

1. protecting the political integrity and the coherence of the internal, social and economic processes of territorial communities from unlawful pressures by other States;
2. establishing the subordinating of national territorial communities to the international community in those social, economic and human rights matters for which the international community has prescribed;
3. establishing the competence of the international community to oblige individual States to act affirmatively or forbear from acting in ways deleterious to others.

If we address ourselves to these questions there is no need to pursue the historical meaning of the term "sovereignty".

Estrella D. Solidum

I would like to address my comments to Prof. Saxena. First, I congratulate him for a paper that has relevance to the theme of our seminar. He has proposed a new world order in the nature of a system characterized by interdependence. Now I would like to raise a few questions which may help us to bring this proposed world system into sharper forms. Is it possible to have a world system order where systematic conditions do not show some probability of development? Some of the conditions are (1) consensus of goals, (2) shared interests, and (3) a certain amount of communication of energy among the member units that makes them interdependent on one another.

On the other hand, is it desirable to have a world system wherein the member units will be vulnerable to the problems of any of them? Is it not wise to prevent conflicts from affecting more member units than necessary by encapsulating the conflict?

If there are disadvantages arising from a world system, conceivably an eclectic form of interdependence could be feasible but yet will not be within a world system.

However, if new conditions which will characterize a world system can be identified, such as the rise of new units different from States with firm claims to sovereignty, downgrading of political relations and increase of functional relations, and the like, it is possible to work towards the new world order. Can law create the conditions for the new world order? Alternatively, will the conditions be brought about by a socialization process over a long period? What kind of world law will maintain the systematic relations in the new world order.

Vojin Dimitrijević

I believe we shall shift our emphasis from independence as a right to independence as a fact.

When independence is juxtaposed with interdependence, which is also a fact, it will be realized that States suffer various and many influences, i. e. emanations of other States' power, not only military power. Independence thus comes to mean unhampered, autochthonos decision-making. Decision-makers adapt to influences and pressures, having theoretically a free choice, but being in fact more independent or less independent. If there is no free decision-making, if it is only rubber-stamping of decisions made elsewhere, there is no independence.

The New International Order should aim to create the conditions for true independence, i. e. for more independence from factual pressures. I do not think this purpose is served if we insist on independence as *a right*. Not only is the right empty if there is no situation of independence, but some paradoxical effects may occur. The right to independence does in fact mean *the* presumption of independence for all duly recognized States. After their recognition, none is allowed to doubt their independence without grave consequences. This has been, then, used by régimes which are not independent, which in fact act as foreign agencies, to use the right to independence as a shield against the legitimate efforts of international organizations to restore true independence.

I believe the above interpretation to be in accordance with Art. 2 (4) of the UN Charter, which refers to political independence as to a basic value, i. e. a situation to be protected by the Organization.

Juan Carlos Puig

I heartily congratulate Professors Gros Espiell and Saxena for their brilliant communications. Specifically, I want to express my agreement, from a formal point of view, with the intelligent and suggestive relationships established by Dr. Gros Espiell and Dr. Saxena about sovereignty, independence and interdependence, a subject matter not clearly disposed of in current doctrinal expositions.

As Dr. Gros Espiell knows perfectly well my position in the matter of the general theory of law, I am sure he is waiting for the comments I am going to make. I think, in effect, that a trialistic approach – i. e. an approach consisting of a contemplation of the phenomenon from normative, sociological and dikelogical perspectives – clears up in a global assessment such a complicated matter.

From the juridical normative standpoint, States are sovereign in the sense that no State may legally intervene in other State's internal or external affairs. That is why national legal orders are only submitted to international law. In fact, following the normativistic approach, internal law derives its validity only from international law, and it is such a criterion that permits to distinguish national law from provincial law within the State.

From the juridical-sociological view-point, it seems to me that States are obviously not sovereign at the present time, since the international order is not a politically coordinated system but a subordinated one. In fact, from the sociological angle what we can find in the international community is a political regime with its own rules, organs of mediation and subjects, as well as supreme criteria of government whether imposed or having arised spontaneously. I realize that this is not the moment to fully develop such an idea, but I have done this in some of my books.

Within the dikelogical (from Dikelogy, the science of justice) perspective, the only absolute thing we can accept is justice itself. Therefore, States are not sovereign either in this field since their internal common good cannot be in opposition to the universal common good. Otherwise, we will find ourselves in a position axiologically, and even logically, impossible to sustain. In such a sense, the States are certainly interdependent.

Andrés A. Aramburu-Menchaca

I wish to congratulate both the distinguished rapporteurs for their talented exposés and to say that I fully share the opinion that to try to eliminate sovereignty is absolutely useless and antihistoric as emphasized by Prof. Gros Espiell.

I am aware of the opinion of many jurists who want to change the word sovereignty for independence which does not generate any conceptual change, and that there are even some who consider that in our time the notion of sovereignty itself has disappeared because it cannot exist with the present interdependence of States that is characteristic of our times.

The matter is one of concern for international lawyers. Ambassador Regnaldo Galindo Pohl as President of the Interamerican Juridical Committee makes it evident by saying that a paramount problem of International Law, in our case, is what we should do with sovereignty as a word and as a concept.

May I very respectfully say that, in my opinion, this problem appears just a semantic question: that sovereignty nowadays cannot be invoked by States as it was in the past. Nevertheless we cannot delete the word from the concept of International Law because it is strongly embedded in the language of international lawyers and in popular language as has been said by Prof. Charles De Visscher.

Sovereignty on the other hand is not opposed to the interdependence that is made evident every day in international relationships because as stated by Ambassador Victor Marirtua, brilliant Peruvian professor of law and diplomat: "Sovereignty leads to international community." I am sure that this will make Professor Saxena happy.

This is true. I, at least, cannot conceive an international community but constituted by sovereign States who use their sovereignty to form such a community and to organize it through their treaty-making power. It is difficult to conceive what treaty-making power represents without accepting the sovereignty of States.

The expression "sovereign equality" inserted in article 2 of the Charter of the United Nations has been the object of severe criticism. It appears strange to use the concept of sovereignty as an adjective of the substantive equality. Nevertheless good reasons can be found that have escaped some of the scholars. States are equal because they are persons, juridical persons subjects of International Law. In such a capacity they are able to organize the community and as members of such a community that have been organized by them using their sovereign rights, they should be recognized as equals.

Another problem raised is the opposition between sovereignty and jurisdiction, but the latter is a right derived from sovereignty. There cannot be jurisdiction without a previous recognized sovereignty. This matter is frequently connected with the reserved domain (for some "domestic jurisdiction"), but this is something else. If something near has to be mentioned with regard to modern International Law it is one of the most relevant phenomena: the transference of competences from the national field to the international field. International Law has now to deal with human rights, education, health and many other things that, not long ago, were exclusive responsibilities of States.

Now I wish to call your attention to some misuses of the concept of sovereignty. I call upon your attention to the drafted as yet non-official convention on the Law of the Sea and the resolution of the General Assembly about natural resources. I will refrain from referring to some political concepts of the sovereignity under certain collective security pacts.

Such draft reference is made to "sovereign rights" with regard to the Economic Exclusive Zone, but there are no such "sovereign rights". Sovereignty is a right that cannot be desintegrated. A State is sovereign or not. The State cannot have sovereign rights for certain purposes or in certain fields. The State enjoys full sovereignty in its territory and cannot exercise such sovereignty "beyond its territory" in an area called territorial waters, as appears in the drafted convention. (Spanish and French text. The English text says "beyond its land territory"). If the so-called "Exclusive Economic Zone" is not recognized as a part of its maritime territory the State cannot exercise its sovereignty or sovereign rights.

In the resolution regarding "Permanent sovereignty of the State over the natural resources located in its territory" another conception appears. I believe in as much as sovereignty is permanent or does not exist. It cannot be temporary. On the other hand there is no State that has ever lost such a right; even in cases where it has lost the certain benefits as a consequence of wrong contract or concession granted to foreigners. Such grants have been accorded by the State in the exercise of its sovereignty.

Allow me to finish with a reference to the Peruvian Constitution, recently enacted. The new Peruvian charter has considered the matter we are dealing with in several provisions but particularly in three. One is article 101 that recognizes that in case of conflict between a national law and a treaty, the latter prevails. The other is article 103 that has made it possible to enter into agreements that are in conflict with the constitution and only requests to follow a special procedure for its approval by the Parliament. The third one is article 136 that has sweetened the restrictions imposed on foreigners dealing with the State, allowing submission of controversies to any judicial organ or tribunal (in the case of financial contracts) and in other cases judicial or arbitration tribunals if constituted by treaties in which Peru is a part. The International Centre for the Settlement of International Disputes (ICSID) of the World Bank was taken into consideration when this provision was approved.

I have brought up this reference as evidence that sovereignty is not consistent with the interdependence that cannot be isolated from the notion of community, and I do this in order to answer a question raised by Professor Grahl-Madsen in one of the papers he has prepared for this seminar.

Gunnar G. Schram (1st intervention)

In the first place I should like to express my thanks to our speakers for their interesting statements. It is my intention to limit myself to a short comment which relates to an analysis of the principle of equality of States which has been mentioned in several contexts by the speakers.

From the point of view of legal analysis it may be important to note that the terms "sovereignty" and "equality" have to be kept apart. While States A and B are sovereign this need not mean that they are in all respects equal even if they may be equal as to their status as sovereign States. In actual fact their rights and duties may differ to a considerable extent. Let me mention as an example the position of the permanent members of the Security Council of the United Nations as compared with the status of all other member States. Here we have an example of the functional inequality of States which reminds me of the old and famous passage in George Orwell's "Animal Farm" which I may be allowed to modify to apply to the relations between States as follows: "All States are equal – some States are even more equal than others".

To return to the "equality of States", I want to stress that we can naturally speak of "equality before the law" as well as of the "sovereign equality of States". However, we cannot regard the latter notion as a valid basis for claims directed at functional equality within the confines of international organizations. The answer to the problem whether States in case enjoy the status of functional equality is to be found following an empirical analysis of the respective international organizations.

In conclusion, I should like to stress that even when the States agree to become members of international organizations, in cases where there is no functional equality of all members, this does not mean that they would have lost their sovereignty. To put it briefly: Sovereignty continues because equality does not mean similarity in all aspects and the States have themselves agreed to become members having the rights and duties in accordance with the constituent document of the particular organization.

Finally, I should like to refer to the paper presented by Professor Saxena, where on page 5 a reference is made to the principle of sovereign equality of States and where it is stated that "one, however, has to admit that general principles expressed in diplomatic documents, are frequently not borne out by specific provisions and they are therefore for lip service rather than as an indication of their strength". Insofar as the doctrine of equality of States is concerned in Article 2, paragraph 1, of the Charter of the United Nations, I do think that if this principle is analysed the way I have tried to do, also by Professor Saxena, the pessimistic conclusion is no longer valid.

Abdullah El-Erian

I wish to make a few brief comments on the concepts of independence and interdependence. – First they should be viewed in their historic context. States are independent in the sense that they are not subject to a higher authority. With the dissolution of the Holy Roman Empire, we saw the emergence of national States in Western Europe. They consisted of new political and territorial units which were not subject to a higher authority, temporal or ecclesiastical. They needed a new law to govern their relations and international law is therefore an inter-State law and not a law dictated by a super-power.

On the other hand those independent States are inter-dependent. They need to enter into relations with each others and cannot live in isolation. Thus political independence counts as a principle of a legal character which has two corollaries. Each State has the right to choose freely its political and economic system. Each State has the duty not to intervene in the affairs of another State. Economic and social interdependence is one of the foundations of the community of nations.

The concepts of independence and interdependence should also be reviewed from the angle of the impact on the orientation of international law and its underlying philosophy. Traditional international law consisted mainly of fragmentary rules of individualistic orientation. They were mainly prohibitive suggestions and regulatory norms of State conduct. Contemporary international law has a changing structure. To the traditional norms were added new cooperative norms. They have as their underlying philosophy the concept of a well-established and relatively developed international order of a universal character with a theory of general interest supplementing and enhancing the interest of the individual States.

J. N. Saxena

There is no doubt that interdependence is a fact and the perception of the world's interdependence is not a new thing. It is also true that it will not always be a boon, as is well exemplified by the national society. But in the recent past this concept has attained a new importance especially after the energy crisis. What is needed is a realization about the pervasive and global nature of the emerging problems which may perhaps best be solved within a broadly cooperative frame of reference. This, in its own turn, may lead to what the Third World Countries demand as "development".

Gunnar G. Schram (2nd intervention)

There seems to be an obvious need for the establishment of a Special Law Committee for the New International Economic Order. Neither the International Law Commission nor the United Nations Commission on International Trade Law (UNCITRAL) are ready to cope with the manifold legal aspects of this extensive and important international issue. A new body should therefore be established which can undertake to develop the legal framework for the New International Economic Order, hand in hand with the implementation of its Action Programme.

Such a Committee could be an organ of the United Nations Economic and Social Council, relying on the Secretariat of UNCTAD, whose reports, through the Board of Trade and Development and the Economic and Social Council, would be considered by the General Assembly.

This proposal is directly related to the decision taken by UNCTAD IV on the establishment of "an appropriate mechanism" for the realization of the goals of the New International Economic Order and the implementation of Article 34 of the Charter of Economic Rights and Duties of States.

It should also be mentioned in this connexion that for the last few years a proposal by the Philippines has been on the agenda of the General Assembly Sixth Committee, requesting that action be taken on the development of international law for the New International Economic Order.

Holger Rotkirch (2nd intervention)

I asked for the floor to support the proposal by Prof. Schram to establish a new permanent body for the progressive development of international economic law. The discussions during this seminar have clearly shown that international lawyers should take a more active part in the development of international economic law. Within the United Nations system many various activities are going on which relate to the New International Economic Order, such as the Conference on the Law of the Sea, the drafting of international industrial development contracts within United Nations Commission on International Trade Law, drafting of rules for the transfer of technology, the conference on new and renewable resources, not to mention the strategy for the second UN Decade of Development and the Global Round of Negotiations within the North-South dialogue. In my opinion an organ of legal experts in international economic law would have an important role both in overseeing the various activities going on within the UN system as well as taking initiatives of its own to promote the establishment of the New International Economic Order. The two existing United Nations legal committees, the International Law Commission (ILC) and the United Nations Commission on International Trade Law (UNCITRAL), would not in my view be suitable to be given this additional task. It would perhaps be better to establish this new organ on international economic law under the Economic and Social Council.

Erik Suy

Within the United Nations, several institutions, bodies and organs have been dealing with the legal aspects of the New International Economic Order. There is not a single organ entrusted with the coordination. The United Nations Commission on International Trade Law (UNCITRAL) made a survey of the trade law aspects and decided to concentrate on industrial development contracts in order to elabortate uniform clauses for the various types of contracts. Moreover, in elaborating international conventions on transport of goods by sea and on the international sale of goods, and in drafting the arbitration rules, UNCITRAL had contributed to some important aspects of the New International Economic Order.

The drafting of a new law of the sea by the United Nations contributed to a large extent to the restructuring of international economic relations. The work of UNCTAD in the field of eliminating the so-called flags of convenience, in setting up a common fund for raw materials, in drafting the various conventions on primary products (commodity agreements), etc., has to be seen as a major contribution to the law of a New International Economic Order.

The Philippines initiated in the General Assembly the codification of all legal rules on the New International Economic Order. This is a very sensitive area and UNITAR has been asked to make a survey of all these legal aspects. One should not politicize this topic in focusing on controversial problems but rather try gradually to build up sets of rules on various topics and aspects. The Charter of Economic Rights and Obligations of States is basically a political instrument which tends to overshadow the real progress made elsewhere.

Natural Resources: Heritage of Nation and Mankind

References:

Gunnar G. Schram

Referring to the report by Achol Deng, I disagree with the idea of declaring natural resources of States the common heritage of mankind. This was a very different matter from Ambassador Pavlos' proposal to the UN General Assembly in 1967 that the seabed area beyond national jurisdiction be declared the common heritage of mankind. That area was not the property of any one nation or under the jurisdiction of any State.

Here the matter was entirely different. The fact was one of extending this principle to natural resources under national jurisdiction.

Such a course of action would be against the best interests of both the developing and the developed States. Furthermore, there was a clear and obvious contradiction between the idea of such a common heritage principle and the UN declarations on Sovereignty and National Resources, which the co-rapporteur had referred to. Applying the common heritage principle to such resources would clearly constitute expropriation without adequate compensation and would thus constitute a violation of international law.

The right way to follow here, on the other hand, was to proceed along the lines Dr. Hossain had suggested for the equitable sharing of global resources for a New World Order.

It was obviously necessary to make an arrangement of resources. International legal action was called for in various areas of common interest. The necessity of conservation and optimum utilization of resources came under this category as also the preservation of the human environment. In such areas of common interest to all mankind, legal planning on a global basis should be enhanced.

Thus the New Economic Order called not only for action in the economic field but also for a legal framework befitting the needs of the new era. The question was: How can this best be achieved?

In this connexion the speaker pointed out that UNCTAD IV had recommended the establishment of "an appropriate mechanism" for realization of the goals of the Action Programme of the New International Economic Order, and for the implementation of Article 34 of the Charter of Economic Rights and Duties of States.

What this really meant was establishing a new Commission for writing the legal guidelines of the New Economic Order. Such a body was needed and this decision by UNCTAD IV should therefore be implemented.

Rup C. Hingorani

I take this opportunity to offer my congratulation to Dr. Kamal Hossain and Mr. Deng for their presentations. The subjects of sovereignty over natural resources and common heritage are of prime importance in today's world community and I am glad to find that they have put up their ideas in such a specific manner.

It is now generally accepted that every State has sovereignty over its natural resources whether these are located within its borders or within its economic resources zone. However, it has been noticed that in the past, developing States have been given a raw deal in respect of natural resources they sold to the developed and industrialized countries. The result was that a small quantity of coca-cola was being sold at higher prices than a litre of petrol. This represented a strange state of affairs. Surprisingly, in 1973 when the oil producing countries began to increase their oil prices, the industrialized countries raised their eyes as if some manipulations had been carried on by the OPEC countries. Sovereignty over natural resources does not only mean symbolic control but also the right to regulate the prices of their commodities. Therefore, when some States tried to threaten the oil producing countries with consequences, it was a misconceived threat. The producer countries have the right to determine the price of their commodities, depending upon supply.

With regard to the problem of the common heritage of mankind, it has been found that there is great confusion over its scope. Some consider it the *communes* property of all – while others consider it as the *nullius* – property of none. States have also thoughts as to the concept which applies in respect of the seabed and ocean floor as well as for celestial bodies. As has been noticed in recent years, the principle of common heritage of mankind has been pricked by industrialized countries by quietly exploiting the seabed and ocean floor which are supposed to be the common heritage of mankind. It will remain to be seen what is the attitude of the two powers who are exploring the celestial bodies. It is hoped that they do not exploit these bodies to the political and economic prejudice of the developing nations.

Luis Gonzales Barros

After listening to the intervention of Dr. Hossain our rapporteur this morning and co-rapporteur Dr. Deng on their very interesting remarks and referring to material, economic and human limits to activities of mankind, indeed they must consider certain elements, one of them even more essential for mankind than energy sources such as oxygen, indispensable element for life.

Indeed, very recent studies by Max Planck Institute indicate that the Amazon forests contributes by itself 50% of the oxygen world wide produced, and that its deforestation may mean a catastrophic menace to the life of human beings at world scale, further consequences are also appreciated such as the increase of the solar reflex incrementing highly the production of carbonic gas in the air. These two effects are susceptible of modifying the climate of the earth provoking an increase of temperature with the resulting consequences on the ecological equilibrium. The Amazon forests are under the jurisdiction of 10 sovereignities of countries that are generally considered underdeveloped, and of course, they need, and naturally plan to use the forests in an economic way, as well as the resources in the underground of the zone, resources to which they are justly entitled, in as much as the OPEC countries are to their oil resources and in certain respects, more.

There is of course an interest of mankind in the preservation of the forests that in certain cases have been estimated as "common heritage of humanity", something that naturally will not be accepted at any stage by the Amazonic nations. Resuming; should it be necessary to keep the Amazonic forest as they are, or not to be utilized by the Amazonic Countries at their will, and should they be used for the benefit and interest of humanity, then the International Community shall study the way of compensating the States of the Amazon region and their populations in an adequate manner. I think it is a matter that should call the attention of the most distinquished jurists that are participating in this meeting as well as the international organizations and public opinion.

Geraldo E. do Nascimento e Silva

In view of the specific reference to the "Brazilian Rain Forests", I feel obliged to clarify the point in short, the principle of the "common heritage of mankind" can only refer to riches outside national jurisdiction; natural resources which are within the border of a given State are subject exclusively to the laws and jurisdiction of that State. In my opinion, the Brazilian Government would never accept any encroachment on its sovereign rights in this case. I would also like to point out that in the recent Treaty on Cooperation in the Amazon an obligation to protect the environment by all means is expressely mentioned. The protection of the Brazilian rain forests is due in great part to the past decisions of the Government not admitting the installation of certain foreign ventures aimed at the commercial exploitations of the timber. If those steps, which were criticized in Brazil and abroad, had not been taken, we would possibly have no rain forest, but another barren waste, as occurred in Africa. Concerning an international control of natural resources I agree with previous speakers that as yet no practical solution had been forwarded and if the lack of enthusiasm shown towards commodity treaties were an indication one could expect a negative approach to the problem.

Leslie F. Manigat

It seems to me that while we are considering the goals and means of the new international economic order, we have also to lay down *the foundations on which to legitimize our search for a new international economic order*. And for me, these foundations can be looked for along three lines which go beyond the idea of a "duty of generosity".

(1) The idea of social justice through a distributive policy: We have to start with the notion of *basic needs* creating a *right*. The analogy with internal law offers the model. When we look back at the literature of the nineteenth century in Europe, we see what were the living conditions of the forest sectors of the population. The evolution of the thinking and the reality of social justice gives the kind of socities where, as in the Scandinavian countries or in Australia or in France or Canada etc. (the western developed democracies), the satisfaction of basic needs is guaranted for all and social justice is largely ensured through distributive politicies. By analogy, we are invited to conceive and organize a new world order in which social justice will inspire policies of distributive justice at international level as the foundation for a new international economic order.

(2) The notion of the *responsibility* of the developed nations creating a right to *compensation* for the developing nations: The idea is that the most developed nations of today reached their prosperity through a type of industrial development which caused pollution, exhaustion of non-renewable resources, loss of natural resources etc., to their exclusive benefit and to the detriment of the other, non-developed societies. To take an example, the German laboratories caused the elimination of indigo and logwood as *resources* for dyeing textiles and removed these products from the international markets. Logwood was the second item in the list of exports of Haiti and ceased to be a "marketable resource". This "spoliation" of the natural environment and natural resources actually benefitted the industrialized nations to the detriment of present developing nations and thus creates a right to compensation from the authors and beneficiaries to the others. It is not the "radical" argument of "culpability of spoliation", it is the notion of responsibility to compensate. This meets the more general framework of the compensation for unequal distribution of gains and losses by the adoption of certain types of technological progress and development.

(3) The deepening and widening of the notion of *security* in the long run: Professor Thomas Franck observed the other day that the United Nations was busy dealing with matters of security concern and now there is a shift towards the substitution of matters of socio-economic concern. May I suggest that perhaps it is not a simple *substitution* but another way to approach the same problem of *security* at a new time and at the level of long duration. Concern for security – the notion of collective economic security – should then be the third foundation for a New International Economic Order (NIEO).

If, looking at the North-South dialogue, we have some pessimism in relation with the prospects for such a NIEO, let us point out that, without considering the alternative, a fruitless spirit of confrontation, a spirit of pressing dialogue is not possible. Let us not forget that is was the conservative Bismarck who inaugurated a legislation (and a policy) of distributive justice in the German empire. Therefore the southern point of the dialogue needs only to meet a reasonable northern point. There may be still a long way to go but it is not any more a Utopian dream or an impossible task, it is a common endeavour "in the cause of humanity".

Otto Kimminich

My report was given a rather lengthy heading by the organizers. Of course the heading came first and the report came later. As I pointed out in the paper the heading served as a guideline. But here I shall have to begin a few explanations in addition to the paper. So in the next twenty minutes I shall try to explain the background of the paper and to summarize its findings.

The paper is oriented towards the aim mentioned in the subtitle: a new economic world order in an ecological context. Thus it is not the concept of limits around which the report has been built up. Of course it would be possible to begin the report with a description of all the dangers, needs and sorrows of our present-day world. There are many amongst us who know these sufferings from their own experience and I am sure that among those present there is nobody who does not know the problems of overpopulation, famine, depletion of natural resources, pollution of air and water, to name only a few. We have been and shall be talking about them for days under different headings. The knowledge about these problems forms the general background of our whole seminar, so-to-speak.

They are human problems throughout. The distinction between material, economic and human factors is dubious. It is human beings who ultimately suffer from the deficiencies of the world monetary system, human beings get poisoned by the products and by-products of chemical industry, human beings are being wounded and killed by what the governments have ordered and bought from the armaments industry and what the arms dealers have distributed around the world. And let us not forget that human beings must work in order to be able to pay taxes to be used for foreign aid, development schemes, common funds for the financing of buffer stocks and so on.

This is perhaps the most striking feature of the latest developments of international law: the human factor has become apparent beyond all doubts, and the considerations concerning it go far beyond the old theoretical discussion about the subjects of international law. We have become aware of the fact that international law must serve the needs of human beings and ultimately derive its normative strength from the convictions of human beings.

At this point there is the temptation to simply deplore a discrepancy in the development of international law: although we recognize the human being as the very foundation of international law and as the ultimate goal of its efforts, its whole organization, its instruments and implementation remain basically State-centered. But it would be completely utopian in this situation to ignore the continued existence of the State as a central institution within the framework of international law or even to develop grand schemes to abolish the State. Those who are prone to criticize international law may argue that here once again the jurists are proving that they are conservative people with an intrinsic aversion against revolution, regardless of their political opinions.

To this we can calmly reply: if and when the day comes, when mankind has found new ways for the organization of relationships between individuals and groups replacing the traditional States, international law will find new adequate rules for the regulation of these relationships or it will fade away because it is no longer needed. But in the meantime we must take the world as it is, with the nation States no longer the sole actors on the international scene but still the most important ones holding and wielding by far the largest proportion of power existent in this world.

To control power and to channel it in beneficial directions are the main functions of law, not to ignore or even destroy power. Therefore law and power should never be seen to stand in opposition against each other. To reconcile them is the task of ethics, and that is the reason why we have discussed the moral basis of international law in this seminar also.

So this is the background of beliefs and convictions behind the report I have the honor to present to you. The intensified awareness of human needs which characterizes the new approach to international law does not mean that the States are substituted by individuals, but it does mean that in applying existing rules as well as in changing old ones and developing new ones we bear in mind that States are creations of human beings. It was not the task of my report to draw any conclusions from this basic approach with respect to humanitarian intervention or the implementation of human rights. The report was limited to the economic field.

The first question arising was whether international law has anything to do with international economic relations. Most textbooks of international law do not even mention this question. Those which do, usually confine themselves to pointing out that public international law provides the framework of stability, reliability and mutual trust which is necessary for the orderly conduct of international economic transactions while private international law is taking care of the details under the umbrella of this protective framework.

This view is no longer satisfying. It does not correspond to developments which have taken place within the body of international law since the end of World War I and it does not meet the demands which are being placed on international law today by extra- or metajuridical factors, so-to-speak from the outside.

The development which I have tried to trace briefly in the report may be illustrated by two concepts which were mentioned yesterday: coexistence and co-operation. It is interesting to note that these concepts have been around for centuries, but it seems justified to say that our century has been marked by the progress from coexistence to co-operation.

It is true that we are still far from knowing in detail all legal obligations which emanate from the general principle of co-operation. But that is exactly the task that lies before us. And it should not be too difficult once we have accepted the basic obligation.

My main proposition therefore is that the quest for a New International Economic Order is not a shocking revolutionary demand, or an outside pressure, but something which comes naturally in the course of developments which started long before the United Nations were founded and which have been fostered by the United Nations for good reasons and so far with good results.

The oral presentation is supposed not to repeat the text of the paper. But I think it is necessary here to mention a few of the findings concerning specific problems, although the summary will be even more superficial than the paper itself.

There is, first of all, the inherent connection between peace and solidarity, which in turn forms the core of all efforts for the New International Economic Order. There is, secondly, the fact that the re-interpretation of sovereignty which the proponents of the new international economic order are calling for has been under way since the end of the first World War. Regardless of whether this is a semantic or a conceptual problem nobody can deny that sovereignty was changed profoundly – or lost its previous meaning – when it no longer meant that the State possessing this legal quality could wage war in order to reach its political goals.

There are other concepts which need re-interpretation in line with the general developments of which the emerging New International Economic Order is only a part. Let me mention the principle of equality. On the one hand it could never be used bringing about equal living conditions for all individuals by all means. On the other hand it cannot be invoked by States against the obligation to bear a heavier burden than other States if that is necessary to help other States.

The same holds true for the principle of reciprocity, which has to be re-interpreted in terms of what has been called "material reciprocity", because it takes into consideration benefits which are outside the narrow limits of formal reciprocity, in which any single advantage of one party has to be matched by an immediate, commensurate advantage of the other party. Material reciprocity takes into account the long-range benefits of seemingly unbalanced relations. On the basis of this approach to reciprocity it is possible to justify preferential treatment within the framework of old instruments adhering to the age-old principle. The best example is, of course, the General Agreement on Tariffs and Trade which in its new articles 34–38 does provide for preferential treatment.

Mentioning the General Agreement on Tariffs and Trade leads us to the really crucial question of the New International Economic Order. The General Agreement is usually seen to symbolize the great attempt to restore a liberal economic order after World War II. There are some – maybe even many – who think that the United Nations Conference for Trade and Development is trying to replace that order by one that would ultimately lead to a planned world economy. Of course there are political opinions involved in such views.

In this seminar we refrain from political statements. But it is not this wise policy which has led me to the conclusion that the New International Economic Order does not necessarily lead to a world without free trade. There will have to be more management in the future. But again, international economic management is not new. Just think of the old commodity agreements, one of which – the sugar agreement – dates back to the 19th century while many where concluded between the two world wars.

Another area in which management is unavoidable is the international monetary system. I think it is Bagehot who coined the phrase: money will not manage itself. It has to be managed. The days when a privately organized central bank – the Bank of England established in 1694 by a group of city merchants and existing in that form until 1946 when it was nationalized – could manage the international monetary system without ever consulting foreign governments or private corporations, or even its own government, are gone and will never return.

The tremendous capital flows which have to be set in motion in order to finance the buffer stocks – which in turn are needed to stabilize the commodity prices – and above all to make investments in countries which lack capital, simply cannot go at random.

Even this brief list of issues to be tackled by the efforts to create a New International Economic Order must be closed now, because there is not enough time. Let me just mention three words which stand for tremendous problems: food, population and migration. They are worldwide problems affecting all countries. The countries with abundant food supply and stable – in some cases even declining – population figures do not only have moral and legal obligations, but they are also directly involved in the problem of migration. Never before in the history of mankind have so many people left their home countries in order to look for a better life in distant parts of the globe. In my opinion the problem of migration is at least as important as oil, energy and raw materials, and I feel guilty that we do not have more time to discuss it.

There is still another complex of problems to be mentioned which was broached upon in the paper, namely ecology. One would think that the protection of the environment is truly a common concern of mankind. A collection of relevant treaties which I have mentioned in the footnotes now contains 600 multilateral treaties. The number of bilateral treaties on pollution control must be far greater. It is probably safe to say that never before in history has the international community responded so extensively to a challenge. But still we do not know whether we did not respond too late. Each month a number of species which have inhabited the world for thousands of years finish their existence for all times, and the rate of extinction is still increasing.

We shall not be able to discuss this whole range of problems. And even with regard to its linkage with the new economic world order I must limit myself to a few sweeping statements. In my paper I have tried to put forward three propositions: Firstly; we should not consider the whole ecological question as a question of limits to desirable activities. Caring for our world – the boat we are sitting in – is a natural obligation, a challenge, an incentive to do certain things. To abstain from others should be an attitude just as natural as our shunning away from objects dangerous to our health. Secondly; there can be no preferential treatment for any country with regard to the protection of the global environment. Thirdly; in spite of that, ecology is not a serious obstacle for the creation of a New International Economic Order.

It is sad, perhaps even tragic, that we must try to solve both problems at the same time. On the other hand it also offers certain opportunities. Only from a shortsighted and superficial viewpoint do the factors creating those problems increase international competition, rat-races, greed and violence. On closer look they should be able to make us realize that we must co-operate and live together in peace as good neighbors. And that is exactly what international law in its present form is aiming at.

Material, Economic, and Human Limits to Activities of Mankind

References:

J. N. Saxena

Prof. Kimminich refers to the food problem and relates it to the population (p. 22), he quotes from Timothy W. Slanley that the developing countries have unlimited demands but entirely limited resources . . . (p. 27). He rightly concludes that in spite of the emerging New International Economic Order, sadness and skepticism are the prevailing emotions, not only because of the deficiencies of the superficial report itself, but also because of the magnitude of the problem still waiting to be solved (p. 33).

In this connection, I would like to draw attention to the concept of distributive justice. Though it embraces "the whole economic dimension of social justice, the entire question of the proper distribution of goods and services within the society", a starting point at the international level may be made under that concept to mean the satisfaction of the basic needs of a State, or minimal utility floor below which no State should be pressed. This is already the commitment of the national State – meeting the minimal needs of its citizens – and has taken the shape of a general principle. The fulfilment of the basic needs of the developing countries has to be recognized as a normal principle and central idea of distributive justice, which, in its own turn, can be a foundation stone for a new world order. Need can be ascertained in an objective way, and there is a widespread consensus on basic requirements of human beings everywhere. Though the criterion of need, it must be admitted, does not provide simple answers even for a single problem like food, it does, however, set a standard, and that can in principle be applied by objective factual engineering.[1]

Gunnar G. Schram

Both the Rapporteurs, and the organizers of the agenda of the Seminar should be congratulated for drawing the attention of the Seminar participants to the importance of adequately dealing with the New Economic World Order in international law.

It is necessary to say that unfortunately international law has, to a large extent, so far bypassed or even neglected the many complicated issues presented by the New Economic Order. These are, however, so important global issues that they should engage the interest of the international lawyer and urge him to work for

1 Schachter, Oscar. *Sharing the world's resources.* New York, Columbia University Press, 1977. 172 p.

applicable and adequate solutions through a new system of legal regulation. To name only a few of these issues one might start with energy, the protection of the environment, raw materials, sovereignty over natural resources and transfer of technology. In spite of laudable efforts of international Organizations in this field and a number of multilateral conventions concluded, we have received information here in Uppsala that 10 000 of the lakes of Sweden have already been destroyed by acid rain coming out of Central Europe, and that 10 000 are now threatened with the same fate. This is certainly not a national problem but an example of a transnational one, which awaits proper solution through legal regulation. The lack of protection of high seas fisheries and the sorry state of the whale stocks are other examples of the same kind.

International lawyers should therefore turn their attention to these new and highly important global issues, and make amends for the inactivity of the past. New approaches and new strategies are therefore called for.

But here the question arises what approaches we should use and which strategies are likely to be most efficient and successful in this respect. One might think of General Assembly Resolutions in the United Nations. Because of their lack of legal binding force, although politically important, this avenue is by itself, not sufficient. Diplomatic conferences, convened under United Nations auspices, are here another way of dealing with the issues on a global scale.

The drawback there is that at such conferences the lawyers tend to be overshadowed by the diplomats and the large number of participants makes for slow progress as so clearly indicated by the Conference on the Law of the Sea eight year track-record.

Another possibility is upgrading the International Law Commission and giving it a new mandate and new issues to deal with. One might also envisage special new law commissions dealing with individual issues. The New World Economic Order certainly seems to merit a law drafting commission on its own, possibly under the directorship of Economic and Social Council. The same applies to the global issue of ecological protection which should be ordained by United Nations Environment Programme.

These are some thoughts on new approaches and strategems for dealing with the legal aspects of the New Economic Order. They are important. But even more important is the realization of international lawyers that these issues are too vital and too vast to be left exclusively to our friends, the economists.

Juan Carlos Puig

Professor Kimminich has given to us the precious gift of a very persuasive and – I should say – unexpected version of the fundamentals of the so-called New International Economic Order. We should all be thankful for such an unusual presentation as well as for Dr. de Seynes's illuminating report.

As it happens with every new theoretical construction, it could be subject to an overall criticism which would take perhaps hours to explain. This is to-day my problem, because I practically disagree with everything he has said. That is why I will only make a few remarks for the sake of brevity.

I agree with Dr. Kimminich (as I do on some points, after all) in his appreciation of the importance of World War I in our times. I personally think, in effect, that that event marked not only the end of an historic era but perhaps the end of a geo-bio-morphological period. Perhaps we are abandoning the metal stage of the quaternary period. In spite of this, however, specifically, the implementation of a New International Order came into being in 1973, with the famous decision of the OPEC countries to raise oil prices.

Why is such a decision so important? Because it meant a change of at least one of the main basic organizational criteria of the international community, the criteria whereby the political power of the States was measured through their potential, what in fact meant their military might.

The day oil was conceived (and implemented) as a new resource of power, the international community was structurally shaken and a new international order was born. None of the events which took place afterwards in the international community find a reasonable explanation without resorting to such a fundamental fact, from Nicaragua to the Iranian hostages and the Polish Solidarity; from stagnation to generalized economic chaos.

I have spoken on purpose of a New International Order without any qualification, because:

1. I think that there is an international regime working as such in the international community. If we apply systemic theories, we can say that the international system contains four subsystems: political, economical, cultural and participational, and in this I strongly disagree with Dr. Kimminich, as well, I should say, the majority of writers on international relations, and
2. because, paradoxically, transformation has operated up to now mainly in the political sub-system, since new resources of power have appeared in the international arena, some of them of an economic nature; some others of a cultural character, such as the religious faith, and there are many more.

Unfortunately, statesmen, diplomats, jurists, even belonging to the so-called Third World countries, do not understand that the very essence of the changes already accomplished is that while we have tried to build a New International Economic Order through declarations, resolutions and conventions, the New Order (in a broad sense) is very healthy and safely works just around the corner.

Finally, I would say that within such a background it is rather useless to find out who was the first to speack of international social justice, solidarity, cooperation, coexistence, and so forth. From the rhetorical viewpoint, it seems to me that everything has already been said, as the Roman saying put it so well: *nihil novum sub sole*, especially when the words in use have broad connotations; when they are "*mots-caoutchouc*" as Louis Le Fur used to say. What really matters from the juridical angle are the new patterns of conduct flowing from social reality. Otherwise, we, the jurists, are – following Kirchmanns's suggestive figure of speech – but vultures flying around the imposing structure of the law until, its flesh having disappeared, the structure itself becomes practically unreal.

D. B. S. Thapa

Having read and heard the paper of Prof. Kimminich on the "New International Economic Order", I would like to express briefly some of the views and aspirations of the small countries of the world like ours which is among the least developed of the developing countries. Prof. Kimminich has in his paper traced the development and analysed the objectives of international relationship among States of the world through periods of peace and war, has shown that as peace had been the ultimate goal of the past days due to several wars fought between the nations, the need of the present day world is for peaceful coexistence and cooperation. To this end economic considerations are as such as important as the political ones.

In the annals of the world, several factors and considerations have dominated and determined mutual relationships between the countries, big and small, rich and poor, developed and underdeveloped, and in their mutual relationship, some apprehensions of fear and suspicion, either real or imaginary, have always existed. Small nations are always found to be the victims of influences or subject to domination of varying nature and magnitude from the rich or big or powerful nations of the neighborhood or vicinity. Fraught by the events of the world and guided by the experience gained by others and of our own, are the small countries which attach much more importance to the peaceful coexistence and economic cooperation between nations. It is true that in our historical past we were no less guided by the principles of peaceful coexistence as contained in the ancient sinon epic called *Mahabharat* of which the *Shanti Parva* (the canto on peace) has dealt most vividly with the nature of the relationship between small and big, strong and weak neighbours during times of war and peace.

Those principles are still equally suitable and worthwhile at the present times amids the principles of modern international law and particularly of importance to a country like Nepal, which is wedged between two highly populated and large neighbours like India and China, for the purposes of survival and maintenance of our national identity.

Despite the variance of size, populations and resources among the nations of the world, the principles of international law require to maintain equality among States; however, the geographical compulsions practically and seriously inhibit the small nations to enjoy such equality in its true sense. So there always exists a sense of dilemma between the ideal law and the facts governing capability. While small developing nations are struggling for survival – the rising number of populations and shortage of food, clothing and shelter aggravated by the lack of resources in terms of wealth, technology and expert hands –, the remarks made in the paper that the developing countries have unlimited demands but extremely limited resources, is most accurate and pertinent. Hence like our old adage that no hungry man knows peace, it is difficult to perceive the maintenance of international peace, when more than half of the world population is living in abject poverty.

The purpose of the new economic order is to help developing nations through a new process of realignment of available resources. But, in actual practice, the norms of relationship are often guided by the selfinterest of the donors, which invariably creates and enhances the spheres of influence and economic control. Such situations are generally seen as the disguised revival of colonialism in a new form, for the donors are more inclined to preserve conditions, often in their own favour, and the receivers are obliged to bear all the burdens arising therefrom. Although the success of its new overture looks rather bleak, this human endeavour designed by and for human beings shall have sufficient support from all corners to make it a successful cause provided it is met with genuine intentions to help.

6.9. Independence and Interdependence
Oral Presentation of the Report of Group II

Endre Ustor (Main Rapporteur of Group II)

The 2nd group has dealt with six papers. Professor Gros Espiell and Professor Saxena submitted papers on sovereignty, independence and interdependence of nations. Professor Kimminich and Professor De Seynes presented papers on the material, economic, and human limits to activities of mankind: legislating for a new economic world order in an ecological context; and lastly Professor Hossain and Minister Deng's papers tackled the problems of natural resources: heritage of nations and mankind.

The rapporteurs and co-rapporteurs presented their papers in the plenary meetings on the 10th, 11th and 15th June; the papers were discussed by the 2nd group on the 11th, 12th and 15th June.

The report of the group will contain the papers submitted in full as well as summary record of the comments and interventions made in the course of the plenary meetings and group sessions.

Owing to the limitations of time my present statement is intended only to give a short review of the main ideas put forward by the rapporteurs and those members of the seminar who participated in the discussions. I do not intend to be exhaustive and I can, of course, in this short statement not refer to all of the views expressed during the debate.

As a general statement, I can say that the views of the rapporteurs and co-rapporteurs do, in most respects, coincide in their basic elements and a remarkable amount of consent as to the basic lines of thought is shown by the interventions also.

In the following, I try to outline very briefly the ideas discussed in Group 2.

According to Professor Gros Espiell, the concept of sovereignty is a necessary and fundamental part of international law and of international life and politics today. To seek to eradicate the concept and confirm its incompatibility with International Law as certain doctrinaire schools have attempted, constitutes according to him a useless and antihistorical effort incompatible with the world as it is and the inescapable and undeniable political and mythical force of the idea of sovereignty.

To seek to eliminate the concept and the term sovereignty is in the view of Prof. Gros Espiell a utopia without sense or reason. To this your rapporteur may add the old saying that the map of the world that does not include utopia is not worth even glancing at.

In the ensuing discussion, Professor Reisman pointed out that the term sovereignty was crafted centuries ago in a different context and for purposes quite different from ours. Jean Boding and Thomas Hobbes, he said, meant something quite different by sovereignty; over the centuries the term had become further encrusted with layer upon layer of connotation. Instead of analytical and etymological exercises, he suggested to eschew the term and to address ourselves to the empirical questions which were really the issue.

As Professor Gros Espiell further explained that sovereignty today does not and cannot mean the ultimate and supreme State power incompatible with the existence of a new international order regulated by law and that it essentially means that other States cannot interfere in its domestic of foreign affairs whatever may be the economic, social or political system which it has adopted – your rapporteur believes that the seeming difference between the views of these two scholars is only of a semantic nature as has been pointed out by Prof. Aramburu-Menchaca in his intervention. A particularly conspicuous case of interdependence was mentioned by Justice Manner who referred to the situation of States whose territories were located in the same international drainage basin. Here, the relevant Helsiniki Rules provide for an equitable utilisation of the waters of the basin. Rules of a similar nature should apply in relation to other resources of the globe such as oil, uranium, food etc. Sooner or later a global approach to the use of resources will be warranted.

The Charter of the United Nations, as pointed out by Professor Gros Espiell, refers to the sovereign equality of all member States, to their territorial integrity and political independence. On the other hand, the term interdependence is not to be found in the language employed by the Charter. Nevertheless, according to him, interdependence forms one of the constitutive elements of the international community and follows from the principle of international cooperation which has been repeatedly invoked by the United Nations Charter.

Equality of States was also brought into the discussion; equality in the sense of Vattel, as your rapporteur ventures to recall, who said that a dwarf is as much a man as a giant, a small republic is no less a sovereign State than the most powerful kingdom. Of course in material powers a great inequality exists between States, there are big and small, rich and poor States alike. This fact gives a special importance to the principle of solidarity of States which commands that the richer ones aid and assist the poor to enjoy an equal dignity in their existence. Hence the reference to Ago's idea that a breath of socialism should penetrate into the international community and inspire the interstate relations to which your rapporteur may add: without prejudice to the special responsibility of the States toward their former colonies.

Professor Saxena pointed out that mankind is entering a new phase in human history depicted by such phrases as the "planetary community", "global village", or "one world". He quoted the opinion of Judge Alvarez of 1948, (as did also the paper of Prof. Gros Espiell), who said that States no longer have an absolute sovereignty but are interdependent. They have not only rights but also duties towards each other and toward this society. International organizations have been playing a vital role in increasing the interdependence among nations and laying down an approach to a different world order in our, and in the next century – says Prof. Saxena. He is, however, somewhat sceptical as to the prospects of the organizations in the near future owing to a sort of lull, which appears to be prevailing now.

He perceives another movement toward the creation of a new world order, namely the systems approach. The basic tenet of this approach would be the unity of the world as a system of interrelated parts and as soon as one part is touched other parts are effected.

Prof. Dimitrijević pointed out that the new international order should aim to create the conditions for true independence of States, that is, for more independence from factual pressures.

Prof. Puig in a modern manner, favoured a trialistic approach to the problems we were dealing with; that is, an approach from normative, sociological and dikelogical perspectives. The latter adjective comes from the noun Dikelogy – the science of Justice, and, according to him, the only absolute thing was justice itself.

Judge El-Erian stated that the concepts of independence and interdependence should also be reviewed from the angle of the impact on the concentration of international law and its underlying philosophy: Traditional international law consisted mainly of fragmentary rules of individualistic orientation. Contemporary international law has a changing nature, having added to the traditional norms, new cooperative norms.

To the topic of material, economic and human limits to activities of mankind Profs. Kimminich and de Seynes made a great contribution. Prof. Kimminich referred to the progress which the world made from the idea of coexistence to that of cooperation, from the simple obligation of refraining from the use of force to the duty to cooperate peacefully. This is precisely what the emerging international law of cooperation wants to facilitate in the economic field. He retraces the idea of solidarity to Vattel who considered it a natural duty of States to help each other in case of famine or other calamities up to the limit of endangering their own existence. At Vattel's time, this was considered an imperfect right of States, it seems, however, logical to press for a transformation of this imperfect right to make it a perfect one. According to Prof. Kimminich a New International Economic Order is not necessarily one without free trade and that is obviously the idea of Prof. Ohlin to whose intervention I shall return later.

Prof. Kimminich particularly stressed the importance of concluding the planned commodity agreements and to complete the other tasks which are inherent in the creation of a new managed world economy.

In the course of the group sessions members particularly stressed the importance of Prof. Kimminich's point concerning the tremendous problems connected with the unheard-of dimension of the migration of populations in our era.

In matters of ecology his paper reminded us of the principles proclaimed at the Stockholm conference of 1972 among which is the dictum that "man has the fundamental right of freedom, equality and adequate conditions of life, in an environment of equality that permits a life of dignity and well-being and he bears a solemn responsibility to protect and improve the environment for present and future generations".

In his intervention Prof. Schram referred also to the questions of ecology, saying that international lawyers should turn their attention to that global issue. He recalled the information received in Uppsala that 10 000 of the lakes of Sweden had already been destroyed by acid rain coming out of Central Europe. New approaches and new strategies were called for to solve the problems of ecology and to make amends for the inactivity of the past.

Ambassador Gonzales Barros referred in this connection to the great forests of the Amazon Basin which probably generate 50% of the world's oxygen.

The exploitation of those forests could cause potentially great harm to the environment within and outside Brazil. This raises the question – what should be the rule of international law for the conservation of forests?

Ambassador do Nascimento e Silva referred in this connection to firm actions taken by the Brazilian government for the protection of the environment. He views this question as a purely internal matter of Brazil. He mentioned, *inter alia* that more than 80% of the pollution of air and water was caused by developed States.

Prof. Grahl-Madsen suggested the possibility of payment for the non-use of certain resources, e. g. rain forests, etc. If such areas and resources were considered the common heritage of mankind, then those who possess them should not foot the bill – the community of States should foot it.

Prof. de Seynes defines ecology as a grandiose mind-expanding concept which, to those who feel responsible for economic policies, may become a veritable nightmare. He referred to new obligations to nature not directly related to human welfare or the enhancement of human rights and dignity. This is, as yet, alien to western culture, although more natural in some civilizations of the East. It involves a belief in the transcendental character of the Laws of Nature supposed to protect ecological cycles and balances.

The treatment of exhaustible resources, although for a long time one of the neglected areas of economic theory, was also a related issue. On the whole, according to Prof. de Seynes, ecology should be seen as a vital element in the renovation of our culture.

He dealt with a number of economic problems facing the world and particularly the developing countries and outlined the debate bearing on the questions, how much trade, how much foreign capital and multinational production, what kind of technology and output-mix, in short what was the desirable degree and nature of the insertion of weak economies in a hostile world system.

He referred to the developing countries self-reliant strategies which, up to now, had been fashioned on the Marxist Model. The cases where such strategies were successful make it probable that only a revolutionary creed is capable of mobilizing the energies needed for a significant transformation. But, according to Prof. de Seynes, it is not a certainty, it may be that this relation is not an inherent one but rather a case of historic accident.

The development of law should also have its rightful place in the investigation of effective poverty-oriented policies. Much research work must be done also in the history of law and its relation to Socialism in general – is Professor de Seynes' conclusion.

The papers of Dr. Hossain and Minister Deng dealt with the problem of natural resources, and of the notion of the common heritage of nations and mankind in a scholarly manner. The authors of the papers tried to solve the antinomy which exists between the notion of the common heritage of mankind and the principle of permanent sovereignty over natural resources.

Prof. Ohlin held that surely there was a conflict between the idea of permanent sovereignty over natural resources and the suggestion to declare such resources the common heritage of mankind. He agreed with Dr. Hossain that such a proposal made no sense. Nor was it necessary, what was involved here was the need for international responsibility that flowed from the unity of the world economy, just as the physical unity of the world raises the need for international responsibility in environmental matters.

The international issues arising from the trade and production of natural resources were extensively considered already in the negotiations leading to the Havana Charter for an International Trade Organization in 1947 and 1948. Some of them survived in the Article of the GATT where, besides access to markets, there is also mention of access to supplies, although this has received little attention. There were good reasons to explain mutually satisfactory ways of increasing the security of investment and supplies in resources; without such security neither producers nor consumers would derive the full benefits from the resources of the world, as shown by the present underinvestment.

This was seen long before the notion of a "common heritage" had emerged to describe resources not yet under any national jurisdiction. Many of the gaps in international economic cooperation might indeed, as Prof. Ohlin suggested, be met by a revival of the International Trade Organization.

Dr. Hossain and Minister Deng found, in the course of the group meetings that the common heritage of mankind can be assimilated to what is called in the national domain public property and the sovereignty over natural resources to that of private property. To this rough division, however, a new category has to be added, namely, that of the social obligations which are connected with the resources belonging to the sovereign domain just as social obligations do burden the private property in progressive legislations of individual countries. Thus the resources under sovereign domain must not be depleted, the environment must not be polluted, raw material must be equitable used. Speaking in general, resources belonging to the sovereign domain must be subject to the duty of international cooperation. This applies also to technology which can be considered as the particular property of a given State. In the field of international cooperation new norms must be introduced to protect the community interest. These norms must include rules applying to contracts which are concluded between States and foreign individuals or companies. These rules must include parts of treaty law which would make it possible to invoke invalidating facts as error, fraud, corruption, coercion etc. or other instances where, by the conclusion of a contract, the community interest was violated.

The establishment of appropritate machinery for the new rules creating a just international economic order was urged by Prof. Schram. He referred to the different legal bodies which are involved with the progressive development of international law and found that the creation of a special new law commission could be envisaged for solving the individual issues of the new world economic order. This could be put, possibly, under the aegis of the Economic and Social Council. According to him these issues were too vital and too vast to be left exclusively to our friends, the economists.

In this connection, Prof. Suy, Under-Secretary-General of the United Nations, indicated first of all that, within the United Nations, several institutions, bodies and organs were dealing with the legal aspects of the New International Economic Order. There was not a single organ entrusted with the coordination. The United Nations Commission on International Trade Law (UNCITRAL) made a survey of the trade law aspects and decided to concentrate on industrial development contracts in order to elaborate uniform clauses for the various types of contracts. Moreover, in elaborating international conventions on transport of goods by sea and on the international sale of goods, and in drafting the Arbitration rules, UNCITRAL had contributed to some important aspects of the New International Economic Order.

Prof. Suy also emphasized that the drafting of a new law of the sea by the United Nations contributed to a large extent to the restructuring of the international economic relations. The work of UNCTAD in the field of eliminating the so-called flags of convenience, in setting up a common fund for raw materials, in drafting the various conventions on primary products (commodity agreements), etc. had to be seen as major contributions to the law of a New International Economic Order.

He finally mentioned the initiation by the Philippines in the General Assembly toward codification of all legal rules on the New International Economic Order. This was a very sensitive area and UNITAR has been asked to make a survey of all these legal aspects. Prof. Suy expressed the view that one should not politicize this topic in focusing on controversial problems but rather try to gradually build up sets of rules on various topics and aspects. The Charter of Economic Rights and Obligations of States was basically a political instrument which tended to overshadow the real progress made elsewhere.

In the course of our group discussion, distributive justice was often referred to. The fundamental human right to food was claimed in the sense that the national level of the poulation should not sink below a certain level. This level should improve proportionally with the increase in production. It is a common responsibility of States that no man remains hungry.

Collective economic security, civil liberties, social justice, are the foundations of international security and of peace which is, in the nuclear age, the most important requirement for the survival of mankind.

In concluding, I would offer my apologies to all those quoted and possibly mis-quoted in this report which, by its very nature, was intended to be only a short outline and which does not replace a more detailed written report which I promise to prepare.

Any member of the seminar who wishes that I correct in the written report anything that I have said, please should not hesitate to inform me orally or in writing of his or her wishes concerning the definitive report.

VII. Sovereignty and Humanity

Working Group III

7.1. A Natural or Moral Basis for International Law

VOJIN DIMITRIJEVIĆ

Notions of nature and morality, referred to in the title, can serve two general purposes. We may examine a natural order of things, or human nature in particular, and moral rules and feelings of equity, as legal phenomena, attaching to them fundamental legal importance with ultimate consequences for the validity of a given rule of international law. Natural or ethical norms thus become supreme legal norms, and, consequently, legal norms of lower order must be denied if contrary to the former. When St. Thomas Aquinas stated that positive law, if not in accordance with natural law, must be deemed invalid, as *legis corruptio*,[1] he brought this position to its logical end in the form of a consistent legal theory of natural law. In such a theory, there is no need for human law-creating agency: the role of the latter can be only secondary and is confined to interpretation and accommodation within limits set by supreme law.

On the other hand, nature and morality can be treated as metajuridical phenomena, without the realm of law, but closely related to it. If we return to our title, the word "basis" in this context would mean that natural laws or moral norms are not a part of international law, that the validity of its rules does not depend on their congruence with some fundamental natural or moral norms, but that the latter influence (or should influence) the creation and interpretation of international legal norms, or that they are the explanation of the validity of international law as a legal order, that they belong, in the words of some authors, to the "material sources" of that law.

It is common to both views presented here that there should be some analogy between something called "nature" and international law, or between moral and international legal norms. Given the fact that there is no central international legislature and that the creation of rules of international law is much more complex than the creation of most municipal law, the barrier between international law and other international normative systems cannot remain absolute: it is rather a delicate membrane filtering new value elements into the sphere of law.

The most formidable logical objection to the theory of natural law has been that there can be no rule without will, and that nature can furnish only facts. Nature contains no inherent preferences, upon which legal norms can be based. In the words of Hans Kelsen: "Daraus, dass etwas ist, kann nicht folgen, dass

1 *Summa theologica*, I–II, 95, 2.

etwas soll, daraus, dass etwas soll, kann nicht folgen, dass etwas ist."[2] The only capacity to will in the cosmology of natural law can belong to God: the validity of natural law stands and falls with the acceptance of the existence of such a unique transcendental being. This argument against naturalist theory has been in the same time the essence of the positivist approach to international law. According to positivists, legal norms cannot be examined as to their "truth", justice, equity, reasonableness, morality etc., but only as to their validity and meaning. If they are willed by the law creating agent (again designed by a valid rule), they are valid, if not, they just do not exist.

To be sure, positivist writers are not necessarily morally indifferent. They only separate – in the Weberian sense – their role as jurists from other roles they play in society. As nonjurists they are free to advocate other contents of legal norms. The concept of *de lege ferenda* allows the positivist to come closer to the naturalist in practice. Still it precludes the influence of his thinking and value judgments on the validity of existing law and, for that matter, the influence of the attitudes and beliefs of anyone else, except the mighty lawmaker, to whom only humble proposals *de lege ferenda* can be made.

Present times are characterized by the dissatisfaction with many rules of international law, many areas of international law, with "classical" or "old" international law altogether. Owing to the importance of this fact I am inclined to interpret the title of our topic as an invitation to examine "nature" and morality as bases for the critique of existing law and the formation of new rules of international law.

*

A strict positivist attitude leads to the glorification of power, even if some positivists hate to admit this. They cannot avoid the objection that, if States can will anything to be law, legal rules would necessarily be arbitrary. The only basis then to criticize a norm is if it affects someone's interests: this critique is futile unless backed by sufficient power to impose a new rule, which now will correspond to the interests of the holder of superior power. In the context of the world we live in, the only position from which to criticize classical international law, established as it was by European powers before the First World War, would be that it was not willed by States which came later into existence and that it is contrary to their particular interests. Certainly, this is a very important objection to the formally existing legal order, but it becomes groundless if the positivist doctrine is pursued too far, that is, if it is maintained that improvement would take place only if the hitherto oppressed and neglected have-nots became powerful enough to impose a set of rules that would correspond to *their* interests, disregarding the interests of other peoples (including former "top-dogs") and to make their will prevail against the will of others. The unrestricted capacity of States to create international law depending solely on the will of their decision makers is apparently an emanation and a confirmation of their sovereignty: in fact, however, the absence of controlling and restrictive superior rules has in most cases amounted

2 Kelsen Hans, Die Grundlage der Naturrechtslehre. In F.-M. Schmölz, *Das Naturrecht in der politischen Theorie.* Wien, Springer, 1963, p. 3.

to the liberty for the more powerful to uphold their interests at the expense of others, especially in bilateral relations. It should not be forgotten that the very "permissiveness" of the old international law is justifiably under attack.[3] The freedom to create law through the pure play of wills has been sought to be restricted by procedural means (coercion of the State) and by controls of substantive nature *(jus cogens)*.[4]

Absence of law, lawlessness, is the best environment for absolute power. The existence of rules, even favourable to the more powerful, increases the predictability of behaviour and thus contributes to some kind of security – no matter how inadequate in its substance. As already stated, the most repugnant features of classical international law are to be found in its condoning the unbridled use and abuse of military and economic power (e. g. treatment of "unicivilized" peoples, occupation of territory, the economic sphere etc.). The results of "free" application of power were later sanctified as customary rules or acquired rights. It is important to note, however, that repeated invocation of the latter indicated the incipient weakening of the political position of European powers. Law is generally perceived by the weaker party as one of its most important weapons. To put it very simply, the present situation is marked by the clinging to "old" international law on the part of the weakening minority of the formerly all-powerful developed States and by the efforts to change and to *strengthen* international law on the part of the hitherto disadvantaged, economically weaker members of the international community. The attitude towards the essential features of the existing and emerging international law is ambivalent at both sides, but there is no denying of the universal acceptance of international law.

Were we still to follow the realist positivist path, we would explain present and nascent international law as a compromise between two opposing wills. In practice, this would mean that we deal only with two groups of States and that international law is but a clear definition of the given balance of power. This cannot be accepted for two reasons. First, we reduce thereby the multitude of international actors, cultures, interests, histories, ideologies, traditions and inspirations to two groups, vaguely defined in crude economic terms. This does not correspond to reality. Second, law conceived and accepted only as compromise is by necessity of short duration: it will be challenged as soon as power relations change. Admittedly, there have been instances where international law performed this – essentially non-legal – function, but law created as compromise is a poor foundation for security and long term policy.

*

International law promises to perform a more meaningful role if the specific attributes of any law are recognized and put to use for good purposes; namely its general abstract character (its formal impartiality) and its normative discrepancy with reality. Law should be formulated to apply to everyone under same circum-

3 See Bedjaoui M., *Towards a New International Economic Order,* Paris, UNESCO, 1979, p. 49.

4 Art. 52 and 53 of the Vienna Convention on the Law of Treaties, 23 May 1969.

stances and to promise a reasonable duration of the consequences of its application. This is the static aspect of law, which binds it to social realities. It is balanced with its dynamic aspect: there is namely no need for law if it is not aimed to change (improve) behaviour. A legal norm is socially meaningless if it is identical with a natural or social fact. Its existence always implies a value, some situation to be brought about, some conduct to be encouraged. Ideally good law is superceded, or dialectically negated, only by its total success, through the disappearance of the behaviour contrary to its rules. The neglect of value-oriented, or future-oriented features of law is a fundamental weakness of naturalism, if we understand natural law to be based on something already existing in nature. Where something exists and there is no need to change it, there is no need for law either. If such need for change (improvement) is felt, the clue cannot be found in already existing reality or in natural laws, which are but descriptions of causality. A similar problem arises for non-naturalists in the treatment of custom as a source of law: if all actors behave uniformly for a long time, and believe to be bound to behave in that fashion, there is a very slight normative load in the rule derived from constant and repeated conduct. It is normative only for newcomers (as in the case of newly independent States), but then it is not a product of their wills, it is not derived from *their* behaviour.

In the above sense, "nature" as a basis of international law is meaningless. However, one should not pretend that it is nature as fact, as neutral reality, which is the core of natural law doctrines. It is rather the belief that nature contains values set by its creator or that it has a hidden purpose, such as the Aristotelan ἐντελεχεία, which is cognizable by human reason ("right reason").[5] Natural law theory is based on the assumption that there are eternal, "true" values, which can be discovered by intelligent people through mental endeavour. Any qualified thinker (the "philosopher" of Plato) will discover the same values, that is, identical rules of natural law. This is a non-ideological view of values, relegating all other "unreasonable" value beliefs to "ideology" in the pejorative sense, ideology influenced by selfishness, emotionality, and ignorance.

Even a superficial acquaintance with values and rules defended and advocated on behalf of "human nature" and "right reason" suffices to show that interpreters of inherent values have adhered to accepted objectives and interests of their cultures and civilizations, that they have belonged to ideologies even while disclaiming this. Thus slavery and servitude were defended as natural. Even Vitoria, who is credited with the important statement that "non-civilized" peoples were members of the human community and had as such an equal status in law, maintained at the same time that, under the natural principles of *Christianitas* and *commercium*, Christian missionaries had the right to freely perform their proselytizing work in the territories of the former. If refused or molested, it was a *casus belli*. If the ruler of the "barbarian" State found, as a result of the mission, an increasing number of Christians in his population, perceived this as a threat,

5 See Midgley E. B. F., *The Natural Law Tradition in the Theory of International Relations*. London, Elek, 1975, passim.

and acted to check the spread of Christianity, his reaction was again a *casus belli.*[6]

The very diversity of cultures coexisting in the world makes it impossible (and dangerous) to assume that there is only one set of *true* values. It is still less acceptable that this set happens to be identical with the value system contained in the religious teachings or ideological traditions, which the interpretor of natural law – be it the statesman, the judge, or the teacher – did in most cases not rationally choose, but which became a part of his personality through socialization in a "we" group. As a rule, we are faced with disguised ideological ethnocentrism of some sort.

Even the denial of all ideology is a form of ideology, generally an ideology of *status quo,* where the value elements of ideology are least perceptible, since there are more possessed values to be protected than desired values to be attained. It is better to face ideology squarely than to pretend it does not exist. Politics, and international politics, cannot be understood without ideology. Paradoxically, rational foreign policy is based on ideology, for if it is not wanted to be a series of reflexes, caused by outer stimuli, it must have clear ultimate goals, that is, must aspire to values. Values are not amenable to scientific scrutiny: it cannot be determined which is "better" or "truer", although there is an intellectual effort involved in determining the hierarchy of values. Any attempt to expel ideology from international relations in the name of reason is thus doomed to failure.

Although some values can be treated as interests, i. e. as "wants and desires of an essentially non-ethical nature"[7], and the distinction between international political and international legal phenomena may be sought along that line, we can reach the tentative conclusion that international law is not influenced by nature, but that it is under the impact of ideologies. Moral attitudes, defending as they do accepted values, are a form of ideology, or at least a normative area most influenced by ideology. As a normative system, morality controls law, even if there are, admittedly, morally indifferent norms in all systems of law (administrative and technical rules etc.). We can safely accept prevailing moral attitudes as a basis for evaluation of international law. Even the naturalist critique has been in fact ideological or moral. We observe today that moral grounds play a prominent role in the denunciation of some rules of "old" international law. While classical international law is seen as unjust,[8] the New International Economic Order (NIEO) is envisioned as "just and equitable" and the Charter of Economic Rights and Duties of States declares the promotion of "international social justice" to be one of the fundamentals of international economic relations.[9]

*

6 Voegelin E. in Schmölz, *op. cit.*, p. 159.

7 Levi, W., The Relative Irrelevance of Moral Norms in International Politics, in J. N. Rosenau, *International Politics and Foreign Policy.* New York, The Free Press, 1969, p. 192.

8 See Bedjaou, *op. cit.*, p. 60 ff, and the literature quoted there.

9 Chapter I of the Charter of Economic Rights and Duties of States, UN General Assembly resolution 3281 (XXIX) of 15 January 1975.

It is much easier to prove that a determining value order does exist and must exist, than to enumerate unequivocal principles and rules of that order. This is the difficulty we share with naturalists, or, for that matter, with anyone trying to establish the material contents of *jus cogens*. The question is, in other words, what are the commonly held values and interests, on the basis of which the existing international legal order should be evaluated, which should be protected and pursued by new international law or, even, which would determine the validity of legal norms?

As stated, the answer is not to be sought primarily in logical deductions, since values, if held, resist scientific analysis. It seems more reasonable to suggest that research be directed toward determining which values are universally held or necessarily follow from the interests generally perceived to be common. Rigorous empirical studies of the world-related values held by large populations all over the globe are still remote, but there has been a number of important contributions, based on limited studies of elites, intelligent insights, informed impressions, and common sense.[10]

*

At this juncture, the distinction between what I propose to call universal and analogous values should be introduced.[11] Universal values are those which cannot be attained within a narrower community and do not belong only to that community but are related to mankind, to the whole world. Analogous values relate to national societies encompassed by States (sometimes wrongly designated by sociologists as "global societies"); they are identical in their appearance but different as to their beneficiary. The cluster of values attached to national security is a good example of analogous values: the survival of the State, its independence, territorial integrity and the like. They are among the most important values held, but they are attached to one's own community: analogous values of some other State may be respected, negated, or viewed with indifference.[12]

Classical international legal order has been based on predominance of analogous values. Originally, this came as a reaction, for Europe had experienced a strong impact of clashing universal values. Owing to religious features of ideologies, mediaeval value systems had had claims to universal validity and had been imposed against any opposition, even by armed force. Value systems originating in the social reality of a certain community had been attributed cosmic validity. The political reality behind this ideological *façade* had been religion used as

10 See e. g. Falk R. A., *A Study of Future Worlds,* New York, The Free Press, 1975, p. 11 ff.

11 This is based on a classification of values developed in Dimitrijević, V., Stojanovic R. *Medjunarodni odnosi.* Beograd, Nolit, 1979, p. 247 ff.

12 A third group of values pertaining to international relations can also be distinguished, that of specific values, which are observed only in some States and are usually attached to the complex of national interest. Specific values do not concern us here, although international law must deal with the harmonization of conflicting specific values. This is generally achieved, however, through the subordination of specific values to some superior commonly held value.

means rather than a sum of ends, universal values had been there to mask specific interests of States, to ennoble their selfishness. After the experience to the Thirty Years War, European States retired into the narrower confines of analogous values. After crusades, indifference was developed toward universalist aspirations and values, which had caused so much harm. At the Congress of Westphalia the principle was established that holders of power in every State had the right to determine the values their subjects were free or encouraged to follow. The individual and his fate ceased to be the concern of world authorities or of universal society: States were the only recognized persons and they aimed at their own, not universal, good. The limits to State egotism have since then been only those set by the legitimate interests of other recognized States, and not by some universal interest. Naturally, the Westphalian system was based on the social similarity of European States: a different treatment was reserved for non-European and non-Christian peoples. The latter had no recognized interest and there was no universal value to protect them. Among the essentially similar fully fledged members of the "international community" common morality was at work – it influenced international law, most notably in the laws applying to wars among them.

The very contrast between the chivalrous elements of the rules of warfare and the irrationality and destructiveness of war itself, to resort to which States were fully entitled, remains as one of the best illustrations of an international legal order based solely on analogy of particular interests. There was no sense of humankind as a whole. States were devoid of their human substance and men and women who remained without links to a certain State, such as refugees, apatrides, or "wild tribesmen" were an irregularity in law, outcasts in real life.

In our century a sudden change in outlooks occurred. I had been prepared by gradual developments in real life. Developments in technology and their effects in political reality had influenced the collective minds. The world has become "smaller", societies more interdependent, peoples closer and better informed. On the one side, this signified the reemergence of the pernicious aspects of ideological confrontations, such as the regressions to cruelty in "international civil wars", but, on the other side, it was realized that the survival and well-being of all depended on something to be protected at the universal level. It became clear that the policies of the international society had to be jointly planned and executed, that the world would not go on existing without something rationally being done about it. Previously undefined values became accutely conspicuous as soon as they were put in jeopardy. Until the most recent times mankind was faced with endless nature. States could wage disastrous wars, but the casualties did not approach the ten percent mark of the total world population. Epidemics exacted millions of victims, but there was always enough remaining biological material to continue the human race. Natural resources had been considered unlimited and earth infinite. It has become clear by now that arms of mass destruction, environmental neglect and pollution can endanger the survival of mankind. The survival of the human race was thus established as the primordial universal value, this time in very concrete and palpable terms. It is not, as for previous generations, a matter depending on superior forces or on nature, the survival of mankind is in human hands.

The construction of biological survival as universal value is not as simple as it may look at the first glance. As a prerequisite for attainment of all other values, it may be posited as supreme. However, the maxim of *primum vivere, deinde philosophari* may turn out to be a philistine and defeatist attitude that, for the sake of survival, realities have to be accepted, no matter how dehumanizing they are. The other extreme amounts to literal comparation with revolutionary situations, where individuals, groups, and entire generations give their lives for the attainment of values which they put above their own existence. Although it is obvious that in the latter case it is the survivors who benefit from the sacrifice, the radicalist view should remind us that life cannot be put at the top of the value system, if it is a life of misery, unworthy of the human being. Such life is a life of despair, and despair does not choose weapons. The unusually long topic, under which international terrorism has been discussed at the UN General Assembly since 1972, is very indicative: "Measures to prevent international terrorism which endangers or takes innocent human lives or jeopardizes fundamental freedoms, and study of the underlying causes of those forms of terrorism and acts of violence which lie in misery, frustration, grievance and despair, and which cause some people to sacrifice human lives, including their own, in an attempt to effect radical changes."[13]

The survival of mankind does not only signify the importance for international law of the effectiveness of the prohibition to use force and measures for disarmament and arms control, or of intense international legislative efforts to protect the common heritage of mankind and save for future generations the unrentable resources of the planet, or of a more equitable distribution of wealth: it also enters the most complex realm of the condition of human beings in their own communities, that is, States.

*

The existence of universal values presupposes mankind as an entity, both an aggregate of all international actors and separate from them. It must be admitted that this is a concept we owe to the classical theory of natural law, irrespective of the application it had to the social and political realities of the times when it was formulated. If we return to the example of refugees, we find that we can better understand the principle of *non-refoulement,* coupled as it is now with the denial of individual right of asylum in a determined country, within the context of Wolff's world community and Jefferson's statement that "every man has a right to live somewhere on the earth", than in the positivist legal order we are accustomed to.

The awareness of universal community has been reflected in a number of recent documents of legal consequence. Let us quote a random sample. The Preamble of the Antarctic Treaty of 1 December 1959, recognizes "that it is in the interest of all mankind that Antarctica shall continue for ever to be used exclusively for peaceful purposes".[14] The States parties of the Convention on Regis-

13 UN General Assembly resolution 3034 (XXVII) of 18 December 1972.
14 *International Legal Materials* 1980, p. 860.

tration of Objects Launched into Outer Space, adopted by the United Nations General Assembly on 12 November 1974, recognize in the Preamble the "common interest of all mankind".[15] In its Draft articles on State responsibility, provisionally adopted in 1977, the International Law Commission defined an international crime as "an internationally wrongful act which results from the breach by a State of an international obligation so essential for the protection of fundamental interests of the international community that its breach is recognized as a crime by that community as a whole".[16]

The signatories of the Bonn Convention on the Conservation of Migratory Species of Wild Animals of 23 June 1979 believe that the earth's natural system "must be conserved for the good of mankind".[17] "The interest of all mankind" is an important consideration in the Preamble of the Convention on the Conservation of Antarctic Marine Living Resources of 20 May 1980.[18] The basis of the whole endeavour to draft a new law of the sea has been the concept of the common heritage of mankind. The informal text of the Draft Convention on the Law of the Sea, prepared by the president of the United Nations Conference in 1980, refers in its introduction to a just and equitable international economic order "which would take into account the interests and needs of mankind as a whole".[19]

The concept of mankind includes future generations. This is explicitely stated in the 1973 Convention on International Trade in Endangered Species of Wild Fauna and Flora ("this and the generations to come"),[20] in the Barcelona Convention for the Protection of the Mediterranean Sea against Pollution of 16 February 1976 ("responsibility to preserve this common heritage for the benefit and enjoyment of present and future generations"),[21] and in the already quoted Convention on the Conservation of Migratory Species, the signatories of which are "aware that each generation of man holds the resources of earth for future generations and has an obligation to ensure that this legacy is conserved and, where utilized, is used wisely".

The importance of the recognition of universal values is not diminished by the observation that States are most ready to concede universal interests when dealing with assets inherited from nature, that they are more prepared to prevent future damage than to correct existing unjustices. Still, one can note common values expanding to the cultural sphere, such as in the form of the right of all peoples to benefit from advances and developments in science and technology, defined in the Draft International Code of Conduct in the Transfer of Technology.[22] In the economic field, conceived in the narrow sense of creation and

15 *International Legal Materials* 1975, p. 44.
16 Art. 19, UN Doc. A/32/183, 30 August 1977.
17 *International Legal Materials* 1980, pp. 15–16.
18 *International Legal Materials 1980*, p. 842.
19 UN Conference on the law of the sea. Informal composite negotiating text/Revision 3. A/CONF. 62/WP. 10/Rev. 3.
20 Preamble, *International Legal Materials* 1973, p. 1088.
21 Preamble, *International Legal Materials* 1976, p. 290.
22 Preamble, 2. TD/CODE TOT/25 of 2 June 1980.

distribution of socially produced wealth, the general idea of NIEO is predominant. It seems, however, that its proponents stress common moral elements rather then the element of the world community. According to the Charter of Economic Rights and Duties of States, the bases of NIEO are "equity, sovereign equality, interdependence, common interest and co-operation of all States". One of the explanations is that the present international economic order can be treated as unjust even by the criteria of existing international law and that small and developing States had to stress their sovereignty *vis-à-vis* the still basically capitalist world economic system and against powerful international agencies trying to impose biased social attitudes in the form of neutral and universally valid economic principles.[23]

*

"International social justice", referred to in the Charter of Economic Rights and Duties of States, is without doubt conceived in terms of just inter-State relations, or inter-society relations, since the same Charter quotes later the "rights of all peoples". This observation brings us back to what we termed the conditions of the human being within his own community. There is some uneasiness reflected in the simultaneous reference to universal values and international social justice, on the one hand, and the jealous protection of State sovereignty, with the implication that States are free to act internally as they see fit. This uneasiness is also demonstrated by the growing preference for the word "people", which carries with it the presumption of popular sovereignty, the distinction between the population and its social superstructure, on the one hand, and the State as an apparatus of power, on the other, a distinction already implied in the famous "We the peoples" opening phrase of the United Nations Charter.[24]

Peoples are assumed to be true international persons in the Universal Declaration on the Rights of Peoples, adopted by a non-governmental gathering in Algiers on 4 July 1976. The wording of the Declaration has a naturalist ring. Its authors believe peoples to have the following fundamental rights and groups of rights: the right to existence, the right to political self-determination, economic rights, the right to culture and the right to environment and common resources, with the rights of minorities treated separately. The Algiers Declaration, in its Art. 7, stresses, however, the so-called "internal" aspect of the right to self-

23 See: No to IMF Meddling. Extract from President Nyerere's New Year Message 1980 to the Diplomats Accredited in Tanzania. *Development Dialogue* (Uppsala), Vol. 2, 1980, p. 7.

24 In fact, "people" is now being used to convey the same meaning "nation" conveyed at the time of the opposition to the absolutist State. This distinction still survives in the terms of national interest and *raison d'Etat*. With the strengthening of the democratic institutions "nation" and "State" became in some important languages synonymous. In some other languages, however, this development did not take place, but the word "nation" or words with the same Latin root have acquired definite ethnical connotations. E. g. the translation of the term "nation" into Serbo-Croat both in the case of the League of Nations and the United Nations has vaccilated between *narod* (closer to "people" and with democratic undertones) and *nacija* ("nation" with an ethnical ring).

determination: "Every people has the right to have a democratic government representing all citizens without distinction of race, sex, belief or colour, and capable of ensuring effective respect for the human rights and fundamental freedoms for all." According to a competent interpreter of the Algiers Declaration, this collective right of the people does not mean only "self-government", that is, non-interference from outside, but "a) the right to choose freely a government, exercising all the freedoms which make the choice possible . . . b) the right that the government, once chosen, continues to enjoy the consensus of the people and is neither oppressive nor authoritorian and c) the right to exercise all the civil and political rights that enable a people to establish and express its will freely and permanently".[25]

The concept of people and the construction of human rights as belonging to group rather than State or individual are meant to reconcile the paradigms of "humankind" and "international community", if the first term is used to designate the society of all human beings, and the second the community of States. In international legal terms, the first one is certainly of mediaeval naturalist origin and the second belongs to the Westphalian positivist image of the world. The conflict of images is politically expressed in the fear of humanitarian intervention and of the propagandistic abuse of alleged violations of human rights, on the one side, and the constatation that the very governments which insist on international justice and inalienable rights of their States sometimes treat their own populations below any acceptable standards, maintaining that even the most heinous atrocities are their internal affairs, or still worse, that such government behaviour belongs to "national culture" and is justified by a certain value system, on the other side. The latter argument is pursued further to juxtapose the lofty proclamations of international treaties and declarations on human rights and the sad facts of massive persecutions, and to inquire whether written law should have predominance over the gruesome "custom".[26]

The complex of human rights is approached with wariness for a very good reason. The position of individuals and groups in society is where universalist ideologies clash most decidedly, sometimes with bloody consequences. Hence any attempt to "deidelogize" international relations tends to leave the "interior" of States blackboxed. The international legal order originating the Treaties of Westphalia left the ethical judgment on the relation between government and its subjects solely as the concern of the territorial State and outside the purview of international law. Until very recently, actions for human rights were of purely municipal nature. In terms of international law, human rights guarantees in some countries were as valid as authoritarian solutions in others and enjoyed the same protection.

When this became intolerable, for reasons I believe to lie in the field of uni-

25 Cassese A., *The Right of Peoples to Political Self Determination: From the UN Charter to the Algiers Declaration*. Mimeographed paper prepared for the Round Table on the Algiers Declaration on the Rights of Peoples. Florence, November, 1976, p. 21.

26 See Watson J. S., Legal Theory, Efficacy and Validity in the Development of Human Rights Norms in International Law. *Law Forum*, 1979, p. 609 ff.

versal values, an explanation was sought and is still being sought within the familiar terms of reference. The positivist rationale for the international concern for human rights has been based on the interpretation of events leading to wars, and especially Second World War. It has thus been held that gross violations of human rights cause aggressive international behaviour of the authorities committing violations in their own countries and thereby endanger *other* nations. Such indirect resoning helped to overcome the objections of domestic jurisdiction and played an important role in bringing the question of apartheid before the United Nations Security Council. In the 1975 Helsinki Final Act, for example, this line of reasoning is reflected in the following statement: "The participating States recognize the universal significance of human rights and fundamental freedoms, respect for which is an essential factor for peace, justice and well-being necessary to ensure the development of friendly relations and co-operation among themselves as among all States."[27]

The important weakness of this position is that so far it has not been proved, to the knowledge of the present writer, that repressive governments are more prone to aggression against other States than those with better domestic human rights records. This observation suggests that prevention of war has not been the ultimate source of concern for human rights but rather it has been a way to present those concerns in the hostile environment of classical international law.

Following natural law thinking, individual human beings derive their rights and freedoms from an order superior to the State, which cannot under any circumstances deprive them of these rights or limit them without their prior consent. In the Helsinki Accord, again, this attitude was expressed in the statement that human rights and freedoms "derive from the inherent dignity of the human person and are essential for his free and full development".[28] The naturalist argument can effectively be used only against encroachments by the State and not when positive action is demanded by it, such as in the case of socioeconomic rights. Furthermore, the concept of human dignity, although markedly present in what we may term UNESCO philosophy,[29] may also prove to be divisive.[30]

*

The unquestioned universal value of the survival of mankind, which was shown not to mean mere vegetation, was translated into a fuller concept of peace, which again is not mere absence of war. The universal adoption of peace as the foremost

27 Declaration on Principles of International law concerning Friendly Relations and Cooperation among States in accordance with the Charter of the United Nations, UN General Assembly resolution 2625 (XXV) of 24 October 1970. Principle VII, para. 5.

28 *Ibid.*, Principle VII, para. 2.

29 See the statements by UNESCO Director-General A.-M. M'Bow, quoted by Bedjaoui, *op. cit.*, p. 73 ff.

30 For the important place human dignity plays in the jurisprudence of Myres McDougal and for his belief that universal legal order is impossible because of the incompatibility of values in the East and in the West, see Falk R., *The Status of Law in International Society*. Princeton. Princeton Univ. Press, 1970, pp. 645, 648.

instrumental (modal) value by all States and all important ideologies shows that ideologies, irrespective of their most fundamental disagreements as to substantive values (interests), can agree on some modal values, that is, conditions under which substantive values are to be pursued. If then peace is to be maintained in its true and full meaning, its consequences on the human conditions within the society must be accepted. Inside societies, modal values are also more influenced by the moral sphere than substantive interest. Thus arise important similarities, or at least common minimal standards, such as strong moral revulsion against certain forms of internal terrorism, torture, abuse of humanitarian feelings etc.

Essentially similar popular attitudes toward the position of the human being in the society, one's own and alien, need only be established and not deduced from eternal attributes of human nature. A simpler and more straightforward explanation is offered by cultural reality, in the prevailing attitudes. People simply do care, they are truly concerned with the fate of distant human beings. It is an empirically verifiable moral reaction, witnessing to a "territorial" expansion of the ethical sphere of the contemporary man and woman.[31] Admittedly, this is still a vague feeling of empathy, but in turn it can be broken down into a cluster of values held indispensable by human beings and peoples. Some of these values seem obvious and can be described in fairly simple terms, for example, life, physical integrity, or health; others can be expressed only through their negation (hunger, pain etc.) while still others defy succint description. Values represent latent, potential, static, as well as dynamic states and situations. It is sometimes difficult to formulate them as "rights", given the fact that this term implies corresponding duties of someone else.

The essence of the international human rights complex is a cluster of universally held values, related to the entire international community, which exist because they are felt by our contemporaries. It is believed that this is a fact, which can be falsified as a fact, but which is independent from support by some superior principles, especially if they belong to heterogenous or obsolete value systems. This situation requires only historical explanation, which I tend to find in the simple statement that in the sphere of public conscience the ideals of humanism have been victorous in the second half of our century and that all ideologies competing for human minds and broad support have a chance only if they show that they aim to the liberation, self-attainment and fulfilment of the human being in a just society. The significance of this victory is in principle not diminished by important differences on how to achieve this final aim, not even by the undeniable fact that humanist ideology can serve as an excuse for the ruling elite to perpetuate its power and to exact severe sacrifices from the present generation for the sake of some ultimate bliss in very distant future. Even the disturbing fact that all regimes tend to style themselves "democratic", that ruthless dictatorships inscribe high-sounding human rights principles in their constitutions and laws, proves, paradoxically, that no claim to legitimacy can be based on the rejection of the humanist ideal. To paraphrase a familiar adage, the victory of an idea is signaled by hypocrites subscribing to it.

31 See Berger P., Are Human Rights Universal? *Commentary*, No 3, 1977, p. 61.

The basis human rights, the political system, and the culture of the society are organically interrelated and interdependent. This truism poses immense problems in the search for a universally applicable definition of human rights. Better adaptations can be made at regional levels, not only in regions marked by pronounced cultural and ideological proximity, but also in those where important differences obtain. Hence the quotations from the Helsinki Accord. The purpose of our gathering seems to me to be to recognize the pressure of the universal moral conscience in this realm, as well as in others, and to attempt to identify universal values, formulate them and examine the contribution international law could make to their attainment and protection. Bearing in mind the complex social fabric in which individual and collective values are perceived, pursued, realized and legally protected, we must very much heed the warning of George F. Kennan: "Do we . . . in undertaking to decide what 'rights' should exist in other countries, propose to tell the peoples and governments of these countries what restraints should also exist? And can one, then, try to tell another country what rights ought to be observed in its society without telling it what sort of government it ought to have?"[32]

32 Quoted by Thompson K., New Reflections on Ethics and Foreign Policy: the Problem of Human Rights. *Journal of Politics*, 1978, p. 1005.

7.2. Le Fondement Naturel ou Moral du Droit International

Alexis Gabou

Le thème à étudier, »Le Fondement Naturel ou Moral du Droit International« pourrait donner lieu à une vaste fresque. Je me bornereai, pour participer à la promotion d'un nouvel ordre juridique international, à donner de ce thème une vision qui s'attache à l'évolution historique des concepts en cause et aux conséquences de cette évolution.

Le naturel, mentionné dans le thème, ne désigne pas la nature minérale ou purement animale, celle qui désigne les choses. Ce naturel ou cette nature, considérés comme fondements du droit international, sont assimilables à la »nature« retenue par l'Ecole du droit naturel.

On peut rappeler que l'on classe dans l'Ecole du droit naturel un certain nombre d'auteures, qui continuent d'une certaine façon une longue lignée de penseurs juristes ou non de l'antiquité gréco-romaine et du moyen-âge européen et chrétien. On y fait place au Hollandais Grotius, au Suédois Puffendorf, au Suisse Vattel, à l'Anglais Locke, à Jean Jacques Rousseau notamment. Ces auteurs détachent le droit de la révélation religieuse, qui cesse de lui servir de fondement, et le rattachent à la nature, à la nature humaine, qui est désormais son soubassement nécessaire et suffisant, du moins pour les naturalistes et, semble-t-il, pour les gens de bon sens. Ces auteurs définissent un état de nature antérieur à toute société humaine et, par conséquent, à la société étatique et à la société internationale et qui est le fondement du droit.

C'est ainsi vraisemblablement que naît l'idée d'un droit tiré de la nature humaine, qui sert de fondement au droit positif et le commande.

A ce fondement du droit et particulièrement du droit international correspond une éthique. Celle-ci sert également de fondement au droit international. Elle est constituée par un ensemble de règles morales qui ont pour caractéristique de tendre à protéger la nature humaine en assurant la sauvegarde de la dignité humaine.

Nature humaine et morale sonst des notions qui relèvent de la philosophie du droit. Celle-ci peut être définie comme l'étude raisonnée d'un certain idéal et de ses implications en vue d'établir un certain ordre juridique, de l'apprécier et de l'explique.[1] De ce point de vue, les notions de nature humaine et de morale

1 Chloros, A. G., Une interprétation de la nature et de la fonction de la philosophie juridique moderne. In: *Le Rôle de la Volonté dans le Droit.* Paris, C.N.R.S., Sirey, 1957. pp. 169–204.

garantissant la dignité humaine constitutent cet idéal téléologique qui commande le droit international et lui sert de fondement.

Elles ne peuvent pas servir de fondement au droit international si, comme tout concept philosophique, elles sonst susceptibles d'interprétations variées et divergentes à un moment donné suivant les utilisateurs. Elles ne peuvent remplir un tel rôle que si, comme le droit international lui-même, elles sonst reconnues et acceptées comme étant le droit par la société internationale. L'insertion de ces notions dans des instruments juridiques applicables leur confère ce caractère obligatoire ainsi qu'une certaine certitude en ce qui concerne leur contenu, leur signification ou leur portée.

De fait, l'historie de l'humanité montre que ces deux notions, aux diverses époques, ont fait l'objet de stipulations dans les instruments juridiques de droit international comme on le verra ci-après. Cette histoire, d'ailleurs, montre que le droit international a toujours eu pour fondement une certaine conception de la nature humaine et une morale correspondante garantissant la dignité humaine.

L'utilisation de ces deux concepts a subi une évolution entrecoupée par une césure qui marque une mutation qualitative. Pendant une longue période, deux notions différentes de la nature humaine et de la moralité correspondante ont coexisté. Les unes, normales, étaient destinées à l'usage des Etats considérés comme les seuls vrais membres de la société internationale, les Etats civilisées, et à leurs sujets. Les autres, restrictives, étaient destinées à régir des pays et peuples considérés comme des objets et non pas des sujets du droit international, les pays barbares et leurs indigènes. L'humanité, divisée contre elle-même et placée sous la férule de la minorité peuplant les Etats civilisés, connaît un droit international à deux volets, le normal et le discriminatoire, qui traduit cette inégalité renforcée et justifiée par la conception dualiste de la nature humaine et de la moralité correspondante. C'est l'ancien ordre juridique international.

La seconde période s'ouvre lorsque la notion de nature humaine et de morale garantissant la dignité humaine acquièrent ce caractère d'universalité qui fait qu'elles embrassent l'humanité entière conçue comme une famille unique. Le droit international qui en découle, valable pour tous les peuples qui composent l'humanité et tous les individus qui constituent ces peuples, est celui qui est en train d'établir le nouvel ordre juridique international plus juste que l'ancien.

I. La conception dualiste de la nature humaine et de la morale, fondement du droit international

La conception dualiste et discriminatoire de la nature humaine et de la moralité internationale correspond à la période des temps modernes antérieure à la décolonisation du XXe siècle dont le temps fort est marqué par l'adoption de la résolution n° 1514 du 14 décembre 1960 de l'Assemblée Générale des Nations Unies sur le droit à l'indépendance des peuples sous domination étrangère. La conception de la nature humaine et de la morale internationale et le droit international, auquel ces notions servent de fondement, sont l'œuvre de la »société européenne et chrétienne du début des temps modernes, qui était demeurée jusqu'à 1939 le noyau solide et central des relations internationales même avec ses multiples ramifications extra-européennes«.[2]

En réalité et pratiquement jusqu'aux années 1960, l'Europe et les pays développés ne sont pas seulement le noyau solide et central des relations internationales, mais encore ils façonnent les relations internationales, fixent le droit international et déterminent les notions de nature humaine et de morale internationale qui lui servent de fondement, le tout à leur profit. En ce qui concerne le fondement du droit international, ils dégagent deux notions differentes de la nature humaine et de la morale correspondante. Les unes, normales, leur sont applicables à eux seuls, et les autres, restrictives, sont destinées à maintenir le reste de l'humanité en état de sujétion et d'exploitation. Les notions normales entraînent le bénéfice des règles normales du droit international pour leurs créateurs. Les notions restrictives entraînent l'assujettissement de leurs destinataires nondéveloppés aux Etats développés.

Quelques instruments juridiques internationaux permettent de saisir la conception dualiste de la nature humaine et de la morale internationale ainsi que ses conséquences discriminatoires dans l'ordre juridique international ancien. On retiendra, à cet égard, le Traité de la Sainte Alliance des 14–26 septembre 1815, l'Acte général de la conférence de Berlin du 26 février 1885, l'Acte général de la conférence de Bruxelles du 2 juillet 1890 et le Pacte de la Société des Nations.

A. Le Traité de la Sainte Alliance

Le Traité de la Sainte Alliance fait état de la fraternité indissoluble unissant les quatre monarques autrichien, prussien, russe et français, de leur devoir d'assistance mutuelle et de leur engagement, en qualité de délégués de la divine providence, à gouverner leurs Etats avec la plus grande bienveillance pour les sujets de ces Etats. A la lumière de la pratique du Concert européen constituée par de multiples interventions armées contre l'instauration de régimes politiques démocratiques en Europe, on considère comme hypocrites les déclarations de fraternité et de sollicitude contenues dans le traité de la Sainte Alliance. L'effet de la morale acceptée internationalement était donc restreint même pour les peuples européens.

B. Les actes généraux coloniaux

Le contenu de l'Acte général de la conférence de Berlin de 1885 et de l'Acte général de la conférence de Bruxelles de 1890 montre que la notion de nature humaine n'est pleinement reconnue qu'aux nationaux des Etats colonialistes de l'époque dont on organisait et garantissait la jouissance de l'égale liberté du commerce et de l'industrie en Afrique, le droit de propriété, le droit de prosélitisme religieux et le droit à l'exploration en vue de l'implantation du système colonial. Le fondement moral du système établi est donné par l'article 10 de l'Acte général de Berlin: »Afin de donner une garantie nouvelle de sécurité au commerce et à l'industrie et de favoriser, par le maintien de la paix, le développement de la

2 Cavaré, Louis, *Le Droit International Public Positif.* 3e édition. Tome 1. Paris, A. Pédone, 1967. p. 78.

civilisation dans les contrées mentionnées à l'article 1er et placées sous le régime de la liberté commerciale . . .«. Les indigènes, à supposer que la nature humaine leur soit reconnue, ne sont guère que des êtres à protéger, les Etats colonialistes s'engageant »à veiller à la conservation des populations indigènes et à l'amélioration de leurs conditions morales et matérielles d'existence et à concourir à la suppression de l'esclavage et surtout de la traite des noirs;« L'objectif moral souligné était de tendre »à instruire les indigènes et à leur faire comprendre et apprécier les avantages de la civilisation«.[3] Tout se résoud en paternalisme.

C. Le droit de la Société des Nations

Le Pacte de la Société des Nations met en œuvre la notion de nature humaine en s'efforçant d'assurer la conservation de l'homme par la paix, la coopération, la sécurité et la justice internationales. Le Préambule du Pacte met à la charge des Etats membres l'obligation de respecter le droit international, de ne pas recourir à la guerre pour régler leurs différences mais, au contraire, de recourir à des moyens pacifiques et notamment à la Cour Permanente de Justice. Ces règles concernent les Etats européens ou développés et leurs peuples.

A l'intention des pays et peuples extra-européens, le droit de la Société des Nations, tout en maintenant la légitimité de la colonisation, crée une notion particulière de nature humaine destinée aux colonies des Etats vaincus durant la première guerre mondiale. Cette notion et la morale qui en découle sont cependant modulées en trois catégories aboutissant à des conceptions restrictives de la nature humaine et de la moralité internationale et dont le caractère restrictif s'aggrave de l'une à l'autre.

La nature humaine se trouve alors classée en trois catégories hiérarchisées suivant la qualité A, B et C des mandats dont font l'objet les peuples auxquels cette nature humaine est reconnue par le droit de la Société des Nations. Sont soumis au mandat A les peuples considérés comme ayant un degré supérieur d'organisation. L'Etat étranger, qui les gouverne, n'a que le droit de maintenir l'ordre et il doit organiser l'administration d'accord avec les indigènes, organiser une bonne justice, garantir la liberté de conscience et de culte, assurer l'égalité économique des ressortissants des membres de la Société des Nations et surtout conduire les indigènes à l'indépendance.

L'humanité inférieure fait l'objet du mandat B. Les Etats étrangers, qui la gouvernent, doivent protéger le travailleur indigène, contrôler le commerce des armes et des spiritueux, supprimer la traite des esclaves, soigner les indigènes, sans pouvoir annexer les pays sous mandat.

L'humanité faisant l'objet du mandat C est, sans doute plus inférieure puisque le régime politique découlant du mandat A est plus restrictif que celui découlant du mandat B.

Au total la conception dualiste de la nature humaine et de la morale internationale apparaît comme génératrice d'un système égoïste profitable à l'Europe et aux pays développés et, en revanche, injuste et empreint de mépris pour le reste

3 Acte général de la Conférence de Berlin du 26 février 1885, article 6. In: Martens, *Recueil Général des traités.* 2e série. Tome X, pp. 414 ff.

de l'humanité, qui, à la limite, est exclue du genre humain et n'est envisagée que comme un agrégat d'objets utilisables avec profit.

II. La conception moniste et universelle de la nature humaine et de la morale, fondement du droit international

La mutation qualitative, constituée par l'adoption de la conception moniste et universelle de la nature humaine, de la morale internationale, commence avec la Charte des Nations Unies du 26 juin 1945 qui lie la nature humaine, sa dignité, ses droits et le devoir des Etats de les sauvegarder. Mais les conditions d'une mutation complète ne sont remplies qu'avec les indépendances des années 1960 et la résolution du 14 décembre 1960 de l'Assemblée Générale de l'Organisation des Nations Unies qui lie la nature humaine, ses droits et sa dignité avec le droit des peuples à l'indépendance. Cette étape permet de continuer le mouvement, amorcé en 1951 au profit du réfugié, tendant à approfondir la conception nouvelle de la nature humaine en descendant du général au particulier pour réglementer la situation d'êtres humains particuliers tels que la femme et l'enfant.

A. L'Etablissement de la conception moniste et universelle

La Charte de l'Organisation des Nations Unies prend ouvertement la nature humaine comme fondement du système des Nations Unies et de son droit. Mais la notion de nature humaine n'est pas adoptée sans précisions. Le Préambule de la Charte donne des précisions qui permettent de saisir les implications de l'adoption de la nature humaine comme fondement du droit international.

Le Préambule de la Charte réaffirme la foi des peuples »dans les droits fondamentaux de l'homme, dans la dignité et la valeur de la personne humaine, dans l'égalité des hommes et des femmes, ainsi que des nations grandes et petites«. Il proclame la résolution des peuples de favoriser le progrès social et d'instaurer de meilleures conditions de vie dans une liberté plus grande, en recourant notamment aux institutions internationales pour favoriser le progrès économique et social de tous les peuples. Ainsi s'établit une conception unique et universellement valable de la nature humaine dont les conséquences sont tirées par le Préambule, lui-même, de la Charte.

L'adoption de la nature humaine comme valeur suprême et fondement du droit international a pour première conséquence que l'on doit assurer la dignité humaine. Celle-ci doit être assurée en l'homme pris individuellement et dans sa collectivité nationale. L'attribution de la nature humaine doit entraîner pour lui, en tant qu'individu, le bénéfice des droits de l'homme, la non-discrimination selon le sexe, une plus grande liberté et un meilleur niveau de vie. L'attribution de la nature humaine aux groupements nationaux ou aux peuples entraîne le principe de l'égalité de toutes les nations, l'inégalité étant assimilable à la discrimination selon le sexe, et la nécessité de favoriser le développement économique et social des peuples en recourant notamment aux organismes internationaux.

Tout ceci implique l'établissement d'une société internationale tout à fait différente de celle de l'époque précédente affligée par une conception dualiste de la nature humaine et considérant comme régulière la domination coloniale d'un peuple sur un autre.

Le nouvel ordre juridique international, qui naît avec la Charte de l'Organisation des Nations Unies, comporte pourtant quelques relents de l'ancien ordre. Ils se manifestent dans les institutions qui maintiennent l'exercice de la compétence coloniale: la tutelle et la notion de territoire non-autonome.

Néanmoins, la Déclaration Universelle des Droits de l'Homme du 10 décembre 1948 reprend et précise la conception moniste et universelle de la nature humaine considérée comme fondement du droit international.

Le Préambule de la Déclaration universelle relève que la famille humaine est une et que la reconnaissance de la dignité humaine et des droits egaux et inaliénables à chaque membre de cette famille est le fondement de la liberté, de la justice et de la paix mondiale. Le Préambule proclame que le plus haut idéal humain est l'avènement d'un monde de liberté, sans terreur ni misère et qu'une conception unique et commune des libertés est nécessaire pour que les Etats puissent assurer »le respect universel et effectif des droits de l'homme et des libertés fondamentales«.

Les conditions de l'émergence complète, en droit, de cette conception moniste et universelle de la nature humaine ne sont remplies qu'avec la résolution n° 1514 du 14 décembre 1960 de l'Assemblée Générale des Nations Unies. Ce texte fondamental proclame le lien entre la dignité humaine, les droits fondamentaux de l'homme, et l'indépendance des peuples. Il affirme que l'assujettissement des peuples à un joug, une domination et une exploitation étrangers constitue la négation des droits fondamentaux de l'homme et une violation de la Charte des Nations Unies. Dès lors la conception moniste et universelle de la nature humaine comme fondement du droit internationale est clairement formulée et peut, en droit, déployer tous ses effets: l'établissement enfin du nouvel ordre juridique international annoncé par la création de l'Organisation des Nations Unies.

B. L'Approfondissement de la conception moniste et universelle de la nature humaine

L'étape suivante, qui dure encore, approfondit la conception moniste et universelle de la nature humaine en y apportant des précisions dans un mouvement qui crée progressivement le nouvel ordre juridique international. On peut distinguer deux aspects dans cet approfondissement de la notion de base. D'un côté, les implications de l'adoption de la conception moniste et universelle de la nature humaine pour l'homme en général sont insérées dans le droit positif. D'un autre côté, la précision est poussée jusqu'à la réglementation de la situation particulière de catégories déterminées d'êtres humains.

Le statut de l'être humain, tel qu'il est établi par la Déclaration Universelle des Droits de l'Homme, devient positiv avec l'adoption des deux conventions du 16 décembre 1966 entrées en vigueur le 3 janvier 1976, le Pacte relatif aux Droits Civiques et Politiques et le Pacte relativ aux Droits Économiques, Sociaux et Culturels. Le système paraît renforcé par le Protocole facultatif se rapportant au Pacte relativ aux Droits Civils et Politiques qui permet aux particuliers de saisir le Comité des Droits de l'Homme de leurs réclamations pour violation des droits de l'homme. Les deux premiers traités mettent en œuvre le statut général libéral reconnu a la personne humaine par la Déclaration Universelle des Droits de l'Homme, en s'appuyant sur la même motivation qui est, en dehors de leurs préambules identiques, contenue dans leur article premier également identique.

Cette argumentation affirme que tous les peuples ont le droit de disposer d'eux-mêmes, de déterminer librement leur statut politique et de promouvoir librement leur développement économique, social et culturel. Ils ont, dans ce but, le droit de disposer librement de leurs richesses et de leurs ressources naturelles, droit assorti de l'interdiction de les priver de leurs moyens de subsistence. L'adoption de la conception moniste et universelle de la nature humaine, lorsqu'elle transforme les droits de l'homme qui en découlent en droits positifs, entraîne ainsi l'institution du lien entre les droits de l'homme politiques, sociaux, économiques et culturels avec les droits collectifs à l'indépendance et à la souveraineté sur les ressources naturelles.

L'approfondissement de la conception moniste et universelle de la nature humaine devient de plus en plus réaliste avec la réglementation de la situation particulière de catégories d'êtres humains dont il est nécessaire d'assurer la dignité humaine. Cette réglementation est faite, d'une part, par les instruments généraux qui réglementent la situation du réfugié, de la femme et de l'enfant et, d'autre part, par les textes régionaux qui tendent à embrasser les mêmes domaines ou le domaine général des droits de l'homme pour les régions considérées.

Le statut des réfugiés du 28 juillet 1951 et le Protocole du 31 janvier 1967 relatif à ce statut, en édictant, sur le plan général, un statut protecteur des réfugiés politiques, se présentent comme l'application particulière, à une catégorie d'êtres humains nécessiteux, du statut général libéral dont doit bénéficier tout être humain. Le préambule du statut des réfugiés de 1951 le rappelle dans ses deux premiers considérants.

Sur le plan général encore, la Déclaration sur l'Élimination de la Discrimination à l'égard des Femmes adoptée par la résolution n° 2263 du 7 novembre 1967 de l'Assemblée Générale des Nations Unies se présente aussi comme l'application, à une catégorie particulière d'êtres humains, du statut général libéral reconnu par le droit international à la personne humaine. L'Assemblée Générale explique la genèse de cette Déclaration par la faiblesse sociale préoccupante de la catégorie considérée et par la constatation de la vanité de tous les instruments juridiques adoptés par l'Organisation des Nations Unies ou ses organismes spécialisés pour éliminer la discrimination dont la femme est partout victime. L'Assemblée Générale justifie ensuite la Déclaration en relevant que le statut général libéral reconnu par le droit international est de droit pour tout être humain et que la discrimination, qui s'exerce contre les femmes, est incompatible avec la dignité humaine.

Une autre catégorie d'êtres humains remarquable par leur faiblesse sociale fait également l'object de la même démarche réaliste d'approfondissement de la conception moniste et universelle de la nature humaine. Il s'agit des enfants, qui font l'object du statut protecteur édicté par la résolution du 20 novembre 1959 de l'Assembléee Générale des Nations Unies. L'Assemblée Générale justifie ce statut particulier de l'enfant par la protection spéciale et les soins spéciaux nécessaires, selon le droit international, à l'enfant en raison de son manque de maturité physique et intellectuelle. L'Assemblée Générale enfin rattache ce statut particulier au statut général libéral reconnu à la personne humaine et dont celle-ci ne peut être privée particulièrement lorsqu'il s'agit de l'enfant.

Les textes régionaux, tels que la Convention de l'Organisation de l'Unité Africaine régissant les Aspects Propres des Réfugiés en Afrique du 10 septembre 1969, le projet de Charte Africaine des Droits de l'Homme du 17 janvier 1981, la Convention Américaine relative aux Droits de l'Homme et la Convention Européenne de Sauvegarde des Droits de l'Homme et des Libertés Fondamentales, participent à l'approfondissement réaliste de la conception moniste et universelle de la nature humaine. Tous ces textes invoquent cette conception formulée par le droit de l'Organisation des Nations Unies et entendent appliquer localement le statut général libéral de la personne humaine résultant de ce droit.

Le Préambule de la Convention Américaine des Droits de l'Homme est particulièrement clair sur ce point. Il proclame que »les droits fondamentaux de l'homme ne découlent pas de son appartenance à un Etat donné, mais reposent sur les attributs de la personne humaine, ce qui justifie leur protection internationale . . .«. Il invoque ensuite la Déclaration universelle des droits de l'homme et le fait que »l'idéal de l'homme libre, à l'abri de la peur et de la misère, ne peut se réalisier que grâce à la création de conditions qui permettent à chaque personne de jouir de ses droits économiques, sociaux et culturels aussi bien que de ses droits civils et politiques«. Ainsi le droit international apparaît bien comme fondé sur la nature humaine et découlant d'une certaine conception de la nature humaine.

Ainsi, le droit international appraît bien comme fondé, à chaque époque historique, sur une conception déterminée de la nature humaine et sur la morale découlant de cette conception. En fait et en droit positif, la conception dualiste de la nature humaine a servi de fondement à l'ordre juridique international ancien, tandis que la conception moniste et universelle de la nature est le fondement de l'ordre juridique international nouveau, qui est valable pour toute l'humanité conçue comme une famille unique et pour chaque élément qui la constitute.

Cette vision du fondement du droit international, outre qu'elle correspond à la vérité historique, comporte quelques avantages *de lege ferenda*. Elle permet de s'arrêter un moment et d'apprécier utilement l'ordre juridique international établi avant d'entreprendre l'action créatrice nécessaire à la genèse du nouvel ordre juridique international. La critère de la nature humaine moniste et universelle, critère relevant du droit positiv international et non pas de la simple spéculation philosophique, permet alors de faire, au sein du droit international existant, la discrimination nécessaire entre les règles inacceptables et à écarter parce qu'elles correspondent à la conception dualiste de la nature humaine et les règles normales à conserver ou à établir parce qu'elles traduisent la conception normale de la nature humaine, l'autre conception.

Le fait que ce fondement du droit international a toujours existé à chaque époque et a effectivement commandé la création du droit international positif est de nature à faciliter la genèse du droit international nouveau. Il est de règle que la logique appliquée sur la base de l'ancienne conception dualiste de la nature humaine doit être également appliquée sur la base de la nouvelle conception moniste et universelle de la nature humaine. Cette logique amène normalement les organes et mécanismes, qui participent de bonne foi à la conception et à la création du droit international, à écarter celles des règles et situations internationales anciennes qui sont discriminatoires et à conserver ou établir les normes et situations internationales nouvelles normales et, pour cette raison, justes. L'adoption d'un tel comportement exclut tout ressentiment et toute violence inutile entre les anciens maîtres du droit international et les nouveaux membres de la société internationale. L'émergence des nouvelles règles internationales ou la suppression des règles et situations anciennes discriminatoires ou inégalitaires ne sont plus la revanche victorieuse des uns ou l'écrasement des autres.

La création du nouvel ordre juridique international est simplement le respect dynamique de la conception moniste et universelle de la nature humaine, conception normale, reconnue et acceptée par le droit international positif.

7.3. Sovereignty and Humanity: Can they converge?*

RICHARD B. LILLICH

The principial thesis of this paper is that the concept of sovereignty in international law is an idea whose time has come and gone. To paraphrase what Dr. Johnson said of patriotism, today it is generally the last refuge of scoundrels,[1] whether powerful regimes relying upon outmoded ideology to justify repression or petty tyrants of what used to be called "banana republics" lining their pockets while depriving their populations of basic human rights. Professor Reisman rightly considers it one of the "inherited impediments"[2] to the achievement of a new world order based upon the human dignity of the individual, urging us to "eschew the term and address ourselves to the empirical questions which are really at issue."[3] Yet the concept lingers on, obscures the real questions at issue, and permits the continuation of great injustices. It has become the example *par excellence* of what the great American jurist Benjamin Cardozo once called "the tyranny of concepts". "A fruitful parent of injustice", he ramarked, "is the tyranny of concepts. They are tyrants rather than servants when treated as real existences and developed with merciless disregard of consequences to the limit of their logic."[4]

In assessing this tyrannical concept, I start with three major premises. The first is that man – or, in the collective sense of my title, "humanity" – is the *raison d'être* of any legal system. It goes without saying, one would think, but it needs saying nevertheless. I studied legal philosophy some years ago under the late Professor Edmond Cahn of New York University, the founder of the "anthropocentric" school of jurisprudence. While he did not deny the importance of legal concepts such as sovereignty, Cahn thought it imperative that "the meaning of any concept, however exalted, [be] investigated by observing the occasions when that concept becomes relevant to the homely experiences of individual

The author would like to express his appreciation to Stephen C. Neff, Esq., his former student and research associate, now UNITAR Research Fellow, Christ's College, Cambridge, for his assistance in the preparation of this paper.

1 Boswell, James, *Boswell's Life of Johnson*. Edited by George Birbeck Hill. Rev. and enl. ed. by L. F. Powell. Oxford, Clarendon Press, 1934, p. 348.

2 Reisman, W. M., International Law and Organization for a New World Order: The Uppsala Model p. 27 of this book, *supra*.

3 *Ibid*., p. 31 *supra*.

4 Cardozo, Benjamin N., *The paradoxes of legal science*. New York, Columbia University Press, 1928, p. 61.

human beings."[5] His observations apply with additional force to the international scene. Indeed, my second premise is that the international legal system for over 300 years, since the Peace of Westphalia, has not been fulfilling what should be its primary function, namely, the protection and development of the human dignity of the individual. Actually, from 1648 until relatively recently it has been structured and administered so that this function would not be fulfilled. How could a system concerned initially (and still primarily, if not exclusively) with the rights and duties of States not "short change" the individual? The individual, as Professor Dimitrijević correctly notes, not only has not received special attention, but he has had to assert himself "in the hostile environment of classical international law."[6] Hence, the divergence suggested in my title, asking as it does whether sovereignty and humanity can converge.

My third and last premise, proceeding from the above, is that any proposed "new world order" should be structured so as to maximize benefits not for States but for the individuals living within States, all the way from freedom of speech and elections, on the one hand, to freedom from hunger and the right to education on the other hand. In my opinion, the oft called for and greatly needed redistribution of power and wealth between States is not enough. Professor Saxena, in a very challenging paper which has been circulated privately, eloquently makes the case for such a redistribution of wealth and other values within States.[7] Surely the international legal system has not addressed this problem adequately to date. Radical restructuring of the international legal order, of the kind advocated by such forward thinkers as Professor Richard Falk,[8] undoubtedly is what the English would call a "non-starter", so suggestions about how "sovereignty" can be restricted ore redefined to achieve grater benefits to "humanity" should be

5 Cahn, Edmond N., *The sense of injustice, a anthropocentric view of law*. New York, New York University Press, 1949, pp. 1–2 (emphasis added): "The purpose of this book is to present an anthropocentric view of the law. Since concepts and abstractions are indispensable instruments of both the regime of law and the pracitce of philosophy, they have understandably engrossed the attention of legal philosophers at the expense of what is vibrant, fleshly, and individual. *An anthropocentric approach, far from banishing concepts, may possibly restore them to their proper dignity – as ministers of the needs and satisfactions of living persons* . . . The abstraction performs an effectual function in the operating machinery of law, but the ultimate consumer of the product will always be some quite concrete individual. In this book, therefore, the meaning of any concept, however exalted, is investigated by observing the occasions when that concept becomes relevant to the homely experiences of individual human beings."

6 Dimitrijevic, V., A Natural or Moral Basis for International Law, p. 297 of this book, *supra*. "At the Congress of Westphalia the principle was established that holders of power in every State had the right to determine the values their subjects were free or encouraged to follow. The individual and his fate ceased to be the concern of world authorities or of universal society: States were the only recognized persons and they aimed at their own, not universal, good."

7 *See* Saxena, J., A Papaya-Seller, Distributive Justice and New World Order, p. 297 of this book, *supra*.

8 *See* Falk, R. A., *A study of future worlds*. New York, Free Press, 1975. xxxiii, 506 p.

modest in ambition and incremental in nature. Since we seem stuck with the Nationstate system, in short, we should direct our efforts to gradual change, change that I believe this paper will demonstrate allready is well underway.

Having set out my thesis and my three major premises, let us proceed to examine aspects of the topic under three general headings: General Survey of the Concept of Sovereignty; Reassessment of the Concept of Sovereignty; and The Concept of Sovereignty in the New World Order.

I. General survey of the concept of sovereignty

The topic posed by the title of this paper is a difficult one with which to come to grips, in no small part because the very terminology is vague and amorphous to international lawyers. Such topics as "The Individual in International Law" have become almost commonplace since World War II, largely because international human rights law has become a distinct sub-discipline in its own right. "Sovereignty and Humanity" suggests territory less well trod. Sovereignty, although much debated, remains somewhat obscure, having both an internal and an external aspect. For present purposes, I shall adopt Brierly's definition that the term "expresses, though in a misleading way, the claims that States habitually make to act as seems good to them without restraint on their freedom."[9] Humanity, though, poses even more problems on the definitional level. Indeed, as a legal term of art the word has no fixed meaning.[10] Moreover, to many persons international law as a discipline might be regarded as singularly ill-equipped to define such a term adequately. Let me explain briefly what I mean by this last remark.

To that ever more elusive character known as the objective observer, it might appear that the entire academic world for the past several generations has been launched on one grand, coordinated crusade against that apparently even more elusive entity known as mankind. Anthropologists, for example, literally never seem to tire of telling us that there is no such thing as human nature: in the light of the constant parade of bizarre and exotic customs and institutions which they are constantly discovering, there appears to be little in the cultural heritage of mankind that may be said to reflect the human essence of man as such.

9 Brierly, J., *The Law of Nations*. 6th ed., Edited by H. Waldock. Oxford, Clarendon Press, 1963, p. 47.

10 In 1900, the Supreme Court of the United States recognized that principles of humanity underlie many areas of international law. See *Paquete Habana*, 175 U.S. 677, 708 (1900). More recently, the International Court of Justice based certain international legal obligations on "elementary considerations of humanity", which it considered as "general and wellrecognized principles". See *Corfu Channel Case*, (1949) I.C.J. Report 1949, pp. 4, 22. Neither tribunal, however, ventured a specific definition of humanity. The International Military Tribunal at Nuremberg, in the context of international criminal law, attempted to formulate a more precise definition of humanity. See Charter of the International Military Tribunal, Art. 6 (c), reprinted in *International Military Tribunal, Trial of the Major War Criminals*, Vol. 1, Nuremberg, 1947. p. 11. The Secretary-General of the United Nations expanded on the results of this attempt. See *The Charter and Judgement of the Nuremberg Tribunal*, U.N. Doc. A/CN. 4/5/1949 (memorandum submitted by the Secretary-General to the General Assembly).

Similarly, think of economics, with its model of man as a rational, calculating, acquisitive, "utility-maximizing" (to borrow the official jargon) person. Or think of sociology or social psychology, which often seem intent on reducing man to ciphers in statistical tables. Even literature, supposedly the most humanistic of fields, is not immune from the contagion: try reading a structuralist analysis of a literary text to see how nearly it approaches a computer program. The most recent assailants on poor hapless humanity are the sociobiologists – first cousins, one might say, to the behavioral psychologists, who are the most notoriously antihuman nature of them all. Except, I schould add, international lawyers of the more traditionalist outlook.

Indeed, traditional international law arguably is the most dogmatically antihumanistic of all the sciences. The reason for saying so is that, unlike the other disciplines mentioned above, which in a sense purport to go beyond the merely human dimensions of the problems they originally faced, traditional international law from its very inception excluded the individual human being from its ambit as a matter of principle. This exclusion is demonstrated most graphically in the tired dictum to the effect that individuals are not subjects, but merely objects, of international law.[11] The historical background to this process of exclusion, dating from the Peace of Westphalia in 1648 to the mid-Twentieth Century, is well known. Rather than review it here, I instead shall comment upon a broader aspect of the subject and then proceed to examine some of the implications my remarks have for what is sometimes called the "real world". What I wish to highlight here is how concerns with humanity as such, at least in Western history, once were lost and then reagained, only to be lost again. The broad question now confronting us is the extent to which such concerns can be regained yet again under a new world order.

The first occasion when humanistic concerns were lost was with the advent of Christianity in the early Middle Ages. Under the heavy hand of the Platonic approaches of Greek philosophy, the belief prevailed that man's humanity or human nature was something to be sloughed off as effectively as possible, something to be denied rather than fulfilled. The most obvious manifestation of this tendency in the socio-economic (and legal) sphere was the exaltation of monasticism as the ideal way of life, with its renunciation of normal family relations, its strict discipline (at least in theory), and so forth. On a different level, though, one also can see this ideal in the institution of baptism, which was a formal renunciation of one's frail and imperfect nature in favor of something more transcendental.

In the context of the times, these Christian concerns might be viewed as very progressive steps. One important reason was the Church's position that all persons on earth, potentially at least, were members of the community of saints. If anything, gospel Christianity even favored the poor and downtrodden over the rich and powerful.[12] Gradually, however, the various strictures of the Church

11 Oppenheim, L., *International Law*. 8th ed., Edited by H. Lauterpacht, Vol. 1, London, Longmans, 1955, p. 639.

12 Consider the famous statement attributed to Jesus that it was easier for a camel to pass

came to be viewed more as incumbrances than anything else. With the slow but steady economic and intellectual development of Europe – both owing a great deal to contact with the neighboring Islamic world – people came to prize freedom, adventure and intellectual curiosity above the supposed certainties of the straight and narrow path to heaven.[13] In Descartes' *Meditations,* to take only one example, one can find almost palpably the heady mixture of loneliness and exhilaration that is so foreign in spirit to the Middle Ages.[14] Man, again, was starting to become the measure of all things.

It is one of the great – and, I believe, tragic – ironies of history that what man did with his new-found humanity was to harness it to another entity, the State, which later did its best to destroy it. This irony emerges most clearly from the writings of Rousseau and Hegel. Indeed, it is the reason that, in the case of Rousseau at least, one is perpetually puzzled as to whether to regard him as the apostle of radical democracy or of fascism.[15] In his notion of the State as a product of the free wills of individuals, Rousseau certainly is the exemplary democrat. Yet the very act of regarding the popular will as the absolute sovereign meant that anything which that popular will chose to create, such as a State, itself became a sovereign of the most absolute and one might even add mystical sort. In fact, we duly find in Rousseau what can best be described as a religious conception of sovereignty as "absolute, sacred and inviolable".[16] The writings of Hegel were later to produce a similar absolutist conception of the State as an entity existing on an altogether different moral, to say nothing of political, plane from the individuals who were its subjects.[17]

through the eye of a needle than for a rich man to enter the kingdom of Heaven. *Mark* 10: 25 (King James).

13 For a famous, if slightly overstated, exposition of the view that the advent of individualism was one of the most distinctive contributions to the Renaissance culture of Italy, see Burkchardt, Jakob, *The Civilization of the Renaissance in Italy, an essay.* London, Phaidon Press, 1960. pp. 81–216.

14 See generally Descartes, René, Meditations of First Philosophy, in: *The Philosophical Works of Descartes,* rendered into English by Elizabeth S. Haldane and G. R. T. Ross, New York, Dover Publications, 1961, pp. 131–139, (particularly *Meditations* I and II, pp. 144–57).

15 For a view of Rousseau as a non-democratic totalitarian, see Crocker, L., *Rousseau's Social Contract.* Cleveland, Press of Case Western Reserve University, 1968, pp. 163–186. See *also* Corban, A., *Rousseau and the Modern State.* 2nd ed. Hamden, Conn., Archon Books, 1964, pp. 99–125.
Gough, J., *The Social Contract: A Critical Study of its Development.* 2nd ed. Oxford, Clarendon Press, 1957, pp. 171–174. On Rousseau's political philosophy generally, see Chapman, J., *Rousseau – Totalitarian or liberal?* New York, Columbia University Press, 1956, VIII, 154 p.; Hall, John C., *Rousseau: An Introduction to his Political Philosophy,* London, Macmillan, 1973, 167 p; Masters, Roger O., *The Political Philosophy of Rousseau,* Princeton, N. J., Princeton University Press, 1968, XXIII, 464 p. and Noone, J. Jr., *Rousseau's Social Contract: A Conceptual Analysis* (1980).

16 Rousseau, J. J., The Social Contract, in: Rousseau, Jean-Jacques, *Political writings.* Translated and edited by F. Watkins. Edinburgh, New York, Nelson, 1953, p. 34.

17 "The State is the divine will, in the sense that it is mind present on earth, unfolding itself to be the actual shape and organization of the world." Hegel, Georg W. F., *Hegel's*

It was in this intellectual atmosphere that the doctrine arose in international law of the individual as an object and not a subject. It was only States, and not the individual or even humanity as such, which were to be clothed in the magic raiment known as sovereignty. "[W]hat was originally an attribute of a personal ruler inside the State," Brierly notes, "came to be regarded as an attribute of the State itself in its relations to other States."[18] This "curious metamorphosis," he remarks, "transformed the doctrine of sovereignty from a principle of internal order . . . into one of international anarchy."[19] For, he explains, "if sovereignty means absolute power, and if States are sovereigns in that sense, they cannot at the same time be subject to law".[20] International lawyers have attempted to reconcile the existence of their subject with the doctrine of the absolute sovereignty of States by various theories of auto-limitation,[21] "which teaches that States are sovereign persons, possessed of wills which reject all external limitation, and that if we find, as we appear to do in international law, something which limits their wills, this limiting something can only proceed from themselves."[22]

This explanation obviously is far from satisfactory insofar as it attempts to explain the role of States within the international legal order. It leaves no doubt, however, that the concept of sovereignty – at least as it was viewed traditionally – renders the individual without much protection on the international as well as the national plane. This development, which I referred to a moment ago, was the second occasion when the concept of humanity was lost, or at least downgraded. Today we still are faced, more urgently than ever in fact, with the problem of overcoming this loss. To this subject I now shall turn, with a few concrete examples that may help to bring the topic closer to earth.

II. Reassessment of the concept of sovereignty

"The sovereignty and equality of States," Brownlie reminds us, "represent the basic constitutional doctrine of the law of nations, which governs a community consisting primarily of States having a uniform legal personality."[23] Such has

Philosophy of right. Translated by T. M. Knox, Oxford, Clarendon Press, 1942, p. 166. This view of the State obviously is quite foreign in spirit to that of contemporary – or even traditional – international law. It may be remarked in passing that Hegel's view of the State differed sharply from Rousseau's in that the former took basically a historicist approach to the question, whereas the latter's social-contract theory was ahistorical and analytical.

18 Brierly, J., *op. cit.* (note 9), p. 11.

19 *Ibid.* p. 45. "The doctrine was developed for the most part by political theorists who were not interested in, and paid little regard to, the relations of States with one another, and in its later forms it not only involved a denial of the possibility of States being subject to any kind of law, but became an impossible theory for a world which contained more States than one." *Ibid.*, p. 45–46.

20 *Ibid.*, p. 16.

21 *Ibid.*, p. 46.

22 *Ibid.*, p. 53.

23 Brownlie, I., *Principles of Public International Law*. 3rd ed. Oxford, Clarendon Press, 1979, p. 287.

been the case for over 300 years, and a radical restructuring of the nation-State system seems unlikely, to say the least, in the near future.[24] Indeed, the decolonization process has spawned a vast number of new States which, in Dr. Dolzer's words, have reemphasized "the concept of State sovereignty to an extent that has not occurred since the end of the last century."[25]

It is not difficult to find illustrations of the metaphysical approach to the concept of sovereignty still at work today. Two examples from Latin America come readily to mind. One was the extensive arguments conducted throughout the negotiations between the United States and Panama as to whether the latter would be accorded "sovereignty" over the Panama Canal. The interesting point is that the concept of sovereignty seemed to be so rarefied and abstract that it was hard to see what it had to do with the practical issues relating to the use and defense of the canal. There was no single, specific right the presence of which meant that Panama was sovereign or the absence of which meant that it was not.[26] Sovereignty, in the best Rousseauian tradition, was something vague, something floating above all of the mundane, day-to-day issues.[27] The second example concerns a matter which still is being hotly debated – the status of the Falkland Islands, in which the protagonists are Argentina and Great Britain. One recent report indicates that Argentina is willing to offer the islanders virtually any degree of autonomy they might demand, asking only one thing in return: sovereignty, whatever that might mean.[28]

Such examples have, or should have, a slightly archaic ring. The reason is that

24 See text at note 8 *supra*.

25 Dolzer, Universalism and Regionalism, p. 525 of this book. Accord, Falk, R., *Human Rights and State Sovereignty*. New York, Holmes and Meier, 1981, p. 153: Territorial sovereignty is the basic characteristic of international relations, has become even more so in recent years as a result of decolonization, and is likely to remain so through the 1980s. Almost every State is zealous of its sovereign rights and places the hightest premium on the protection of its polity against various forms of encroachment."

26 For an illustration of the difficulties involved in squeezing the various issues involved in the Panama Canal problem into the traditional categories of international legal thinking, see Lopez Guevara, Negotiating a Peaceful Solution to the Panama Canal Question, *New York University Journal of International Law and Politics*, Vol. 9, 1976, p. 1; Shay, The Panama Canal Zone: In Search of a Juridical Identity, *Ibid.*, p. 15.

27 Consider, for example, Rousseau's remark concerning the application of the general will of a society to particular issues: "[T]he general will . . . changes its nature when directed toward a particular object, and cannot, without ceasing to be general, pronounce on any individual or fact." Rousseau, *op. cit. supra* (note 16), ii. 32.

28 One member of the Falkland Islands Council gave the following description of offers made by Argentina early in 1981: "We were asked what did we want, presuming we agreed to cede sovereignty. Would we draw up a list of our requirements . . . We said, well, we have a democratic form of government, a different legal system from yours, different customs, a different form of education. And they told us that all these things could be guaranteed for some considerable length of time. The only thing they wanted was sovereignty." *The Times* (London) 3 March 1981, p. 6., col. 1. On the concept of autonomy in international law, see text at and following note 58 *infra*. In the event, of course, Argentina tried to establish its alleged sovereignity over the Falklands by the use of force, with tragic consequences.

the old religious mystical concept of sovereignty as being something which is "absolute, sacred and inviolable" already has lost much of whatever relevance it once may have had. The Rousseauian notion may have the force of pure logic behind it, but in this area logic has been largely overtaken by experience (to paraphrase a famous remark by Mr. Justice Holmes of the United States Supreme Court).[29] The fact of the matter is that sovereignty today – like its corollary, autonomy – is an extraordinarily flexible, manipulative concept. From the practical perspective of the international lawyer it is no longer "a metaphysical concept, nor is it part of the essence of statehood; it is merely a term which designates an aggregate of particular and very extensive claims that States habitually make for themselves in their relations with other States."[30] The point is aptly illustrated by Dr. Hans Blix. "Sovereignty," he writes,

> need not be anything mystic and indivisible. Historically it was the plenary internal power of the King. It consisted in his freedom of action in various fields. As ownership is described as a bundle of rights, sovereignty may perhaps be described as a bundle of competences. There is no inherent reason against the voluntary acceptance [*quaere:* or involuntarily imposition?] of limitations upon the freedom of action in one field or in several fields, upon one or more of the competences in the bundle. Of course, such limitations do reduce the freedom of action of the State and thereby nibble at the sovereignty – as the concept is defined here.[31]

The key question facing the world community today is: in whose favor will this "nibbling process" take place? Will it be in the interests of this creature called humanity, which has been hibernating for several centuries but which gradually has aroused itself since World War II, or will it be in favor of what might be called darkly "other interests"?[32]

29 Holmes, Jr., Oliver Wendell, *The common law*. Boston, Little, Brown and Co, 1881, p. 1.

30 Brierly, J., *op. cit. supra* (note 9), p. 47. "To the extent that sovereignty has come to imply that there is something inherent in the nature of States that makes it impossible for them to be subjected to law, it is a false doctrine which the facts of international relations do not support. But to the extent that it reminds us that the subjection of States to law is an aim as yet only very imperfectly realized, and one which presents the most formidable difficulties, it is a doctrine which we cannot afford to disregard." *Ibid.*, pp. 47–48.

31 Blix, H., *Sovereignty, Aggression and Neutrality*. Stockholm, Almquist and Wiksell, 1970. pp. 11–12.

32 That the "nibbling process" already is underway seems scarcely debatable. "The negative repercussions which have accompanied the basic concept of absolute State sovereignty for international relations have been gradually perceived by the international community, and slowly a more relative notion of State sovereignty has gained acceptance." Dolzer, *supra*, (note 25), pp. 526 f. But see Falk, R. *op. cit. supra* (note 25), p. 99: "For [Third World] societies, the State as a political actor has achieved important goals, and is regarded by all parts of the political spectrum as a positive phenomenon. Such governing elites are nor ready to relinquish their sovereignty to any external actor, whatever the global relationale, not to diminish their internal control, even on behalf of ethnic groups pressing their own claims for autonomy and self-determination."

Right now, I wish to mention just a few of the more important ways in which the concept of sovereignty has been compelled to accommodate itself to the contemporary "real world".

First and foremost is, of course, the mere existence of the vast bulk of norms, customary as well as conventional, that make up international law. To be sure, there still is some dispute as to whether a State is bound by international law otherwise than by its own consent, whether express or implied.[33] I shall not attempt any resolution of that debate here – I have no doubt that it will continue to mislead some people for many years to come. It is fundamentally misleading because it is not descriptive of how States function in the day-to-day world. Even if one accepts the argument – which I do not – that in principle a State is bound by international law rules only by consent, the fact remains that in literally every walk of international life – from racial discrimination to civil aviation to diplomatic relations to the law of the sea – States have accepted limitations on their freedom of action. These limitations are found not only in conventional international law, from which most of the above examples are taken, but in customary international law as well. The claim that before States accepted this array of limitations they were free not to accept them, even if true, is little more than a scholastic quibble in light of what States have done in fact during the past century.[34]

The existence of regional arrangements in various parts of the world certainly has accelerated this process. The best known of these arrangements is undoubtedly the EEC in Western Europe, but there are a host of other ones which have appeared in all ideological groupings, at all levels of economic development and in all parts of the world. The Andean Pact in South America is one ready example. One also could point to the Central American Common Market, the OAS, the Economic Association of West African States, the African and Malagasy Union, the OAU, the Council of Europe, COMECON in Eastern Europe, the Arab League and ASEAN.

Few observers appreciate just how fundamental some of the aspects of sovereignty that have been nibbled away by such arrangements are. Consider, for example, the traditional international law rule that a State has absolute discretion whether to admit aliens into its territory.[35] It might be thought that one could hardly expect to find a more venerable or unchallenged rule, and, in a sense, such is the case. That is to say, no one doubts that in principle, in the abstract, that rule still holds with all its rigor and austerity.

When one steps out of the world of blackletter law, however, and observes just what States have been doing in fact, one finds something very different. One finds, indeed, a whole array of exceptions to this supposedly "absolute, sacred and inviolable" rule, to recall Rousseau's expression. Perhaps the most obvious

33 *See, e. g.*, Guha, Roy, Is the Law of Responsibility of States for Injuries to Aliens a Part of Universal International Law?, *American Journal of International Law,* Vol. 55, 1961. p. 863.

34 *See* Blix, H., *op. cit. supra* (note 31), p. 11.

35 Oppenheim, L., *Op. cit. supra* (note 11), pp. 67–76.

example is the free movement of labor provisions of EEC law,[36] but other examples abound. For instance, in Africa the Economic Association of West African States now has a free movement of labor arrangement, whereby citizens of the 16 member States are allowed to cross freely into the territories of other member States without visas and remain for 90 days (longer with permission of the host State).[37] The Charter of the Union of Central African States also has free movement provisions.[38]

Even in the sphere of bilateral arrangements, there are significant derogations from the traditional international law rule that have not yet attracted general attention. The various Western European countries, for example, have set up mechanisms with a number of developing countries over the past 25 years or so for the recruitment and admission of alien workers.[39]

The argument will no doubt be made – and therefore I shall take the precaution of anticipating it – that all of the above derogations arise only by the free choice of the State concerned, and that they therefore do not in any way compromise the substantive rule involved. (A similar argument has been made against the significance of lump sum agreements, by which States have settled wealth deprivation claims for compensation generally less than the "prompt, adequate and effective" amount said to be required by traditional international law.)[40] The problem with this argument, persuasive as it is at first glance, is that it assumes what it is attempting to prove: it assumes that voluntary departures from established rules cannot, by their very nature, eventually work to modify those rules. However, that is hardly an answer. On the contrary, that is the very question at issue: is international law generally – and the doctrine of sovereignty particularly – to remain a static, closed system, or is it to function as a tool for dealing with the seemingly infinite exigencies of today's world, where humanity increasingly seeks to assert itself against the State? Merely to invoke abstract doctrines like the

36 See Mathijsen, Pierre S., *A Guide to European Community Law*, London, Sweet and Maxwell, 1972, pp. 130–37.

37 Divorce Averted, *The Economist*, 11 April 1981, p. 55, col. 1.

38 Article 26 (c) of the Charter of Union, in: *Basic Documents of African Regional Organisations*, L. B. Sohn (ed.), Vol. 2, Dobbs Ferry, N. Y., Oceana Publications, 1972, pp. 776, 775.

39 Between 1954 and 1971, 16 such treaties were registred with the United Nations. The labour-importing States involved were France, Australia, Belgium, and the Netherlands. The labour-exporting States were Greece, Yugoslavia, Tunisia, Algeria, Morocco, Italy, Spain and Portugal. In July 1981, the US announced the decision to implement a pilot scheme for the admission of 50,000 "guest workers" from Mexico, as part of an effort to deal with the problem of illegal immigration from Mexico to the US *The Times* (London), 31 July 1981, p. 6, col. 2.

40 On the question of the emergence of customary international law norms from a pattern of *ad hoc* treatments of issues through the bilateral treaty mechanism, see Baxter, R. R., Treaties and Custom, *Recueil des Cours, Académie du droit international*, Tome 129, 1970, I, pp. 25, 75–91. For a detailed analysis of one area of the law in which general norms have emerged from a network of bilateral treaties, see Lillich, R. & Weston, B. H., *International claims: their Settlement by Lump-Sum Agreements*. Charlottesville, University of Virginia Press, 1975, 2 v.

right of States to exclude all aliens absolutely really begs the question. What is at issue is not just the content of rules, but rather their relevance to the demands individuals now are making on the international legal order. Repeated derogations, moreover, often lead to the reformulation or even rejection of established rules.

Another area in which State sovereignty certainly has been severely circumscribed is the area of international human rights. Norms in this area, flowing from customary international law (*e. g.*, many of the provisions contained in the Universal Declaration of Human Rights) and from multilateral (*e. g.*, the two United Nations Covenants) and regional (*e. g.*, the American and European Conventions on Human Rights) conventions, greatly restrict the traditional right of States – emanating from their unbridled sovereignty – to treat their citizens (or, for that matter, aliens) as they like.[41] To enforce this developing body of international law, the international community relies upon a wide range of sanctions, ranging from gentle persuasion at one end of the continuum to humanitarian intervention at the other end.[42] The latter doctrine permits intervention by the United Nations when human rights deprivations within a State constitute a threat to the peace.[43] Whether collective intervention by a group of States or unilateral invervention by a single State for humanitarian purposes is permissible under international law, however, raises different and more difficult questions.

Humanitarian intervention by the United Nations, although by traditional lights an infringement upon a State's sovereignty, clearly is contemplated and authorized by the United Nations Charter (Articles 2 (7), 39, 41 and 42). Collective or unilateral humanitarian intervention, equally an infringement upon a State's sovereignty, undoubtedly was recognized by traditional international law,[44] but its critics contend that it is now prohibited by Article 2 (4) of the Charter, which enjoins States "from the threat or use of force against the territorial integrity or political independence of any State, or in any other manner inconsistent with the Purposes of the United Nations."[45]

41 For a collection of documents containing the basic norms in this area of international law, see Lillich, R. *International Human Rights Instruments* (forthcoming). The normative bite of these norms is considered in Lillich, R. B. & Newman, F. C., *International Human Rights: Problems of Law and Policy*, chs. I–IV. Boston, Little, Brown and Co., 1979. XVI, 1030 p.

42 For one State's practice in this regard, see Lillich R., A United States Policy of Humanitarian Intervention and Intercession, in: *Human Rights and American Foreign Policy*. Komers, D. P. & Loescher, G. D., eds. Notre Dame, University of Notre Dame Press, 1979, p. 278.

43 See generally *Humanitarian Intervention and the United Nations*. (Ed. by Lillich R. B.), Charlottesville, Univ. of Virginia Press, 1973. XII, 240 p.

44 For an annotated bibliography of material in support of the proposition that such intervention was lawful under pre-Charter customary international law, see Stowell, E. C., *Intervention in International Law*, Washington D. C., J. Byrne & Co., 1921, pp. 461–540.

45 Opposed to the idea that collective or unilateral humanitarian intervention is lawful under contemporary international law, see Brownlie, T., Humanitarian Intervention,

These critics rely not only upon a literal reading of Article 2 (4), but also upon a concept of sovereignty that by its very nature is "absolute, sacred and inviolable". Such an argument, however, only gives rise once again to the question of whether the spinning out, gossamer-style, of the logical consequences of the Rousseauian approach to sovereignty has anything to do with the actual problems of coping with life – and death – in the real world today. Would we, as international lawyers, really wish to turn a blind eye, as a matter of principle (not even of expediency), to the events in East Pakistan in 1971 and thereafter in Uganda under the rule of Idi Amin, and say that a collective or unilateral intervention in either of those situations would have been *ipso facto* illegal under contemporary international law?[46] I am not, I should emphasize, attempting to justify the policies and practices of India and Tanzania in these two cases. Rather, I am subjecting to criticism an attitude towards the concept of sovereignty that holds that anything which India and Tanzania could have done must have been unlawful.[47] Here as elsewhere, in my opinion, a functional rather than an inflexible attitude must be taken in regard to the claims of State sovereignty *vis-à-vis* the claims of human rights.[48]

III. The concept of sovereignty in the new world order

We now may take a very cautious look towards the future to see some of the other issues likely to arise in this field in the coming years.

One important area to watch surely will be the treatment of aliens, which I have mentioned already but now will develop in more detail.[49] Aliens are the

in: *Law and Civil War in the Modern World* (J. N. Moore ed.) Baltimore, Johns Hopkins University Press, 1974, p. 217. For a rejoinder, see Lillich, Humanitarian Intervention: A Reply to Dr. Brownlie and a Plrea for Constructive Alternatives, *Ibid.*, p. 229.

46 Yet as Falk points out, many States today advance an outmoded concept of State sovereignty to preclude action in such situations, probably "for the dubious reason for insulating their [own] domestic rule from outside criticism." Falk, R., *op. cit. supra* (note 25), p. 65. One reason States accord such high priority to the non-intervention concept, he explains, is that "(g) overnments seem wary that the sword used against others today could be turned against them tomorrow. Hence, there is a reluctance about any undertaking that could be generalized beyond a particular situation and turned into a precedent. In this regard, antiapartheid intervention gathers widespread support because the situation in South Africa seems *sui generis*, whereas anti-Amin intervention was impossible to organize because it would have created a precedent perceived as dangerous." *Ibid.*, p. 153–54.

47 Compare the views of Professor Tom Farer, once a staunch critic of collective and unilateral humanitarian intervention, who now endorses "a quiet tolerance of intervention in extreme cases, rather as jurists will sometimes refuse to convict in certain cases of euthanasia," T. Farer, Sovereignty and Humanity: The Suppression of Tyranny, p. 429 of this book, *supra*.

48 For a generally pessimistic answer to the question of whether the present State system is compatible with the substantial realization of human rights, see Falk, R., *op. cit, supra* (note 25), pp. 63–66, 98–99, 153–57, 178–82 *passim*.

49 On the protection of aliens under traditional international law (i.e., as a sub-category of the law of State responsibility), see Borchard, E., *The Diplomatic Protection of Citizens*

weathervane which reveals how international law treats the claims of humanity at any given period. By definition, aliens do not possess that important nexus of nationality with the State in which they reside, and hence historically often were (and, to some extent, remain) the objects of widespread discrimination. Yet a body of law called State Responsibility for Injuries to Aliens – a limited precursor to today's international human rights law – evolved to afford aliens a modicum of protection against deprivations caused by their host States. This body of law currently is being reformulated by the United Nations General Assembly as it continues its effort, begun in 1980, to draft a Declaration on the Human Rights of Individuals Who Are Not Citizens of the Country in Which They Live.[50] This trend towards reinforcing the protection accorded aliens – or, conversely, to limit the sovereign discretion of States over aliens – also is evident in the recent upsurge of interest in migrant workers problems by both the International Labour Organisation and the United Nations.[51]

There are many more sovereignty-limiting developments, however, which to date have received scant attention. I already have mentioned the various free movement of persons provisions of some of the regional groupings of States. Another important line of attack, which may become more significant in the future, is the development of various domestic law restrictions on sovereign prerogatives, which ultimately may influence customary international law norms in this area. It is fitting in this respect that this seminar should be taking place in Sweden, since it is one of a handful of States where aliens have been accorded the right to vote in certain elections.[52] Also noteworthy is the fact that the Labour Party in Great Britain now supports bestowing a limited franchise upon aliens,

Abroad; or the Law of International Claims, New York, Banks Law Publishing Co., 1915. XXXVII, 988 p; Dunn, F., *The Protection of Nationals; a study in the application of international law.* Baltimore, Johns Hopkins Press, 1932, X, 228 p; Freeman, A., *The International Responsibility of States for Denial of Justice,* London, Longmans, Green and Co., 1938. XIX, 758 p; and Jessup P. C., Responsibility of States for Injuries to Individuals, *Columbia Law Review,* Vol. 46, 1946, p. 903. For a discussion of the protection of the civil rights of aliens under contemporary international law (*i.e.,* including international human rights law), see Lillich, R. B., Duties of States Regarding the Civil Rights of Aliens, *Recueil des Cours, Académie du droit international,* Tome 161, 1978 III, p. 329.

50 See Elles, *International Provisions Protecting the Human Rights of Non-Citizens,* UN Doc. E/CN. 4/Sub. 2/392/Rev. 1 (1980). A preliminary review of this effort may be found in Lillich & Neff, The Treatment of Aliens and International Human Rights Norms: Overlooked developments at the UN, *German Yearbook of International Law,* Vol. 21, 1978. p. 97.

51 See, e.g., the recent ILO Migrant Workers (Supplementary Provisions) Convention 1975 (No. 143), and Migrant Workers Recommendation, 1975 (No. 151). For a summary of UN activity in the area of migrant workers, see *Measures to Improve the Situation and Ensure the Human Rights and Dignity of All Migrant Workers,* UN Doc. E/CN. 4/1325, pp. 6–17 (1978). At the present time, the UN is considering the adoption of a multilateral convention on the human rights of migrant workers.

52 See Hammar, Tomas, The First Immigrant Election, *International Migration,* Vol. 15, No. 23, 1977. p. 153.

and that a similar proposal has been advanced in Spain.[53] In the Council of Europe, there have been initiatives of a similar nature.[54]

In the United States, perhaps more than elsewhere, there is a body of case law building up which extends to aliens an ever-larger array of domestic constitutional rights, including access to most of the professions and to social security and other welfare benefits.[55] These rights have been extended very recently, in two cases now before the United States Supreme Court, to illegal aliens. Two lower courts, in *Doe* v. *Plyler*[56] and the *Texas Schoolchildrens Case*,[57] decided in 1980 that the State of Texas could not deny the benefits of free primary school education to the children of Mexican workers illegally residing in the United States. In Opinions that go well beyond the general nondiscrimination norm contained in the United Nations Charter, the Court ruled that Texas had run afoul of the Fourteenth Amendment to the United States Constitution which guarantees any person within the United States "the equal protection of the laws".

A second area, in addition to the treatment of aliens, where the claims of humanity will assert themselves ever more strongly against the views of doctrinaire international lawyers involves the interrelated questions of self-determination and autonmy.[58] The outstanding recent example in this respect, of course, is the peace treaty between Egypt and Israel in 1979. Whether the two countries will fill the Camp David Framework with substance still remains to be seen, but the trend towards autonomy has been manifested worldwide of late. I already have referred to the Falkland Islands, where Argentina has offered the inhabitants autonomy of the most far-reaching kind (in exchange for that philosopher's stone known as sovereignty). Numerous other examples can be cited.[59]

The problem of autonomy inevitably raises the broader issue of self-determination. In the past, at least some international lawyers thought they knew what they were talking about when they used that facile expression: the liberation of all peoples of the world from colonial rule. Zimbabwe is the most recent triumph of

53 Spain May Give Vote to Foreigners, *The Times* (London), 5 February 1981, p. 4, col. 8.

54 Voting Rights for Europe's Immigrant Workers Urged, *The Times* (London) 15 December, 1980, p. 4, col. 3. See also Sica, Mario, Involvement of the Migrant Worker in Local Political Life in the Host Country, *International Migration*, Vol. 15, No. 23, 1977. p. 143.

55 These cases are collected and discussed in Muthrika, A. P., The Alien under American Law: text, materials, cases. Dobbs Ferry, N. Y., Oceana Publications, 1980, 2 v.

56 458 F. Supp. 569 (E.D. Tex. 1978), *aff'd*, 628 F. 2d 448 (5th Cir. 1980), *prob. juris. noted*, 101 S.VCt. 2044 (1981).

57 501 F. Supp. 544 (S. D. Tex. 1980).

58 See generally Hannum, H. & Lillich, R., The Concept of Autonomy in International Law, *American Journal of International Law*, Vol. 74, 1980, p. 858. reprinted in *Models of Autonomy* (Y. Dinstein ed.) 1981. p. 215.

59 For an example of some innovative legal steps which have taken place recently in the area of autonomy, see Armstrong, The Negotiations for the Future Political Status of Micronesia, *American Journal of International Law*, Vol. 74, 1980, p. 689.

self-determination, with Namibia, it is hoped, next on the list, followed eventually by South Africa.

The virtual ending of the colonial era, however, has not resolved by any means the problem of the self-determination of peoples. On the contrary, it has raised questions conveniently ignored during the past quarter century. Did the people of Biafra, for instance, have a legally cognizable right to become independent of the rest of Nigeria in 1966–1970? Or the people of Bangladesh from Pakistan in 1971? What about the people of the Western Sahara, studiously ignored by the United Nations despite the International Court of Justice's Advisory Opinion rendered in 1975? Looking ahead, what about the people of Quebec in Canada, the Basques in Spain, the Kurds in various Middle Eastern States, the Shaba in Zaire, or the Eritreans in Ethiopia? Does the principle of self-determination apply to these peoples, or will it be consigned to the juridical dustbin after it has served to liberate peoples in the traditional colonial, white-exploiting-black context?[60]

Until the international community comes to grips with such issues, the tough problems of today's and tomorrow's "real world", international law will continue to merit the criticisms to which it has been so often subjected in the past. We have all heard the apostles of *realpolitik* scornfully demand: who pays attention to international law anyway? The way to counter such criticism is not to burrow about like moles in search of odd corners of international life that still conform to the concepts and doctrines of the past. The challenge is to reformulate and develop international law so that it pays greater attention to the aspirations and hopes of individual human beings.

The final point I wish to make is that international law actually may be responding, in a sense, better than many international lawyers themselves realize. A whole substructure of rules and principles have been building up from beneath, so to speak, in the various regional organizations, in the domestic laws of various States, in State practice emanating from bilateral treaties, and also of course in the numerous international human rights instruments upon which ever-increasing reliance is being placed. Initially, therefore, we need only to open our eyes and see the many ways in which the international community already has evolved away from the abstract doctrine of sovereignty into a more flexible and variegated system of arrangements between and within States aimed at enhancing the rights of individuals.

Our task for the future is two-fold: first, to make sure that contemporary international law takes full cognizance of those changes that have been occurring all around us for at least a generation; and second – and more important – to

60 On the principle of self-determination, see generally Emerson, R., *Self-Determination Revisited in an Era of Decolonization*, Cambridge, Center for International Affairs, Harvard University, 1964. 64 p., Rigo-Sureda, A. *The Evolution of the Right of Self-Determination, A Study of United Nations Practices*, Leyden, Sijthoff, 1973, 397 p. *Self-Determination: National, Regional and Global Dimensions* (Alexander, Y. & Friedlander, R., eds.) 1980; and Chen, Self-Determination as a Human Right, in *Toward World Order and Human Dignity: essays in honour of Myres S. McDougal* (Reisman W. & Weston B. eds.), New York, Free Press, 1976. p. 198.

solidify and carry those changes yet further in the coming years. For that task, skill and imagination, hard work and perseverance will be required. Much discouragement and many setbacks inevitably will and must be met. We have no choice but to shoulder this task, however, if the discipline of international law is to be fashioned into a tool for the achievement of social justice and the fulfillment of humanity rather than remain a captive of yesterday's tyrannical concepts such as sovereignty.

7.4. Sovereignty and Humanity: The Suppression of Tyranny

Tom J. Farer

I. The question of definition

There is at least a little bit of tyranny at work in the day-to-day operations of every political order. What country does not have its isolated minorities whose members congregate disproportionately in the prison and the poor house? What country has entirely cleansed its police of sadists who would administer backroom justice with fists and feet? What country can take pride in the quality of its prisons, including the means by which they are ruled? And where except in dreams does democracy penetrate the workplace?

The ubiquity of small tyrannies is a secret known best to the popular classes, that great mass of humanity so rarely encountered by those who govern or who, as scholars, study the process of governance.

But though tyranny is everywhere, we rightly assume differences of degree that at some point become distinctions of quality: Great tyrannies spilling over the frontier of insentivity and cynicism which are the natural products of observation and experience.

The traditional conservative – as distinguished from the actors, used-car salesmen, jumped-up greengrocers and supplyside economists who have recently appropriated the term (at least in my country) – would say that suppressing little tyrannies requires eradicating human beings all of whom, being congenitally flawed, will go on creating new tyrannies at least as fast as the old ones disappear.

Liberals and socialists may take a less lugubrious view of human potential. But one and all will agree that under present and foreseeable circumstances, if we are to move with any effect against tyranny, we must negotiate with the lesser ones lest the general vulnerability of States to indictment unite all in a pact of self-defence against the curators of conscience. Thus any practical efforts to reduce the incidence and truncate the tenure of tyranny must begin with the drawing of bright lines between the common run of regimes and the isolable group of authentically distinguished thugs.

Achieving agreement among those at least nominally hostile to tyranny about the identity of the prime delinquents has proven rather more difficult than a simply humane man or woman, without any particular ideological commitments, might have supposed. Today the United States is the scene of a furious debate about precisely this issue. A curious assortment of human baggage that has acquired a degree of influence in recent years claims that the fundamental moral distinction lies between conservative, "merely authoritarian" and "modestly repressive" regimes, on the one hand, and "totalitarian revolutionary regimes" on the other. The former may be defined as those governments which repress parties of the left and act as if they believed that wealth is the surest sign of virtue.

A leading proponent of this view is the present US Permanent Representative to the United Nations, Mrs. Jeanne Kirkpatrick. In a 1979 article which apparently helped catapult her to her present altitude, she set out in detail the assumptions of her intellectual clique. She conceded, to begin with, that absolute monsters such as Hitler and Stalin or Pol Pot and Papa Doc Duvalier will occasionally appear at both ends of the political spectrum. What concerns her, however, are the systemic differences between traditional and revolutionary autocracies that have a predictable effect on their degree of repressiveness. Generally speaking, traditional autocrats tolerate social inequities, brutality, and poverty while revolutionary autocracies create them.

"Traditional autocrats . . . do not disturb the habitual rhythms of work and leisure, habitual places of residence, habitual patterns of family and personal relations. Because the miseries of traditional life are familiar, they are bearable to ordinary people who, growing up in the society, learn to cope, as children born to untouchables in India acquire the skills and attitudes necessary for survival in the miserable roles they are destined to fill."

The other presumed moral advantage of anticommunist autocracies is their capacity for evolution toward more humane societies.

"Although there is no instance of a revolutionary "socialist" or Communist society being democratized, right-wing autocracies do sometimes evolve into democracies – given time, propitious . . . circumstances, talented leaders, and a strong indigenous demand for representative government.

Nothing so well illustrates the stupefying power of dogma than this attribution of permanence to revolutionary regimes and of an always latent fluidity to most conservative ones. In any fair test of durability, the latter make an impressive showing. The Somoza family, for example, lasted forty-five years. By monopolizing so much of the nation's economy, it had, by the time of its overthrow, actually reduced the possibility of democratic evolution.

Military rule in El Salvador, to take another current example, has endured since Franklin Delano Roosevelt's first election. If we use a measure more relevant to human rights and equate the "regime" with a very rigid structure of power and wealth and opportunity, then El Salvador had a stable autocracy from its independence in the early nineteenth century at least until the armed forces coup of 1979.[1]

What was characteristic of this period was not "evolution" toward democracy but prevention of that evolution. In Peru, one hundred and fifty years of oligarchic control ended in 1968, not through democratic evolution but by means of reforms imposed by the armed forces.

1 As president of the Inter-American Commission on Human Rights, I cannot comment on post-coup developments in El Salvador which we are now monitoring very closely.

Authoritarian governments of every ideological hue extend their jurisdiction as far as necessary to achieve their ends. They tolerate autonomous activity outside the formal State structure only when it is harmless or when it is informally but effectively integrated with the regime. In El Salvador before 1979, the military government and a small group of capitalists ("the fourteen families") consciously shared virtually the same interests and acted together. Though the press was nominally free, mass circulation newspapers in San Salvador conformed to the policies of the ruling groups.

"Preserving the existing distribution of wealth and power and poverty" is a deceptive summary of the goals of Kirkpatrick's "traditional autocrats". It is deceptive in that it implies that Third World nations exist in a state of muscular placidity, as if society were ruled by a group of not necessarily good-natured but decidedly unambitious thugs who have no serious ambition beyond retaining control of their privileges and extorting protection money, and are willing to live and let live. When threatened by violent assault, of course they will actively hurt people – the violent malcontents and their sympathizers. But once the problem is liquitaded, the "ordinary people" who want only to be left alone will come out of the cellar, where they have been hiding to avoid getting caught in the cross-fire, and docilely resume their "habitual rhythms."

This image is unreal because it misses the dynamic character of many contemporary Third World societies. When the masses are quiet, unambitious rulers can be placid. Today their serenity is constantly disturbed. All the interconnected tendencies of recent years – urbanization, industrialization, rapid population increase, the vast spread of TV and transistor radios, revolutionary ideas about man and society – have unleashed a torrent of demands that may seem all the more terrifying because they cannot be suppressed by a government's administering exemplary punishment from time to time. Feeling a consequent need for sterner and more sweeping measures, rulers claim that national security requires them to impose comprehensive surveillance and more tightly controlled social institutions by increasing the power and reach of public authority.

This political project is "corporatism", fascism's cousin. As the Yale political scientist Alfred Stepan notes in his penetrating study of Peru's corporatist experiment,[2] it has two poles.

At the "inclusionary pole", the State offers working-class groups positive inducements to take part in its political and economic plans, as did the first Perón regime in Argentina, Lázaro Cárdenas in pre-war Mexico, and Peru's military government before it turned to the right in 1975. At the "exclusionary pole", the State elite relies heavily on coercion to break up existing working-class organizations and then to institutionalize docility. Chile under Pinochet is a particularly harsh example.

When the second of the two patterns predominates, as in Brazil and Chile following their respective military coups,[3] it follows that universities are purged,

2 Stepan, Alfred C., *The State and Society: Peru in Comparative Perspective*. Princeton, Princeton University Press, 1978. XIX, 348 p.

3 Brazil in 1964 and Chile in 1973.

political parties dissolved, unions reorganized, dissidents murdered, the Church harassed, all as part of a huge effort first do demobilize the popular classes, and then to direct and strain their demands through new, purified institutions subject to manipulation by the State. In this effort, which has been analysed with particular brilliance by the Argentine social scientist Guillermo O'Donnell,[4] the ruling groups can be said to be following, consciously or not, the example of empires like that of Rome which for several centuries aggressively expanded its domain in a furious effort to liquidate threats to the *status quo* before they became unmanageable.

Seeking to preserve their own *status quo*, uncompromising right-wing governments ape the comapagns of classical revolutionary regimes to remove every source of dissent. They call themselves conservative. They are anticommunist. They will say nice things about the Free World. And contrary to Kirkpatrick's optimistic speculations, they often take society on a road without any democratic exit.

The defense of right-wing authoritarian regimes finds a receptive, uncritical audience among many Americans because deeply ingrained ideological commitments affect their moral sensitivity. Anyone familiar with conditions in Haiti, for example, knows that its desperately hungry people would emigrate *en masse* if only a country able to provide life's basic needs would open its doors. Although poverty and the nature of the Duvalier regime are linked, since that autocracy is noncommunist the US government presumes that its refugees who reach our shores merely flee economic "conditions" and must therefore be turned back. On the other hand, practically all Cubans who arrive here are presumed to be fleeing political persecution rather than economic privation.

Another case of selective perception: If a revolutionary State commands people to move from one section of a country to another, we naturally condemn this ugly act as violating the right to travel freely and choose one's place of residence. But if the State enforces an absentee landowner's decision to expel sharecroppers who have tilled the land for generations, and if the landowner's choice was a rational response to market forces, even if those forces were themselves determined by political decisions about subsidies or the tariff on imported farm equipment, many economists will applaud ist. Farming will be more efficient, free marketeers will say, and sharecroppers will eventually find employment in more productive and hence better-paying activities. Or at least, it is claimed, they would if only markets could be manipulated to function in accordance with theory.

The account of the Third World provided by Kirkpatrick and those who think like her obscures the realities of life under authoritarian governments – not only the torture and murder of political dissidents but also the more subtle yet often more comprehensively destructive acts carried out through the operation and manipulation of economic forces in societies with vast gaps between the power

4 O'Donnell, Guillermo, *Modernization and Bureaucratic Authoritarianism: Studies in South American Politics*. Institute of International Studies, University of California, 1979.

and education and wealth of a relatively few people and the rest of the population, a pattern of inequality often inherited from a precapitalist era.

Acting through the State, the few can require proof of land tenure which illiterate peasants cannot produce. They can manipulate the exchange rate to encourage high technology imports at the expense of high employment. They can prohibit strikes and hold wage increases below the rate of inflation. They can subsidize large-scale agriculture and monopolize irrigation, while withholding subsidies for basic consumption goods. They can and do intervene in a thousand ways which have the predictable effect of uprooting whole communities, because neither they nor the State apparatus is a neutral arbiter guided by some abstract calculus of national interest. One certainly need not be a Marxist to see this. And one needs only a minimum of candor to admit it.

If Mrs. Kirkpatrick's formula for distinguishing greater and lesser tyrannies will not do, and it will not, what alternative might command support? I think that in most of the world the closest thing to a consensus would converge around the idea that the peculiarly awful delinquents are those that institutionalize violations of rights relating to personal security: The rights not to be summarily executed, not to be tortured, not to be incarcerated for long periods of time without prior conviction by a fair procedure and the right not to be detained at all under brutal conditions. However, while governing elites hardly ever question openly the categorical character of these rights, in the codewords of diplomacy and the special conventions of domestic political discourse, governments sometimes appear to justify the suspension of human rights generally as necessary means for combatting "terrorism".

Insidious under any circumstances, this form of justification for atrocious behavior threatens human rights on an enormous scale particularly because the term "terrorism" is now employed with a total lack of discrimination. Historically it referred to certain intolerably cruel and viciously indiscriminate methods that even in the midst of civil or international wars were forbidden. These methods have been used by subversive enemies of governments and also by governments attempting to repress opposition.

It is certainly true that in the life of any nation, threats to the public order or to the personal safety of its inhabitants, by persons or groups that use violence, can reach such proportions that even authentically democratic governments may feel compelled to suspend the exercise of certain rights. The International Bill takes account of such emergencies. Article 4 of the Political and Civil Covenant allows participating States:

"In time of public emergency which threatens the life of the nation . . . to take measures derogating from their obligations under the present Covenant to the extent strictly required by the exigencies of the situation . . ."

Restrictions may, for example, be imposed on the freedom of information or the right of association. In rare and extreme cases persons may be detained for short periods without specific charges being brought against them. Such measures inevitably endanger the rule of law; but that danger can normally be contained by responsible governments: If they register arrests and inform the families of the detainees of the detentions; if they issue strict orders prohibiting torture; if they carefully recruit and train security forces, weeding out sadists and psychopaths; and lastly, if there is an independent judiciary to correct swiftly any abuse of authority.

Certain fundamental rights, however, can never be suspended, among these, the right to life, the right to personal security and integrity, and the right to due process. In other words, under no circumstances may governments employ summary execution, torture, inhumane conditions of detention, or conviction by a process which does not adequately distinguish guilt from innocence.

In this regard, it is useful to recall words spoken by His Holiness Pope John Paul II to the Organization of American States on 6 October 1979. After acknowledging that at times special measures may be adopted, he added the following:

". . . they never, never justify an attack on the inviolable dignity of the human person and on the authentic rights that protect this dignity.

If certain ideologies and certain ways of interpreting the legitimate concern for national security were to result in subjugating man and his rights and dignities to the State, they would to that extent cease to be humane and would be unable, without gross deception, to claim any Christian reference . . . A kind of security with which people do not identify, because it does not protect them in their very humanity, is only a farce; as it grows more and more rigid, it will show symptoms of growing weakness and rapidly approaching ruin."

Each government that confronts a subversive threat must choose, on the one hand, the path of respect for the rule of law, or on the other hand, the descent into State terrorism. The violation of basic human rights is the essence of terrorism whether the violation is perpetrated by private entrepreneurs of atrocity or by governments themselves.

Politically-motivated terrorism is carried out in democratic societies with the precise intention of provoking a terrorist response from the security organs of the State. Such a response tends to polarize the society and fuel sympathy for subversives.

A just and self-confident society has the toughness and resilience to fight back within the limits of law and morality. In waging war against a society which honors those limits, the terrorist campaign manages only to consolidate the community and to reinforce its values and its morale. The campaign must therefore fail.

A society already divided by injustice and riddled with merited guilt will usually respond with counter-terrorism and thereby fertilize subversion while sapping the strength and authority it struggles to preserve.

II. What is to be done?

In this case, defining may be the largest part of doing. Monsters find shelter in ideological cleavages. Amin exemplified this game, presenting himself first as an associate of Israel and the West against Third-World socialism, then as the ruthless counterthrust of a liberated Africa, and finally as an Islamic zealot. If his successive metamorphoses did not ultimately save his regime, his last one permits him the pleasures of an affluent retirement rather than the welldeserved hangman's noose.

Ideological cleavage persists, exemplified these days by the endless debate over measures to reduce "terrorism". One group of States want virtually to equate it with rebellion against non-Marxist regimes. Another would exempt every rebellion against pro-Western regimes whatever its methods. States and intellectuals too debate whether the term should be applied exclusively to private entrepreneurs of violence or to all persons using brutal and indiscriminate methods whether in the name of or against recognized governments.

Neither genius nor any special degree of imagination is required for the assembly of great lists of potential sanctions for the suppression of tyranny. The problem is one of will, not technique. Hence the practical importance of struggle on behalf of a definition of tyranny which will transcend ideological differences to the extent that is possible in such a divided world. The great texts of the human rights movement at least nominally record such a consensus. Hence the need to place them at the center of our effort to spur action.

National governments remain the preeminent instruments for the application of incentives and sanctions. But those assets which can arguably be deployed within the constraints of formally-acknowledged international law seem progressively less useful. Military and economic aid can still be granted or withheld largely if not entirely as a matter of national discretion. But a diminishing number of States are significantly dependent on bilateral assistance. In a world of proliferating arms manufacturers, tyrants can satisfy their needs on the open market even in the rare cases of an embargo authorized by a regional organization or the United Nations. And modern technologies of repression facilitate the extraction of that economic surplus required to continue purchasing the technology and the loyalty of the private army required to deploy it.

Tyrannies with broader ambitions than survival need capital. Today most of it flows through private channels, and much of the rest through transnational institutions, primarily through the World Bank and the IMF, which have thus far refused to incorporate human rights into their lending criteria.

The international financial institutions (IFIs) claim that their characters preclude the application of "political" criteria. The obvious answer is that human rights are legal, not political, criteria and, at least in the case of fundamental rights, are an essential element of international public policy. As the international lawyers like to put it, they are overriding norms, *jus cogens*. Hence every international agreement should be construed so as to avoid conflict between its terms and the defense of human rights. And where such conflict is indisputable, then the agreement must yield to public policy. If a State committed an open act of aggression against a neighbor, I believe that the Bank and the Fund would assume the impropriety of acting in ways which might be thought to facilitate the aggression. The same assumption should operate when a regime aggresses against its own subjects. Individual States could act on the same rationale to restrain private capital flows.

The principal legal doubt affects not the means but their intended end. Most butchery is gratuitous only at the margin. Great tyrannies employ it as a rational, necessary means. Great delinquencies therefore imply the existence of powerful opposition to the tyranny's projects. Hence State terrorists often cannot go beyond a few cosmetic adjustments without a consequent relinquishment of their central purposes. Initially those purposes may have been grand reasons of State, attainable only on the assumption of international indifference to the means employed. But even when that assumption fails, and the delinquents redesign their ends in a way more acceptable to the society, they may need brutal means more than ever simply to survive in the face of the hatred engendered by their earlier crimes. In short, once begun, great tyrannies can often be terminated only by the removal of the tyrants, who are recognized governments.

Although certain means at the disposal of national States and international institutions may in themselves be legimate, when employed for the purpose of unseating a regime hitherto in effective control and widely recognized, they come into conflict with the normative policy, dominant since the Second World War, of preserving ruling elites at least from external opponents. Until recently, and outside the context of decolonization, whenever the international community of existing regimes has had the chance to express a preference, it has apparently subordinated human rights to elite self-preservation. For instance, when India invaded what was then East Pakistan, responding to the consequences of West Pakistan's campaign of extermination against local Bengali elites and Hindus in general, overwhelming majorities in both the Security Council and the General Assembly refused to treat the deprivation of human rights in Bangladesh as an issue appropriate for consideration in connection with Pakistan's claim against India. In the General Assembly, after a debate dominated by the concepts of territorial integrity, sovereignty and national independence, by a vote of 104 in favor to 11 against, with ten abstentions, the member States called for an immediate cease fire and mutual (i.e. Indian) troop withdrawal.

Yet perhaps the result is not quite as categorical as the vote alone suggests. In assessing the views of reigning governments, one might also want to take into account the roughly coincident decision of the Aid-to-Pakistan Consortium formed by the major industrialized States not to renew its assistance program until the internal conflict was satisfactorily resolved, an act which, because of its timing, could easily have been construed as an implied critique of the method of resolution employed by Pakistan's Government.

One might also note that the General Assembly did not censure India for its initial use of force or its subsequent refusal to cease firing until it had attained its political and militariy objectives.

More recent examples of "Humanitarian Intervention" go further in suggesting a quiet tolerance of intervention in extreme cases, rather as juries will sometimes refuse to convict in certain cases of euthanasia. Tanzania's removal of Amin hardly rippled the surface of diplomacy. And France's replacement of the equally ineffable Bokassa, its former puppet, was a non-event. The muted reaction to Israel's Entebbe rescue mission – in contrast, for example, to the aftermath of the 1964 Belgian-American Stanleyville "rescue operation", which was, after all, legitimated by the nominal authorities in Leopoldville – also implies some shift in perspective. Admittedly, however, the shift may as easily be cited to evidence greater tolerance of force in international relations as to demonstrate enhanced concern for the defense of human rights. My own judgment is that perspectives have shifted on both issues.

Perhaps the least dangerous way to accommodate the interest in suppressing tyranny with that of preserving national independence is by means of a doctrine and a procedure for withdrawing recognition from regimes guilty of grave and systematic violations. The political will necessary for such a development does not yet exist either at the United Nations or among regional organizations. But scholars and leaders of non-governmental organizations in the field of human rights and the small but growing number of sympathetic States can begin to lay the psychological foundations for a formal normative shift by an all-out assault on the legitimacy of tyrranical governments.

As a complementary measure and one more likely to command political support today, the transnational community of human rights advocates should launch a major campaign for the punishment of government officials, high and low, directly involved in gross violations of human rights. By analogy to pirates, war criminals and aerial hijackers, those who order torture and murder and those who execute those orders should be subject to trial and punishment wherever they may be found. Cooperation against private terrorists should be linked explicitly to the adoption of measures against the public variety. And the suggestion that concern over terrorism and concern over the violation of human rights are somehow in competition for attention and resources should be exposed as malicious nonsense. We will move forward more easily if we first clear hypocrisy from the path.

7.5. Suppression of Tyranny: A Feasible Task?

Issa Diallo

It seems utopian to think that tyranny can be eliminated from the practice of governments. It is, however, possible to oppose tyranny legally by outlawing it. Legal means to this effect already exist. Once tyranny is outlawed, it then becomes possible to envisage applicable sanctions against offenders of the law.

1. Tyranny is an abuse of power, an illegal act, perpetrated against the rights of individuals in a society. It is of little importance if the act of tyranny is committed by an isolated group, by a party or by a political regime; responsibility for the act is incumbent on the government. If we attribute the concept of tyranny to a specific political regime, ideology, culture or to a specific group of countries, developed or developing, we adopt the double standard frequently used by politicians. Tyranny is not a question of degree within a political system. It is also not a question of the difference between conservative, authoritarian and modestly repressive regimes on the one hand and totalitarian, revolutionary regimes on the other as the US Permanent Representative to the United Nations, Jeane Kirkpatrick, recently defined it.

2. We concur with Vattel on the illegal nature of tyranny *(Le Droit des gens ou Principes de la loi naturelle appliqués à la conduite et aux affaires des Nations et des Souverains).* Tyranny has no legitimization in international law. Governments which practice tyranny, thus acting in violation of the law, are guilty and subject to sanction because the State is not above the law.

3. Because a uniform, universal definition of the concept of sovereignty does not exist, concepts of the exercise of sovereign power formed by lawyers and States are not always in harmony. This divergence of opinion on the concept of sovereignty has led certain governments to evoke the absolute nature of the State's sovereign power as a means of justifying acts of tyranny both within and without their borders. It is in this way that authoritarian governments of every ideological tendency extend their jurisdiction beyond the law which governs the society. They do not tolerate any sort of autonomous activity nor any deviation from the policies of the group in power. By means of such interpretations of sovereignty the State tends to monopolize power by its police force and to monopolize the law-making process. Sovereignty is not a raw fact, but rather an historical assumption about authority. Furthermore, the ultimate aim of sovereignty is the community; the exercise of this sovereignty cannot be carried out if it is at odds with the only source which legitimizes it, that is the individual. Within the community, man and freedom on the one hand cannot be regarded as equal to the concept of sovereignty on the other hand, for man is all important. A

legal basis for acting against tyranny exists, first of all, in the nature, inherently legal, by which individuals delegate their sovereignty to the State. Every State in the exercise of sovereignty is bound by the legal nature of this delegation of power. Sovereignty cannot be used as a legal argument against man. In fact, humanity must be encourged, developed and recognized in international law. Secondly, sovereignty is not an unlimited power as it is bound by international legal instruments such as treaties and conventions. The more such agreements are developed in international relations, the less are States sovereign. The sovereignty of the State is today a necessity which must recognize the reality of present international relations in a world divided culturally and ideologically. States are obliged to cooperate in promoting human rights and the protection of individuals. Opposing the right to tyranny implies, first of all, the creation of legal instruments capable of rendering tyranny illegal and the anticipation of sanctions against the authors of tyranny.

A legal basis for acting against tyranny exists:

a) In the legal nature by which individuals delegate their sovereignty to the State

Among the parameters put forward in some interpretations of sovereignty is the concept of sovereignty defined by Hobbes (in *Leviathan*) and Rousseau (in the *Social Contract*) for whom sovereignty is directly linked to authority. It is the absolute authority beyond any other.

The position which is put forward here is that freedom must be limited. Hobbes states that "people are to conferre all their power and strength upon one Man, or upon one Assembly of men, that may reduce all of their Wills, by, pluarality of voices, into one Will . . . I authorize and give up my Right of Governing myselfe . . ." In other words, man living in a commonwealth surrenders his conscience to the law. Jean-Jacques Rousseau later uses this approach as the national postulate for his *Social Contract*.

Although there have been attempts to overcome and hence make more explicit the limits of sovereignty, namely by Bodin *(De la République)*, Grotius *(De Jure Belli ac Pacis)* and Vattel *(Le Droit des Gens)*, this interpretation of sovereignty continues to be put forward whenever necessary by some States to justify their actions internally or externally. This concept of sovereignty denies the conceptual potentiality of man's freedom to exist beyond that of the sovereign State. The logical implication here is to shatter the notion of community and its grounding in man as man. Man and States have become two distinct breeds operating in different logical universes, governed by different equations. Sovereignty has been elevated to the level of an intrinsic right in international relations where it is seen as the guarantor of freedom.

What States decide among themselves can either become law or go beyond the law. i.e. States are above moral and political restraints when it comes to determining a higher order of the notion of Good. – Freedom is viewed as a product of sovereignty; i.e. freedom is obtained when a new State via diplomatic recognition enters the States system. Consequently, equality among States derives from the equality of their autonomy in this system.

This interpretation of the concept of sovereignty which favours the removal of man as the subject and source of law and which surrenders to the State the law-making process, thereby situating it above and beyond the law obviously poses a threat to human rights. This interpretation leads us to ask in particular:

- if we can accept the idea of the existence of two sovereignties – man, on the one hand, and the State on the other – which are two entirely different entities invested with different powers.
- if the State can deny man his sovereignty in the international arena when, in fact, the sovereignty of the State has man as its source at the national level.

The response to these questions must be no. Sovereignty is an historical assumption about authority. Its logical conceptual implications are directly grounded in historical choices. It was during the revolt of the various European principalities against Papal supremacy that the concept of sovereignty became historically dominant. At that time, the debate on the nature of the concept of sovereignty centered on God and his realm. There seemed a need for some absolute authority beyond reach of all other authority. Sovereignty is not an end in itself. If viewed this way, serious repercussions and detrimental effects upon the freedom of man and community result. The source of sovereignty and its legitimizing force is man. The sovereignty with which governments are empowered is a mandate which they are not, however, free to interpret at will and use against the very source which legitimizes it, that is against man.

Moreover, the concepts of liberty, community and sovereignty are intimately linked and cannot be dissassociated from one another in man's existence. One of the dominant factors of man's existence is the fact of his *becoming*. Man is not satisfied simply to *be*, because what he also wants is to *become*. "It is not being alive that one should value most, but making a proper use of being alive." (Socrates from *Crito*)

Intrinsic to the notion of man who wants to become is the notion of community. The State in its multiple and varied forms is an expression of man's behavior. Freedom is the underpinning of the range of man's possibilities. Freedom, in other words is not choice itself, but represents the possibility of choice. Freedom is not a right in itself; freedom of choice produces the conditions for the emergence of other rights. For example, man by chosing to live in society rather than in isolation, creates by his choice a situation which is new for him and which, in turn, requires the establishment of new rights. Sovereignty in this context is the *what*, not the *how* of man's becoming. The exercise of the principle of sovereignty by the State must in no event deny the supremacy of man's relationship with freedom and community.

b) In a number of international legal instruments created to protect human rights

A legal basis for acting against tyranny exists as well in a number of international and regional legal instruments which limit the concept of sovereignty and protect human rights. The dualistic concept of international law which views States as the only recognized members of the society of nations, favours a restrictive interpretation of human nature and of international morality. The adoption of the monist concept which considers human nature and morality as the basis of international law and which links humanity, its dignity, its rights and the duty of States to safeguard them, will favour the protection of human rights. Indeed, the adoption of the principle of human nature as one of the bases of international law implies that States must ensure the dignity of man both as individual and in his national collective. Today, these concepts have been included in a number of applicable legal instruments – a phenomenon which has greatly contributed to their importance, and better still, which has confered upon them an obligatory character.

The Charter of the United Nations which adopts human nature as its basis figures among these instruments. The preamble to the Charter, in fact, sets forth the faith of peoples "in fundamental human rights, in the dignity and worth of the human person, in the equal rights of men and women and of nations large and small". Furthermore, it proclaims the will of nations to facilitate social progress and to introduce better living standards and more freedom. Likewise, Resolution 1514 of 14 December 1960 of the General Assembly of the United Nations proclaims the link between human dignity, the basic rights of man and the independence of nations.

The Universal Declaration of Human Rights of 10 December 1948 had already set forth the same approach. Its preamble stresses the necessity of recognizing human dignity and the equal and inalienable rights of the human family taken as one. It links peace among nations to the universal and genuine respect of human rights and basic liberties.

The specific situation of certain determined categories of human beings has also been the object of reglementation in international law. There is, most notably, the case of the Covenant on Civil and Political Rights and the Covenant on Economic, Social and Cultural Rights which have been in effect since 3 January 1976. The Statute of Refugees of 28 July 1951 and the Protocol of 31 January 1967 related to this Statute also ensure the protection of a specific category of human beings. In the same way, the Declaration on the Elimination of Discrimination against Women adopted by the General Assembly of the United Nations on 7 November 1967 constitutes an aspect of the general evolution of international law favouring the protection of human dignity and freedom. On the regional level, this effort was followed by instruments such as the Convention of the Organization of African Unity, dated 8 September 1969, on the specific aspect of refugee problems in Africa; the draft African Convention on Human Rights of 17 January 1981; the American Convention on Human Rights; and the European Convention for the Protection of Human Rights and Fundamental Freedoms.

All these efforts taken together, and created thanks to the monist concept of human nature, undertaken on a world-wide as well as on a regional level, are particularly indicative of the orientation of the new international legal order to oppose tyranny. This orientation, however encouraging, is not necessarily enough by itself to suppress tyranny. It indicates, however, that it is possible to place tyranny outside the law. The American Convention for the Protection of Human Rights and Fundamental Freedoms is, for example, quite explicit on this point since it affirms in its preamble that "Recognizing that the essential rights of man are not derived from one's being a national of a certain State, but are based upon attributes of the human personality, and that they therefore justify international protection in the form of a convention reinforcing or complementing the protection provided by the domestic law of the American States . . . that . . the ideal of free men enjoying freedom from fear and want can be achieved only if conditions are created whereby everyone may enjoy his economic, social, and cultural rights, as well as his civil and political rights . . ."

Since the legal bases for outlawing tyranny and appropriate legal instruments to this effect already exist, the question of applicable sanctions can now be raised.

7.6. Human Rights in Developing Countries

RUP C. HINGORANI

One of the important accomplishments of the United Nations has been bringing about the consciousness regarding human rights by the world community and its peoples. For the first time in world history, States swore in the name of their peoples and reaffirmed faith in fundamental human rights and the dignity and worth of the human person. One of the purposes of the United Nations has been to promote and encourage respect for human rights. This was followed by adoption of the Universal Declaration of Human Rights and the Genocide Convention commended by the General Assembly in 1948. In 1966, two International Covenants on Economic, Social and Cultural and on Civil and Political Rights were commended. These Covenants became effective in 1976. Besides, many other instruments concerning various aspects of human rights have been concluded at different levels.

For the Third World, it was an augury of a new era. Self-determination being one of the purposes of the United Nations, about 100 new States have sprung up since 1945 by a process of decolonisation and transformation from colonial or trust territory status. Third World countries have been very vocal in the spread of the gospel of human rights. Surprisingly, however, while these new States have championed the cause of human rights in world forums, some of them have denied human rights within their national borders. This is despite the fact that some of these States have incorporated human rights in national constitutional documents. My attempt in this paper is to study the trends of these developments in new States.

1. Right to peace

Developing countries have won the freedom but not the peace. Up to 1945, these countries enjoyed comparative peace and were away from war zones. Today, Asia and Africa have been the main theaters of war. It is estimated that out of little more than 100 wars since 1945, about 90 wars have been fought in Asia and Africa. Tribal, ethnic and religious hatreds have engulfed these regions into theaters of war which have threatened their fragile economy and their recently acquired freedom. Ideological differences and border disputes are equally responsible for some wars. The recent Iran-Iraq war portrays the tragedy of the day.

The United Nations was established to save the succeeding generations from the scourge of war. Members agreed to refrain from use of force against the territorial integrity and political independence of any State. Armed force was not to be used except in the common interest. Yet, nations have preferred to resort to use of force at the slightest pretext.

The crying need for the Third World is to practise tolerance and live together in peace with one another as good neighbours. Nations should shun use of force for settlement of internal or border disputes. Proxy wars should be avoided and big Powers warned against pumping instability in the region by supplying their discarded arms to one State to the prejudice of another State. Big Powers should be told to leave us alone and let us live in peace.

2. Right to development

Until the mid-twentieth century, Third World countries were exploited by the Western world. The colonial countries exploited the natural resources and raw material of their colonies in Asia and Africa to develop and enrich themselves. Even non-colonies of the Third World were exploited by the Western countries through economic subjugation by multinationals like ARAMCO and Anglo-Iranian Oil Company. Surprisingly then, a bottle of coca cola was costing more than a litre of petrol. The process has been going on for the last few centuries.

Now the Third World has awakened and become its own master. It seeks quick development of its depleted economy. It would not brooke any more its economic exploitation by the Western World. The preamble of the United Nations Charter envisages promotion of the economic and social advancement of the peoples through international machinery. The United Nations General Assembly has commended the Charter of Economic Rights and Duties of States in 1974. There has been a North-South dialogue on New International Economic Order. There has been some breakthrough under the UNCTAD auspices, but a New International Economic Order has yet to crystalize.

Development and peace are two wheels of the cart. There can be no peace without development of the Third World and no development without peace. Unfortunately, States from the Third World are more embroiled in internal strifes and border disputes which motivate them to spend more in armament than they invest in development. The world is spending about 500 billion dollars annually on armament. This would mean that the world is spending about one million dollars every minute on armaments. The Third World countries do not lag behind in military expenditure. This is indeed very unfortunate. What is needed is disarmament and development and not armament. These nations should better settle their disputes around the table rather than on the battlefield. They should not stick to false notions of national prestige at the expense of welfare of their peoples. In India, there is an impression that the poor man wastes his money on litigation and marriage. This seems to be equally true in respect of poor nations which waste their resources in mini wars and grandeur plans.

3. Political detentions

News regarding political detentions in newly independent countries are causing great concern among world elites. It is unfortunate to notice that political leaders of these new States use the scepter of preventive detention which they had earlier condemned while they were fighting for the independence of their country. It is indeed agonising that while they swear by democracy, they do not tolerate dissent at home. Resultantly, political dissenters are muzzled and detained, mostly without trial. The phenomenon is too obvious in a number of developing countries in Asia, Africa and Latin America.

The phrase "political detention" may be defined as detention of political opponents of the regime or dissenters from the political philosophy of the ruling party. Perhaps, ruling parties in newly independent countries do not tolerate any kind of political opposition or dissent within their territories. The intensity of these practices has invited world-wide concern among world elites. Some countries like Chile, Uruguay, Nicaragua, Uganda under Amin and Equatorial Guinea have become proverbial in their detention of political dissenters.

There is an International Covenant of Civil and Political Rights of 1966 which became effective in 1976. Article 19 of the Covenant gives the right of holding any opinion. No one should be detained for political dissent. Unfortunately, one finds prisons filled with political dissenters in the developing countries. Ruling elites should develop a sense of tolerance for political dissent which may be considered as a healthy sign. Therefore, no one should be detained for opposing the ruling party. Developing countries which indulge in political detentions should make necessary amends and free them forthwith. The tragedy sometimes is that governments commit themselves solemnly to international agreements which they seek to violate with impunity at home. We should make efforts to highlight incidents of political detention and build up world opinion to see that these detentions are discontinued.

More than political detention, there is the problem of the living conditions in prison camps. It has been found that a number of political detainees are lodged in ordinary prisons along with hardened criminals and lunatics. Efforts are made to break their will by subtle psychological methods. They are pressurized through their families and friends to follow the line of conformity. Many of them are kept incommunicado without information to their families or friends. Their solitary confinement is motivated to break their will to follow an independent path. Often, they are condemned on paltry evidence which cannot be sustained in well-established democracies under normal canons of law.

Something should be done to ameliorate the lot of political detainees. It is necessary to prescribe that no person should be arrested except on a clear charge of violation of a law which entails arrest. Invariably, a detainee must be produced before a magistrate within twenty four hours of his arrest and charges communicated to him. A detainee should be given the right of defence and the services of a competent lawyer. Detainees should be taken to distant places where they could be kept incommunicado. The provisions of Article 9 of the International Covenant on Civil and Political Rights should be scrupulously observed.

There should be minimum standards of treatment of political detainees. As provided by Article 10 of the Covenant, they should be treated with humanity and inherent dignity of the human person. They should not be kept in ordinary jails and in any case they should not be lodged with hardened criminals and lunatics. They should be given facilities compatible with their social status.

Trials of political detainees should be expedited. They should be tried before ordinary courts and not before special courts. Special courts are not a welcome category of courts and their use should be discouraged as far as possible.

Detainees should be given the right of defence by a competent lawyer. If the detainee is not financially capable to organize his defence well, he should be provided with the services of a competent lawyer free of cost by the government. There should be no cooked-up charges nor cooked-up confessions which are sought to be extracted from them by using third degree methods against them.

There should be no summary trials of political detainees. All normal procedures of law and evidence must be observed in order to ensure for trial and determine the guilt of the detainee, if any. Any summary trial under the pretext of expeditious disposal should be discouraged.

In so far as sentence is concerned, there should be a ban on death sentence being passed on political detainees. Holding of dissenting opinion should not be considered as a crime. All normal avenues of appeal should be made available to the political detainees as well. They should not be discriminated against.

In between arrest and trial, the detainee should have the facility for moving the court for habeas corpus for determining whether detention is in conformity with law or otherwise. As far as possible, a detainee should be released on bail unless his release would cause grave threat to internal security or there is reasonable apprehension of jumping the bail.

4. Torture

State torture has become an institutionalised affair. Amnesty International Reports show that some seventy States, mostly developing States, practise torture against their political detainees. Whether it is Bokassa's Central Africa, Amin's Uganda, Macia Ngvema's Equatorial Guinea or the Shah's Iran or Pol Pot's Khmer Republic, these States have surpassed all past perpetrators of torture. As President Hay of the International Red Cross once remarked: Torture has become scientific, systematic and State-controlled. Ironically, torture is resorted to by the very State officials who are entrusted with the responsibility of maintaining law and order within the society. In some States, torture of political opponents is a regular mode of governing the country and over-awing its people. Torture seeks to transform the victim into a worn-out wreck often irreparably damaged in body and mind.

Article 7 of the International Covenant on Civil and Political Rights prohibits torture. So do the European Convention of Human Rights and the Inter-American Convention of Human Rights. The latter two Conventions are confined to the Council of Europe and the Organization of American States respectively. Need for separate conventions is felt in order to emphasise upon the intensity of the infection and the effort to control it immediately and abolish it eventually.

The United Nations has expressed its great concern over the increased incidence of torture. There is a United Nations Declaration of 1975 on Torture. In 1977, the UN General Assembly asked the Commission on Human Rights to prepare a Draft Convention Against Torture. The Swedish Committee of Human Rights has prepared a Draft Convention against torture and other cruel, inhuman or degrading treatment or punishment. There is also a Draft Optional Protocol to the Draft International Convention Against Torture prepared by the International Commission of Jurists. The UN Commission on Human Rights is seized of these documents.

Torture is proscribed by all world legal systems. About fifty five States ban torture under their national constitutions. Unfortunate part of the story of torture is that while every State condemns torture in public, some of the States practise it in private as an effective instrument of its policy to eliminate opposition through torture. Recent disclosures of torture by the Colombian army indicate how innocents are harassed in an effort to control guerilla activity. There are, of course, individual sadistic instances of torture by State officials as in the case of blindings in Bhagalpur (India). While the latter category of torture can be remedied through judicial machinery within the country, international elites are more concerned with the first category of State-sponsored torture.

State torture should be considered as an international crime like piracy and hijacking subject to jurisdiction of any State where the perpetrator of the crime is found. The perpetrator should not be treated as a political offender. It is, therefore, gratifying to find that an American court has recently held that torture is a violation of international law and its perpetrators may be punished in the United States regardless of where the violation occurred. The action was taken by the Federal Judge under the United States Statute giving federal courts jurisdiction in respect of international torts. The matter related to the killing of a 17 year old boy in Paraguay in 1976 by Pena, Inspector General of Police, Paraguay!

The effort should be to bring to book not only the perpetrator of the crime of torture but also the State functionaries who instigate, encourage or condone the crime to extract information, false confession or cause intimidation. State functionaries charged with the crime should be summarily dismissed under Departmental Discipline Rules, irrespective of judicial proceedings. The perpetrators may only be proxy for the main accused. Unfortunately, the Human Rights Committee appointed under Article 28 of the International Covenant on Civil and Political Rights has not been able to do much in respect of complaints of State Torture against Uruguay under Article 2 of the Optional Protocol.

5. *Involuntary disappearances*

Closely allied with political detentions and torture is the problem of involuntary disappearance. Rulers of the Day resort to detention of their political opponents and torture them to conform. Failing all this, they are eliminated. In many cases, political opponents are removed from their homes during night by uniformed persons or toughs. No one hears of them later on. The Government shows ignorance of such events and disowns any responsibility for such disappearances. After a lapse of a few years, they are declared dead to the discomforture of family members and friends. These things normally happen where one man rules through decrees.

The UN Commission on Human Rights has received a number of complaints regarding involuntary disappearances. Sometimes, the idea of international habeas corpus is floated to enable production of persons kept incommunicado. But there is the problem of implementation. The Commission on Human Rights has decided to establish a Working Group on Disappeared Persons and the General Assembly has asked the Secretary General to use his good offices with the regimes where such things happen to preserve life and integrity of individuals.

6. Right of self-determination

The principle of self-determination is enshrined in the UN Charter as well as in the two Covenants of 1966. Article I gives the right of self-determination to peoples to determine their political status and pursue their economic, social and cultural development. However, what has been granted to them at an international level has been denied to them at a national level. Colonies have become independent but their peoples have been deprived of their right to choose their political status.

It is indeed shocking to learn that out of more than 100 new States, a very few of them have a working democracy within their territories. Some have a semblance of democracy with one-party system and the virus is spreading. Others have naked dictatorships. Unfortunately, authoritarian regimes seem to thrive mostly in Third World countries.

Self-determination is as much necessary at the national level as it is at the international level. People should have the right to choose their own form of government at regular intervals as envisaged under Article 21 of the Universal Declaration of Human Rights and Article 25 of the International Covenant of Civil and Political Rights. The will of the local people should be the basis of authority of government; not the will of the self-seeking and self-appointed authoritarian. The advent of democracy will greatly reduce the incidence of political detentions, torture and involuntary disappearances which are off-shoots of authoritarian rule.

7. Right to stay in one's own country

Independence of colonial territories has brought in its trail a number of local problems within the borders of newly independent States. The worst thus created has been the emergence of tribal, religious, racial and lingual differences between the local sects of society. This has given rise to the feeling of majority and minority tribe, majority and minority community, majority and minority racial group and majority and minority lingual group. A sort of fear psychosis subsists among the minority groups who feel insecure or humiliated. Old frontiers were arbitrarily fixed by the colonialists. With the exit of colonialists, the ruling group behaves like a big brother, thus straining the relations between different sections of the society. The idea of new frontiers would only aggravate the situation instead of solving the problem.

Free Africa has been the center of emotional eruptions. This has resulted in large scale migration from the country of origin. It is estimated that about ten million refugees have been uprooted in this way throughout the world. Africa alone accounts for 5 million refugees. Ironically, poor neighbouring countries bear the brunt of refugee exoduses through no fault of theirs.

There is great sympathy evinced among world elites for the welfare of the uprooted refugees. The UN High Commissioner for Refugees started with a paltry annual budget of a few million dollars in 1951. Today, its annual budget has swollen to 500 million dollars, besides *ad hoc* arrangements. Recently, the Organization of African Unity convened a meeting of potential donors in Geneva and asked for 1.2 billion dollar aid for African refugees who constitute 50% of the total world refugee population. However, only 560 million dollars were collected at the April 1981 Conference. Amazingly, twenty-five poor countries from Africa are looking after the refugees there.

While sympathy for refugees is welcome, no one seems to bother or think seriously to remove the underlying causes which motivate such large scale exoduses. The World community should concern itself to see what can be done to allay the fears of potential refugees who seek to leave their own country in the hope of getting better treatment in an alien land. Refugees are strewn everywhere, whether they are boat refugees from Vietnam or other refugees from Kampuchea, Afghanistan, Chad, Ethiopia, Zaire, Nigeria, Equatorial Guinea and a few other countries.

There must be compelling reasons for people to leave their hearths and homes. No one would wish to leave his country for the love of it. But when this happens, no accusing finger is raised against the Government whose policies motivate mass exodus from within its territory. People should have the right to live in their own country and be free from fear and a sense of insecurity. The dawn of freedom is not meant for the ruling group only. The minority group is as much entitled to stay at home and enjoy the fruits of freedom as the majority group. Otherwise, the dawn of freedom would mean a dawn of disaster for the minority group. Persecution on ground of religion, language, tribe, ethnic or racial group must stop. There should be a spirit of tolerance and accommodation for different ideologies, different languages, different tribes and ethnic groups in a multiple society. Independence does not mean heaven for some and hell for others. All the local groups should reap the fruits of independence and self-government without excluding the other. Peaceful co-existence is as much essential within national borders as beyond these borders.

There should be concerted action by the world community to pre-empt situations warranting refugee migration. This attitude has been singularly wanting. States should strive to see that situations are not created which cause refugee movements. The problem may be political but world community should be prepared to tackle political problems like these.

It is, therefore, suggested that the refugee problem should not be looked into in isolation. The underlying causes responsible for such exodus should be determined and efforts made by world elites to remove these causes in the form of either persuading the defaulting State to make amends or taking other measures as the situation may demand. In appropriate cases, States may be asked to take back its nationals and grant them civil and political rights, besides a sense of security. Else, it may be asked to compensate for the losses suffered and properties left behind by fleeing refugees.

8. Minority rights

When one considers a multiple or plural society, one comes across a number of minority sections within the country. There may be a racial minority, a lingual minority, a tribal minority, a religious minority or an ethnic minority. Here one does not take into consideration a political minority which is bound to happen in a democratic set-up.

The tragedy of the post-independence era in developing States has been the lack of national intetration of various sections of society within the territory. Nurtured in the midst of the principle of self-determination which has been the catchword for decolonisation, some groups seek to stretch the principle to the farthest end which may result in fragmentation which may be worse than Balkanisation. One has witnessed attempts at secession in Zaire, Ethiopia, Nigeria, Chad, Sudan, Lebanon, Thailand, the Philippines and India, to mention only a few examples.

One good thing which has emerged from the United Nations practices is the recognition of each member-State as a single unit whose disintegration is discouraged by the United Nations. In the process, an atmosphere of mutual trust should be created within the country where minorities should feel secure and their traditional rights be protected. In turn, minorities should join the mainstream of national life without getting themselves isolated.

It has been noticed that in a number of countries, minorities seek trans-border affiliation which causes loss of mutual trust among various sections of society. Perhaps, it may be desirable to try local solutions for national problems rather than to complicate the issue by involving foreign elements in the problem. Mutual trust will facilitate the solution of any intricate problem.

9. Right to basic necessities of life

Most of the Third World countries suffer from proverbial poverty amidst plenty in the world. These States are poor and their peoples still poorer. The World Bank Report of 1979 lists 21 countries which have less than 200 dollars per capita income per annum. Not surprisingly, budgets of many of these States are less than the budgets of some of the giant multinationals.

Traditional human rights of liberty and free expression have no meaning for these States and their peoples. Their first priority is basic necessities of life. These are bread, clothing and shelter. These necessities of life could be termed as basic human rights for them. Pope John Paul II, while addressing the United Nations General Assembly in 1979, said that right to food, clothing, housing and sufficient health care are inalienable rights of man.

There should be an international effort to see that no one dies because of food starvation and malnutrition. It is indeed a shocking revelation that about 35 000 children die every day due to want of basic nutrition, elementary health care and plain drinking water. It is further estimated that by the turn of the century, there will be about 800 million people in a state of abject poverty. Some of these people cannot afford to have even one loaf of bread in a day. The people should have at least two stomach-filling meals a day, plain drinking water, some minimum clothing and shelter to sleep, relax and protect their body from inclement weather. Otherwise, all this tall talk of human rights would become a sham.

10. Rights of persons under trial

It has been noticed that in a number of developing countries, prisons are filled with persons under trial. Many of them remain detained for years, in some cases for longer periods than the maximum periods of punishment prescribed for crimes attributed to them. In 1980, the Supreme Court of India ordered release of 34 undertrials on personal bond for being in prisons for two to ten years without facing any trial.

In India, which may be typical of any developing country, there are 150 000 undertrials in 1220 jails. There is over-crowding, poor food and lack of minimum medical care. There is no jail for women, children and juveniles. There are five million cases pending before Indian courts, including 68 000 cases involving serious offences. Jails are treated as government run slums manned by toughs.

Police is in no hurry to bring the accused before the trial magistrate. The magistrate is in no mood, and perhaps overworked, to complete the trial. The undertrial has no money to pursue the trial and defend himself effectively. In some cases, he has no desire to be out of jail because freedom does not promise him anything good. Some prefer to remain in jail because that ensures them some food, clothing and roof, howsoever bad these may be.

There are no scientific methods of investigation. In their absence, third degree methods are resorted to compel the suspects to admit their guilt, supposed or real. In some cases, suspects consider false confession as a lesser evil than prolonged third degree methods practised on them. Non-cooperative suspects are liquidated in alleged encounters during so-called mob fury.

It is no use paying lip service to human rights where undertrials are subjected to all types of deprivations. Undertrials are as much human as anyone else. There is a saying that everyone is presumed to be innocent unless it is proved otherwise. But in developing countries, undertrials are persecuted before they are prosecuted. In some cases, they languish in police custody or jails for years without being brought before trial courts.

It may, therefore, be suggested that all persons arrested under charge of any crime should be brought before the magistrate within twenty-four hours from the time of his arrest but excluding the journey period. Any deviation from this rule should be considered as a dereliction of duty for which the officer responsible may be penalised. There should be education of law-enforcing authorities which should behave as welfare agencies and not as repression agencies.

Initial trial should be completed within two years from the date of the arrest of the accused. The Supreme Court of India has held in 1980 that expeditious trial of the accused is an essential part of fundamental rights in India.[2] During the pendency of trial, bail should invariably be given except in case of habitual offenders. In between arrest and release on bail, the accused should be humanely treated and

1 *Filartega* v. *Pena*, I.C.J. Reports December 1980, pp. 62–3.
2 *Hussainara Khatoon* v. *State of Bihar*, AIR 1980 S.C. 83.

lodged under hygienic conditions. Handcuffing of prisoners has been treated as degrading treatment and therefore criticised by the Supreme Court of India.[3] Even convicts should be sought to be reformed rather than hardened. The Supreme Court of India has remarked that imprisonment should aim at rehabilitation of the prisoner who should turn out of jail as a willing member of a law-abiding society.[4]

Legal aid should be given to needy undertrials. There is a sense of inequality in criminal cases where the State is the prosecutor and its personnel is the judging authority. Besides, while the State is rich and can afford to engage the best prosecutor at the people's cost, the poor accused may not be in a position to engage even an average lawyer, not to say a good lawyer. Legal aid cells should operate at trial courts to evaluate instances of inequality at prosecution-defence level. Whenever necessary, accused should be provided with a competent lawyer to defend him. It has been noticed that an indigent accused dosed not get a competent and motivated lawyer. Lawyers should consider this as a moral duty, irrespective of whether fees are paid to them by the State exchequer or by litigants.

11. Implementation

Recognition of human rights alone is not enough. For that reason, many national constitutions of new States contain provisions regarding recognition of human rights. Yet, these are the very countries where human rights are violated. What is required is an impartial machinery to prevent or redress violation of human rights. This can be done at three levels, national, regional and international.

a) National level

Victims of violations of human rights should have right to seize their courts for vindication and protection of their rights. For this, there should be right of access to justice within the country and the judiciary should be impartial and free from pressure of the executive wing of the government.

While many States have provision for right of access to justice, the provision is either suspended on ground of national emergency or even the substantive right is itself suspended. In other cases, a subservient judiciary toes the line of the government. This makes any judicial remedy difficult or diluted. In many cases, particularly in cases of State repression, redress for violation of human rights at the national level becomes a farce. In such circumstances, redress may be sought at regional and international levels.

b) Regional level

Redress of violation of human rights may be possible at regional level if there is any regional Convention for protection of human rights. Two such regional conventions operate – one in Western Europe and the other in the American continent.

3 *Prem Shanker Shukla* v. *Delhi Administration,* AIR 1980 S.C. 1535.
4 *Sunil Batra* v. *Delhi Administration,* AIR 1980 S.C. 1600.

There is a European Commission of Human Rights under the Rome Convention of 1950. The Commission has two-fold jurisdiction. It has compulsory jurisdiction in respect of complaints preferred by any contracting State against another contracting State. It may also have optional jurisdiction under Article 25 in which case any individual, organization or group may refer complaint to the Commission. While there are very few complaints preferred by one State against another, optional jurisdiction has been conferred by only 14 out of 21 contracting States. The Commission investigates the complaints it receives and tries for friendly settlement under Article 28 of the Convention. In its absence, it may report to the Committee of Ministers which may take decision on the report.

The matter may also be referred to the European Court of Human Rights under Article 46 of the Convention which is optional. So far, sixteen States have accepted the jurisdiction. The Court's decision is binding on States party to the case. The Committee of Ministers supervises the excution of the decision under Article 54 of the Convention.

There is an Inter-American Convention of Human Rights of 1969. The Inter-American Human Rights Commission is entitled to take action on individual petitions under Article 45 which is optional. The Commission can make binding decisions. The Inter-American Court of Human Rights has an optional jursdiction. But once the jurisdiction is conferred, it can work like a national court by giving redress and awarding damages for any violation of human rights.

Unfortunately, there are no regional human rights conventions or commissions and courts in the developing regions of Asia and Africa. The Organization of African Unity is preoccupied with the process of decolonisation and apartheid and colonial policies of South Africa. The League of Arab States is equally occupied with its conflict with Israel and violation of human rights in occupied territories.

The Asian continent does not have any regional organization like the Council of Europe, the Organization of American States or the Organization of African Unity. There is a small group of States called the ASEAN countries in the South East Asian region. These States are mostly concerned with the problem of security in the face of expansionist policies of neighboring countries. There is LAWASIA – an organization of Asian lawyers – which does not have the official status which is necessary for bringing about regional cooperation on human rights. Perhaps the Afro-Asian Legal Consultative Committee may be the right organization to take up the issue of two regional conventions on human rights in Africa and Asia.

c) International level

The Covenant of Civil and Political Rights envisages establishment of the Human Rights Committee under Article 28. Like the European Commission of Human Rights, the Human Rights Committee may hear complaints by one State against another State. It may also hear individual petitions against the State which has ratified the Optional Protocol.

The function of the Committee is limited. It can lend its good offices to amicably settle the matter. In its absence, it can only give statement of facts without giving its own opinion. The Committee may appoint a Conciliation Committee with the prior approval of the disputing States. The Commission may give its findings on matters of fact to the Committee without giving its opinion on whether they constitute breach of the Covenant.

The Human Rights Committee may hear individual petitions under the Optional Protocol. These petitions are to be considered after hearing from the State against whom the complaint has been received. No oral hearings are allowed, nor any sponsored petitions by Amnesty International, the International Commission of Jurists or such other organizations. The Committee hears such complaints in closed door meetings. Apart from the fact that the Optional Protocol has been ratified so far by 12 States only, the Committee has no power to give any relief.

Human right violations have been considered at various levels at the United Nations. The Sub-Commission on Prevention of Discrimination and Protection of Minorities has considered a number of situations involving violations of human rights. The Commission on Human Rights has also considered human rights violations in different countries regarding which complaints have been received. The Economic and Social Council also receives periodic reports regarding progress of human rights in the territories of member States. It must, however, be admitted that apart from high-lighting the violations of human rights by some countries, the results of discussions at the UN level have not been very fruitful.

Conclusions

Above have been discussed some of the pertinent human right problems which are confronting the Third World countries. Of course, traditional human rights are important. But it is a question of priorities. For Third World countries, priority is given to the new category of human rights like the rights to peace and development. No State can progress in the midst of war which consumes all energies of the State. It must feed its people rather than fight. Peace is a must for these countries.

Developing States have also witnessed the emergence of authoritarian forces within their frontiers. This does not give any chance to their people to freely choose their government and participate in national administration. Non-exercise of the right of self-determination at the national level causes a string of problems like political detentions, torture of political opponents and exodus of various minorities. The right of a people to freely choose their government should be considered as sacrosanct.

Other human rights should also be enjoyed by the peoples of the Third World. There should be a judicial guarantee for the vindication of human rights. Unfortunately, it has been noticed that very few countries of the Third World have ratified the two Covenants and fewer States have ratified the Optional Protocol which gives the right of individual petition.

At the same time, there needs to be a caveat here. It has been often noticed in developing countries, that freedom is misconstrued and often abused. Rights are claimed in isolation without being conscious of one's responsibilities. Strikes are rampant and loss of work-hours colossal. This hampers national development. People should do their work conscientiously and help in the development of the national economy instead of engaging in unnecessary agitations and strikes.

Finally, some suggestions follow:

1. Article 4 of the UN Charter should be suitably amended to include that States seeking membership should ratify various human rights conventions and abide by them.
2. States which violate human rights persistently may be suspended or expelled from the United Nations according to the gravity of the violations;
3. In each country, there should be a Human Rights Commissioner to monitor the implementation of various human rights conventions at the national level and look after individual complaints regarding violations of human rights. He should have powers to redress such violations;
4. Periodic seminars should be held in different regions to highlight the importance of human rights and focus on countries in the region where human rights are grossly violated;
5. The Asio-African Legal Consultative Committee should be requested to work towards conclusion of regional conventions on human rights in Asia and Africa;
6. The Human Rights Committee should be given more powers in respect of individual complaints of human right violations under the Covenant.

7.7. Sovereignty and Humanity
Interventions at Plenary and Group Sessions

A Natural or Moral Basis for International Law

References:

7.1. Vojin Dimitrijević 383
7.2. Alexis Gabou 397

Philippe de Seynes

1. Dr. Gabou approaches the issue of the new international legal order in a historical context which is one of "assymetry". The rest of us have adopted a broad and inevitably somewhat loose view of international law. The new international legal order is incomplete unless you relate it to history and sociology.

2. There is another distinction that should be mentioned. That between those who make the law or apply it and those who say what it is in an oracle-like fashion. Are these jurists playing the role they should be playing in a modern world, in an assymetric world?

Eduardo Jimenez de Aréchaga

I wish to commend Prof. Dimitrijević's report for emphasizing that contemporary International Law is a value-oriented instrument of change.

Lawyers are accustomed to distinguish between *'lege lata'* and *'lege ferenda'* and dismiss the latter provisions, such as programatic rules, as not being legal norms and presenting no interest for the jurist.

This is a wrong approach, which takes an instantaneous view of the legal system and disregards the importance of the time element in the evolution and development of the law. All legal systems aspire to enjoy a certain permanence, and this cannot be achieved without becoming a more just system. Thus, it is due to this aspiration to last that justice and other values are incorporated, often slowly and with difficulties, into the existing fabric of the law.

A consequence of the foregoing is the importance that should be attributed by jurists to programatic provisions which establish the goals and determine the orientation that is to be followed in the process of legal development.

To be more concrete, I wish to give an example – related to the main objects of this seminar.

The Charter of Economic Rights and Duties of States contains certain provisions which codify existing rules of International Law; others which crytallize emerging rules, such as those proclaiming permanent sovereignty over natural resources and establishing a system of compensation (which was the only provisions opposed by developed countries) and, finally, a large number of programatic provisions, with the purpose of generating a practice of States which could, in due course, harden into customary rules; these are, for instance, the provisions proclaiming the need to introduce equity in the terms of trade between developed and developing countries; to control transnational enterprises and to ensure an equitable transfer of technology. The importance of these programatic provisions is that they define certain objectives, and in view of the consensus of States in respect of these provisions, they place those objectives above further discussion. Thus, the purposes and objectives of the new economic order have been agreed by all States.

The question which remains to be settled, not an easy one, concerns the methods and means for achieving these objectives; for instance what type of instrument should be adopted in respect of transnational companies; what should be the economic importance of the Common Fund for stabilizing prices of raw materials etc.

This is important because it signifies that the Third World can no longer be described, as it has been, as an *"ordre mendicante"* asking for charity, but as a large group of States demanding justice on the basis of objectives defined and agreed by all.

William Michael Reisman

In a period of rapid and disjunctive change, such as we find ourselves in, one of the functions of the jurist is to facilitate and participate in the clarification of community goals, which guide the modification and innovation of law. I applaud the inclusion of this subject in the agenda of the Seminar and the 2 papers we have heard. But I regret the use of the words "natural law". As Professor Dimitrijević observed, nature *is*, while law involves *choices* about how it is to be used. No law is natural. In this regard I would add three observations:

1. Law and its goals do not "evolve". The passive voice is wholly inappropriate. Changes in the law have been proposed and agitated for by individuals. Future law will be formed by the same process. The human agency in the process must be emphasized.
2. International goal clarification is much more than a search for values common to the diverse cultures of the world. While commonality is relevant, goals are invented, especially in radically new situations.
3. Appropriate goals for the world community need not be universal at the time of their postulation. One should bear in mind that many of the values expressed in the Universal Declaration of Human Rights in 1948 were far from universal at that time. Some, alas, are still not accepted everywhere.

The point of emphasis is the need for the international lawyer to accept the manifest function of clarifying goals for the world community and to discharge it with vigor.

Juan Carlos Puig

I have been thoroughly impressed by Professor Dimitrijević's communication, certainly a masterpiece of legal and philosophical reasoning, as well as by Dr. Gabou's report. Although I agree with them in many aspects as to what they have said, perhaps some new elements may be useful.

First of all, let me say that Professor Dimitrijević has elaborated his communication taking into account mainly the problem of the substance, the content, of justice. But it seems to me that the problem of the formal structure of justice is equally relevant and important. In other words, Professor Dimitrijević has lectured us on the matter of what is justice nowadays. But we should also say something about the problem of how justice has to be done. This is a very important matter since it is here where the problem of the relativity of justice appears.

Justice is an absolute value from the standpoint of its substance but it is relative and contingent from the viewpoint of its structure. Within this perspective, justice is a pantonomous category, and this means that in order to establish permanent justice in this world, it is necessary to be initiated into all forms of conduct, past, present and future. As this is obviously impossible for a human being, what in fact is done is to select "relevant" conduct. The method of selective apportionment enables us to retain those known forms of conduct which the adjudicator in a broad sense (judge, State, individual, etc.) should take into account in order to reach a "just" decision. Normally, the discussion as to whether a decision is just or unjust is, in this sense, a discussion of the "relevancy" of conducts envisaged by the adjudicator to arrive at his ruling.

Moreover, I would like to comment upon the somewhat contingent and transitory character attributed by the rapporteur to natural law, or, in Dr. Gabou's words to the "*conception moniste et universelle de la nature humaine*".

It seems to me that there always was a shared feeling of what is the content of justice. Let me recall only one example. Aristotle admitted slavery but he did not say that having slaves was just. In fact, instead of giving a real basis for his contention, he asked himself a question. If the slaves are freed, who else will do the work? It was, then, a matter of interest, not a matter of justice.

Géza Herczegh

I have to express my gratitute towards our two distinguished rapporteurs for the excellent papers they prepared for us. I fully agree with the great majority of their statements and it is not in order to oppose their conclusions that I asked the floor but to underline some of them, which seem to me of major importance.

I belong to a legal school prevailing in Hungary and also in other countries of Eastern Europe, to the Socialist school, according to which the essence of any kind of law is to be found not in the norms themselves but in their relations to the human behaviour they try to regulate. What kind of society established and developed the law in question, and does this law exercise a real regulating effect on the society from which it emerged? Even if some scholars may qualify these questions as being alien to the proper realm of jurisprudence, I think without answering them, no legal theory can pretend to be complete. This " sociological" approach has to be applied also in studies concerning values. Every legal system is not only a set of rules emanating from the will of the appropriate organs, it must be just, that is, conform to the values the society in question respects. As professor Dimitrijević has put it, "the existence of a legal norm implies a value, a situation to be brought about". But we should never forget that values are changing with the social evolution. What seems to be just now may become a striking injustice tomorrow and even the rank of order of the values may be different in coexisting socieites (States). According to Mr. Gabou the international law of the period of colonialism was based on a dualist conception of human nature and morals, I would rather say it applied a double standard of values.

It is necessary to underline this, because in many cultures there are trends to express values as being universal and eternal – sometimes as commands of God – with the aim to give them in this way greater authority. But the great religions, philosophies and moral teachings all have their social context, their own history which is essentially a permanent process of adaptation to changing realities.

I think everyone among us will agree that our international law must express the values that mankind – despite its division by economic, social and political and other kinds of differences – respects, and without any doubt there would be unanimity on such principles as the preservation of peace, self-determination of peoples, respect of human rights and so on. But is this enough to maintain and to develop an international legal order?

The famous *De jure belli ac pacis* of Grotius was based on three pillars: values and cases taken from the Greek, the Roman and the Hebraic tradition and literature. Grotius' followers in the 20th century have a bigger task and they have to make comparative inquiries and analyses on a much broader base taking into account – now that international law has become really universal – all social systems, cultures, nations, regions of the World with their positive legal rules, institutions, with their legal traditions. Specialists will soon discover a great number of common principles in the various legal systems, but they will eventually be disappointed in concluding that despite their similar appearances they have not the same meaning in their respective societies. The sociological approach can clarify the causes of the differences and can demonstrate when and where to we have to do with real identity, and also help to decode the meaning of far remote teachings.

What I advocate is the promotion of studies of a rather neglected field, the elaboration of a general sociology of international law. Of course it is a great task that only a generation of specialists from many countries can fulfill, but I think that UNITAR, the famous University of Uppsala and even our seminar can raise interest in this respect, encourage inquiries and in this way promote our common aim.

Tom J. Farer

What values have infused the international system during the past several decades?

At the level of formal international law, i.e. the level of governing elites, there has been one preeminent value:

To stabilize the State system (e.g. no more divisions of Poland et al.) and the tenure of reigning elites.

As a functional corollary, the system has worked to restrict foreign intervention, particularly the use of force.

But with one exception: Decolonization.

Query: Why did influential sectors within the colonialist States gradually accept this exception?

1. Intelligent conservatives had their own, distinctive reasons. In essence, they did their sums and concluded that the exercise of direct political control was an inefficient means for protecting economic and residual political interests. And the cost-benefit ratio would worsen as a progressively larger proportion of the colonized populations could be marshalled by local elites for acts of resistance.

2. "Liberals" (i.e. those persons more-or-less deeply invested with humanistic values) had very different reasons, although they no doubt accepted as accurate the pedestrian, amoral calculations of the conservatives. Liberals equated decolonization with heightened realization of human rights. Why?

Colonial government was authoritarian, hierarchic, anti-egalitarian.

Hierarchy reflected ascriptive characteristics (race, culture, etc.), not intrinsic merit (e.g. bureaucratic efficiency, integrity, commitment), *hence* the ablest local people could not aspire to the highest positions in colonial life.

Metropolitan governments were inevitably more responsive to the needs and preferences and prejudices of the population at the Imperial core. The more democratic the Imperial Government was in its home base the more insensitive it would have to be to the conflicting interests of colonized peoples (e.g. relatively poor voters in London were unlikely to applaud welfare expenditures in the colonies, expenditures benefiting people deemed alien and inferior).

As the acid of modernity ate away the passivity of the colonized peoples more and more ruthless methods of repression would be required.

The failure of the majority of decolonized societies to evolve along the democratic, pluralistic and relatively egalitarian lines envisioned by liberals has had at least two important consequences:

1. Disillusioned liberals have become skeptical about the possibility of enhancing human rights by means of the transfer of wealth to Third World governments.
2. Liberals (again, for the limited purpose of this intervention I use liberal and humanitarian interchangeably) are less inclined rigidly to oppose intervention and the use of force. Rather they are more inclined to consider on its case-by-case merits the argument that highly coercive intervention may be justified on humanitarian grounds.

Certain reasons why liberal exceptions were disappointed:

1. Post-colonial governing elites were likely to be more insecure than their predecessors.
2. Their experienced model of government was, as noted above, authoritarian and inegalitarian.
3. New elites would step into the institutional shoes of their predecessors.
4. Within the colonized society, there usually were a variety of ascriptive groups with little in common to offer than the experience of colonial domination. Colonial rulers had in many cases exploited and aggravated ethnic, tribal, racial and religious differences ("divide and rule").

Florentino P. Feliciano

Apropos the suggestion that humanistic values express the ultimate goals of law, domestic or international, it should be noted that there are differing conceptions of the nature of man and of the proper relationship of man to his fellow man, and of man to nature and to the universe. These varying conceptions embedded in the law and culture of distinct societies commonly contribute to differences in the specific interpretations of the requirements of humanistic values. We have often seen how the same verbal symbols used in the process of carrying out the same material operations, may result in different consequences for the value positions of persons and nations. Our hope is that agreement may be reached on prepositions concerning human rights which are relatively specific and which can be supported and implemented by most nations regardless of their differences in ideology or ultimate philosophy.

One may express the hope that Prof. Dimitrijević would comment on Ambassador Theutenberg's observation that "Eurocentric" international law had lost its original moral and/or religious moorings and needed to reestablish, as it were, contact with "higher values".

Suppression of Tyranny: A Feasible Task?

References:

7.4. Tom J. Farer 422
7.5. Issa Diallo 431

William Michael Reisman

I find the term "tyranny" too vague and subjective to be used as a legal standard for the appraisal of regimes in a multiculutral world with many different conceptions of authoritative power. I would recommend instead that governmental acts be tested for lawfulness against the basic international documents expressing human rights. They enjoy wide acceptance.

I must disagree with my friend Professor Franck with regard to his conception of humanitarian intervention. Law is authoritative power and all law is backed up by force. If one begins by saying that commitment to human rights notwithstanding coercion will never be used, violatives will ignore the protest. Of course, force should only be used *in extremis* and only if no other alternatives obtain.

Enoch Dumbutshena

My intervention is substantially in agreement with the substantive submissions so ably presented by Professor Tom Farer and Dr. Issa Diallo. There are however constraints in the suppression of tyranny by those countries which are capable of imposing sanctions on those governments which are tyrannic both in theory and in practice and which openly deny fundamental human rights to large sections of their own people. The constraints are brought about by the dictates of the law of necessity or ordinarily speaking self-interest.

It may, for instance, not be in the interest of the super powers, viz. the USA and the USSR, to impose sanctions against the Republic of South Africa because, in the case of the USSR, of some open or secret trade links with South Africa which are of greater importance to the Soviet Union than the imposition of sanctions against South Africa. And in the case of the United States, it may be because South Africa is of importance in its global military strategy and also because the whole of Southern Africa is rich in minerals and therefore of economic importance to the USA. These national self-interests may be more fundamental to these countries than the punishing of South Africa for infringing human rights.

One question of national self-interest supercedes, in some cases, the often openly proclaimed resolutions of the United Nations Assembly.

In the case of the Colony of Southern Rhodesia, now the independent Republic of Zimbabwe many members of the United Nations, big and small, traded with Rhodesia in an open violation of the United Nations imposed mandatory sanctions. Petroleum and petroleum products were shipped to Rhodesia, a country that had been declared an enemy of the international community because of its unilateral declaration of independence on 11 November 1965. Members of the United Nations turned a blind eye to the resolutions imposing sanctions because of national self-interest and in some instances out of greed. A lot will be revealed when the documents on sanctions are published.

These two cases are but some of the many instances and difficulties encountered by the international community in its attempts to make international law binding on each and every country. Until international lawyers find some method for imposing sanctions on those countries that contravene international law and universally accepted practices, there will always be open disregard of human rights and the practice of torture. I am afraid that in the international sense, the desire for military or political dominance or the fight for survival by the poorer States, will remain an incentive to the breaching of international law especially when it is clear that such breaches are not attended by sanctions.

Florentino P. Feliciano

(1) You will probably have substantial practical difficulties in determining when a government is pursuing a *deliberate policy* of violating human rights. It will be an inept government which reduces such a policy (if it is following one) to explicit pronouncements or written statements. In practice, in applying a hypothetical international legal norm prohibiting tyranny, it may become necessary to fall back upon a doctrine of command responsibility, the same doctrine under which Generals Yaarashita and Homma were hanged after World War II.

(2) Does the international community need a new and separate norm against tyranny? It may be well to consider whether the proposed convention against the use of torture, for instance, may be adequate, along with other conventions against specific violations of human rights. Such conventions commonly focus upon individuals, for instance, who apply torture; and to focus upon individuals rather than upon governments may be useful and often certainly advantageous. Thus, a government should be able to dissociate itself from the acts, perhaps unauthorized and unlawful under internal laws, of particular police or army officers and then to take action against the offending individuals.

(3) If the proposed legal norm against tyranny were to materialize, it may result in a difference in legal status between a revolutionary or rebel guerilla fighter who explodes a bomb in a cathedral killing a hundred persons and a police officer who applies torture to extract a confession from a respected rebel. The former would be a political offender, not subject to extradition, and probably able to claim refugee status. The latter would be guilty of a crime under international law or a crime against mankind and, under Prof. Farer's proposals, liable to prosecution and punishment wherever he might be found, under the principle of universality of jurisdiction over certain offenses. This difference in legal status would seem unreasonable and eccentric.

(4) The suggested convention against tyranny raises among others, a problem of determining who should properly be liable for tyranny under the convention. The Head of State? The Prime Minister? The Party Secretary? The Cabinet? The Minister of Police? Police Colonels? Army Captains? How far down the ladder of authority should such a convention be able to reach and for what particular purposes? Perhaps Prof. Farer might wish to comment on these questions.

J. N. Saxena

I would agree with Dr. Diallo's observation that the idea that State's is the only source of power to break the human rights is not correct. As such the suggestion of Prof. Farer that those (individuals or groups) who order torture (or other inhuman acts) should be subject to trial, may not be workable in every case, e.g. in India in spite of the fact that the Government is trying its best and there is legislation to that effect that bonded labour or intouchability is prohibited, quite some people still practice it and this can be eradicated more by social workers than legal sanction.

Sovereignty and Humanity: Can They Converge?

JUAN C. PUIG

I have really enjoyed Dr. Lillich's and Dr. Saito's papers and speeches and I must confess that I have learned a great deal from them. I agree in general with them, especially with Prof. Saito's approach to the matter of justice in international law.

I would only like to come to the rescue of Jean-Jacques Rousseau, and to the rescue of Argentines and Panamanians.

As to Rousseau, it is true that Rousseau considered sovereignty as an "absolute, sacred and inviolate" thing, because sovereignty of the people was for him a political liberal tool against the absolute will of the King. But when he takes up the matter of democracy he says quite a different thing.

I have been always fascinated by that chapter of the *Contract Social* where Rousseau explains, first, how the majority rule constitutes a democratic device through the fiction of the *volonté de tous* (the "will of the whole"). Before the assembly meets – he says, if I recall well – every participating member has anticipated his vote in favour of what the majority will decide, and therefore, the majority will express the will of the whole *(la volonté de tous)*. But, after having said that, he continues his reasoning on the true meaning of the *volonté de tous* and, as a conclusion, he says that sometimes the *volonté de tous* does not reflect the *volonté générale* (the "general will") of the people.

How is it that the will of the whole does not reflect the general will? In my opinion, following Goldschmidt's remarks on the subject, there is only one possible answer. It seems to me that the "general will" expresses the "just" will and that is why, even in Rousseau's reasoning, sometimes the "*volonté de tous*", that is to say, the sovereignty of the people, could be unjust and hence could not reflect the "*volonté générale*". Sovereignty of the people is still not absolute from a democratic point of view, but submitted to justice. The Rousseaunian approach to sovereignty, thus, has much to do with the actual problems of life and death of humankind.

As to Argentines and Panamanians, I should say that for them sovereignty is not something vague, something floating above all of the mundane day-to-day issues. It is a formidable normative tool. But this is not a capricious standing: it derives from international law.

Leaving aside sociological and dikelogical considerations (I have already talked of them in this seminar), from the normative point ov view, we all know that after the famous ruling in the *Lotus* case, sovereignty means that a State is permitted to do under the law everything except what is expressly prohibited by the Law of Nations. Once you have said that a State is sovereign in a particular region or in a particular subject, there is nothing to be added from a normative angle. You are permitted to do anything but not what has been expressly prohibited. And this is of course a very important issue when the interpretation of a treaty is at stake.

Autonomy, on the contrary, is a status regulated by national law. So, autonomous entities could do only what is expressly permitted to them. That makes the difference, from the normative standpoint and that explains, too, why the Argentines are so eager to grant autonomy and so excited about acquiring sovereignty.

Rudolf Dolzer

I should like to congratulate the two rapporteurs for their inspiring presentations. My main comment, however, relates to the direction which the discussion has taken. I feel that the interventions so far made do not fully reflect the attitudes which have been expressed in the earlier reports and discussions of the Conference.

More specifically, I agree with Prof. Lillich when he suggests that the topic of this session could well serve as the background upon which all or most other subjects areas covered in the Seminar could be viewed. Thus, it would not appear particularly helpful strictly to confine the discussion to the existing dominating role of national sovereignty in international relations. One may not agree with the two rapporteurs in every detail concerning the degree to which sovereignty could or should be given up in the future; so far, no other unit than the State has emerged which can effectively guarantee the security and well-being of the peoples. Nevertheless, it will also be recognized that the progress made in international law in the past decades toward a more peaceful and just world order has only been possible due to the fact that States have gradually given up their sovereign rights in important areas. The prohibition of the use of force was the most striking example. In the area of human rights and the treatment of aliens, the progress made has eroded the traditional rights of States to act solely on the basis of the will of existing governments. Also, the acceptance of the juridical settlement of disputes by international courts and tribunals has only been possible where States have been willing to renounce unilateral modes of solving problems. Finally, inasmuch as any change has occurred in the international economic order, this has been due to the fact that States have in fact recognized the existing interdependence and the obstacles which might be posed in the future in case States would insist on their sovereign rights in the economic area. Viewed in context, all these developments illustrate the fact that the concept of sovereignty will have to be at the center of future deliberations on an improved world order. It is true that there is no clear indication that all States are at present willing to consider changes in international relations involving a partial abandonment of sovereign rights, and it is therefore essential for a progressive world order that the trend of the past decades to reconsider the importance and the implications of absolute sovereignty, should be emphasized and strengthened rather than ignored in international legal thinking.

Geza Herczegh

I have to congratulate Professor Lillich and Professor Saito for their outstanding reports even if I can hardly agree with what they said on the relevance of sovereignty of States. Since my youth I have read countless numbers of books and papers stating that State sovereignty is the source of all kinds of cost, the main obstacle of an efficient international legal order and even its notion is obsolete, a remnant of a bygone age. But what can we see? The sovereignty of States resisted quite well the attacks of the theorists and despite their concentrated and seemingly convincing arguments its legal and political importance has not diminished during the last fifty years. There is a reality behind this notion, the division of States by economic, social, political and other factors. What is good for one country is not necessarily also good for others and it is quite impossible to regulate the details of human relations by a unique legal system all over the world. State sovereignty is not good or bad in itself, but it is the necessary,the inevitable consequence of the factual diversity of mankind. We have to accept it and to live with it as long as its social, economic and political foundations will exist. Some among us would qualify my approach as traditionalistic, I would rather call it a realistic one.

Richard B. Lillich

I should like to direct my comments to the remarks of Prof. Herczegh, who if I heard him correctly made these points:

1. State sovereignty has not lessened at all during recent decades; 2. it is impossible for the international community to legislate in any detail since there are so many different social systems among States; and 3. the traditional approach to State sovereignty is the realistic approach to international law. I believe he is absolutely wrong on the first two points and certainly reveals an unnecessary acceptance of the *status quo* on the third.

In the first place we have heard from Judge Lachs and many other speakers at this conference countless instances when States – generally voluntarily but often involuntarily – have relinquished sovereignty in many areas. I gave numerous examples in my group, and Dr. Dolzer has furnished us with additional examples in the discussion. Thus it is simply impossible for anyone today to contend seriously that State sovereignty is still what it was before the United Nations Charter.

Secondly international legislation, even when spelled out in detail, is not impossible for the international community to prescribe when there is consensus underlying the norm being spelled out. The ICAO convention and regulations thereunder are detailed and yet no State objects to all of its sovereignty thereunder. The international norm against torture, first mentioned in the Universal Declaration and now a part of customary international law, is a detailed prescription that undoubtedly will be further clarified when the UN finally adopts its Convention Against Torture. No State that I know of argues that a provision of the draft convention is too detailed for adoption and application by States.

Obiously, where there are divergencies of opinion about a particular norm the chances of international legalization are more remote but the fact that a norm is spelled out in some detail does not necessarily hinder its adoption with the consequent impingement upon the sovereignty of States.

Finally, in view of the abuse of sovereignty well known to us all and the criticism of the State system manifested directly and indirectly at this conference, are we really so satisfied with the *status quo* that we regard the traditional approach to be any longer a realistic approach? I doubt it, if by "realistic" we mean an approach which will provide both the international and internal distributive justice we have talked about this past week. The present interventional system, like the federal system in the United States which left wider power to the various States, has been tried and found wanting. For the foreseeable future nation States under the rubric of State sovereignty, will contrive to have wider power of action, but the trend is towards the "nibbling away" of these facilities and eventually as Prof. Reisman has suggested towards a world order system in which various groupings of States – or regions – would have wider autonomy on many matters but far less sovereignty than States have today. As we grope towards such a régime, one should bear in mind that sovereignty is a flexible and not an absolute concept, and that in an international language one should seek to use it only to guarantee the basic rights and satisfy the basic needs of humantiy.

VIII. International Organisation for a New World Order

Working Group IV

8.1. New Ways for Treaty-Making and International Legislation

Geraldo E. do Nascimento e Silva

1. Introductory remarks

At the 35th Session of the General Assembly of the United Nations the question of the "Review of the Mulilateral Treaty-Making Process" was studied by the 6th Committee, where the question had been initially brought up. As a result of the discussions which were held, a resolution was adopted on 15 December 1980, in which, *inter alia*, the General Assembly requested the Secretary-General to "make his report and its addenda widely available to the interested organizations which are active in the preparation and study of multilateral treaties, and to invite them to comment on the subject of the report".

In other words, JUS 81 is faced with a very positive question and not with an academic one and should give its collaboration on the subject to the world community.

This task comes at a particularly fortunate moment, and the observations of Judge Manfred Lachs also apply to this problem: "This is a timely mission at a period when international law is being subjected to challenge from so many quarters, when its very existence is being questioned not only by laymen but even by some lawyers, and when its relevance to international relations and to the regulation of concrete problems between States is constantly belittled."

Thus, JUS 81 is in a position to "provide a chance for a reassessment of our situation and perhaps a modest beginning for a new and very necessary more constructive multilogue" on this subject. One should therefore try to establish before 31 July 1981 some guide-lines, taking into account the question raised in Section 4 of the report of the Secretary-General on the subject (Doc. A/35/312).

Even though we should emphasize the question on the elaboration of multilateral treaties by United Nations and other members of the United Nations family, it must be pointed out that the theme, as raised in our programme has a wider scope: it does not limit the problem to multilateral treaties and also mentions the questions related to international legislation.

We should also study the treaty-making process of other international organizations such as the Organizations of American States which began as far back as 1902 the codification of international law, following up a suggestion made by the Brazilian Delegate José Hygino. However, I feel that we should limit ourselves to the United Nations approach to the question.

2. Overall approach of the subject by JUS 81

In order to link this paper with the overall philosophy of the Seminar, I feel that some preliminary remarks are in order. A lot of emphasis is being placed on the role of the so-called new-States, whose history, in many cases, can be traced to a pre-Christian era. With the acceptance of these new States by the United Nations, there occurred a change in the geography of international law, i.e. the necessity of making it really universal. In many cases, the legal background of these States had developed prior to that of the European nations. As Ambassador Bo Johnson Theutenberg points out, "we must also remember that in the past law and religion were one and the same. Religion shaped and sanctioned the law."

3. Universalism and regionalism

If we accept the idea that this international law of non-European nations exist, we are faced by another problem raised by JUS 81, namely the existence of a universal international law in contrast to regional international law. In other words should we admit the possibility of conflicting rules of international law. In our view, certain principles accepted in a given region and which are not in harmony with international law as understood by scholars, should be placed under the heading "international policy". The existence of an American (or Latin American) international law distinct from European international law was the object of controversy in South America, where the opinion that finally prevailed was that the civilized world must recognize the same supreme rules of justice and the same essential or fundamental juridical principles. However there is no doubt that in certain geographical regions, social and economic circumstances, or even political circumstances, may induce to the adoption of certain particular rules for that region. But these rules cannot be contrary to general or universal international law.

International law which was accepted before World War II was of European inception and in most cases coincided with the political and economical interests of European States. The birth of so many new States, especially after the sixties, brought in its wake an over-reaction by many of them, aimed at a recognition of their legal systems which were systematically condemned until World War I by most European jurists and States, which placed emphasis on the law of civilized nations. This idea was even endorsed by the Statute of the Permanent Court of International Justice and was maintained in that of the International Court of Justice under Article 38, that one shall apply "the general principles of law recognized by civilized nations". This reference to *civilized nations* is an anachronism and takes us back to a period that precedes the First World War when international law was of Western European inspiration. If we consider the spirit which prevails in the United Nations in favour of the independence of all non-governing territories, the limitation is completely out of place. The phrase *civilized nations* originally was meant to exclude the application of the general rules of certain nations which at present are part of the United Nations family. In other words, the general rules of law which exist in a State member of the United Nations must be deemed as acceptable by the Court and in those very few territories which do not possess an international statute it is doubtful if such a thing as general rules of law exist.

4. Bi-lateral treaty-making process

The United Nations' aim is to review the multilateral treaty-making process, but the theme placed on our programme has a wider scope. The bi-lateral treaty-making process is equally complex and also places a burden on Governments, their legal advisers and on the Parliament of those countries where every treaty is subject to approval.

When we consider that there are at present more than 150 countries in the world, all of them with capacity to sign treaties, we realize the incredible network of treaties which must be enacted. In the case of extradition, to quote an example, many countries only grant it if they are bound to do so by a valid treaty. The result of such a policy is that the number of havens for criminals and even terrorists is on the increase. In the present situation, the ideal solution is the liberal approach adopted by some countries that grant extradition as long as a declaration of reciprocity is forthcoming.

Since treaties can be signed on such a variety of subjects and with so many countries, the recourse to multilateral treaties remains the ideal solution, especially for smaller nations that do not dispose of qualified experts in all the fields.

In the case of extradition, to return to the previous example, the Hague Convention for Suppression of Unlawful Seizure of Aircraft, of 7 December 1970, contains in Article 8 sensible rules aimed at getting around this difficulty: 1. The offence shall be deemed to be included as an extraditable offence in any extradition treaty existing between Contracting States. Contracting States undertake to include the offence as an extraditable offence in every extradition treaty to be concluded between them. 2. If a contracting State which makes extradition conditional on the existence of a treaty receives a request for extradition from another Contracting State with which it has no extradition treaty, it may at its option consider this Convention as the legal basis for extradition in respect of the offence. Extradition shall be subject to the other conditions provided by the law of the requested State."

5. Multilateral treaty-making process

The innumerous multilateral treaties signed under the aegis of the United Nations play a dual role: not only do they contribute to the progressive development of international law and its codification, but they also give the new emerging nations an opportunity to participate in the elaboration of conventions which they consider to be of European inception. Those delegates who had the opportunity to accompany the international conferences held in Vienna, especially those on diplomatic relations, consular relations and the law of treaties, were able to appreciate the work of the representatives of some of these new countries. Their proposals and amendments to the ILC draft and the apposition of their signatures to the conventions finally drafted, transformed, in a certain sense, those rules into really universal rules of international law. In most cases, however, we are forced to admit that the texts which were sanctioned follow very closely classical international law.

But the fact remains that the proliferation of multilateral treaties has become a very serious problem to the community of State and one can state that the avalanche of treaties and proposals is more than it can digest.

The work load is enormous and the costs involved in certain conferences are draining the financial resources not only of the United Nations but also of member States.

Faced by this problem, the Sixth Committee of the General Assembly deems it advisable that the United Nations carry out a review of the many methods of multilateral treaty-making, especially with a view to determining whether the methods employed are as efficient and economical as the needs of the world community require and circumstances permit.

The General Assembly adopted, on 15 December 1980, a resolution in which it invited not only governments and international and inter-governmental organizations to submit their observations to the questionnaire submitted by the Secretary-General (annexed to this Report), but also invited other organisations to do likewise.

In the opinion of the rapporteur, additional study should be made. There is no doubt that the work of treaty-making is a heavy one; that the elaboration of certain treaties could be postponed in order to avoid overlapping; that the General Assembly could create a body to coordinate the treaty-making activity, setting out priorities; that the responsibility of the ILC in this field could be increased.

Be it as it may, the United Nations in going about this problem must act with extreme caution in order to avoid the creation of yet another body which might, in the long run, hinder what is being done.

6. *Other forms of international legislation*

At the present stage, treaties are the principal source of international laws, since among other qualities, they determine in a clear or in a relatively clear manner the rights and duties of States which ratified them.

The value of treaties is such that Paul de Visscher, a staunch defender of Custom, comments that it may seem out of place in today's international law. But Custom still plays an important role, especially when transplanted to a resolution dealing with a specific problem of international law. The question of *resolutions* is one of the most complex with which international lawyers have had to deal with. However, I feel that a correct approach to the value of resolutions or recommendations can be reduced to two situations.

If a recommendation embodies a rule of international law already considered as such (and we return here to the continuing importance of Custom), it means that the United Nations is merely recognizing it officially. In this case the rule of international law stands, even though resolutions are not considered obligatory. If on the other hand no rule of international law exists on the subject matter, the recommendation is not obligatory. In this case, a resolution may exert a certain political pressure on member-States and play an important role acting *de lege ferenda* when it establishes guide-lines for new juridical problems.

The General Assembly has on more than one occasion enunciated future law and the recent "Charter of Economic Rights and Duties of States" is a good example.

In resolution 1721 (XXI), the General Assembly commends to States "for their guidance and exploration and use of outer space" certain principles. Two years later, acting *de lege ferenda*, it proclaimed their legal value. This cycle was completed by the treaty on the "Principles Governing the Activities of States in the Exploration and Use of Outer Space, including the Moon and other Celestial Bodies".

The United Nations Conference on the Human Environment held in Stockholm in 1972 is another important example. The Declaration which was adopted then embodies certain principles which were already *de lege lata* and others that were *de lege ferenda*. Some of these principles have already been incorporated into various international treaties, as in the case of the pollution of the sea; others are acquiring international standing, others continue to be wishful thinking.

I feel that those doubts which existed as to whether a declaration is the right kind of instrument to embody rules of international law should be considered a thing of the past. We must find new ways to render international law more precise and to try to utilize all the instruments at our disposal, ignoring past restrictions.

7. Conclusions

It is not our aim to answer here the Secretary-General's questionnaire on the treaty-making processes, and it will be otiose to tread on the ground already covered by his report; we shall simply put forth some suggestions on the subject as well as on the use of resolutions.

The treaty-making process is chaotic. The initiative can be in a number of different ways; the procedure varies from the careful approach we find in the International Law Commission to efforts aimed at creating instant international law; important subjects are put aside in favour of others which at a given moment are important; other subjects which are not ripe for codification are, with the positive vote of member States, the object of protracted and extensive international conferences.

The Secretariat of the United Nations should draw up a list of subjects which could be codified, mentioning the body that should be charged with the task. In the case of matters exclusively within the domain of international law, the International Law Commission should be the competent body. In order to abbreviate the work, the International Law Commission could establish three or four working groups whose decisions would be approved by the International Law Commission in full.

Other subjects of scientific or technical nature could be entrusted to the specialized agencies that have already given proof of their capacity in this field.

In certain cases the international community should adopt a less ambitious approach and suggest a mere restatement of the law or a code as was suggested by

Sir Gerald G. Fitzmaurice with regard to the Law of Treaties. In this case, it would suffice to draw up a code of a given subject, in which the difficulties could not be summarized in a few sentences, which could be more explicit.

A draft prepared by the International Law Commission, UNCITRAL, *ad hoc* committees or one of the specialized agencies should be submitted to the General Assembly, which would then present it in the form of a Declaration, which could be *de lege lata, de lege ferenda* or a combination of both.

Unfortunately, the value of United Nations resolutions has been undermined, and the democratic principles which are followed in most parliamentary systems, by which a vote of the majority is accepted by the minority, is simply ignored by some States which in the domestic scene are staunch defenders of the democratic process. Even though the rule *pacta sunt servanda,* enshrined in the UN Charter and in Article 26 of the Convention on the Law of Treaties is aimed at treaties, we feel that it is valid in international relations and in the case of the United Nations resolutions that they should be performed in good faith.

Annex

Questionnaire of the Secretary-General of the United Nations on the review of the multilateral treaty-making process

(UN document A/35/312: Excerpts)

IV. Questions to be considered

63. Taking into account the above-mentioned and other examples of treaty-making practices, the observations of Governments and of the International Law Commission, it is suggested that the Sixth Committee might address itself to some or all of the following questions raised therein:

A. *Additional studies*

1. Should an attempt be made to solicit additional responses from intergovernmental organizations that did not respond or that did not respond in sufficient detail to the Secretary-General's first request?
2. Should the responses of intergovernmental organizations be published in some form, perhaps in a separate volume of the *Legislative Series* (in which other documentation relevant to this item might also be included)?
3. Should the Secretariat prepare a detailed description of all significant multilateral treaty-making techniques, perhaps in the form of an annotated manual?
4. Should the Secretariat assist in the formulation of the formal clauses of multilateral treaties by:
   (a) Updating the *Handbook of Final Clauses* and extending it to additional categories of formal clauses?
   (b) Formulating sets of model clauses?

B. *Over-all burden of multilateral treaty-making process*

1. Is the burden of the treaty-making process too great for:
   (a) The personnel that States can make available to participate in expert and representative organs?
   (b) The personnel and budgets of the intergovernmental organizations concerned?
   (c) The domestic legal resources of States that must consider the ratification of duly formulated treaties?

2. To the extent that the burden of the current treaty-making process cannot be reduced through making it more efficient, should the international community seek:
   (a) To reduce the number of treaties being formulated (i.e. should the formulation of certain treaties be postponed temporarily or indefinitely) by setting priorities?
   (b) To increase the resources available, nationally and internationally as required, for multilateral treaty-making?

C. *Over-all co-ordination of multilateral treaty-making*
1. Should the General Assembly assume a co-ordinating role in respect of multilateral treaty-making activities of:
   (a) All United Nations organs?
   (b) All organizations of the United Nations system?
   (c) All intergovernmental organizations?
2. Should such a co-ordinating role by the General Assembly be:
   (a) Restricted to the gathering and dissemination of data about all treaty-making activities within the sphere specified under C.1 above?
   (b) Extended to influencing, through decisions in respect of United Nations organs and through recommendations addressed to other intergovernmental organizations, the treaty-making process, such as by proposing subjects to be considered and identifying the organs or organizations most suitable to do so?
3. If such functions are to be exercised by the General Assembly, should this most suitably be done through the Sixth Committee?

D. *General improvements of the treaty-making process in the United Nations*
1. Before embarking on the formulation of a particular treaty should more extensive efforts be made, in general, to:
   (a) Collect legal and factual data relevant to the proposed treaty?
   (b) Ascertain the potential interest of States in the proposed treaty?
   (c) Consider the utility of some less binding instrument (e.g., a declaration)?
2. Should the preliminary formulation of the text of a treaty generally or in respect of certain categories be entrusted to:
   (a) A representative organ?
   (b) An expert organ?
   (c) The Secretariat?
3. Should an effort be made to reduce the number of treaty-making organs and procedures in the United Nations by concentrating them?
4. Should an effort be made to achieve in some or all treaty-making organs and procedures a more structured approach, aiming at completing some or all steps of the process within specified periods of time? To what fields might such an approach most profitably be applied?

E. *Work of the International Law Commission*
1. Possible structural changes
   (a) Should the ILC be converted into a full-time organ, whose members would be appropriately remunerated?
   (b) Should the honorarium or the *per diem* of ILC members be increased?
   (c) Should the Special Rapporteurs work and be remunerated on a full-time basis?
   (d) Should Special Rapporteurs occasionally be drawn from outside the Commission?
   (e) Should the Special Rapporteurs be supported by experts working under their direction on a full-time basis?
2. Possible changes in agenda
   (a) Should certain questions not be referred to the ILC or should certain additional questions be referred to it?

(b) Should the ILC have a heavier or a lighter agenda?
(c) Should the ILC concentrate more on specific topics, restricted in scope, that may constitute only part of a larger subject area?

3. Possible procedural changes
(a) Should the ILC make more of an attempt to complete all its work on each subject within the five-year term for which its members are elected?
(b) Should Governments be consulted more or less frequently during the progress of work by the ILC on a particular draft?
(c) Should there be working groups that meet intersessionally – with perhaps a reduction in the length of Commission sessions?
(d) Should the ILC formulate preambles and final clauses for the draft articles it submits to the General Assembly?
(e) Should the ILC prepare alternative texts of particularly controversial provisions?
(f) Should the ILC consider the possibility of "restating" areas of customary international law as an alternative to codification?
(g) Should the ILC consider drafting texts for instruments other than treaties?

F. *Final negotiation and adoption of multilateral treaties*

1. Should the negotiation of multilateral treaties of concern to the General Assembly, such as those emanating from the ILC or UNCITRAL, normally be completed in a Main Committee of the General Assembly, or is it preferable to convene *ad hoc* plenipotentiary conferences?
2. If negotiations are normally to be completed in the General Assembly:
(a) Will it be necessary or desirable to extend the preliminary preparatory stage so as to submit to the Assembly more nearly completed texts?
(b) Should special procedural rules be adopted to assist the Assembly in acting as a treaty-formulating organ, e.g., providing for the participation of non-member States, special voting procedures, the establishment of drafting committees, etc.?
(c) Should the Sixth Commitee normally be involved in such a process, even if the substance of the treaty is considered by some other Main Committee (e.g., disarmament in the First Committee; economic relations in the Second; human rights in the Third):
(i) Through joint meetings of the Sixth with other Main Committees?
(ii) Through the consideration of all formal and legal clauses by the Sixth Committee?
(iii) Through the review of the text as a whole by the Sixth Committee?
3. To the extent the completion of multilateral treaties is assigned to plenipotentiary conferences:
(a) Should such conferences be scheduled for longer periods, to make it less likely that additional sessions would need to be convened, or does a series of successive sessions enable preparation of a better text supported by a broader consensus?
(b) Should uniform or model rules of procedure be established for such conferences?
(c) Should such rules provide for the establishment of negotiating committees?
(d) Should there be intersessional meetings of certain conference bodies (negotiating or drafting committees)?
(e) Should formal debate at conferences be restricted as much as possible to group spokesmen?
(f) Should there be provision for more extensive participation of intergovernmental and non-governmental organizations at plenipotentiary conferences?

G. *Drafting and languages*

1. Should an international legislative drafting bureau be created?
2. Should drafting committees generally be given more extensive functions?
3. Should treaties continue to be formulated simultaneously in all languages in which their text is to be authentic, or should they originally be formulated in only one or two languages, with additional versions established by a special procedure later?
4. If negotiation in multiple languages is to continue, should the example of the Third United Nations Conference of the Law of the Sea be followed, of establishing a subgroup for each language, whose co-ordinators meet from time to time to resolve any interlingual and general questions about the text?

H. *Records, reports and commentaries*

1. To what extent should verbatim or summary records be maintained by organs formulating multilateral treaties:
   (a) Expert groups?
   (b) Restricted representative groups?
   (c) Various organs of plenipotentiary conferences:
      (i) Main committees?
      (ii) Negotiating committees?
      (iii) Drafting committees?
2. Whether verbatim or summary records are kept and especially if they are not, should certain organs and conferences prepare more complete records of their negotiations, indicating various positions taken and the reasons for changes in the text? Who should prepare such reports?
3. Should commentaries normally be prepared on draft treaty texts formulated:
   (a) By expert groups?
   (b) By representative organs?
4. Should a systematic effort be made to prepare and publish the *travaux préparatoires* of most or all multilateral treaties? If so, should this primarily be done by:
   (a) The secretariat unit concerned?
   (b) UNITAR?

I. *Post-adoption procedures*

1. Should the United Nations consider and take any action in respect of the procedures by individual States to ratify and bring into force multilateral treaties formulated under its auspices?
2. Should a questionnaire be addressed to States as to why they fail to become parties to multilateral treaties?
3. Should the United Nations seek to establish a legal régime, following the example of some intergovernmental organizations, under which it could require:
   (a) A commitment from each Member State that it will submit treaties to the appropriate domestic organs with a view to authorizing ratification?
   (b) Periodic reports concerning the steps taken towards ratification?
4. Should special rapporteurs or other experts who helped in negotiating a treaty be made available to assist States with their internal ratification procedure?
5. Should an attempt be made, in respect of certain categories of treaties, to provide for their automatic entry into force except in respect of States that voted against adoption or that submit an opting-out notice?
6. Should treaties or certain categories of treaties normally provide for provisional entry into force, at least among those States that voted for their adoption and that do not submit an opting-out notice?

J. *Treaty-amending procedures*

1. Should certain categories of treaties provide for simplified forms of amendments?

2. Should certain categories of treaties provide for automatic supersession in respect of States parties that later become parties to other treaties in respect of the same subject?
3. Should greater use be made of framework treaties, whose substantive provisions are set out in separate annexes that may be adopted or changed by an organ established by the treaty or by the organization that promulgated it?

8.2. The Charter Review: Some Reflections on Concepts and Trends

NABIL A. ELARABY

I. San Francisco revisited: failure to carry out key Charter concepts

When the Charter of the United Nations was being drafted at San Francisco in 1945, it was generally believed that the wartime alliance would continue to function in peacetime. An attempt was made to introduce an effective and credible international collective security system. To provide this new machinery with a fair chance to function properly the Charter emphasized the political rather than the legal approach to the problem of preserving world peace.[1] The maintenance of international peace and security was therefore entrusted to the Security Council which was empowered to unleash the collective security system with the concurrence of Five Permanent Members.[2] Post World War II developments, however, did not conform to the San Francisco expectations. Cold war rivalry resulted in deep-seated suspicions that in turn made agreements on many crucial aspects of the collective security system within the realm of the unattainable. As the late Secretary-General U Thant once pertinently remarked:

> "The Chapter VII arrangement had been designed with Manchuria and the Nazi and Fascist aggressions of the 1930's especially in mind, for situations where aggressors could be easily identified and where the "good guys" of the international world would have no moral doubts about collectively fighting the "bad guys". But the situation that has prevailed since World War II defied such simplifications. It is worth remembering that United Nations enforcement measures were actually suggested as early as 1948 when war broke out in the Middle East. But this suggestion quickly lapsed when it was found impossible to answer even the simplest questions about such a United Nations force. Which way, by what criteria and at whom would it shoot, and who would give the command to shoot? On what ground would the force take its stand? What countries, indeed, would be prepared to lend their soldiers to such a force in such a situation?"[3]

When the Security Council was rendered inactive due to the aforementioned considerations, a basic Charter postulate crumbled, and the whole UN system

1 Art. 1, para. 1.
2 Chapter, V, in particular Articles 24 and 27.
3 Secretary-General U Thant, United Nations Press Release SG/SM/1177, 28 October 1969.

had to undergo far-reaching transformations. Member States searched for new relationships under the Charter provisions.

The historical account of the attempts to provide the UN with the military might required to discharge its Charter responsibilities, is beyond the scope of this paper.[4] The point to be emphasized, however, is that since its inception the UN was unable to maintain international peace and security through taking the effective collective measures referred to in Article 1 and outlined in Chapter VII.[5]

The experience of the last three decades have provided ample confirmation that the original concepts and perceptions that prevailed at San Francisco would continue to be elusive. Today's world power structure and pattern of inter-State conduct promises to continue the trends that have impeded the realization and development of the original intent of the UN founding fathers.

The question thus arises whether it has become imperative to strive for Charter review. The purpose of this paper is to examine the attitude of the UN membership towards Charter review. Its scope does not go beyond assessing the feasibility of a formal Charter review at the present time. The consideration of the various dimensions of this issue require an examination of some of the most salient developments that affected the constitutional evolution of the UN and have ushered subtle improvisations that, in a sense, amount to an informal review of the Charter.

II. Is a Charter review a feasible proposition?

To begin with it might be appropriate to recall that the Charter provides that if no attempt to convene a general Conference of UN members for the purpose of reviewing the Charter is made before the tenth annual session of the General Assembly, "the proposal to call such a Conference shall be placed on the Agenda of that session of the General Assembly and the Conference shall be held if so decided by a majority vote of the members of the General Assembly and by a vote of any seven members of the Security Council."[6] Thus the Charter expressly provides for, and even encourages, Charter review. A Charter review, however, is fraught with unknown consequences. The insurmountable obstacle will be securing the approval of the Security Council's five permanent members, each of whom enjoys a veto power over the Organization's decisions to amend the Charter. Though these five members cannot prevent the convening of a general conference for Charter review, each of them has the power and authority, under

4 Cf. Seyersted, Finn, *United Nations Forces in the law of peace and war*. Leyden, A. W. Sijthoff, 1966. 447 p.

5 Article 1, paragraph 1, states "To maintain international peace and security, and to that end: to take effective collective measures for the prevention and removal of threats to the peace, and for the suppression of acts of aggression or other breaches of the peace."
Chapter VII entlitled "Action with respect to threats to the peace, breaches of the peace and acts of aggression" spells out in detail how the collective security system was to function.

6 Article 109, para. 3.

the Charter, to block the adoption of amendments to the Charter. Thus the so–called "unanimity rule" bodes ill for the prospect of meaningful amendments to the Charter.

So far no–one can detect the emergence of a consensus, or even a significant trend in favour of a general conference for the purpose of changing the existing UN system.[7] It is submitted that the reluctance of States to espouse this cause is based on a realistic assessment that at least one of the five permanent members will oppose any proposed change. This however has not prevented member States from seriously examining the nature, scope and dimensions of changes. Indeed the General Assembly has, as a consequence, established several subsidiary organs to explore ways and means to improve and strengthen the United Nations discharge of its responsibilities in the maintenance of international peace and security. So far the area of international peace and security has figured highly on the General Assembly's priorities in establishing Committees whose mandate encompassed issues relevant to improving the Charter system. However, it cannot be said that the members of these subsidiary organs have favoured amending the Charter. It should nevertheless be borne in mind that the consideration in such subsidiary organs of matters pertaining to improving the UN system and enhancing the effecitiveness of the Organization, could, in due course, create an irresistable momentum to undertake such a review. It is moreover submitted that the annual mushrooming of resolutions pertaining to the maintenance of international peace and security is concrete evidence of a genuine conviction to consider reforming the existing system. A relevant example would be the item entitled "The strengthening of international security" which was inscribed in 1969 on the Agenda of the General Assembly.[8] Each year the General Assembly goes through the ritual of adopting an omnibus resolution on the subject. Last year's resolution referred in clear terms to the fact that "the Security Council increasingly has not been able to act in accordance with its mandate under the Charter".[9] Another relevant example is the establishment of the Special Committee on the Charter of the UN and the Strengthening of the Role of the Organization. Following the consideration of the report of the Special Committee, the General Assembly adopted a resolution, which requested the Special Committee, *inter alia*, "to accord priority to its work on the proposals regarding the question of the maintenance of peace and security, with a view to listing and examining all proposals, including those relating to the *functioning of the Security Council*,"[10]

7 6th Summit Conference of the Heads of State and Government of the Non-Aligned Movement that met in Havana, Cuba in 1979 adopted resolution no. 7 which called on the non-aligned countries to participate "actively in the efforts to amend the Charter of the United Nations, particularly its provisions relating to the right of veto . . ." Document A/34/542 dated 11 October 1979, page 188. Non-aligned States, however, have not adopted a uniform position on this matter in the UN.

8 The USSR proposed the inscription.

9 Resolution 35/158 adopted on 12 December 1980.

10 Resolution 35/164 adopted on 15 December 1980 (emphasis added). The proposals relating to the functioning of the Council will be discussed and analysed later.

It should not, therefore, be ruled out that sooner than generally expected it would become inevitable to examine how the UN handles its primary responsibility to preserve world peace. The creation of such Committees confirm that the system requires if not radical changes, then at least major improvements. Hence the real issue which should be addressed becomes whether a Charter review is feasible and not whether it is necessary.

On the basis of the adamant and forceful opposition from some permanent members, it would seem rather far–fetched to entertain, in the not so distant future, the possibility of convening the General Conference referred to in Article 109 para. (3).[11] A modest starting point seems to be the convening of a Special Session of the General Assembly to be devoted to a comprehensive examination of all the dimensions of the maintenance of international peace and security including the increased non–compliance with UN resolutions.[12]

The General Assembly could thus serve as a clearing house for the evaluation of the feasibility of pursuing a formal Charter review. The thrust of engaging the General Assembly in such a comprehensive examination is to provide clear evidence of the real intention of the UN membership before embarking on the course prescribed by the Charter, namely, formal amendment. Such a course will also offer an opportunity to undertake the studies necessary to form the drafting of the required reforms.

Difficult as the obstacles may be, there are many who believe that Charter amendment is necessary. For example, Richard Hudson of the Center for War/Peace Studies has made proposals for amendments to Articles 18 and 13, which he believes would enable the UN to cope far more effectively not only with peace and security questions, but all other global issues as well.[13]

11 Article 109 (3) states that "If such a conference has not been held before the tenth annual session of the General Assembly following the coming into force of the present Charter, the proposal to call such a conference shall be placed on the agenda of that session of the General Assembly, and the conference shall be held if so decided by a majority vote of the members of the General Assembly and by a vote of any seven members of the Security Council."

12 The Foreign Minister of Egypt proposed last year that this matter should be considered: A/35/PV.16 of 30 September 1980.

13 His two amendments, which he calls the Bind Triad, are: – Article 18, which establishes the one nation, one vote system for the General Assembly, would have its key sentence changed to read: "Decisions of the General Assembly on important questions shall be made by a two-thirds majority including members representing a two-thirds majority of the population of the members present and voting, and including members representing a two-thirds majority of the contributions to the regular Organization budget of the members present and voting." – Article 13, which states that the General Assembly "shall initiate studies and make recommendations", would be changed to begin: "The General Assembly shall have the power to enact binding resolutions, to be interpreted if necessary by the International Court of Justice, and to be overseen and carried out if necessary be peace-keeping units . . ." – Other changes declare that the General Assembly cannot adopt binding decisions that would "intervene in matters which are essentially within the domestic jurisdiction of any State" and cannot "have

III. The development of new trends and concepts

It is now proposed to examine the development of some newly emerged trends and concepts that have a direct bearing on the constitutional process of the UN. It is worth noting that, in general, the origin of these trends and concepts could always be traced to the inability of the Security Council to function properly in accordance with the Charter provisions.

The shortcomings and failures of the UN have triggered a variety of responses. During an earlier period attempts were made to circumvent the oft-abused veto power. The frequent use of the veto to abort action by the Security Council necessitated the exploration of other means by which the UN would maintain world peace. The most notable, and still most controversial of these devices was General Assembly resolution 377(V) entitled "Uniting For Peace". In that resolution the General Assembly, at the behest of the US, resolved "that if the Security Council, because of lack of unanimity of the permanent members, fails to exercise its primary responsibility for the maintenance of international peace and security in any case where there appears to be a threat to the peace, breach of the peace or act of aggression, the General Assembly shall consider the matter immediately with a view to making appropriate recommendations to members for collective measures, including in the case of a breach of the peace or act of aggression the use of armed force when necessary, to maintain or restore international peace and security."[14]

The rationale for adopting that resolution was to provide an alternative source to authorize UN action when the Security Council is unable to act. In retrospect the device established in the "Uniting For Peace" resolution for convening Emergency Special Sessions, proved practical and useful. Seven such sessions have hitherto been convened.[15] This device was also incorporated in the General Assembly rules of procedure.[16] Even the Soviet Union, the vocal and firm advocate of the strict interpretation of the Charter, opted, under the pressure of circumstances, to call for the convening of an Emergency Special Session of the General Assembly in June 1967.[17] The point to be stressed, however, is that the substantive aspects of the "Uniting For Peace" resolution were hardly used. The General Assembly recommended only once, during the 1956 Suez tripartite attack on Egypt, the type of action originally envisioned by the authors of resolution 377A(V). By resolution 1000(ES–1) a United Nations Emergency Force was established "to secure and supervise the cessation of hostilities. . ." No other peace–keeping force was ever created by the General Assembly.

After entertaining various attempts to assign a more active role to the General Assembly, it became apparent that this channel had its limitations. Suffice it to

the power to employ military forces, which is the prerogative of the Security Council under Chapter VII".

14 UN General Assembly resolution 377 A (V) of 3 November 1950: "Uniting For Peace".

15 The first was in November 1956 during the Suez Crisis.

16 Rule 8B and Rule 9B.

17 UN Document A/6717 dated 13 June 1967.

refer to the 1964 so–called financial crisis when the opposition of certain States who wield considerable influence prevented the development of a consensus to have recourse to the General Assembly on a regular basis to authorize peace–keeping operations when the Council is in no position, for a variety of reasons, to undertake this action. This particular episode indicates that the arguments advanced by the International Court of Justice in its 1962 Advisory Opinion in the Certain Expenses Case have not been totally acceptable.[18] It is submitted that it would be erroneous to rule out the possibility of a future change of heart. The assignment of a more active role for the Assembly, with certain limitations, could well be explored in future crises. A relevant example would be a situation where opposition to the Security Council action emanates from a non-super–power.

From its very inception the Council has, for all practical purposes, been unable to avail itself of this vast and unparalleled power. It is relevant to point out, by way of illustration, that according to a recent statement by the UN Legal Counsel, Chapter VII has been expressly invoked in but three cases since the inception of the UN In response to a request submitted by me the UN Legal Counsel stated on 16 March 1981 the following in the Special Committee on the UN Charter: "in response to the Egyptian delegation's question regarding cases when the Security Council had passed resolutions referring expressly to Chapter VII of the Charter, he said that it had done so in three cases. Firstly, in connexion with the question of Palestine, in resolutions 54 and 62 (1948); secondly, in the numerous resolutions adopted from 1966 to 1979 on the situation in Southern Rhodesia; and finally, in resolutions 418 and 421 (1977) concerning the question of South Africa. Other Security Council resolutions did not mention Chapter VII specifically, but clearly derived from Article 39, such as the Complaint of Aggression upon the Republic of Korea in resolutions 82 through 84 (1950) and resolution 146 (1960) on the Congo question".[19] I responded in the same meeting by stating, *inter alia*, that "When the Security Council failed repeatedly to take effective action under Chapter VII, and to discharge its responsibility to remove threats to international peace and security, it gave serious cause for concern, and the reasons for that failure should be examined. My delegation therefore hoped that the Special Committee would make a definitive and clear statement to the General Assembly on the reasons why the system had failed." The irony is that what was invoked was the language of Chapter VII and not the required enforcement

18 The most relevant part of the Advisory Opinion was that the Court noted that, while the Security Council has the primary responsibility for matters involving international peace and security, the General Assembly is also concerned with such matters. Thus, the Court found nothing in the provisions of the Charter dividing authority and responsibilities between the General Assembly and Security Council to indicate that the General Assembly does not have the authority to decide on questions relating to expenditures for the maintenance of international peace and security.

19 Statement delivered by UN Legal Counsel at Fourth Session of Committee on Enhancing the Effectiveness of the Principle of Non-Use of Force in International Relations.

action that should accompany non–compliance with a Security Council decision.

Through trial and error the UN was forced to undergo, in a pragmatic and sometimes improvised manner, many changes. The pressure of circumstances dictated that the UN membership abandon some of the original Charter concepts and seek ways and means to adjust to the future requirements of the international community. As far back as 1959, the late Secretary-General Hammarskjöld recognized the inevitability of change to cope with the dilemma confronting the UN. He wrote in his 1959 Introduction to the Annual Report that "The Charter as an international treaty establishes certain organs which the Member States may use in their cooperation towards these goals. The statement of objectives in the Charter is binding and so are the rules concerning the various organs and their competence, but it is not necessary to regard the working methods as indicated in the Charter as limitative in purpose. Thus, they may be supplemented by others under the pressure of circumstances and in the light of experience if these additional procedures are not in conflict with what is prescribed."

The working methods contained in the Charter have indeed taken turns away from the original plan. Some of these trends have ceased to be relevant. Others however are very much alive and all indications point out that they are now permanent features of the system. The following is a brief outline of the most relevant emerging trends.

A close examination of the pattern followed in UN organs clearly indicates that the UN has come to be ragarded as the most convenient diplomatic forum to confer or deny legitimacy on government policies. The overriding consideration to be ascertained before referring a particular issue to the UN is no longer what effective action is to be expected, but rather whether a resolution shall be adopted. As if by dint of adoption the course of events will be accordingly altered. The emphasis has thus shifted from striving for conflict resolution to verbal approval or denial of a policy. The repetition of adopting a resolution that commands no-compliance and even scarce attention has gravely eroded the credibility of the UN. The Charter created an action–oriented Organization. Yet in practice all that the UN can realistically dispense is verbal condemnations. This function has been accurately described as collective legitimization, a phrase coined by Professor Inis Claude who wrote some years ago that "the world Organization has come to be regarded and used as a dispenser of politically significant approval and disapproval of the claims, policies and actions of States."[20] Professor Claude very convincingly expounds his theory by stating that "collective legitimization is an aspect of the verbal rather than the executive functioning of the United Nations, and in some sense it is a result of the Organization's incapacity for decisive intervention in and control of international relations."[21]

The implications of this development surfaced slowly and soon permeated the whole spectrum of UN consideration of all politically oriented issues. How can

20 Claude, Inis, L., *The changing United Nations.* New York, Random House, 1967, p. 73.
21 *Ibid.*, p. 88.

the UN be used to promote a particular view–point has regrettably become the criterion for submitting issues to its various organs.

Another relevant development relates to the decision-making process. In both the General Assembly and the Security Council, as well as in other organs, consultations with a view to adopting resolutions through consensus became a main feature of everyday activities.

In the General Assembly, members have become in general more inclined to undergo lengthy, informal drafting with a view to harmonizing the positions of States. Voting on certain issues is not nowadays resorted to until all other measures to harmonize have been exhausted.[22]

In the Security Council the same practice prevails and a substantial number of important resolutions have been adopted unanimously. In addition, some important decisions have been agreed upon through a "consensus statement" read by the President of the Council.

In the final analysis this shift from block–voting to consensus is also a by–product of the inability to resuscitate the collective security system. Under the Charter system very limited measures are available for ensuring compliance with the resolutions of the deliberative organs. When it was recognized that the enforcement measures were not applicable to Security Council decisions, it gradually became more relevant to seek agreement through reconciliation. In other words, coercion gave way to persuasion. The study of the various ramifications of this new trend is beyond the scope of this paper. It is noted here merely to underline its emergence and probe its effect on enhancing the prospects of securing implementation of resolutions. In theory the nature of the decision-making process as well as the size of the votes cast in support of a given resolution should serve as an indication of the possibility of ultimate compliance.

In reality, however, the size of the support behind a resolution does not always correspond to the prospects for implementation at the present stage of evolution in the United Nations. No doubt it could be construed as evidence of the importance attached by the members to the discharge of the relevant provisions, thus reflecting their insistence to pursue the matter further until full implementation has been achieved.[23]

The support of the Super Powers to a resolution in the United Nations might also prove inadequate unless their support is grounded in unison with objectives and actions outside the United Nations as well as inside it. This point is well demonstrated by the two Super Powers' verbal support for the now famous Security Council resolution 242 (1967) and their actual contradictory views on how to implement it.

It is therefore submitted that the new trend to reconcile views before adopting resolutions should facilitate the implementation process. However, with regard to resolutions which contain provisions unaccepted by certain States, it is doubt-

22 It might generally be stated that "speedy voting" is still employed in the Third and Fourth Committees. Items on the agenda of the First and Special Political Committees are usually subjected to harmonization before voting takes place.

23 The repetition of resolutions on the Southern African problems is a good example.

ful that this procedure will be sufficient to overcome the rejection of the parties concerned. Likewise this developing trend might give rise to genuine impediments with far-reaching implications whenever a given resolution is anchored on the lowest common denominator. Subsequent disagreement on interpreting such resolutions could ensure their indefinite non–implementation.[24]

On the operational side the UN was able to devise an effective machinery to function with the consent of the concerned parties. Beginning with the establishment of UNEF in 1956, the United Nations devised a new type of machinery to maintain peace and security. The concept of peace–keeping is based on the consent of the concerned parties and particularly the host country. Under the generally recognized principles of international law the stationing and operation of such forces are dependent on the consent of the territorial sovereign. The mandate for peace–keeping forces usually embraces supervising the cessation of hostilities, manning buffer zones, and other related third party interposition functions. Several criticisms have been levelled at this device. The most notable would be its inadequacy as a deterrent force.[25] Others consider that the inadequacy emanates from the effect of freezing a given situation without injecting elements of peace-making. Be that as it may, no one seriously doubts the usefulness of the UN peace–keeping operations in controlling violence and conflicts. In point of fact the emergence and subsequent development of peace–keeping is universally recognized as one of the major UN achievements which demonstrate the Organization's ability to respond to changes.

What is relevant to this paper is the emergence of a new concept which was not envisaged when the Charter was drafted. The controversial issues relating to peace-keeping which, *inter alia*, encompass the role of the Security Council versus the Secretary-General, have not yet been resolved. This, however, has not hampered the viability of such a useful concept. It might be illuminating to bear in mind what Hammarskjöld wrote in another context with respect to the lessons to be drawn from a previous peace–keeping operation:

> "In view of the impossibility of determining beforehand the specific form of a United Nations presence of the type considered in this report, which would be necessary to meet adequately the requirements of a given situation, a broad decision by the General Assembly should attempt to do no more than endorse certain basic principles and rules which would provide an adaptable framework for later operations that might be found necessary. In a practical sense, it is not feasible in advance of a known situation to do more than to provide for some helpful stand–by arrangements for a force of similar forms of a United Nations presence."[26]

Another major shift occurred with respect to disarmament. Originally the consideration of the regulation of armaments was one of the principal functions

24 Security Council resolution 242(1967) is a relevant example.

25 The UNIFIL operation in Lebanon is a case in point.

26 United Nations Emergency Force, Summary Study of the experience derived from the establishment and operation of the force. UN General Assembly, A/3943, 9 October 1958, para. 154.

which the Charter assigned to the Security Council.[27] Yet, as a result of the quasi–paralysis of the Council practically all matters related to disarmament were shifted to the General Assembly. At present the General Assembly has clearly eclipsed the Council as the focal point for disarmament activities and as a consequence tilted the balance established by the Charter for handling disarmament matters.[28]

IV. The significance of the emerging trends and concepts

The emergence of new trends and concepts to cope with the changing realities of our contemporary international society is, no doubt, a welcome sign of maturity. Such trends and concepts are clearly within the framework defined in objectives and principles contained in the Charter. It might therefore be appropriate to stress that notwithstanding the changes in perception and the shift from collective security to collective legitimization, the maintenance of international peace and security remains the foremost objective and the primary responsibility of the UN The emphasis in discharging this function is now channelled into new techniques based on persuasion, mediation and interposition of UN peace–keeping forces.

Indeed one can detect no graphic evidence of serious efforts to reverse this trend and revert to the coercive measures outlined in the Charter. As a corollary it would be naive, at this stage, to expect the UN to promptly take the "effective collective measures" referred to in Article 1 whenever peace is shattered. Yet one should not exclude the possibility of a meaningful UN involvement to perform preventive diplomacy as well as peace–keeping and peace–making functions. This mirrors the stage of development of international organizations at this juncture in history.

It ought to be recognized that the Charter is a dynamic constitutional instrument, capable of evolution. Member States could always re–direct the constitutional development of the Charter with a view to ensuring the proper functioning of the United Nations. This point was pertinently made by the late Secretary-General Hammarskjöld in 1961, when he stated "it is clearly for the Governments, Members of the Organization, and for these Governments only, to make

27 Article 26 stipulates that "In order to promote the establishment and maintenance of international peace and security with the least diversion for armaments of the world's human and economic resources the Security Council shall be responsible for formulating, with assistance of the Military Staff Committee referred to in Article 47, plans to be submitted to the Members of the United Nations for the establishment of a system for the regulation of armaments."

28 Very few disarmament issues are now referred to the Council. An important exception is Security Council Resolution 255(1968) of 19 June 1968, concerning security assurances for non-nuclear weapon States party to the Non-Proliferation Treaty. A further exception is to be found in the Egyptian initiative in the General Assembly to establish a nuclear-weapon free zone in the Middle East. General Assembly Resolution 35/147 establishes a role for the Security Council by inviting the concerned States of the region to deposit a declaration with the Council for "consideration as appropriate".

their choice and decide on the direction in which they wish the Organization to develop."[29]

It might be appropriate to conclude this point by stating that, in a sense, member States have reviewed many aspects relating to the role and functioning of the UN This informal review was carried out through subtle and consistent change of emphasis. It necessitated resort to innovative and pragmatic measures. A general operational pattern, not tailored according to some of the original ideals of 1945, has been stablished. The edifice is modest and imperfect. It requires further development and elaboration. It also requires an open-minded and pragmatic approach. The creation of a general awareness for the need to institutionalize some, if not all, of the emerging trends and concepts would contribute positively to the achievement of an enhanced UN.

V. Some practical suggestions

The aforementioned trends were introduced and developed without formal Charter amendment. I am convinced that several more reforms of relevance and value could very well be introduced without amending the Charter. Any far–reaching and ambitious reforms will, no doubt, be opposed by powerful and influential States who have no interest in strengthening an independent UN. It is thus necessary to conceive of certain limited reforms. The general orientation of such reforms, in my view, should be practical and pragmatic and aim at building upon the newly emerged trends and concepts. The objective would be to supplement and enhance the effect of the limited development that has become accepted practice. Thus entertaining hopes that it would be possible to revitalize the collective security system, should be recognized as a non–starter.

In this context I would like to advance some proposals to three vital areas which, in essence, symbolize the UN system. *First the Security Council.* At present there are no Charter provisions which define the scope of application of the unanimity rule. The rules of procedure of the Security Council do not shed any more light on this point.

An examination of the reasons behind the failure of the Security Council to perform its primary responsibility as the guardian of world peace would undoubtedly point out the abuse of the veto. Hence it would be a logical point of departure to explore ways and means to limit the scope of application of the unanimity rule to certain activities of the Council. The availability of facts would seem to be a pre-requisite for its proper functioning. Experience has shown that when conflicts erupt, the Council is usually unable to determine the veracity of the allegations and counter-allegations presented by the parties.

It might therefore be desirable to consider how to ensure that the veto would not apply to the following:

(a) issues which are confined to ascertaining facts and providing the Security Council with the necessary information to discharge its functions;

29 This quote is from the Introduction to the Annual Report of the Secretary-General, on the work of the Organization, 16 June 1960 to 15 June 1961. *General Assembly, Official Records: 16th session.* Supplement No 1 A (A/4800/Add. 1), p. 1.

(b) dispatch of UN observers with the consent of the host country to observe and report impartially and accurately to the Council;
(c) entrusting the Secretary–General with certain functions in dispute settlements, in accordance with Article 98 of the Charter and Rule 23 of the Provisional Rules of Procedure of the Security Council.

The modalities for incorporating and reflecting such proposals require further negotiation and sharpening in order to be agreed upon. It is submitted that they could be inserted in the Rules of Procedure of the Security Council and become operational without Charter amendments.[30]

Second. As for the General Assembly, an area that requires urgent attention is the reporting system, it should be pointed out that, at present, whenever a resolution is adopted the practice has been for the Secretary–General to transmit the text of the resolution to member States. The replies and comments by States are subsequently included in a report to be submitted to the Assembly for its consideration. Such a reporting practice requires radical changes in order to create a degree of accountability for non-implementation. It might be necessary to consider conferring a more active role regarding its ability to pursue the implementation of its resolutions. A shift of emphasis should be produced reflecting the necessity to consider that States are responsible for informing and providing answers to the whole membership on non-compliance. In particular, when a State casts a positive vote in favour of a given resolution, it should be considered as politically and constitutionally committed to honour its vote by adhering to the provisions of the resolutions. It is therefore proposed that the Assembly should not confine itself to the response and comments of States, it should focus its attention on non-compliance and why States do not respond.

Third. The Secretary-General's authority to pursue the implementation of resolutions will be drastically enhanced if he is empowered to improve the reporting system as outlined above. Thus the Secretary-General would include in his report to the Assembly the lack of progress in carrying out a given resolution and the names of States who have not taken action to carry out the resolution. It is hoped that the adoption of such a procedure would be considered as an added incentive to prompt States to publicly confirm their adherence to the adopted resolutions. He should be empowered to recommend deferral of consideration of certain items when the provisions of the adopted resolution have not been fully carried out. A more active role for the Secretary-General in dispute settlement should be accepted, since in practice his office does perform many functions relating to preventative diplomacy. A formal recognition of this development could be of great assistance in the future. The U.N. can be more effectively used as an instrument of preventative diplomacy.

The rationale behind the resort to the Secretary-General is to benefit from, *inter alia*, the flexibility and pragmatism innate in his Office. The main attraction

30 In the course of the deliberations of the Special Committee on the Charter 1980, 14 non-aligned States submitted more elaborate proposals: Document A/AC. 182/WG/46/Rev. 1 and 2. In the course of the 1981 meeting of the Committee, Egypt submitted a revised version of such proposals: Document A/AC.182/WG/50.

of the Office of the Secretary-General is its proven ability to innovate discreetly.

In conclusion it is submitted that, in the final analysis, the original Charter design has been altered. Many of the Charter concepts proved impractical and have been tacitly abandoned. New trends and concepts have emerged and gained acceptance through gradual evolution. The major flaw in the evolutionary process is not only that it is painstakingly slow. What is more serious is that such a process, by necessity, deals with isolated issues. The lack of a comprehensive perception would result in the continuation of gaps and loopholes in the system.

The well advertized shortcomings of the UN should be jointly addressed and suitable measures to ensure a more effective system should be decided upon. What is argued in this paper is the feasibility of realizing genuine reforms through measures that fall short of formal Charter review. The interaction between the emerging trends and concepts and such limited proposals could create auspicious conditions for a more effective and responsive UN.

8.3. Organs for Conflict Resolution and Execution

Bengt Broms

I. Introduction

In his background paper for the Joint UNITAR-Uppsala University Seminar on International Law and Organization for a New World Order (JUS 81), Professor Atle Grahl-Madsen points out, quite correctly, that the resort to orderly procedures for conflict resolution and execution is of great importance for the effectiveness of international law. The specific problems to be discussed under Theme No. 4, Subject No. 2, have been listed by Grahl-Madsen as follows: "What is the status in this respect today? And what can be done in this field? Is it possible to get more States to trust the judicial or abritral process? What else can be done?" To clarify the slight discrepancy between the heading of Subject No. 2 and the list of specific problems it has been indicated orally that the group should discuss the pacific settlement of disputes in the light of the facilities offered by the United Nations and by arbitral and judicial process.

II. The United Nations and the International Court of Justice

Turning to the present status of the organs for the pacific settlement of disputes, the system created by the Charter of the United Nations deserves to be dealt with first. While Chapter VI of the Charter deals with the pacific settlement of disputes, Chapter VII includes the provisions on the action by the United Nations with respect to threats to the peace, breaches of the peace, and acts of aggression.[1] It is but natural that States should, in the first place, resort to the provisions of Chapter VI and that, in all those cases where this is not enough, the United Nations will make use of the provisions of Chapter VII.

Article 33 of the Charter underlines the duty of all the parties to such disputes which are likely to endanger the maintenance of international peace and security to resort, first of all, to "negotiation, enquiry, mediation, conciliation, arbitration, judicial settlement, resort to regional agencies or arrangements, or other peaceful means of their own choice". The wording of Article 33 makes it clear that the list is not exhaustive. In accordance with Article 33, paragraph 2, the Security Council shall, when it deems necessary, call upon the parties to settle their dispute by peaceful means indicated in the first paragraph.

The duty of the Security Council to call upon the parties is in the nature of a

1 As to the division of powers between the General Assembly and the Security Council in the field of pacific settlement of disputes see Broms, Bengt, *The Doctrine of Equality of States as Applied in International Organizations*. Vammala, 1959, pp. 235–239.

recommendation, which is less than what the Security Council is expected to do in a situation falling under Article 39 of the Charter, whereby the Security Council shall determine the existence of any threat to the peace, breach of the peace, or act of aggression and shall make recommendations, or decide what measures shall be taken in accordance with Articles 41 and 42 of the Charter to maintain or restore international peace and security.

Article 38 of the Charter makes it possible for the Security Council to make recommendations to the parties with a view to a pacific settlement of the dispute without prejudice to the other provisions of Chapter VI. This is, however, possible only under the condition that all the parties to the dispute so request. So far the parties to disputes have preferred the normal procedure under Chapter VI in the pacific settlement of their disputes. This attitude is apparently to be seen against a psychological background in so far as the parties know the limits of the powers belonging to the General Assembly, whereas the possibility of resorting to Article 38 may lead to unforeseen consequences.

A survey of the United Nations practice indicates that there are cases which have been handled solely by the General Assembly and cases which have been dealt with by the Security Council.[2] In some cases both of these principal organs of the United Nations have handled the issues. The main emphasis has been placed on the Security Council which is a natural consequence of the wider powers of this organ as compared with those of the General Assembly.

When the Security Council takes up a case the normal procedure is that the parties to the dispute and the members of the Security Council explain their views. The publicity which is focused on the meetings of the Security Council forces the parties to the dispute to try to justify their actions and views the best way they can. In many cases the next step to be taken by the Security Council will be the setting up of a commission or a committee to investigate the dispute. This is often necessitated already by the differing views of the parties themselves. Once a commission has investigated the dispute its report will be discussed by the Security Council which, at this stage, may also reach the conclusion that no further action is to be taken or required by the Charter of the United Nations.

Another alternative, which may follow the discussion of the report issued by the commission, is to make a recommendation to the parties to the dispute to make use of the means mentioned in Article 33 of the Charter in order to solve the dispute. At this stage there is also another alternative, *i.e.*, a reference to Article 36, paragraph 3, of the Charter. By doing this the Security Council is entitled to take into consideration that legal disputes should, as a general rule, be referred by the parties to the dispute to the International Court of Justice.

As a third alternative the Security Council may make a recommendation indicating to the parties what they are expected to do to solve their dispute. Before giving such a recommendation the Security Council is expected to investigate the

2 On the practice of the General Assembly and the Security Council see Broms, Bengt, *Yhdistyneet Kansakunnat*, 2nd ed., Helsinki, Suomalainen Lakimiesyhdistys, 1976, pp. 206–211.

dispute as fully as possible. Once such an investigation has been carried out the Security Council is free to decide, taking into account the particular circumstances relating to each case, the contents of the recommendation.

The fourth alternative is a decision by the Security Council whereby a special organ is set up to find a solution which is acceptable to the parties. In this context it is also possible to nominate only one person to act as a mediator between the parties. If this does not leads to a positive result, the Security Council is entitled to choose some of the other means mentioned in Chapter VI of the Charter. None of the alternative solutions is exhaustive in so far as the other alternatives are concerned.

In case the Security Council cannot reach a decision, there is also the possibility of removing the issue from the agenda. Once this has been done the General Assembly becomes entitled to include the same issue on its agenda. The General Assembly may, however, only make recommendations. In comparison with the powers of the Security Council those of the General Assembly are more limited.

It is always to be hoped for that the efforts of the Security Council or the General Assembly will lead to the pacific settlement of a dispute. In general the results have been satisfactory, even if there are cases where the Security Council has not been able to prevent the parties from resorting to force.

At the San Francisco Conference the establishment of a judicial system under the aegis of the United Nations was regarded as a matter of primary importance. According to Article 92 of the Charter the International Court of Justice was to be the principal judicial organ of the United Nations. All members of the United Nations were to be *ipso facto* parties to the Statute of the International Court of Justice and each member of the United Nations undertook to comply with the decision of the International Court of Justice in any case to which it is a party. The Security Council of the United Nations was empowered to make recommendations or decide upon measures to be taken to give effect to the judgments of the International Court of Justice if a party to a case had recourse to the Security Council after the other party to the case had failed to perform the obligations incumbent upon it under a judgment rendered by the Court.

In accordance with Article 95 of the Charter the members of the United Nations are not prevented by the provisions of the Charter from entrusting the solution of their differences to other tribunals by virtue of agreements already in existence or agreements which they were to conclude in the future.

Regardless of its position as the principal judicial organ of the United Nations it is well known that the International Court of Justice has not been utilized as often as could have been expected. Relatively few States have accepted the optional clause in accordance with Article 36, paragraph 2, of the Statute of the International Court of Justice.[3] Furthermore, many of the States who have ac-

3 There are now 47 States which have made declarations under Article 36, paragraph 2 of the Statute of the International Court of Justice or whose declarations made under

cepted the optional clause have made so extensive reservations that the importance of their acceptance becomes questionable.[4]

There is no simple and easy answer to the question why this is so. There seems to exist still a basic mistrust in the judicial process in general and this leads many States to rely rather on their own diplomatic efforts in the pacific settlement of their disputes. Unless the State concerned is reasonably certain of winning a case it will consider the possibility of turning to the International Court of Justice rather as the last resort.

While this is true of the contentious cases that have been submitted to the International Court of Justice, it seems as if the record of the Court would be more encouraging in the field of the giving of advisory opinions.[5] While it was decided in San Francisco that only States could become parties to contentious cases before the Court, it was also decided that only the General Assembly and the Security Council as well as other organs of the United Nations and specialized agencies, which have been so authorized by the General Assembly of the United Nations, may turn to the Court for an advisory opionion on any legal question. Practice has shown that the wisdom of limiting the right to request an advisory opinion of the Court in this way is open to criticism.

III. Arbitration

The adjudication of disputes differs in some respects from arbitration, both being parts of the machinery for the pacific settlement of disputes. Although arbitration has been resorted to by the parties to international disputes for a long time, the principles governing arbitration in general were first codified in the Hague Conventions for the Pacific Settlement of International Disputes of 1899 and 1907. The Permanent Court of Arbitration was established by the Hague Convention of 1899 as a model for the future. Regardless of its name it is only a panel of arbitrators whom the parties may ask to act as arbitrators in particular disputes. Arbitration tribunals include normally two arbitrators elected by each party together with an umpire. The parties are entitled to agree among themselves as to exceptions to the rules of procedure which the arbitration tribunal is to follow.

After an initial active period of work the Permanent Court of Arbitration has

Article 36, paragraph 2, of the Statute of the Permanent Court of International Justice are deemed to be acceptances of the compulsory judisdiction of the International Court of Justice.

4 The United States declaration provides that it does not apply to disputes essentally within the domestic jurisdiction of the United States "as determined by the United States". The Secretary of State of the United States admitted in 1978 that "in regard to any American proposals to expand the use of and strengthen the Court, we are likely to hear that reform should begin at home". The Department of State, *Selected Documents*, No. 8, 1978, p. 17. As to a promise by President Carter to request, at an appropriate time, the Senate to reexamine the Connally Reservation see *ibid.*, p. 7.

5 On the practice of the International Court of Justice in giving advisory opinions see Broms, Bengt, *Yhdistyneet Kansakunnat,* 2nd ed. Helsinki, Suomalainen Lakimiesyhdistys, 1976, pp. 547–559.

since 1932 dealt with only three cases. The General Assembly of the United Nations took note of this and in 1949 the International Law Commission chose arbitration as one of its topics for codification. After a lengthy preparation the International Law Commission presented in 1953 to the General Assembly a draft text on arbitration together with a proposal to convene a diplomatic conference to prepare a Convention on Arbitral Procedure. The General Assembly, however, did not agree with this proposal and by Resolution 797 (VIII) it was merely decided that the draft convention was to be sent to the member States for their opinions. Two years later the General Assembly adopted Resolution 989 (X) and returned the matter to the International Law Commission for further preparation.

At this stage the International Law Commission relinquished the idea of a new convention and decided, instead of the convention, to prepare model rules for arbitration.[6] The model rules were adopted by the International Law Commission in 1958, and upon having considered the issue the General Assembly decided by Resolution 1262 (XIII) to send the model rules to all member States asking for their views. However, the member States showed no interest in this issue and the General Assembly has not returned to it.

One of the provisions provoking opposition in the debates of the General Assembly was the provision which had been included by the International Law Commission in the model rules and which made it possible for the President of the International Court of Justice to nominate the members of the arbitral tribunal in case the parties could not within three months agree among themselves on its composition. One of the parties to a dispute was to be entitled to ask the President of the International Court of Justice to make the nominations. A majority of the members of the General Assembly were not prepared to accept this proposal because they feared that such an alternative would limit the right of the States to decide freely whether they wanted to enter into arbitration proceedings.

There were, however, two important suggestions in the model rules created by the International Law Commission which did not meet with any strong opposition. One of these suggestions was that the parties were recommended to indicate in each particular case those legal principles which they wanted the arbitral tribunal to apply. The other suggestion was that the parties should decide already in advance those instances where the arbitral tribunal would be entitled to decide *ex aequo et bono.*

While the efforts to develop arbitration by the General Assembly of the United Nations were not carried out, it is worth noting that since the end of the Second World War, due to the great increase in international commerce, there have been many regional conventions on arbitration.[7] From the point of view of

6 The idea of mere model draft articles has been praised by Berber, Friedrich, *Lehrbuch des Völkerrechts*, III. Band, München, C. H. Beck, 1964, pp. 47–48.

7 As early examples of regional conventions one may refer to the European Convention for the Peaceful Settlement of Disputes of 29 April 1957 and the Protocol of the Commission of Mediation, Conciliation and Arbitration of the Organization of African Unity of 21 July 1964.

international law the most important effort to develop arbitration was the Convention on the Settlement of Investment Disputes between States and Nationals of Other States, which entered into force on 14 October 1966. At 30 June 1980, there were 79 contracting States. Forty-four States had, pursuant to Article 13, paragraph 1, of the Convention designated 148 persons to serve on the Panel of Conciliators and 146 persons to serve on the Panel of Arbitrators. One arbitrator has been designated by the Chairman of the Administrative Council pursuant to Article 13, paragraph 2, of the Convention. The contracting States include among their group all important industrialized States and a great number of developing States.

On the basis of the Convention an International Centre for the Settlement of Investment Disputes (ICSID) was set up to facilitate and provide facilities for conciliation and arbitration of investment disputes between the contracting States and nationals of other contracting States. The Centre has been endowed with the full international status of a juridical person. While the Centre has been established at the main office of the International Bank for Reconstruction and Development in Washington, DC, the Centre is not dependent on any of the Specialized Agencies of the United Nations.

The Centre offers to parties to the Convention facilities to solve their investment disputes with nationals of other contracting parties in an international forum by making use of either a Panel of Conciliators or a Panel of Arbitrators. The Centre acts as an administrative organ which sees to it that the proceedings are conducted in accordance with the Convention. The principal organ of the Centre is the Administrative Council which is composed of one representative of each contracting State. The President of the World Bank acts as the Chairman of the Administrative Council. The Centre has a Secretariat which is headed by a Secretary-General elected by the Administrative Council by a majority of two-thirds of its members.

The jurisdiction of the Centre covers all legal disputes which may arise directly out of investments between a contracting State and nationals of another contracting State and which the parties to the disputes submit in writing to the Centre.[8] Once the consent has been given by a party, it cannot be withdrawn. The parties are entitled to choose between the conciliation and the arbitration procedure.

In case the parties have chosen the conciliation procedure, the dispute will be registered by the Centre and the parties are expected to agree on the composition of the conciliation commission. This may consist of a sole conciliator or an uneven number of conciliators in accordance with the agreement of the parties. In case the parties cannot agree on the composition of the conciliation commission within 90 days after the dispute has been registered, the Chairman of the Administrative Council is entitled, upon a request by any of the parties to the dispute, to nominate the members.

The task of the conciliation commission is to investigate the dispute and to

8 On the International Centre for the Settlement of Investment Disputes see Broms, Bengt, *Kansainvälinen oikeus*, Helsinki, Suomalainen Lakimiesyhdistys, 1978, pp. 479–484.

propose an agreement which the parties are able to accept. Once such an acceptance has been given the conciliation commission draws up a report, which includes a statement as to the agreement of the parties or their failure to reach an agreement. The parties cannot refer in any subsequent court procedure or arbitration procedure to the statements or admissions which have been made during the conciliation procedure.

In case the parties to a dispute have chosen the arbitration procedure, the setting up of an arbitral tribunal adheres mainly to the principles followed in the setting up of a conciliation commission. The powers of the arbitral tribunal are extensive as the tribunal is the judge of its own competence. In case the parties have reached an agreement as to the legal principles which they want to see applied in the arbitral award the tribunal is bound to act accordingly. In case there is no such agreement between the parties, the tribunal has to apply the legislation of the party concerned, including the relevant principles of private international law and the relevant principles of international law. The tribunal cannot reach a *non liquet*-decision and the tribunal is entitled to decide the dispute *ex aequo et bono* in case the parties so agree.

The tribunal reaches its award by a majority vote and the members of the tribunal are entitled to present their dissenting opinion in case they want to. As a rule the awards of the arbitral tribunal are final and binding on the parties. They are not subject to any appeal or to any other remedy except those which have been provided for in the Convention. The parties shall abide by and comply with the terms of the award unless the Convention provides otherwise.

The Convention has not been used very often. In most cases the parties that have submitted cases to the conciliation or arbitration procedure have been investment companies which have sued States.[9] A very positive sign is the willingness of the developing States to agree to the submission of cases. The procedure is sufficiently elastic to be a good example for other new specialized arbitration and conciliation organs. It seems also that the number of cases that are being submitted to the conciliation or arbitration procedure is growing together with the number of parties to the Convention. On the basis of the past practice one may draw the conclusion that many States seem to be more prepared to allow a specialized arbitral tribunal handle a dispute to which it is a party than to submit a dispute to judicial process. The reason for this may be found in their reluctance to trust a judicial organ which consists mainly of judges who represent different legal systems. In an arbitral tribunal the party is entitled to nominate some members of the tribunal and due to the neutral chairman the award is likely to be neutral. This factor seems to serve as an inducement to favour arbitration.

The above conclusion does not apply to any particular group of States. There are several Great Powers which usually try to avoid judicial settlement while they are likely to agree to an arbitral process. The fact that nationals of these States are members of international courts like the International Court of Justice does not seem to diminish their unwillingness to resort to the judicial process. This atti-

9 The Government of Gabon instituted arbitration proceedings against Société SERETE S. A., Case ARB/76/1.

tude is rather surprising because the developing States have often mistrusted the impartiality of the International Court of Justice due to the composition of the Court which is said to favour the Great Powers.

IV. Resolutions of the General Assembly of the United Nations

Already in 1949 the General Assembly of the United Nations decided to discuss the pacific settlement of international disputes when, in the course of its study of methods for the promotion of international co-operation in the political field, the General Assembly decided to restore to the General Act for the Pacific Settlement of International Disputes of 26 September 1928 its original efficacy by introducing amendments to the original text taking into account the fact that the League of Nations and the Permanent Court of International Justice no longer functioned.

The Revised General Act includes provisions especially on conciliation, judicial settlement and arbitration.[10] In accordance with Article 1 disputes of every kind between two or more parties to the General Act, which it has not been possible to settle by diplomatic means, are to be submitted to the procedure of conciliation. The parties are expected to set up a permanent or special conciliation commission within a period of six months from the day when such a request has been made by one of the contracting parties to another party. The General Act includes provisions concerning the composition and procedure of the conciliation commissions.

Chapter II of the General Act deals with the judicial settlement, which means both arbitral tribunals and the International Court of Justice. Specific rules as to arbitration follow in Chapter III, which includes the principles as to the composition and functioning of an arbitral tribunal. Chapter IV of the General Act includes general provisions which apply to the means chosen in a particular case by the parties to the dispute.

Although the provisions of the General Act were revised in order to help States in their efforts to solve international disputes, only five States have so far acceded to it. Two States have accepted parts of the General Act which entered into force on 20 September 1950, the nineteenth day following the receipt by the Secretary-General of the United Nations of the second instrument of accession.

At the same time, with the adoption of the General Act by Resolution 268 A (III), the General Assembly adopted Resolution 268 D (III) which led to the creation of a Panel for Inquiry and Conciliation. Each member State was invited to designate from one to five persons who, by reason of their training, experience, character and standing, are deemed to be well fitted to serve as members of commissions for inquiry or of conciliation and who would be disposed to serve. The Secretary-General of the United Nations was requested to take charge of the administrative arrangements.

10 The Revised General Act is open to accession by the members of the United Nations, by the non-member States which shall have become parties to the Statute of the International Court of Justice or to which the General Assembly of the United Nations communicates a copy for this purpose. Article 43, paragraph 1, Revised General Act for the Pacific Settlement of International Disputes.

In addition to any States involved in controversies also the General Assembly, the Security Council and their subsidiary organs were expected to make use of the Panel for Inquiry and Conciliation. The Secretary-General compiled the Panel and fifteen member States nominated their representatives. The last time this list was reviewed was in 1961 and neither the States nor the principal organs of the United Nations have ever made use of the Panel when setting up organs for investigation or mediation.

During the following session the General Assembly adopted Resolution 297 B (IV). The preamble to this Resolution includes a reference to the pacific settlement of international disputes in accordance with the Charter of the United Nations. The Resolution requests the Secretary-General to establish and maintain a list of persons qualified to assist United Nations mission in the functions of observation and supervision. Such persons are to be called to service in response to a specific resolution by a competent organ of the United Nations. The list was to be known as the United Nations Panel of Field Observers. In actual practice this Resolution has never been implemented.

In 1963 the General Assembly adopted Resolution 1967 (XVIII) concerning the question of methods of fact-finding. The preamble recalls the principle that States shall settle their international disputes by peaceful means in such a manner that international peace and security and justice are not endangered. To this it is added that an important contribution to the peaceful settlement of disputes and to the prevention of such disputes could be made by providing for impartial fact-finding within the framework of international organizations and in bilateral and multilateral conventions. The member States were subsequently invited to submit in writing their comments and in 1966 the Secretary-General prepared a report on this issue. After a lengthy debate during the following session the General Assembly adopted Resolution 2329 (XXII).

According to this Resolution the Secretary-General was requested to prepare a register of experts, in legal and other fields, whose services the States parties to a dispute may use by agreement for fact-finding in relation to the dispute. The member States were requested to nominate up to five of their nationals to be included in the register. The experts were expected to represent such disciplines as the legal profession, economics, technical expertise, military research or other comparable fields. The member States were urged to make more effective use of the existing methods of fact-finding and they were expected to turn to the experts mentioned in the register asking them to carry out fact-finding in connection with a particular dispute. Upon the completion of the fact-finding the parties to the dispute were to take note of its results when they continued their negotiations.

The Secretary-General of the United Nations compiled the register of experts for fact-finding on the basis of the nominations by 42 member States which had nominated by 1969 in all 189 experts. During the following year some corrections were still made to the list, but since then the register has remained the same. States have not even once resorted to the fact-finding procedure in accordance with Resolution 2329 (XXII) and no fact-finding organs have been set up in accordance with this Resolution. This is a somewhat surprising outcome as at the time of the adoption of this Resolution the members of the Sixth Committee of the General Assembly considered the plan as an important step forward in the pacific settlement of international disputes.

The last-mentioned efforts by the General Assembly to develop the organs for the pacific settlement of international disputes cannot be regarded as successful. It is difficult to understand why some of these resolutions, even after they have been adopted with some enthusiasm, have not induced States to resort to the facilities provided for. By now these resolutions have been almost forgotten and one is inclined to think that the legal departments of many Foreign Offices have long ago forgotten that they ever existed. This raises, however, the following question: Is the follow-up of these resolutions, among many other comparable resolutions which require action by the member States to be properly implemented, too poorly executed? Should the Secretariat of the United Nations not see to it better that the member States are at reasonable intervals of time reminded of this type of resolution? Or, could it be the case that the legal departments of Foreign Offices should do their homework better than has been the case up until now?

In any case, it seems as if at least Resolution 268 A (III) and Resolution 2329 (XXII) belong to such resolutions which merit attention even today. At least they ought to be carefully reviewed once again to see whether they could still be utilized either in their old form or whether they should be brought up-to-date.

V. Proposals by the Special Committee on the Charter of the United Nations and the Strengthening of the Role of the Organization

As JUS 81 is intended to look into the future to try to find new solutions to some of the old problems of international law I should like to point out that, in so far as the pacific settlement of disputes is concerned, several new ideas have been put forward in connection with the work of the Special Committee on the Charter of the United Nations and the Strengthening of the Role of the Organization.[11] Many members of the Special Committee have expressed the idea that, regardless of the progress in the pacific settlement of international disputes during the existence of the United Nations, further progress is still urgently needed.[12] In this context a reference has often been made to the proliferation of conflicts throughout the world.

One of the proposals which have gained almost unanimous support is a suggestion that the General Assembly ought to adopt a declaration on the peaceful settlement of disputes. During its two last sessions the Special Committee has

11 The establishment and first sessions of the Special Committee have been described by Broms, Bengt, The Special Committee on the Charter of the United Nations and the Strenghtening of the Role of the Organization. *German Yearbook of International Law*, vol 20, 1977, pp. 77-102.

12 On 24 March 1978 the Chairman of the Special Committee presented a compilation of 51 proposals on the peaceful settlement of international disputes. See UN, General Assembly, Off. Rec., A/33/33, pp. 63–69.

directed its main attention to the drafting of this declaration.[13] Several member States have expressed the opinion that, once the declaration has been adopted by the General Assembly, it should be followed by a treaty on the same subject. For the time being, however, many members have presented their objections to the proposal aiming at a later drafting of a treaty.

Romania, among other members, has been continuously a warm supporter of the idea that the General Assembly should appoint a permanent commission to fulfil the functions of mediation, good offices and conciliation. Past presidents of the General Assembly have been mentioned as examples of the type of persons that should be appointed to serve in this commission.

Wide support exists in favour of a recommendation to be presented by the General Assembly of the United Nations to all member States to the effect that they should always include into their bilateral and multilateral treaties compromissory clauses conferring compulsory jurisdiction on the International Court of Justice or other judicial bodies in the event of a dispute between the parties concerning the interpretation or application of the treaty. It has also been suggested that States should make wider use of the regional machinery pursuant to Article 52 of the Charter of the United Nations and that *ad hoc* and specialized settlement procedures should be further developed. A list should be prepared of authorities which would be willing to appoint arbitrators or chairmen of arbitral tribunals.

The representative of France has made a proposal that a practical United Nations manual on the settlement of international disputes should be prepared. This manual should include all relevant information on the existing methods for the pacific settlement of international disputes together with other useful information for the consideration of the governments of member States. This proposal has gained unanimous support among the members of the Special Committee.

Among the numerous proposals concerning the functioning of the Security Council in the field of the pacific settlement of disputes it has been suggested that the Security Council should take a more active role in applying Article 33 of the Charter. It has been said that the Security Council should consider greater use of informal consultations to consider possible difficulties before they get out of hand.

As to the working methods of the Security Council it has been suggested that ministerial meetings should be held and that meetings of the Security Council should be convened at times in places where an unresolved international dispute threatens peace and security in the world. The last proposal has raised some opposition by those who regard the proposal as somewhat impractical. Another suggestion is that the Security Council should hold periodic meetings in order to review the progress achieved with regard to the elimination of tensions and international crises. Such a review is seen as a preventive factor. It has also been proposed that the Security Council should be encouraged to consider the establishment of a standing committee of experts in the techniques of fact-finding and mediation.

13 For the texts of the first draft declarations on the peaceful settlement of international disputes see UN, General Assembly, Off. Rec., A/35/33, pp. 63–82.

In view of the expected difficulties to amend the Charter of the United Nations or the Statute of the International Court of Justice it has been proposed that the General Assembly should adopt a resolution whereby an appeal would be directed to the permanent members of the Security Council to reach an understanding on the non-use of the veto in matters pertaining to the pacific settlement of disputes. This understanding would make a normal amendment of the constituent documents unnecessary. So far the permanent members of the Security Council have not been prepared to accept this proposal.

One of the suggestions that has been directed to the General Assembly and the Secretary-General as well as to the Security Council is that they should in the future make more efficient use of expert groups and fact-finding panels. The Secretary-General should also be entitled, at the request of a member State, to send observers to the territory of such a requesting member State which considers that there exists a situation or controversy which may endanger the maintenance of international peace and security. The observers would then keep the Secretary-General continuously informed so that the machinery mentioned in Article 99 of the Charter could be made use of more effectively than it has been up to now.

Many proposals have been directed to changing the role of the International Court of Justice. A basic proposal, which seems to belong rather to the class of confidence-building measures, is to enlarge the composition of the International Court of Justice by electing a certain and so far unspecified number of new judges from different legal and political systems of the world. Those who have made this proposal explain that its adoption should result in more frequent recourse to the International Court of Justice.

Another proposal is that the consultative role of the International Court of Justice should be enhanced and, to this end, methods should be studied in order to entitle States parties to a dispute to ask for an advisory opinion of the International Court of Justice. It has also been suggested that the general role of the International Court of Justice in the solution of disputes should be strengthened and, to this end, a binding system of pacific settlement of disputes should be established.

Several other proposals have been made to encourage States to make more frequent use of the International Court of Justice. Some of these proposals may be traced back to the debates of the Sixth Committee of the General Assembly when the item concerning the review of the role of the International Court of Justice was discussed in 1970-1974.[14]

VI. The Draft Convention on the Law of the Sea

In this context one should not forget that the draft Statute of the International Tribunal for the Law of the Sea, which has been drafted by the Third United Nations Conference on the Law of the Sea, provides for the establishment of a

14 See Resolution 3232 (XXIX) of 12 November 1974 on the Review of the role of the International Court of Justice. In this Resolution the General Assembly recognized the desirability that States study the possibility of accepting, with as few reservations as

specialized new judicial tribunal.[15] The suggested tribunal shall be open to the States parties to the Convention on the Law of the Sea as well as to other entities in accordance with special provisions, and the jurisdiction of the tribunal shall comprise all disputes and applications submitted to it in accordance with the Convention on the Law of the Sea and all matters specifically provided for in other agreements.

An investigation of the draft Statute reveals that the tribunal is to be composed of twenty-one members whose qualifications are comparable with those of the members of the International Court of Justice.[16] The tribunal will be capable of working in four chambers, composed of three or more members, as the tribunal may deem necessary for dealing with particular categories of disputes.[17] The Sea-Bed Disputes Chamber of the International Tribunal for the Law of the Sea is an example of the specialization of the subordinate organs.[18] It is worth noticing that the Sea-Bed Disputes Chamber will be entitled to give advisory opinions when requested to do so by the Assembly or the Council of the International Sea-Bed Authority on legal questions arising within the scope of their activities.[19]

Assuming that the Convention on the Law of the Sea will be adopted in due course there will exist, once the Convention enters into force, a specialized system of organs for the settlement of international disputes in the field of the law of the sea. From the point of view of the development of the international judicial system this may be regarded as a welcome innovation. It gives also rise to the question whether there will be in the future other comparable specialized judicial organs created to form a decentralized system of international courts?

A proposal to establish an International Criminal Court has been discussed by various organs of the United Nations for a long time. Relatively few States have supported this idea during the recent past and, therefore, it may presumably take considerable time until this court can be created. But other comparable proposals may be forthcoming for other fields, for instance, for economic problems and human rights. Here, again, a decentralized regional system may be a better alternative. In the light of the recent debates in the Sixth Committee of the General Assembly there is a likelihood of some pressure being put on the United Nations to see to it that the pacific settlement of disputes be developed through the creation of new either univeral or regional courts and tribunals. We seem to be approaching the threshold of a stronger system of judicial process in the field of international law.

possible, the compulsory jurisdiction of the International Court of Justice. Furthermore, the attention of States was drawn to the advantage of inserting in treaties, in cases considered possible and appropriate, clauses providing for the submission to the International Court of Justice of the disputes which concern such treaties.

15 See Annex VI to the Draft Convention on the Law of the Sea, doc. A/CONF. 62/WP.10/Rev. 3, pp. 165–175.

16 Article 2, paragraph 1, of the Draft Statute.

17 Article 15, paragraph 1, of the Draft Statute.

18 As to the proposed jurisdiction of the Sea-Bed Disputes Chamber see Article 187 of the Draft Convention on the Law of the Sea.

19 Article 189 of the Draft Convention on the Law of the Sea.

VII. Why do States not trust the judicial or arbitral process?

This leads one into the problem, what good does a fully developed system of courts, tribunals and arbitration organs do, in case it is not sufficiently used by States? Past experience indicates that States, in general, are hesitant to resort to the judicial process and that they prefer other pacific means to solve their disputes.[20] A recent ecample is the dispute between Norway and the Soviet Union concerning the division of the continental shelf in the Barents Sea. The parties have been negotiating for over a decade without reaching an agreement. Nevertheless, neither party seems to be willing to submit this dispute either to arbitration or to the International Court of Justice, although both would be meaningful alternatives from the procedural point of view at least. Another recent example is the refusal of Iceland to participate in the proceedings on the *Fisheries Jurisdiction* cases before the International Court of Justice.

In many instances the reluctance to submit international disputes to the judicial process is due to the fear that the somewhat unsettled state of the law in a particular case makes the submission risky.[21] Likewise, in some cases the parties or some of them seem to think that it is wiser at least to postpone the handling of a dispute until a later date hoping that the law which is going through a period of formation will be changed to a more favourable one from the point of view of the reluctant party. This may be understandable from the tactical point of view, but it may also be counterproductive in those cases where the other party loses its patience.

Fortunately, international law as a whole has reached another and more advanced stage than during the period before the Second World War. At that time it was quite usual that governments were suspicious of the standard of the international law provisions concerning many specific problems. Many rules were held to be unclear or under a continuous process of formation. Therefore, it was often difficult to forecast the contents of a judgment or award in those cases where a dispute would be submitted to a judicial or arbitral process.

Many governments were not confident in so far as their own facilities as a party to a dispute were concerned as it was feared that the leading experts on international law questions who often represented important States would put their case

20 When speaking of the present crisis of the International Court of Justice Eduardo Jiménez de Aréchaga points out that "it is understandable that States, like individuals, prefer to negotiate and compromise rather than to go to Court for a 'win or lose' decision; Foreign Offices wish to retain their control over the ultimate disposal of a controversy rather than relinquish that power to the Court". International Law in the Past Third of a Century, *Recueil des Cours, Académie de droit international,* Tome 159, 1978, I, p. 168.

21 When discussing the argument that governments do not take cases to the International Court of Justice because the outcome is unpredictable R. Y. Jennings points out, correctly, that "if the outcome of litigation were predictable, there would be no cases at all for any court lacking compulsory jurisdiction, save where one party had by chance been uncommonly badly advised". The Discipline of International Law, Lord McNair Memorial Lecture, *International Law Association, Report of the 57th Conference,* 1976, p. 12.

more effectively in court proceedings. Some important arbitral awards were also likely to lead to a similar conclusion.

When that situation is compared with the present stage of international law one has to admit that the situation has changed. In the first place the bulk of international law has greatly grown as a result of the extensive codification work which has been undertaken mainly by the United Nations.[22] It may suffice to refer, as an example, to the Convention on the Law of Treaties, which has already entered into force, and which forms a most important source of international law to all those who have to interpret problems of treaty law either in arbitral or judicial process. States need not fear anymore that the uncertainty of the law as such would lead to unwelcome surprises in case an arbitration or adjudication process is resorted to.

Another factor which has apparently undermined the confidence of especially new States is their fear that the International Court of Justice, due to the division of the seats, will not apply the legal principles to a case in a manner which would properly reflect their own regional rules.[23] This is still a problem and it may be the cause, or one of them at least, why especially Socialist States and new States have not been interested enough to submit their disputes to the International Court of Justice. Strange as it may seem, some Great Powers, whose nationals have continuously served as Judges of the Court, have not either shown any enthusiasm over the facilities offered by the Court. Instead, States like the United States have shown a distinct preference for various modes of arbitration. Needless to say, States which prefer arbitral process should include to their treaties provisions which cover the handling of possible future disputes.[24]

VIII. Conclusions

On the whole it seems as if the prerequisites for a more effective utilization of the arbitral and judicial process in the field of pacific settlement of disputes do exist and that, furthermore, in so far as the choice of various means is concerned, the situation is significantly better than ever before. There is no reason to become as

22 See Broms, Bengt, *Kansainvälisen oikeuden erikoisluonne*, Suomalainen Suomi, 1963, pp. 151-155.

23 T. O. Elias thinks, however, that the present number of judges is correct. In his opinion the point of increasing the membership from fifteen to twenty-five "does not appear to be the most urgent facing the Court today". *New Horizons in International Law*, Alphen aan den Rijn, Sijthoff and Noordhoff, 1980, pp. 79–80. Nevertheless Elias has suggested that Article 9 of the Statute of the International Court of Justice should be construed as "not emphasizing the principal legal 'systems' in the traditional sense, but rather the distinctive legal 'cultures' which had grown beyond the range of civil law and common law systems". Elias suggests that the clearly distinguishable cultures that have been devloping within Latin America, Asia and Africa should be given as fair representation as possible. Elias, T. O., *op. cit.*, pp. 83–84.

24 In view of the limited space available, it has not been possible to discuss the treaties on settlement of disputes, treaties which impose a general obligation to settle all disputes by peaceful means and treaties providing for an obligation to resolve the differences arising out of particular treaty arrangements.

discouraged as Vilhelm Lundstedt, a well-known Swedish author on legal problems, who in 1937 published in Uppsala a book called *Folkrätten – en livsfara för folken, i.e.*, "International Law – a Mortal Danger for Peoples".

In conclusion, I would like to say that JUS 81 is a forum which is especially well suited to discuss problems concerning the pacific settlement of disputes. As the participants come from different parts of the world their views are likely to reveal the reasons behind the reluctance of States to resort to arbitral or judicial process and to guide us in trying to find remedies to the existing dilemma. Although it has not been possible to deal above with the regional arbitral and judicial systems this is also a problem area on which views would be appreciated. It is submitted that regional solutions might be particularly well suited for the settlement of certain international disputes and that, similarly, a centralized system need not be the best solution for all international disputes. It is to be hoped for that the debate will cover these problems as well.

In the light of the basic views it may be possible to decide whether there is a continuing need for new organs for the conflict resolution or whether the presently existing ones offer a satisfactory network of means? Should some of the older resolutions by the General Assembly of the United Nations be carefully looked into? Do the proposals that have been presented during the work of the Special Committee on the Charter of the United Nations and the Strenghtening of the Role of the Organization merit support or are there other and more effective proposals in this field?

8.4. Organs for Conflict Resolution and Execution

Winston A. Tubman

A main argument of those who would deny the status of law to international law rests on the alleged absence of courts and law enforcement officers as found within States from the community of nations. The world court at the Hague, this argument goes, may be a Court of Justice, but it is not a court of law. Whatever merits this contention may have, it demonstrably goes against the practice and behaviour of States in their regard for International Law and makes claims for the role of courts and officers of law enforcement within a State that are greater than the actualities warrant. The prevalence of courts and of law enforcement agents reflects the existence of law and not the other way around. More than courts and policemen result from the existence of law. The phenomenon of law – i.e. norms which by tradition and consent are considerd as binding – employs numerous devices and instruments by which to hold sway over the conduct of a society. Indeed the more law abiding a society, the less conspicious will be the role of courts and policemen because public opinion and sentiment – forces more powerful than courts or law officers – ensure respect for law.

When the States of Africa were, with one or two exceptions, the colonial possessions of a few European Powers, the situations for conflict among and between them were much less than is the case today when there are more than fifty sovereign States on the continent. Besides this increase in numbers which has multiplied the potential for conflict, one needs to be reminded that the struggle against colonialism was not only the resistance of alien rule, it was most importantly a struggle aimed at colonial borders which often divided people of the same ethnic origins or split up into separate jurisdictions important natural resources and valuable lands in a manner which now hold fertile seeds for conflicts.

With the achievement of decolonization and the departure of the colonial overlords, many of the problems that went with the territories have remained and are the cause and source of constant conflicts among and between the States of Africa.

But while the conflicts among the African States are many and continue to grow in number and seriousness the organs for conflict resolution and execution in Africa, which is the focus of this brief paper, are not easy to identify.

There are, strictly speaking, no specific continental functioning organs within Africa that are charged unambiguously with conflict resolution and execution. The organs of the United Nations having conflict resolution and execution powers have effect within the African context by virtue of the acceptance by African

States of the requisite obligations under the United Nations Charter. Beyond this, the organs of the OAU which may bear resemblance to conflict resolution and execution organs are upon examination seen to be much less than that.

The obligations assumed by African States under the Charter of the Organization of African Unity (OAU) have definite legal import; but such import does not exceed the objectives laid down in the OAU Charter, the preamble of which states that signatores were "inspired by a common determination to strengthen understanding and co-operation among our States in response to the aspirations of our peoples for brotherhood and solidarity in a larger unity transcending ethnic and national differences".

These sentiments are lofty and well stated, but in terms of what they create by way of obligations laid down, one is left with a sense of vagueness. The vagueness is confirmed when the organs of the OAU and the powers vested in them are examined. Let us look at those organs briefly: The OAU Assembly of Heads of State and Government which is referred to by the Charter as the supreme organ is vested with power simply to discuss matters with a view to "co-ordinating and harmonizing the general policy of the Organization". The second tier organ of the OAU, its Council of Ministers, composed of the Foreign Ministers of member States, has been vested by the Charter simply with responsibility for preparing Conferences of the Assembly and for implementing Assembly decisions.

The apparent severe limitation of the OAU's powers under its Charter to impose a particular course of conduct upon its members has been brought out starkly in the issue now being debated within the Organization concerning the establishment of a Security Council type organ within the Organization of African Unity with powers of conflict resolution and execution.

The attempt to draw parallels from the United Nations Charter within the Organization of African Unity is not surprising because the maintenance of international peace and security – the primary objective of the United Nations – cannot be discharged in isolation. Member States of the UN are obligated whether in the UN or in their regional organizations or even bilaterally not to use force to settle disputes. No compulsory settlement of disputes is permissible under the scheme of the United Nations Charter except by Security Council action. Even when the International Court of Justice has been seized of a matter and has rendered a judgment, enforcement of that judgment depends ultimately upon the actions by the Security Council. Self-defence measures which States by virtue of Article 51 of the UN Charter may undertake in situations of urgency cease to be permissible unless the Security Council is, as soon as possible, brought into the picture.

Non-intervention in the affairs of sovereign States is a basic principle of both the Organization of African Unity and the United Nations. Constant conflict among a large number of relatively weak and small States such as the States of Africa often provides the pretext for intervention in the affairs of the continent by outside forces including the Super Powers, and serve to undermine the exercised right to self-determination and independence by leading to the return of the former colonial Powers to a Continent they once ruled.

The importance therefore which must be attached to the development of means of conflict resolution and execution within Africa cannot, as the conflict in Southern Africa centered around the issue of Apartheid and the numerous border disputes demonstrate, be overstressed.

If the Security Council is the model which the OAU would follow in an attempt to provide an effective organ for conflict resolution and execution, one faces immediately the very serious weakness in this regard which has been uncovered in the Security Council. Proposals before the Security Council in order not to be frustrated by the use of the veto must invariably wind up as weak compromises. When eventually such compromises assume the status of Security Council Resolutions the record of compliance with them has been far short of impressive. The institution of sanctions against South Africa on account of its racial policies, the oil embargo against Rhodesia on account of its illegal unilateral declaration of independence, the Security Council's Plan for the transition to independence by Namibia are all cases which come to mind. In all of these cases, the strict compliance with the Council's decision or sanctions has been unimpressive. Certainly States' conduct has been influenced by the Security Council resolutions, but instances of noncompliance and breaches have been numerous and startling.

Returning to the OAU Charter – under whose authority OAU members are being pointed to the Security Council's role and example in conflict resolution and execution – there exists no obligation to respect decisions of the OAU Assembly or Council paralleling that pertaining to the Security Council. The OAU Charter does not merely omit to concern itself with collective compulsion to respect obligations assumed under the OAU Charter or the will of the majority, rather its main thrust has been to leave OAU members free except through persuasion and a sense of the greater good of the group to comply or not comply with OAU principles and decisions. Compliance therefore rests upon and must be implemented by the same feeling of common ideals and aspirations which give rise to the creation of the OAU itself.

The principles set out under Article III of the OAU Charter – e.g. noninterference in each other's affairs, abhorrence of political assasinations – as well as the resolution of the Organization's 1974 Cairo Summit by which all member States pledge themselves to respect the borders existing on their achievement of national independence, the intent of all of these are clear enough but the means by which the OAU ensures compliance with them are weak or almost nonexistent. The OAU Charter does not provide for what is to follow when obligations under it are breached. Article XIX does contain a pledge by member States to settle all disputes among themselves by peaceful means. It further provides for the establishment of a Commission of Mediation, Conciliation and Arbitration. The Commission has been set up for quite a few years now and its members appointed, but thus far it has built up no enviable record of activity in conflict resolution and execution among OAU member States. The commission simply has not been used. The same is true of the Committee of Jurists established under the aegis of the OAU.

In the years since 1963 when the regional Organization was established, numerous conflicts have been brought before its organs. Those organs, particularly the Assembly and the Council as well as sub-organs established by them, have exerted much effort at conflict resolution and execution. Equally important – perhaps more so – has been the role played by mediation and good offices undertaken from time to time by African Heads of State to resolve conflicts on the continent. The OAU Charter does have limitations but because African States meet frequently and do so at the level of Heads of State, the decisions which they take at such meetings invariably acquire an import which go beyond the strict framework of the OAU Charter. Herein perhaps lies the most effective organ for conflict resolution and execution within Africa.

It is perhaps true that in no other region of the world have the mediation and good offices modalities of peaceful settlement of disputes been used with greater frequency and success than in Africa. Traditional African societies were quite accustomed to peace making through the mediation of elders and other respected personalities. The town meeting of elders, the palaver house, the veneration of elders and respect for tradition are features from African societies since time im-memorial that are being reflected today in inter-State conduct as pertains to conflict resolution and execution.

Frequent use of the informal flexible processes of mediation and good offices however indicates that the organs and formal structures for conflict resolution and execution are not rapidly being developed. The highly personalized and *ad hoc* nature of mediation and good offices elude systematization and militates against the urgent need which exists and which otherwise might have been felt a compelling argument for strengthening the OAU's organs for conflict resolution and execution.

Conclusion

The organs for conflict resolution and execution on the African scene are very rudimentary and still to be developed. The existence of the OAU as a regional Organization with Heads of States meeting at least once a year provides a pragmatic and workable modality for conflict resolution and execution which promises to grow in importance as the ideals of African unity commonality of interests and brotherhood continue to assert themselves. The growth of those ideals however would definitely be facilitated by functional, less ponderous organs for conflict resolution and execution.

8.5. Remarks on the Problem of Universalism and Regionalism

Ludwik Gelberg

Contemporary international law applies to all nowadays existing States. Universal development of economic, political and cultural relationships between States caused that international law regulating such relationships, encompasses today the surface of all the world. What is more, vivid development of contemporary technology enabling conquering outer-space and exploitation of formerly inapproachable regions, such as, e.g., sea and oceanbeds or deep-sea territories, caused that international law covers those above mentioned areas as well.

However, not all international law rules are of the same legal force, if regarded from the point of view of their applicability in space. International law is of universal, global, general character if it binds legally all the States belonging to the international community. Some authors are inclined to see the difference between universal law binding all States without exception, and general law binding a great number of States including the Great Powers (Oppenheim). However, general international law thus understood always shows a great tendency to transform into universal law. Therefore it would seem to us too pedantic and practically too difficult to establish, whether a given legal rule is recognized by all the States without exception, or by the majority only.

Until now international general or universal law has been in its greater part composed of customary law rules since only a few treaties binding all or almost all States of the world existed. As a result of active work in the field of codification undertaken on the basis of the UN initiatives, the situation in the last 25-years period has been substantially changed. Among the rules of general international law we should first of all mention the UN Charter, and especially the principles and purposes proclaimed in the introduction and Chapter I of the Charter. These principles are directly or indirectly recognized by all States of the modern world. Now, the preponderant majority of States belongs to the United Nations Organization and the scarce ones which are not its members have bound themselves to comply with the purposes and principles declared in the Charter in other acts of a normative character. So did, e.g., both German States not yet being members of the UN (GFR in a declaration of 3 October 1954 made during the London Conference, and GDR in an introduction to the Warsaw Treaty of 1955).

Besides universal international law there exists also regional law (of more local character) binding a certain number of States only, and therefore having limited special applicability. By this we mean first of all the law of the treaties, although regional customary law exists as well as a result of practice and legal consciousness of States linked by common economic and political interests and one geographical region (e.g. American States, West-European or Arab States, or States belonging to the Socialist community). Often the limits of international general law and regional rules are not distinct, since regional rules – at first binding only a limited number of States – may transform into generally recognized norms when the number of States accepting them increases.

Recently, the role of universal and regional organizations as well as their mutual relationships are vividly discussed in the doctrine and practice of many States. Such organizations act simultaneously on the international arena, and therefore the policy of their members, and especially those playing leading roles, naturally influence the appraisal of their activity.

From the point of view of a hierarchy, regional law may be placed as far as interested States are concerned before general law, since States – as subjects of international law – are able to enter into agreements of any possible contents. They cannot, however, conclude agreements violating basic principles and rules of general law (e.g., prohibition of using force, principle of non-intervention, etc.), which are of peremptory character *(ius cogens)* and therefore have priority over any particular law (article 53 of the Vienna Convention of the Law of Treaties).[1] Thus, the UN Charter (article 103) belongs to the rules of peremptory character *(ius cogens)*; we should also mention the prohibition to use force or threat of its use, rules of a humanitarian character contained in the Geneva Conventions of 1949 concerning war prisoners, rules prohibiting certain acts such as genocide, slave-trade or piracy. The role of particular norms in international law is great. The norms of general international law are in many instances not sufficient to govern relations between individual States having particular problems to be solved. Particular norms are often indispensable for the proper functioning of norms of general international law. The effective functioning of these norms in many instances depends upon the creation by the States concerned of particular legal norms based on norms of universal international law (Tunkin). States of some regions often regulate common matters by way of concluding particular regional treaties. It is worth nothing here that lately the Baltic States have concluded treaties in Gdańsk (1973) and in Helsinki (1974) with the purpose of protecting their interests in using the Baltic Sea resources.[2] All the 7 Baltic States are parties to these treaties, even though 5 of them belong today to the two powerful and opposed political and military groupings: the GDR, Poland and USSR are members of the Warsaw Treaty, whereas Denmark and the GFR are members of the NATO; while Finland and Sweden remain outside the blocs,

1 "A peremptory norm of general international law is a norm accepted and recognized by the international community of States as a whole as a norm from which no derogation is permitted and which can be modified only by a subsequent norm of general international law having the same character."

2 These issues were discussed in my work: Gelberg, L., *Cooperation of the Baltic States. Legal Problems.* Wroclaw, Ossolineum, 1981. 180 p., in chapter VI: Problems of the Conservation of the Living Recources in the Baltic Sea, pp. 82-104, and chapter VII: Protection of the Maritime Environment of the Baltic Area, pp. 105 – 120.

with their consequent policy of neutrality and disengagement. This was the Gdańsk Convention of Fishing and Conservation of the Living Resources in the Baltic Sea and the Belts concluded in September 1973 and the Helsinki Convention on the Protection of the Marine Environment of the Baltic Sea Area from March 1974. The two Conventions did not create any new regional organizations being subjects of international law, though there is a possibility that with the growing cooperation between the Baltic States in fishing, conserving the living resources of the Baltic and protecting the environment in this region the States concerned will reach the conclusion that it is necessary to establish a regional organization possessing appropriate permanent organs for the implementation of the aims and tasks envisaged by the two Conventions. The concluding of both the above mentioned treaties caused that the relations between the Baltic States are normalized and maintained in an atmosphere of cooperation and mutual understanding, and that the issue of elaborating a "Baltic Code" appeared. Undoubtedly, the crisis of the modern law of the sea and the difficulties in reaching a generally recognized agreement thereon are particularly favourable to such a regional solution.[3]

It should be mentioned here that the Gdańsk and Helsinki Conventions are regarded by many as a model of regional cooperation, applicable to other geographical regions as well. Both conventions can be considered to be a beginning of the "Baltic Sea Regionalism" which was a political product of the détente in this part of Europe. Today, there exist firm foundations for a further development and consolidation of the cooperation between the Baltic States in various fields, beneficial to all the participants. The conclusion of the two conventions started the process of introducing new legal rules into the Baltic region, which would settle all questions of the proper use of this sea. These include: co-ordination and concentration of scientific research, unification of navigation marking systems, tracing out and organization of ship traffic (including containers), common exploitation of the sea-bed resources, as well as unification of regulations concerning salvage operations, etc. We may assume that a regional law of the sea for the Baltic basin would to some extent serve as a pattern for the regulation of similar questions in other regions.

It is worth noting that the Baltic States, while concluding regional agreements, have decided not to abandon the universal principles and rules of the law of the sea, both those binding today and those that will probably be codified by the Third UN Conference on the Law of the Sea.[4]

3 A. A. Hermann states in his article "Oil Companies and the Law of the Sea" that: "if a compromise is not reached in the basic issues soon, there is a real danger that the international law of the sea will desintegrate and that each region or closed sea will make its own rules". See Hermann, A. A., Oil Companies and the Law of the Sea. *Fairplay International Shipping Weekly*, Vol. 250, No 4, 723, 28 February 1974, pp. 5-6.

4 This has found its expression in Article 21 of the Helsinki Convention. As envisaged, the provisions of the Convention "shall be without prejudice to the rights and obligations" of the signatories, ensuing from "the treaties concluded previously as well as treaties which may be concluded in the future, furthering and developing the general principles of the Law of the Sea that the present Convention is based upon".

A question arises how was the issue of universalism and regionalism treated in the UN Charter. The main purpose of the UN Organization was " to save succeeding generations from the scourge of war, which twice in our lifetime has brought untold sorrow to mankind" (from preamble), "to maintain peace and security" (article 1) by way of creating an effective world system of collective security. That system was supposed to prevent formation of blocs or political and military groupings of States, since – as we learn from experience of the inter-war period – they always lead to competition between the blocs and finally to their confrontation. The UN Charter shifted primary responsibility for the maintenance of international peace and security to the Security Council (article 24), which is the only competent organ to apply force in case of necessity on behalf of the UN. The Charter also allows for the existence of regional arrangements and agencies for dealing with such matters relating to the maintenance of international peace and security as are appropriate for regional action (article 52). They may cooperate in settling regional disputes although without the authority of the Security Council they are not allowed to apply force. A question arises, how in the light of the above provisions are we to value the formation and functioning of political and military organizations such as NATO, SEATO, CENTO and the Warsaw Pact. From a geographical point of view NATO, formed in 1949, can hardly be considered a regional organization. It covers the surfaces of States belonging to three continents, separated from each other by thousands of kilometers. Thus, e.g., the smallest distance between the territories of Canada and Turkey, two NATO members exceeds 6000 kilometers. From a geographical point of view, the notion of regionalism was in the NATO brought to absurdity. On the other hand, the Warsaw Pact covers the territories of States of Eastern and Middle Europe, all having borders with each other. The NATO recalls in its text the UN Charter and declares that it was concluded exclusively with the aim of individual and collective self-defence mentioned in article 51 of the Charter. There is no doubt about the fact that a preponderant majority of European States joining the NATO considered this Organization an instrument serving purely defensive purposes. We should remember, however, that declarations of some politicians and military officials of the leading NATO members do not always confirm purely peaceful intentions of this Organization. It is also difficult to forget that in the past quite a few treaties and peaceful declarations served only as a cover for not entirely peaceful purposes. It is difficult to maintain as well that political and military blocs help to strengthen general peace and safety. In 1955, i.e. 6 years after the NATO was signed and as an answer to it, the Warsaw Pact was concluded. At first, it was not thought of as an Organization uniting Socialist States only. There are no such words in its text as "Socialist internationalism" or "Marxist-Leninist principles" usually found in agreements concluded between the Socialist countries. The Warsaw Pact was "open for joining by other States without regard to their social or State structure" (article 9). Rather, the Pact was a warning in the face of a possible division of Europe into two blocs and a call to restore its unity.

This was the matter dealt with in article 11 (2) which states that "in case a system of collective safety in Europe or an all-European treaty with this purpose is signed, the Warsaw Pact will loose its legal force . . ." Naturally, the Warsaw Pact was transformed into a regional defensive Organization of the European Socialist countries[5].

If the situation allowed to conclude an all-European treaty concerning collective safety, i.e. the treaty which would naturally lead to the liquidation of both opposing Organizations, the interests of peace and safety would be well served. And even more positive effects would be the result of a development of international relations which would allow the UN to strengthen its importance, and bring to proper proportions the role of regional treaties and organizations as far as their relationship to the UN is concerned, since the latter is an effective organ of general collective safety in the world.

One of the key-problems of contemporary international relations characterized by total liquidation of the colonial system, is the problem of quick and effective assistance for the States which have only lately gained their independence, after centuries of slavery. Such States may gain strength only when their political independence is accompanied by economic independence, by economic and social restoration, and by breaking loose from long-lasting underdevelopment inherited after the colonial period. The necessity of assisting such States in their development is at present a generally accepted principle of international politics. Elementary equity requires that first of all the rich States participate in the realization of this principle. This concerns especially States which had for long years governed colonial territories and owe a part of their riches and welfare directly to colonial exploitation. Assistance in liquidation of the economic, technical, social and cultural backwardness of the States of Africa, Asia or Latin America would certainly constitute a partial restitution of material goods taken away by force from the nations of such countries by the nowadays highly developed Western States. However, this assistance cannot be linked with any political or military conditions, economic privileges or concessions, otherwise it would only mean another form of neo-colonialism. The process of compensating damages done in the past to the nations of the developing countries was to be carried on within the frames of a new economic order supported by these States. It is a difficult process because a new economic order naturally requires the introduction of changes or corrections into non-existing political and legal structures formed during the peaceful period of co-existence and co-operation of States belonging to different social and political systems. Some steps undertaken within the frames of the new economic order, aimed at assisting the countries of the Third World, did not bring the expected effects. As an example we may cite a proposition made in the field of the law of the sea, to create 200-miles economic zones in order to protect the economic interests of developing coastal States by preventing exploitation of adjoining maritime zones by highly developed States. This proposition was supported by Socialist and other States, however in practice it brought great profits to the richest States of the world, such as e.g. USA,

5 Legal analysis of this treaty is presented in a monography of Gelberg, Ludwik, *Uklad warszawski; studium prawnomiedzynarodowe*. Wyd. 1. Warszawa, Panstwowe wydawn. naukove, 1957. 202 p.

Canada, Japan, Australia: in the form of economic zones they took over vast territories constituting until now parts of the open seas (over 80 per cent of the whole of this new category of maritime territories). At present, there is a fight going on in order to ensure to a greater extent the interests of the developing countries in exploitation of sea-beds and deep-sea territories, i.e. areas beyond the jurisdiction of these States and considered "common heritage of mankind". Rich, highly industrialized States attempt with various methods to avail themselves of this issue without due consideration to the interests of developing countries. But although the question is of great importance we cannot forget that assistance for the developing States is necessary right away, when millions of people face the danger of hunger. In this action of assisting the developing countries undertaken in result of the program of the new economic order, and including a new division of wealth and technology transfer, regional organization such as the Organization of African Unity or the Arab League may play an important role. However, the role of the United Nations as a universal Organization, must always be decisive, since the future of the international world community depends upon the way one of those two international key-problems is solved.

The most important issue of the contemporary world is that of war and peace, i.e. the problem of life and death of hundreds of millions of people who would undoubtedly become the victims of thermo-nuclear war. The vivid development of war techniques, especially those using nuclear power and missiles, must act as a deterrent to any plan of beginning a war. As a matter of fact, such a war would only become a modern form of a collective suicide. It seems that the present division of forces on the international level made avoidance of war possible. The existing strong group of Socialist States constitutes a decisive element acting in favor of peace. The number of States which broke their colonial fetters is constantly growing. Also the number of States of Africa, Asia and Latin America, vividly interested in preserving peace, has substantially increased. Masses of people of imperialistic States rise against war. Many governments of States, which because of various reasons found themselves in military blocs and saw exclusively their peaceful aims, are decidedly against politics which might lead to war. To-day, a group of disengaged States plays an important role strengthening an already wide movement in favour of peace and anti-imperialism. In the present configuration of forces declaring themselves in favour of war or peace, the latter decidedly prevail, and in our opinion are able to eliminate the danger of war and enforce world peace; war, which was formerly considered inevitable because of existing imperialism. The main means to ensure peace and prevent war are: peaceful methods of settling disputes, strengthening of the system of collective security; steps aimed at weakening international tensions; total liquidation of colonialism and opposition to all possible forms of neo-colonialism; and most important, refraining from further armament. General disarmament, liquidation of the material and technical basis necessary to lead a war, and in particular destruction of terrible weapons of mass extermination, would constitute the most important guarantee for preserving peace. Even if we assume that none of the governments of the Great Powers give the first order to make use of such weapons, it may result from pure accident. As experience teaches us, even the best machines fail sometimes, and so does the nervous system of a man. Keeping of hundreds of rocket launchers aimed at the densely populated, most important centers of other States, constant flights of bombers equipped with deadly nuclear cargos, constitute a real and great danger for all the world. Explosion of even one nuclear bomb on the territory of another State (if only by accident) may cause a disaster probably not to be prevented by a hot line linking chiefs of the governments of the Super Powers. On the other hand, avoidance of such a catastrophe may undoubtedly be attained in case of total liquidation of these weapons in all States possessing them. In other words this means total disarmament.

Beyond that, the present state of armaments causes serious problems to all States. If military expenses of all the States in the world rose up to 4.2 billion dollars in 1929, they increased up to 120 billion dollars in 1961, 388 billion in 1976 and up to the almost astronomical sum of 550 billion dollars in 1980. This means more than 1 million dollars for every single minute (as counted by the Swedish SIRPI). The sum of annual expenses on armament rises up to two-thirds, or – according to others – equals the financial value of the combined national incomes of all underdeveloped States. As stated by a group of UN experts, there is no doubt about the fact that using for peaceful purposes all the resources now designed for defence, would serve the interests of all States and lead to improvement of economic and social conditions all over the world. Also, general and total disarmament would be beneficial to all mankind. Even a partial reduction of armaments, especially if carried out by the Great Powers, would release important material means which might be used in favour of and to the advantage of underdeveloped countries facing the danger of hunger; to increase the standard of their living.

All these most important issues, world peace and international safety, as well as the organically linked issue of disarmament and the banning of the use of nuclear weapon, naturally require universal regulation including participation of all States, and especially that of the great atomic Powers.

Certain achievements in this domain may be already mentioned, such as the Moscow Treaty of 5 August 1963 banning nuclear weapons in the atmosphere, outer space and under water; and the Treaty of 1 July 1968 on the non-proliferation of nuclear weapons. Of great importance is also the Treaty of 27 January 1967 on principles governing the activity of States in the exploitation and use of outer space including the moon and other celestial bodies, which contains an obligation not to introduce nuclear weapons and other kinds of mass extermination weapons into outer space. All these treaties show a clear tendency to transform restrictions on nuclear weapons into norms of universal law. Their weak side, however, is that two atomic States, such as the People's Republic of China and France, have not yet joined them.

On the other hand, a clearly positive role of regional agreements should be noted here. Thus, e.g. fourteen States of Latin America have signed on 14 February 1967 a Treaty banning storage, use and production of nuclear weapons in Latin America. Further seven States have recently joined this Treaty.

8.6. Universalism and Regionalism

Rudolf Dolzer

Introductory remarks

The width of the topic assigned to me suggests that the pre-conditions for the functioning of universally and regionally oriented models be studied, that possible variations of models containing elements of both concepts are examined and that the implications of the relevant major types of orders for the stability and justice of a world order[1] are outlined.[2] A comprehensive study of these broader topics would also have to address existing arrangements, a spectre of conceivable models for world order, and an examination of the relationship between these models and the existing order. In the following remarks, no such comprehensive approach to the topic can be offered.[3] The aim here is limited to point out some of the key problems that exist in this area. This necessarily involves both normative reasoning and speculative thinking.

1 The term "world order" is here used in a normative-analytical rather than an empirical-descriptive sense; for the ambivalence of the term as it is used in practice, see Hoffmann, Stanley, Report of the Conference on Conditions of World Order, in: *Conditions of World Order* (Hoffmann, Stanley, ed.), Boston, Houghton Mifflin, 1968. p. 2.

2 For more recent studies of world order, see Hoffmann, Stanley, *Primacy or World Order*, New York, McGraw-Hill, 1978. pp. 105–200; at times more extravagant Falk, R., *A Study of Future Worlds*, New York, Free Press, (1975), 506 p. For a brief discussion of world order models, see Pickus, R. and Woito, R., Five Approaches to World Order: The Idea and Discussion in the US, in: Clark, G. and Sohn, L., *World Peace through World Law* (as revised by Sohn, L.). Cambridge, Mass., Harvard University Press, 1973, pp. 66 ff.

3 The major studies prepared in this field: Nye, Joseph S., Jr., *International Regionalism*. Boston, 1968; Fenwick, Charles C., *The Organization of American States*. Washington, D. C., 1963; The Inter-American Institute of International Legal Studies, *The Inter-American System*. Dobbs Ferry, 1966; Thomas, Ann Van Wynen and Thomas, A. J., Jr., *The Organization of American States*. Dallas, 1963; Macdonald, Robert W., *The League of Arab States*. Princeton, 1965; Frey-Wouters, Ellen, The Prospects for Regionalism in World Affairs, in: Falk, Richard and Black, Cyril (eds.), *Trends and Patterns*, Vol. 1, The Future of the International Legal Order. Princeton, 1969, p. 463; Miller, Lynn H., The Prospects for Order Through Regional Security, in: Falk, Richard and Black, Cyril (eds.), *Trends and Patterns*, Vol. 1, The Future of the International Legal Order. Princeton, 1969, p. 556; Korbonski, Andrew, The Warsaw Pact. *International conciliation*, May 1969, p. 573; Claude, Inis L., Jr., The OAS, the UN and the United States. *International Conciliation*, March 1964, p. 547; Boutros-Ghali, Boutros, The Addis Ababa Charter. *International Conciliation*, January 1964, p. 546; Boutros-Ghali, Boutros, The Arab League: 1945–1955. *International Conciliation*,

With respect to the terminology used in the following remarks, it must be pointed out that the concept of regionalism is understood here in a broad sense. It would not appear to be helpful to limit the definition so that only arrangements falling under Chapter VIII of the UN Charter would be covered; the phenomena which occur in fact and which bear upon the present topic are not confined to the narrow issues of peacekeeping which are addressed in Chapter VIII. A wide definition of the kind suggested here has its disadvantages inasmuch as it becomes necessary thereby to examine in each specific normative context whether a more specific use of the terms is called for. However, in order to allow an adequate perspective of the broad topic, this consequence must be admitted.

1. The UN Charter: regionalism subordinate to universalism

The choice between regionalism and universalism as alternative routes for the preservation of world peace was a main theme in the negotiations leading up the adoption of the UN Charter. The views held on this point were widely divergent in the international community. Whereas in the Arab world, in Australia, and, in particular, in Latin America it was felt that an emphasis upon regionalism would strengthen the aspirations toward world peace, the great powers favoured a system in which all the basic decisions on matters of war and peace were to be made on the universal level; however, even the countries victorious in World War II were divided among themselves on this issue, at least during the earlier part of the discussions. The British Prime Minister did not fully share the preference for universalism, nor did France. As a result of this constellation of views, the UN Charter was finally phrased in a way which combines elements of universalism and regionalism. The composition and the voting rules of the Security Council as

May 1954, p. 498; Ved Nanda, P., The United States Action in the 1965 Dominican Crisis: Impact on World Order – Part II. *Denver Law Journal*, Vol. 44, No. 2, Spring 1967, p. 225; Halderman, John W., Regional Enforcement Measures and the United Nations. *Georgetown Law Journal*, Vol. 52, No. 1, Fall 1963, p. 89; Slater, Jerome, The Limite of Legitimization in International Organizations: The Organization of American States and the Dominican Crisis. *International Organiszation*, Vol. XXIII, No. 1. Winter 1969, p. 48; Wild, Patricia Berko, The Organization of African Unity and the Algerian-Moroccan Border Conflict: A Study of New Machinery for Peacekeeping and for the Peaceful Settlement of Disputes among African States. *International Organization*, Vol. XX, 1966, p. 18; Wilcox, Francis O., Regionalism and the United Nations. *International Organization*, Vol. XIX, 1965, p. 789; Padelford, Norman J., The Organization of African Unity. *International Organization*. Vol. XVIII, 1964, p. 521; Mecker, Leonard C., Defensive Quarantine and the Law. *American Journal of International Law*, Vol. 57, No. 3, July 1963, p. 515; Bebr, Gerhard, Regional Organizations: A United Nations Problem. *American Journal of International Law*, Vol. 49, No. 2, April 1955; Moore, J., The Role of Regional Arrangements in the Maintenance of World Order, in: *The Future of the International Legal Order* (Falk, Richard and Black, C., eds.) Vol. 3, Princeton, N.J., Princeton University Press, 1969, p. 122, note 2. For earlier studies of the problems, see Hoyt, Albert Jonathan, Regionalism and the United Nations. Los Angeles, Calif., microfilm copy of typewritten manuscript, negative, (1954) 522 p. Vellas, P., *Le régionalisme international et l'Organisation des Nations Unies*, Paris, A. Pedone, 1948, 166 p.

determined by Art. 27 of the Charter indicate the strength of the views held by the powers favouring universalism; on the other hand, the provisions contained in Arts. 51 to 54 of the Charter show that regionalism was by no means fully rejected in 1945. The precise legal significance of these latter Articles has never since been fully established: The ambiguities inherent in the wording of the Charter made it possible for international lawyers after 1945 to emphasise the subordination, the autonomy or even the superiority of regional principles *vis-à-vis* the universalist elements of the Charter if they so desired. Looking back at the original intentions of those who drafted the Charter, it is nonetheless safe to assume that regionalism was not meant to receive the same weight in the legal structure of the United Nations as universalism: In fact, regionalism was introduced as a subordinate element in the global framework of the Charter, more meant rather to strengthen than to weaken the fundamental decision in favour of universalism.[4] This view is supported most clearly by Art. 53 Section 1 sentence 2 according to which enforcement action shall not be taken under regional arrangements without the authorisation of the Security Council.

2. Definitional issues

After 1945, the debate on universalism and regionalism was continued, not surprisingly in the light of the flexibility which the wording of the Charter had left for future developments. Most of the discussions were carried on within the precincts of political science; the description of actual developments, its implications for world order and potential alternative routes have held less attractions as a topic of research for international lawyers. In keeping with the task of normative reasoning, the lawyers have focused on the specific meaning of Art. 51 to 54; however, it would appear that in doing so they have not entirely lost sight of the political implications of the various interpretations which they have set forth.

Definitional issues have not been prominent in legal analysis.[5] The UN

4 Thus, on the basis of the UN Charter, there is no necessity or desirability of a choice between regionalism and universalism; the issue is that of the appropriate balance. Also, this issue cannot be said to pose the same question in all areas; whereas, for instance, the preservation of peace has become an inherently global task, economic regional cooperation is fostered by the United Nations, at least to a certain extent.

5 The desirability of a consensus regarding the definitional issue was expressed in General Assembly Resolution 32/197 of 20 December 1977, Point 22.
For proposals in the literature, see Akindele, R., *The Organization and Promotion of World Peace: A Study of Universal-Regional Relationships*, Toronto, Buffalo, University of Toronto Press, 1976. p. 9 Andemicael, B., Foreword, in: *Regionalism and the United Nations.* (Andemicael, B., ed.) Dobbs Ferry, N. Y., Oceana Publications, 1979. p. 8; Frey-Wouters, Ellen, The Prospects for Regionalism in World Affairs, in: *The Future of the International Legal Order* (Falk, R. and Black, C., eds.). Vol. 1. Princeton, N. J., Princeton University Press, 1969. p. 466; Moore, J., The Role of Regional Arrangements in the Maintenance of World Order, in: *The Future of the International Order* (Falk, Richard, and Black, C., eds.) Princeton, N. J., Princeton University Press, 1969, pp. 142 f.; Nye, J. Regional Institutions, in: *The Future of the International Legal Order* (Falk, R. and Black, C. eds.), Vol. 4. Princeton, N. J., Princeton University Press, 1969. pp. 425, 429 ff.; Smithers, P., Toward Greater Co-

Charter itself does not spell out the constitutive elements of a "regional arrangement" or a "region".[6] Some attempts to delineate the meaning of the concepts used in the Charter were made in order to characterise specific groupings after World War II. A particularly difficult legal problem exists where there is a need to distinguish collective self-defence organisations set up under Art. 51 from regional arrangements falling under Art. 52.[7] The organisations concerned have themselves usually preferred a status under Art. 51: The exercise of self-defence does not require prior authorisation by the Security Council, nor are collective self-defence organisations required (as regional arrangements under Art. 54) to keep the Security Council "at all times . . . fully informed" of their activities.

It appears that three elements have presented particular problems in a legal definition of a "region". Firstly, it is not clear whether geographical proximity is a constitutive element of any region. Could a grouping involving, for instance, the Soviet Union, Cuba, Ethiopia and Mongolia qualify as a regional arrangement? Even though the original intentions of 1945 were probably not directed at such forms of regional grouping, it is far from clear that the Charter would prohibit a construction permitting such a regional arrangement.

A second point which is open to discussion relates to the purposes of a "region". Is it enough for a grouping to qualify when the scope of cooperation in the field of preservation of peace is very loose? Is it perhaps even sufficient, for some purposes, that the grouping's chief purposes be not at all related to issues of peace but, for instance, to environmental issues?

The third area which has not been exhaustively discussed concerns the question as to the subordination of the grouping under the terms of the rules established by the grouping itself. Could a regional group within the meaning of Chapter VIII of the Charter set up a rule implying that the group assumes permanent exclusive jurisdiction over all issues pertaining to its area? It would hardly seem possible to construe the Charter correspondingly, but neither has it been required in practice that a grouping explicitly recognises any specific subordination to the United Nations before being granted the status of observer at the United Nations.[8]

herence Among Intergovernmental Organizations through Governmental Control, in: *Regionalism and the United Nations* (Andemicael, B., ed.), Dobbs Ferry N.Y., Oceana Publications, 1979. pp. 26–36; Virally, M., Les relations entre organisations régionales et organisations universelles, in: *Régionalisme et universalisme dans le droit international contemporain* (Société Française pour le Droit International, ed.), Paris, A. Pedone, 1977. pp. 147, 148 ff. – For a most useful general survey of characteristics of regional organisations and their functioning, see Fried Esterbauer, *Grundzüge der Formen regionaler Gliederung im Regionalismus*. 1978. pp. 43 f.

6 Jenks, C. W., Co-ordination: A New Problem of International Organization, *Recueil des Cours, Académie de Droit International*, Tome 77, 1950, II, pp. 157–302.

7 Miller, Lynn, The Prospects for Order through Regional Secuirity, in: *The Future of the International Legal Order* (Falk R. and Black, C. eds.), Vol. 1, Princeton, N. J. Princeton University Press, 1969. pp. 556–560.

8 See General Assembly Resolution 253 (III) (concerning OAS); 477 (V) (concerning the League of Arab States); UN Doc. S/2988, S/3232, A/4543, A/4701 (concerning OAU).

One may well speculate whether definitional problems of the kind mentioned do not reflect a more fundamental issue in the present context: Has the concept of a "regional group" acquired at all that degree of specificity which makes it useful as an element of consideration in legal thinking about problems of world order? Most legal thinking about regionalism in fact stops after describing the composition, functions and organs of a regional arrangement, modes of cooperation with the United Nations and situations of confrontation which have evolved in practice. Apart from the fact that thinking in terms of world order may not in all corners be considered very rewarding, is there a substantive point indicating that regional groups have a specific role to play in the building of a future world?

From an empirical viewpoint, the frequency and the weight of phenomena usually described as regional cooperation certainly would permit such a conclusion. The pervasiveness of regionalism as a principle of present international cooperation does not find adequate emphasis in current legal thinking. Virtually all States are today involved in regional planning and cooperation. Nordic cooperation, for instance, between Denmark, Finland, Iceland, Norway and Sweden has advanced to an extent hardly realised in many quarters. The Group of 77 of course has become a powerful new force in the past decade which might well, in a broad definition of regionalism, also have to be taken into account here; the older regional institutions such as the OAS, the OAU or the European institutions have not lost their attractiveness. Looking at substantive areas of regional cooperation, an increase of activities will also be discerned. Efforts at cooperation in the human rights area in Africa and in the Arab States deserve particular mention;[9] a considerable part of international efforts in the environmental field takes place in regional groupings. Efforts toward more regional cooperation in the civilian use of nuclear energy may soon be under way,[10] to mention just one more field. The point here is not to describe the diversity of regional cooperation, but to recall the intensification which has taken place. Given this strong current trend, it is essential to reconsider international legal thinking about regionalism and its implications for world order.

One appropriate way of reassessing the "regional choice" is to contrast it with the elements of universalism as they have evolved since 1945. In this context, it is first necessary to recall the organisational manner in which universalism was conceived and fashioned in 1945. Universalism as understood in 1945 was in a sense a misnomer for the solution intended. Certainly, universalism was meant to indicate a "universal" solution inasmuch as major decisions were to be made not on the regional, but on the global plane. However, universalism was not meant to imply that the decision-making process on the global level was to occur in a "universal" body in which all States members of the UN were equally represented. On the contrary, the major peace-keeping institution was to be arranged

9 With respect to a regional approach to human rights, see: *Regional Promotion and Protection of Human Rights*, Twenty-Eighth Report. New York, Commission to the Organization of Peace, 1980.

10 Concerning problems of sovereign equality in the nuclear world, see Graf Vitzthum, W., Weltnuklearordnung und Staatengleichheit, in: *Festschrift Wilhelm Grewe* (Kroneck, S. and Oppermann, T., eds.) (forthcoming).

so that those powers who had won the war would also have a special responsibility and a correspondingly privileged position.[11] A considerable amount of thinking about regionalism and universalism has been misplaced because this specific meaning of "universalism" as a form of centralised structure of collective hegemony has not always been heeded. The Allied Powers made it very clear during the negotiations on the UN Charter that this specific version of universalism was an indispensable pre-condition for their cooperation in a future world organisation.[12] Thus, it is clear that the major body responsible for peacekeeping was set up on the assumption that the "veto States" would share a common interest in the future world order and in the working of the United Nations.[13] Opting for universalism in effect meant rather opting for great-power cooperation than for equal participation of all States on the global level. Against the background of this understanding of universalism, the concept of regionalism acquires a more distinct meaning: It signifies a preference, negatively speaking, for a geographical – perhaps also a substantive – limitation of great-power politics; of course this may in practice also mean that regionalism might be viewed by great powers as a form of delimiting spheres of influence. At the same time, regionalism has always relied on the assumption that peacekeeping is a concern which should and can be geographically limited; the same is true for fields of cooperation other than the key issue of peace.

3. Regionalism as a functional substitute for universalism?

Due to the ideological rift between the Soviet Union and the United States, the universalist element of the Charter has never been transformed into the practical operation of the United Nations. In a few instances, the Security Council did perform its envisaged function. In general, however, this was not true. The UN forces, a key element of peacekeeping in the Charter's system, were never established according to Art. 43 of the Charter, and the existence of the veto of the great powers meant in practice that their own activities were exempt from the supervision of the Security Council. Generally, the Council was paralysed whenever one of the great powers felt that any point on the agenda, irrespective of the regional area concerned, touched negatively upon its vital interests.

11 Claude Jr., Inis L., The United Nations and the Use of Force, *International Conciliation*, No. 532, 1961., p. 329: "The veto rule is an explicit declaration that the framers of the Charter rejected the idea of making . . . the United Nations an instrument of collective security in cases involving aggressive action by great powers".

12 For a history of the veto, see also Russell, R., *A History of the United Nations Charter: The Role of the United States, 1940–45*. Washington, Brooking Institutions, 1958. pp. 713–749; Akindele, *op cit. supra* (note 5), pp. 46 ff.; Askin, N., Le droit de "veto" au Conseil de Sécurité, in: *Thesaurus Acroasium, The Law of the United Nations*. vol. II. Institute of Public International Law and International Relations of Thessaloniki (Session September 1973), 1976 pp. 405–416; Wilcox, F., The Yalta Voting Formula. *American Political Science Review*, 1945. p. 954.

13 With respect to the model of world order which underlies in large part the UN Charter, see Ducci, R., The World Order in the Sixties, in: *The Strategy of World Order*, Vol. I, Toward a Theory of War Prevention. (Falk, R. and Mendlovitz, S. eds.), New York, World Law Fund, 1966. pp. 175 f.

Not surprisingly, regional tendencies filled the vacuum which was created by this failure of the universalist element in the United Nations.[14] When we look at the composition of the Security Council, at the personnel policy in the UN Secretariat, or at the election process used for offices of the General Assembly, it will be easily discerned that regionalism plays a much greater role than could have been assumed in 1945.[15] More recently, this trend was in a certain sense confirmed in the Third United Nations Conference on the Law of the Sea.[16] Whenever procedural questions were under consideration, the regional groups were the organisational units upon whose preferences the decisions were in fact based. In a real sense, regionalism has become an operational basis upon which the United Nations builds its functions.[17]

14 For specific examinations of the development of regionalism in the various areas of the world, see the essays in: *Régionalisme et universalisme dans le droit international contemporain*, Paris, A. Pedone, 1977. Jiménez de Aréchaga, E., L'évolution récente du régionalisme interaméricain, pp. 45–60; Boutros-Ghali, B., Le système régional africain, pp. 61–72; Isoart, P., Le régionalisme en Asie du Sud-Est, pp. 73–112; Andréani, J., La Conférence sur la sécurité et la coopération en Europe, pp. 113–128. For the causes of the growth of regional bodies, see Smithers, *op. cit. supra* (note 5), pp. 29 ff. See also Moore, *op. cit. supra* (note 3), pp. 127 ff. It would be worth a separate study to examine in detail both the positions of the big and the smaller States *vis-à-vis* regionalism; these positions have shifted in the post-war period. Yalem, R., Regionalism and World Order, in: *The Strategy of World Order*, Vol. 1 (Falk, Richard A. and Mendlovitz S., eds.), New York, World Law Fund, 1966, pp. 214 ff., suggests that regionalism is a response to the decline of the territorial State "in which changing technological conditions have rendered the State more penetrable and less secure than at any other period in modern history", p. 218; see also Nye, *loc. cit. supra* (note 5), p. 434. For a recent discussion of the development of substantive regional international law, and its relationship to universal law, see Golsong, H., Le développement du droit international régional, and Dubois, L., Les rapports du droit régional et du droit universel, both in: *Régionalisme et universalisme dans le droit international contemporain*, Paris, A. Pedone, 1977, pp. 221–242 and pp. 263–288.

15 According to Art. 23 Section 1 sentence 3 of the UN Charter, "equitable geographical distribution" is one of the considerations guiding the elections of the nonpermanent members of the Security Council. Regional considerations have also been prominent in elections for the UN Economic and Social Council, for the International Court of Justice and various UN committees; in some cases, the relevant procedure has been formalised, see, e.g., General Assembly Resolution 1192 (XII) and 1991 (XVII). The groups established within UNCTAD must also be mentionned here. Regional groupings have been referred to explicitly in the General Assembly Resolution, enlarging the Security Council and the Economic and Social Council, General Assembly Res. 1991 (XVIII), 17 Dec. 1963; see on this point also Mosler, H., The International Society as a Legal Community, Alphen A. D. Rijn, Sijthoff & Noordhoff, 1980, pp. 184 ff.

16 See on this point Graf Vitzthum, Wolfgang, *Peaceful Change through International Lawmaking, Law and State*, 1981. pp. 7, 17 f. With respect to regional chambers of the International Court of Justice, see the reports by Garcia-Amador, F., and Golsong, H. in: *Judicial Settlement of International Disputes* (Mosler, H. and Bernhardt, R., eds.) Berlin, Heidelberg, New York, Springer, 1974, pp. 83–98, 99–118.

17 See Gautron, J., Le fait régional dans la Société internationale, in: *Régionalisme et*

The question which must necessarily arise from the viewpoint of world order in the light of the decline of the universalist element and the dominance of regionalism relates to the functional implications for the UN as a whole: Has regionalism only replaced the universalist element in an organisational sense, or have the regionalist forces also entered into the existing vacuum in a functional sense?[18] Legally speaking, the preconditions for effective peacekeeping through regional groupings have never existed inasmuch as the Charter's basic structure was never adapted to the developments occurring after 1945.[19] Apart from the legal aspects, have the regional groupings been able in fact to perform peacekeeping functions which had been assigned to the Security Council in San Francisco? It appears helpful to distinguish between intra-regional and trans-regional peacekeeping functions in this respect. It was certainly not to be expected that trans-regional situations could as rule be effectively dealt with by regional organisations. In the few instances in which such situations occurred, it indeed becomes apparent that regional groupings had no strong potential to contribute toward peaceful solutions. However, the record of regional groupings in preventing or solving intra-regional disputes has not been fully satisfactory either.[20] Most of the numerous violations of the prohibition of force as enshrined in Art. 2 (4) have occurred in such disputes. No discernible consistent pattern in the approach to solving such disputes on an organised international level has emerged. When such a dispute was placed on the agenda of the Security Council there has been a tendency to refer it to the regional organisations concerned. However, the effective power of these organisations to influence their members has not always

universalisme dans le droit international contemporain, Paris, A. Pedone, 1977, pp. 5 ff. Regionalism has become a major organisational means of achieving influence within the United Nations; see also Virally, *op.cit. supra* (note 5), p. 149.

18 Thinking about universalism and regionalism has become more important after it became clear that the premises of functionalism may not turn out to be correct; this seems to be true at least from a European viewpoint. For a variety of theories of a "functional" view of world order, see the essays collected in: *Functionalism* (Groom, A. and Taylor, P., eds.) New York, Crane Russak, 1975. It is remarkable that there has been no clear tendency of bloc voting in the International Court of Justice; for some statistical material, see Hensley, T., Bloc Voting on the International Court of Justice, *the Journal of Conflict Resolution* Vol. 22, 1978, pp. 39.

19 For the early discussion, see van Kleffens, E., Regionalism and Political Pacts, *American Journal of International Law*, Vol. 43, 1949, p. 668; see also: Potter, P., Universalism versus Regionalism in International Organization, *American Political Science Review*, Vol. 63, 1943, p. 852, Bebr, Gerhard, Regional Organizations, A United Nations Problem, *American Journal of International Law*, Vol. 59, 1955, p. 168, Goodrich, L., Regionalism and the United Nations, *Columbia Journal of International Affairs*, Vol. III, 1949, p. 8.

20 For instance, with respect to the achievements of the OAU in peacekeeping, Andemicael, The Organization of African Unity and the United Nations, in: *Regionalism and the United Nations* (Andemicael, B. ed.), Dobbs Ferry N.Y., Oceana Publications, 1979, correctly concludes for the period after 1973: "Its main achievement has been in helping to reduce tensions between members, but it has done little to resolve the disputes or to remove the problems which caused the tensions", p. 258.

sufficed to intervene in a decisive manner.[21] Nor even has the will of the regional organisations to do so been always shown. The cases in which the activities of a regional organisation had a positive result have been less numerous than those in which an ambivalent result or none at all was reached.[22] Seen from this perspective, the regional organisations have sometimes assumed a kind of exculpatory function for the United Nations without in fact contributing to effective solutions. This aspect of modern regionalism may well represent its most negative contribution to the well-being of the international community, in particular when the subordination of one State in the region by forceful intervention of a more powerful State was involved. At the same time, one must also accept the fact that the Security Council has been aware in such cases of the course of action but did not intervene. The point here, however, is that regionalism has not been able to play the role of a substitute element of peacekeeping in the past decades. The original decision in favour of universalism and against a priority for regionalism has in this light not been proven wrong by the history of peacekeeping since 1945.

Turning away from peacekeeping, it must also be asked in our context how regional organisations have been cooperating and interacting with parts of the United Nations in other areas. The most important field to be mentioned here is of course that of economic cooperation.[23] The Economic Commissions set up by the United Nations after the war have not everywhere, again due to ideological rifts, been able to operate on the scale originally planned;[24] this is true in particular for the Economic Commission for Europe. Regional economic forms of cooperation have been much more effective in this area.

Where ideological obstacles to activities of regional branches of the United Nations were not present, the States involved nevertheless preferred in most areas to establish in addition ways of cooperation among themselves which had parallel functions. Of course, this presented the problem of reducing and avoid-

21 With respect to the relationships between the major regional organisations and the United Nations, see the following essays in: *Regionalism and the United Nations*, (Andemicael, B., ed.). Dobbs Ferry, N.Y., Oceana Publications, 1979: Andemicael, B., *loc.cit. supra* (note 20), pp. 225–298; Hassouna, H., The League of Arab States and the United Nations, pp. 299–338; Levin, A., The Organization of American States and the United Nations, pp. 147–224. This volume, published by UNITAR, contains also valuable studies relating to problems of coordination between the United Nations and the other major regional groupings now in existence.

22 With respect to general problems of regionalism in peace-keeping, see also Zacher, M.W., International Conflicts and Collective Security, 1946–77. New York, Praeger, 1979, 297 p.

23 With respect to considerations relating to a reorganisation of the United Nations in the area of economic activities, see Doc. E/5172, Nov. 72; E/5727; JIU/REP 75/2, 1975; Res. 3362 (S–VII); Res. 32/197 of 20 Dec. 1977 (Restructuring of the Economic and Social Sectors of the United Nations System).

24 With respect to the UN Economic Commissions, see Fagen, M. and Siotis, J., Les Commissions économiques régionales de Nations Unies, in: *Régionalisme et universalisme dans le droit international contemporain*, Paris, A. Pedone, 1977, p. 167.

ing duplications of functions and eliminating frictions.[25] In general, the necessary cooperation has in fact been achieved, mainly due to the influence which the members of the regional group exerted upon the universal level toward adapting the activities of the United Nations to the needs as perceived by the region in question. Such interaction between universalism and regionalism may well be viewed as a positive factor inducing effective action on the regional level; at the same time it cannot be overlooked that if the influence of the regional group upon the universal body becomes too strong, it could imply that the broader aspirations of the international community as a whole could, in case of divergent views, no longer be transformed into operational programs.[26] Whereas this aspect might appear to be more of an academic nature, it would be much more disquieting from a universal viewpoint for the regional forces to become so strong as to effectively replace the functions of the universal organisation; tendencies in this direction have not been entirely lacking in the past.

The foregoing observations have been primarily directed at those areas in which regional organisations have been active even though the United Nations has a mandate to act in these areas as well. Another, in a sense more important, way of viewing the alternatives of universalism and regionalism in the present context consists in assessing the regional groupings in terms of their general attitude toward the importance and the functioning of the universal order. In other words, can we perceive any general sign that regions are in fact positive elements of world order which serve universal peace in a manner consistent with the purposes and principles of the United Nations?

The idea of regionalism as a necessary and desirable element of world order, in the sense of a subsidiary level of global organisation and cooperation, occurs in theoretical thinking about world order and has also played a certain role in the evaluation of existing regional arrangements. At the same time, regionalism may be seen as the modern version of traditional power politics involving sometimes shifting and basically unstable systems of rival alliances; within regional groupings, the danger of the domination by one power has not always been averted.

25 With respect to problems of duplication, see Smithers, P., *loc.cit. supra* (note 5), pp. 13, 25. During the 1930's, for instance, the Chaco dispute was under consideration not only of the League of Nations, but also of regional groupings; there was a lack of coordination, and the efforts toward a peaceful settlement were hindered and delayed.

26 For clear evidence of existing competition and rivalry between universal and regional organisations in the economic field, see Newman, P., Regionalism in Developing Areas: United Nations Regional Economic Commissions and their Relations with Regional Organizations, in: *Regionalism and the United Nations* (Andemicael, B., ed.), Dobbs Ferry N.Y., Oceana Publications, 1979, pp. 350 ff., 375 ff. See on this point also UN Doc. E/5727, 69. For the relationship of European regional organisations and the United Nations, see Lukin, L., The Council for Mutual Economic Assistance and the United Nations; Robertson, A., The Council of Europe and the United Nations; de Gara, J., The European Economic Community and the United Nations, all in *Regionalism and the United Nations* (Andemicael, B., ed.), Dobbs Ferry, N.Y., Oceana Publications, 1979, pp. 449–488, 489–542, 543–586.

The ambivalence of regional groupings from the viewpoint of a global order, which becomes apparent from such conflicting perspectives, however, is not of a nature which prohibits any attempt at assessing the roles which existing groupings play for the stability of the global order. In a sense, the international lawyer is in a better position to discuss this issue than colleagues from other disciplines: From a global viewpoint, the willingness of regional organisations to refer issues of global interest to the global level, the readiness to defer to decisions made on the global level within the region, and the effective implementation of functions assumed within the framework of the global organisation are those elements which divide regional groupings in the sense of subsidiary elements of global organisation from traditional alliances. Of course, the strength of the mechanisms intended for effective interaction between the global and the regional level must also be considered in this context.

Looking at existing arrangements in the light of such criteria yields no clear picture. Whereas the constitutions of some organisations explicitly refer to cooperation with the United Nations, others do not. The fact that the major regional groups have been admitted as observers within the United Nations does not weigh heavily enough to allow a conclusion in this context. The difficulty here in reaching a globally oriented judgment is again related to the partial inefficiency of the universal institutions within the United Nations: Inasmuch as no effective decision-making body exists at the global level, regional organisations do not have to take a firm position in their attitude toward interregional cooperation. Altogether, it appears for these reasons difficult to make any general statement about the willingness of regional groupings to synchronise their activities with the global interests as determined by a universal organisation.[27] From a normative rather than descriptive viewpoint, the judgment can hardly be evaded that contemporary regional groupings are so diverse in their structure,[28] their objectives of cooperation,[29] in their attitude to world order[30] and their attitude

27 For the ambivalence of regionalism, see also Lang, W., Internationaler Regionalismus, in: *Regionalismus* (Esterbauer, F., ed.), 1978, pp. 83 f.

28 Whereas some regional organisations, in particular OAS and OAU confer a right of membership to all States situated within their geographic sphere, most constituent instruments of regional groupings provide that a positive decision by the major organ is required.

29 See, for instance, on the divergent motives behind the various regional organisations in Asia, Hass, M., Asian Intergovernmental Organizations and the United Nations, in *Regionalism and the United Nations* (Andemicael B., ed.), Dobbs Ferry, N.Y., Oceana Publications, 1979, p. 403. The major arguments advanced in favour of regionalism are the necessity of smaller States to retain their independence and influence by organising in a common framework, the requirements of a stable economic system and the flexibility of a world order needed to permit peaceful change, see Frey-Wouters, E., *loc.cit. supra* (note 5), p. 465.

30 The OAS Charter reaffirms the principles and purposes of the United Nations in its preamble; it also states, in Art. 1, that the OAS is a regional agency within the framework of the United Nations; in the OAU Charter (preamble) it is stated that "the UN provides . . . a solid foundation for peaceful and positive cooperation among States", but otherwise no clear-cut position is expressed. The Covenant of the League of Arab

toward other regional institutions that it is not possible to speak globally of regionalism as an element of world order.[31]

4. States as dominant actors in regional and universal organisations

Looking back from a broader perspective at trends in universalism or regionalism as they have evolved since 1945, it is essential to realise one aspect which so far has not been mentioned explicitly: When the choice between universalism and regionalism was discussed in 1945, there was a widerspread willingness to look at both concepts in terms of their meaning for the global order and to adapt and modify both of them to global needs. Both were seen as alternative, perhaps complementary, models of world order. In the light of this fundamental global dimension in the juxtaposition "universalism versus regionalism", the basic change in the developments since 1945 becomes apparent. Universalism in this sense is no longer today a topic of discussion in terms of practical political orientation and substantive organisational thinking and planning. This is not only true for the activities of the Security Council; more far-reaching in terms of the general functioning of the United Nations is that tendencies to view and use the United Nations more as a convenient forum for multilateral diplomacy than as a centre of global orientation and decision-making have grown and in some areas become dominant over the past decades.[32] Looking, on the other hand, at

States, set up in March 1945, has never been amended with respect to the relationship to the United Nations, although Art. 3 explicitly leaves room for such a change. Virally, *loc.cit. supra*, (note 5), p. 149, suggests that the distinction between "universal" and "regional" organisations should be abandoned in favour of "limited" ("*partielles, ou restreintes*") and "universal" organisations.

31 See on this point also the encyclical letter of Pope John XXIII, *Pacem in Terris/Peace on Earth*, Lyon, Chronique Sociale de France, 1966, 141 p., No. 135: "It can be said, therefore, that at this historical moment the present system of organization and the way its principle of authority operates on a world basis no longer correspond to the objective requirements of the universal common good". – There is no reason to assume that the "Cunning of Reason" operates so that the present regional blocs will later form the basis for a more unitary order. – For a negative assessment of regionalism, see Gaitskell, H., An Eight Point Programme for World Government, reprinted in: *The Strategy of World Order*, vol. 1 (Falk, Richard A. and Mendlovitz, Saul H., Eds.), New York, World Law Fund, 1966., pp. 117 ff.; Yalem, R., *loc. cit. supra* (note 14), p. 222. For some general thoughts on the reconsideration of issues concerning universalism and regionalism, see Smithers, P., *loc cit. supra* (note 5), p. 36. Smithers rightly suggests that regional tendencies in the economic sphere have encroached upon the universal jurisdiction of the United Nations; he recognises, at the same time (pp. 67 ff.) that inefficiency of the United Nations has contributed to this development. For a policy-oriented analysis of issues of universalism and regionalism in the field of security, see Moore, J., *loc. cit. supra* (note 3).

32 See on this point Mosler, H., *op. cit. supra* (note 15), p. 176. The only UN organ which can be presumed to express the common interest is the Office of the Secretary General. Of course, its powers have been limited. Further legal analysis is needed to establish the type of actions in which the Secretary General may act independently as he did, for instance, in the Iran crisis in early 1980. – With respect to recent discussions on the

regionalist thinking, we have seen that regionalism has in fact again become a strong force in international relations, but that it has received its main impetus and significance from sources not specifically related to categories of global thinking. In this sense, to overstate the point, "universalism or regionalism" has been a mode of political and legal thinking which was specific to the historical period immediately following the end or World War II, but which in subsequent years lost its dynamic force. "Universalism or regionalism" from a contemporary viewpoint has virtually become a nontopic: The common underpinning of global thinking is in general no longer discernible practice, and the same is true, to a certain extent at least, with respect to legal analysis. Of course an analysis of the variety of sources which may have led to this situation is beyond the scope of the specific topic to be discussed here. However, in thinking about the past and the future of universalism and regionalism it is indispensable that one touches, at least briefly, upon the major category of international law which has been at the basis of the developments here discussed: I speak of course of State sovereignty.

Thinking about "regionalism and universalism" implies a readiness on the part of States to abandon parts of their sovereign power which they enjoy under traditional international law. It is thus no surprise to find that the decline of global thinking in terms of universalism or regionalism has been accompanied by a re-emphasis of the concept of State sovereignty to an extent that has not occurred since the end of the last century.[33] To mention just one important area: The attempts at peaceful settlement of international disputes by means of international arbitral bodies or courts were stronger in the period before World War I, and between the two Wars, than they have generally been after World War II. The emphasis upon State sovereignty on the part of Communist States after World War II has been an integral part of their view of international law. At the

desirability of a stronger position of the Secretary General, see UN Doc. A/34/33, Supplement No. 33, pp. 6, 8; A/35/33, Supplement No. 33, pp. 12, 22. For two useful short studies on the Secretary General's position, see Gordenker, L., The Secretary General, in: *The United Nations: past, present and future:* (Barros, J., ed.), New York, Free Press,1972. p. 104; Alexandrowicz, Charles, The Secretary-General of the United Nations, in: *The Strategy of World Order*, (Falk, R. and Mendlovitz, S. eds.), vol III, New York, World Law Fund, 1966; see also Gordenker, Leon, *The UN Secretary-General and the Maintenance of Peace*, New York, Columbia University Press, 1967, 380 p.; Petrolia-Ammaniti, M., The Position of the Secretary-General of the UN in the Organization and in the International Community, in: *Thesaurus Acroasium, The Law of the United Nations*, vol. II. Institute of Public International Law and International Relations of Thessalonika (session Sept. 1973), 1976, pp. 351–368.

33 For issues relating to the basic problems relating to the effects of the concept of sovereignty upon modern international relations, see, for instance, Doehring, K., Internationale Organisationen und staatliche Souveränität, in: *Festgabe für Ernst Forsthoff*; Hinsley, Francis Harry, *Sovereignty*, London, C. A. Watts, 1966, 255 p.; *Between Sovereignty and Integration* (Ionescu, Ghita, ed.), London, Croom Helm, 1974; *In Defence of Sovereignty* (Stankiewicz, W., ed.), New York, Oxford University Press, 1969, 305 p.; Passerin d' Entrèves, Alessandro, *The Notion of the State: an introduction to political theory.* London, Oxford University Press, 1967, 233 p.

same time, the new States which have emerged from colonial domination in the past decades have relied heavily upon the traditional categories of international law.[34] During their struggle for decolonisation, they have placed emphasis upon the principle or self-determination which developed within the confines of international law after World War I. When independence was achieved, the units were formed as States in the traditional sense; and after the establishment of statehood, these States placed heavy emphasis in their international relations upon the principle of State sovereignty. Let me illustrate this in one area, that of State responsibility for the treatment of alien property: Whereas international law had gradually established international standards in this field, the opaque concept of "Permanent Sovereignty over Natural Resources"[35] was used to deny in effect the relevance of international law in this area and to re-allocate the rule-making power exclusively to State organs.

More broadly speaking, the emphasis upon State sovereignty found its corollary in heavy attacks upon the system of traditional international law, even though that very system had permitted and facilitated the birth and development of the new States. The major ground on which these attacks were placed related to the historical fact that traditional international law had developed within Europe. From this historical fact it was concluded that the values supported by traditional international law originated in a specific European culture. Although this may be so in specific areas, the arrgument in principle has no solid foundation. International law as it has developed in the past centuries grew out of the age of Enlightenment when it became necessary to develop rules governing the relations of independent States. According to patterns of rational thinking, the rules of traditional international law emerged, leaving internal aspects, their legal and cultural systems to these States;[36] it was only to govern the more technical aspects of relations between the States. It is because of this functional basis of traditional international law that, as a system, it cannot be termed as outdated under modern circumstances.

The negative repercussions which have accompanied the basic concept of absolute State sovereignty for international relations have been gradually percevied by the international community, and slowly a more relative notion of State

34 See Mosler, H. *op. cit., supra* (note 15), p. 11: "The movement towards independence has not furthered the process of unification, though a tendency of larger unions of States and world organisations towards federal organisation seems to have arisen from the terrible lesson taught by the two World Wars, which were caused by anarchy among the existing group of States." See also L'Connell, D., The Role of International Law, in: *Conditions of World Order* (Hoffmann, Stanley, ed.), Boston, Houghton Mifflin, 1968, pp. 49, 50.

35 Dolzer, R., New Foundations of the Law of Expropriation of Alien Property, *American Journal of International Law*, vol. 75, 1981, p. 553.

36 See on this point Mosler, H., *op. cit. supra* (note 15), pp. 3 ff.; Nussbaum, Arthur, *A Concise History of the Law of Nations*, New York, MacMillan, 1947 & 1954, 376 p. Ruddy, Frank Stephen, *International Law in the Englightenment: the background of Emmerich de Vattel's Le Droit des Gens*. Dobbs Ferry N.Y., Oceana Publications, 1975, 364 p.

sovereignty has gained acceptance. The trend away from sovereignty toward notions of international cooperation has not been strong enough, but it will not suffice in the future to express disapproval of existing international law and simultaneously to re-emphasise a concept of sovereignty which has little to offer in terms of guidance for actions taken in global rather than national interests. These observations are not meant to allocate any specific value judgment upon particular States or groups of States: The record in terms of insistence upon sovereign rights would be much too eomplex to address it comprehensively in a few sentences. To mention one important element which indicates a significant trend and which would not correspond with the foregoing general remarks: The record of the Third World in terms of submitting to the compulsory jurisdiction of the International Court of Justice compares quite favourably with that of the developed States. The intention here was merely to point out the relationship between the decline of regionalism and universalism and the resurgent trend of legal thinking in terms of State sovereignty.

In terms of regionalism and universalism as current categories of global thinking, the resurgence of the concept of State sovereignty and the limitations which it has placed upon considerations of the interests of the international community, one effect must be considered as particularly unfortunate. The decision in favour of States and the emphasis upon sovereignty clearly reflects a view that no other form of organisation affords the same well-being and security as the traditional concept of the State. One aspect of this attitude is that alternative forms of organisation, for instance in supranational or federal arrangements, have not long existed. The trend away from international forms of organisation which we have observed in the post-war period in some areas will probably reinforce the widespread feeling that a State in its traditional form is the ideal form of organisation for each independent community.

One development within States needs further consideration in this context. One main topic of political thinking – practical and theoretical – about the future of States has been the concern about the "ungovernability" of larger States, i.e. a feeling that the diversity of interests and the intensity with which they are faced presents problems of manageability which might grow ever more serious;[37] the fact that (for instance) virtually all European States with centralist constitutions are plagued by problems of separation of ethnic groups is only one facet of the growing problems of "governability", or rather "ungovernability". One might speculate whether this phenomenon, if it should continue to develop, could have an impact upon the broader aspects of the organisation of the international community.[38] It would seem at present that some individual States might be weakened by this trend, but there is no sign at the moment that the concept of the State would in a general sense be modified by such developments. In a sense,

37 See on this point Crozier, M. et al., *The Crisis of Democracy (Report on the Governability of Democracies to the Trilateral Commission)*, New York, New York University Press, 1975, 220 p.

38 See on this point Allemann, F., Aufstand der Regionen, in: *Regierbarkeit*, vol. II (Hennis, W. et al., eds.), 1979, pp. 279–309.

problems of "governability" may well serve to point out that the traditional notion of the State has its very basis in the desire to preserve order and human dignity.[39] Hobbes' theory of the State today still deserves close attention. The State, at least when it functions, must so far still be viewed as the most effective way of organising peace and justice,[40] ritual attacks upon the State notwithstanding.[41] Alternative models of world order must be measured on this yardstick before they can be accepted and implemented.[42]

5. *Universalism, regionalism and the United Nations Charter: a contemporary perspective*

The Charter of the United Nations was the product of the specific historical situation as it had developed up to 1945.[43] The major concern toward which the deliberations in San Francisco were directed and which is addressed in the Charter's provisions is the avoidance of another World War II, another situation as it developed up to 1939. The factors dominating present international relations are of course by no means identical with those of 1939 or 1945. The stability of international peace is today basically a question of the ideological rift which developed after 1945. The emergence of new States and their aspirations to restructure the existing international society were of no dramatic concern in 1945, but it is today the single most important issue in the practical work in the United Nations. Of course, such a situation has provoked allegations that the Charter has become an outdated instrument and that it needs to be redrafted in the light of current realities. The composition of the Security Council and the voting rules of Art. 27 (3) of the Charter have been the most frequent target of criticism.

One aspect of the Charter and its implications which has been less frequently discussed, but which needs further consideration in the future, shall be briefly sketched here. It has become virtually a commonplace statement in current pol-

39 It must not be overlooked that the sovereignty of the State is the basic principle upon which the UN Charter (see Art. 2) was built. The view that there is today an international obligation to cooperate, in the absence of a specific treaty obligation, is at best questionable; the provisions of the Charter have been phrased too vaguely to permit a different conclusion.

40 See also Mosler, H., *op. cit. supra* (note 15), p. 15: "It is certainly true that the era of the nation State will last for a long time yet. It is therefore . . . not by working for the disappearance or transformation of the nation State that progress will be made, but by accepting it as the milieu within which international law and the international legal system must endeavour to reach maturity."

41 Wright, Q., Toward a Universal Law for Mankind, *Columbia Law Review*, Vol. 63, 1963, p. 440, has rightly suggested that lasting forms of government depend on processes of communication, acculturation and cooperation.

42 van Benthem van den Bergh, G., Contemporary Nationalism in the Western World, in: *Conditions of World Order* (Hoffmann, S., ed.), Boston, Houghton Mifflin, 1968, pp. 76, 101, suggests that nationalism may contribute to break up the present blocs and thus contribute to world order.

43 See Scheuner, U., Aufgaben- und Strukturwandlungen im Aufbau der Vereinten Nationen, in: *Die Vereinten Nationen im Wandel* (Kewenig, W., ed.), Berlin, Duncker & Humblot, 1975, pp. 189, 190.

itical thinking, echoed by numerous speeches and reports at the highest levels, that the problems which the world faces have acquired a much more international profile than was true in the past; global interdependence has become a main topic of political reasoning, both in practice and in scholarly discussions.[44] In fact, this is easily justified in terms of international peacekeeping; given the present military technology and the weapons of mass destruction of ever-increasing "sophistication", it is disquieting that there is hardly any place on earth which the great powers do not consider as important from their own perspective. In the economic sphere, it is well recognised that existing problems can only be solved by way of global cooperation. The discussions on the changing international economic order are nearly always informed by this understanding. A recent aspect to be mentioned here is the policy of the oil-producing countries and their impact upon the structures of the international monetary system. The list of global issues is in fact much more extensive; let me merely mention, as a last point, the concerns for the stability of an international ecological order.

The call which has so often been sounded is that we need more institutions in which the global interest is reflected. The point that has to be made in this context is that this need is felt even though the United Nations Charter was envisaged as a constitution for a global order, but that this global dimension of the United Nations has more and more lost its dynamic force. To put it more distinctly: Whereas the substantive problems of the international community have become more and more international, the existing body for securing a global order has more and more become the forum of traditional diplomacy, in other words of national interests.

The conclusions which may be drawn from this paradoxical disharmony between the global scope of substantive issues and the national perspective of the global institutions are not easily decided. It appears that in practice the most important result was in fact to seek solutions outside the United Nations. The response which has been far less frequently given is that a renewed effort should be made to make effective use of the universal perspective which has organisationally been built into the United Nations. At a time when global perspectives are indeed needed so urgently, the universalist element of the United Nations has become almost anachronistic. Looking at the Charter in this perspective, one might well conclude that it reflects a hope for the future rather than the disappointments of the past. The United Nations Charter appears in this light as a document which is more attuned to the future than most other models of political planning presently in vogue. It is most doubtful whether a document of the same global orientation as the Charter would be agreed upon today, if a new conference of State representatives were to meet and decide again. The fact that the Charter has become ineffective in key areas should, from this perspective, not

44 For a general study on modern problems of interdependence, see Keohane, Robert Owen & Nye, Joseph S., *Power and Interdependence: world politics in transition.* Boston, Center for International Affairs, Howard University, Little Brown, 1977, 273 p. See on this point also Scheuner, U., Die internationalen Probleme der Gegenwart und die nationale Entscheidungsstruktur, in: *Regierbarkeit*, (Hennis, W. et al., eds.). Vol. I, 1977, pp. 255, 265 ff.

lead to an abandonment of the Charter's structures, but to ways of thinking how to revitalise the Charter. The widespread disappointment and frustatrion with the institutions and the work of the United Nations has its roots less in the structure of the global organisations set up in 1945 than in the attitude of the actors called upon to use the machinery agreed upon. One is strongly reminded in this context of the fact that the law does not only create an order, but that it is also a function of the political order; this is true in the decentralised international legal system even more so than in national orders.

6. *Changing the United Nations Charter?*[45]

If the above diagnosis is correct, the United Nations Charter has a global orientation that is in many respects stronger than that of the major political forces today at work within the United Nations.[46] This observation will serve in itself as a sign of caution against reform plans seen from the viewpoint of global thinking, be it of a more regional or universal character.[47] In this respect it may not be so unfortunate as it may at first appear that attempts directed at major reforms of the principal organs have met with strong objections from those States whose positions were at stake.[48] When the voting rules of the Security Council were under

45 The following remarks only relate to those provisions of the Charter which deal with the structure of the Security Council and the General Assembly; the desirability of a change may be assessed differently in such areas as the jurisdiction of the International Court of Justice and the outdated provisions regarding enemy States (Arts. 53, 107). Also, it should be further studied whether consensus can be reached among the permanent members of the Security Council with respect to refraining from using the veto in certain areas. For proposals to alter the structure of the Security Council and the General Assembly, see *The United Nations: The Next Twenty-Five Years*, Twentieth Report of the Commission to Study the Organization of Peace, New York, 1969, pp. 56 ff. For a proposal to amend the law-making power of the United Nations along the lines accepted in the International Civil Aviation Organization and the World Health Organization ("opting out"), see *The United Nations: The Next Twenty-Five Years*, Twentieth Report of the Commission to Study the Organization of Peace, New York, 1969, p. 18.

46 It must be recognised in this context that the emphasis in the activities of the United Nations has gradually shifted in the past decades from peacekeeping to economic development; this has had an impact upon the relative weight of the Security Council and the General Assembly. See Goodrich, L., *The United Nations in a Changing World*, New York, Columbia University Press, 1974, pp. 56 ff.; Scheuner, U., Wandlungen im Aufgabenbereich und Struktur der Vereinten Nationen, in: *Die Vereinten Nationen und die Mitarbeit der Bundesrepublik Deutschland* (Scheuner, U. and Lindemann, B., eds.), München, R. Oldenbourg, 1973, pp. 15–44.

47 The fact that the United Nations have so far been functioning as it did, in spite of existing tensions between big powers, must be attributed to a large extent to its special constitutional structure.

48 See also Goodrich, L., The Security Council, in: *The United Nations: past, present and future* (Barros, J., ed.), New York, Free Press, 1972, pp. 16, 39, 59. It is remarkable that US President Carter suggested in March 1977 that Japan might become a permanent member of the Security Council, see *Department of State Bulletin*, Vol. 71, 1977, p. 375.

discussion in the past years in the Special Commitee on the Charter of the United Nations and on the Strenghening of the Role of the Organization,[49] all permanent members (with the exception of China)[50] made it clear beyond doubt that they intended to use their veto when reforms requiring Charter amendment were under discussion;[51] it is also not so long ago that a President of the General Assembly firmly rejected any discussion of the concept of weighted voting for this organ.[52]

Looking more specifically, as the Chairman has suggested, at proposals to rearrange the distribution of permanent seats in the Security Council according to a regional formula[53] and to permit an opting-out for individual regions, it would indeed appear today that the permanent seats as they were allocated in San Francisco need to be reconsidered from a contemporary viewpoint. But it must also be observed here that the regional elements have in fact been strengthened and that the Third World already has a strong voice in the Security Council. All efforts which would lead to a strengthening of the "veto arrangement" in the Security Council have to face the powerful argument, from a global perspective, that the Security Council at this point of historical development has become a

49 For a lucid analysis of the origins of the Special Committee on the Charter of the United Nations and on the Strengthening of the Role of the Organization and its activities up to 1976, see Broms, B., The Special Committee on the Charter of the United Nations and the Strengthening of the Role of the Organization, *German Yearbook of International Law*, Vol. 20, 1977, pp. 77–102. According to Broms (then Chairman of the Committee), England, France, the Soviet Union and the United States viewed proposals to change the composition of the Security Council "with the utmost abhorrence" (p. 78) from the beginning of the discussions in the Committee, see also Broms, *loc. cit.*, pp. 96 f. With respect to the general progress made by the Committee, see its Reports, General Assembly, Official Records, Thirty-Fourth Session, Supplement No. 33 (A/34/33); Thirty-Fifth Session, Supplement No. 33 (A/35/33). For summaries of recent initiatives, with further references, see the reports of Klein, Eckart, Tätigkeit der Vereinten Nationen in völkerrechtlichen Fragen, in: *Archiv des Völkerrechts*, vol. 18, (1980), pp. 408 ff., vol. 18, (1980), pp. 196 ff., vol. 17, (1978), pp. 382 ff., See also Gunter, M., Recent Proposals in the United Nations to Amend the Charter, *Case Western Reserve Journal of International Law*, Vol. 10, 1978, p. 763.

50 China supports a review of the Charter "with a view to changing the unjustifiable situation of super-Power manipulation of the United Nations and implementing the principle of the equality of all States", UN Doc. A/AC. 182/SR. 12, 27.

51 According to Art. 108 of the Charter, amendments to the UN Charter are dependent upon the approval of all permanent members of the Security Council.

52 In September 1973, the President of the General Assembly declared: "The idea of weighted voting would spell the final overthrow of the organization . . .", *UN Monthly Chronicle*, Vol. 10, 1973, p. 20.

53 The general problem of the relationship between the competence of regional organisations was again discussed in the Special Committee on the Charter of the United Nations and on the Strengthening of the Role of the Organization, see UN Doc. A/34/33, Supplement No. 33, pp. 6, 15; A/35/33, Supplement No. 33, pp. 16, 19. No common view emerged. In some statements, the favouring of regionalism apparently is viewed as a viable means to circumvent the provisions of the Charter.

relatively weak organ and that additional elements of a centrifugal nature might paralyse it even more.[54]

Another point which needs to be considered here is the often overlooked fact that, historically, international law has always had its foundations in a certain political power basis as set up by the internationally dominant forces; here again it must be recognised that law is largely a function of political notions of order.[55] The Uniting for Peace Resolution and other attempts at shifting responsibilities from the Security Council to the General Assembly appear questionable in this light; in the same vein, it must, however, be recalled here that the privileged position of the permanent members entails a corresponding obligation on their part, in a political sense, to cooperate in the maintenance of peace. Finally, the idea of an opting-out system in the Security Council could appear as an escape from the paralysis caused by individual vetos. However, any movement toward majority voting in the Security Council might present at least as many problems as the present voting rules. Compliance and enforcement problems, for instance, would raise delicate issues in the case that one of the great powers might actively oppose the majority in the Security Council. Dangerous forms of fragmentation might soon have to be faced.

These provisional remarks, of course, do not do full justice to the existing proposals for a reform of the Charter.[56] My own view of the discussions on this point is that they deserve special attention because they reflect discontent with the present global system and thus indicate lines along which future changes might be made. With respect to the near or middle future, however, there are strong arguments against any change of the Charter, because it reflects a global way of thinking which is at present hardly discernible in the main stream of

54 For a recent attempt to broaden the jurisdiction of the General Assembly, see Broms, *loc. cit. supra* (note 49), p. 95.

55 With respect to the powers of the big States, and the corresponding international division of labour, it must be observed that international law cannot evade the consequences of given political factors; see on this point Mosler, H., *Die Großmachtstellung im Völkerrecht*, Heidelberg, 1949, p. 10, (Süddeutsche Juristen-Zeitung. Schriften. Hft. 8). The dangers arising from the abuse of powers by the big States and from a lack of cooperation between them will in themselves not suffice to disregard such factors *a priori* within the system of international law. On the relationship of international law to the development of international relations, see O'Connell, P., *loc. cit. supra* (note 34), p. 51.

56 It is true that the United Nations has not yet found a voting procedure which allows both efficiency and a protection of minorities. Whereas the voting in the Security Council has shown elements of a tyranny of a minority, voting in the General Assembly in certain instances has had the characteristics of a tyranny of the majority; for a most useful study of the problems involved, see Tomuschat, C., Tyrannei der Minderheit? Betrachtungen zur Verfassungsstruktur der Vereinten Nationen, *German Yearbook of International Law*, Vol. 19, 1976, p. 278. – The practice of "consensus" has not fully solved the issues concerned; it appears that the shortcomings of this practice have been increasingly recognised; see also Suy, E., Innovations in International Law– Making Processes in: *International Law and Policy of Human Welfare*, (MacDonald R. et al., eds.), Alphen a.d. Rijn, Sijthoff and Noordhoff, 1978, p. 187.

current political and legal thinking.[57] To use phraseology coined by a German jurist in the 19th century: It is doubtful whether the international community in this specific period of history has any vocation to legislate on a new international order.

57 The current problems in the functioning of the United Nations mainly stem from the fact that the States concerned feel that the Charter in some areas provides for weighty limitations which they are not willing to accept under all circumstances. Given this situation, it appears more useful to consider imaginative proposals for the enforcement of the existing Charter than to think about such revisions of the Charter which would in effect limit the States concerned in an even stronger fashion.

8.7. International Organization for a New World Order

Interventions at Plenary Sessions

New Ways for Treaty-Making and International Legislation

References:

VOJIN DIMITRIJEVIĆ

Dwelling on the second part of Ambassador do Nascimento e Silva's excellent report, it seems to me worth while to consider the creation of international law through so called "instant" custom. This has been referred to in the reports of Professors Jiménez de Aréchaga and Suy, as well as by other speakers. It has been observed that some decisions of universal international organizations create principles or rules of international law. Such rules are supposed to be customary, but in this case the *opinio juris*, expressed in the resolution of the UN or some other organization is – to paraphrase Suy – so strong that the time element, the uniform practice of States, can be very short, or none at all. Confirming that this tendency is present, I cannot help putting the following unorthodox question: Why call it custom? The latter term, in many languages, implies long and consistent conduct and does not sound very convincing when applied to future-oriented decisions, which aim at preventing possible harmful behaviour in the future (e.g., in outer space, in the sub-soil, etc.).

The next question is: are we not too positivistic as regards sources of international law? Art. 38 of the International Court of Justice, though constitutional in nature, is, after all, binding only on the Court. The existence of a new source is possible, and ought not be deduced from a positive rule of international law, but from the observation of international reality. If it is discovered that rules recognized as obligatory come into existence by the expression of consensus in an international organization, and that no subsequent practice is needed, it would be theoretically "cleaner" to call this by its own name. The important task would then remain to determine under which circumstances "ordinary" resolutions acquire this force.

Unfortunately, the International Court of Justice is not in a position to determine this, neither can its decisions be quoted in support of the creation of a principle or rule through a decision of an international organization. The Court is bound by its Statute and its members must make the mental effort to construe such a new rule as a customary rule; otherwise they could not be able to apply it.

Finally, I share Ambassador do Nascimento e Silva's view that too often it is insisted only on the non-binding character of UN resolutions. By saying that a resolution of a universal international organization is legally non-binding, we are saying what it *is not*, and not what *it is*.

Juan Carlos Puig

I agree with everything Ambassador do Nascimento e Silva has said in his stimulating speech and his valuable paper. I would only like to push his argument further, on the one hand, and to make a brief comment on the democratic principle as applied to the international decision-making process, on the other.

In the first place, if the problem is the number of international conferences, special sessions of the General Assembly, and so forth, perhaps the best way to get rid of such time- and money-consuming procedures would be to make the General Assembly a permanent body, and to decide that everything related to codification and progressive development of international law should be treated in the General Assembly.

It seems to me that we are facing a pattern of concentration, not of coordination. Perhaps the worst thing to do would be to create a coordinating committee. According to UN experience, in general, coordination bodies to not coordinate anything owing to the interests at stake, and then it is necessary to create another body to discoordinate what has been wrongfully coordinated.

In the second place, I think, that one of the reasons for some of the failures of such a legislative procedure is the fact that up to now it has been managed by governments representatives. If we take into account that approximately 60% of governments are dictatorships, the real question is how can we possibly have a fair legislative or quasi-legislative process on the international level when the majority of the legislators are not representing peoples but a dictator's will?

The problem becomes still more acute when we observe that, perhaps owing to such a lack of genuine representation, the vacuum has been filled by a curious and sometimes useful – I should confess – relationship between diplomats and international civil servants which in fact is working as an international subsystem of political participation with its own rules and practices.

Perhaps one of the feasible ways to correct such a distortion would be to supplement the governments' role with a kind of functional representation such as the one practiced in the International Labour Organisation.

Finally, as to the application of the democratic principle to international decision-making, I have always thought that we are confronted here with an undue extrapolation. Democracy is a form of government for individuals. According to it, a government is more democratic when more people are willing to support it. But, in addition to the democratic principle we normally have, too, the liberal principle, whereby the minority is protected against the majority, through principles like fundamental rights, division of power, equality under the law, etc. Precisely, the equality of States is not an expression of the democratic principle, but of the liberal one. The real problem is that we do not have, up to now, a fair expression of the democratic principle in international organizations, with the obvious exception of the European Communities.

This is perhaps a naive assumption but it is nonetheless unvoidable if one seeks to understand the real role the equality of voting is playing in the international community.

Nabil A. Elaraby

The point of departure of any discussion on the review of the UN Charter should be that the Charter provisions presuppose that the Charter would, in the light of developments and according to a specified procedure, be amended. So there is nothing sacrosanct about the Charter review. What is relevant is how to improve the existing UN system and how to enhance the effectiveness and credibility of the UN.

What is also of relevance is how to approach the required reforms within the constitutional limitations regarding the vast and unprecedented power conferred on the permanent members of the Security Council. It is therefore necessary and timely to consider ways and means to improve the system. One of the most important topics which the UN Special Committee on the Charter is considering is how to limit the scope of application of the so-called "unanimity rule" or veto power. The Charter did not provide an indication. The provisional rules of procedure of the Security Council have not clarified this matter. Thus, the so-called double veto may still be invoked by the permanent members when they base their position on the Four Sponsoring Powers Statement submitted in San Francisco in 1945.

Taking into account the inability of the UN to carry out the Charter provisions relating to the maintenance of international peace and security, it seems appropriate to explore ways and means to improve the functioning of the Security Council. Certain areas, such as ascertaining facts and settlement of disputes, should be considered outside the scope of the veto in order to encourage referring disputes and conflicts to the Security Council. A group of non-aligned States have submitted such proposals to the Special Committee on the Charter.

In conclusion, it is submitted that the majority of the UN members, in particular the new States, consider that the trend of the attempts to reform and improve the UN should be to attempt to render the UN more effective. Issues like redistributing permanent seats in the Security Council are of marginal importance if not completely irrelevant. A cautious, step by step approach is, therefore, more realistic. It might be also appropriate to convene a special General Assembly session to discuss these issues.

Finn Seyersted

I agree with Ambassador Elaraby that the veto-power went too far and ought to be limited. However, I want to emphasize that even today the veto-power is not unlimited. It is clear from the documents from the San Francisco conference that the veto was not to be used for procedural decisions. Consequently, if a permanent member of the Security Council were to use the double veto to subject a clearly procedural matter to the veto, this would constitute an abuse and the majority of the Council and the other organs of the Organization should treat the majority decision as valid, despite the negative vote of the permanent member. If that member would insist on its right to veto, an advisory opinion could be requested from the International Court of Justice. It should be noted, moreover, that, whereas there has been political abuse of the veto power on substantive issues, there has not been any legal abuse of the double veto on procedural matters. Moreover, the practice of abstention has been used in many cases to avoid even political abuse of the veto, indeed this practice now constitutes in effect an amendment of article 27 (3) of the Charter by customary law.

Organs for Conflict Resolution and Execution

References:

8.3. Bengt Broms 486
8.4. Winston A. Tubman 502

Holger Rotkirch

I would like to thank both rapporteurs for their interesting and thought-provoking presentation of the item under discussion. The purpose of my intervention is to make a few additional comments.

My first comment relates to Art. 33 of the Charter concerning methods for the peaceful settlement of disputes such as mediation and conciliation as well as resort to regional arrangements.

As Ambassador Tubman spoke of regional arrangements in Africa, I believe it would be of interest to mention that within the follow-up process of the Conference of Security and Co-operation in Europe (CSCE) an effort has been undertaken to develop methods for peaceful settlement of disputes among the participating States. The basis is a very elaborate Swiss initiative, and one meeting of governmental experts has been held in Montreux in 1978. Another meeting of experts to continue the work will probably be convened by the meeting of Governments at present going on in Madrid.

Another method which I think ought to be mentioned in this context when we consider methods for settlement of disputes under the UN Charter is he use of the good offices of the Secretary General. These are not expressly mentioned in the Charter but I believe there is general agreement that this function is considered to belong to the inherent powers of the Secretary General.

Under these powers the Secretary General can use his good offices at the request of the parties to a dispute. However, he may also take an active role and offer his good offices on his own initiative. To make use of the Secretary General's services in this respect may be very effective as it does not have to become public knowledge and thus, psychologically difficult questions of prestige may be avoided.

On the whole I believe that we should undertake efforts to develop the various methods mentioned in Art. 33 of the Charter which do contain a third party involvement, but not a final outcome which is binding on the parties to the dispute, such as mediation, conciliation, various regional arrangements and other peaceful methods. It is often advocated that we should strive to agree on methods where the parties to the dispute beforehand agree to be bound by the decision. However, this very fact frequently prevents the dispute from being submitted to settlement. Further, there is no guarantee that the party against whom the decision goes will accept the decision. As an example could be mentioned the Beagle Channel case. In my opinion, the most important thing is to get the parties to agree to submit the dispute to third party settlement. Even if the result is only a recommendation, if this is considered just by the States involved, chances are that they will accept it, like Finland and Sweden did in the Åland Islands case.

My second point refers to the settlement of disputes according to the draft Convention on the Law of the Sea. I think it ought to be noted that the system provided by the draft Convention is more complex than what Prof. Broms referred to in his short description. In addition to the Law of the Sea Tribunal special arbitration organs are set up for certain types of disputes such a fisheries, maritime matters, pollution and scientific research. The parties to a dispute may choose to resort to the International Court of Justice, the Law of the Sea Tribunal, general arbitration, one of the specific arbitration procedures or any other method they agree upon.

Concerning settlement of disputes relating to delimitation of marine boundaries concilitation is to be utilized. It is impossible to go into further details in this brief intervention. I only wanted to point out the very complex structure of settlement of disputes under the draft Law of the Sea Convention. In this connection it should also be noted that many questions are in the Convention considered to belong to the internal matters of a State and, accordingly, they cannot be subject to the settlement of disputes under the Convention. In my view, this is very much to be regretted as it thus opens possibilities for future conflicts between the parties for which no procedures for the settlement of such disputes have been agreed upon.

Taslim O. Elias

I wish to make only a few remarks on the very able and interesting reports submitted to us this morning by our two Rapporteurs – Prof. Broms and Ambassador Tubman. Each of them spoke on topics which touched me on certain significant points.

With regard to the International Court of Justice, I consider Prof. Broms' reference to the adjudicatory role of the Court to be of crucial, contemporary relevance. As we all know, the problem of enforcement of the judgments of the Court is of great concern to the whole of the international community, particularly in relation to the duty laid upon the Security Council by Article 94, paragraph 2, of the Charter of the United Nations. This provision requires the Council to make recommendation or take steps that should lead to the execution of a judgment of the Court at the instance of one of the parties to the case where the other party would not fulfil the obligation imposed upon it by a judgment of the Court. In the recent case concerning the dispute between the United States and Iran over the illegal seizure by the so called militants of the United States Embassy and Consulates and the taking of 52 American hostages in Iran, the Security Council adopted a unanimous resolution condemning Iran for its violation of diplomatic law by both its action and its inaction. When the matter later came before the Court, Iran was unanimously held to have violated its international obligations under the two Vienna Conventions on Diplomatic and Consular Relations of 1961 and 1963 respectively. The United States again took the matter to the Security Council for enforcement action under Article 94 of the Charter, but the necessary steps towards execution of the judgment were blocked by the use of the veto involved by one of the Great Powers in the Security Council. It seems to me wrong that the Power that vetoed the proposed resolution, having previously joined in the Security Council resolution that had condemned Iran and noting that the Court's judgment had been unanimous in ordering Iran to release both the hostages and the American Embassy and Consulates in Teheran, should have turned round to block the only legal means of enforcing the judgment of the Court. The use of the veto should never be in such cases. Article 94 (2) requires the Security Countil to help enforce the Court's judgments, not to block them.

As regards the Organization of African Unity, I agree with Ambassador Tubman that the Commission of Conciliation, Mediation and Arbitration has remained moribund since its inception in September 1965 when the judges of the tribunal were appointed in Accra following the formal adoption of its constitutive Protocol by the Summit of the Heads of State and Goverment in Cairo the previous years. As one of the drafters of both the Protocol (of which I was chairman in Cairo) and the OAU Charter out of which the Commission grew, I must deplore the circumstance that has rendered this dispute-settlement body so far inoperative. The OAU Charter had such high hopes for the International Court of Justice as it does not provide for its own judicial mechanism, but relies on the Court for final settlement of its disputes. Instead, it provides for the establishment of the Commission for regional disputes of a domestic character. After establishing the necessary machinery for the purpose, the OAU shied away from it and began to deal with the types of disputes envisaged under the Protocol by establishing *ad hoc* committees to deal with them as soon as they have arisen. One of the latest occasions for the use of an *ad hoc* committee has been in respect of the Western Sahara Case in which the ICJ ordered a referendum for the people to exercize its right to self determination under United Nations auspicies. The OAU has since been seized of the matter by means of an *ad hoc* committee of some five Heads of State, which is still trying to grapple with the problem. It is a question whether the OAU Commission might not have been more successful had it been supported and used at the appropriate stage.

Eduardo Jimenez de Aréchaga

I wish to commend the excellent report submitted by Prof. Broms, which combines his learning as a distinghished professor with his practical experience as President of the Committee of the General Assembly on reform of the UN Charter.

He rightly points out the difficulties in the way of ratification of amendments to the Charter, and indicates that one of the methods open for improvement is the interpretation of Charter provisions.

In this respect it seems to me that a proper interpretation of the UN system of peaceful settlement, as intended at San Francisco, and as established in the Charter, would yield better results than the incorrect interpretation which has been followed in practice in recent years.

That practice considers that the formula in article 33, "peaceful means of their own choice", also applies to recommendations of procedures or methods of pacific settlement under article 36. In other terms, that both parties to a dispute have to agree beforehand on a particular method before any recommendation is made to those parties by the UN organs competent in the field of peaceful settlement. This naturally causes frequent deadlocks in the process of peaceful settlement since the parties, already opposed on the merits of their dispute, are hardly in agreement as to a particular method of solving that dispute.

However, from a legal point of view, and in a correct interpretation of the system of the Charter, the choice required by article 36 as to the appropriate method of settling a dispute is not one to be made by the parties in agreement, but it should be made by the competent UN organs (Security Council, General Assembly, even the Secretary General). According to the Charter they must decide in each case on the basis of objective criteria (such as, for instance, the legal character of a dispute) which is the most appropriate method or procedure to deal with the merits of a particular dispute, and make that recommendation disregarding the preference of one of the parties, or even, of both of them.

The confirmation that this is the system of the Charter as intended at San Francisco, may be inferred from the proviso at the end of art. 27 par. 3, according to which a permanent member cannot veto the recommendation of a method of peaceful settlement made in respect of a dispute to which it is a party. This is an important provision of the Charter which was obtained with great difficulty during the San Francisco Conference.

Now, if a permanent member of the Security Council cannot veto a recommendation of a method of peaceful settlement in its own dispute, this should be the case, *a fortiori*, of non-permanent members. It would be absurd to interprete the context of the Charter as allowing non-permanent member a power of veto denied to the permanent member.

ANDRÉS A. ARAMBURU-MENCHACA

I meet all our colleagues that have previously taken the floor in the congratulations and gratitude expressed by them to Prof. Broms and Ambassador Tubman for their talented reports.

My intervention, at this time, will be limited to Prof. Broms' report and to a very concise point of that report: the International Center for the Settlement of Investment Disputes (known as ICSID within the frame of the World Bank).

My first point is to stress the need to make a very clear distinction between political disputes and economic disputes. Any dispute brought before the International Court of Justice is a political case because both parties are States, even when the dispute is of an economic character and has been generated by a private foreign person (individual or corporation) receiving diplomatic protection of the State of its nationality. This statement is valid for arbitration cases when the two parties are States.

The case loses such political character if the parties in the juridical or arbitration case are on one side, a State, and a foreign private person on the other. An arbitration case brought to ICSID has no political character because such character cannot be recognized to a dispute between the State and a private person in connection with economic interests. Moreover by bringing the case before an ICSID tribunal a political dispute (or diplomatic dispute) between States would be avoided.

This distinction becomes relevant nowadays having in mind the entrepreneurial activities of States, a new phenomenon whose effects are evidenced every day in political and economic relations, either domestic or international.

It is important to recall that ICSID is the first authentic international center of arbitration of the kind we are referring to: the arbitrations between a State and a foreigner.

None of the other existing centers are really international in spite of their names as is the case for the international Chamber of Commerce (ICC). All the existing centers have been organized under the laws of a certain country and therefore have the nationality of such country. Here we find one of the reasons why States or entities of public law cannot accept arbitration outside and why they consequently force foreigners contracting with them expressly to submit any dispute to the national courts of justice in accordance with their constitutional provisions inspired in Calvo's doctrine born more than a hundred years ago under very different circumstances.

Arbitration settlements through ICSID have three advantages that it is necessary to point out:

1. One is that the awards will not need exequatur in the country of execution because they are not foreign awards;
2. Another is that they will not be in conflict with any internal rule inspired in nationalistic doctrines about the national jurisdiction in as much they are based in a treaty and treaties are a part of the law of the land; and
3. Finally, the settlement of disputes in accordance with ICSID's rule will avoid a diplomatic claim.

All these points have been considered by the new Peruvian Constitution in its article 13 that allows the State or entities of public law to agree about settlement of disputes through judicial or arbitral tritunals constituted by treaties to which Peru is a party.

The President of the Council of Minister, Mr. Manuel Ulloa has therefore recently, in a meeting in Paris, stated that Peru will ratify the Convention of the ICSID. This relevant declaration indicates a change in the attitude until yet followed by the Latin-American countries.

Universalism and Regionalism

References:

8.5. Ludwik Gelberg 506
8.6. Rudolf Dolzer 513

Richard B. Lillich

I should like to supplement and comment briefly upon two points raised by Dr. Dolzer with respect to State sovereignty and regionalism.

In the first place, talking about the negative repercussions of absolute State sovereignty, Dr. Dolzer rightly concludes that "it will not suffice in the future to express disapproval of existing international law and to re-emphasize a concept of sovereignty which has little to offer in terms of guidance for actions taken in global rather than national interests". I agree with this statement completely and would like to illustrate, by reference to the law governing the treatment of aliens, how misguided notions about absolute State sovereignty, at least until recently, have retarded and prevented the progressive development of this body of law.

Specifically, the various (successful) attempts to modify and reformulate the traditional international law of nationalization and compensation, based as they have been on the concept of absolute State sovereignty over natural resources, have had as an unfortunate byproduct the weakening of support for the entire body of State Responsibility for Injuries to Aliens law, 90 percent of which concerns personal rather than property rights. States and commentators, invoking absolute State sovereignty as justification for their view that the law needed changing, have not distinguished between the taking of property norms that no doubt did need changing and other aspects of the law governing the treatment of aliens. Thus absolute State sovereignty unfortunately and unnecessarily has contributed to undermining treatment of aliens law – one of the first fields of international law designed to protect the rights of individuals.

Somewhat ironically, since the recession that began following the Arab oil embargo of 1973–1974 many of the same States whose overreliance on absolute State sovereignty worked to undermine treatment of aliens law in the first three decades after World War II have found that they needed this law to protect their own citizens who had gone to other countries to seek employment and, following the recession, had been thrown out of work. All of a sudden these States – which included Algeria, Mexico and Yugoslavia – have ceased relying upon absolute State sovereignty and have invoked and even pressed for codification of treatment of aliens law. At the present time two such efforts are underway at the United Nations General Assembly: The first is the attempt to draft a convention spelling out the rights and duties of States with respect to migrant workers. The second is the attempt to draft a declaration governing the treatment of aliens generally.

These two efforts, both of which of necessity involved codifying and even progressively developing limitations upon absolute State sovereignty are good examples of how the international legal system should approach problems from the point of view of the individual person rather than abstract legal theory. They demonstrate a realistic taking into account of the inclusive interests of all States. They show that absolute State sovereignty is an outmoded juridical concept that should be used more carefully than it has been in the past. To repeat what Dr. Dolzer has said, it "has little to offer in terms of guidance for actions taken in global rather than national interests".

Secondly, when discussing regionalism Dr. Dolzer first mentions peacekeeping and then refers to what he considers the next most important function of regional organizations – economic cooperation. He does not mention what I consider to be an equally important function – the protection of human rights. At present there exists a European Convention on Human Rights and an American Convention on Human Rights. 1981 apparently will see the signing of an African Convention on Human Rights, while efforts are afoot to generate an Asian Convention on Human Rights. Some observers have suggested that the fifth area of the world – the Communist countries – adopt a similar conventional approach to protecting human rights.

These regional conventions and the procedures established thereunder eventually may become far more significant than the UN Covenants and procedures. Indeed, it can be argued that at present both the European and the American regional systems offer more effective and certainly more depoliticized systems of human rights enforcement. Moreover, these conventions contain norm-generating provisions that already have contributed to the development of customary international law which binds all States. In the United States where the American Convention has not been ratified and hence is not the law of the land it has been cited (along with the European Convention and other human rights instruments) to establish that both torture and arbitrary detention violate not only conventional but also customary international law. In *Filartiga* v. *Plena-Irala* and *Fernandez v. Wilkinson* US courts have held that customary international law, stemming in part from regional conventions, constituted a binding rule of decision enforceable against not only the importance of regional organizations should not overlook their potential contribution in the field of human rights.

Bengt Broms

While thanking for the most interesting papers presented by Professor Gelberg and Dr. Dolzer I would like to make some comments on the last chapter of the paper by Dr. Dolzer. In this chapter he is dealing with the changing of the Charter of the United Nations. The issue is topical and I note with great pleasure that this issue is, thus, subjected to a debate.

Ever since the San Francisco Conference there have been proposals to amend the Charter of the United Nations and some of these proposals have, indeed, been adopted in the past. In 1970 the Government of Colombia presented an item on the need to revise the Charter of the United Nations to the agenda of the General Assembly. After a lengthy debate the General Assembly eventually, in 1974, adopted a Resolution to set up an *Ad Hoc* Committee for the Review of the Charter. The following year this *Ad Hoc* Committee was replaced by the Special Committee on the Charter of the United Nations and on the Strengthening of the Role of the Organization. During those years the matter was hotly debated by the General Assembly and I do still recall a statement by the representative of the Soviet Union, Ambassador Malik, when he called the Foreign Minister of the Philippines, General Romulo, by the name of Taras Bulba who killed his own son, as General Romulo had earlier during the debate spoken warmly in favour of amending the Charter and mentioned that he belonged to the founding fathers of the Organization as he had participated in the San Francisco Conference.

The reason why I want to comment on Dr. Dolzer's paper is that he reaches on page 532–533 a somewhat pessimistic conclusion when he says that "with respect to the near or middle future, however, there are strong arguments against any change of the Charter, because it reflects a global way of thinking which is at present hardly discernible in the main stream of current political and legal thinking."

In view of this conclusion I would like to say something of the work of the Special Committee on the Charter of the United Nations and on the Strengthening of the Role of the Organization. In the first place I want to underline the fact that the mandate of the Special Committee includes, in addition to the proposals to amend the Charter, also all other proposals which may strengthen the role of the Organization without amending the Charter.

During its sessions the Special Committee has covered in two readings an analytical summary presented by the Secretary-General including all past proposals. These include, among others, proposals concerning all the main organs of the United Nations, the relationship between the General Assembly and the Security Council, the peace-keeping system, the peaceful settlement of disputes, the maintenance of international peace and security, the position of the Secretary-General and the Secretariat as well as also the procedure of the General Assembly and its subordinated organs. With reference to the last mentioned topic the Special Committee adopted a number of proposals at its Geneva session in 1979 and forwarded them to the Secretary-General of the United Nations. Many of those proposals have already been acted upon by the General Assembly. During the last two years the work has concentrated on the drafting of a declaration on the peaceful settlement of international disputes and on problems related to the maintenance of international peace and security.

During the last three years it has been noted that important changes have taken place in the attitudes of even those Great Powers who originally were most strongly against even the possibility of amending the Charter. Once it was seen that the States that have been advocating amendments to the Charter have not insisted on such amendments which would revolutionize the entire Charter the attititudes have become softer. By now all members of the Special Committee are prepared to stress that the United Nations should be strengthened and the differences of opinion concentrate rather on the issue whether or not this requires amendments to the Charter or should the work be done merely by putting new life to those provisions of the Charter which have remained a dead letter – and I may mention Article 43 on the military agreements as an example – and by more elastic interpretation of other provisions of the Charter. One should not forget that the Charter has already been amended and that it is not sacrosanct. If there are proposals which are generally recognized as reasonable the members should not fear their adoption. On the other hand one has to remember that the Charter is probably the best legal document among the constituent documents of the international organizations since the Second World War and that there is no reason to change the Charter merely for the sake of making amendments.

In conclusion I would like to express the view that all the proposals to review the Charter or to strengthen the role of the Organization merit careful consideration with an open mind. Once this is done, and once it is clear that a complete revision of the Charter is not unnecessarily intended, the prospects for a compromise solution warrant Dr. Dolzer's pessimism in his interesting paper, less.

Gunnar G. Schram

I want to make a few remarks, based on the content of Professor Gelberg's report.

Firstly, I want to state, for the record, that what was said in the report on the aims of the North Atlantic Treaty Organization (NATO) and how it came into being, was somewhat misleading and biased. I do not intend to enter into a discussion with Professor Gelberg on the matter as the Rules of Procedure forbid any discussion of political issues at the Seminar.

I refer now to the statement that some steps, taken within the framework of the new economic order, and aimed at assisting the Third World countries, had not brought the results expected. The 200 mile economic zone had instead brought great profits to the richest States of the world, who had extracted 80 per cent of the whole of this new category of marine area. Such allegations were not quite to the point.

It was, indeed, the developing nations themselves who in 1970 pressed through the UN General Assembly a decision to redraft the law of the sea in its entirety, against the advice of a number of the developed nations. The 200 mile economic zone had always been a crucial part of the new ocean law revision, championed by the developing countries (and Iceland as the only European country at the time) but firmly opposed by the great majority of the rich countries of the world. It would be rather naive to surmise that the developing countries had not at that time recognized the benefits they would derive from such an economic zone. They had, indeed, already benefitted greatly from this new and extensive jurisdiction and their share of the maritime area was much larger than 20 per cent.

According to the data provided by the Trilateral Commission less than half (46%) of the exclusive economic zones belongs to the developed countries but 54% to the developing world.

Thirdly, I draw attention to the fact that the new Law of the Sea Draft Convention has now gained acceptance by consensus of perhaps 95% of its provisions. This could only be described as a major achievement, even though one Government has asked for more time to analyse some of the draft articles and thus postponed final agreement on the Draft Convention.

It is important to remember that the draft grants the developing nations, as it stands, valuable benefits from exploitation of the deep sea-bed area. Large benefits will accrue to these nations through operations licensed by the Sea-Bed Authority, which will enhance their economic and social development in years to come. In this respect it is clear that the developing nations will be the gainers and not the loosers, and it should not be made to look otherwise.

Indeed, the new Law of the Sea Convention opens up new vistas and new opportunities for the Third World countries which they may utilize through transfer of technology and joint ventures with entities in the developed countries.

Rudolf Dolzer

It is necessary to recognize the ambivalence which is inherent in an evaluation of regional customary law from the viewpoint of a coherent system of international law. It was indeed correct that regional law had a potential to support and strengthen existing norms of universal law. However, this was not necessarily the case under all circumstances. The possibility that regional law could in effect weaken the consensus reflected in rules of universal law should always be kept in mind: recognition of the danger of a fragmentation of the international legal system and the weakening of the contribution of international law to the preservation of a global order through a tendency to recognize regional law in an unqualified manner should be needed. In fact, developments within the last decades have revealed this danger. In the area of customary law, the universal rules governing the use of force have been challenged on the ground of regional peculiarities. In the area of treaty law, similar problems have occurred when regional organizations occasionally have made it difficult for the Economic Commissions of the United Nations to perform their functions. Thus, it is necessary in every individual instance to examine carefully whether a regional norm was in fact consistent with the principles and purposes of existing universal law; in case of a discrepancy the member States of the United Nations are bound under Art. 103 of the Charter to recognize and observe the applicable rule of universal law.

IX. Legal and Organizational Problems of Mini-States

Working Group V

9.1. The Problems of Mini-States in International Law

PHILIP K. A. AMOAH

In considering the problems of "mini-States" one has to begin first with the problem of definition. What is a mini-State? So far no attempt has been made to define it. The closest one can get is the definition of "micro-States" which have been described as "entities which are exceptionally small in area, population and human and economic resources".[1] Although a few mini-States share those characteristics, several of them cannot be described in those terms at all. A more acceptable definition has to be found.

This paper attempts to examine the problems of such nations from two separate but inter-related perspectives, viz. problems of economic development and those related to their membership of international organisations in general and the UN in particular.

Although a good deal of literature has appeared in recent years which deals with the developing nations in general, scant attention has been paid to the peculiar problems of very small nations. This is hardly surprising. Their smallness – in area, population, natural resources, and infrastructure – puts them on the sidelines. They simply do not possess the strategic and news-making resources of their more powerful brethren. This is unfortunate because in fact such small nations, particularly those which are also land-locked, epitomize the problems of the Third World. They present interesting issues and provide unique opportunities for a rewarding study of the development problem. Recent interest shown by Sussex University's Institute of Development Studies in the special problems of very small nations is a major step forward. In its Report the Institute comments on the internal structures of small nations and their relations with the world system in terms which throw some light upon their role in international affairs.

"Small countries are likely to be more closely concerned with the world system than large countries. This connection may take the form of heavy dependence on imports and exports, on a few transnational corporations, on external labour markets and on foreign institutions. Such dependence will be reflected in internal economic and social structures. Specific areas of international policy where small nations may face special problems include relations with import supplies, with commodity markets, with transnational enterprises, with sup-

1 Introduction to the Annual Report of the Secretary-General on the work of the Organisation, 16 June 1966–15 June 1967. *General Assembly, Official Records, 22nd session, Supplement No 1A (A/6701/Add. 1)*, p. 20.

pliers of tastes and standards, and with 'donor' governments and aid agencies".[2]

The dependence of small nations on more powerful neighbours[3] or former colonial masters and other donor governments and aid agencies is fraught with difficulties and has been considered unsatisfactory in many respects. First, the uncertainties resulting from changes in donor governments or their aid policies can be quite unsettling for smaller client nations. Secondly, some of the conditions attached to the use of certain types of aid funds are so onerous that small nations are deterred from using them. Thirdly, some developing nations hold the view such aid compromises national independence and sovereignty. It is argued that the aid is not motivated by any sense of solidarity but it has been a means of exerting influence on smaller nations and thereby perpetuate the dependence relationship. The writings of Abi-Saab reflect this view: "Aid, especially bilateral aid, is a very important tool of influence in contemporary international relations. It has been, and continues to be, used to keep the States of the Third World politically in line and to make sure they behave, in their internal economic policies, in a manner consistent with the interests of the capital exporting countries."[4]

In such a state of affairs, very small nations have found themselves in a dilemma. Being very small and considering themselves fragile, vulnerable and liable to be overrun by more powerful neighbours they are jealous of their national independence and would like to behave like other States. Consequently they undertake very ambitious nation-building and sometimes prestigious projects, maintain diplomatic missions abroad, set up an elaborate public service and a national university at the same time as they attempt to satisfy the basic needs of the population. Without the capacity to bear the costs involved they have had to rely more and more on the goodwill of the international community. Thus support for multilateral negotiations through membership of international organisations is seen as an effective method of achieving the two major goals of all the small nations of the developing world, namely, safeguarding their independence and territorial integrity and finding lasting solutions to their economic problems without compromising their national independence. The concerns of the small States have been aptly described by Abi-Saab in the following words: "In these circumstances what they need most is protection from foreign intervention and undue influence and at the same time maximum help in the form of transfer of resources and know-how to ease the strains of nation-building and development"![5]

2 University of Sussex, Institute of Development Studies, Brighton, England: *Annual Report*, 1979 p. 57.

3 A typical example of such dependence is the situation that exists in the relationship between South Africa and Botswana, Lesotho and Swaziland. The latter countries heavily depend on the former, *inter alia*, for mine employment, trade and transport.

4 Abi-Saab, G., The Third World and the Future of International Legal Order. *Revue Egyptienne de Droit International*, Vol. 29, 1973, p. 34.

5 *Ibid.*, p. 37.

The issue of the membership of small nations of international organisations and the UN has been of interest to many scholars beginning from the early sixties. That period coincided with the efforts of the UN itself in the decolonization process which launched several "micro States" into independent statehood.[6] In his 1967 Annual Report the Secretary-General of the UN made a distinction "between the right to independence and the question of full membership in the United Nations".[7] Following the Report a number of studies have been conducted into the problems of very small nations.[8] In spite of their problems, as Harris observed, in 1970, "... microstates are being admitted – the latest being Equatoral Guinea – and it is arguable whether these precedents preclude the United Nations from limiting further memberships."[9] Having admitted the Republic of Nauru (population 6,000) the UN would be hard pressed to find the justification for denying membership on the ground of population to new sovereign independent States desirous to join.

Unless a revision of the UN Charter is contemplated with a view to changing the status of very small nations in the UN any discussions of the problems of their membership must either be of academic interest or for the benefit of prospective applicants. That very small nations have problems associated with their membership in the UN and other International Organisations cannot be denied. Such problems fall into two broad categories. In the first category may be placed the nation's own perception of its problems while the second is concerned with what outsiders perceive as the nation's problems. Those relating to a State's inability to fulfil the obligations of membership, difficulties in sending suitably qualified representatives, and the like are of the first type. This is illustrated by Mendelson in his examples of Tonga (population 75,000; area 699 km^2) and

6 G. A. Resolution 1514 (XV) of 14 December 1960: Declaration on the Granting of Independence to Colonial Countries and Peoples. The Resolution provides, inter alia:
1. The subjection of peoples to alien subjugation, domination and exploitation constitutes a denial of fundamental human rights, is contrary to the Charter of the United Nations and is an impediment to the promotion of world peace and cooperation.
2. All peoples have the right to self-determination; by virtue of the fact that they freely determine their political status and freely pursue their economic, social and cultural development.
3. Inadequacy of political, economic, social or educational preparedness should never serve as a pretext for delaying independence ...

7 Introduction to the Annual Report of the Secretary-General on the work of the Organization, 16 June 1966–15 June 1967. *General Assembly, Official Records, 22nd session, Supplement No 1 A (A/6701/ Add. 1)*, par. 164.

8 Writing under the title Harris, William I., Microstates in the United Nations: A Broader Purpose, in the *Columbia Journal of Transnational Law*, Vol. 9, No 1, 1970, p. 26. William Harris refers to a 1969 study by *UNITAR: Status and Problems of Very Small States and Territories*, New York, Unitar, 1969. (Unitar Series No. 3) and an article by Rapoport, J. G., The Participation of Ministates in International Affairs. *American Society of International Law. Proceedings.* 1968, pp. 155–156.

9 Mendelson, M. H., Diminutive States in the United Nations. *International and Comparative Law Quarterly*, Vol. 21, 1972, p. 617.

Western Samoa, both independent States which have not sought admission to the UN, the latter because "she has been unwilling to incur the expense involved in UN membership".[10]

What outsiders consider as a nation's problems in relation to its membership of international organisations are strictly speaking no problems at all but criticisms of or objections to membership.

The major criticisms are as follows:

(a) That the present system of equal voting rights in the General Assembly makes it possible for a group of very small nations to dominate the Assembly and to commit the Organisation to costly enterprises for which they are not financially responsible.
(b) Membership is said to impose obligations which are too onerous for very small nations.
(c) That the "invasion" of very small nations in the halls of the General Assembly may lead to a weakening of the United Nations itself.
(d) A great strain on the resources of the UN is said to be the result of the influx of these States in terms of seating capacity, documentation, duration of meetings, reimbursement of travel expenses of delegates, and so on.

System of equal voting rights

Much criticism has been directed at the Charter provisions which provide for the one-State-one-vote principle.[11] This has been found to be unsatisfactory in many respects. For one thing it is said to create equalities between large and small States. The voting system accords with the equality of States principle of the Charter. Any system of weighted voting or relegation to observer States would call for a Charter amendment and seriously undermine the basic philosophy underlying the establishment of the Organisation.

Without the concurrence and the financial support of the Super-Powers any resolution and action of the general Assembly is never going to be implemented. In any case that argument accords a status upon the Assembly which goes beyond the power to discuss and recommend as provided for in the Charter. In the history of the UN any actions of the Organisation initiated by the Assembly have been endorsed by the Security Council or been tacitly supported by a Super-Power.

A statement which Haldeman attributes to an official of the United States Department of State clarifies the position:

"Anyone who believes that United States influence in the United Nations is measured by the fact that it has less than one-hundredth of the votes in the General Assembly fails completely to understand the realities of power as they are reflected in the World Organisation. These realities include the fact that the US is the principal contributor to the UN's regular budget and by far the largest supporter of the UN's peace keeping and development programs, and that the US

10 *Ibid.*

11 UN Charter Article 18, para. 1: "Each member of the General Assembly shall have one vote".

is making by far the largest individual contribution to the defence and development of the non-Communist World. On UN decisions of vital importance to the United States, the voting of other countries has been considerably influenced by US views."[12]

The real centres of power are located in the Security Council which is dominated by the five permanent members. So far no 'mini-State' has been elected to the membership of the Council.

Unless one is excessively concerned with formal equality of States as opposed to real disparity of power which the Charter itself provides for in the allocation of power between the Assembly and the Council, the argument about equal voting rights does not take cognizance of the real centres of power in the UN system. Perhaps it is fair to conclude that he who possesses the veto controls the Council and he who controls the Council controls the Assembly.

Obligations of membership

The main obligations are: contribution to the budget of the Organization, the provision of military personnel and other forms of assistance in UN peacekeeping services and enforcement actions, and the question of sanctions.

It is often assumed that because very small nations have meagre resources they will not be able to contribute to the regular budget of the Organisation and for that reason full membership status should not be accorded upon them. When a sovereign State consciously applies for membership of any organisation it must be taken to be conversant with the obligations attendant to membership status and the consequences of failure to fulfil them. In the UN system failure to pay contributions may result in loss of voting rights. Any member failing to do so must face the consequences. Indeed such action was contemplated by the Assembly against the Congo and the Central African Republic in 1976.[13] Since this built-in deterrent is provided for in the Charter, the justification for denying small nations membership on the grounds of inability to contribute is questionable.

The provision of military personnel and other forms of assistance in peacekeeping services and enforcement actions may certainly be an onerous burden on some very small nations. For one thing they may not have established military systems and defence forces themselves. For another their population (like that of Nauru, 6000) may be such that it would be almost impossible to send part of the population out. Perhaps consolation must be taken in the fact that such operations necessitating the involvement of personnel from all member States rarely occur. In any case failure to provide such assistance cannot be expected of very

12 Halderman, John W., *The United Nations and the rule of law.* Dobbs Ferry, New York, Oceana Publications, 1966 p. 228.

13 Special authorisation had to be given by the Assembly to enable the two nations to vote in accordance with the second sentence of Article 19, during the brief period before their contributions reached the Secretary-General. By letters dated 22 and 24 September 1976 the Secretary-General informed the Assembly that the States in question had paid the amounts required to reduce their arrears below the limit specified in Article 19.

small nations alone. In the past some more powerful nations, abstaining from or voting against certain actions have refused to assist in such operations.

Unless small nations are dependent on larger States upon whom sanctions are imposed or find themselves in the unique position of Botswana, Lesotho and Swaziland in relation to South Africa,[14] sanctions or threats thereof do not present much difficulty to very small nations. Their support can be total. They simply do not possess the resources and facilities for sanction-busting.

Weakening of the Organization

It is arguable whether an Organisation committed to the maintenance of international peace and security need to be exclusively composed of Super-Powers. To dismiss small nations as irrelevant in the peace process is to undermine the very foundation of the United Nations itself. Although it has to be a strong organisation capable of dealing with its manifold problems, its strength does not lie exclusively in its composition or domination by powerful States.

The presence of large and small, rich and poor in a single world forum is a reminder that global problems are not a monopoly of any particular States or group of States.

A strain on the resources of the Organization

A view held by those who see the United Nations as the special preserve for the rich and the powerful members of the world community is the one which charges that the membership of very small nations imposes a strain on the resources of the Organisation. This view is supported by references to expenses incurred in terms of seating capacity, documentation, duration of meetings, reimbursement of travel expenses of delegates, and so on.[15] Delegates from very small States will obviously increase the numbers in the halls of the UN. To speak of a strain on resources is an exaggerated view of the situation. Delegations from these nations tend to be small – they occupy only one or two seats compared to the fifty or sixty from large nations.

A considerable proportion of the UN budget is devoted to the work of the Secretariat and the specialised agencies. In view of the serious manpower problems experienced by very small nations, they are hardly represented in those important aspects of the work. The problem is particularly serious in Africa. In 1970 James Magee found that in the Economic Commission for Africa only 62% of the professional staff was African.[16] The weakness of their delegations and the fact that they are seldom represented in UN committees conspire against the effectiveness of very small nations in the UN. If their membership in international organisations is to be meaningful proposed solutions of their problems must aim, *inter alia*, at strengthening their participation.

14 Supra, note 3.

15 Mendelson, M. H., Diminutive States in the United Nations. *International and Comparative Law Quarterly*, Vol. 21, 1972, p. 623.

16 Magee, James S., ECA and the Paradox of African Cooperation. *International Conciliation*, No. 580, Nov. 1970, page 30, note 27.

Conclusion

In sum, my submission is that definite and more realistic solutions to the problems of very small nations (whether they are perceived as problems from within or from without) can only emerge from a study of the larger processes of the complex United Nations system within which the narrow issue of the concerns of or concerns about the membership of very small nations is located.

In dealing with international organisations in general and the UN in particular, which represent all shades of political opinion and diverse interests due attention must be paid to changing expectations and the demands of all groups represented. Any proposed solutions therefore must address such issues as: the concept of sovereign equality of States, the ineffectiveness of very small nations in influencing world affairs, the desirability of a forum truly representative of all nations and international peace and security.

A number of proposals have been put forward in the past. These have included limited membership, associate membership, weighted voting[17] and proportional representation.[18] These are all very carefully thought out solutions which require closer scrutiny. The difficulty with most of them is that they tend to emphasise the economic and population factors at the expense of the independent and sovereign status of the individual State members. Another attractive idea is one which emphasises cooperation among small States in the creation of a joint secretariat which provides the delegates from small nations with facilities in the pursuit of their common interests.

Very small nations undoubtedly do possess the capacity and the desire for cooperation as shown by their membership of the UN and in some cases their association with regional organisations such as the EEC. Some difficulties have also been encountered, particularly in the field of education in Southern Africa. As to whether they have common interests is an open question. Further research into the possibilities of regional cooperation involving small nations will be a step in the right direction.

17 Clark, G. and Sohn, L. B., *World Peace Through Law: Two Alternative Plans.* Cambridge, Mass., Harvard University Press, 1966, p. 26.

18 The former regional University of Botswana, Lesotho and Swaziland (UBLS) was an exercise in such cooperation. It broke up in October 1975 largely as a result of problems concerning the distribution of facilities and the desire to establish national universities.

9.2. Legal and Organizational Problems of Mini-States

GUNNAR G. SCHRAM

In the last two decades we have seen scores of States gain freedom and independence. As a mark of their independence the great majority of these States have requested to join the United Nations as full-fledged members with all the rights and duties which go with full membership.

Many of these States are mini-States with total population figures far below the 1 million criterion, e.g. the Maldive Islands (population 101 000) admitted in 1965, Barbados (population 245 000) admitted in 1966 and Quatar (population 180 000) admitted in 1971.

When discussing the legal and organizational problems of mini-States the question of definition immediately crops up. What States should be classified as mini-States? The answer is that no such commonly accepted definition exists today, either in international law or United Nations practice. When discussing the membership of mini-States a decade ago the Security Council eschewed any attempt of a definition of such States. For the purpose of this paper we will therefore consider a mini-State any State which has a population of less than 1 million, although it may well be quite large in area, e.g. Iceland which is somewhat larger that Ireland but has only 225 000 inhabitants. By applying this criterion we find that the number of such States, who have become members of the United Nations, is now just over thirty.

Analysing the legal and organizational problems of mini-States presents considerable difficulties as their legal and social conditions are not of a homogeneous nature. True, most of them are young developing countries who have through the UN decolonization process recently gained independence and full statehood. But this does not apply to all mini-States. If we take for example the mini-States of Europe we find that both Luxemburg and Iceland are highly developed States with one of the highest per capita incomes in the world. This same income factor applies also to e.g. Quatar, Bahrein and the United Arab Emirates. The smallness of the mini-States' population is however a binding common denominator which makes it both logical and imperative to analyse the problems and prospects of these States under a common heading. Their importance in international relations will undoubtedly increase in years to come, as we may shortly see a number of non-independent territories gain statehood and want to take their place in the international arena.

For the purpose of this report we will first discuss the important issue of whether United Nations membership should be limited in the case of mini-States or micro-States (those having less than 100 000 inhabitants), both on the grounds that they are unable to fulfill their obligations under the Charter and also because they present a disruptive threat to the decision-making process of the Organization.

In the second part attention will be given to how mini-States can collaborate among themselves on matters of common interest and how the United Nations system could provide aid and assistance through new approaches which will contribute to the development of the States in question.

1. United Nations membership and the mini-State

The international problems created by the existence of mini-States can be approached from two different angles. (1) Firstly from the angle of the international community and the relevant international organizations. Are mini-States fully qualified for membership in such organizations as the U.N. and the Specialized Agencies? Doubt has been cast on the participation of mini-States in the UN in past years and attempts have been made to find new solutions which would fit the mini-States in the arena of the UN.

The disadvantages for the UN in admitting the mini-States have often been stressed in the recent past. M. H. Mendelson pointed out in 1972[2] that most large territories are now independent, but if all of the 70-odd remaining dependent territories of population of less than one million became independent and were admitted to the UN, their combined voting strength would constitute a "blocking third" in the General Assembly, even though their combined populations would amount to no more than that of one medium-sized normal State. In alliance with another group they could easily dominate the Assembly; but though they could commit the Organization to various sorts of action, including the undertaking of heavy financial or even military responsibilities, their contribution to carrying out these decisions would necessarily be very small. Nearly a decade has passed since these doubts were expressed but in the interval we have not seen such a bloc-formation by the mini-States in the UN and it may be questioned whether it will ever happen.

On the other hand the question can also be approached from the viewpoint of the mini-State itself and its immediate international interests. The attractions of UN membership for mini-States are obvious and substantial. Admission to the world political organization endorses a State's political independence and enhances its prestige. It provides them with a platform for airing their grievances and affords them the protection that goes with participation in a block of States at the UN.

Before taking a closer look at these arguments for a full or restricted membership of mini-States in the UN, it is necessary to refer briefly to the role of the UN in facilitating the establishment of mini-States in the past decades.

1 UNITAR, *Status and Problems of Very Small States and Territories*, New York, Unitar, 1969. (UNITAR Series No. 3), p. 2.

2 Cf. Mendelson, M. H., Diminutive States in the United Nations. *The International and Comparative Law Quarterly*, Vol. 21, 1972, pp. 622–23.

2. The creation of mini-States and the role of the UN

The UN itself has in past years encouraged and facilitated the creation of mini-States through its active role in decolonization. The Organization took one of its most important steps in that field by the adoption of resolution 1514 (XV) of 14 December 1960 (Declaration on the Granting of Independence to Colonial Countries and Peoples). The first three operative paragraphs are here of particular relevance:

[The General Assembly] Declares that

1. The subjection of peoples to alien subjugation, domination and exploitation constitutes a denial of fundamental human rights, is contrary to the Charter of the United Nations and is an impediment to the promotion of world peace and co-operation;
2. All peoples have the right to self-determination; by virtue of that right they freely determine their political status and freely pursue their economic, social and cultural development;
3. Inadequacy of political, economic, social or educational preparedness should never serve as a pretext for delaying independence.

Although resolution 1514 (XV) is not particularly concerned with small territories it is, however, on the basis of this resolution that scores of mini-States have gained their independence in the last two decades.

The UN has concerned itself in other ways with the mini-States problem. General Assembly resolution 2105 (XX) of 20 December 1965 contained a request to the Special Committee of Twenty-Four:

"To pay particular attention to the small territories, and to recommend to the General Assembly the most appropriate way, as well as the steps to be taken, to enable the populations of these territories to exercise fully their right of self-determination and independence."

The Committee of Twenty-Four has also recognized that there are special problems when a very small territory is concerned and the United Nations has special responsibilities in that respect, as indicated in one of its resolutions:

"The United Nations should take appropriate steps to ensure that the people of these [small] territories are enabled to express themselves freely on their future status and in full knowledge of the options available to them."[3]

It may be said that through its work on decolonization the UN has given impetus to the establishment of new independent States, small as well as large. The question may therefore be asked whether through these actions the Organization has not committed itself to granting full membership rights to mini-States as well as larger States who want to join.

3. Legal restrictions on UN membership of mini-States

In the past attempts have been made to devise a special membership for mini-States in the United Nations, constructing a legal basis for participation in the

3 UN Doc. A/6300/Rev. 1. Report of the Special Committee on the situation with regard to the Implementation of the Declaration on the Granting of Independence to Colonial Countries and Peoples; pp. 769–770.

Organization that falls short of full membership. Although this is mostly past history, it still remains the most important venture in giving the mini-States a legal status different from that of larger States within the Organization.

In 1967, Secretary General U Thant made a statement in which he asserted that "it appears desirable that a distinction be made between the right of [mini-State] independence and the question of full membership in the United Nations" recommending that the Organization should "undertake a thorough and comprehensive study" of the situation.[4]

Two years later, in 1969, the Security Council established a Committee of Experts (The Mini-State Committee) to study the question and report back its recommendations. This Committee did not reach an agreement upon a final report and although it could theoretically be called back into session and has yet to submit a final report, it is understood that the issue, if not the problem, is dead.[5]

It is, however, relevant to take note of the two main proposals that were put before the Committee. These were a US and a British proposal. The US proposal envisaged the establishment of a category of associate membership. The British proposal contained a voluntary renunciation of certain rights and obligations by a State upon admission as a full member.

Under the US proposal a mini-State associate member would:

(a) enjoy the rights of a member in the General Assembly except to vote or hold office;
(b) enjoy appropriate rights in the Security Council upon the taking of requisite action by the Council;
(c) enjoy appropriate rights in the Economic and Social Council and in its appropriate regional commission and other sub-bodies, upon the taking of requisite action by the Council;
(d) enjoy access to United Nations assistance in the economic and social fields;
(e) bear the obligations of a member except the obligation to pay financial assessments.

The admission to associate membership in the United Nations would be effected in accordance with the same procedures provided by the Charter for the admission of members. States which opt for associate membership would submit to the Secretary-General a declaration of willingness to abide by the principles of the United Nations, as set forth in the Charter.

The British proposal was drawn up in the form of a declaration which a mini-State could make:

"The State of . . . hereby applies for membership of the United Nations in accordance with Article 4 of the Charter.

4 Introduction to the Annual Report of the Secretary General on the Work of the Organization, 16 June 1966–15 June 1967. *UN General Assembly, Official records: 22nd Session. Supplement No. 1A (A/6701/Add. 1).*

5 Gunter, M. M., What happened to the United Nations Ministate Problem? *American Journal of International Law*, Vol. 71, January 1977, p.–123.

In submitting this application, the State of . . . expresses its desire to enjoy the privileges and assume the obligations of membership of the United Nations and to be accorded the protection and assistance which the United Nations can provide, in particular with regard to the maintenance of its territorial integrity and political independence;

and declares that it does not wish to participate in voting in any organ of the United Nations, or to be a candidate for election to any of the three Councils established by the Charter or to any subordinate organ of the General Assembly.

On this basis and on the understanding that the assessment of its financial contribution would be at a normal level, the State of . . . declares that it accepts the obligations contained in the Charter of the United Nations and solemnly undertakes to fulfill them."

Later, when it was argued that a State which had voluntarily renounced its right to vote ought to be able to recover it, the United Kingdom added the following paragraph to its formula:

"The State of . . . further understands that it may at any time, after the expiration of one year's notice to the Secretary-General of its intention to that effect and after its acceptance of a revised assessment of its financial contribution, avail itself of those rights of membership the exercise of which it has hereby voluntarily renounced."

Consensus was not achieved in the Committee on these proposals and it was decided to seek the advice of the UN Legal Counsel on the compatibility with the Charter of both the US and the British proposals. His opinion on the US proposal was the following:

"Article 4 of the Charter [which defines the conditions for admitting new members to the United Nations] makes no reference to "associate membership" or to "associate members", nor do these terms appear elsewhere in the Charter . . . It is not possible, without Charter amendment, to create some other means of becoming a party to that instrument or of becoming a party in a capacity other than that of a Member."

As for the British proposal the Legal Counsel conceded that it did not present the same difficulties as the US proposal in respect of Article 9 of the Charter concerning the composition of the General Assembly in that the British suggestion admitted the mini-States concerned to full membership of the Organization. The Legal Counsel, however, queried whether the British proposal would be compatible with Article 4 of the Charter.

These efforts represented the last attempts of UN members to devise a new category for the mini-State, short of full membership. They did not result in any concrete action by the UN on the issue. That, by itself, makes it less likely that another attempt will be made to reduce the status of mini-States within the UN system in the near future.

As we have now seen, the efforts of the Secretary General and the Security Council have not resulted in any action taken on the participation of mini-States in the UN on a different footing from that of larger States. In the writers' view this only reflects the fact of the equality of independent sovereign States, long since recognized in international law. If a State fullfills these objective criteria, albeit how small, it should be able to participate on an equal footing in the world Organization, if it so chooses.

If the criteria of independence and sovereignty are fullfilled it would be unjust, in the writer's opinion, to exclude any State from full membership in the Organization.

4. Possibilities of voluntary limited membership

Having submitted the foregoing conclusion, it must be pointed out that it seems sensible that in the future provisions be made for a limited participation in the UN of newly independent small territories if they themselves so desire, either out of financial or other reasons.

The following options could here be envisaged:

1. *Observer status*, similar to that of Switzerland, where a country does not desire active participation.
2. *Limited membership*. San Marino, Monaco and Liechtenstein have participated in some Specialized Agencies of the UN without full membership. This would enable the mini-State to avail itself of the vast field of services of the UN, e.g. in the technical aid and economic field and thus meet their most immediate interests.
3. *Joint membership*. This does not seem to be a very viable alternative because of organizational problems such a scheme will create. The participation of unions of States in recent years in UN conferences and activities such as the European Economic Community, might, however, give new life to this old idea.

5. Organizational problems of mini-States and dependent territories

Turning now to some of the organizational problems of small States, it is evident that these States are faced with situations created by their particular size and not encountered by larger States. Their smallness does not make them as economically viable entities as larger States on the whole, although the oil-rich mini-States are here the exception.

Lack of an adequate number of qualified personnel, both in administration and the civil service sector, presents here another problem. The mini-State must maintain a similar infrastructure, social services and educational facilities as larger States, but sheer lack of manpower, expertise and financial resources often makes this difficult. The fact that most of the mini-States have only become independent in the last decade or two, and are still in the developing stage, underlines these difficulties. In most sectors funds for technical development are needed, but also for education, public administration and assessment of national resources which need to be explored and which can lay the foundation for economic progress and social development.

With respect to such organizational problems, which characterize mini-States more extensively than larger States, two ideas or approaches come to mind which might prove of some value in the development and cooperation of such States within a New World Order. They will now be briefly explained and discussed as a basis for further elaboration at the Seminar.

6. *Conferences on problems of mini-States*

Although in many respects heterogeneous, mini-States have many common economic, social and political factors. It might therefore be worthwhile to convene from one time to another Conferences of Mini-States, where common issues and problems are discussed and evaluated. The experience of one State can in many ways benefit other States, who face similar situations and conditions. This would not be an alliance or political grouping of mini-States, as their political framework is much too varied for that, ranging from non-aligned States to members of NATO.

It would rather be a forum for exchanging ideas and advice on problems of common interest and possibly formulating guidelines for the international community and the United Nations as regards policymaking towards the mini-State.

A proposal of this nature was brought forward by Yugoslavia in the UN General Assembly in 1966, but received little discussion and was not adopted. It was then foreseen that such Conferences could *inter alia* discuss problems of (a) smallness of dependent territories as it affects self-determination, (b) smallness after independence, (c) problems of smallness on a regional basis, (d) public administration, social and educational aspects of smallness, (e) participation of mini-States in international relations and international assistance granted them.

With increasing number of mini-States this idea seems timely and could be of considerable benefit to the nations concerned. By far the most expedient method would be to convene such a Conference under the auspices of the United Nations, be it on a regional basis or a general international gathering of mini-States.

7. *Special assistance to very small States and territories*

Many of the mini-States have only recently gained independence and are among the least affluent in the family of nations. This applies also to a number of territories. now.on the verge of achieving statehood.

Not only does this pertain to national income and financial resources for development, but in many instances is there also a severe shortage of skilled manpower needed for dealing with the manifold objectives a small newly independent State is confronted with through all strata of society.[6] The question therefore merits consideration whether there should be established within the UN framework special services and assistance to very small States and territories, as a part of an organization for a New World Order. It is of course well known that valuable aid is granted through UNDP and other organs of the United Nations in the field of development. But as here has been underlined, the problems of these States and territories are in many respect *sui generis* and call for special approaches and special treatment, because of the very smallness of these societies.

A mini-State has for example greater difficulties than larger nations in building

6 This question is discussed in UNITAR: *Status and Problems of Very Small States and Territories*, New York, UNITAR, 1969. (UNITAR Series No. 3) V, 230 p.

and maintaining efficient services in the following fields: public administration, communication and coordination, civil service, local government, public finance and information on external contacts and availability of technical assistance from a multitude of sources.

Advice on constitutional problems and processes and the conduct of foreign relations might here also be of considerable value. The information flow from United Nations bodies has grown to such an extent in recent years that much larger nations have difficulties in filtering and utilizing such data which may be of value to them in different categories.

It is therefore a matter for discussion whether there is not a need for a special unit within the United Nations system which would act as an advisor and coordinator for mini-States and small dependent territories to be called upon at will as the need may arise. In the field of technical aid duplication must be avoided, but such a service could well be located within the UNDP, or as a special unit in the Secretariat.

When organizing for the future and a New World Order, these are a few thoughts on the problems and interests of ministries which merit consideration at this particular time.

9.3. Legal and Organizational Problems of Mini-States
Interventions at Plenary Session in Mariehamn, Åland

References:

William Michael Reisman

There are 4 problems pertinent to the formulation of future policy about mini-States:

1. Should mini-States that now exist be deprived *ex post facto* of the rights of an existing State?
2. Should mini-States be admitted – and under what terms – to the United Nations and other international organizations?
3. How should mini-States that lack the infra-structural capacity to fulfill the basic requirements of their citizens be helped, by other States and by the international community?
4. Should very small territorial communities be encouraged in the future to seek full statehood?

The first three questions have been thoroughly discussed in the papers and comments. The fourth – which may be the most important – has been ignored. I submit that we should no longer think that the principle of self-determination must invariably lead to full statehood. Since international law now has a welfare function which establishes as of right human standards, a question is whether a candidate community has the capacity to provide its inhabitants with those minima. If not then that community should be urged to achieve self-determination in a different fashion: association, autonomy, integration, minority guarantees and so on. One should always remember that the real thrust of policy is self-determination of peoples and not of States.

J. N. Saxena

I congratulate Prof. Amoah and Dr. Schram on their very interesting papers. But I would like to make the following observations:

On Prof. Amoah's paper on page 5 under the heading "Obligations of Membership", I would like to point out one more very important obligation of the membership, viz. settlement of disputes by States by peaceful means. Even the non-members are under an obligation not to disturb the peace of the world [Art. 2(6)]. But I think the purpose of the Charter would be better served if even the mini-States are members of the United Nations.

Even if the membership goes up in the General Assembly, the power of the Security Council, the main executive body is not touched, and the policies of the big powers are not very much affected as we find at present. In spite of the group of 77 (now more than 100), the effectiveness of the General Assembly resolution on New International Economic Order is nowhere in sight. Similarily the fate of the Law of the Sea Conference hangs in balance though the vast majority of the United Nations members would very much like it to succeed.

So I submit, besides the economic considerations which will be the mini-States' own concern, there should be no attempt to block the membership of such States.

Gunnar G. Schram

When I started to write this paper on mini-States, at the request of our genial host Atle Grahl-Madsen, there were two things that astonished me and which I am going to tell you about. I suddenly realized that I had all my life been living in a place that unmistakably was a mini-State – without ever knowing it.

The other thing was that nowhere, absolutely nowhere, could I find a legal definition of *what* States are supposed to be mini-States, not even in the excellent 34th floor law library of the UN in New York. I was therefore faced with the dilemma of writing about a juridical entity of the most uncertain dimensions – which only Atle Grahl-Madsen seemed to be sure about.

Should we define the mini-State by population, *per capita* income or geographical area? No definite answer is available and this seminar would gain an even larger place in legal history if it were also to come up with an acceptable definition before Thursday next. For the time being I have arbitrarily defined a mini-State for the purpose of this paper as any State having a population of less than 1 million inhabitants.

A few years ago an economic theory was advanced whose main tenet was: *Small is beautiful.* According to that the mini-States whould be in an enviable position in the contemporary world. This theory was, however, based on a specific value judgement made by its author and can unfortunately not be transferred *in toto* and made to apply to the societies of the mini-States or the micro-States of the world.

When we discuss and analyse the role and the position of the mini-State in the New World Order, we can approach the issue from different points of view. There is to begin with the question of the independence and sovereignty of mini-States. Are mini-States viable entities in the world today or is their independence merely an empty shell, covering the fact that many of them can only survive by the aid and assistance of larger neighbouring States?

Then there is the question of the role of the mini-State in international relations. What place should they take in the New World Order and how can they best influence the conduct of world affairs – if they can influence it at all? Lastly, how can the New World Order aid the micro-States and mini-States in solving their own particular problems both in the field of law and social progress.

These are a few of the issues that come to mind when one contemplates the legal and organisational problems of mini-States and which I have outlined in my report.

It has been said in the debates of this seminar that independence is a right and interdependence is a fact. I submit that this is especially true of the mini-States. Most of them have been created through the decolonization process, initiated by the United Nations. Their independence is therefore a real, if a precarious right, which the New World Order must *recognize* and *support*. But because of their smallness, the mini-States have a greater need for security and interdependence than other States in the community of nations. An integrated world community is therefore of vital importance for the survival of the mini-State in the world today. Many of them are poor with scant natural resources and many have no armed forces at all, like my own country Ireland, to defend their interests and independence. This is why the collective security of international organizations, like the United Nations, is especially valuable to the mini-State, as are the prospects offered by the New International Economic Order.

My conclusion on this point is therefore that the New International Economic Order, which we are debating here at this Seminar, is even more important for the very small States than the larger and more powerful ones.

In recent years the debate on legal aspects of mini-States has chiefly been concerned with the question whether legal restrictions should be put on their UN membership, especially by limiting their right to vote in the General Assembly and other organs of the UN. I have discussed this question in some detail in my Report and will therefore only briefly refer to it here.

Richard B. Lillich

Prof. Broms stated facetiously in his introductory remarks that it might be considered inappropriate to hold a session on this topic at this place, since the Åland Islanders "may get some ideas" and presumably demand mini-State status. On the other hand, quite seriously, I would suggest that we might get some good ideas from them, since the Åland Islands is the classic example of an autonomous entity, linked to a sovereign State, which has achieved the maximum of rights – civil and political, as well as economic, social and cultural – for its inhabitants. Indeed, these islands might serve as a model for other small territories or areas of existing States currently flirting with the idea of seeking independent State status.

The two main papers today both assume that small territories emerging from colonial or quasi-colonial status should seek sovereign State status and admission to the UN, the OAS and other international and regional organizations. Oftentimes, while appealing to the elites of such territories, statehood carries few benefits and many burdens for their inhabitants. Also, having exceptionally small States in the UN or the OAS frequently distorts the voting patterns and the activities of such international organizations. Consequently, seeking a reasonable degree of autonomy within the formal legal structure of an existing sovereign

State – as the Ålanders have done – may present a more appealing and certainly more rational alternative to statehood in many if not all cases. At the very least, entities contemplating statehood also should consider the option of autonomy, which can be tailored to suit the size, needs and values of the inhabitants of the areas concerned.

Finally, Prof. Reisman says, and I agree, that there can be no "rollback" or revocation of statehood status already accorded to existing mini-States, nor can they easily be dropped from membership in the UN or the OAS. However, they certainly should be encouraged, politically and financially, to relinguish statehood in their own interests and in the overall interests of the international community. I realize that this recommendation may seem utopian to many participants of this conference and certainly will not bear fruit in the near future, but I nevertheless believe it to be a sound and ultimately necessary step if we are to construct an effective, as opposed to just a new, world order.

Enoch Dumbutshena

During the last two decades, many small States have emerged as independent nations and have become members of the family of nations. Undoubtedly, this emergence has changed the world situation fundamentally. In the United Nations system, it caused some serious considerations including measures to classify the membership into different categories. In my view such measures would amount to a kind of discrimination. However small those States may be in view of their size and population, if such States are determined to fulfill their obligations under the Charter of the Organization and under the principles of international law, there should be no other criterion to put them in a category different than others and they should not be discriminated by denying the equality of treatment. Any such measure would itself be contradictory to the basic purposes and principles of the Charter. Any consideration on the capacity of such a State to fulfill the obligation would be a pre-admission procedure and the General Assembly can take it into consideration prior to recommending for membership, but once, if it finds satisfactory and agrees to admit any State within its fold, that State should receive complete equality in all respects without any discrimination, like the domestic relationship of a person in the family; i.e., we cannot deny to any subsequently born son of our parents the rights of brotherhood, so is the case of a State and each such State has an equal right to and become a full member of the family of nations.

Leslie F. Manigat

The problem raised in the title "Independence and Interdependence" is related to a concrete specific case. I would like to suggest right now that we clarify the implications of our discussion A. We are witnessing in the Caribbean the creation of new small States (Grenada 100 000 inhabitants etc.). With the independence of the other small islands, one after the other, we have a list of *micro-States* in the

Caribbean which changes, for example, the majority within the Organization of American States (OAS). This has raised 2 questions; (1) Is there a *threshold* for the credibility and variability of independence for a micro-State? (2) Is it possible, as Argentina seems to have tried to suggest, to make a grouping of micro-States with one vote for the group?

We have to face the full consequences of our principles: one State, one vote, which is the expression of the norm of equal sovereignty of the States. May I suggest, moreover, that the resolution from independence to interdependence (as qualified previously) seems to be the best context to make credible and viable the micro-State, since, in an interdependent world, their independence may best be ensured when certain functions and obligations can rely on common links? Therefore I see a new legitimacy for the independence of the new micro-States in a world context of interdependence.

Geraldo E. do Nascimento e Silva

The question of the definition of "mini-State" is irrelevant and the same applies to that of "super-powers", "principal powers", etc. When a State applies for membership of the United Nations and is accepted, it becomes a member State like all the others with the same rights and duties. The legal equality of States is based precisely on this idea. Therefore it is up to the States not to diminish their status by speaking only of their rights but not of their duties. It is up to them not to act as mini-States. There is also the problem of mini-States in the Organization of American States where the majority are Latin-American States, but the admission of many new small States of the Carribean area has created problems due to their different approach to the inter-American problems. But that is a problem which is being satisfactorily solved with a certain amount of give and take.

Annexes

Officers and Staff of the Seminar

Officers

Honorary President:

H. E. Judge GUNNAR LAGERGREN, Marshal of the Realm, Chairman of the Board of the Swedish Institute of International Law (SIFIR)

Honorary Vice-Presidents:

H. E. Dr. DAVIDSON NICOL, Under-Secretary-General of the United Nations, Executive Director of the United Nations Institute for Training and Research (UNITAR)

H. E. Judge MANFRED LACHS, International Court of Justice

Honorary Officers:

Professor MARTIN H:SON HOLMDAHL, Rector Magnificus of Uppsala University

Professor STIG STRÖMHOLM, Vice-Rector of Uppsala University

Professor ANDERS AGELL, Dean of the Faculty of Law, Uppsala University

Guests of Honour:

Archbishop OLOF SUNDBY, Primate of Sweden

Mr. INGEMAR MUNDEBO, Governor of the County of Uppsala

Dr. HANS BLIX, Under-Secretary of State, Swedish Ministry for Foreign Affairs

Professor emeritus TORGNY T:SON SEGERSTEDT, former Rector of Uppsala University

Mr. ANDERS FORSSE, Director-General of the Swedish International Development Agency (SIDA)

Ms. BRITA NORDLANDER, Mayor of the City of Uppsala

Uppsala Organizing Committee:

Executive Board:

Professor STIG STRÖMHOLM, Vice-Rector of Uppsala University (Chairman)

Professor ATLE GRAHL-MADSEN, Director of the Swedish Institute of International Law (SIFIR), Seminar Director (Vice-Chairman)

Dr. ÅKE VINTERBÄCK (Secretary-General)

Advisory Members:

Ambassador BO JOHNSON THEUTENBERG, The Legal Adviser, Swedish Ministry for Foreign Affairs

Dr. ZDENEK ČERVENKA, Director of Research, Scandinavian Institute of African Studies

Mr. SVEN HAMRELL, Executive Director, Dag Hammarskjöld Foundation

Dr. SVEN LUNDSTRÖM, Head of Information Office, Uppsala University

Ms. ULLA STRÖM, Head of Legal Division, Swedish International Development Authority (SIDA)

Ms. LENA WALLENSTEEN, Information Secretary, Information Office, Uppsala University

Professor PETER WALLENSTEEN, Director of Department of Peace and Conflict Research, Uppsala University

UNITAR Liaison Committee:

Professor THOMAS M. FRANCK, Director of Research, UNITAR

Dr. ABDUL-GHANI AL-RAFEI, Director of Training, UNITAR

Dr. ISSA DIALLO, Assistant Director of Training, UNITAR (Deputy Seminar Director)

Åland Host Committee:

Mr. OLOF JANSSON, Speaker of the Province Parliament of Åland

Mr. MARTIN ISAKSSON, Governor of the Province of Åland

Mr. FOLKE WOIVALIN, Head of the Province Government of Åland

Ambassador OSMO LARES, Head of the Legal Division, Ministry for Foreign Affairs of the Republic of Finland

Mr. KARL-GUNNAR FAGERHOLM, Deputy Speaker

Mr. JAN-ERIK LINDFORS, Deputy Speaker

Ms. GUNNEVI NORDMAN, Member of the Province Government of Åland

Mr. KLAS EKLUND, Mayor of the City of Mariehamn

Mr. GUNNAR JANSSON, Permanent Secretary of the Province Government of Åland

Mr. CHRISTER JANSSON, Chief Legislative Officer

Mr. LARS-INGMAR JOHANSSON, Principal Executive Officer (Secretary to the Committee)

Mr. GÖRAN LINDHOLM, Legal Officer (Executive Assistant to the Seminar Director, Liaison Officer)

Principal Officers:

Seminar Director: Professor ATLE GRAHL-MADSEN
Deputy Seminar Director: Dr. ISSA DIALLO
General Rapporteur: Professor WILLIAM MICHAEL REISMAN
Assistant General Rapporteur: Dr. JIRI TOMAN
Secretary-General: Dr. ÅKE VINTERBÄCK
Programme Co-ordinator: Dr. ZDENEK ČERVENKA
Information and Press Services: Dr. SVEN LUNDSTRÖM, Ms. LENA WALLENSTEEN
Library Services: Mr. RAFAL LEKACH
Report Co-ordinator: Mr. ERIK BRANDEL
Head of Secretariat: Ms. INGRID FAGERSTRÖM
Reception Committee: Mr. BELATCHEW ASRAT, Mr. ABDUL-KARIM TIKRITI
Transportation: Mr. LARS WAHLUND
Executive Assistants to Seminar Director: Mr. MAGNUS BEER, Mr. GÖRAN LINDHOLM

Working Group I: "International Law in a Multicultural World"

Presiding Officers:
H. E. Judge SHIGERU ODA
Professor FRANCISCO V. GARCIA-AMADOR

Main Rapporteur:
H. E. Judge TASLIM O. ELIAS, President of the International Court of Justice

Rapporteurs and Co-Rapporteurs:
A Realistic Approach to International Law
H. E. Judge MANFRED LACHS
Rector, Professor YORAM DINSTEIN
Growth of the International Community and Qualitative Shift in International Legal Relations
Professor EDUARDO JIMÉNEZ DE ARÉCHAGA
Professor THOMAS M. FRANCK
Customary Law: From "Universal" in a European System to "Regional" in a World System
Professor FLORENTINO P. FELICIANO
Professor ALLAN ROSAS

Assistant to Main Rapporteur:
Dr. OVE BRING

Working Group II: "Independence and Interdependence"

Presiding Officers:
Mr. Justice Dr. EERO J. MANNER
Hon. Justice CHRISTOPHER O. E. COLE

Main Rapporteur:
H. E. Ambassador ENDRE USTOR

Rapporteurs and Co-Rapporteurs:
Sovereignty, Independence and Interdependence of Nations
Professor HÉCTOR GROS ESPIELL
Professor J. N. SAXENA
Natural Resources: Heritage of Nation and Mankind
Dr. KAMAL HOSSAIN
Mr. ACHOL DENG
Material, Economic and Human Limits to the Activities of Humankind
Professor OTTO KIMMINICH
Professor PHILIPPE DE SEYNES

Assistant to Main Rapporteur:
Ms. ANNE STOCKER

Working Group III: "Sovereignty and Humanity"

Presiding Officers:
H. E. Judge ABDULLAH EL-ERIAN
Hon. Secretary DHRUBA B. S. THAPA

Main Rapporteur:
Professor HERNAN MONTEALEGRE

Rapporteurs and Co-Rapporteurs:
A Natural or Moral Basis for International Law?
Professor VOJIN DIMITRIJEVIĆ
Procureur-Général Dr. ALEXIS GABOU
Sovereignty and Humanity: Can They Converge?
Professor RICHARD B. LILLICH
Professor YASUHIKO SAITO
Suppression of Tyranny: A Feasible Task?
Professor TOM J. FARER
Dr. ISSA DIALLO

Assistant to Main Rapporteur:
Mr. PAUL RENÉ

Working Group IV: "International Organization for a New World Order"

Presiding Officers:
Professor JUAN CARLOS PUIG
Professor GEZA HERCZEGH

Main Rapporteur:
H. E. Ambassador MUSTAFA KAMIL YASSEEN

Rapporteurs and Co-Rapporteurs:
New Ways for Treaty-Making and International Legislation
H. E. Ambassador GERALDO E. DO NASCIMENTO E SILVA
H. E. Ambassador NABIL A. ELARABY
Organs for Conflict Resolution and Execution
Professor BENGT BROMS
H. E. Ambassador WINSTON A. TUBMAN
Universalism and Regionalism
Professor LUDWIK GELBERG
Dr. RUDOLF DOLZER

Assistant to Main Rapporteur:
Ms. MICHELLE ROSS

Working Group V: "Legal and Organizational Problems of Mini-States"

Presiding Officer:
Professor SHENG YU

Rapporteur and Co-Rapporteur:
Professor PHILIP K. A. AMOAH
Professor GUNNAR G. SCHRAM

Staff

Secretariat:

Ms. Vera Červenka
Ms. Karin Fjällström
Ms. Ewa Hodell
Ms. Kerstin Kvist
Ms. Ann-Sophie Ylander

Students and Post-graduate Students who volunteered in various capacities:

TAHIR BABAR
FREDRIK BOHEMAN
EDWARD CARLESSON
INGRID DAHLSTEDT
MAJA ERIKSSON
GERASSIMOS FOURLANOS
EYASSU GAYIM
ANDERS HAGSGÅRD
GERDA HEIDEL
LARS HENRIKSSON
FRANK HORN
GUNNAR IVARSSON
BIRGITTA JAHRESKOG
PECKA JANSSON
MIKAEL MÅNSSON
FARHAD MALEKIAN
FREDRIK MALMBERG
HOMAYOON MOUSSAVIAN
KERSTIN NORDLÖF
BIRGITTA NYLUND
HÅKAN OLOVSSON
SUPAVAS PHUNWUT
SUSANNE ST. CLAIRE RÉNARD
GUNNEL STENBERG
INGEMAR STENBERG
BJÖRN-URBAN SYRÉN
CHRIS VEERABUTHRO

Participants

AGELL, ANDERS, Professor
Dean of the Faculty of Law, Uppsala University
Box 512, S-751 20 Uppsala, Sweden

AMOAH, PHILIP KOFI ADJAPONG, Professor
Head of Law Department
University College of Swaziland
Kwaluseni, Swaziland

ARAMBURU-MENCHACA, ANDRÉS, Professor
Faculty of Law, University of San Marcos
(Mailing address:) Plaza Grau 291, 16th floor,
Lima-01, Peru

ASRAT, BELATCHEW, B. C. L.
Swedish Institute of International Law (SIFIR),
Box 1611, S-751 46, Uppsala

BERNHARDT, RUDOLF, Professor
Max-Planck-Institut für ausländisches öffentliches Recht und Völkerrecht
Berliner Strasse 48, D-6900 Heidelberg, Fed. Rep. of Germany

BLIX, HANS, Director-General
International Atomic Energy Agency
P. O. Box 100, A-1400 Wien, Austria

BROMS, BENGT, Professor
Faculty of Law, University of Helsinki
(Mailing address:) Rådmansgatan 2,
SF-00140 Helsinki 14, Finland

ČERVENKA, ZDENEK, Director of Research
Scandinavian Institute of African Studies
Box 2126, S-750 02 Uppsala, Sweden

CHANDRAHASAN, NIRMALA, Professor
Head, Department of Law, University of Colombo
Colombo 3, Sri Lanka

COLE, CHRISTOPHER O. E., Hon. Justice,
10 Laminah Sankoh Street,
Freetown, Sierra Leone

DENG, ACHOL, Ministre plenipotentiaire
Résidence Universitaire, App. G 105,
F-92160 Antony-Paris, France

DIALLO, ISSA BEN YACINE, Principal Officer
Cabinet of the Secretary-General of the United Nations
(Mailing address:) 304 East 20th Street,
New York, NY 10003, USA

DIMITRIJEVIĆ, VOJIN, Professor
University of Beograd
(Mailing address:) Bulevar JNA 139,
YU-11040 Beograd, Yugoslavia

DINSTEIN, YORAM, Professor
Rector, Tel-Aviv University
Tel-Aviv 69978, Israel

DOLZER, RUDOLF, Dr.
Max-Planck-Institut für ausländisches öffentliches Recht und Völkerrecht
Berliner Strasse 48, D-6900 Heidelberg, Fed. Rep. of Germany

DUMBUTSHENA, ENOCH, Hon. Mr. Justice
Zimbabwe High Court
P. O. Box 8050, Causeway, Harare, Zimbabwe

ELARABY, NABIL A., H. E. Ambassador
Mission of Egypt to the United Nations
36 East 67th Street, New York, NY 10021, USA

EL-ERIAN, ABDULLAH, H. E. Judge
International Court of Justice
(deceased)

ELIAS, TASLIM O., H. E. Judge
President, International Court of Justice
Peace Palace, Carnegieplein 2,
NL-2517 KJ 's-Gravenhage, The Netherlands

FARER, TOM J., Professor
School of Law, The State University of New Jersey (Rutgers)
Fifth and Penn Streets, Camden, NJ 08102, USA

FELICIANO, FLORENTINO P., Attorney, Professor
University of the Philippines
(Mailing address:) SYCIP, P. B. 4223,
Manila, The Philippines

FRANCK, THOMAS A., Professor,
Director of Research, UNITAR
801 United Nations Plaza, New York, NY 10017, USA

GABOU, ALEXIS, Procureur Général
Supreme Court
Brazzaville, People's Republic of Congo

GARCIA-AMADOR, FRANCISCO V., Professor
University of Miami
(Mailing address:) 8500 SW 104th Street,
Miami, FL 33156, USA

GELBERG, LUDWIK, Professor
Institute of State and Law,
Polish Academy of Sciences
Al. 1 Armii WP 11, 00-580 Warszawa, Poland

GONZALES BARROS, LUIS, H. E. Ambassador
Colombian Embassy
Casilla de Correos 2923, Quito, Ecuador

GRAHL-MADSEN, ATLE, Professor
Department of Public and International Law, University of Bergen
Allègaten 34
N-5014 Bergen-Universitetet, Norway

GROS ESPIELL, HÉCTOR, H. E., Secretary-General
Cerrada de Monte Camerun, No. 42, Piso 11,
Mexico 10, D. F., Mexico

HAMRELL, SVEN, Executive Director
Dag Hammarskjöld Foundation
Övre Slottsgatan 2, S-752 20 Uppsala, Sweden

HERCZEGH, GÉZA, Professor
Faculty of Law and Political Science, University of Pécs
(Mailing address:) Váci Mihely utca 6,
H-7624 Pecs, Hungary

HINGORANI, RUP C., Dean,
Faculty of Law, University of Patna,
Patna 800 006, India

HOSSAIN, KAMAL, Dr.
Chamber Building, 122-124 Motijheel C. A.,
Dacca-2, Bangladesh

JIMENEZ DE ARÉCHAGA, EDUARDO, Professor
Faculty of Law, University of Montevideo
18 de Julio Nro. 1824
Montevideo, Uruguay

KASME, BADR, Dr.
Deputy Chief Librerian, United Nations Library
Palais des Nations, CH-1211 Genève 10, Switzerland

KIMMINICH, OTTO, Professor
University of Regensburg
(Mailing address:) Killermannstrasse 6,
D-8400 Regensburg, Fed. Rep. of Germany

LACHS, MANFRED, H. E. Judge
International Court of Justice
Peace Palace, Carnegieplein 2
NL-2517 KJ 's-Gravenhage, The Netherlands

LAGERGREN, GUNNAR, H. E., Marshal of the Realm
Riksmarskalkämbetet
Kungl. Slottet, S-111 30 Stockholm, Sweden

LILLICH, RICHARD B., Professor
School of Law, University of Virginia
Charlottesville, VA 22901, USA

MANIGAT, LESLIE F., Professor
Simón Bolivar University
(Mailing address:) Residencias Monte Carlo, Ato 11 B,
Avenida Monte Sacro, Colinas de Bello Monte,
Caracas 1041, Venezuela

MANNER, EERO, Mr. Justice Dr.
Supreme Court of Finland
Länsitie 9, SF-02160 ESPOO 16, Finland

MONTEALEGRE, HERNÁN, Director
Instituto Interamericano de Derechos Humanos
Apartado Postal No. 10081,
San José, Costa Rica

DO NASCIEMENTO E SILVA, GERALDO E., H. E. Ambassador
Brazilian Embassy
Prinz Eugen Straße 26,
A-1040 Wien, Austria

NICOL, DAVIDSON, H. E. Dr., Under-Secretary-General
Executive Director of UNITAR
801 United Nations Plaza, New York, NY 10017, USA

NOBEL, PETER, Attorney
Box 1203, S-751 42 Uppsala, Sweden

ODA, SHIGERU, H. E. Judge
International Court of Justice
Peace Palace, Carnegieplein 2,
NL-2517 KJ 's-Gravenhage, The Netherlands

OHLIN, GÖRAN, Professor
Uppsala University
(Mailing address:) Strandpromenaden 10,
S-131 50 Saltsjö-Duvnäs, Sweden

PUIG, JUAN CARLOS, Professor
Simón Bolivar University
(Mailing address:) Apartado 17.271, El Conde,
Caracas 1015 A, Venezuela

REISMAN, WILLIAM MICHAEL, Professor
Yale Law School
(Mailing address:) 127 Wall Street,
New Haven, CT 06520, USA

ROSAS, ALLAN, Professor
Faculty of Law, Åbo Akademi
Gizeliusgatan 2, SF-20500 Åbo 50, Finland

ROTKIRCH, HOLGER, Deputy Director
Head of International Law Division,
Ministry of Foreign Affairs,
Helsinki, Finland

RUDOLF, DAVORIN, Professor
Faculty of Law, University of Split
(Mailing address:) Slavicéva 39,
YU-58000 Split, Yugoslavia

SAITO, YASUHIKO, Professor
Tokyo University of Foreign Studies
51-21 Nishigahara, 4-chome,
Kita-ku, Tokyo 114, Japan

SAXENA, JAGDISH NARAIN, Professor
Jawaharlal Nehru University
(Mailing address:) B1/34, Model Town
Dehli 110 009, India

SCHRAM, GUNNAR G., Professor
Faculty of Law, University of Iceland
Sudurgata, IS-101 Reykjavik, Iceland

SEYERSTED, FINN, Professor
Department of Public and International Law, University of Oslo
Karl Johans gate 47, Oslo 1, Norway

DE SEYNES, PHILIPPE, Director
UNITAR Project on the Future
801 United Nations Plaza,
New York, NY 10017, USA

SHENG YU, Vice-Director
Institute of Law, Chinese Academy of Social Sciences
15, Sha Tan Bei Jie, Beijing, China

SOLIDUM, ESTRELLA, Professor
303 Letcher Avenue,
Lexington, VA 24450, USA

STRÖMHOLM, STIG, Professor
Vice-Rector, Uppsala University
(Mailing address:) N. Rudbecksgatan 5,
S-752 36 Uppsala, Sweden

SUY, ERIK, H. E., The Legal Counsel
United Nations
New York, NY 10017, USA

THAPA, DHRUBA B. S., Secretary
Ministry of Law and Justice
Babar Mahal, P. O. Box 828,
Katmandu, Nepal

THEUTENBERG, BO JOHNSON, Ambassador
The Legal Adviser, Ministry for Foreign Affairs
Box 16121, S-103 23 Stockholm, Sweden

TOMAN, JIRI, Dr.
Deputy Director, Institut Henry Dunant
Case postale 11, CH-1211 Genève 21 (Sécheron), Switzerland

TUBMAN, WINSTON, H. E. Ambassador
Ministry of Foreign Affairs
Capitol Hill, Monrovia, Liberia

USTOR, ENDRE, H. E. Ambassador, Professor
Karl Marx University of Economic Sciences
(Mailing address:) Fodor utca 73,
H-1124 Budapest, Hungary

WALLENSTEEN, PETER, Professor
Department of Peace and Conflict Research
Box 278, S-751 04 Uppsala, Sweden

YASSEEN, MUSTAFA KAMIL, H. E. Ambassador
(deceased)

Rules of Procedure

§ 1. During the Seminar there will be a Steering Committee, consisting of the Seminar Director, the Deputy Seminar Director, and the Programme Co-ordinator.

§ 2. The presiding officer of each session appears in the programme. In the case of a vacancy, the Steering Committee may appoint another presiding officer for any particular session.

§ 3. The agenda of the Seminar is laid down in the programme. No subject which is not in the programme shall be added to the agenda or discussed at the Seminar except with leave of the Steering Committee.

§ 4. Discussion of political issues as such in the sessions of the Seminar is strictly out of order.

§ 5. All sessions of the Seminar shall start and end strictly on time.

§ 6. Rapporteurs are allotted 25 minutes and co-rapporteurs 20 minutes. Others wishing to speak should make a request in writing to the presiding officer of the session within five minutes before it starts or during the session. The presiding officer may limit the time available to each speaker but not to less than five minutes, if this should be necessary on the basis of the number of persons wishing to speak. Such limitation may be introduced at any time and shall be strictly observed. If in a plenary session there are more persons wishing to speak than the available time allows, the presiding officer shall give priority to two speakers from each region (Africa, Asia, Latin America, Socialist countries, Western Europe and others).

§ 7. No person other than those listed as participants may address any session of the Seminar, except upon the invitation of the Steering Committee.

§ 8. Discussions in the Seminar will be conducted in English, and all papers should be submitted in this language. Only in exceptional cases and with the express permission of the Steering Committee, may a speaker use any other language.

§ 9. No resolutions or recommendations will be adopted by the Seminar.

§ 10. No tape-recording of proceedings will take place, except at direct request by the speaker concerned.

§ 11. The secretary of each session will make a record of the names of all speakers in the session.

§ 12. Speakers are invited to summarize their interventions in writing for inclusion in the Seminar report. Such summaries should normally not exceed two typewritten A4-pages with 1½ spacing. The Seminar secretariat will assist in typewriting the manuscripts of speakers. The Assistant General Editor is responsible for collecting the summaries.

§ 13. Administrative and economic questions arising in the course of the Seminar are handled by the Executive Board of the Organizing Committee, which plans to meet every day during the Seminar.

Abbreviations

A/CN. 4	International Law Commission (ILC)
A/CONF. 62	Third United Nations Conference on the Law of the Sea, 1974–82 (UNCLOS III)
A/RES	General Assembly resolution
ASEAN	Association of South-East Asian Nations
BRD	Federal Republic of Germany (GFR)
CENTO	Central Treaty Organization
CMEA	Council for Mutual Economic Assistance (COMECON)
COMECON	Council for Mutual Economic Assistance (CMEA)
CSCE	Conference on Security and Co-operation in Europe
DDR	German Democratic Republic (GDR)
E/CN. 4	United Nations Commission on Human Rights (UNCHR)
EC	European Communities
ECA	Economic Commission for Africa (United Nations)
ECAFE	Economic Commission for Asia and the Far East (United Nations)
ECE	Economic Commission for Europe (United Nations)
ECLA	Economic Commission for Latin America (United Nations)
ECOSOC	Economic and Social Council (United Nations)
EEC	European Economic Community
FAO	Food and Agriculture Organization
GA	General Assembly (United Nations)
GATT	General Agreement on Tariffs and Trade
GDR	German Democratic Republic (DDR)
GFR	Federal Republic of Germany (BRD)
HCR	United Nations High Commissioner for Refugees (UNHCR)
IAEA	International Atomic Energy Agency (United Nations)
IATA	International Air Transport Association
ICAO	International Civil Aviation Organization
ICC	International Chamber of Commerce
ICJ	International Court of Justice
ICSID	International Centre for Settlement of Investment Disputes between States and Nationals of Other States
IDA	International Development Association
IFI	International financial institution(s)
IGO	Intergovernmental organization
ILC	International Law Commission (A/CN. 4)
ILO	International Labour Organisation
IMF	International Monetary Fund

INGO	International non-governmental organization
JUS 81	Joint UNITAR-Uppsala Seminar on International Law and Organization for a New World Order, Uppsala 9–18 June 1981
NATO	North Atlantic Treaty Organization
NGO	Non-governmental organization
NIEO	New International Economic Order
OAS	Organization of American States
OAU	Organization of African Unity
OECD	Organisation for Economic Co-operation and Development
OPEC	Organization of Petroleum-Exporting Countries
PCIJ	Permanent Court of International Justice
Res. (RES.)	Resolution
SALT 2	Strategic Arms Limitation Talks, Second Strategic Arms Limitation Treaty
SEATO	South East Asia Treaty Organization
SWAPO	South-West African People's Organization
UBLS	University of Botswana, Lesotho and Swaziland
UN	United Nations
UNCHR	United Nations Commission on Human Rights (E/CN. 4)
UNCITRAL	United Nations Commission on International Trade Law
UNCLOS III	Third United Nations Conference on the Law of the Sea, 1974–82 (A/CONF. 62)
UNCTAD	United Nations Conference on Trade and Development
UNDP	United Nations Development Programme
UNEF	United Nations Emergency Force, 1956
UNESCO	United Nations Educational, Scientific and Cultural Organization
UNHCR	United Nations High Commissioner for Refugees
UNIDO	United Nations Industrial Development Organization
UNIFIL	United Nations International Force in Lebanon
UNITAR	United Nations Institute for Training and Research
US	United States of America
USA	United States of America
USSR	Union of Soviet Socialist Republics, Soviet Union
WP	Warsaw Pact
WP	Working paper

Index

Kolibri 360 GmbH
Ferdinand-Jühlke-Straße 7
99095 Erfurt, Deutschland
produktsicherheit@kolibri360.de